*The*

# LEXHAM
# OLD TESTAMENT
# APOCRYPHA

D1664550

*The*

# LEXHAM
# OLD TESTAMENT
# APOCRYPHA

*Introduced by*

## DAVID A. DESILVA

LEXHAM
ACADEMIC

*The Lexham Old Testament Apocrypha*

Copyright 2023 Lexham Press

Lexham Academic, an imprint of Lexham Press
1313 Commercial St., Bellingham, WA 98225
LexhamPress.com

All rights reserved. You may use brief quotations from this content
in presentations, books, and articles. For all other uses,
please write Lexham Press for permission. Email us at
permissions@lexhampress.com.

Print ISBN 9781683596615
Digital ISBN 9781683596622
Library of Congress Control Number 2022942957

Lexham Editorial: Douglas Mangum, Lynsey Stepan, Kelsey Matthews
Cover Design: Joshua Hunt
Typesetting: Jessi Strong, Abigail Stocker

# CONTENTS

# ACKNOWLEDGMENTS

*The Lexham Old Testament Apocrypha* uses translations from the *Lexham English Septuagint*, edited by Ken M. Penner (2019), a translation of H. B. Swete's edition of the Septuagint—*The Old Testament in Greek According to the Septuagint* (1909). The book of 2 Esdras is not included in the *Lexham English Septuagint*, so the translation here is adapted from public domain English translations that were primarily based on the Vulgate, especially the World English Bible, *The Cambridge Paragraph Bible: Of the Authorized English Version* (1873), and the Revised Version (1895). This translation mainly reflects the Latin text of the Clementine Vulgate though the text of a Latin critical edition from 1895 was also consulted on occasion. The passage at 2 Esdras 7:36–106 is missing from the Clementine Vulgate, but it appears in the 1895 critical edition and was translated in the Revised Version of 1895. Jacob N. Cerone wrote the headings to 2 Esdras, and Cerone and Douglas Mangum both worked on revising the translation. The general introduction and the book introductions for *The Lexham Old Testament Apocrypha* were written by David A. deSilva.

# THE APOCRYPHA:
# ITS ORIGINS, CONTENTS, AND VALUE

David A. deSilva

The writings grouped in the collection known as "The Apocrypha" represent a broad sampling of Jewish texts from the Second Temple Period, more specifically ranging from about 300 BC to AD 100. Within the collection are books revisiting biblical and post-biblical history (1 Esdras, 1 and 2 Maccabees); edifying historical fiction (Tobit, Judith, 3 Maccabees, the episodes added to Esther and Daniel); wisdom, philosophical, and polemical literature (Wisdom of Ben Sira, Wisdom of Solomon, Letter of Jeremiah, 4 Maccabees); liturgical texts (Prayer of Azariah, Song of the Three Young Men, Psalm 151, Prayer of Manasseh); a quasi-prophetic text (Baruch); and an apocalypse responding to the theological challenges posed by the destruction of Jerusalem by Rome in AD 70 (2 Esdras). A good number of these were composed in Hebrew and in the land of Israel, such as the Wisdom of Ben Sira, 1 Maccabees, and Judith, and reflect the social, political, and ideological tensions in Greek-dominated Judea. Some were composed in Greek in the lands of the diaspora, such as Wisdom of Solomon, 3 Maccabees, and 4 Maccabees, and reflect more directly the challenges facing pious Jews in that setting. Some represent Greek translations of texts that were originally composed in Hebrew (and Aramaic) and that were substantially expanded along the way to their final Greek form, such as Greek Esther with its multiple additions and Greek Daniel with its additional liturgical pieces and episodes.

All of these texts, however, share two things in common. The first is that each reflects the perspective and agenda of a pious Jewish author who, in some fashion, seeks to promote steadfast fidelity to the Mosaic covenant, continued pride in the heritage of Israel, and the conviction that God remains deeply concerned about the fate of God's people, both collectively and individually. The second is that each text survived into modernity not because it was particularly valued by the Jewish community but because it had been embraced by the early Christian community as an important resource for *its* reflection on God and the way of life that pleases God—that is, for its theology, ethics, and piety. Indeed, the Apocrypha exists as a discrete and identifiable collection only as a consequence of the differing positions taken in regard to this literature and its authority and proper use in the synagogue and in varying Christian circles from the earliest period through the modern age.

By the end of the first century AD, Jews both in Israel and throughout the diaspora had essentially embraced as their canon of Scripture the books known by Protestant Christians as the Old Testament. There continued to be some discussion about the status of Esther and Ecclesiastes, on the one hand, and the Wisdom of Ben Sira on the other. Yet, by and large, a consensus had already emerged by the time of Josephus (*Against Apion*

*The Origins of the Apocrypha and the Question of Authority*

1.38) and the author of 2 Esdras 3–14 (see 14:45) that only those books composed in Hebrew (allowing for some Aramaic portions) and ostensibly prior to the Persian period were to be granted the status of authoritative scripture. The early church, on the other hand, was showing a greater openness to texts beyond that number. This can be seen first and foremost in the circulation and treasuring of letters from the circle of apostles and, eventually, the Gospels. But it is also seen in their willingness to read, use, and appeal to pre-Christian Jewish texts that, while read and valued in some Jewish circles (like Tobit, Wisdom of Ben Sira, and Wisdom of Solomon), did not attain the status of holy scripture in the synagogue. As the early church also quickly became a predominantly Greek-speaking phenomenon, the Greek versions of the books of the Hebrew canon were naturally the versions it embraced (thus the longer editions of Esther and Daniel).

The authoritative status of these additional Jewish texts—and even of the Greek editions of Hebrew texts—was by no means uniformly upheld at any point during the history of the Christian movement. Origen, Augustine, and John Chrysostom championed a broader Old Testament canon than the synagogue had embraced; Athanasius, Jerome, and Gregory Nazianzus promoted the narrower canon of the synagogue as the church's Old Testament. The Roman Catholic Church would not make a formal pronouncement concerning the matter until the Council of Florence (1442), more famously reaffirmed by the Council of Trent (1546) as a definitive response to the position taken by Protestant Christians in favor of the shorter Old Testament canon.

It is this centuries-long debate and difference in liturgical practice (for the issue was always one concerning what texts were to be read in public worship as *scripture*, not what texts were valuable for private study) that allowed a discernible collection of texts to emerge as "Apocrypha." These would be the texts that were *not* affirmed as scripture by the Jewish community, by some sectors of the Catholic and Orthodox communions, and by the vast majority of Protestant Christians, but that *were* affirmed as scripture by the majority of Catholic and Orthodox circles throughout the period of the church's existence. The preferred term for this collection among the latter groups would be "Deuterocanonical" books—a term that acknowledges the fact that these texts are both generally later than the books of the shared canon of synagogue and church and decisively emerged as canonical later as well. The term, however, does not imply a "secondary" status for these books any more than "Deuteronomy" implies a secondary status for its legal contents vis-à-vis Exodus through Numbers. The word "Apocrypha" is a transliteration of a Greek word meaning "hidden things." This term was originally applied to these Jewish texts in the context of discussions concerning the propriety of reading them *as Scripture* in public worship or retiring them from the repertoire of Old Testament scriptures and the practice of public reading. The term only began to take on its decisively negative hue among Protestants in the centuries following the Reformation as the original Reformers' positive commendation of these texts faded and prejudice against all things Catholic prevented a nuanced view of the books that distinguished the Catholic Bible from the Protestant Bible.

We must at this point, however, reckon with the differing contents of *The Contents* various collections of "Apocrypha." The term traditionally has referred to *of the* those books or parts of books that appeared in the Roman Catholic Old *Apocrypha* Testament canon but not in the Jewish canon. Thus, the contents would include Tobit, Judith, Wisdom of Solomon, Wisdom of Ben Sira, Baruch, Letter of Jeremiah, 1 Maccabees, 2 Maccabees, as well as the longer versions of Esther (thus with "the additions") and Daniel (thus with the Prayer of Azariah, Song of the Three Young Men, Susanna, and Bel and the Dragon). These books constituted "The Apocrypha" in Martin Luther's German Bible of 1534 and the King James Version of 1611. This tradition continued through the publication of the Revised Standard Version with Apocrypha of 1957. More recently, the Apocrypha has been expanded to include also those books regarded as canonical in Greek Orthodox churches (1 Esdras, Prayer of Manasseh, Psalm 151, and 3 Maccabees) as well as books included as appendices in the Latin Vulgate (2 Esdras) and the Greek Bible (4 Maccabees). This is the collection of Apocrypha represented, for example, in the New Revised Standard Bible of 1989 and Common English Bible of 2011.

*The Lexham Old Testament Apocrypha* (LOTA) includes this broader collection and adds two further, significant texts: the Psalms of Solomon, reflecting concerns of a pious circle of Judeans in the mid-first century BC, and portions of 1 Enoch, an influential apocalypse the oldest layers of which date to the mid-third century BC. All of these texts, with the single exception of 2 Esdras, are represented in the manuscript tradition of the Septuagint, the Greek Bible used by the early church. Indeed, the three major codices of the Greek Bible from the fourth and fifth centuries—Codex Sinaiticus, Codex Vaticanus, and Codex Alexandrinus—reflect something of the variation in local practice where the books now designated "Apocrypha" are concerned. The fifth century Codex Alexandrinus includes within its Old Testament *all* of the books of the expanded Apocrypha save for the apocalypse, 2 Esdras. Based on the appearance of the Psalms of Solomon in the table of contents, it can be presumed to have contained this as well as an appendix. Codices Sinaiticus and Vaticanus are more conservative in their contents. The former includes only Tobit, Judith, 1 and 4 Maccabees, Wisdom of Solomon, Wisdom of Ben Sira, and Greek Esther. The codex probably also contained Daniel with its additions as well as the "Additions to Jeremiah," namely Baruch and Letter of Jeremiah, but these sections have not survived. Vaticanus includes Tobit, Judith, Wisdom of Solomon, Wisdom of Ben Sira, Baruch, Letter of Jeremiah, and the fuller Esther and Daniel, but none of the books of the Maccabees. *The Lexham Old Testament Apocrypha*, following *The Lexham English Septuagint*, takes as broad an approach to its contents as the Septuagint manuscript tradition allows, even going so far as to include the portion of 1 Enoch represented in the sixth-century Codex Panopolitanus—a fortunate inclusion given its importance generally as well as its canonical status in the Ethiopic Orthodox Church.

Although there was significant variation in opinion concerning the status of each or all of these additional books as far as canonical authority was concerned, for the first sixteen centuries of the church's history there was near unanimity as far as their *value* was concerned. This was famously true of the leading voices of the Protestant Reformation both on the continent of Europe and in England. The value that Martin Luther placed on these texts is evident from the fact that he took the pains to translate them into German. He took the innovative step of culling them from the Old Testament and placing them in a separate section between the Testaments as a means of highlighting their secondary status, but, in the title to his Apocrypha translation, he promoted them as "useful and good to read" even though they are "not held equal to the Scriptures."[1] In his prefaces to the Apocryphal books, he highlighted their value. He particularly commended the Wisdom of Solomon: "There are many good things in this book, and it is well worth reading. ... This is the foremost reason why it is well to read this book: that one may learn to fear and trust God."[2] He promoted the reading of 1 Maccabees as a "very necessary and helpful" book, particularly as background to understanding the vision in Daniel 11.[3]

Ulrich Zwingli commended the books of the Apocrypha as offering "much that is true and useful—that serves piety of life and honesty" (preface to the 1531 Zurich Bible[4]), though he also cautioned his readers to be discerning and critical in their engagement with these texts. John Calvin took a similar position, though he became decidedly less enthusiastic about them in response to the Council of Trent's formal endorsement of the Apocryphal books as canonical for Roman Catholic Christians. The Thirty-Nine Articles of the Church of England commended the books of the Apocrypha for "example of life and instruction of manners" (article 6), and readings from several of these books continued to be read in public worship, making their inclusion in the first decades of printings of the King James Version a matter of course.

*The Value of These Texts*   The value of these texts is apparent, first and foremost, in the windows that they open up for us into the history, social and political tensions, theological and ethical reflection, and religious practice of the Jewish people throughout the latter half of the Second Temple Period. First and Second Maccabees introduce us to the events and dynamics of the hellenizing reform and Maccabean revolt of 175–141 BC that would significantly shape Jewish consciousness for more than two centuries to come, particularly where the value of keeping covenant and the hope for political independence were concerned. They also introduce us to the tensions that the Jewish people faced as they navigated their varying paths between assimilation to gentile practice as a path to individual success and commitment to the distinctive Jewish way of life as the path of virtue and the enjoyment of divine favor, tensions that run throughout this literature (quite prominently, for example, in Wisdom of Solomon, 3 Maccabees, and 4 Maccabees). Tobit and the Wisdom of Ben Sira offer compendia of Jewish ethics and practice during this period. The Prayer of Manasseh, Prayer of Azariah, Song of the Three Young Men, and the prayers that appear in Tobit, Judith, the Greek version of Esther, and 3 Maccabees introduce us to the piety of the period. Baruch, Ben Sira, and 4 Maccabees, in particular,

---

[1]  Martin Luther, *Luther's Works*, vol. 35 (Philadelphia: Fortress Press, 1960), 337n1

[2]  Luther, *Luther's Works*, vol. 35, 343, 345

[3]  Luther, *Luther's Works*, vol. 35, 350

[4]  *Die gantze Bibel: der ursprünglichen ebraischen und griechischen Waarheyt nach auffs aller treüwlichest verteütschet* (Zurich: Froschouer, 1531), 4r–v [editor's translation]

alert us to the ways in which the Law of Moses was regarded by its prac-
titioners not as a burden nor as an impossible yoke but rather as God's
generous and gracious gift to Israel, capable of leading God's people to
wisdom and practical virtue. Several of these texts also bear witness to
significant developments in both personal and national eschatology that
more directly informed the (Jewish) audiences of Jesus or his apostles than
what one finds in the Hebrew Bible alone.

These texts are also valuable to students of the New Testament because
Jesus and his earliest followers clearly valued much that is now found not
only in the Hebrew Bible but also in the Apocrypha, for some poignant
teachings in the Apocrypha are echoed in the New Testament. Some schol-
ars will assert that Jesus, Paul, and James "quoted" the Apocrypha and did
so in a manner similar to their quoting from the books of the Hebrew Bible.
Such a statement, however, calls for significant nuancing, for it depends
upon a very loose definition of "quoting." If we think of quoting as calling
attention specifically to another's words, then no New Testament author
"quotes" from a book now found among the Apocrypha. No such text is
ever introduced with the words "as it is written in Tobit," "as Ben Sira says,"
or even, "as someone somewhere has said" (e.g., Heb 2:6). This suggests,
at the very least, that the New Testament authors did not expect that an
explicit appeal to one of these texts would carry unquestioned authoritative weight at the level of an appeal to a book that would emerge as part
of the Jewish canon, from which quotations *are* regularly introduced with
such call-out formulas. It might suggest, at the very most, that the New
Testament authors themselves were not aware that a particular ethical
teaching derived from a particular text from the Apocrypha. The New Testament authors would have learned about these texts indirectly as select
contents from the Apocryphal books became part and parcel of the cultural milieu in which they were raised. (The sole exception to this is the
Letter of Jude, whose author quotes 1 Enoch 1:9 while explicitly referring
to the source as "Enoch, the seventh from Adam" [Jude 14–15].)

Those cautions noted, however, the impact of the Apocryphal books
upon the writers of the New Testament and even upon the Jesus tradition transmitted therein, which, whether directly or indirectly absorbed, is
significant and pervasive. The Jerusalem-based sage Ben Sira, for example,
taught his students:

Forgive your neighbor his injustice,
    and then when you pray, your sins will be pardoned.
A person holds anger against a person—
    and he seeks healing from the Lord?
He has no mercy for a person like himself—
    and he petitions regarding his sins? (Sir 28:2–4 LOTA)

If one expects God to forgive sins—that is, offenses against God's dignity
that would rightly provoke God's anger—then one had better also forgive
one's fellow humans when they sin since it would be wrong to treat one's
own honor as more inviolable than the honor of God! This is an ethical
concept that appears prominently in Jesus' own teaching, first and most

famously in the prayer that he taught his followers to pray and in his explanation of this striking petition:

> Forgive us our debts,
>   as we also have forgiven our debtors. (Matt 6:12 ESV)

> For if you forgive others their trespasses, your heavenly Father will also forgive you, but if you do not forgive others their trespasses, neither will your Father forgive your trespasses. (Matt 6:14–15 ESV)

The concept also provides the logic undergirding Jesus' severe parable of the unforgiving servant and its explicit moral (Matt 23:18–35). The greater-to-lesser argument in Ben Sira (if one expects God to forgive affronts to his incomparable honor, one must be willing to forgive affronts to one's own significantly inferior honor) is not found in the Hebrew Scriptures and may be original to him. As a revered teacher whose material continues to surface in rabbinic texts many centuries after his death, Ben Sira was well poised to impact the ethical heritage of the Jews in Israel and, through his grandson's translation efforts, Greek-speaking Jews throughout the diaspora as well. It appears that his teaching on forgiveness made its way into the thinking of Jesus and was embraced by him as a tenet worth continuing to promote.

As a second example, we might consider the instructions concerning charitable giving found in Ben Sira as well as in Tobit, another book that clearly enjoyed circulation within the land of Israel (witness the five manuscripts discovered in the caves around the Qumran settlement).

> Help a poor man for the sake of the commandment,
>   and do not turn him away empty according to his need.
> Lose your silver for a brother and a friend,
>   and do not let it rust under a stone for destruction.
> Set your treasure according to the commandments
>     of the Most High,
>   and it will profit you more than gold.
> Deposit alms in your storehouse,
>   and this will deliver you from every affliction. (Sir 29:9–12 LOTA)

> According to the abundance you have, give alms from them in proportion to the abundance. If you possess a little, do not be afraid to give alms in proportion to the little, for a good treasure you store up for yourself against a day of necessity. For giving alms delivers one from death and will not allow that one to go into darkness. (Tob 4:8–10 LOTA)

Almsgiving, of course, had been a mainstay of the ethics of Israel promoted throughout the Hebrew Bible, notably in Deuteronomy (15:1–18; 24:9–12; see also, e.g., Prov 14:21, 31; 21:13; 28:27). Nevertheless, Tobit and Ben Sira introduce a number of new ideas in support of the ethic of generosity. What one gives away to the poor becomes the treasure one has laid up for oneself—a treasure that will prove more valuable than the wealth one might have squirreled away. Such wealth runs the risk of being wasted ("rusting") while the wealth spent on the poor endures. These are concepts that appear also in, and otherwise distinguish, Jesus' instructions promoting charitable giving and sharing with one's poorer neighbors.

> Do not lay up for yourselves treasures on earth, where moth and rust destroy and where thieves break in and steal, but lay up for yourselves treasures in heaven, where neither moth nor rust destroys and where thieves do not break in and steal. (Matt 6:19–20 ESV)

> Sell your possessions and give to the needy. Provide yourselves with moneybags that do not grow old, with a treasure in the heavens that does not fail, where no thief approaches and no moth destroys. (Luke 12:33 ESV)

Once again, it might go beyond the evidence to claim that Jesus valued Ben Sira and Tobit *per se*, but it *is* clear that he valued some of the material that Ben Sira and Tobit had contributed to the cultural heritage of Jewish ethical thought available to him as he "increased in wisdom and in stature and in favor with God and man" (Luke 2:52 ESV).

Such examples are but the tip of the iceberg of the Apocryphal books' impact on the ethical teaching of the New Testament. Many more such examples await the careful reader of the Gospels, Paul, and James, among others. It is important to acknowledge, however, that material found in some of the books of the Apocrypha contributed to the early church's *theological* reflection as well. For example, in light of their sense of Jesus' unique relationship to and even participation in the very being of God, Paul, the author of Hebrews, and John all appear to have found traditions about the figure of Wisdom useful as they sought to give voice to their insights. The author of Proverbs had already spoken of "Wisdom" in highly personified terms as a being present with God from before creation itself and active alongside God in the work of creation (Prov 8:22–31). By the turn of the era, however, the author of Wisdom of Solomon could speak in much more exalted and specific terms concerning the essential relationship of Wisdom to God:

> for wisdom, the artisan of all, teaches me. ...
> she pervades and penetrates everything because of her purity.
> For she is the vapor of the power of God
>     and the emanation of the pure glory of the Almighty;
>         because of this nothing defiled creeps into her.
> For she is the brightness of the eternal light,
>     and the spotless mirror of the activity of God,
>         and the image of his goodness. (Wis 7:22, 24–26 LOTA)

Wisdom is still God's partner in creation. The precise relationship of Wisdom to God, however, is now defined as akin to the relationship between the radiance emitted by a light source and the light source itself, between a reflected image and the thing itself that is being reflected. To perceive Wisdom is, in effect, to perceive God. Early Christian writers appear to have found in such statements the language they needed to talk about the relationship they perceived Jesus to have with the Father. Thus, Paul says of Jesus:

> He is the image of the invisible God, the firstborn of all creation; for in him all things in heaven and on earth were created, things visible and invisible ... all things have been created through him and for him. He himself is before all things, and in him all things hold together. (Col 1:15–17 NRSV)

Similarly, the author of Hebrews speaks of:

> the Son, whom [God] appointed heir of all things, through whom he also created the worlds. He is the reflection of God's glory and the exact imprint of God's very being, and he sustains all things by his powerful word. (Heb 1:2–3 NRSV)

Important here is not only ascribing to the pre-incarnate Son the work of creation alongside the Father, as was formerly predicated of Wisdom, but also the specific language of the Son as the image of God's character, glory, and essence such that, once again, to have seen the Son would be to have seen the Father (cf. John 1:18; 14:9).

The Church Fathers would draw more explicitly and extensively upon the language of Wisdom of Solomon 7–9 as they continued to explore the divine nature of Christ and the relationship of the persons of the Trinity. Since the Son was the radiance of God's glory, the Son must share the same fundamental essence of and be co-eternal with the Father since radiance is coeval with light (Dionysius of Alexandria, *To Dionysius of Rome* 4). At the same time, the Son and the Father must share an essential unity since a light source and the radiance it emits, while they can be distinguished from each other, cannot be divided or separated into two different entities (Ambrose, *On the Christian Faith* 1.7.48–49). As a light source is always generating radiance, so the Father could be said to be ever begetting the Son. Several clauses of the Nicene Creed ("of one being with the Father," "eternally begotten of the Father"), that fundamental statement of the Christian faith, owe a debt therefore to early christological readings of passages in Wisdom of Solomon alongside the New Testament. One could also point to passages in Baruch and Ben Sira that came to bear similarly important theological weight in the Nicene and post-Nicene periods.

Finally, many of the books of the Apocrypha have intrinsic spiritual and inspirational value. Christians have been emboldened to face both the threat *and* the reality of martyrdom by the courage and witness of Eleazar, the seven brothers, and the mother of the seven whose contest is related in 2 and 4 Maccabees, whether used for this purpose by Origen and Cyprian in the third century or by Menno Simons in the sixteenth. Indeed, the author of Hebrews had already held up these martyrs as exemplars of faith-in-action for his Christian audiences in the mid-first century (Heb

11:35b). Since the third and fourth centuries at the latest, Christians have learned to confess their sins and seek God's forgiveness using the words of the Prayer of Manasseh. Others have sung God's praises and invited all of creation to do the same using the words of the Song of the Three Young Men in the expanded Greek version of Daniel. Indeed, these liturgical pieces continue to this day to have a place in Anglican and Episcopal services of Morning Prayer. The visions of the post-mortem vindication of the righteous and distress of the ungodly in Wisdom of Solomon and the assurance of the hope of the resurrection in 2 Maccabees have encouraged Christians, particularly when suffering disgrace for their confession, to persevere in faithfulness even when extremely costly in this life. As we read the Apocrypha, we too might discover them, with Joachim Morgenweg who thus commended them in his 1708 Hamburg Luther Bible, to contain inspiring stories and discourses that offer "a mirror of divine providence and help, Christian wisdom, good household discipline and wholesome moral teaching."[1] We are, at the same time, instructed to do so ever with the blend of appreciation and discernment that Ulrich Zwingli had recommended in the preface to his 1531 Zurich Bible—so that one could drink in the clear water provided in these texts while avoiding the areas where the water is a bit disturbed and muddied. There is much here to drink in, alongside Jesus, James, Paul, and the many important voices of the early church that were also refreshed by these streams. Even those passages that fall short of the best of the Jewish and Christian tradition can be instructive to us, who are no less liable to the impulses to ethnocentrism, chauvinism, and disdain for "the other" that occasionally surface even in the wisest of teachers among the authors of the Apocrypha.

RECOMMENDED RESOURCES ON THE APOCRYPHA AND ITS CONTEXT

Collins, John J. *Jewish Wisdom in the Hellenistic Age.* Louisville: Westminster John Knox, 1997.

A specialized study worthy of attention for its excellent treatment of both Wisdom of Ben Sira and Wisdom of Solomon, two of the most important books of the Apocrypha in terms of overall influence.

deSilva, David A. *Introducing the Apocrypha: Message, Context, and Significance.* 2nd ed. Grand Rapids: Baker Academic, 2018.

An in-depth introduction to each of the books of the (expanded) Apocrypha treating historical context, literary features, textual transmission, and influence along with the particular themes and contributions of each text. Includes extensive and up-to-date bibliographies.

---

[1] Klaus Dietrich Fricke, "Apocrypha in the Luther Bible," in *The Apocrypha in Ecumenical Perspective*, ed. Siegfried Meurer (New York: United Bible Societies, 1991), 46–87, quote from 65

deSilva, David A. *The Apocrypha*. Core Biblical Studies. Nashville: Abingdon, 2012.

> A brief, thematic introduction to this corpus focusing on the themes of God, law, covenant, ethics, spiritual practices, and ethnic tensions in the Apocrypha along with an accounting of their impact on the early church and place in the canon.

Dunn, J. D. G., and J. W. Rogerson, eds. *Eerdmans Commentary on the Bible*. Grand Rapids: Eerdmans, 2003.

> A one-volume commentary that includes treatments of all the books of the (expanded) Apocrypha as well as 1 Enoch, each contributed by a recognized expert.

Harrington, Daniel J. *Invitation to the Apocrypha*. Grand Rapids: Eerdmans, 1999.

> A brief introduction to each book of the (expanded) Apocrypha with a particular interest in how each text deals with the themes of suffering and divine justice.

Helyer, Larry R. *Exploring Jewish Literature of the Second Temple Period: A Guide for New Testament Students*. Downers Grove, IL: InterVarsity, 2002.

> An accessible treatment of the major books of the Apocrypha alongside other Second Temple Jewish texts that lays out their historical significance and value for students of the New Testament.

McDonald, Lee M. *The Biblical Canon: Its Origin, Transmission, and Authority*. Rev. ed. Peabody, MA: Hendrickson, 2007.

> A thorough study of the formation of the canons of the Old and New Testaments, the former being particularly relevant to the varying status of the Apocrypha.

Metzger, Bruce M. *An Introduction to the Apocrypha*. New York: Oxford University Press, 1957.

> A dated but classic introduction to the (shorter) Apocrypha along with brief essays on their impact on the New Testament and Western culture as well as their place in the Christian canon throughout history.

Meurer, Siegfried, ed. *The Apocrypha in Ecumenical Perspective.* New York: United Bible Societies, 1991.

A helpful and detailed collection of essays (apart from the problematic contribution by Oikonomos) exploring the reception of the Apocrypha in various Christian traditions.

Oegema, Gerben, ed. *The Oxford Handbook of the Apocrypha.* New York: Oxford University Press, 2021.

A reference work containing essays on the setting, theology, and impact of the Apocrypha as well as essays on each of the texts themselves written by a team of specialists in the field.

Schäfer, Peter. *The History of the Jews in the Greco-Roman World.* Rev. ed. with correction. London: Routledge, 2003.

A credible and relatively concise reconstruction of the history of the Jews under Greek and Roman rule from Alexander through the Arab conquest of Palestine.

Tcherikover, Viktor. *Hellenistic Civilization and the Jews.* Philadelphia: Jewish Publication Society of America, 1959. Repr., Peabody, MA: Hendrickson, 1999.

A classic and thorough study of the impact of Hellenism on Jewish life both in Judea and the diaspora, particularly important for its detailed reconstruction of events in Judea from 175 through 141 BC.

Voicu, Sever. *Apocrypha.* Ancient Christian Commentary on Scripture. Downers Grove, IL: InterVarsity, 2010.

A compendium of excerpts from comments made by the early church fathers through the eighth century on texts from the Apocrypha (apart from 1–4 Maccabees), showing the contribution of these texts to early Christian ethics and theology.

*Introduction to*

# TOBIT (SHORTER VERSION)

T HE BOOK OF TOBIT presents an entertaining fictional story that also
serves as a vehicle for communicating theological convictions and
promoting ethical practices. The interwoven stories of two branches of
a larger family, each facing a significant crisis, show how God intervenes
to bring deliverance to, and a future for, the righteous among his people.
The speeches of the father Tobit to his son Tobias and the actions of the
main characters reinforce values and practices essential to Jewish identity
and community by word and example. The book was composed in either
Aramaic or Hebrew, probably at some point during the third century BC. It
is not clear whether it originated in the land of Israel or in the eastern diaspora; the blunders concerning the geography of the Persian Gulf region
might argue against the latter. In any event, Tobit enjoyed a sufficiently
broad reception for fragments of five manuscripts (four in Aramaic, one in
Hebrew) to have made their way to the caves around Qumran.

Of particular importance for background to the New Testament are the
book's depictions of the activity of angels and demons, its promotion of
almsgiving as the manner in which to lay up a good treasure for the future
and to attract God's favorable attention, its view of God's responsiveness
to the prayers of the righteous, and its well-developed expectations for
God's future interventions in the history and restoration of political sovereignty to Israel. Tobit's ethical admonitions also continue to adorn early
second-century Christian texts like the Didache and the Letter of Polycarp.
Tobit has been passed down in a longer and a shorter version. The shorter
version presented here is translated from Codex Vaticanus.

—D. A. deSilva

# Tobit (Shorter Version)[a]

*Introduction*

**1** The book of the accounts of Tobit son of Tobiel, son of Hananiel, son of Aduel, son of Gabael, son of Raphael, son of Raguel, from the descendants of Jahzeel, from the tribe of Naphtali, ²who was taken into captivity in the days of Shalmaneser, king of the Assyrians, from Thisbe, which is to the right of Kedesh of Naphtali, in upper Galilee above Asher toward the west, left of Peor.

*Tobit's Righteousness and Captivity in Nineveh*

³I, Tobit, walked in the ways of truth and in righteousness all the days of my life, and I performed many charitous acts for my brothers and for my people who went with me into captivity in the region of the Assyrians, that is, to Nineveh. ⁴Now when I was in my region in the land of Israel, and when I was young, the whole tribe of Naphtali, my father, withdrew from the house of David, my father, and from Jerusalem, the city—from all the tribes of Israel, for the purpose of sacrificing for all the tribes of Israel, and the temple of the resting place of God was consecrated there, and it was made into a permanent building in that place for all generations forever. ⁵All my brothers and the house of Naphtali, my father, sacrificed to the calf that Jeroboam the king of Israel fashioned in Dan on all the mountains of Galilee. ⁶But I went often completely alone to Jerusalem during the feasts, as it is written for all Israel in an everlasting decree. I would run off to Jerusalem, taking the firstfruits and the firstlings and the tithes of the flocks and herds and the first cut of the sheep. ⁷And I would give them to the priests, that is, the sons of Aaron, at the altar, and also the tenth of the wine and the grain and olive oil and pomegranates and the rest of the fruits to the sons of Levi, to the attendants in Jerusalem. And I would save for payment in money a second tithe for six years, and I would go and spend it in Jerusalem every year. ⁸And I would give them to the orphans and to the widows and converts having devoted themselves to the sons of Israel. I would bring it, and I would give it to them in the third year, and we would eat them in accordance with the ordinance commanded concerning them in the law of Moses and in accordance with the commands that Deborah the mother of Hananiel gave our father, for my father left me to be an orphan and died. ⁹And when I became a man, I took a woman from the descendants of our people, and I bore a son by her, and I called his name Tobias. ¹⁰After being taken into captivity into Assyria, and when I was brought as a prisoner, we went into Nineveh, and all my brothers and those who belonged to my people ate the food of the Gentiles. ¹¹But I guarded my soul so as to not eat the food of the Gentiles. ¹²And when I remembered my God with all my soul, ¹³and the Most High God gave to me good favor and a good impression before Shalmaneser, and I used to buy for him all things for his use. ¹⁴And I used to go into Media and buy goods for him from there until he died. And I entrusted money bags with Gabael the brother of Gabri in the region of Media totaling ten talents of silver.

---

[a] This is a translation of Swete's alternate version of Tobit from Codex Sinaiticus

[15]But when Shalmaneser died, and Sennacherib, his son, ruled in his *Burying*
place, and the roads of Media went away, then I was able no longer to go *the Dead*
into Media. [16]In the days of Shalmaneser, I performed many merciful acts
for my brothers who were from my people. [17]I would give my food to those
who were hungry and clothes to the naked, and if I should notice that
someone from my people died, and had been thrown out beyond the walls
of Nineveh, I would bury him. [18]And if Sennacherib killed someone when
that one departed, fleeing from Judah in those days of judgment, which
the King of Heaven determined for him concerning the blasphemous
words which he was speaking slanderously, I buried him. For because of his
wrath, he killed many people who belonged to the sons of Israel, and I stole
their bodies, and I buried them. And Sennacherib searched for them, but
he did not find them. [19]Then a certain one from Nineveh went and made it
apparent to the king the matter concerning me, namely, that I was burying
them, and I hid myself. And when I came to know that the king learned
about me and that I was being pursued so that I might die, I was afraid,
and I ran away. [20]And everything was seized, whatever belonged to me, and
nothing was left for me that was not taken into the royal treasury, except
Hannah, my wife, and Tobias, my son. [21]And forty days did not pass before
the time when two of his sons killed him, and they fled to the mountains
of Ararat. And Esar-haddon, his son, ruled after him and appointed Ahikar,
the son of my brother, Hanael, over all the accounts of his kingdom, and
he had authority over the whole administration. [22]Then Ahikar made a
case encouraging good favor for me, and I returned to Nineveh, for Ahikar
was the chief cupbearer and the one over the signet and administrator
and accountant for Sennacherib, king of the Assyrians. And Esar-haddon
positioned him second in command. He was my nephew and from the
same family as me.

**2** And at the time of the reign of King Esar-haddon, I returned to my *Tobit*
house, and my wife, Hannah, and my son, Tobias, were returned to me. *Goes Blind*
And at the time of Pentecost, our feast that is during sacred weeks, a deli-
cious dinner was made for me, and I sat down to eat it. [2]And the table was
set before me, and a large amount of cooked food was set before me, and
I said to Tobias, my son, "Child, go, and whomever you find that is needy
among our kin from the Ninevite prisoners who remembers the Lord with
all his heart, bring him, and he will eat together with me. And take notice,
I will wait for you, child, until you come back." [3]And Tobias went to look for
some needy person from our people and, having returned, he said, "Father!"
And I said to him, "Look! It is me, child." And, having answered, he said,
"Father, look! Someone who belongs to our people has been murdered
and was thrown into the marketplace, and there now he lies, strangled."
[4]And, having jumped up, I abandoned the dinner before I even tasted it,
and I carried the body away from the open space. And I put it into one of
the small houses until the sun had set and I could bury it. [5]Then, having
returned, I washed and ate the food in sorrow. [6]And I remembered the
saying of the prophet Amos, that he spoke against Bethel, saying, "Your festivals shall be turned into mourning and all your roads into lamentation."[a]

---

[a] Amos 8:10

⁷And I wept, and when the sun had set, I went out and dug a hole, and I buried him. ⁸And my neighbors mocked me, saying, "Is he not even afraid now?" (For already I was sought after to be killed concerning this matter.) "And he ran away!" And again, "Look, he is burying the dead bodies!" ⁹And the same night I washed myself, and I went into my courtyard. And I fell asleep by the wall of the courtyard. Now, my face had been exposed due to the scorching heat. ¹⁰And I did not know that there were sparrows on the wall above me; and their warm droppings came down onto my eyes, and it produced white films. And I went to physicians to be cured, and the more they treated me with medications, so much more my eyes were made blind on account of the white films until I was completely blinded. And I was without use of my eyes for four years, and all my brothers were grief-stricken over me. And Cyaxares tended to me for two years until he went to Elymais. ¹¹And at that time, Hannah, my wife, earned money by feminine work. ¹²And she used to send what she made to the owners of them,ᵃ and they would give her the payment, and on the seventh day of Dystros, she cut the piece of woven cloth, and she sent it to the owners, and they gave her the whole payment. And they gave her a kid of goats for the hearth. ¹³And when she came toward me, the kid began to bleat, and I summoned her, and I said, "From what place is this goat? It is not stolen, is it? Give it back to its owners, for we do not have the authority to eat anything stolen." ¹⁴But she said to me, "It was given to me for a gift over and beyond my wages." But I did not believe her, and I told her to return it to the owners. And I became red in the face with anger toward her because of this. Then, answering, she said to me, "And where are your merciful acts? Where are your righteous deeds? See! Such things are known about you."

*Tobit Prays for Death* **3**And I was deeply grieved in my soul. And I groaned and wept, and I began to pray with moans, ²"You are just, Lord, and all your deeds are just, and all your ways are mercy and truth. You judge the world. ³And now, you, Lord, remember me and look after me. And do not punish me according to my sins and because of my mistakes and those my fathers sinned against you. ⁴And I disobeyed your commands. And you gave us over into plunder and captivity and death, and to be a proverb and a byword, and a disgrace in all the nations among whom you scattered us. ⁵And now, your many judgments are fair, which you carry out against me concerning my sins, for we have not obeyed your commands and not walked faithfully before you. ⁶And now, do with me according to that which is pleasing to you, and order my spirit to be taken away from me so that I may be released from the face of the earth and that I may become dust. Therefore, it is more profitable for me to die than to live because I have heard false insults, and much grief is with me. Command, Lord, that I might be set free from this distress; deliver me into the eternal place, and do not turn away your face, Lord, from me. Therefore, it is more profitable for me to die than to see so much distress in my life, that is, to not hear such insults."

*Raguel's Daughter Is Falsely Accused* ⁷On this same day it happened that Sarah, the daughter of Raguel, was in Ecbatana of Media, and she was listening to insults by one of the maidservants of her own father. ⁸For she was given in marriage to seven men, but Asmodeus, the evil demon, killed them before they could be with her as it is fixed by custom for wives. And the maidservant said to her, "You are the one who killed your husbands. Look! Already you have been given in marriage to seven men, and you have not been named by one of them. ⁹Why do you whip us because of your husbands, that is, because they died? Go off with them, and may we not see a son nor a daughter for eternity." ¹⁰On that day she was grieved in her soul, and she wept. And she ascended into an upstairs room belonging to her father, and she wanted to hang herself. And she reconsidered and said, "May they not ever revile my father and say to him, 'You had one beloved daughter, and she hanged herself because of her troubles.' So I will bring my aged father down with sorrow into Hades. It is more profitable for me not to hang myself but, instead, to pray to the Lord so that I might die and no longer listen to insults in my lifetime." ¹¹At the same time, when she stretched out her hands toward the window, she prayed and said, "Blessed are you, God of merciful acts, and blessed is your name for eternity, and may you bless all your works for eternity. ¹²And now, I have set my face and my gaze toward you. ¹³Speak out so that I may be set free from the earth and I will not hear insults any longer. ¹⁴You know, Master, that I am clean and innocent of all impurity from a man. ¹⁵And I have not defiled my name nor the name of my father in the land of my captivity. I am my father's only child, and he has no other child that can be an heir for him. Nor does he have a brother close to him or another relative that I should keep myself for him as a wife. Already seven husbands have died because of me, and what purpose do I have to live any longer? If it does not seem good to you to kill me, Lord, now listen to the insult set upon me."

¹⁶At the same time, the prayer of both was heard before the glory of God. *The Prayers* ¹⁷And Raphael was sent to heal the two: Tobit by removing the white films *of Tobit* from his eyes so that he might see with his eyes the light of God; and Sarah, *and Sarah* the daughter of Raguel, by giving her to Tobias, son of Tobit, as wife, and by *are Heard* separating Asmodeus, the evil demon, from her. For Tobias was appointed to take possession of her beyond all those who were wanting to take her. At that time, Tobit went back from the courtyard into his house, and Sarah, the daughter of Raguel, also came down from the upstairs room.

**4** On that day, Tobit remembered the money that he entrusted to Gabael *Tobit's* in Rages of Media. ²And he said in his heart, "Look! I asked for my own *Instruction* death. Why should I not summon Tobias, my son, and I will inform him *to His Son* about this money before I die?" ³So he summoned Tobias, his son. And he came to him, and Tobit said to him, "Bury me appropriately and honor your mother. And do not abandon her all the days of her life. And do what is pleasing before her, and do not grieve her spirit in any matter. ⁴Remember her, dear child, because she has seen much distress on account of you while you were in her womb. And whenever she dies, bury her alongside me in one grave. ⁵And all your days, dear child, remember the Lord, and do not promote desires to sin and transgress his commands. Perform righteous deeds all the days of your life, and do not walk according to the ways of the unrighteousness. ⁶For the ones who carry out covenantal faithfulness will be made prosperous in their works. And to all those who do righteousness,*ᵃ*

---

*ᵃ* Codex Sinaiticus omits verses 7b–18, but the Gk. reads smoothly from verse 6 to verse 19, allowing continuous translation

[19]the Lord will give good counsel to them, and whomever he wishes, the Lord brings down to the very bottom of Hades. And now, dear child, remember these commands, and let them not be erased from your heart. [20]And now, dear child, let me inform you that I entrusted ten silver talents to Gabael, son of Gabri, in Rages of Media. [21]And do not fear, dear child, as if we have become poor. There are waiting for you many good things if you fear God and flee from every act of sin. And do good things before the Lord your God."

*Tobias and the Angel Raphael*

**5** Then Tobias answered and said to Tobit, his father, "All that you have commanded me I will do, father. [2]But how will I be able to take it from him since he does not know me and I do not know him? What sign should I offer to him such that he might acknowledge me and believe me and give me the money? Also, I do not know the way to Media so that I may travel to that place." [3]Then, answering, Tobit said to Tobias, his son, "He gave his bond to me, and I gave my bond to him. And I divided his into two parts, and we took each one part. And I put my part with the money. And now, look, it is twenty years after which I set aside this money. And now, dear child, seek out for yourself a trustworthy person who will go with you, and we will pay to him wages until whatever time you come back. But take back from him this money." [4]So Tobias went out to find a person who would go with him to Media, who had knowledge of the way. And he went out and found the angel Raphael standing in front of him. But he did not know that he was an angel of God. [5]And he said to him, "Where are you from, young man?" And he said to him, "From the sons of Israel, your brothers, and I came here to work." And he said to him, "Do you know the way to go to Media?" [6]And he said to him, "Yes, I have gone there many times. And I am experienced in and know all the roads. I have gone many times to Media, and I have lodged with Gabael, our brother, who lives in Ecbatana of Media. And it is a distance by road two full days from Ecbatana to Garras. For Ecbatana lies on the mountain in the middle of the plain." [7]And he said to him, "Wait for me, young man, until the time when I have gone inside and should tell my father. For I have a need for you to go with me, and I will pay you your wages." [8]And he said to him, "Look, I am going to wait alone; do not take too long."

[9]And when he went inside, Tobias told his father, Tobit, and said to him, "Look! I found someone among our brothers, from the sons of Israel." And he said to him, "Summon this person for me so that I may know what is his heritage and from what sort of tribe he originates, and if he is trustworthy so that he might travel with you, dear child." And Tobias went out and summoned him and said to him, "Young man, my father is summoning you." [10]And he went to him, and Tobit greeted him first. And he said to him, "May there be great joy for you." But answering, Tobit said to him, "What joy still remains for me? I am a man without use for my eyes, and I cannot see the light of heaven. Instead, I lie in the darkness as the dead who can no longer see the light. Though living, I am among the dead. I hear the voice of human beings, but I do not see them." And he said to him, "Take heart, it is nearly time for you to be healed by God. Take heart!" And Tobit said to him, "Tobias, my son, desires to go to Media. Are you able to go along with him and direct him? Then I will give you your wages, brother." And he said

to him, "I will be able to go with him, and I know all the directions. And I have gone to Media many times, and I have traveled through all its plains. And I know the mountains and all its roads." <sup>11</sup>And he said to him, "Brother, from what family do you originate? And from what tribe? Explain to me, brother." <sup>12</sup>And he said, "What need do you have in knowing my tribe?" And he said to him, "I wish to know who you truly are, brother, and what your name is." <sup>13</sup>And he said to him, "I am Azariah, son of Hananiah the Great, one of your brothers." <sup>14</sup>And he said to him, "In good health may you go and be protected by God, brother. And do not be angry with me, brother, because I wanted to know the truth even about your family. Now you happen to be a brother. And you are from a good and respectable lineage. I knew Hananiah and Nathan, the two sons of Shemeliah the Great. And they used to go with me to Jerusalem and worship with me there, and they were not led astray. Your kin are good men. You are from a good stock. And may you go with joy." <sup>15</sup>And he said to him, "I am giving to you the wage of a drachma per day, and what is necessary for you in equivalence to my son. So go with my son, <sup>16</sup>and I will be before you for pay." And he said to him, "I will go with him. Do not be afraid! In good health we will depart, and in good health we will return to you, for the path is safe." <sup>17</sup>And he said to him, "May there be a blessing on you, brother." And he called his son and said to him, "Dear child, prepare whatever you need for the road and go out with your brother. And may the God who is in heaven preserve you there, and may he bring you back to me safely. And may his angel accompany you for your safety, dear child." And he went out to proceed on his way, and he kissed his father and mother. And Tobit said to him, "Go in good health." <sup>18</sup>And his mother lamented and said to Tobit, "Why is it that you have sent my child? Is he not the staff of our hand as he goes in and goes out before us? <sup>19</sup>Money should not precede money, but let it be treated like refuse for our child! <sup>20</sup>As it has been given for us to live before the Lord, this is enough for us." <sup>21</sup>And he said to her, "Do not worry,[a] our child will go in good health, and in good health he will come back to us. And your eyes will see him on the day that he returns to you well. You have no reason; do not be afraid about them, sister. <sup>22</sup>For a good angel will accompany him, and

**6** his way will be made clear, and he will return safely." <sup>1</sup>And she became quiet, no longer lamenting.

<sup>2</sup>And the son went out, and the angel along with him, and the dog came out with him and went along with them. And they both went along, and it became one night. And they spent the night alongside the Tigris river. <sup>3</sup>And the son stooped down to wash his feet in the Tigris river, and a great fish leapt out of the water and tried to swallow the young man's foot, and he cried out. <sup>4</sup>And the angel said to the boy, "Grab hold and take possession of the fish!" So the boy overpowered the fish and brought it up onto the bank. <sup>5</sup>And the angel said to him, "Tear apart the fish and remove the gall bladder and the heart and its liver. And set them aside for yourself, and discard the entrails. For it can be a useful drug, the gall bladder and the heart and its liver." <sup>6</sup>And after the boy tore apart the fish, he collected the gall bladder and the heart and the liver. And he cooked the fish and ate some of

*Tobias and the Fish*

---

[a] Lit. "Do not have a word"

it and left the rest of it to be salted. And they both carried on together until they drew near to Media. ⁷And then the boy asked the angel and said to him, "Azariah, my brother, what sort of drug is found in the heart and the liver of the fish, and in the gall bladder?" ⁸And he said to him, "As for the heart and the liver of the fish, you must make a smoky fire before a man or a woman who has happened upon a demon or evil spirit, and every effect will disappear from him. And they will not remain with him for eternity. ⁹And as for the gall bladder, you must rub the eyes of a person where white films have appeared upon them. Blow on them, upon the white films, and they will be healthy."

*Raphael's Counsel to Tobias* ¹⁰And when he entered into Media and drew near already to Ecbatana, ¹¹Raphael said to the boy, "Tobias, my brother." And he said to him, "Look! Here I am." And he said to him, "We must stay in the home of Raguel this night. And this man is your relative, and he has a daughter whose name is Sarah. ¹²And he has no male son nor a daughter of his own other than Sarah, and you, a close relative to her, are first before all other men to make a hereditary claim over her. Also, it is appropriate for you to inherit that which belongs to her father. And the young lady is sensible and courageous and very beautiful, and her father is respectable." ¹³And he said, "It is appropriate for you to take her in marriage. Now listen, my brother, and I will talk to the father about the young lady this very night so that we may take her for you as a bride. And when we return from Raguel, we will perform the wedding celebration for her. I know that Raguel will not be able to distance her from you or to set her up with another man except under penalty of death according to the judgment of the book of Moses—and because he knows that the inheritance belongs to you so that you may take his daughter in the first place beyond all other men. And now, listen to me, brother, and let us speak about the young lady this night, and we will seek her out in marriage for you. And when we return from Rages, we will take her and lead her away with us to your house." ¹⁴Then Tobias answered and said to Raphael, "Azariah, my brother, I have heard that she has been given in marriage already to seven men and they died in their bridal chamber. On the night when they went in to be with her, they died. And I have heard people saying that a demon killed them. ¹⁵And now I am afraid because it does not mistreat her, but whoever wishes to come close to her, it kills that very person. I am the only son of my father. I should not die and bring down the life of my father and my mother into their grave with grief on account of me. For there is no other son of theirs to bury them." ¹⁶And he said to him, "Do you not remember the commands of your father that he gave you to find a wife from the house of your father? And now, listen to me, my brother, and do not have concern over this demon, and accept this young lady. I know that this night a wife will be given in marriage to you. ¹⁷And when you go into the bridal chamber, take some of the liver of the fish and the heart and set them on the ashes of the incense, and the aroma will circulate. ¹⁸And the demon will catch wind of it and flee, and he will no longer appear around her for all eternity. And when you are about to be intimate with her, both of you should stand up first and pray and ask the Lord of heaven that he may have mercy and bring safety to you. Do not fear. For she was set apart for you before eternity. And you will rescue her, and she will go with you. And I am confident that children will be produced for you by her, who will be like brothers to you. Have no concern!" And when Tobias heard these words of Raphael, namely, that she is a female relative of his from the descent of the house of his father, he fell deeply in love with her, and his heart clung to her.

**7** And when he entered Ecbatana, he said to him, "Azariah, my brother, *In the Home* take me directly to Raguel, our brother." So he took him to the house of *of Raguel* Raguel, and they found him sitting by the door of the courtyard. And they greeted him first, and he said to them, "A welcome to you, great brothers. It is nice that you have come in good health!" And he led them into his house. ²And Adnah, his wife, said, "This young man looks just like Tobit, my brother." ³And Adnah asked them and said to them, "Where are you from, my brothers?" And they said to her, "We are from the sons of Naphtali; we are among the captives in Nineveh." ⁴And she said to them, "Do you know Tobit, our brother?" And they said to her, "We do know him." And she said to them, "Is he well?" ⁵And they said to her, "He is in good health and alive." And Tobias said, "He is my father." ⁶And Raguel leapt up and embraced him and wept. ⁷And he opened his mouth and said to him, "May a great blessing be upon you, my child! You are one from a noble and respectable father. O what wretched wickedness, that a man was blinded who is righteous and performs merciful acts." And clinging to the neck of Tobias, his brother, he wept more. ⁸And Adnah, his wife, wept because of him, and also Sarah, their daughter, wept. ⁹And he slaughtered a ram from the flock and welcomed them readily.

And when they had bathed and washed themselves and sat down to *Tobias and* eat dinner, Tobias said to Raphael, "Azariah, my brother, talk to Raguel so *Sarah Wed* that he will offer to me Sarah, my kinswoman." ¹⁰And Raguel heard the conversation and said to the boy, "Eat and drink and have joy this night. For there is no man who waits to take Sarah, my daughter, before you, my brother, just as also I do not have the authority to give her to another man before you. For you are the closest relative of mine, and I will tell you the whole truth, my child. ¹¹I have given her in marriage to seven men of our brothers, and all of them died on the night when they went to be with her. And now, my child, eat and drink, and the Lord will work among you." And Tobias said, "I will not eat right now nor will I drink until you resolve the problems that pertain to me." And Raguel said to him, "I will do so. She is to be given to you according to the judgment of the book of Moses, and by heaven it has been decided that she is to be promised to you. Take your kinswoman as your wife. From now on, you are her brother, and she is your sister. She has been promised to you from today and onward to eternity. And the Lord of heaven will make you prosperous, my child, this night. And may he bestow on you mercy and peace." ¹²And Raguel summoned Sarah, his daughter, and she came to him. And, taking her hand, he gave her over to him and said, "Accept her as your wife according to the law and according to the judgment that has been written in the book of Moses to give you a wife. Take her and lead her away to your father safely, and may the God of heaven bless you with peace." ¹³And he summoned her mother and said, "Bring a scroll." And he wrote a contract of a scroll of cohabitation in marriage. And so he gave her to him as a wife according to the judgment of the law of Moses. ¹⁴From that time he began to eat and to drink. ¹⁵And Raguel called Edna, his wife, and said to her, "Sister, prepare the other chamber, and take her there." ¹⁶And she went to make up the bed for the chamber as he told her, and she led her there. And she wept for her and dried her tears and said to her, ¹⁷"Be brave, dear daughter. May the Lord of heaven give you joy in place of your sorrow. Be brave, dear daughter." And she went out.

**Tobias Defies the Demon** 8And when they were done eating and drinking, they wanted to go to bed. So they directed the young man and took him into the inner room. ²And Tobias remembered the words of Raphael, so he took the liver of the fish and the heart from the bag that he carried. And he put the parts on the ashes of the incense. ³And the aroma of the fish restrained the demon, and he fled upwards to the remotest parts of Egypt. And Raphael went and bound his feet there and tied him up at once. ⁴And the parents went outside and shut the door of the inner room. And Tobias got up from the bed and said to her, "Sister, stand up; pray and ask our Lord that he may bestow on us mercy and well-being." ⁵And she stood up, and they began to pray and to ask the Lord that they would have safety. And he began to say, "Blessed are you, O God of our fathers, and your name is blessed for all eternities of the generation. Let the heavens bless you and your whole creation for eternity. ⁶You created Adam and made for him a helper, a supporter, his wife Eve, and from both of them came the seed of the human race. And you said, 'It is not good for the man to be alone. Let us make for him a helper like him.' ⁷And now, I did not take this kinswoman of mine for the sake of sexual gratification, but rather out of faithfulness. Grant that mercy may be shown upon her and me and that we may grow old together." ⁸And they said together, "Amen." ⁹And they fell asleep for the night.

But after Raguel stood up, he called the household servants to himself. And they went out and dug a grave. ¹⁰For he said, "Perhaps he died and we might become a laughingstock and a cause for insult." ¹¹And when they finished digging the grave, Raguel went into the house and summoned his wife. ¹²And he said, "Send one of the maidservants. And let her go inside and see whether he is alive. But if he has died, we should bury him so that no one may know." ¹³And they sent the maidservant, and she lit the lamp and opened the door. And she went in and found them lying down and fast asleep together. ¹⁴And when the maidservant came out, she told them that he was alive and there was no problem. ¹⁵And they blessed the God of heaven and said, "Blessed are you, O God, with every pure blessing; let them bless you for all eternities. ¹⁶And blessed are you because you made me glad; and it did not happen as I had presumed, but, according to your abundant mercy, you acted in such a way toward us. ¹⁷And blessed are you because you had mercy on two only children. Grant to them, Master, mercy and safety; and fill up their lives with joy and compassion." ¹⁸Then he said to his household servants, "Cover up the grave before dawn has come to be."

¹⁹And he told his wife to make plenty of bread; and walking to the herd, he led two oxen and four rams. And he said to kill them, and they started making preparations. ²⁰And he summoned Tobias and said to him, "Do not leave here for fourteen days, but here you will remain, eating and drinking with me. And you will gladden the soul of my daughter, a life that has been much afflicted. ²¹And whatever I have, take at once half and go in good

health to your father. And whenever I along with my wife die, the other half will be yours. Take heart, my child, I am your father and Adnah your mother; and we are with you now, as well as your kinswoman. We will be from now to eternity. Take heart, my child!"

**9** Then Tobias called Raphael and said to him, ²"Brother Azariah, take with you four servants and two camels, and go to Rages. And go to Gabael and give him the bond. Take the money and bring him with you to the wedding. ⁴For you know that my father will be counting the days, and if I waste a single day, I will put him in much distress. ³And you see what Raguel swore, and I am not able to break his oath." ⁵And Raphael set out along with the four servants and the two camels to Rages of Media, and they stayed with Gabael. And he gave him his bond, and he told him about Tobais, the son of Tobit—namely, that he took in marriage a wife and that he was inviting him to the wedding. And he stood up and counted over to him the money bags with the seals. And they set them upon the camels. ⁶And they both rose early in the morning and went to the wedding celebration. And they arrived at the house of Raguel and found Tobias seated at a table. And he jumped up and greeted him, and Gabael wept and blessed him. And he said to him, "Good and noble man, descended from one who is good and noble, righteous and generous in merciful acts, may the Lord grant you a blessing from heaven and to your wife and your father and the mother of your wife. Blessed be God because now I have seen Tobit, my cousin, that is, one who is close in appearance to him."

*The Money Is Recovered*

**10** Each day after day, Tobit kept track of the days—in how many for Tobias' going and in how many for his returning. And when these days had passed and his son did not arrive, ²he said, "Perhaps he was delayed there? Or perhaps Gabael died and there was no one to give him the money?" ³And he began to grieve. ⁴And his wife, Hannah, said, "My child has been killed, and he remains no longer among the living!" And she began to lament and to wail for her son and said, ⁵"Woe to me, my child, for I let you leave, O light of my eyes!" ⁶But Tobit was saying to her, "Quiet down. Do not have concern, my sister. He is fine. Indeed, some distraction came upon him there. And the man who went with him is reliable and one of our brothers. Do not grieve for him, my sister. He is already coming back." ⁷And she said to him, "You should be quiet before me! And do not deceive me. My child has died." And every day she would leap up and scan the road on which her son departed. And she was not consoled by anyone. And when the sun had set, she would go back inside and wail and lament throughout the whole night, and she had no sleep.

*Tobias' Parents Grow Anxious*

And when the fourteen days of the wedding celebration had passed, which Raguel had sworn to observe for his daughter, Tobias went to him and said, "Send me back. For I know that my father and my mother do not believe that they will see me again. And now I entreat you, father, hoping that you will send me back and I can go to my father. I explained already to you how I left him." ⁸And Raguel said to Tobias, "Stay here, my child. Stay with me, and I am going to send messengers to your father, Tobit, and they will explain to him about you." ⁹And he said to him, "Certainly not! I entreat you to send me back from here to my father." ¹⁰And Raguel stood up and handed over to Tobias his wife Sarah and half of all that belonged to him:

servants, maidservants, cows, sheep, donkeys, camels, clothing, silver, and furniture. ¹¹And he sent them off safely. And he embraced him and said to him, "Farewell, my child. Go in good health. May the Lord of heaven give you success and also your wife, Sarah. And may I see children of yours before I die." ¹²And he said to his daughter, Sarah, "Go to your father-in-law, because from now on they are your parents as if they had begotten you. Go in peace, dear daughter. May I hear about you a good report as long as I live." And saying farewell, he sent them away. And Adnah said to Tobias, "My child and beloved brother, may the Lord bring you back so that I may see your children as long as I am alive and the children of Sarah, my daughter, before I die. Before the Lord, I entrust to you my daughter as a deposit. Do not cause grief for her all the days your life, my child. Go in peace. From now on I am your mother, and Sarah is your sister. May we prosper all together*a* for all the days of our life." And she kissed both of them and sent them off with good wishes. ¹³And Tobias went away from Raguel well and with joy. And he was blessing the Lord of heaven and earth, who is king over all, because he blessed his way. And he said to him, "May it be prosperous for you to honor them all the days their of life."

*The Journey Home* **11** And as they drew near to Kaserin, which is opposite Nineveh, ²Raphael said, "You know how we have left your father. ³Let us run ahead of your wife and prepare the house to which they are coming." ⁴And they both went along together, and he said to him, "Hold the gall bladder in your hands." And the Lord went along with them from behind him and her son. ⁵And Hannah sat down, scanning the road for her son. ⁶And she noticed him coming and said to his father, "Look! Your son is coming along with the man who went with him." ⁷And Raphael said to Tobias before he drew near to his father, "I know that his eyes will be opened. ⁸Smear the gall bladder of the fish on his eyes, and the medicine will spread, and the white films will peel off of his eyes. And your father will look up again and see the light." ⁹And she ran and clung to the neck of her son and said to him, "I have seen you, my child. Now I may die." And she wept. ¹⁰And Tobit stood up and stumbled on his feet. And he went out of the door of the courtyard. And Tobias proceeded toward him, ¹¹and the gall bladder of the fish was in his hand. And he blew on his eyes and held him. And he said, "Take heart, father." And he set the medicine on him and applied it. ¹²⁻¹³And he peeled each of them with his hands from the corners of his eyes. And he clung to his neck ¹⁴and wept and said to him, "I have become able to see you, my child, the light of my eyes!" And he said, "Blessed be God, and blessed be his great name. And blessed be all his holy angels. May his great name be upon us, and blessed be all the angels for all eternity, ¹⁵because he afflicted me, but look, I see Tobias, my son." And Tobias went in rejoicing and blessing God with his whole body, and Tobias showed his father that his journey had gone well and that he had brought the money, and how he had taken Sarah, Raguel's daughter, as wife, and that look, she was on her way, and she was close to the gate of Nineveh.

*Tobit's Sight Restored* ¹⁶And he went out to meet his bride, and he was rejoicing and blessing God as he went toward the gate of Nineveh. And those inhabitants in

---

*a* Lit. "in the same thing"

Nineveh saw him coming, and he was crossing over with his full strength and with no one leading him by hand; and they were amazed. [17]And Tobit confessed before them that God had mercy on him and opened his eyes. And Tobit approached Sarah, the wife of Tobias, his son, and he blessed her and said to her, "Come in as you are welcome, daughter. Blessed be your God who brought you to us, daughter. And blessed is your father, and blessed is Tobias, my son, and blessed are you, daughter. Enter into your house, as you are welcome, with praise and delight. Enter, daughter." On this same day there was rejoicing among all the Jews who were in Nineveh. [18]And Ahikar and Nadab, his relatives, were there rejoicing with Tobit.

**12** And when the wedding celebration had ended, Tobit summoned Tobias, his son. And he said to him, "My child, see to it that you give the payment to the man who went with you, and add extra for him toward his payment." [2]And he said to him, "Father, how much should I give to him for the payment? It would not hurt to give him half of the goods that have come back with me. [3]He brought me back safely, and he helped my wife, and he carried the money with me, and he healed you. How much more should I give to him for payment?" [4]And Tobit said to him, "It is justifiable for him, my child, to receive half of all of which he carried when he returned." [5]And he summoned him and said, "Take half of all of which you carried when you came back as your payment, and go in good health." [6]Then he called the two aside privately and said to them,

*Raphael Discloses Himself*

> "Bless God and acknowledge him before all the living,
>> what good things he has done for you.
> Bless and sing about his name.
> Declare the acts of God to all mortals with honor,
>> and do not hesitate to acknowledge him.
> [7] It is good to hide the secret of a king,
>> but it is good to acknowledge and to disclose the works of God
>> and confess them with honor.
> Do what is good, and evil will not find you.
> [8] Prayer with faithfulness is good,
>> but mercy with righteousness is better;
> or wealth with wrongdoing is good for oneself,
>> but to perform an act of mercy is better,
>> or better than to store up gold.
> [9] Merciful acts rescue one from death, and it cleanses all sin.
>> Those who perform acts of mercy are filled with life.
> [10] Those who do what is sinful and who perform acts of injustice are
>> enemies of their own lives."

[11]"I will tell you the whole truth, and I will not hide from you even one word. Already I have shown you, and I said, 'It is good to hide a secret of a king but better to disclose the works of God with honor.' [12]And now, when you prayed along with Sarah, it was I who brought the record of your prayer before the glory of the Lord, and similarly when you buried the dead bodies. [13]And when you did not hesitate to stand up and to abandon your dinner and used to go and bury the dead, [14]then I was sent to you to

test you. And, at the same time, God sent me to cure your daughter-in-law, Sarah. ¹⁵I am Raphael, one of the seven angels who stand close by and enter before the glory of the Lord."

¹⁶And the two men were shocked and fell on their faces and were afraid. ¹⁷And he said to them, "Do be not afraid! Peace be with you. Bless God for all eternity. ¹⁸As for me, when I was with you, I was not with you for my own profit, but rather according to the will of God. Bless him throughout all the days. Sing praises to him. ¹⁹And look at me; I did not eat anything, but a vision was seen by you. ²⁰And now bless the Lord on the earth, and acknowledge God. Look, I am going up to the one having sent me. Record all these things that have happened to you." And he ascended.

²¹And they stood up, and they were not able to see him any longer. ²²And they were praising and singing songs to God and acknowledging him concerning these great works of his, as an angel of God appeared to them.

*Tobit's Prayer of Thanksgiving*

**13** And he said,

"Blessed be the living God and his kingdom for eternity.
² For it is he who afflicts and shows mercy.
He leads people down to Hades, in the lowest parts of the earth,
and it is also he who brings people up out of the place of great
destruction;
and there is not anything that will escape from his hand.
³ Acknowledge him, you sons of Israel, before the nations,
for it is he who scatters you among them.
⁴ Even in that place, he showed you his greatness.
Now exalt him before every living being,
as he is our Lord, and he is our God, and he is our Father,
and he is God for all eternity.
⁵ He will afflict you for your wrongdoings,
and he will have mercy on all of you out of all the nations
among whom you have been scattered.
⁶ When you turn toward him
with your whole heart
and with your whole soul
to demonstrate before him your faithfulness,
then he will turn toward you,
and he will never hide his face from you anymore.
And now look at what he has done for you,
and acknowledge him with all your voice,
and bless the Lord of righteousness,
and exalt the King of the ages.
¹⁰ And again your tent will be built in you with joy—
and may he give joy to all the captives among you,
and may he love all those who suffer among you and all
generations of eternity.
¹¹ A bright light will shine, reaching all the ends of the earth.
Many nations will come from far away,
and he will cause all the farthest regions of the land to dwell
with your holy name,

carrying their gifts in their hands for the King of heaven.
Generations upon generations will give expressions of joy for you,
    and the name of the chosen for the generations of eternity.

12 Cursed will be all those who speak a harsh word against you;
cursed will be all who cut you down
    and who pull down your towers
    and all those who overthrow your towers
    and who set ablaze your houses.
And blessed will be all those who fear you for eternity.

13 Then go and be glad for the sons of the righteous,
    for all will be gathered together, and they will bless the Lord of
        eternity.

14 Blessed are those who love you,
    and blessed are those who rejoice on account of your peace.
And blessed are all the people who are grieved over you for all
        your afflictions,
    for in you they will be glad and will see every joy from you for
        eternity.

15 My soul praises the Lord, the great King.

16 For Jerusalem will be built into a city,
    his house for all eternity.
I will be blessed should the remnant of my seed come to see your
        glory
    and acknowledge the King of heaven.
And the gates of Jerusalem will be built with sapphire and
        emerald,
    and all your walls with precious stone.
The towers of Jerusalem will be built with gold,
    and their outer fortifications with pure gold.

17 The streets of Jerusalem will be paved with ruby and with the
        stone of Ophir.

18 And the doors of Jerusalem will speak forth with songs of joy,
and all her houses will say:
    'Hallelujah! Blessed be the God of Israel!'
And the blessed will bless his holy name for eternity and beyond."

**14** And the words of Tobit's thanksgiving ended. And he died in peace *Tobit's Parting* when he was one hundred and twelve years old. And he was buried *Counsel* with honor in Nineveh. ²Now he was sixty-two years old when he became handicapped with his eyesight. And after he could see again, he lived in prosperity and performed acts of mercy and still continued to praise God and acknowledge the greatness of God. ³And when he was about to die, he summoned Tobias, his son, and commanded him, saying, "My child, take your children ⁴and hurry off to Media, for I believe the word of God upon Nineveh, which Nahum professed, that all these things will happen, and it will fall upon Assyria and Nineveh. And whatever the prophets of Israel whom God sent have spoken, all these things will happen. And not even one thing will be overlooked out of all of the sayings, and everything will happen in their appointed times. And in Media there will be more safety than in

Assyria and in Babylon. Therefore, I know and I believe that all things that God proclaimed will be fulfilled and will come to pass, and absolutely no word will be in vain out of the words. And our brothers who live in the land of Israel, they will be considered from all, and they will be taken captive out of the good land. And the whole land of Israel will be desolate, and Samaria and Jerusalem will be desolate. And the house of God will also be burned with grief for a time. 5And again God will show them mercy, and God will return them to the land of Israel. And they will again build the house, and not like the first one, until the time when the time of the seasons should be fulfilled. And after these things, they will all return from their captivity, and they will build Jerusalem with honor. And the house of God will be built in it as the prophets of Israel proclaimed concerning it. 6And all the nations that are in all the land, they will all turn around and fear God genuinely. And they will abandon all their idols that led them astray into their vain deception. 7And they will bless the God of eternity in righteousness. All the sons of Israel who are saved in those days and who are mindful of God with sincerity will be gathered together, and they will come to Jerusalem and will live throughout eternity in the land of Abraham with security. And it will be given over to them, and those who love God with sincerity will rejoice, but those who commit sin and acts of injustice will vanish from the whole land. 9And now, my child, I am commanding you: commit yourself as a slave to God in sincerity, and do what is pleasing before him. And for your children, the command is given to submit themselves to do what is righteous and to perform acts of mercy, and that they should be mindful of God, and they should bless his name in every season with sincerity and with all their strength. 8And now, as for you, my child, go away from Nineveh, and do not stay here. 10On whatever day you bury your mother with me, on that same day do not spend the night in its regions. For I see that there is too much wrongdoing in this place, and so much deceit is worked out here. And they are not ashamed. See, my child, what Nadab did to Ahikar, who raised him. Was he not brought down while still alive into the earth? And God repaid the dishonor to his face, and Ahikar went out into the light, but Nadab went into the darkness forever because he desired to kill Acheikaron. Because he showed me mercy, he escaped from the trap of death that Nadab had set for him, and Nadab fell into the trap of death, and it destroyed him. 11And now, my child, observe what mercy accomplishes and what wrongdoing accomplishes, such that it destroys! And, look, my life is ending." And he laid him on his bed, and he died and was buried with honor.

12And when his mother died, Tobias buried her with his father. And they went away, he and his wife, to Media, and he settled in Ecbatana with Raguel, his father-in-law. 13And he cherished them in old age with honor and buried them in Ecbatana of Media. And he inherited the house of Raguel and also the house of Tobit, his father. 14And he died with honor when he was one hundred and seventeen years old. 15And before he died, he saw and heard about the destruction of Nineveh. And he saw its captives being led into Media, whom Cyaxares, the king of Media, took prisoner. And he blessed God for all that he had done for the sons of Nineveh and Assyria. He rejoiced over Nineveh before he died and blessed the Lord God for the eternities of the eternities. Amen.

*Introduction to*

# TOBIT (LONGER VERSION)

T OBIT HAS BEEN PASSED down in two primary forms—a longer and shorter version. The longer version presented in translation here is best attested in the fourth century AD Codex Sinaiticus, itself only rediscovered in the nineteenth century. The shorter version enjoys the wider manuscript support and broader reception. It would, in general, be preferred as the more original since the tendency of scribes and copyists is to expand rather than abbreviate a document. However, the fragments of Tobit discovered among the Dead Sea Scrolls tend in the main to agree with the longer version and, thus, to confirm it as the more original form. The shorter version arose as a result of intentional attempts to improve the literary style of the book, both through eliminating Semitisms and crafting a more concise narration.

—D. A. deSilva

# Tobit (Longer Version)

**1** The book of the words of Tobit the son of Tobiel, the son of Hananiel, the son of Aduel, the son of Gabael, from the seed of Jahzeel, from the tribe of Naphtali, ²who was taken prisoner in the days of Shalmaneser, the king of Assyria, from Thisbe, which was to the right of Kedesh of Naphtali, in the Galilee above Asher.

³I, Tobit, was walking in the ways of truth and with righteousness all the days of my life, and I did many acts of mercy for my brothers and the people who proceeded with me into the territory of Assyria, into Nineveh. ⁴And when I was in my territory, in the land of Israel, being in my youth, all the tribe of Naphtali, my ancestor, withdrew from the house of Jerusalem, which was selected from all the tribes of Israel to sacrifice for all the tribes. And the sanctuary of the habitation of the Most High was sanctified and was built up for the whole generation of eternity. ⁵And all the tribes, and the house of Naphtali my ancestor, had joined in apostasy to sacrifice a heifer to Baal. ⁶And I went alone frequently into Jerusalem to the feasts, as it is written for all Israel as an eternal ordinance, having the firstfruits and the tithe of the produce and the first shorn. ⁷And I gave these things to the priests, to the sons of Aaron, at the altar. I gave the tithe of the produce to the sons of Levi who were attending in Jerusalem, and the second tithe I sold. Then I went, and I expended these things in Jerusalem according to each year. ⁸And the third tithe I gave to those to whom it belonged, as Deborah the mother of my father had commanded, because I was left an orphan by my father. ⁹When I became a man, I took Hannah as a wife from the seed of our father, and I begot Tobias from her. ¹⁰And when we were taken prisoner to Nineveh, all my relatives and those from my family were eating from the bread of the nations. ¹¹But I kept my spirit from eating it, ¹²for I had remembered God with my whole soul. ¹³The Most High granted favor and a good appearance before Shalmaneser, and I was his slave in charge of provisions. ¹⁴I went to Media, and I entrusted to Gabaelos the brother of Gabria at Rages in Media ten talents of silver. ¹⁵And when Shalmaneser died, Achereil his son became king in his place, and his roads became unstable, and I was no longer able to go to Media.

¹⁶In the days of Shalmaneser I did many acts of mercy to my brothers. ¹⁷I gave my bread to those who were hungry and clothing to the naked, and if I beheld anyone from my race who had died and who had been thrown behind the wall of Nineveh, I buried him. ¹⁸And if Achereil the king killed anyone when he came fleeing from Judah, I buried them by stealth, for he killed many in his anger. And the body was sought by the king, but it was not found. ¹⁹But one of those in Nineveh went to inform the king concerning me, that I buried them, and I hid. But after discovering that I was being sought for to be killed, I withdrew, terrified. ²⁰And all the things that were mine were plundered, and nothing was left to me except Hannah my wife and Tobit my son. ²¹Fifty days did not pass until his two sons killed him, and they fled into the mountains of Ararat. And Esarhaddon his son became

king in his place, and he appointed Ahikar the son of Hanael, my brother, over all the accounts of his kingdom and over the whole administration. ²²And Ahikar asked about me, and I came to Nineveh. Now Ahikar was cupbearer, keeper of the signet ring, administrator, and accountant; and Esarhaddon, the son from the second, appointed him; he was my nephew.

**2** When I returned to my house and when Hannah my wife was restored to me with Tobias my son on the feast of Pentecost (which is the holy Feast of Seven Weeks), there was a good dinner prepared for me, andI reclined to eat. ²And I saw a numerous variety of dishes and said to my son, "Go and bring whom you may find of our brothers in need who is mindful of the Lord; and behold, I shall wait for you."

³And when he came back, he said, "Father, one of our people, after he had been strangled, he was thrown away in the marketplace." ⁴Then, before I tasted the food, I jumped up and carried him away into a certain room until the sun went down. ⁵And after I returned, I washed myself and ate my food in sorrow. ⁶Then I remembered the prophecy of Amos just as he said,

> "Your feasts will be turned into mourning
> and all your merriment into lamentation."

⁷And I cried. When the sun had set I went and dug a grave and buried him. ⁸And the neighbors laughed, saying, "No longer does he fear to be killed concerning this thing he is doing, and yet he fled, and now behold, once more he is burying the dead!"

⁹And in the same night I returned from burying the dead, I also fell asleep alongside the wall of the courtyard being defiled, and my face was uncovered. ¹⁰I did not know that sparrows were on the wall; my eyes being uncovered, the sparrows discharged warm dung into my eyes, and white spots appeared in my eyes. And so I went to physicians, but they did not help me. And Ahikar took care of me until I had gone into Elymais. *Tobit Goes Blind*

¹¹And my wife Hannah was earning money by women's work. ¹²She would send off to the owners, and they paid her. And in addition to her wages, they gave her also a young goat. ¹³But when it came to me, it started to bleat, and so I said to her, "Where did the goat come from? It's not stolen, is it? Give it to its owners,ᵃ for it is not lawful to eat what is stolen." ¹⁴But she said, "It was given as a gift to me in addition to the wages." But I did not believe her and said, "Return it to the owners!" And I blushed at her; but replying, she said to me, "Where are your alms and your righteous deeds? Behold, all things are known with you!"

**3** And so being distressed I wept and prayed in grief, saying, ²"You are righteous, O Lord, and all your works and all your ways are mercy and truth, and you judge true and righteous judgment for eternity. ³Remember me and look upon me. Do not punish me for my sins and my oversights and those of my fathers who sinned before you, ⁴for they paid no attention to your commandments. You gave us over to plunder, captivity, and death, and made us a proverb of disgrace to all the nations among which we were dispersed. ⁵And now your many judgments dealing with *Tobit Prays for Death*

ᵃ Lit. "the lords" (also in verse 14)

me are true because of my sins and those of my fathers; for neither have we observed your commandments, nor have we walked in faithfulness before you. ⁶So now deal with me as you see fit. Command to take up my spirit that I may be released and may become dirt, since it is more profitable for me to die than live. For I have heard untrue reproaches, and much grief is within me. Command that I be released of the distress immediately into the eternal place. Do not turn your face away from me."

*Raguel's Daughter Is Falsely Accused* ⁷On the same day at Ecbatana in Media it happened that Sarah the daughter of Raguel was also reproached by her father's maidservants, ⁸because she was given seven husbands but Asmodeus the evil demon killed them before they could be with her as with a wife. And they said to her, "Are you not aware that you have strangled your husbands? You have had seven already, and you have not benefited from any one of them! ⁹Why do you whip us? If they died, go with them! May we never see a son or daughter of yours for eternity!"

¹⁰After she heard these things, she became very distressed so as to hang herself. And she said, "I am the only child of my father. If I do this, it will be a reproach to him, and I will bring down his old age in sorrow to Hades."

*Sarah's Prayer* ¹¹Then she prayed toward the window and said, "Blessed are you, O Lord my God, and blessed be your holy and honorable name for eternities! May all your works bless you for eternity! ¹²And now, O Lord, I set my eyes and my face toward you. ¹³Say to release me from the earth so I may no longer hear a reproach. ¹⁴You know, O Lord, that I am pure from any sin and being with a man, ¹⁵and neither have I defiled my name nor my father's name in this land of my captivity. I am an only-begotten child to my father, and neither is there to him a young child who will become his heir, nor a close relative. Nor yet does he have a descendant for whom I may keep myself for a wife. Seven of mine are already dead! So then why should I live? Now if it does not seem right for you to kill me, command that regard be had on me and show mercy to me that no longer may I hear a reproach."

¹⁶And the prayer of both of them was heard before the glory of the great Raphael. ¹⁷And he was sent to cure the two, to peel off Tobit's white spots and to give Sarah, daughter of Raguel, as a wife for Tobias son of Tobit and to bind Asmodeus the evil demon; for Tobias was entitled to inherit her. At the same time, Tobit returned and entered to his house, and Sarah the daughter of Raguel came down from her upstairs room.

*Tobit's Instruction to His Son* **4** On that same day Tobit remembered about the money that he deposited with Gabael in Rages of Media. ²And he said to himself, "I have asked for death. Why not call Tobias my son so that I can explain to him before I die?" ³So having called him, he said, "Child, if I should die, bury me and do not neglect your mother; honor her all the days of your life and do what pleases her and do not grieve her. ⁴Remember, child, that she experienced many dangers because of you when you were in her belly. When she dies, bury her beside me in the same grave. ⁵Child, be mindful of the Lord our God all the days. Do not want to transgress against his commandments; practice righteousness all the days of your life and do not walk in the ways of unrighteousness. ⁶For when you practice fidelity, there will be successes in all your works and in all your doings of righteousness. ⁷Give alms from your possessions and do not let your eye be envious when you give alms. If you do not turn your face back from any poor individual, then the face of God will not be turned back from you. [8]According to the abundance you have, give alms from them in proportion to the abundance. If you possess a little, do not be afraid to give alms in proportion to the little, [9]for a good treasure you store up for yourself against a day of necessity. [10]For giving alms delivers one from death and will not allow that one to go into darkness. [11]Indeed, almsgiving is a good gift for all who practice it in the sight of the Most High.

[12]"Take heed to yourself, child, to stay away from every kind of fornication. First of all, take a wife from the seed of your fathers, and do not take a foreign wife who is not from the people of your father because we are the sons of the prophets Noah, Abraham, Isaac, Jacob—our fathers from eternity. Remember, child, that they all took wives from their own brothers, and they will be blessed continually with their descendants, and their seed will inherit the earth.

[13]"And now, child, love your brothers and do not behave arrogantly in your heart toward your brothers and the sons and daughters of your people in taking for yourself a wife from them. For in arrogance there is ruin and much confusion, and in worthlessness there is loss and dire poverty, for worthlessness is the mother of hunger.

[14]"Do not delay the wages of every person who may work for you, but pay him right away. If you serve God, it shall be repaid back to you. Take heed to yourself, child, in all your deeds, and be disciplined in all your conduct. [15]And what you hate do to no one. Do not drink wine for drunkenness, and do not let drunkenness go with you on your way. [16]Give[a] some of your bread to the person who is hungry and some of your clothing to those who are naked; and give what is a surplus for you as alms and do not let your eye be envious in your alms giving. [17]Pour out your bread upon the grave of the righteous and do not give it to sinners. [18]Seek counsel from every wise person and do not think lightly about any useful counsel. [19]And bless the Lord God on every occasion, and request from him that your ways be made straight and all the paths and plans be made prosperous. For every nation does not have counsel, but the Lord himself gives all good things, and he makes low whom he wants as he wishes.

"Now, child, remember my commands and do not let them be erased from your heart. [20]And now I should show to you concerning the ten talents of silver that I entrusted to Gabael,[b] the son of Gabri, at Rages of Media. [21]Do not be afraid, child, that we have become poor, for you have many things, if you fear God and depart from all sin and do what is pleasing before him."

**5** Then Tobias answered and said to him, "Father, I will do all things that you have commanded me. [2]But how will I be able to get the money and yet not know him?" [3]So he gave him the certificate and said to him, "Seek for yourself a person who will go with you, and I will pay him wages as long as I live; now go get the money."

[4]And he went to look for a person and found Raphael, who was an angel (but he did not know it). [5]And he said to him, "Am I able to go with you to Rages of Media, and are you acquainted with those places?" [6]And the angel said to him, "I will go with you; I am acquainted with the route, and I have

*Tobias and the Angel Raphael*

lodged with Gabael our brother." ⁷And Tobias said to him, "Wait for me, and I will say it to my father." ⁸And he said to him, "Go, and do not spend too much time there."

⁹And when he went in he said to his father, "Behold, I have found someone who will go with me." And he said, "Call him to me so that I may know from which tribe he comes and whether he is reliable enough to go with you." ¹⁰Then he called him, so he came in, and they greeted one another. ¹¹And Tobit said to him, "Brother, from what tribe and from what country are you? Tell me." ¹²And he said to him, "Are you looking for a tribe and a family or to hire someone who will go along with your son?" And Tobit said to him, "I wish to know, brother, your people and your name." ¹³And he said, "I am Azariah of Hananiah the Great, your brother." ¹⁴And he said to him, "Welcome, brother, and do not be angry with me, because I sought to know your tribe and your lineage. You happen to be my brother from a good and noble family, for I knew Hananiah and Jathan the sons of Shemaiah the Great when we used to travel together into Jerusalem to worship, offering the firstborn and the tithes of the produce, and they did not go astray in the deception of our brothers. You are from a good stock, brother. ¹⁵But say to me what sort of wages I shall pay you—a drachma per day and the things necessary for you, as also for my son? ¹⁶And moreover, I will give something to you in addition to the wages if you both return safely." ¹⁷So they agreed.

Then he said to Tobias, "Get ready for the trip, and may both of you have a successful journey." And his son prepared the things for the journey. And his father said to him, "Go with this person, and God who dwells in the heaven will help both of you on the journey. Let also his angel go along with you both." Then the two of them went out and departed, and the young man's dog was with them.

¹⁸And Hannah his mother cried and said to Tobit, "Why have you sent our child away? Isn't he the staff of our hand in his going in and going out before us? ¹⁹Don't let money overtake money; rather, it should be an offscouring in comparison to our child! ²⁰For as it has been given us to live by the Lord, this is sufficient for us." ²¹Then Tobit said to her, "Don't worry,ᵃ sister, he will come back safely, and your eyes will see him again. ²²For a good angel will go along with him, and his journey will be successful; he will return safely." ¹And so she stopped crying.

*Tobias'*
*Journey to*
*Rages*

**6** ²As they went along the way, they came at evening to the Tigris River and camped there. ³Then the young man went down to wash himself, and a fish leaped out from the river and wished to swallow the young man. ⁴The angel said to him, "Catch the fish!" And so the young man grabbed the fish and threw it on the ground. ⁵Then the angel said to him, "Slit open the fish and remove the heart, liver, and gall. Set them safely aside."

⁶So the young man did as the angel told him. After roasting the fish, they ate it. And both of them continued traveling until they drew near to Ecbatana. ⁷Then the young man said to the angel, "Brother Azariah, what are the liver, heart, and gall of the fish for?"

⁸And he said to him, "As for the heart and the liver, if a demon or evil spirit troubles someone, so let these things make smoke before a man or

---

ᵃ Lit. "Do not have a word"

woman, and no more will the person be troubled. ⁹The gall is for anointing a human who has white spots on his eyes, and he will be healed."

¹⁰And when they drew near to Rages, ¹¹the angel said to the young man, "Brother, today we will lodge with Raguel, for he is your relative, and he has a daughter named Sarah. ¹²I shall speak about her that she be given to you for a wife because her inheritance is entitled to you. For you alone are of her people, and the girl is beautiful and sensible. ¹³So now hear me, and I shall speak to her father, and when we return from Rages we should make the wedding. For I know that Raguel can never give her to another man according to the law of Moses or he shall be liable to death, for the inheritance belongs to you to take her as a bride more than any man." *Raphael's Counsel*

¹⁴Then the young man said to the angel, "Brother Azariah, I have heard the girl has been given seven husbands, and all died in the bridal chamber. ¹⁵And now I am the only one left to the father, and I am afraid, lest going in I may die just as also the former, because a demon loves her who does not harm anyone except those who approach her. So now I am afraid lest I may die and bring down my father's and mother's life with sorrow to their grave because of me, for there is no other son to them who will bury them."

¹⁶The angel said to him, "Don't you remember the words that your father charged you, about you taking a wife from among your people? Now listen to me, brother, because she will become a wife to you. Take no account of the demon, for this very night she will be given to you as a wife. ¹⁷And when you enter into the bridal chamber, you will take coals of incense and place upon them some of the heart and liver of the fish and burn them into smoke. ¹⁸Then the demon will smell the smoke and flee and not return for eternity of eternity. And when you approach her, both of you should arise and cry out to the merciful God, and he will deliver you both and have mercy. Do not be afraid, for she has been prepared for you from eternity. So you will deliver her, and she will go with you, and I suppose that you will have children from her." And when Tobias heard these things, he loved her, and his soul clung to her very much.

**7** Then he came to Ecbatana and arrived at the house of Raguel. And Sarah met him and greeted him, and he them. Then she brought them into the house. ²And he said to Adnah his wife, "How the young man resembles Tobit my cousin!" ³Then Raguel asked them, "Where are you from, brothers?" And they said to him, "We are from the sons of Naphtali, the captives from Nineveh." ⁴Then he said to them, "Do you know Tobit our brother?" ⁵And they said, "He is both alive and well." Then Tobias said, "He is my father." ⁶Then Raguel jumped up and kissed him and cried ⁷and blessed him. Then he said to him, "You are the son of a noble and good man!" And when he heard that Tobit lost his own eyes, he grieved and cried. ⁸Also Adnah his wife and Sarah his daughter cried, and they welcomed them warmly. *In the Home of Raguel*

⁹Then they killed a ram from the flock and set out much food. And Tobias said to Raphael, "Brother Azariah, speak concerning the things that you talked about on the journey, and let the matter be settled." ¹⁰So he shared the matter with Raguel, and Raguel said to Tobias, "Eat, drink, and be merry, for you have the right to take my child in marriage. But I will declare the truth. ¹¹I have given my child to seven husbands, and when they *Sarah and Tobias Wed*

went in to her, they died during the night. Nevertheless be merry for now!" But Tobias said, "I am not tasting anything here until you make a binding agreement with me."[a] So Raguel said, "Take her as a wife from this present time according to the judgment. You are her brother, and she is yours. And the merciful God will prosper you both with the best things." ¹²Then he called Sarah his daughter and, taking her hand, he gave her over to Tobias as a wife, and he said, "Here she is; according to the law of Moses, take her as a wife and bring her to your father." And he blessed them. ¹³Then he called Adnah his wife and, taking a document, he wrote a contract and they closed it with their seals. ¹⁴Then they began to eat. ¹⁵And Raguel called Adnah his wife and said to her, "Dear, prepare the other room and bring her in." ¹⁶So she did as he requested and brought her there, and she cried and understood the tears of her daughter and said to her, ¹⁷"Take courage, child; may the Lord of heaven and earth grant you favor in place of this sorrow of yours. Take courage, daughter!"

*Tobias Defies*
*the Demon*
**8** When they finished dining, they brought Tobias in to her. ²As he went, he remembered the words of Raphael; so he took the coals of the incense and placed on them the heart of the fish and the liver and made them smoke. ³And when the demon smelled the odor, it fled to the upper parts of Egypt, and the angel bound it.

⁴And when they were shut in together, Tobias rose from the bed and said, "Arise, sister, and let us pray that the Lord shows us mercy." ⁵Then Tobias began to pray, "Blessed are you, God of our fathers, and blessed be your holy and glorious name into the eternities! Let the skies and all your creatures bless you! ⁶You made Adam and gave him a helper and support: Eve, his wife. From them has come the seed of humans. You said, 'It is not good for the man to be alone; let us make for him a helper like himself.' ⁷And now, Lord, not on account of lust do I take this kinswoman of mine, but on the basis of fidelity. Grant mercy on me that I may grow old together with her." ⁸And she said with him, "Amen!" ⁹Then both of them fell asleep for the night.

But Raguel rose up and went and dug a grave, ¹⁰saying, "Lest even this one die." ¹¹Then Raguel went into his house, ¹²and he said to Adnah his wife, "Send off one of the maidservants and let them see whether he is alive, and if he is not, that we may bury him, and no one may know about it." ¹³And having opened the door, the maidservant went in and found the two asleep. ¹⁴So when she came out, she told them that he was alive.

¹⁵So Raguel blessed God, saying, "Blessed are you, O God, with every blessing. And let your saints bless you, and all your creatures; all your angels and your chosen ones, let them bless you for eternities! ¹⁶Blessed are you because you have made me glad, and it did not turn out for me as I was expecting, but according to your abundant mercy you have dealt with us. ¹⁷Blessed are you because you have shown mercy on two only-fathered children! Show them mercy, O Master; fulfill their life in health with gladness and mercy!" ¹⁸And then he ordered the servants to fill in the grave.

¹⁹And he made for them a wedding feast for fourteen days. ²⁰And before the days of the wedding feast had come to an end, Raguel swore to him by

---

[a] Lit. "until you establish and are established toward me"

oath that he should not depart from it until the fourteen days of the wedding feast be fulfilled, ²¹and at that time he should take half of his property and go in health to his father. "The rest you will get when I and my wife die."

**9** Then Tobias called Raphael and said to him, ²"Brother Azariah, take with you a servant and two camels and go to Gabael in Rages of Media. Also get me the money and bring him to me to the wedding feast. ³For Raguel has sworn that I should not leave, ⁴and my father is counting the days; so if I should delay much longer, he will be greatly distressed." ⁵So Raphael went and stayed with Gabael and gave him the certificate, and Gabael brought out the sacks with their seals and gave them to him. ⁶Together they rose up early and went to the wedding feast. And Tobias blessed his wife. *The Money Is Recovered*

**10** Now his father Tobit counted each day. And when the days of the journey had ended and he was not coming, ²he thought, "What if they have been put to shame? Or what if Gabael died and no one is giving him the money?" ³So he grieved very much. ⁴And his wife said to him, "The child has perished; that is why he has delayed." Then she began to mourn for him and said, ⁵"Does it not concern me, child, that I sent you, the light of my eyes, away?" ⁶But Tobit said to her, "Quiet! Don't worry;ᵃ he is safe." ⁷But she said to him, "Shut up! Do not deceive me! My child has perished." And every day she would go by the path outside by which he had departed. She would not eat food during the days, and during the nights she would not cease mourning for Tobias her son until the fourteen days of the wedding feast had ended, which Raguel had sworn to make him spend there. And Tobias said to Raguel, "Send me back because my father and my mother no longer hope in seeing me." *Tobias' Parents Grow Anxious*

⁸And his father-in-law said to him, "Stay with me, and I will send messengers to your father, and they will explain to him the things concerning you." ⁹But Tobias responded, "Send me back to my father." ¹⁰And so Raguel stood up and gave to him Sarah his wife and half of his property, slaves,ᵇ livestock, and money. ¹¹And when Raguel blessed them, he sent them away, saying, "The God of heaven will prosper you, children, before I die." ¹²And he said to his daughter, "Honor your in-laws; they are now your parents. May I hear good news about you." Then he kissed her.

Then Adnah said to Tobias, "Beloved brother, the Lord of heaven will restore you, and may he grant me to see your children from Sarah my daughter so that I may rejoice before the Lord. Now behold, I entrust to you my daughter as a pledge. Do not grieve her."

**11** After these things Tobias went forth, blessing God, because he prospered his way. He also blessed Raguel and Adnah his wife. So he went until he drew near to Nineveh. *The Journey Home*

²Then Raphael said to Tobias, "Don't you know, brother, how you left your father? ³Let us run ahead of your wife and prepare the house. ⁴Now take in your hand the gall of the fish." So they went, and the dog came along behind them. ⁵And Hannah sat and kept looking at the path for her child. ⁶Then she noticed him coming. She said to his father, "Look! My son is coming and the man who went with him!" ⁷And Raphael said, "I know

---

ᵃ Lit. "do not have a word" ᵇ Lit. "bodies"

that your father will open his eyes. [8]You, smear the gall into his eyes, and when it bites, he will rub hard, and he will throw away the whiteness. Then he will see you."

*Tobit's Sight Restored*
[9]And Hannah ran to her son, fell on his neck, and said to him, "I have seen you, child; from now on I am ready to die!" And both of them cried. [10]Then Tobit began toward the door but stumbled. And the son ran to him [11]and took hold of his father and sprinkled the gall on his father's eyes, saying, "Take courage, Father!" [12]And when they started to sting, he rubbed his eyes hard, [13]and the white spots scaled off from the corners of his eyes. Then seeing his son, he fell upon his neck [14]and cried and said, "Blessed are you, O God, and blessed is your name for eternities, and blessed are all your holy angels. [15]For you flogged me, but showed mercy. Behold, I see Tobias my son!" And his son went in rejoicing and announced to his father the magnificent things that happened to him in Media.

[16]Then Tobit went out to meet his daughter-in-law at the gate of Nineveh, rejoicing and praising God. Now those who saw him as he was walking to the gate were astonished because he could see. [17]And Tobit gave thanks before them because God had been merciful to them. Then as Tobit approached Sarah his daughter-in-law, he blessed her, saying, "May you come in good health, daughter. Blessed be God who brought you to us, and blessed be your father and your mother." And there was joy among all his brothers in Nineveh. [18]And Ahikar was present, and Nadab his nephew. [19]Then the wedding feast of Tobias was held with gladness for seven days.

**12** Then Tobit called to his son Tobias and said to him, "My child, see to the wages for the man who went with you; it is necessary to add something extra for him." [2]And he said, "Father, it is no harm to give him half of what I have brought back, [3]for he has brought me safe to you, attended to my wife, brought my money, and likewise he attended to you." [4]Then the old man said, "That is the right amount for him."[a]

*Raphael's Hymn*
[5]So he called the angel and said to him, "Take half of all that you have brought back." [6]And when he had called the two privately, he said to them,

> "Bless God and acknowledge him!
> Ascribe greatness to him,
>> and acknowledge to him before all the living concerning
>>> what he has done for you!
> It is good to bless God and to lift up his name,
>> declaring honorably the accounts of the works of God.
> Now do not hesitate to acknowledge him!
> [7] It is good to conceal the mystery of a king,
>> but it is glorious to reveal the works of God.
> Do what is good, and evil things will not befall you.
> [8] Prayer is good with fasting, almsgiving, and righteousness.
>> Better little with righteousness than much with
>>> unrighteousness.
> It is better to practice almsgiving than to store up gold.

---

[a] Lit. "It is justified for him"

9 Almsgiving delivers from death, and it will cleanse every sin.
   Those who practice almsgiving and righteousness will be filled
      with life.
10 But those who sin are enemies of their own life.
11 I will not conceal anything from you! I have already proclaimed,
   'It is good to conceal the mystery of a king, but it is
      glorious to reveal the works of God.'"

12"And now during the time when you prayed, and your daughter-in-law *Raphael* Sarah prayed, I brought to remembrance the prayer of both of you before *Reveals His* the Holy One; and when you would bury the dead, likewise, I was present *True Self* with you. 13And during the time when you did not hesitate to rise up and leave your meal to go and bury the dead, the good deed was not hidden from me, but I was with you. 14And now God sent me to heal you and Sarah your daughter-in-law. 15I am Raphael, one of the seven holy angels who present the prayers of the saints*a* and enter before the glory of the Holy One."

16Now the two of them were troubled and fell on their face because they were afraid. 17And he said to them, "Do not be afraid! Peace will be with you, and praise God for eternity. 18For it is not by any grace of my own but by the will of your God. Therefore praise him for eternity. 19All the days I appeared to you and neither ate nor drank, but you were seeing a vision. 20And now acknowledge God, because I am going up to the one who sent me. Now write all the things that have been accomplished in a document." 21Then they stood up and did not see him. 22So they continued to acknowledge his great and wonderful works when the angel of the Lord appeared to them.

# 13 Then Tobit wrote a prayer for rejoicing and said,

*Tobit's Prayer of Thanksgiving*

"Blessed be the living God and his kingdom for eternities.
2    For he afflicts and shows mercy, he leads down to Hades
         and brings up from the grave,
      and there is no one who will escape from his hand.
3    Acknowledge him, O sons of Israel, before the nations,
         because he has scattered us among them.
4    There declare his greatness;
         exalt him before every living being.
      For he is our Lord and God;
         he is our Father for all eternities.
5    And he will whip us in our wrongdoings
         and yet again show mercy and gather us out from all
            the nations
         among which you have been scattered.
6    If you turn to him with your whole heart and with your
            whole soul,
         to act in truth before him,
      then he will turn to you
         and not hide his face from you.
      And behold how he will deal with you.
         Then acknowledge him with your whole body;

all that Jonah the prophet has spoken concerning Nineveh, that it will be overthrown. But in Media there will be peace for a time instead. For also our brothers in the land will be dispersed from the good land, and Jerusalem will be desolate, and the house of God in it will burn down and be desolate for a time. ⁵Then again God will show mercy on them, and he shall bring them to the land. And they will build the house, not like the former one, until the times of eternity are fulfilled. Then after these things, they will return from their captivities and build Jerusalem honorably, and the house of God will be built in it honorably just as the prophets spoke concerning it. ⁶And all the nations will turn to truly fear the Lord God; they will bury their idols. ⁷So all the nations will bless the Lord. And his people will acknowledge God, and the Lord will exalt his people. And they will rejoice, all those who love the Lord God in truth and righteousness, showing mercy to our brothers.

⁸"And now, child, depart from Nineveh, for all that the prophet Jonah said will happen. ⁹But you, keep the law and the commandments and be merciful and righteous so that it is well with you. ¹⁰Also bury me properly, and your mother with me. And dwell no longer in Nineveh. Child, consider what Adam did to Ahikar, who had brought him up—how he brought him from the light into the darkness, and all that he requited him. Now Ahikar he has saved, but that other one was rendered his due recompense, and he went down into the darkness. Manasseh gave alms and was delivered from the snare of death that he set for him, but Adam fell into the snare and perished. ¹¹And now, children, see what almsgiving accomplishes and righteousness delivers." And when he had said these things on his bed, his soul came to an end. And he was one hundred fifty-eight years old. And he buried him honorably.

¹²And when Hannah died, he buried her with his father. Then Tobias departed with his wife and his sons into Ecbatana to Raguel his father-in-law. ¹³And he grew old honorably and buried his in-laws honorably, and he inherited their property and also that of Tobit his father. ¹⁴Then he died one hundred seven years old in Ecbatana of Media. ¹⁵Yet before he died, he heard of the destruction of Nineveh, which Nebuchadnezzar and Ahasuerus captured. Before he died, he rejoiced over Nineveh. Amen.

## Introduction to

# JUDITH

**B**Y MEANS OF ITS obvious anachronisms, the book of Judith presents itself as an explicitly fictional version of the kinds of perennial challenges that gentile rulers and their military commanders had posed to the honor of Israel's God and the well-being of the nation, the harrowing circumstances that resulted, and the deliverance that God would ultimately grant. Affronts to God's honor come from outside Israel (in the person of Holofernes, who claims there to be no god greater than his king, Nebuchadnezzar) and from within Israel (in the decision of the besieged elders to surrender their city to Holofernes if God does not deliver them within a particular time frame). Nevertheless, God raises up a heroine, Judith, who will teach both the gentiles and the Israelites that God is supreme—and supremely reliable.

The book was long thought to have been composed in Hebrew but may in fact have been originally composed in Greek—the language in which it had also survived from antiquity. The author appears to have been familiar with a number of episodes from Greek history that have helped shape the dramatic plot of the narrative. Its composition is often dated to the period of the later Hasmonean dynasty. It is of particular interest in its affirmation of the Deuteronomistic view of history, its portrait of Achior (an Ammonite who becomes a full convert to Judaism), and, of course, its heroine's execution of her dangerous stratagem to deliver her people.

—D. A. deSilva

# JUDITH

*The Threat of Nebuchadnezzar* **1** It was the twelfth year of the reign of Nebuchadnezzar, who ruled over Assyria in the great city of Nineveh. In those days, Arphaxad ruled over Medes in Ecbatana. ²And he built in Ecbatana fortification walls round about out of hewn stones, three cubits wide and six cubits long. He also made the wall seventy cubits high and fifty cubits wide. ³And he built towers at the gates a hundred cubits high, and he laid its foundation at sixty cubits. ⁴And he made its gates, being built seventy cubits high and its width forty cubits, for the going out of his mighty force and the deployment of his infantry. ⁵In those days, King Nebuchadnezzar made war against King Arphaxad in the great plain (that is the borders of Reu). ⁶And all the people living in the hill country joined together with him and all the people living beside the Euphrates and the Tigris and the Hydaspes and the plain of Erich, king over the Elymeans. Many nations gathered together to join forces with the sons of the Chaldeans.

*Nebuchadnezzar's Call to Battle* ⁷Then Nebuchadnezzar, king of Assyria, sent to all the people living in Persia and to all those living in the west, those living at Cilicia and Damascus, Lebanon and Antilebanon, and all those living along the face of the coast, ⁸and those among the nations of Carmel and Gilead and upper Galilee and the great plain of Esdraelon, ⁹and all those in Samaria and its cities and on the other side of the Jordan as far as Jerusalem and Bethany and Chelous and Kadesh and the river of Egypt and Tahpanhes and Rameses and the whole land Goshen, ¹⁰as far as and beyond Zoan and Memphis and all those living in Egypt, as far as the borders of Ethiopia. ¹¹But all the people living in the whole land ignored the word of Nebuchadnezzar, king of Assyria, and did not gather together with him in battle because they did not fear him; rather he was like an equal man to them. And they turned back his messengers empty, with dishonor before their face.

*Defeat of Arphaxad* ¹²Then Nebuchadnezzar was very angry at this whole land, and he swore by his throne and kingdom that he would indeed take revenge against all the borders of Cilicia and Damascus and Syria, and that he would kill them by the sword, against all those living in the land of Moab and the people of Ammon and all Idoumaia, and everyone in Egypt, as far as the borders of the two seas. ¹³So in the seventeenth year he organized his army against King Arphaxad, and he was strengthened in the battle and overthrew the whole army of Arphaxad and all of his cavalry and all of his chariots. ¹⁴Thus he took control of his cities and went as far as Ecbatana and captured the towers and looted its broad streets, and its honor he made for its reproach. ¹⁵Then he captured Arphaxad in the mountains of Reu and shot him with his hunting spears and utterly destroyed him until this day. ¹⁶Then he returned with them, he and his force for one hundred and twenty days.

*Expedition against the West* **2** In the eighteenth year on the twenty-second day of the first month, there was talk in the house of Nebuchadnezzar, king of Assyria, of exacting vengeance on the whole land just as he said. ²And he convened all of his attendants and all of his great men, and he set his secret plan before them and completed all the wickedness of the land out of his mouth. ³And then they determined to destroy all flesh who did not obey the word of his mouth.

⁴And it came to pass that as he brought his counsel to a close, Nebuchadnezzar, king of Assyria, called Holofernes, commander-in-chief of his army, being second in command after him, and said to him, ⁵"Thus says the great king, the lord of the whole earth: 'Look, you will go out from my face, and you will take with you men confident in their strength, one hundred and twenty thousand foot soldiers and a multitude of horses with riders, one hundred and twenty thousand. ⁶And you will go out to meet in battle all the western land that resisted the word of my mouth, ⁷and to prepare earth and water, because I shall come out in my anger against them, and I shall cover the entire face of the earth with the feet of my force, and I shall hand them over as plunder by them. ⁸And their wounded will fill their ravines and the swollen streams, and the river shall be filled to overflowing with their corpses. ⁹I shall lead their captives to the ends of the whole earth. ¹⁰After going out, you will seize for me all of their borders, and they will surrender themselves to you. Then you will keep them for me until the day of their punishment. ¹¹But for those who resist you, your eye shall not refrain to deliver them over to slaughter and looting in all of your land. ¹²Because I live, and by the power of my kingdom, I have spoken; thus I shall do this with my hand. ¹³Even you—you shall not deviate from any of the commands of your lord, but in accomplishing you shall accomplish them, exactly as I assigned you, and you shall not delay to do it.'"

¹⁴So Holofernes went out from the face of his lord, and he called all the commanders and generals and officers of the army of Assyria. ¹⁵He also mustered choice men for an army exactly as his lord commanded him, up to one hundred and twenty thousand soldiers and twelve thousand archers on horseback. ¹⁶And he arranged them in the way that great war is organized. ¹⁷He took camels and asses and mules for carrying their baggage, a very great number, as well as sheep and oxen and goats for their provision, which were innumerable, ¹⁸and a great number of provisions for each man and very much gold and silver from the house of the king.

*The Campaign of Holofernes*

¹⁹So he went out with all his power to advance a march before King Nebuchadnezzar and to cover the whole face of the earth to the west, with chariots and horsemen and a land-force of their chosen soldiers. ²⁰And a large mixed group like a swarm of locusts went out with them even like the sand of the earth, for their multitude was innumerable. ²¹And they attacked from Nineveh for three days to the face of the plain of Bectileth; and they camped opposite Bectileth close to the mountain on the left of upper Cilicia. ²²And he took his whole army, his infantry and horsemen and chariots, and he departed from there to the hill country. ²³He cut through Put and Lud and they plundered all the people of Rassis and the people of Ishmael along the desert to the south of the Chaldeans. ²⁴And then he passed alongside the Euphrates and went through Mesopotamia and dug through all of the high cities by the brook of Abron as far as the sea. ²⁵And he seized the borders of Cilicia and killed everyone who resisted him, and he went as far as the border of Japheth toward the south along the face of Arabia. ²⁶He surrounded all the sons of Midian and burned their tents

and plundered their sheepfolds. <sup>27</sup>And then he went down to the plain of Damascus during the days of the wheat harvest and burned all of their fields. And he gave their flocks and herds for destruction, and he plundered their cities and destroyed their plains and struck all their young men with the edge*a* of the sword.

<sup>28</sup>And then fear and terror of him fell upon those living along the seacoast, those in Sidon and Tyre, and those living in Shur and Ocina; and everyone living in Jamnia and in Ashdod and Ashkelon feared him very much.

*Entreaties for Peace* **3** So they sent messengers to him with words of peace, saying, <sup>2</sup>"Look, we the servants of Nebuchadnezzar, the great king, prostrate ourselves at your face. Treat us just as it is pleasing in your presence. <sup>3</sup>Look, our dwellings and our every field of wheat and flocks and cattle and all the sheepfolds of our tents lie before your face; use them according to what would please you. <sup>4</sup>Look, even our cities and those dwelling in them are your servants; come deal with them as seems good in your eyes." <sup>5</sup>The men approached Holofernes and reported to him these words.

<sup>6</sup>Then he went down to the seacoast, he and his army, and guarded the high cities, and they took from them chosen men for allies. <sup>7</sup>And these people and all their surrounding country welcomed him with crowns and dancing and tambourines. <sup>8</sup>And he broke down all their borders, and he cut down their groves since it was given to him to destroy all the gods of the earth so that all the nations should worship only Nebuchadnezzar, and all tongues and their tribes might call upon him as god. <sup>9</sup>And then he went down by the face of Esdraelon close to Dothan, which is opposite the great mountain ridge Judah. <sup>10</sup>And they set up camp between Geba and Scythopolis, and he was there a month of days in order to gather all the baggage of his army.

*Judah Prepares for War* **4** And the sons of Israel living in Judah heard about all the great things Holofernes, the commander-in-chief of King Nebuchadnezzar of Assyria, did to the nations and the way in which he plundered all of their temples and gave them over to destruction. <sup>2</sup>Thus they were very, very afraid from his face, and they were disturbed for Jerusalem and the temple of the Lord their God. <sup>3</sup>For they had recently returned from the captivity, and just now all the people of Judah had gathered together, and the vessels, the altar, and the house had been dedicated from their profanation. <sup>4</sup>So they sent to every border of Samaria, Kona, Beth-horon, Belmain, and Jericho, and to Hobah, Aesora, and the valley of Salem. <sup>5</sup>And they seized in preparation all the highest points of the high mountains, and fortified the villages in them, and put aside provisions in preparation for war since their fields were only recently harvested. <sup>6</sup>And then Jehoiakim, the high priest who was in Jerusalem in those days, wrote to those living in Bethulia and Betomesthaim, which is opposite Esdraelon and faces the plain near Dothan, <sup>7</sup>saying, "Hold fast the ascent of the hills." For through them was the entrance to Judah, and it was easy to hinder them from ascending, since the approach was only wide enough for two men. <sup>8</sup>Thus did the sons of Israel, just as Jehoiakim the high priest and the senate of all the people of Israel, which is seated in Jerusalem, ordered them.

---

*a* Lit. "the mouth"

⁹And then every person of Israel cried out to God in great intensity and humbled their souls with great earnestness. ¹⁰They and their wives and their infants and their livestock, and every resident alien or hireling and their purchased servants, put sackcloth around their loins. ¹¹And every man and woman of Israel and child living in Jerusalem fell down at the face of the temple, and cast burnt ashes upon their heads, and spread out their sackcloth at the face of the Lord. ¹²They even wrapped the altar with sackcloth and cried aloud earnestly to the God of Israel in one accord, that their children be not delivered as plunder, and women as booty, and the cities of their inheritance over to destruction, and the sanctuary to profanation and reproach by the malicious joy of the Gentiles. ¹³So the Lord listened to their voice and saw their affliction; for the people were fasting many days in all Judah and Jerusalem before the sanctuary of the Lord Almighty. ¹⁴And Jehoiakim the high priest and all those who stood before the Lord as priests and ministered to the Lord, having girded their loins with sackcloth, offered the daily burnt offering and prayers and free-will gifts of the people. ¹⁵And there were ashes upon their turbans, and they were crying out to the Lord with all of their strength to look upon all the house of Israel with favor.

5 And it was reported to Holofernes, the commander-in-chief of the army of Assyria, that the sons of Israel had prepared themselves for war and had closed the passes of the hills and fortified every highest point of the highest mountains and set in place traps on the plains. ²And then he was very wrathfully angry, so he summoned all the rulers of Moab and the generals of Ammon and every governor of the seacoast, ³and he said to them, "Tell me the truth, sons of Canaan: What people is this seated in the hill country? And which cities do they inhabit? And what is the multitude of their force? And how much power and strength do they have?ᵃ And who stands over them as king, leading their army? ⁴And why have they alone who dwell in the west not agreed to come meet me?" *The War Council against Israel*

⁵And then Achior, the leader of all the sons of Ammon, said to him, "Let my lord now hear a word from the mouth of your servant, and I shall report to you the truth concerning the people who dwell in the hill country and live in the area near to you. And no lie shall come out of the mouth of your servant. ⁶These people are descended from the Chaldeans. ⁷They formerly dwelt in Mesopotamia because they did not wish to follow the gods of their fathers who were in the land of the Chaldeans. ⁸They departed from the way of their ancestors, and they worshiped the God of heaven, the only God whom they acknowledged, and the Chaldeans drove them out from the face of their gods. Then they fled to Mesopotamia and dwelt there for many days. ⁹And then their God said to come out of their exile and to go into the land of Canaan. So they settled there and prospered in gold and silver and very many livestock. ¹⁰And then they went down into Egypt because a famine had spread over the face of the land of Canaan, and they dwelt there until which time they were nourished. There they became a great number, and their race was innumerable. *Achior Advises against War with Israel*

ᵃ Lit. "in what is their power and their strength"

[11]"So the king of Egypt rose up against them, and they dealt craftily with them with hard work and brick; he humbled them and placed them in servantry. [12]Then they cried out to their God, and he struck the land of Egypt with plagues for which there was no healing, and the Egyptians drove them from their face. [13]Then God dried up the Red Sea before them. [14]And he led them by way of Sinai and Kadesh-barnea, and he drove out all those who lived in the wilderness. [15]Then they occupied the land of the Amorites, and they destroyed all the Heshbonites by their strength; and after crossing the Jordan, they gained possession of all the hill country. [16]And they drove the Canaanite and the Perizzite and the Jebusite and Shechem, and all the Girgashites out of their face and they lived in it for many days.

[17]"As long as they did not sin against their God, good things were with them, because the God who hates iniquity is with them. [18]But when they turned away from the way that was established for them, they were utterly defeated in very many battles, and they were taken as prisoners to a land not their own. Even the temple of their God became a foundation, and their cities were conquered by their enemies.

[19]"And now having returned to their God, they have come up from the dispersion from which place they were scattered, occupied Jerusalem where their sanctuary is located, and settled in the hill country because it was desolate. [20]Now, then, O lord my master, if there is a fault of ignorance among this people and they sin against their God, and we should observe that there is this offence among them, then we shall go up and engage them. [21]But if there is no lawlessness in their nation, let them pass by now, O lord, lest their Lord and God protect and defend them. For then we shall be as a reproach before the whole world."

[22]And it came to pass that as Achior ceased saying these words, all the people encircling the tent and standing around murmured, and the noble men of Holofernes and all those dwelling along the seacoast and in Moab command that he be cut down. [23]"For we shall not fear the sons of Israel. Look! They are a people in whom there is neither power nor strength to make war. [24]Therefore surely we shall go up, and they shall be as a thing devoured by all of your army, master Holofernes."

*Rejection of Achior's Council*

**6** And when the disturbance made by the men standing around the council ceased, Holofernes, commander-in-chief of the army of Assyria, said to Achior before all the foreign people, [2]"And who are you, Achior, also with all the sons of Moab and the hirelings of Ephraim, that you prophesy among us today and say not to make war with the nation of Israel because their God will protect them? And who is god except Nebuchadnezzar? He will send his forces and will destroy them from the face of the earth, and their God shall not rescue them. [3]But we, his servants, will strike them as one person, and they will not be able to resist the might of our cavalry. [4]For with them we shall burn them. And their borders will be drunk with their blood, and their fields will be full of their corpses. Not even the tracks of their feet will be able to resist our face. But they will be annihilated by destruction. So says King Nebuchadnezzar, lord of the whole earth. For thus he commanded, and his words shall not be made futile. [5]But you, Achior, hireling of the Ammonites, you spoke these words on the day of your iniquity. You shall not see again my face from this day until which time I avenge myself upon this race that came out of Egypt. ⁶Then the sword of my army and the troops of my attendants will go through your side, and you will fall among their wounded when they return. ⁷And my servants shall restore you to the hill country and put you in one of the cities along the passages. ⁸And you will not perish until which time you perish with them. ⁹But if you really hope in your heart that they will not be taken, do not let your face fall. I have spoken, and none of my words shall fail."

¹⁰Then Holofernes commanded his servants, who were attending him in his tent, to take hold of Achior and to bring him to Bethulia and to hand him over into the hands of the sons of Israel. ¹¹And his servants took hold of him and led him out of the camp, into the plain, and away from the middle of the plain into the hill country, and they arrived at the springs that were below Bethulia. ¹²And when the men of the city saw them on the top of the mountain, they took up their weapons and attacked out of the city on the top of the mountain, and all the slingers held control of the top of the mountain and threw stones at them. ¹³But after going under a mountain for shelter, they bound Achior and left him thrown by the base of the mountain and departed to their lord. *Achior Delivered to Israel*

¹⁴Now when the sons of Israel came down from their city, they came to him. After unbinding him, they led him into Bethulia and brought him before the rulers of their city ¹⁵(who were, in those days, Uzziah the son of Micah from the tribe of Simeon, and Chabris the son of Othniel, and Charmis son of Malchiel). ¹⁶And he convened all the elders of the city, and all their young men and women ran together to the assembly, and they stood Achior in the midst of all their people, and Uzziah asked him about what happened. ¹⁷He answered and announced to them the decisions of the council of Holofernes and all the words he had spoken in the midst of the ruler of the sons of Assyria and how greatly Holofernes boasted against the house of Israel. ¹⁸Then, falling down, the people worshiped God and cried aloud, saying, ¹⁹"Lord God of heaven, look down upon their arrogance and show mercy upon the humiliation of our race; and look upon the faces of those dedicated to you this day."

²⁰Then they encouraged Achior and praised him very much. ²¹And Uzziah took him from the assembly into his house and gave a banquet for the elders, and they called upon the God of Israel for help that whole night.

**7** On the next day, Holofernes ordered all of his army and all the troops who joined his alliance to break camp, move against Bethulia, seize the ascents of the hill country, and make war with the sons of Israel. ²So all their mighty men broke camp on that day, and the power of their warriors was one hundred and seventy thousand foot soldiers and twelve thousand cavalry, apart from the baggage of the men who were infantry among them, a very great multitude. ³And they set up camp in the valley near Bethulia by the spring, and they spread out breadth near Dothan as far as Balbaim, and in length from Bethulia as far as Cyamon, which is opposite of Esdraelon. ⁴And when the sons of Israel saw the great number of them, they were very troubled, and they said each one to his neighbor, "Now these men shall lick up the face of the whole earth, and neither the high mountains nor the ravines nor the hills will be able to stand up under their *Holofernes Campaigns against Israel* weight." ⁵Then each man took up his implements of war, and after lighting fires on their towers, they stood fast, keeping guard that whole night. ⁶On the second day, Holofernes led out all of his cavalry before the face of the sons of Israel who were in Bethulia. ⁷And he inspected the ascents of their city, he visited the springs of water, and he seized them and placed over them a detachment of warriors. Then he returned to his troops.

⁸All the rulers of the sons of Esau and all the leaders of the people of Moab and the commanders of the seacoast came to him and said, ⁹"Let our master hear now a word, so that defeat does not come to your army. ¹⁰For this people, the sons of Israel, do not rely on their spears but on the height of their mountains in which they dwell, since it is not easy to ascend to the top of their mountains. ¹¹And now, master, do not make war against them as war happens in a battle array, and not a single man from your people will fall. ¹²Wait in your camp, keeping watch over all the men of your army. And let your servants keep control of the spring of water that goes out from the base of the mountain, ¹³since all those dwelling in Bethulia draw water from there. Then thirst will kill them, and they will surrender their city. And we and our people will go up on the tops of the surrounding mountains and will camp before them as protection for not one man to leave the city. ¹⁴They shall waste away in their hunger, both their wives and their children, and before the sword comes upon them, they shall be spread out in the streets of their dwelling. ¹⁵Thus you will pay back to them a repayment of evil because they rebelled and did not meet your face in peace."

¹⁶Their words satisfied Holofernes and all of his attendants, so he gave orders to do just as they had said. ¹⁷So the sons of Ammon moved away from the camp, and with them five thousand of the sons of Assyria. And they set up camp in the valley and seized the water supply and the springs of the sons of Israel. ¹⁸And the sons of Esau and the sons of Ammon went up and camped in the hill country opposite Dothan, and they sent some men from them toward the south and the east opposite of Egrebeh, which is near to Cush, which is on the brook of Mochmur. The rest of the Assyrian army set up camp on the plain and covered all the face of the land, and their tents and baggage camped in a large crowd, and they were a very great multitude.

*The Israelites Besieged* ¹⁹The sons of Israel cried out to the Lord their God because their spirit was discouraged; for all their enemies surrounded them, and there was no way to flee from them. ²⁰And the whole camp of Assyria, their infantry and chariots and cavalry, remained circled around them for thirty-four days, and all the water vessels belonging to those living in Bethulia came to an end. ²¹The cisterns were being emptied out, and they did not have enough water to drink for even one day because it was given to them in measure to drink. ²²Their children were disheartened, and the women and the young fainted*ᵃ* from thirst and were falling in the streets of the city and in the passage ways of the gates. Indeed, there was no strength left in them.

²³Then all the people, the young, the women, and the children, gathered together around Uzziah and the rulers of the city, and they cried out with

---

*ᵃ Lit. "failed"*

a great voice and said before the elders, ²⁴"O God, judge between you and us! For you did great injustice against us by not talking peace with the sons of Assyria. ²⁵And now, there is no help for us; but God has sold us into their hands in order to spread us out before them in thirst and great destruction. ²⁶Now, call them and surrender the whole city to the troops of Holofernes and all of his army for plunder. ²⁷For it is better for us to become plunder for them, for then we will be in servantry, and our soul shall live and not see the death of our infants with our eyes, as well as our women and children giving up their lives. ²⁸We call to witness against you heaven and earth, and our God and Lord of our fathers, who punishes us according to our sins and according to the sins of our fathers, that he might not do according to these words today." ²⁹Then there happened a great weeping in the midst of the assembly, and everyone with one accord cried aloud to the Lord God with a great voice. ³⁰And Uzziah said to them, "Take courage, brothers; let us hold on another five days, in which time the Lord our God will turn his mercy upon us. For he will not forsake us in the end. ³¹But if these days go by and help should not come to us, I shall do according to your words." ³²And he dispersed the troops to each of their posts, and they departed to the walls and the towers of their city. And he sent away the women and children to their homes, and there was much humiliation in the city.

**8** And in those days, Judith heard about these things. She was the daugh- *The Story* ter of Merari son of Uz, son of Joseph, son of Uzziel, son of Hilkiah, son *of Judith* of Elijah, son of Hilkiah, son of Eliab, son of Nathanael, son of Shelumiel, son of Sarasadai, son of Israel. ²Her husband was Manasseh of her tribe and family, and he died in the days of the barley harvest. ³For he stood over the binding of the sheaf in the field, and the burning heat came upon his head, and he fell upon his bed and died in Bethulia, his city. So they buried him with his fathers in the field between Dothan and Balamon. ⁴And Judith was living as a widow in her house for three years and four months.

⁵She made for herself a tent on the roof of her house, and she placed around her loins sackcloth, and the garments of her widowhood were on her. ⁶And she was fasting all the days of her widowhood except for the day before the Sabbath and the day of the Sabbath, and the day before a new moon and the holidays and joyful days of the house of Israel. ⁷And she was shapely in form and very beautiful in appearance. And her husband, Manasseh, left for her gold and silver and male and female servants and livestock and fields, and she continued to live on them. ⁸There was no one who brought an evil word against her because she feared God very much.

⁹Now she heard the evil words of the people against the rulers because *Judith's* they were faint over the lack of water. And Judith heard all the words *Appeal to* that Uzziah spoke to them, who swore to them to surrender the city to *the Elders* the Assyrians after five days. ¹⁰So she sent her maid, the one who was set over all of her possessions, to summon Chabris and Charmis, the elders of her city. ¹¹They came to her, and she said to them, "Hear me, O rulers of those who dwell in Bethulia! For the words that you spoke before the people on this day are not right. You confirmed the oath that you spoke between God and you, and you promised to surrender the city to our enemies unless in these days the Lord should turn and help you. ¹²Now,

who are you who put God to the test on this very day and stand in place of God in the midst of the sons of humans? [13]Now you can scrutinize the Lord Almighty, and you will learn nothing until eternity. [14]Since you cannot discover the depths of the heart of humanity, and you cannot comprehend the deliberations of his thoughts, how will you search out God, who made all these things, and learn his mind, and comprehend his reasoning? By no means, brothers, provoke to anger the Lord our God. [15]For if he should not wish to help us in the course of the next five days, he has the power to protect us on the day he wants, or even to destroy us before the face of our enemies. [16]But, as for you, do not demand surety for the counsel of the Lord our God. For God is neither like a human to be threatened, nor like a son of humanity to be turned by entreaty. [17]Therefore, while waiting for deliverance from him, let us call upon him to rescue us, and he will hear our voice, if it were pleasing to him. [18]For it has not occurred in our generation, nor is there today any tribe or family or people or city from among us who has worshiped gods made by hand as happened in the former days. [19]That is why our fathers were given over to the sword and to plunder, and they suffered a great calamity before our enemies. [20]But we have not acknowledged any other God except him, the one from whom we hope that he will not disregard us or any from our nation. [21]Because when we are taken in this way, all Judah will be seated, and our sanctuary will be plundered, and he will seek our blood for their profanation. [22]And the slaughter of our brothers, the captivity of the land, and the desolation of our inheritance will return upon our heads among the Gentiles wherever we serve, and we shall be there an offense and a reproach before those who acquire us. [23]For our servantry will not lead us to favor, but the Lord our God will turn it into dishonor.

[24]"Now, brothers, let us set an example for our brothers, because their lives depend upon us, and the sanctuary, both the house and the altar, rest upon us. [25]Apart from all this, let us give thanks to the Lord our God who tests us just as also our fathers did. [26]Remember all that he did with Abraham and how greatly he tested Isaac and all that happened to Jacob in Mesopotamia of Syria, while tending the sheep of Laban the brother of his mother. [27]For just as he did not burn them for the affliction of their heart, and he also did not punish us; but the Lord whips those who draw near to him, for admonition."

[28]And Uzziah said to her, "All that you said you spoke with a gentle heart, and there is no one who opposes your words. [29]For on this day your wisdom is not manifest beforehand, but from the beginning of your days all the people have perceived your understanding, because the disposition of your heart is good. [30]But the people thirsted very much, so that they forced us to do just as we said to them and to bring upon us an oath that we cannot break. [31]Now pray for us, because you are a pious woman, and the Lord will send rain to fill up our cisterns. Then we will no longer be coming to an end."

[32]So Judith said to them, "Hear me. I shall do the deed that shall extend unto generations of generations through the children of our nation. [33]You shall stand at the city gates this night, and I shall go out with my devoted servant, and within the days after which you promised to surrender the

city to our enemies, the Lord will restore Israel by my hand. <sup>34</sup>But you shall not discover my deed, for I will not speak to you until that which I am about to do is accomplished."

<sup>35</sup>Uzziah and the rulers said to her, "Go in peace, and may the Lord God be before you for vengeance on our enemies." <sup>36</sup>Then they returned from the tent and went to their positions.

**9** Then Judith fell upon her face and put ashes upon her head, and she took off the sackcloth that she had withdrawn. At the same time the incense offering of that evening was being brought into the house of God in Jerusalem, Judith cried out with a great voice to the Lord and said, <sup>2</sup>"O Lord, God of my father Simeon, who gave into his hand a sword for taking revenge on strangers; who opened the womb of a virgin to defilement, uncovered her thigh to disgrace, and polluted the womb to reproach her—for although you said such a thing ought not to happen, still they did it. <sup>3</sup>Because you gave their rulers over to slaughter and their bed, which was ashamed of their deceit, to blood; and you struck servants along with masters and princes upon their thrones. <sup>4</sup>And you gave their wives for plunder and daughters into captivity and all the spoils for distribution among your beloved sons, who also were moved with zeal by your zeal and were sickened by the defilement of their blood and called upon you for help. God, my God, also listen to me, a widow! <sup>5</sup>For you did for those who came before and those also who came afterward; and you intended also the things that are about to happen now, and you planned that which has happened. <sup>6</sup>And those things that you planned were presented and said, 'Look, here we are!' For all of your ways are at hand, and your judgment is with foreknowledge. <sup>7</sup>Look, the Assyrians multiply in their power; they take pride in their horses and riders; they exalt in the strength of their infantry; they put their trust in shield and spear and bow and sling, and they do not know that you are the Lord who crushes wars. <sup>8</sup>The Lord is your name. Dash their strength by your power and destroy their might in your wrath, for they plan to profane your sanctuary, to defile the tabernacle, the repose of your glorious name, to cut down the horn of your altar with a sword. <sup>9</sup>See their arrogance; send your wrath upon their heads. Give into my hand, a widow, the strength for that which I have planned. <sup>10</sup>By the lips of my deceit strike the servant along with the ruler and the ruler along with his attendant; break down their pride by the hand of a woman. <sup>11</sup>For your strength does not depend on numbers, nor your power on those who are strong. But you are the God of the humble, a helper of the inferior, a protector of the weak, a shelter for the forsaken, a savior to those who despair. <sup>12</sup>Yes, yes, God of my father and God of the inheritance of Israel, master of the heavens and the earth, creator of the waters, king of all your creation, give ear to my prayer. <sup>13</sup>Give my words and deceit to wound and bruise those who have planned harsh things against your covenant and your consecrated house and Mount Zion and the house your sons possess. <sup>14</sup>Make your whole nation and every tribe know and see that you are the God of all power and might and there is no other who protects the nation of Israel except you."

**10** And it came to pass that when Judith ceased crying out to the God of Israel and finished all these words, <sup>2</sup>she rose up from lying prostrate and summoned her maid and went down to the house in which she lived

*Judith's Prayer*

*Judith Prepares Her Plan*

during the days of the Sabbaths and during her festal days. ³And she took off the sackcloth that she had been wearing, and she took off her garment of widowhood, washed her body with water, and anointed it with rich perfume. She also arranged the hair of her head and put a headband upon it, and she put on her clothes of merriment, with which she used to clothe herself in the days of the life of her husband, Manasseh. ⁴And she put sandals upon her feet and put on ankle bracelets and rings and earrings and all her jewelry, and she made herself very beautiful for catching the eyes of men, as many as might see her. ⁵Then she gave her maid a skin of wine and a flask of oil and a leather pouch full of grain and dried fig cakes and pure bread; and she wrapped all her vessels and gave them to her.

*Judith Departs for Holofernes' Camp* ⁶Then they set out for the gates of the city of Bethulia, and they found Uzziah and the elders of the city, Chabris and Charmis, waiting for her. ⁷When they saw her—that her face was altered and clothing changed—they marveled at her beauty even very much more, and said to her, ⁸"May the God of our fathers give you favor to accomplish your plans for the exaltation of the sons of Israel and the exaltation of Jerusalem." And she worshiped God. ⁹Then she said to them: "Order that the gates of the city be opened for me, and I shall go out in order to accomplish the things that you spoke of with me." And they ordered the young men to open the gates for her just as they spoke. ¹⁰And they did so, and Judith went out, she and her maid with her. And the men of the city watched her until she had gone down the mountain, until she went through the valley and they could no longer see her.

¹¹And they were walking in the valley in a straight path, and a guard of the Assyrians met her. ¹²And he took hold of her and inquired, "Who are you, and from where do you come, and where are you going?" And she said, "I am a daughter of the Hebrews, and I am escaping from their face because they are about to be handed over to you to be devoured. ¹³And I am going to appear to the face of Holofernes, commander-in-chief of your army, to announce true words and to show before his face a way down that he might go and become master of all of the hill country, and not a single one of his men shall risk body nor the breath of life." ¹⁴And when the men heard her words and observed her face (for she was very marvelous in beauty before them), they said to her, ¹⁵"You have saved your life by hastening to come down to the face of our lord. Now, go to his tent, and some from among us shall conduct you until they hand you over into his hands. ¹⁶And when you stand before him, do not be afraid in your heart; instead, report according to your words, and he shall treat you well."

¹⁷Then they chose from among them one hundred men to accompany her and her maid, and they led them to the tent of Holofernes. ¹⁸And an excited crowd of people formed in camp, for her arrival was proclaimed in the tents; and coming they surrounded her as she stood outside the tent of Holofernes while they reported to him about her. ¹⁹They marveled at her beauty and wondered about the sons of Israel from her appearance. And each one said to his neighbor, "Who can despise this people who have among them a woman such as this? It is not good to allow one single man among them to remain alive, for they will be able to deal craftily with the whole world."

²⁰Then the bodyguards of Holofernes and all of his attendants went out and led her into the tent. ²¹Holofernes was resting upon his bed under a canopy, which was woven from purple and gold and emeralds and costly stones. ²²Then they reported to him about her, and he came out to the entrance of the tent with torches of silver carried before him. ²³And when Judith came before his face and that of his attendants, they all marveled at the beauty of her face; and falling upon her face, she worshiped him. But his servants rose her up.

**11** Then Holofernes said to her, "Take courage, woman, do not have fear in your heart, because I have mistreated no person who has chosen to serve Nebuchadnezzar, king of all the earth. ²Even now, if your people who dwell in the hill country had not despised me, I would not have taken up my spear against them. But they have done these things to themselves. ³And now, tell me, why have you escaped from them and come to us? For you have come to deliverance. Take courage! You shall live through this night, even the nights remaining. ⁴For there is no one who will injure you, but rather you shall be treated well just as happens to the servants of my lord, King Nebuchadnezzar."

*Judith and Holofernes*

⁵Judith said to him, "Accept the words of your servant and let your servant speak to your face, and I shall not report a lie to my lord this night. ⁶If you follow the words of your servant completely, God will bring about something through you, and my lord will not fail in his mission. ⁷For as Nebuchadnezzar, king of all the earth, lives, so also his power lives which he sent you to correct every living being. For not only do humans serve him on account of you, but even the beasts of the field and the livestock and the birds of the air shall live under Nebuchadnezzar and all his house on account of your strength. ⁸For we have heard about your wisdom and the great deeds of your life; and it was reported in all the land that you alone are good in the whole kingdom and mighty in skill and marvelous in the campaigns of war.

⁹"Now, as for the words which Achior spoke in your council, we have heard his words since the men of Bethulia preserved him, and he reported to them all that he spoke to you. ¹⁰Therefore, lord and master, do not ignore his word, but place it in your heart because it is true. For our nation cannot be punished, nor can the sword overpower them, unless they should sin against their God. ¹¹And now, in order that my lord might not become frustrated and unsuccessful, death will fall upon their face; for a sin has seized them in which they will anger their God, at which time they would commit wickedness. ¹²For since the provisions failed them and all water has become scarce, they are planning to lay hands upon their livestock, and all that God has forbidden them in his laws not to eat they are planning to consume. ¹³And the firstfruits of the grain and the tithes of the wine and the olive oil that they closely guarded, having dedicated it to the priests who stand in Jerusalem before the face of our God, they have determined to consume, that which is not permissible for those among the people to touch with their hands.

¹⁴"And they have sent men to Jerusalem, since even those who dwell there have done these things, those that dwell with them for permission from the council of elders. ¹⁵And it shall be when it is reported to them

and they do it, they shall be given over to you for destruction in that day. ¹⁶Therefore I, your servant, having witnessed all these things, escaped away from their face, and God sent me to accomplish with you deeds at which the whole earth will be confounded, as many as would hear about them. ¹⁷For your servant is pious and attends to the God of the heavens night and day. And now I shall remain beside you, my lord, and your servant shall go out each night into the ravine, and I shall pray to God, and he will tell me when they have committed their sins. ¹⁸And after returning, I shall report to you, and you will go out with all your army, and there is not one from among them who shall resist you. ¹⁹Then I shall lead you through the midst of Judah until you come before Jerusalem, and I shall set your seat in the midst of it. Indeed, you will lead them like sheep for whom there is no shepherd, and no dog shall growl with its tongue before you because this was told to me according to my foreknowledge; it was announced to me, and I was sent to report it to you."

²⁰And her words pleased Holofernes and all his attendants, and they marveled at her wisdom, and they said, ²¹"There is no woman such as this from one end of the earth to the other, in beauty of face and intelligent words." ²²And Holofernes said to her, "God has done well, sending you before the people for strength to be in our hands, but for destruction among those who despise my lord. ²³And now, you are pretty in your appearance and wise in your words; for if you do just as you spoke, your God will be my God, and you shall be seated in the house of King Nebuchadnezzar and will be famous before all the earth."

*Holofernes Makes Judith His Special Guest* **12** Then he commanded to lead her where his silver plates were being set and ordered to prepare some of his food and his wine for her to drink. ²And Judith said, "I shall not eat of them so that I might not cause offence, but it shall be provided from that which has accompanied me." ³Then Holofernes said to her "But if your things come to an end, from where shall we bring things like them to give to you? For there is no one from your nation with us." ⁴Judith said to him, "As your soul lives, my lord, your servant will not consume my things until he does what he has planned by my hand." ⁵And the attendants of Holofernes led her into the tent, and she fell asleep until the middle of the night, and she rose up toward the morning watch. ⁶And she sent to Holofernes, saying, "Permit me now, lord, to allow your servant to go out for prayer." ⁷And Holofernes commanded the bodyguards not to hinder her. And she remained in the camp three days, and she went out each night into the valley Bethulia and immersed herself at the spring of water. ⁸And when she came up, she would ask the Lord God of Israel to direct her path for the raising up of the children of his people. ⁹Then entering clean, she would remain in the tent until she took her food toward evening.

¹⁰And it came to pass that on the fourth day, Holofernes made a drinking party for his servants only, and he did not summon for service any of those on duty.*a* ¹¹And he said to Bagoas, the eunuch who was over all of his things, "Go now, persuade the Hebrew woman who is with you to come to us and eat and drink with us. ¹²For look, it is causing shame to our face

---

*a* Lit. "those at the needs"

if we allow a woman such as this to leave, not having had her company, because if we do not gain her she will laugh at us."

¹³Then Bagoas went out from the face of Holofernes and entered toward her and said, "Let not this beautiful young girl hesitate now from coming to my lord to be honored before his face, and to drink wine with us for merriment, and to become in this day like a daughter of the sons of Assyria who attend in the house of Nebuchadnezzar." ¹⁴And Judith said to him, "And who am I to oppose, my lord? For hastening, I shall do all that is pleasing in his eyes, and this shall be a great joy to me until the day of my death." ¹⁵And rising up, she was adorned with clothing and every feminine ornament, and her servant girl went ahead and spread on the ground before Holofernes the sheepskins that she had received from Bagoas for her daily use in order to eat while reclining upon them. ¹⁶And when Judith entered, she reclined, and the heart of Holofernes was beside itself for her. His spirit was shaken, and he was very eager to have sex with her and was watching for an opportunity to seduce her from the day he saw her.

¹⁷Then Holofernes said to her, "Drink now, and become merry with us." ¹⁸And Judith said, "I shall drink now, lord, because my life has been exalted in me today more than all the days of my birth." ¹⁹And taking that which her servant girl had prepared, she ate and drank before him. ²⁰And Holofernes was delighted by her and drank very much wine; he drank more than he had ever drank in one day since he was born.

**13** And when evening had come, his servants made haste to depart; and Bagoas closed the tent from outside and shut off the attendants from the face of his lord. Then they departed for their beds, for they were all weary since the drinking party had been going on for a long time. ²Judith was left alone in the tent, and Holofernes had fallen upon his bed, for the wine had overcome him. ³And Judith had told her servant girl to stand outside of her bedchamber and to look out for her departure, as on each day; for she said she would be going out for her prayers. She spoke also to Bagoas according to these words. ⁴And everyone departed from the face, and no one was left in the bedchamber from small to great; and Judith, standing beside his bed, said in her heart, "Lord God of all power, look in this hour upon the works of my hands for the exaltation of Jerusalem. ⁵Because now is the time to lay hold of your inheritance and to complete my mission for the destruction of the enemies who rose up against us."

⁶Then, approaching the post of the bed that was close to the head of Holofernes, she took down his straight sword from it. ⁷And drawing near the bed, she grasped the hair of his head and said, "Strengthen me, God of Israel, in this day." ⁸And she struck at his neck twice with her strength, and she took his head. ⁹Then she rolled his body from the bed and took the curtains from the pillars. After a little while she went out and gave to her maid the head of Holofernes, ¹⁰and she threw it into her food bag. Then the two went out together as was their custom, and passing through camp, they circled that valley and went up the mountain of Bethulia, and they came to her gates.

*The Beheading of Holofernes*

¹¹And Judith said from afar to those watching over the gates, "Open, open now the gates! Our God is with us still to build strength in Israel and power against our enemies, just as he did also today." ¹²And it came to pass that when the men of her city heard her voice, they hurried to get down to the gates of their city, and they called the elders of the city together. ¹³And they all, from the least to the greatest of them, ran together because it was incredible to them for her to return. Then they opened the gates and accepted them; and lighting a fire for light, they circled around them.

¹⁴And she said to them with a great voice, "Praise God, give him praise! Praise God, who did not remove his mercy from the house of Israel, but rather broke our enemies into pieces through my hand in this night." ¹⁵Then she brought forth the head from the bag and showed it, and she said to them, "Look, the head of Holofernes, commander-in-chief of the army of Assyria; and look, the curtains in which he was lying in his drunkenness. The Lord struck him by the hand of a woman. ¹⁶And as the Lord lives, who watched closely over me in my way which I went, because my face deceived him for his destruction, he committed no sin with me for defilement and shame." ¹⁷All the people were very amazed, and bowing down, they worshiped God and said in one accord, "Blessed are you, our God, the one who has brought the enemies of your people to naught today." ¹⁸Then Uzziah said to her "Blessed are you, O daughter, to God Most High, above all the women upon the earth, and blessed be the Lord God who created the heavens and the earth, who guided you to wound the head of the ruler of our enemies. ¹⁹For your hope will not depart from the hearts of humans, who remember the strength of God until eternity. ²⁰And may God make them for you an eternal honor, visiting you with good things. Because you did not spare your life on account of the humiliation of our nation, but rather you went out to face our calamity by making a straight path before our God." And all the people said, "Let it be so! Let it be so!"

*Judith's*
*Battle Plan*
**14** Then Judith said to them, "Hear me now, brothers, and take this head and hang it upon the battlement of your wall. ²And it shall be whenever the daybreak dawns and the sun comes out over the land, each one of you will take up your implements of war, and every man of strength will go out of the city. And you will put a leader over them as if you were going down on the plain against the front guard of the sons of Assyria, and yet you will not go down. ³Then, after they take up their armor, they will go to their camp and will awaken the generals of the army of Assyria; and they will run together to the tent of Holofernes, and they will not find him. And fear will fall upon them, and they will flee from your face. ⁴Then, after pursuing them, you and all those dwelling in every border of Israel will slay them on their paths. ⁵But before doing these things, call to me Achior the Ammonite so that, seeing, he might identify the one who disparaged the house of Israel and sent him to us, as if unto death."

⁶So they summoned Achior from the house of Uzziah. And when he came and saw the head of Holofernes in the hand of one of the men in the assembly of the people, he fell upon his face, and his breathing was weakened. ⁷And when they picked him up, he fell at the feet of Judith and did reverence to her face and said, "You are praised in every tent of Judah,

and in every nation, anyone hearing your name will be troubled. ⁸And now, recount to me all that you have done in this day." And Judith reported to him in the midst of the people all that she had accomplished from that day she departed until which time she was talking to them. ⁹And when she ceased speaking, the people raised a cry with a great voice and gave a merry cry in their city. ¹⁰Achior, seeing all that the God of Israel had accomplished, trusted in God very much and circumcised the flesh of his foreskin; and he was added to the house of Israel until this day.

¹¹And when the dawn arose, then they hung up the head of Holofernes from the wall, and every man of Israel took up his weapon, and they went out by divisions to the ascents. ¹²When the sons of Assyria saw them, they sent for their leaders, and they went for the generals and captains and to all of their rulers. ¹³Then they came to the tent of Holofernes and said to the one who was over all of his things, "Awaken our lord now, because the servants have dared to come down against us for battle, so that they might be destroyed in totality." ¹⁴And Bagoas entered and knocked on the curtain of the tent, for he suspected he was sleeping with Judith. ¹⁵And when no one responded, tearing them open, he entered into the bedchamber and found him dead, thrown on the threshold and his head removed from him. ¹⁶And he cried out in a loud voice with weeping and moaning and a mighty cry, and he tore his garments. ¹⁷And he entered into the tent where Judith was staying, and he did not find her; and he leapt out to the people, crying aloud, ¹⁸"The servants have acted treacherously: one woman of the Hebrews has brought disgrace to the house of King Nebuchadnezzar. For look, Holofernes is on the ground, and his head is not on him." ¹⁹And when the rulers of the army of Assyria heard the words, they tore their garments, and their soul was very troubled. And there came from among them shouting and a very loud cry in the midst of the camp.

*Holofernes' Head Presented to His Camp*

**15** When those who were in the tents heard, they were amazed at the things that had happened. ²Then trembling and fear fell upon them, and there was no person remaining before the face of his neighbor yet; but, pouring out with one accord, they fled on every path of the plain and the hill country. ³Those encamped in the hill country around Bethulia also turned to flee. And then the sons of Israel, every man a warrior from among them, poured out upon them. ⁴And Uzziah sent to Betomasthaim and Choba and Chola and to every border of Israel those bringing news about the things that had been accomplished and that all should pour out against the enemy for their destruction. ⁵And when the sons of Israel heard, with one accord they all fell upon them and struck them as far as Hobah. And likewise even those from Jerusalem and from all of the hill country were present, for they had reported to them the things that had happened in the camp of their enemies. And those in Gilead and those in Galilee outflanked them with a great blow until they passed by Damascus and its borders. ⁶And the rest of those dwelling in Bethulia fell on the camp of Assyria. Then they plundered them and became very rich. ⁷When the sons of Israel returned from the slaughter, they took control of the rest, and the villages and hamlets in the hill country and on the plain held much spoil, for there was a very great number.

*The Assyrians Flee*

⁸And Jehoiakim, the high priest, and the elders of the sons of Israel who live in Jerusalem came to look the good that the Lord had done for Israel and to see Judith and to speak peace with her. ⁹And when they came to her, they all blessed her in one accord and said to her, "You are the exaltation of Jerusalem; you are the great pride of Israel, and you are the great boast of our nation. ¹⁰You did all these things by your hand; you accomplished good things with Israel, and God was well pleased on account of them. Be blessed before the all powerful Lord for eternal time." And all the people said, "Let it be so!" ¹¹All the people plundered the camp for thirty days; and they gave to Judith the tent of Holofernes and all the silver plates and couches and bowls and all of his preparation. And taking it, she placed it upon her mule, hitched her wagons, and piled the things upon them.

¹²Then every woman of Israel ran together in order to see her; and they blessed her, and some from among them performed a dance for her. Then she took wands in her hands, and she gave them to the women with her. ¹³And they crowned themselves with olive branches, she and those with her, and she went before all of the people, leading all the women in a dance, and every man of Israel followed, wearing armor with crowns and with hymns in their mouth. ¹⁴Then Judith began this confession in all Israel, and all the people were singing loudly this praise.

*The* **16** Judith said,
*Deliverance*
*Hymn of*        "Go out to my God with tambourines;
*Judith*              sing to the Lord with cymbals.
            Create for him a psalm and a song of praise; exalt and call upon
                  his name.
      2    For the Lord is a God who crushes wars;
                  for into his encampments, in the midst of the people, he
                        removed me
                  from the hand of those pursuing me.
      3    Assyria came from the mountains of the North;
                  he came with the myriads of his forces,
            of whom their great number blocked up the winter streams,
                  and their horses covered the hills.
      4    He said he would set my mountains on fire
                  and kill my young men with the sword
            and put my suckling babies to the ground
                  and deliver up my infants for plunder
                  and despoil virgins.
      5    The Lord Almighty set them aside by the hand of a woman.
      6    For their mighty one did not fall by young men,
                  nor did the sons of the Titans strike him,
                  nor did tall giants set upon him,
            but Judith, a daughter of Merari,
                  brought him down with the beauty of her face.
      7    For she took off the garment of her widowhood for the exaltation
                        of those who suffer in Israel.
                  She covered her face with an anointing,

8 and she tied her hair with a headband,
   and she took a linen garment for charming him.
9 Her sandal ravished his eye,
   and her beauty captured his soul;
   the sword went through his neck.
10 Persia shivered at her boldness,
   and Media was struck by her courage.
11 Then my humble ones raised the war cry,
   and my weak ones were terrified and scared.
   They raised up their voice, and they were turned back.
12 Sons of girls cut them down,
   and, wounded like children of fugitives,
   they perished from the battle line of my Lord.
13 I shall sing a new song to my God:
   O Lord, you are great and glorious,
   marvelous in strength, unsurpassable.
14 Let all of your creation serve you,
   for you spoke, and they came into being.
   You sent your spirit and established it.
   And there is none who can resist your voice.
15 For the mountains will be shaken from their foundations together
         with the waters,
   while the rocks shall melt like beeswax away from your face.
   And yet to those who fear you,
   you are merciful to them.
16 For every sacrifice for sweet smell is a small thing,
   and all fat for a whole burnt offering is insignificant to you.
   But the one who fears the Lord is great forever.
17 Woe to the nations rising up against my race.
   The Lord Almighty shall punish them in the day of judgment;
   he will send fire and worms for their flesh,
   and they will weep in full knowledge until eternity."

18 When they came to Jerusalem, they worshiped God. And when the people were purified, they brought their burnt offerings and their freewill offerings and gifts. 19 And Judith dedicated all the vessels of Holofernes, which the people gave to her, and the curtains that she herself took from his bedroom, she gave them to God for a votive offering. 20 And the people were continually celebrating in Jerusalem at the face of the sanctuary for three months. And Judith remained with them.

21 And after these days, each one returned unto his inheritance, and *Epilogue* Judith departed for Bethulia and remained on her property. In her time she was honored in all the land. 22 Many desired her, but no man knew her all the days of her life from that day her husband, Manasseh, died and she was added to his people. 23 And she was increasing very much, and she grew old in the house of her husband, one hundred and five years. And she set her favorite servant free.*a* She died in Bethulia, and they buried her in the cave

*a* Lit. "she loosed her favorite servant for freedom"

of her husband, Manasseh. <sup>24</sup>And the house of Israel mourned her seven days. She divided her property<sup>a</sup> before she died among all the relatives of Manasseh, her husband, and to those nearest her family. <sup>25</sup>And there was no one who terrified the sons of Israel again in the days of Judith, nor for a long time after she died. Amen.

<sup>a</sup> Lit. "the things belonging to her"

*Introduction to*

# GREEK ESTHER

**P**RAYER, THE INTERVENTION OF God, and any interest in particularly Jewish practices are all notable for their absence from the Hebrew version of Esther. The reader of the Greek version of Esther is immediately struck by the abundant remedy of these deficiencies, especially through the introduction of additional episodes. An opening vision and a concluding interpretation of that vision introduce the strongly theistic frame of God's imparting revelation and God's activity behind the scenes working to assure the deliverance of his people, the Jewish nation. Mordecai and Esther now bathe their circumstances and actions with lengthy and well-crafted prayer. Yet even those parts of Greek Esther that represent translations of Hebrew Esther now include explicit references to God, praying, and Torah-observance. Two further additions provide the text of Haman's edict and its retraction, the former offering a further window into the sources of gentile anti-Jewish prejudice. The result is a version of Esther in which God is fully present and the distinctiveness of Jewish practice is clearly acknowledged.

Some of the additions may well have been composed in Hebrew and added to a version of Esther prior to the translation of the whole into Greek. The additions containing the edicts appear to have been originally composed in Greek. A postscript to Greek Esther points to a time of composition either in the late second century or early first century BC; it was clearly completed well before Josephus turned to it as a source for his *Jewish Antiquities* around AD 90. The work is of interest as an expression of God's providential care for God's people and his special care for this people over against the gentile nations.

—D. A. deSilva

# ESTHER

A *a*In the second year of the reign of Ahasuerus the great king, on the first of Sivan, Mordecai the son of Jair, the son of Shimei, the son of Kish, of the tribe of Benjamin, saw a dream. ²He was a Judean man living in the city of Susa, a great man, attending in the courtyard of the king. ³He was of the body of captives that had been taken prisoner by Nebuchadnezzar, king of Babylon, from Jerusalem with Jeconiah, the king of Judah. ⁴And this was his dream: Behold, voices and clamor, thunders and earthquake, confusion upon the earth. ⁵Behold, two great dragons, both came forth prepared to struggle and a great voice came from them. ⁶And at the sound of their voice, every nation was prepared for war, so that they made war against the righteous nation. ⁷Behold, a day of darkness and gloom, affliction and distress, ill-treatment and great tumult upon the earth. ⁸And the entire righteous nation was troubled, fearing evil things upon themselves. They prepared to be killed ⁹and called to God. And from their cry there appeared, as it were, from a small spring a great river, with much water. ¹⁰Light appeared, and the sun arose, and the humble were exalted and devoured the honorable. ¹¹And having awoken, Mordecai, the one who had seen this dream and what God planned to do, held it in his heart. And with all his reason, he wanted to interpret until the night.

¹²Now Mordecai kept quiet in the courtyard with Gabatha and Harbona, two of the king's eunuchs, who guarded the courtyard. ¹³And he heard their plans and scrutinized their ambitions, and he learned that they were preparing to lay their hands upon King Ahasuerus; and he warned the king about them. ¹⁴Then the king questioned the two eunuchs, and after they confessed, they were led away. ¹⁵And the king wrote these words for a memorial; Mordecai also wrote about these things. ¹⁶Then the king ordered Mordecai to attend in his courtyard, and he gave him gifts because of these things. ¹⁷Now Haman the son of Hammedatha, the Bougaios,*b* was an honored man before the king, and he desired to harm Mordecai and his people on account of the two eunuchs of the king.

1 And it happened after these matters in the days of Ahasuerus—this Ahasuerus ruled over one hundred and twenty-seven territories from India—²in those days, when King Ahasuerus was enthroned in the city of Susa, ³in the third year of his reign, he prepared a banquet for his friends, and for the rest of the nations, and for the honored of Persia and Media, and for the rulers of his satrapies. ⁴And afterward, after he had shown the riches of his kingdom and the glorious splendor of his wealth over one hundred and eighty-four days, ⁵when the days of the wedding feast were completed, the king held a drinking party for the people who were found in the city. It lasted for six days in the courtyard of the king's house. ⁶The courtyard was adorned with fine linen and cotton cloths that were stretched by cords of

---

*a* The Septuagint version of Esther includes six major additions to the Hebrew text, identified as sections A–F
*b* Heb. of 3:1 has "Agagite"

fine linen and purple, fastened to rings of gold and silver on pillars of marble and stone. There were couches of gold and silver on a precious pavement of emerald, pearl, and marble, and diaphanous mattresses, variously adorned with flowers, and roses were scattered round about. ⁷The drinking vessels were of gold and silver, and there was a small cup of carbuncle, an exhibit worth thirty thousand talents. There was abundant sweet wine, which the king himself drank. ⁸Now this drinking party did not take place according to prescribed law, but as the king wanted, and he commanded his stewards to fulfill his and his peoples' desire. ⁹Queen Vashti also held a drinking party for the women in the palace where King Ahasuerus dwelt.

¹⁰Now on the seventh day, when he was merry, the king told Mehuman, Biztha, Harbona, Bigtha, Zethar, Abagtha, and Carcas, the seven eunuchs who were the court servants of King Ahasuerus, ¹¹to bring in the queen before him so that she might reign and put on her diadem, and so that she might show the rulers and the people her beauty, because she was beautiful. ¹²But Queen Vashti refused to come with the eunuchs; and the king was grieved and angry. ¹³Then he said to his friends, "Because of these things that Vashti has spoken, make a law and judgment concerning this matter." ¹⁴So Arkesaios and Sarsathais and Malesear, the rulers of the Persians and the Medes, who were near the king, the first in importance, the ones who sat beside the king, came to him. ¹⁵And they reported to him according to the laws how it was necessary to deal with Queen Vashti, because she had not done the things which were commanded by the king through the eunuchs. ¹⁶Then Memucan said to the king and the rulers, "Queen Vashti has not wronged only the king, but also all the king's rulers and leaders." ¹⁷(In fact he detailed for them the words of the queen and how she had opposed the king.) "Therefore as she has opposed King Ahasuerus, ¹⁸so, today the rest of the princesses of the rulers of the Persians and the Medes, having heard the things that were said by her before the king, will dare likewise to dishonor their husbands. ¹⁹If therefore it seems good to the king, let him prescribe a royal decree, and let it be written corresponding to the laws of the Medes and Persians, and do not let it be used otherwise, and do not let the queen go in to him any longer, and let the king give her queenship to a woman more worthy than she. ²⁰And let the king's law be obeyed, which, if it should work in his kingdom in this way, all the women will show honor to their men, from the poor to the rich." ²¹And the word pleased the king and his rulers, and the king did just as Memucan said. ²²And he sent word throughout all the kingdom, in every territory in their language, so that there would be fear for the men*a* in their houses.

**2** Now after these things, the king ceased from his anger and no longer was mindful of Vashti, recalling what she had said and how he had condemned her. ²And the servants of the king said, "Let uncorrupt and beautiful maidens be sought for the king. ³And the king shall appoint commissioners in all the territories of his kingdom and allow them to choose young maidens, beautiful in appearance, for the harem in the city of Susa, and let them be handed over to the king's eunuch, the guard of the women; and let cosmetics and such other things as needed be given to them. ⁴And

*Esther Chosen as Queen*

---

*a* Lit. "them"

the woman who pleases the king shall reign instead of Vashti." And the command pleased the king, and he did accordingly.

⁵Now there was a Judean in the city of Susa whose name was Mordecai, who was the son of Jair, the son of Shimei, the son of Kish, from the tribe of Benjamin. ⁶He was a captive from Jerusalem, which Nebuchadnezzar, king of Babylon, had captured. ⁷And he had a foster child, the daughter of Abihail, the brother of his father, and her name was Esther. Now when her parents died, he raised her for himself as a wife; and the maiden was beautiful. ⁸So when the ordinance of the king was heard, they gathered together many girls in the city of Susa under the hand of Ai; and he brought Esther to Ai, the guard of the women. ⁹And the maiden pleased him and found favor with him, and he hastened to give her cosmetics and her allotment, and the seven girls appointed for her from the king, and he cared well for her and her maids in the harem. ¹⁰Esther did not reveal her race or her country, for Mordecai had ordered her not to tell. ¹¹And every day, Mordecai walked through the women's courtyard to observe what might happen to Esther. ¹²Now this was the appointed time for a girl to go in to the king, when she had completed twelve months thusly: for the days of treatment comprised six months of being anointed in oil made from myrrh and six months with aromatic spices and women's cosmetics. ¹³And then she goes in to the king; and whatever she asks will be given to her to take with her from the harem into the palace. ¹⁴She enters in the evening and toward morning she hurries away into the second women's apartment, where Ai, the king's eunuch, is the guard of the women; no longer does she go in to the king, unless he calls her by name.

¹⁵And when the time was completed for Esther, the daughter of Abihail, the brother of the father of Mordecai, to go in to the king, the eunuch who guarded the women refused nothing that she commanded, for Esther found favor from all who saw her. ¹⁶And Esther went in to Ahasuerus the king in the twelfth month, which is Adar, in the seventh year of his reign. ¹⁷And the king loved Esther, and she found favor more than all the other virgins, and he placed the queen's crown upon her. ¹⁸Then the king held a drinking party for all his friends and for those with influence; for seven days he celebrated his marriage to Esther and granted rest to those under his reign. ¹⁹Now Mordecai was attending in the courtyard. ²⁰And Esther had not revealed her country, for Mordecai had commanded her to fear God and to keep his commandments, as when she was with him, and Esther did not change her way of life. ²¹But the two eunuchs of the king, the chiefs of the bodyguard, were distressed because Mordecai was promoted, and they were seeking to kill King Ahasuerus. ²²And the matter was revealed to Mordecai, and he made it known to Esther, and she reported the plot to the king. ²³Then the king examined the two eunuchs and hanged them. And the king ordered that a memorial be recorded in the royal library in praise of Mordecai concerning his goodwill.

*Haman's Plot* **3** And after these things, King Ahasuerus exalted Haman son of Hammedatha, a Bougaion,*ᵃ* and he elevated him, and he assumed the first seat among all the friends of the king. ²And all the men in the courtyard

---

*ᵃ* Heb. "the Agagite"

bowed low to him, for thus the king ordered that they do. But Mordecai did not bow down to him. ³And the men in the courtyard of the king said to Mordecai, "Mordecai, why do you disobey the orders spoken by the king?" ⁴Every day they asked him, and he did not listen to them. So they informed Haman that Mordecai was resisting the commandments of the king, and Mordecai pointed out to them that he was a Judean. ⁵Now when Haman learned that Mordecai did not bow down to him, he became very angry; ⁶and he resolved to destroy all the Judeans under the reign of Ahasuerus. ⁷And he made a decree in the twelfth year of the reign of Ahasuerus, and he cast lots day after day and month after month in order to destroy the race of Mordecai in one day; and the lot fell on the fourteenth of the month of Adar. ⁸Then he spoke to King Ahasuerus, saying, "There is at your disposal a nation, which is dispersed among the Gentiles throughout your entire kingdom, and their laws are more peculiar than all the laws of the Gentiles, and they disobey the laws of the king; it is not advantageous to the king to allow them to do this. ⁹If it seems good to the king, let him command to destroy them, and I will draft ten thousand talents of silver for the treasury of the king." ¹⁰And the king removed his ring and placed it in the hand of Haman to seal concerning the things written against the Judeans. ¹¹And the king said to Haman, "You hold the silver, and deal with the nation as you wish." ¹²Then the scribes of the king were summoned in the first month, on the thirteenth day, and they wrote as Haman ordered to the generals and to the rulers over every territory—from India to Ethiopia—to the one hundred and twenty-seven territories and to the rulers of the nations, according to their language from Ahasuerus the king. ¹³And he sent by letter-carriers throughout the kingdom of Ahasuerus that they should destroy the Judean race on the first day of the twelfth month, which is Adar, and that they should plunder their possessions.

¹⁴And copies of the letters were posted publicly in each territory, and it was commanded that all the nations be prepared for this day. ¹⁵And the deed was hastened even in Susa. The king and Haman were getting drunk, but the city was troubled.

**B** ¹And this is a copy of the letter: The Great King Ahasuerus writes these things to the rulers in the one hundred and twenty-seven territories from India to Ethiopia and the governors placed under them: ²"Governing many nations and prevailing over all the world, I do not wish to act haughtily, with arrogant authority, but always considerately and with kindness, to make the lives of my subjects continually calm, to render my kingdom both civilized and passable to its boundaries, and offering to restore the peace desired by all humanity. ³But after inquiring of my advisors how this should be brought to conclusion, Haman—who excels among us in sound judgment, and is distinguished by his unchanging goodwill and steadfast faithfulness, and has obtained the second post of honor in the kingdom—⁴pointed out to us that a certain hostile people is mixed together in all the tribes throughout the world, who are opposed in their laws to every nation and are steadfastly neglecting the ordinances of the kings, so that the common government, administered blamelessly by us, is not established. ⁵Therefore, having comprehended that this nation alone is set continually in opposition to every person, changing

*Haman's Letter*

laws and having entertained a strange way of life, being ill-disposed to our affairs, and is actually accomplishing the most injurious things against the stability of our kingdom; ⁶therefore, we have assigned those who were signified to you in the letters written by Haman, who is set over state affairs and is our second father, to utterly destroy all—along with their wives and children—by the swords of their enemies, without pity and sparing of any, on the fourteenth day of the twelfth month, Adar, of the present year, ⁷so that those people who have long been and are at this very time enemies of the land, having gone down violently into Hades in a single day, may render hereafter to us a continually firmly based and steady public affairs."

*Mordecai Encourages Esther to Act* **4** Now when Mordecai discovered what was being perpetrated, he tore his own garments and put on sackcloth and sprinkled himself with ashes and rushed out through the streets of the city, crying out with a great voice, "A nation which has done nothing unjust is to be destroyed!" ²And he came as far as the gate of the king and stood, for it was not lawful for him to enter into the courtyard wearing sackcloth and ashes. ³And in every territory where the letters were being posted publicly, there was shouting and weeping and great mourning among the Judeans; they brought down sackcloth and ashes for themselves. ⁴Then the queen's maids and eunuchs came in and reported to her, and she was troubled when she heard what had taken place. So, she sent to clothe Mordecai and to take away his sackcloth, but he was not persuaded. ⁵Then Esther summoned Hachratheus, her eunuch who attended her, and she sent him to find out for her from Mordecai the exact situation. ⁷And Mordecai revealed to him what had happened, and the promise which Haman gave to the king of ten thousand talents for the treasury so that he might destroy the Judeans. ⁸He also gave him the copy of the letter that had been published in Susa concerning their destruction to show to Esther, and he told him to command her to go in and entreat the king, "Beg him for our people. Remember your days of low estate, how you were sustained by my hand, because Haman, who is second to the king, has spoken against us for death. Call upon the Lord and speak to the king for us, to deliver us from death." ⁹So Hachratheus went in and told her all these words. ¹⁰Then Esther said to Hachratheus, "Go to Mordecai and say, ¹¹'For all the people of the kingdom know that every man or woman who goes in to the king in the inner court unbidden has no deliverance, however, to whom the king extends the golden scepter, this person will be safe. And I have not been called to go in to the king these thirty days.'" ¹²So Hachratheus told Mordecai all Esther's words. ¹³Then Mordecai said to Hachratheus, "Go and say to her, 'Esther, do not say to yourself that you alone will be saved of all the Judeans in the kingdom. ¹⁴For if you do not listen at this time, there will be help and shelter for the Judeans from another place, but you and the house of your father will be killed; and who knows whether you are queen for this time?'" ¹⁵Then Esther sent him who had come to her to Mordecai, saying, ¹⁶"Go, convene the Judeans who are in Susa and fast for me, and do not eat nor drink for three days, night and day, and I, indeed also my maids, shall fast, and then I shall go into the presence of the king contrary to the law, even if I die."

¹⁷And Mordecai went and did all Esther commanded him.

C¹Then he begged the Lord, remembering all the Lord's works. ²And he *Mordecai's* said, "Lord, Lord, King who rules over all things, for everything is in *Prayer* your power, and there is none who opposes you when you want to save Israel, ³because you made the heaven and the earth and everything that is wonderful under heaven. ⁴And you are Lord of all, and there is none who will oppose you, Lord. ⁵You know all things; you know, Lord, that it was not in insolence, not in arrogance, nor in love of honor that I have done this, to refuse to bow down to the arrogant Haman, ⁶for I would be well pleased to kiss the soles of his feet for Israel's deliverance. ⁷But I did this in order that I might not place the glory of a person above the glory of God, and I will not worship anything except you, my Lord, and I will not do these things in arrogance. ⁸And now, Lord God, the King, the God of Abraham, spare your people, because they look upon us for destruction, and they desired to destroy your inheritance from the beginning. ⁹Do not disregard your portion, which you redeemed for yourself from the land of Egypt. ¹⁰Hear my prayer and be merciful to your lot; and turn our mourning into feasting in order that, living, we may sing of your name, Lord; and do not destroy the mouth that is praising you." ¹¹And all Israel cried out from their strength because their death was before their eyes.

¹²And Esther the queen fled to the Lord, seized in deathly anxiety.[a] ¹³And *Esther's* removing her garments of glory, she put on the garments of distress and *Prayer* grief, and instead of impressive spices, she covered her head with ashes and dung, and she humbled her body very much; and every part that she loved to adorn[b] she covered with her tangled hair. ¹⁴And she petitioned the Lord, God of Israel, and said, "My Lord, you alone are our king. Help me, the one who is alone, not having a helper except you, ¹⁵because my danger is in my hand. ¹⁶I have been hearing from birth in my paternal tribe that you, O Lord, took Israel out of all the nations, and our ancestors from all their forebears, for an eternal inheritance, and that you did for them everything you promised. ¹⁷And now we have sinned before you, and you have delivered us into the hands of our enemies ¹⁸because we glorified their gods. You are righteous, O Lord! ¹⁹And now they are not satisfied with our bitter slavery, but they have placed their hands ²⁰to remove the decree of your mouth and to destroy your inheritance and to stop the mouths of those praising you and to quench your altar and the glory of your house ²¹and to open the mouth of the nations for the wondrous deeds of vain idols and to have a mortal king be marveled at for eternity. ²²O Lord, do not give over your scepter to those who have no being, and do not let them laugh at our downfall, but turn their plan against themselves, and make an example of the one who began this against us. ²³Remember, O Lord; make yourself known in the time of our affliction and encourage me, O King of the gods and Master of all dominion. ²⁴Give eloquent speech into my mouth before the lion and change his heart to hate the one who is fighting against us, to the end of him and of those who agree with him. ²⁵But rescue us by your hand, and help me, the one who is alone and not having a helper except you, O Lord. You have knowledge of all things, ²⁶and you know that I hate the splendor of lawless ones and abhor the bed of the

---

[a] Lit. "a struggle of death"  [b] Lit. "every place of adornment of joy of her"

uncircumcised and of any alien. [27]You know my necessity, that I abhor the sign of my proud position, which is upon my head on days of my appearance. I abhor it like a menstrual rag, and I do not wear it on the days of my rest. [28]And your servant has not eaten at Haman's table, and I have not honored the feast of the king, nor have I drunk the wine of libations. [29]And your servant has had no joy from the day of my transition until now, except in you, O Lord, the God of Abraham. [30]O God, the one who is mighty over all, hear the voice of the despairing, and deliver us from the hands of evildoers, and deliver me from my fear."

*Esther Approaches the King*

**D**[1a]Then it happened on the third day, when she had ceased praying, she took off the garments of her service and put on her glorious clothes. [2]And having become resplendent, after she had called upon God, the Overseer and Savior of all, she took her two devoted slaves, [3]and she leaned upon one, as though she were delicate, [4]and the other one followed, bearing her train. [5]And she was blushing in the flower of her beauty, and her face was cheerful, as to be beloved, but her heart was distressed from fear. [6]And when she had come through all the doors, she stood before the king. He was sitting upon the throne of his kingdom, and he had put on every vestment of his majesty, covered all over with gold and precious stones, and he was very dreadful. [7]And when he lifted up his face, resplendent with glory, he looked with intense rage. Then the queen fell, and her complexion changed in faintness, and she bowed down upon the head of the slave who went before her. [8]And God changed the spirit of the king to gentleness, and being distressed, he sprang from his throne and took her up into his arms until she stood. Then he comforted her with peaceable words [9]and said to her, "What is the matter, Esther? I am your brother. Be bold. [10]You shall not die, for our ordinance is public. [11]Draw near." [12b]Having raised his golden scepter, he laid it upon her neck and greeted her and said, "Speak to me." [13]Then she said to him, "I saw you, lord, like an angel of God, and my heart was terrified for fear of your glory. [14]For you are wonderful, lord, and your face is full of grace." [15]And while she was speaking, she fell from faintness. [16]And the king was troubled, and all his staff comforted her.

*Esther's Invitation*

**5**[3]Then the king said, "What do you want, Esther? What is your petition? Even up to half my kingdom, and it will be yours." [4]And Esther said, "Today is my significant day. If therefore it seems good to the king, let both he and Haman come to the banquet that I shall prepare today." [5]And the king said, "Hasten, Haman, that we may do Esther's request." And both arrived for the banquet that Esther requested. [6]And during the drinking party, the king said to Esther, "What is it, Queen Esther? And it will be as much as you ask." [7]And she said, "This is my request and petition: [8]If I have found favor before the king, let both the king and Haman come again tomorrow to the banquet that I shall prepare for them, and tomorrow I shall do these things."

[9]So Haman went out from the king overjoyed and celebrating, but when Haman saw Mordecai the Judean in the courtyard, he became very angry. [10]And when he entered into his own home, he summoned his friends and Zeresh, his wife. [11]And he told them about his wealth and the glory that the

---

*a* Swete D:1 = Heb. 5:1 *b* Swete D:12 = Heb. 5:2

king had invested in him and how he had made him to have the first place and to lead the kingdom. ¹²And Haman said, "The queen did not invite anyone to the banquet with the king but me, and I have been invited for tomorrow. ¹³And yet these things do not please me whenever I see Mordecai the Judean in the courtyard." ¹⁴Then his wife, Zeresh, and his friends said to him, "Let a pole of fifty cubits be cut down for you, and at daybreak speak to the king, and let Mordecai be hung on the pole. Then go to the banquet with the king and celebrate." And what was said pleased Haman, and the pole was prepared.

**6** But the Lord withdrew sleep from the king that night, so he called his teacher to bring the written daily memoranda to read to him. ²And he found the letters that were written concerning Mordecai, how he informed the king about the two eunuchs of the king when they were guards and sought to lay their hands upon Ahasuerus. ³Then the king said, "What honor or favor have we made for Mordecai?" And the servants of the king said, "You have not done anything for him." ⁴And while the king was inquiring about the goodwill of Mordecai—behold, Haman was in the courtyard. Then the king said, "Who is in the courtyard?" And Haman entered to tell the king to hang Mordecai on the pole that he prepared. ⁵And the servants of the king said, "Behold, Haman is standing in the courtyard." And the king said, "Summon him." ⁶Then the king said to Haman, "What shall I do for the person I want to honor?" And Haman said to himself, "Whom does the king want to honor if not me?" ⁷So he answered the king, "As for the person the king wants to honor: ⁸Let the servants of the king bring a stole of fine linen, which the king wears, and a horse upon which the king rides ⁹and give it to one of the honored friends of the king, and let him dress the person whom the king loves, and let him mount him upon the horse, and let him proclaim through the broad streets of the city, saying, 'So it will be for every person the king exalts.'" ¹⁰And the king said to Haman, "You have spoken rightly. Do so for Mordecai the Judean, who attends in the courtyard, and don't let one word that you have said fall away." ¹¹So Haman took the stole and the horse, and he adorned Mordecai and mounted him upon the horse, and he passed through the broad street of the city, and he proclaimed, saying, "So it will be for every person the king wants to honor!" ¹²Then Mordecai returned to the courtyard, but Haman turned back to his own home distressed, his head covered. ¹³And Haman related the things that had happened to him to Zeresh, his wife, and his friends. Then his friends and his wife said to him, "If Mordecai is of the Judean race, and you have begun to be humbled before him, when falling, you will fall and not be able to withstand him, for the living God is with him." ¹⁴While they were speaking the eunuchs arrived, urging Haman to the drinking party that Esther had prepared.

*Ahasuerus Honors Mordecai*

**7** Now the king and Haman entered to drink together with the queen. ²Then the king said to Esther on the second day during the drinking party, "What is it, Queen Esther? What is your request, and what is your petition? Let it be yours, up to the half my kingdom." ³And she answered and said, "If I have found favor with the king, let my life be given for my request, and my word for my petition. ⁴For we have been sold, both I and my people, for destruction, and plunder, and slavery, we and our children

*Haman's Execution*

for servants and maidservants, and I took no heed, for the slanderer is not worthy of the court of the king." ⁵Then the king said, "Who is this, whoever dared to do this thing?" ⁶And Esther said, "The person, the enemy, is Haman! This is an evil man." Then Haman was terrified by the king and the queen. ⁷And the king stood up from the symposium and went into the garden, but Haman was begging the queen, for he saw himself in trouble. ⁸Then the king returned from the garden, but Haman had fallen upon the couch, begging the queen. And the king said, "So, you assault even my wife in my house?" And when Haman heard this,ᵃ he was confounded in his face. ⁹Then Bougatha, one of the eunuchs to the king, said, "Behold, Haman prepared a pole for Mordecai, who spoke on behalf of the king, and a pole fifty cubits high has been set up at the house of Haman." And the king said, "Let Haman be crucified upon it." ¹⁰So Haman was hanged upon the pole which was prepared for Mordecai, and the king ceased his anger.

*Mordecai's Elevation*

**8** And on that day King Ahasuerus bestowed upon Esther whatever possessions belonged to Haman the slanderer, and Mordecai was summoned by the king, for Esther made it known that he was related to her. ²Then the king took the ring that he had taken from Haman and gave it to Mordecai, and Esther appointed Mordecai over all of the things that had been Haman's. ³And having advanced toward the king, she spoke and fell before his feet, and she begged him to take away the evil of Haman, as great as he had done to the Judeans. ⁴Then the king stretched out the golden scepter to Esther, and Esther raised up to stand near the king. ⁵And Esther said, "If it seems good to you, and I have found favor, let letters be sent to return the letters which were sent by Haman, the letters that were to destroy the Judeans who are in your kingdom. ⁶For how can I bear to see the oppression of my people? How can I dare to be saved amidst the destruction of my country?" ⁷Then the king said to Esther, "If all the possessions of Haman I gave to you, and I showed kindness to you, and I hanged him upon a pole because he laid his hands upon the Judeans, what more do you seek? ⁸Likewise you write in my name as seems good to you and seal it with my ring, for whatever is written from the king, being enjoined and sealed with my ring, it is not for them to oppose." ⁹So the scribes were summoned in the first month, which is Sivan, on the twenty-third day of the same year, and it was written for the Judeans whatever had been commanded to the stewards and the rulers of the satraps from India to Ethiopia, one hundred and twenty-seven satrapies, territory by territory, in the language of each. ¹⁰And it was written through the agency of the king, and it was sealed with his ring, and they dispatched the letters by letter-carriers, ¹¹that he commanded them to use their laws in each city, both to aid them and to help them, against their opponents and those who resist them, as they wish, ¹²in one day in all the kingdom of Ahasuerus, on the thirteenth day of the twelfth month, which is Adar.

*The King's Letter*

**E** ¹The following is a copy of this letter: "The Great King Ahasuerus, to the rulers in the one hundred and twenty-seven satrapies within the territories from India to Ethiopia, and to those who share our purposes, greetings. ²Many men, frequently being honored with the greatest generosity of their benefactors, are presumptuous, ³and not only do they seek to harm our subjects, but not being able to bear prosperity, they endeavor to plot against their own benefactors. ⁴Not only are they canceling the gratitude of people, but, being carried away by the boasts of those who are strangers to goodness, they suppose they shall escape the evil-hating justice of the God who always sees all things. ⁵Furthermore, often encouragement has involved many who have been appointed to offices and entrusted to handle the affairs of friends, in fatal circumstances, having made them accomplices of shedding*a* innocent blood. ⁶By the lying deception of malevolence, men have led astray the innocent goodwill of those who govern. ⁷And it is possible to observe this not so much from the ancient accounts as we have handed down, as it is close to hand, when you observe what has been accomplished wickedly through the pestilent condition of those who rule unworthily. ⁸And for the future, we shall offer to make the kingdom undisturbed, peaceful for all persons, ⁹dealing with the changes and always judging what is to come by its appearance, with a more moderate reply. ¹⁰For when Haman the son of Hammedatha, a Macedonian who was in truth a foreigner to Persian blood and standing far apart from our kindness, though having been hospitable to us, ¹¹obtained the benevolence that we hold for every nation to such a degree that he was publicly proclaimed as our father, and, continuing as the second face from the royal throne, he was worshiped by all. ¹²But not restraining his pride, he attempted from the beginning to deprive us even of our spirit, ¹³of both Mordecai, our savior and perpetual benefactor, and Esther, the blameless companion of our kingdom, along with all their nation. With the ingenious deceptions of stratagems, he asked for their destruction. ¹⁴For by these methods he imagined that he would catch us defenseless, to transfer the dominion of the Persians to the Macedonians. ¹⁵But we find that the Judeans, who were betrayed by this thrice-sinful man for destruction, are not malefactors, but are living by the most righteous laws ¹⁶and are sons of the living God, the most high and greatest, who guides the kingdom both for us and for our ancestors, in the most excellent arrangement. ¹⁷Therefore, do honorably; do not put to use the letters sent by Haman son of Hammedatha, ¹⁸because he who worked out these things was crucified at the gates of Susa with his whole household—God, who rules over all things, having swiftly repaid him a worthy judgment. ¹⁹And openly publishing a copy of this letter in every place, permit the Judeans to use their own laws, ²⁰and join in helping them, so that on the thirteenth day of the twelfth month, Adar, on the same day, they may defend themselves against those who attack them in a time of oppression. ²¹For in place of the destruction of his chosen race, God, who rules over all things, has made this a time of merriment for them. ²²Therefore, you also, among your named feasts, celebrate a notable day with all good cheer, ²³so that both now and afterward it may be a day of deliverance for us and for those favorable Persians, but for those who contrived against us, a memorial of destruction. ²⁴And every city and territory, without exception, that does not act accordingly shall be consumed with

---

*a* Lit. "throwing around"; a term elsewhere used to signify clothing oneself

wrath by spear and fire. It shall be rendered not only desolate for humans, but also hateful for beasts and birds for all time."

*The Publication of the Letter* **8** <sup>13</sup>And the transcript was posted publicly, conspicuously, in all the king-dom, and all the Judeans were prepared on this day to make war on their enemies.

<sup>14</sup>Accordingly, the horsemen went out, hastening to fulfill the orders by the king, and the ordinance was publicized even in Susa. <sup>15</sup>And Mordecai came out adorned in the royal robe and wearing a golden crown and a diadem made of fine purple linen, and the people in Susa rejoiced when they saw him. <sup>16</sup>Then light and merriment appeared for the Judeans <sup>17</sup>throughout every city and territory, wherever the ordinance was publicized. Wherever the proclamation was publicized, there was joy and merriment for the Judeans, feast and mirth. And many of the Gentiles were circumcised and lived as Judeans, for fear of the Judeans.

*The Jews Destroy Their Enemies* **9** For in the twelfth month, on the thirteenth day of the month that is Adar, the letters that had been written by the king arrived. <sup>2</sup>On this day, those who opposed the Judeans were destroyed, for no one withstood, fearing them. <sup>3</sup>For the rulers of the satraps and the tyrants and the royal scribes honored the Judeans, for fear of Mordecai weighed upon them. <sup>4</sup>For the ordinance of the king became known; it was remembered in all the kingdom. <sup>6</sup>And in it, the city, the Judeans killed five hundred men, <sup>7</sup>including Parshan and Nestain and Dalphon and Aspatha <sup>8</sup>and Poratha and Adalia and Aridatha <sup>9</sup>and Parmashta and Arisai and Aridai and Vaizatha, <sup>10</sup>the ten sons of Haman, the son of Hammedatha, the Bougaios, the enemy of the Judeans, and they plundered <sup>11</sup>on the same day. And the number of those who were destroyed in Susa was given to the king. <sup>12</sup>Then the king said to Esther, "The Judeans killed five hundred men in the city of Susa and in the surrounding area. How do you imagine they suffered? What therefore do you deem worthy still to ask? It will be done for you." <sup>13</sup>And Esther said to the king, "Grant the Judeans to do in like manner tomorrow, so that they may hang the ten sons of Haman." <sup>14</sup>So he permitted it to happen in this way, and he published for the Judeans of the city to hang the bodies of the sons of Haman. <sup>15</sup>And the Judeans in Susa were assembled on the fourteenth day of Adar, and they killed three hundred men, but no one plundered. <sup>16</sup>Then the remainder of the Judeans who were in the kingdom were assembled, and they helped themselves and ceased from their warring activities, for they had killed fifteen thousand of them on the thirteenth day of Adar, but no one plundered. <sup>17</sup>So they rested on the fourteenth of the same month and observed the same as a day of rest with joy and merriment. <sup>18</sup>And the Judeans who were in the city of Susa gathered as well on the fourteenth day and rested, but they observed also the fifteenth day with joy and merriment. <sup>19</sup>Therefore, on account of this, the Judeans who are scattered abroad in every territory on the outside observe the fourteenth day of Adar as a good day; with merriment they send portions, each to his neighbor. But those who dwell in the mother-city also observe the fifteenth of Adar for good merriment, also sending forth portions to their neighbor.

*The Feast of Purim* <sup>20</sup>Now Mordecai wrote these words into a document and sent it to all the Judeans in the kingdom of Ahasuerus, to those near and to those far away, ²¹to establish these as good days, to observe both the fourteenth and the fifteenth days of Adar, ²²for in these days the Judeans rested from their enemies, and to observe the entire month, which was Adar, in which it changed for them from grief to joy and from pain to a good day, all the good days of feasting and merriment, to send portions to their friends and to the poor. ²³So the Judeans accepted it just as Mordecai wrote for them, ²⁴how Haman the son of Hammedatha, the Macedonian, made war against them, how he set a decree and a lot to destroy them, ²⁵and how he went to the king, saying that he should hang Mordecai, but as much as he made an attempt to bring evil things upon the Judeans, they came upon him, and he was hanged, and his children. ²⁶On account of this, these days were called Purim because of the lots that in their dialect are called Purim, on account of the words of this letter, and as much as they suffered on account of these things, and as much as happened to them. ²⁷And the Judeans established it and took it upon themselves and upon their seed, and upon those they handed it after them, so that they would not celebrate the month differently, and so that these days would be kept as a remembrance, throughout generation after generation, by city, and family, and territory. ²⁸And these days of Purim will be celebrated for all time, and their remembrance will not come to an end from the generations. ²⁹Then Esther the queen, the daughter of Abihail, along with Mordecai the Judean, wrote all that they did, and the confirmation of the letter concerning Purim. ³⁰ᵃᵇAnd Mordecai and Esther the queen established themselves privately, and then they stood according to their own health and their plan. ³¹And Esther established it by command for eternity, and it was written for a memorial.

**10** Now the king inscribed upon his kingdom, by land and by sea, ²both his strength and bravery, and the wealth and glory of his kingdom; behold, it is written in the document of the kings of the Persians and the Medes for a memorial. ³And Mordecai was next in rank to King Ahasuerus, and he was great in the kingdom and was honored and loved by the Judeans. He told his way of life to all his people.

*Mordecai's Greatness*

**F** ¹And Mordecai said, "These things have come from God. ²For I remembered about the dream that I saw concerning these things, for no item of them failed. ³There was the small fountain that became a river, and there was light and the sun, and much water. Esther is the river whom the king married, and he made her queen. ⁴And the two dragons are I myself and Haman. ⁵And the nations are those that had been gathered together to destroy the name of the Judeans. ⁶But my nation, this is Israel, the people who cried to God, and we were saved, and the Lord saved his people, and the Lord rescued us out of all these afflictions, and God performed signs and wonders, great things that have not been done among the nations. ⁷Therefore he made two lots, one for the people of God and one for all the nations. ⁸And these two lots came for a season and a time and for a day of judgment before God, and for all the nations. ⁹And God remembered his people and justified his own inheritance. ¹⁰And these days in the month of Adar, the fourteenth and the fifteenth of the same month, shall be for

*The Interpretation of Mordecai's Dream*

---

ᵃ Swete 9:30–31 = Heb. 9:31–32  ᵇ The Septuagint does not include Heb. 9:30

them days with a gathering, and joy, and merriment before God, through-out the generations, for eternity among his people Israel."

[11]In the fourth year, while Ptolemais and Cleopatra were reigning, Dositheos, who said he was a priest and Levite, and Ptolemy, his son, brought in to Egypt the preceding letter concerning Purim, which they had affirmed and had been translated by Lysimachus, the son of Ptolemais, one of those in Jerusalem.

*Introduction to*

# WISDOM OF SOLOMON

WISDOM OF SOLOMON WAS composed in well-crafted Greek by a Greek-speaking Jew adopting the literary persona of Solomon, the patron saint of wisdom, as it were. There are hints in the book that the author had personal knowledge of Egyptian religious practice, suggesting composition in a Jewish community there, perhaps even the metropolis of Alexandria (where it exercised particularly early acceptance and authority among Christians like Clement and Origen). The appearance of certain terms and the presentation of the cult of the ruler particularly suggest that the book was composed at some point during the reign of Augustus (31 BC–AD 14) or very shortly thereafter. The author combined a good knowledge of Greek philosophy and ethics with a deep commitment to obey—and to promote obedience to—the commands of the God of Israel.

The book falls into three major sections which are also skillfully woven together. The first section focuses on the oppression that the godly suffer at the hands of those who are not mindful of God's law and the assurance of God's vindication of his righteous ones in the life beyond death. The second offers a greatly expanded version of Solomon's prayer for wisdom (see 1 Kgs 3:4–14) in which the figure and activity of Wisdom are developed in ways that would become formative for the early church's reflection on the person and work of the Son and the relationship of the Son to the Father. The third is a retelling of the story of the plagues that befell Egypt in the course of God's liberation of his people, incidentally, providing lengthy treatments of the origins of idolatry and the consequences of the same for the morality of the gentile nations (containing striking parallels to Paul's treatment of the topic in Rom 1:18–32).

—D. A. deSilva

# WISDOM OF SOLOMON

*Seek Wisdom*
*Not Death* **1** Love righteousness, rulers of the earth.
　　Think about the Lord in goodness,
　　　and seek him in simplicity of heart.
2　Because he is found by those who do not test him,
　　and he is shown to those who do not mistrust him.
3　For perverted reasonings separate people from God,
　　and when the power of God is tested, it rebukes the foolish.
4　For wisdom will not enter into a treacherous soul,
　　nor will it dwell in a body involved in sin.
5　Because a holy spirit of discipline will flee deceit,
　　and depart from thoughtless reasoning,
　　and rebuke the coming of unrighteousness.
6　For the spirit of wisdom is kind
　　and will not leave a blasphemous person unpunished
　　　for his lips,
　　because God is a witness of his kidneys,
　　and the true overseer of his heart,
　　and hearer of the tongue,
7　because the spirit of the Lord has filled the whole world,
　　and the one who holds together all things has knowledge
　　　of every voice.
8　Because of this, no one who speaks unrighteous things will escape
　　　notice;
　　and surely justice, when it rebukes, will not pass by him.
9　For in the counsels of the ungodly there will be close examination,
　　and a report of his words will be presented to the Lord
　　for reproof of his iniquities.
10　Because an ear of jealousy hears all things,
　　and the sound of complaints is not hidden.
11　Therefore guard against useless complaining,
　　and spare the tongue from slander;
　　because a secret utterance will not proceed without result,
　　and a lying mouth destroys the soul.
12　Do not strive for death in the deception of your life,
　　or invite destruction by the works of your hands,
13　because God does not cause death
　　or delight in the destruction of living ones.
14　For he created all things to exist,
　　and the generations of the world bring salvation,
　　and there is no poison of destruction in them,
　　and the kingdom of Hades is not on the earth,
15　　for righteousness is immortal.

16 But the ungodly, by their hands and words, summoned it;
    considering it a friend, they pined away
and made a covenant with it,
    because they were worthy to take part with it.

# 2

For they said in themselves, having reasoned incorrectly,
    "Our life is short and painful,
and there is no healing in the death of a human,
    and no one has been known who returned from Hades.

*The Reasoning
of the Ungodly*

2 Because we were fathered by chance,
    and after this we will be as those who never existed,
because the breath in our nostrils is smoke,
    and the word is a spark in the beating of our heart,
3 when it is extinguished, the body will become ashes,
    and the spirit will be dissolved like empty air.
4 And our name will be forgotten in time,
    and no one will remember our works;
and our life will pass away like the track of a cloud,
    and like a mist it will be scattered,
pursued by the rays of the sun
    and oppressed by its heat.
5 For our life is the passing of a shadow,
    and there is no return from our death,
because it is sealed up and no one returns.
6 Come, therefore, and let us enjoy the good things that exist,
    and let us use the creatures hastily as in youth.
7 Let us be satiated with expensive wine and perfumes,
    and let no blossom of air pass us by;
8     let us crown ourselves with rosebuds before they wilt.
9 Let none of us be without a share of our revelry;
    let us leave everywhere signs of merriment,
    because this is our portion and this is our lot.
10 Let us oppress a poor righteous person;
    let us not spare a widow
    or respect the ancient grey hairs of an old man.
11 But let our strength be the law of righteousness,
    for what is weak shows itself to be useless.
12 Let us lie in ambush for the righteous person, because he is
        burdensome to us,
    and he opposes our works,
and he reviles us for our sins against the law,
    and he accuses us of our sins against discipline.
13 He claims to have knowledge of God,
    and he calls himself a child of the Lord.
14 He has become a reproof to us of our thoughts;
    *a*he is burdensome for us even to see,

---

*a* 2:15 begins here in Heb.

15 because his life is unlike others,
    and his ways are strange;
16 we are considered base by him,
    and he distances himself from our ways as from impurity.
He calls the end of the righteous blessed,
    and he boasts of God as his father.
17 Let us see if his words are true,
    and test the outcome of his life,[a]
18 for if the righteous is the son of God, he will help him
    and rescue him from the hand of those who resist him.
19 Let us examine him by insult and torture,
    that we might know his gentleness
    and judge his patience.
20 Let us condemn him to a shameful death,
    for his examination will be by his words."
21 They considered these things and were misled,
    for their evil blinded them,
22 and they did not know his mysteries,
    or hope for a recompense of piety,
    or consider the reward of blameless lives.
23 Because God created humanity for incorruption,
    and he made it an image of his own peculiar nature;
24 but through the envy of the devil, death entered into the world,
    [b]and those who are party with him experience it.

**The Fate of the Righteous and the Ungodly**

3 But righteous souls are in the hand of God,
    and torment will never touch them.
2 They seemed to have died, in the eyes of the foolish,
    and their departure was considered to be oppression,
3 and their journey from us to be an affliction;
but they are at peace.
4 For even if they are punished in the sight of people,
    their hope is full of immortality;
5 and having been disciplined a little, they will receive great good,
    because God tested them
    and found them worthy of himself.
6 He tested them like gold in a smelting furnace,
    and he received them like a whole burnt offering of sacrifice.
7 And in the time of their examination they will shine out,
    and they will run around like sparks in straw.
8 They will judge nations, and they will rule over peoples,
    and the Lord will reign over them for eternities.
9 Those who trust him will understand truth,
    and the faithful in love will remain with him,
    because grace and mercy belong to his chosen ones.

[a] Lit. "the things in his outcome" [b] 2:25 in Heb.

¹⁰ But the ungodly will have punishment according to what they
reckoned,
those who neglected the righteous and deserted the Lord.
¹¹ For the one who disdains wisdom and instruction is miserable,
and their hope is vain, and their labors are unprofitable,
and their works are useless.
¹² Their wives are foolish
and their children wicked,
and their lineage is cursed.
¹³ Because the blessed is the undefiled barren woman
who has not experienced intercourse in transgression;
she will have fruit at the examination of souls.
¹⁴ And blessed is the eunuch who worked no transgression by hand
or considered evil things against the Lord;
for because of his faithfulness, there will be given to him
choice favor
and a delightful share in the temple of the Lord.
¹⁵ For the fruit of good labors is glorious,
and the root of understanding is infallible.
¹⁶ But children of adulterers will be unable to reach maturity,
and the seed of unlawful intercourse will perish.
¹⁷ For even if they become long-lived, they will be reckoned as
nothing
and dishonored at the end of their old age.
¹⁸ Even if they die quickly, they have no hope
or comfort in the day of decision,
¹⁹ for the ends of an unrighteous generation are grievous.

**4** Better is childlessness with virtue,
for immortality is in the memory of it,
because it is known both by God and humans.
² When it is present, they imitate it,
and they desire it when it is gone;
and it parades in eternity wearing a crown,
having won the fight for the undefiled prizes.
³ But the prolific multitude of the impious will be useless,
and from illegitimate seedlings it will not send roots into
the depth
or establish a secure footing.
⁴ For even if a branch might shoot up again for a time,
standing insecurely, it will be shaken by the wind,
and by the force of the winds it will be uprooted.
⁵ Immature twigs will be broken off,
and their fruit will be useless, unripe for eating
and useful for nothing.
⁶ For children born from lawless sleep
are witnesses of wickedness against their parents at their
examination.

7   But the righteous person, if he predecease others, will be in rest.
8   For a respectable old age is not longevity,
       nor is it measured by number of years;
9   but understanding is grey hair for humans,
       and a spotless life is the maturity of old age.
10  One who was pleasing to God was loved,
       and one who lived between sinners was transferred.
11  He was taken away so that evil would not change his
           understanding
       or treachery deceive his soul.
12  For the envy of worthlessness obscures the good things,
       and roving lust mines an innocent mind.
13  Being perfected in a short time, he fulfilled a long time,
14  for his soul was pleasing to the Lord;
       because of this he hastened out of the middle of wickedness.
   *But the people despite seeing and not understanding,
       or thinking about it,*
15  that grace and mercy are among his chosen ones,
       and examination is among his holy ones.
16  But the righteous dead will condemn the ungodly who live,
       and youth quickly perfected will condemn the great old age* of
           the unrighteous.
17  For they will see the demise of the wise,
       and they will not understand what he planned for him
       and for what purpose the Lord secured him.
18  They will look and despise them,
       but the Lord will laugh at them;
19  and after this they will become a dishonored corpse
       and an insult among the dead throughout eternity,
   because he will break them face down and speechless,
       and he will shake them from their foundations.
   And to the end they will be left dry and barren,
       and they will be in pain,
           and their memory will perish.
20  They will come, fearful, when their sins are calculated,
       and he will rebuke them in opposition because of their
           transgressions.

The Final  **5**  Then the righteous will stand in great confidence
Judgment of          against the face of those afflicting him
the Unrighteous          and those rejecting his labors.
2   When they see it, they will be stirred up with terrible fear
       and be amazed at the unexpected salvation.
3   They will say among themselves, repentant,
       and groan because of the distress of their spirit:
   "This was he whom we once held in derision,

---

*a* 4:15 begins here in Heb. *b* Lit. "setting such a thing in mind" *c* Lit. "will condemn the old age of many years"

and in a proverb of disgrace; ⁴we fools
considered his life madness
and his death dishonored.

5 How was he counted among the sons of God,
and his share is among the saints?

6 So we were misled from the way of truth,
and the light of righteousness did not illuminate us,
and the sun did not rise on us.

7 We were filled in the ways of lawlessness and destruction,
and we traveled through desolate deserts;
but we do not know the way of the Lord.

8 What has arrogance gained us?
And what has wealth with boastfulness benefited us?

9 It passed by all those things like a shadow,
and like a rumor slipping away.

10 Like a ship moving through billowing water,
of which, when it has passed, no track is to be found,
nor the path of its keel in the waves;

11 or, like a bird flying through the air,
no sign of its journey is found,
but the light wind, beaten by the stroke of oars
and split by the force of the rushing,
was traversed by moving wings,
and after this no sign of approach was found in it;

12 or, like an arrow shot at a target,
the air, when pierced, is immediately returned into itself,
so as to be unaware of its passage.

13 In this way also we who were born came to an end,
and indeed, we have no sign of virtue to show,
but we were consumed in our evil."

14 Because the hope of an impious person is like dust being carried
by the wind,
and like frost driven away by a storm,
and like smoke dispersed by the wind,
and, like the memory of a day guest, passes by.

15 But the righteous live for eternity,
and their reward is in the Lord,
and their care is with the Most High.

16 Because of this, they will receive the majestic palace,
and the beautiful diadem from the hand of the Lord,
because he will shelter them with his right hand,
and he will protect them with his arm.

17 He will take zeal as his armor,
and he will make creation a weapon for vengeance against his
enemies.

18 He will put on righteousness as a breastplate
and wear impartial judgment as a helmet.

<sup>19</sup> He will take holiness as an unconquerable shield
<sup>20</sup> and sharpen his severe wrath into a sword,
and the world will fight with him against those with no sense.
<sup>21</sup> Well-aimed arrows of lightning will come,
and they will leap from the clouds to the target as from
a well-drawn bow,
<sup>22</sup> and hailstones full of wrath will be thrown from a catapult;
the water of the sea will be angry against them,
and rivers will overwhelm them relentlessly.
<sup>23</sup> A powerful wind will blow against them,
and like a storm, it will winnow them;
and lawlessness will desolate all the earth,
and wrongdoing will overturn the thrones of the rulers.

*The Judgment*
*of Rulers* **6** Listen, then, O kings, and understand!
Learn, judges of the ends of the earth!
<sup>2</sup> Pay attention, rulers of a multitude,
and those who exalt themselves over crowds of nations.
<sup>3</sup> Because power was given to you from the Lord,
and sovereignty from the Most High,
who will test your works and will search your plans.
<sup>4</sup> Because although you were servants of his kingdom, you did not
judge rightly,
or keep the law,
or proceed according to the plan of God.
<sup>5</sup> He will come upon you terribly and swiftly,
because severe judgment comes on those highly placed.
<sup>6</sup> For the least is pardoned with mercy,
but the mighty will be strenuously tested.
<sup>7</sup> For the Master of all will not withdraw his face
or reverence greatness,
because he himself made great and small,
and he regards all alike.
<sup>8</sup> But a strong inquiry will come upon the mighty.
<sup>9</sup> To you, then, O tyrants, are my words,
so that you may learn wisdom and not fall away.
<sup>10</sup> For those who guard holy things devoutly will be declared holy,
and those who have been taught them will find a defense.
<sup>11</sup> Therefore set your desire on my words;
long for them, and you will be disciplined.

*Finding*
*Wisdom* <sup>12</sup> Wisdom is radiant and unfading,
and she is observed easily by those who love her;
<sup>13</sup> she anticipates those desiring to be known beforehand.
<sup>14</sup> The one who rises early upon her will not labor,
for he will find her sitting beside his gate.
<sup>15</sup> For to ponder about her is the perfection of understanding,
and one who is vigilant because of her will quickly be free
from care,

16 because she goes about seeking those worthy of her,
    and appears to them graciously in their paths,
    and meets them in every thought.
17 For her truest beginning is the desire for discipline,
18     and care of discipline is love;
    and love is the keeping of her laws,
    and attention to laws is confirmation of incorruption,
19 and incorruption brings near to God.
20     So the desire of wisdom leads up to a kingdom.
21 If, then, you delight in thrones and scepters, O tyrants of the
        peoples,
    honor wisdom so that you may rule for eternity.
22 But I will announce who is wisdom and how she came to be,
    and I will not hide the mysteries from you,
    but I will trace her from the beginning of her origin,
    and I will make the knowledge of her into what is manifest,
    and I will never disregard the truth.
23 Nor, indeed, will I travel with wasting envy,
    because this will have no share in wisdom.
24 But the multitude of the wise is the salvation of the world,
    and a prudent king is the stability for a people.
25 Therefore be disciplined by my word, and you will benefit.

**7** Even I am certainly a mortal the same as everyone,
    and offspring of the first-formed earthborn;
and I was shaped into flesh in my mother's belly

*Solomon's
Wisdom*

2     in ten months' time, established in blood
    from the seed of a man and the pleasure of coming together
        in sleep.
3 And when I was born,*a* I drew in the common air
    and fell upon the same earth,
    crying with my first sound the same as everyone.
4 I was nursed in baby clothes and with care.
5 For no king had any different beginning of existence;
6     but there is one entrance into life for all and an identical exit.
7 Because of this I prayed, and understanding was given to me;
    I called upon God, and the spirit of wisdom came to me.
8 I preferred her to scepters and thrones,
    and I considered riches nothing in comparison to her.
9 Nor did I compare her to priceless stone,
    because in her view all gold is like a little sand,
    and silver will be considered as clay before her.
10 I loved her more than health and beauty,
    and I chose to have her instead of light,
    because her light never rests.
11 But all good things together came to me with her,
    and countless wealth is in her hands.

---

*a* Lit. "And I, becoming,"

<sup>12</sup> And I rejoiced about everything because wisdom leads them;
   but I did not know her to be their family.
<sup>13</sup> And I learned honestly, and I shared ungrudgingly;
   I do not hide her wealth,
<sup>14</sup> for it is an unfailing treasure for people,
   which they that use it obtained friendship with God,
   commended because of the gifts of discipline.
<sup>15</sup> But may God grant me to speak with purpose
   and to think worthily of what is granted,
   because he is both the guide of wisdom
   and the corrector of the wise.
<sup>16</sup> For in his hand are both we and our words,
   and all understanding and skill in crafts.
<sup>17</sup> For he gave me truthful knowledge of the things that are,
   to see the structure of the world and the operation of the
      elements,
<sup>18</sup> the beginning and ending and middle of times,
   the changes of cycles and changes of the seasons,
<sup>19</sup> the cycles of the year and the positions of stars,
<sup>20</sup>    the nature of animals and the wrath of beasts,
   the forces of spirits and the reasonings of humans,
   the varieties of plants and the powers of roots.
<sup>21</sup> And I know whatever is hidden and visible,
<sup>22</sup>    for wisdom, the artisan of all, teaches me.

*Wisdom's*
*Power*

For in her is a spirit that is intelligent, holy,
   unique, manifold, gentle,
movable, clear, undefiled,
   distinctive, invulnerable, loving goodness, sharp,
unhindered, beneficent, <sup>23</sup>humane,
   steady, secure, free from care,
all powerful, overseeing all,
   and penetrating through all spirits
   that are intelligent, pure, gentle.
<sup>24</sup> For wisdom is more mobile than any motion,
   and she pervades and penetrates everything because of her
      purity.
<sup>25</sup> For she is the vapor of the power of God
   and the emanation of the pure glory of the Almighty;
   because of this nothing defiled creeps into her.
<sup>26</sup> For she is the brightness of the eternal light,
   and the spotless mirror of the activity of God,
   and the image of his goodness.
<sup>27</sup> But although she is one, she is able to do all things;
   and although she remains in herself, she renews all things;
   and although she enters into holy souls throughout generations,
   she makes them to be friends of God and to be prophets.
<sup>28</sup> For God loves no one except the one who lives with wisdom.

29 For she[a] is more beautiful than the sun
 and above every constellation of the stars;
compared with the light, she is found to be foremost,
30  for night succeeds this,
 but evil does not prevail against wisdom.

# 8

But she reaches strongly from end to end of the world,[b]
 and she manages all things well.

2 I had affection for this one, and I sought her out from my youth,
 and I sought to take her to myself as a bride,
 and I became infatuated with her beauty.

*Wisdom, the Companion for Life*

3 She glorifies her noble birth by living with God,[c]
 and the master of all loved her.
4 For she is a mystic of the knowledge of God
 and a chooser of his works.
5 But if wealth is a desirable possession in life,
 what is richer than wisdom, the maker of all things?
6 And if understanding is productive,
 who more than she, artisan of the things that exist?
7 And if anyone loves righteousness,
 her labors are virtues,
for she teaches moderation and understanding,
 righteousness and virtue,
 of which nothing is more useful in life to humans.
8 And if also anyone desires great experience,
 she knows the things of old and how to conjecture the things
  to come;
she understands the subtleties of words and the solutions to
  riddles;
 she knows in advance signs and wonders
 and the outcomes of the seasons and times.
9 Therefore I decided to bring her to live with me,
 knowing that she would be a counselor of good things for me,
 and a comfort of cares and sorrows.
10 Because of her I will have glory among the crowds,
 and as a young man, I will have honor among the elders.[d]
11 I will be found to be sharp in judgment,
 and I will be admired by the rulers.
12 When I keep silence, they will wait for me; and when I speak,
  they will pay attention;
 and when I speak at length,
 they will lay a hand over their mouth.
13 I will have immortality because of her,
 and I will leave an eternal memory for those after me.
14 I will govern peoples, and nations will be subject to me.

---

[a] Lit. "this" [b] Lit. "limit to limit" [c] Lit. "She glorifies nobility of birth, having a living with God" [d] Lit. "the young, honor beside elders"

15 Horrible tyrants will be afraid when they hear of me;
    I will appear good in the crowd and virtuous in battle.
16 When I enter my house, I will rest with her,
    for companionship with her has no bitterness
        and living with her no pain,
        rather gladness and joy.
17 When I considered these things in myself
        and reflected in my heart—
        that immortality is in kinship with wisdom,
18 and in her friendship is good delight,
        and in the labors of her hands is unfailing wealth,
    and in the exercise of conversation with her is understanding,
        and prominence in the sharing—I went around her words,
            seeking how I might take her for myself.
19 But I was a clever child,
        and I was appointed to be of a good soul;
20 or rather, being good, I came into an undefiled body.
21 But knowing that I would not otherwise be in possession of
            wisdom unless God gave her to me,
        and this was a matter of understanding to know whose gift she
            was,
    I appealed to the Lord, and I beseeched him,
        and from my whole heart I said:

*Prayer for* **9** "God of my fathers and Lord of your mercy,
*Wisdom*         who made all things by your word,
2 and by your wisdom made humankind
        that it might have mastery of the creation you made
3 and manage the world in holiness and righteousness
        and make judgments in uprightness of soul,
4 give me the wisdom that sits beside your throne,
        and may you not reject me from your children.
5 For I am your slave and the son of your servant girl,
        a weak and short-lived human
        and inferior in understanding judgment and laws;
6 for even if someone is perfect among the sons of humans,
        he will be considered nothing apart from your wisdom.
7 You chose me to be king of your people
        and judge of your sons and daughters.
8 You said to build a temple on your holy mountain
        and an altar in the city of your habitation,
        a copy of the holy tent that you prepared beforehand from the
            beginning.
9 And wisdom is with you, who knows your work
        and was present when you were making the world,
    and who understands what is acceptable in your eyes
        and what is right in your commands.
10 Send her out from the holy heavens,
        and send her from your throne of glory,

so that, being present with me, she might labor,
  and I might know what is pleasing with you.
11 For she knows and understands all things,
  and she will lead me in my actions wisely,
  and she will watch me in her glory.
12 And my works will be acceptable,
  and I will judge your people correctly
  and be worthy of the thrones of my father.
13 For what human will know the plan of God?
  Or who will ponder what the Lord wants?
14 For mortal reasonings are worthless,
  and our intentions are likely to fail.
15 For the corruptible body weighs down the soul,
  and the earthly tent burdens the mind full of thoughts.
16 And we can hardly envision the things on the earth,
  and we find the things at hand with labor,
  but who has traced out the things in the heavens?
17 But who would know your plan, unless you gave wisdom
  and sent your Holy Spirit from the most high places?
18 And so the paths of those on earth were made straight,
  and humans were taught the things that please you,[a]
  and they were saved by wisdom."

**10** Wisdom[b] protected the first-formed father of the world
  who alone was created,
  and she delivered him out of his own transgression,
2   and she gave him power to rule over all things.
3 But when the unrighteous one left her in his anger,
  he perished by his brother-murdering wraths.
4 On account of whom wisdom again preserved the earth when it
      flooded,
  piloting the righteous one through worthless wood.
5 Wisdom also, when the nations in evil agreement were confused,
  found the righteous one and kept him blameless before God,
  and guarded him strong against compassion for his child.
6 Wisdom rescued a righteous man when the ungodly were being
      destroyed;
  he fled the fire descending upon Five Cities,
7 of which still as evidence of the wickedness,
  appointed a smoking barren land,
  and plants bearing fruit unripe at their seasons,[c]
  a pillar of salt set up as a monument to an unfaithful soul.
8 For, disregarding wisdom,
  they were hurt, not only from not knowing good,
  but also, they abandoned life; a memorial of their thoughtlessness,
  lest they be able to forget the things by which they fell.
9 But wisdom rescued from labors those who attended to her.

*Wisdom
from Adam
to Moses*

---

[a] Lit. "your acceptable things"  [b] Lit. "This" (throughout ch. 10)  [c] Lit. "unripe in hours; fruit-bearing plants"

10 A righteous fugitive from his brother's wrath
   Wisdom led in straight paths.
   She showed him the kingdom of God
      and gave him knowledge of holy things.
   She prospered him in his toils
      and multiplied his labors.
11 When greed overpowered him, she stood by him,
      and she made him rich.
12 She guarded him from his enemies,
      and secured him from those lying in wait for him,
   and in his mighty struggle she ruled in his favor,
      so that he might know that piety is stronger than everything.
13 Wisdom did not desert the righteous one when he was sold
      but rescued him from sin.
14 She descended with him into the well,
      and she did not abandon him in his chains
   until she brought him the scepter of the kingdom
      and the authority of those ruling over him,
   and showed those finding fault with him to be false
      and gave him eternal glory.
15 Wisdom rescued this holy people and blameless seed out of a
      nation of oppressors.
16 She entered into the soul of the servant of the Lord
      and stood against fearsome kings in wonders and signs.
17 She paid the holy ones the reward of their labors;
      she led them in a wonderful road
      and became for them a shelter by day
      and a flame of stars by night.
18 She carried them across the Red Sea
      and led them through much water.
19 But she flooded their enemies,
      and she threw them up out of the depth of the abyss.
20 Because of this, the righteous plundered the ungodly,
      and they sang hymns, Lord, to your holy name,
      and they praised your defending hand with one accord,
21 because wisdom opened the mouths of the mute
      and made the tongues of infants clear.

*Wisdom* **11** She prospered their works by the hand of a holy prophet.
*through Moses* **11** 2 They traveled through an uninhabited desert
      and pitched tents in untraveled places.
3    They resisted hostile people and defended against enemies.
4 They became thirsty and called on you,
      and water was given to them out of a sharp rock,
      and a remedy for thirst out of hard stone.
5 For through the things by which their enemies were punished,
      through these same things when they were in need, they
         benefited.

⁶ Instead of a fountain of an ever-flowing river,
    stirred up in defiled blood
⁷ in rebuke of the edict of killing children,
    you gave to them abundant water unexpectedly, ⁸showing
    through the thirst at that time how you punished the opposing
    people.
⁹ For when they were tested, although they were the ones being
    trained in mercy,
    they knew how the impious were tortured, being judged
    in wrath.
¹⁰ For you tested these people like an admonishing father,
    but you examined those people like a severe, condemning king.
¹¹ Whether absent or present,ᵃ they were distressed alike.
¹² For a double sorrow took them,
    and a groaning of memories of what had passed.
¹³ For when they heard that through their own punishments
    they were doing well, they understood that it was of the Lord.
¹⁴ For they mockingly renounced him who had long before been
    thrown down to be exposed;
    on the completion of the outcomes they were amazed,
    when they thirsted unlike the righteous.
¹⁵ But instead of their thoughtless reasonings of unrighteousness,
    by which they were misled and were worshipping unreasoning
    reptiles and vile vermin,
    you sent upon them a horde of unreasoning animals for
    punishment,
¹⁶ so that they might know that through the things one sins,
    through these things one is punished.
¹⁷ For your hand, which is all powerful
    and created the world out of formless matter,
    lacked nothing to send a horde of bears or fierce lions
    upon them,
¹⁸ or newly created unknown prey full of anger,
    whether puffing a fire-breathed blast
    or scattered belches of smoke
    or flashing fearful sparks from their eyes,
¹⁹ of which not only would the injury be able to destroy them,
    but even the frightening sight to destroy them.
²⁰ But also apart from these things, they were able to fall by one
    breath when pursued by justice
    and when scattered by the breath of your power;
    but you ordered all things by measure and number and weight.
²¹ For great strength is always present with you,
    and who will resist the strength of your arm?
²² Because the whole world is like the movement of a scale
    before you,
    and like a drop of morning dew coming down on the earth.

ᵃ Lit. "But both being absent and being present"

23 But you have mercy on all because you are able to do all things,
and you overlook the sins of humans for their repentance.
24 For you love all things that exist, and you detest nothing that you
made,
for you would not build anything if you hated it.
25 But how would anything remain if you did not want it,
or what was not called by you be preserved?
26 But you spare all things because they are yours, Master, lover of
souls.

**12** For your incorruptible spirit is in all things.
2 Therefore you discipline those fallen away little by little,
and you admonish them, reminding them of their sins,
so that, being set free from wickedness, they might trust upon
you, Lord.

*Wisdom in*    3 For also the old inhabitants of your holy land,
*the Holy Land*    4     hating them because of their hostile practices, works of
sorceries
and unholy rites, 5 and a merciless murderer of children,
and a feast of eating the entrails of human flesh and blood,
the initiates from the middle of a revelry,
6 and parents who are murderers of helpless souls,
you wished to destroy them through the hands of our ancestors,
7 so that the land, most precious of all before you,
might receive a worthy colony of the children of God.
8 But even some of these you spared as humans,
and sent off wasps as forerunners of your army,
so that they might destroy them little by little,
9 though you were not unable to place the impious under the
authority of the righteous in battle
or to rub them out at once by terrible beasts or a sharp word.
10 But judging little by little you kept giving them a place of
repentance,
not being unaware that their generation was evil,
and their evil implanted,
and that their reasoning would not be changed for eternity.
11     For it was a cursed seed from the beginning;
and not because you feared someone did you keep giving
pardon for their sins.
12 For who will say, "What have you done?" Or who will resist your
judgment?
And who will accuse you for the destroyed nations that you
made?
Or what avenger of the unrighteous person will come to stand
against you?
13 For is there no god besides you who has concern for everything,
so that you might show that you did not judge unrighteously;

¹⁴ and there is no king or tyrant who will be able to confront you
        about those whom you punished.
¹⁵ But because you are righteous, you manage all things righteously,
        considering it foreign to your power to condemn
        one who does not deserve to be punished.
¹⁶ For your strength is the beginning of righteousness,
        and your rule of all things makes you spare all.
¹⁷ For you show strength when people disbelieve the completeness
        of your power,
        and you refute the audacity among those who know it.
¹⁸ But although you master by strength, you judge in gentleness,
        and you manage us with much forbearance;
        for the power to act is there for you whenever you want.
¹⁹ But you taught your people through such works,
        because the righteous must be kind,
    and you made your sons hopeful
        because you grant repentance for sins.
²⁰ For if you took vengeance with such great care and entreaty
        against the enemies of your children and those deserving
            death,
        giving them a time and place by which they might be set free
            from evil,
²¹ with what strictness have you judged your sons,
        to whose ancestors you gave oaths and covenants of good
            promises?
²² Therefore while disciplining us, you flog our enemies ten
            thousand times,
        so that when we judge, we may be concerned about your
            goodness;
        but when we are judged, we may expect mercy.
²³ Therefore also those who lived unrighteously in thoughtlessness
        of life,
        you tortured through their own abominations.
²⁴ For they also were led far astray in the ways of deception,
        taking up as gods the things dishonored even among the
            animals of their enemies,
        being deceived like foolish children.
²⁵ Because of this, as if to unreasoning children,
        you sent judgment to mock them.
²⁶ But those who ignored the gentle rebuke
        will experience the judgment worthy of God.
²⁷ For when they, suffering, became indignant
        at these things which they were imagining to be gods, when
            they were punished for them and saw, they began to
            recognize the true God whom formerly they kept refusing
            to know.
    Therefore also the most extreme judgment came on them.

Nature
Worship **13** For all people who are ignorant of God were fruitless by nature,
and neither could they know the one who exists by seeing good
things, nor by having the advantage of his works did they
recognize the Artisan.

2 Rather, they supposed that either fire or wind or swift air
or the circle of stars or violent water
or the luminaries of the heavens were gods, presiding over
the world.

3 If it was because they were delighting in their beauty that they
supposed them to be gods,
let them know how much better than these things is the Master,
for the originator of beauty created them.

4 But if it was because they were amazed by their power and
activity,
let them know how much stronger than they are is the one
who made them.

5 For from the greatness and beauty of what was created,
correspondingly their originator is seen.

6 Nevertheless on these persons is little fault,
for perhaps they are also led astray
while seeking God and wanting to find him.

7 For while they live among his works, they keep searching
and trust what they see,[a] because the things they see are
beautiful.

8 But, again, neither are they excusable;

9 for if they could know so much
that they could calculate eternity,
how did they not find the master of these things sooner?

Ridiculous
Idols

10 But miserable are they, and in dead things is their hope,
who called the works of human hands gods,
gold and silver artistic works[b]
and representations of animals
or useless stone, the work of an ancient hand.

11 But if also some woodworker, after sawing down an easily
moved tree,
skillfully stripped off all its bark,
and after crafting it beautifully,
made a useful vessel for the service of life;

12 but after using the cast-off pieces of the work for the preparation
of food, he was satisfied;

13 but the piece cast off from them, useful for nothing,
wood growing crooked and knotty,
he took and carved with care in his leisure,
and he formed it by experience of rest,
he fashioned it in the image of a human,

---

[a] Lit. "the appearance" [b] Lit. "exercise of crafts"

14   or he made it like some worthless animal,
    painting it with red paint and coloring its skin red,
    and painting every spot on it,
15   and making it a home worthy of it,
    he put it on a wall, securing it with iron.
16   Therefore, lest it fall down, he provided for it,
    knowing that it could not help itself,
    for it is also an image, and it needed help.
17   When praying for his possessions and marriages and children,
    he is not ashamed, though addressing the lifeless thing,
    and he calls upon what is weak regarding his health.
18   He entreats what is dead about life;
    he asks what is ignorant for help,
    what is not able to make use of its feet*a* about a journey,
19   for gain and production and success of his hands;
    from the thing whose hands are most powerless, he asks for
      strength!

**14** Again someone preparing a voyage and about to travel through
      raging waves
    calls on wood more rotten than the ship bearing him.
2   For desire for gains planned that ship,
    but wisdom the artisan made it.
3   But your provision, father, pilots the ship,
    because you have given it a path in the sea
    and a safe track in the waves.
4   You show that you are able to save from every danger,
    so that even someone without skill can put to sea.
5   But you do not want the works of your wisdom to be ineffective;
    because of this, people entrust their lives to the smallest piece
      of wood, and they are preserved, passing through the
      waves on a raft.
6   For even in the beginning when arrogant giants were perishing,
    the hope of the world, taking refuge on a raft,
    guided by your hand, left a seed of generation for eternity.
7   For blessed is the wood through which righteousness comes.
8   But the handiwork: accursed be it and the one who made it,
    because he made it and called what is perishable a god.
9   For hateful to God in equal measure is the ungodly and his
      ungodliness.
10   For what is done will be punished together with the one who
      did it.
11   Because of this, there will be an examination of the nations even
      among the idols,
    because they became an abomination among God's creations
    and scandals for the souls of humans
    and a trap for the feet of fools.

---

*a* Lit. "base"

*The Origins*
*of Idolatry*

12 For the idea of idols was the beginning of prostitution, and the
    invention of them was the corruption of life;
13 for they did not exist from the beginning, and they will not exist
    for eternity.
14 For through human vanity they entered into the world,
    and because of this their shortened end has been planned.
15 For a father, distressed by untimely grief,
    making an image of the child so quickly taken away,
    at that time honored the dead person as a god
    and handed on the mysteries and worship to his dependents.
16 Then the ungodly practice, strengthened over time, was guarded
    as a law,
    and the carved images were worshiped by the command of
    tyrants—
17 who, because people could not honor them by sight because they
    lived far away,
    and they imagined their appearance from a distance,
    they made a visible image of the honored king,
    so that through zeal they might flatter the absent king as if
    present.
18 But the ambition of the artisan encouraged
    even the ignorant into increasing the intensity of the worship.
19 For he, possibly wanting to please the ruler,
    with skill forced the likeness toward what is beautiful;
20 and the crowd, being attracted by the grace of the work,
    now considered what shortly before was honored as a human to
    be an object of worship.
21 And this became an ambush for life,
    because humans, enslaved to misfortune or tyranny,
    assigned the unshareable name to stone and wood.

*The*
*Consequences*
*of Idolatry*

22 Then it was not sufficient to stray from*a* the knowledge of God,
    but even though living in great strife from ignorance,
    they call such great evils peace.
23 For while celebrating either child-killing rites or secret mysteries
    or raving revelries of special rituals,
24 they no longer keep their lives or marriages pure,
    but one destroys another by ambushes or grieves another by
    adulteries.
25 But all have a confusion of blood and murder, theft and treachery,
    destruction, unfaithfulness, disturbance, perjury,
    confusion of good things, 26forgetting of gifts,
    defilement of souls, perversion of procreation,*b*
    disorder of marriages, adultery and licentiousness have
    everything in a confusion.
27 For the worship of nameless idols
    is the beginning and cause and end of every evil.

*a* Lit. "to wander around" *b* Lit. "change of birthing"

28 For they either rave in rage, or they prophesy false things,
or they live unrighteously or quickly perjure themselves;
29 for those who trust lifeless idols,
swearing evilly, expect not to be injured.
30 But righteous things will come upon them regarding both of
these things:
because they thought wrongly about God, offering to idols,
and they swore unrighteously in deceit, despising holiness.
31 For it is not the power of that by which they swear,
rather the penalty against those who sin
that always pursues the transgression of the unrighteous.

**15** But you, our God, are kind and true,
patient and administering all things in mercy.

*The Foolishness
of Idolatry*

2 For even if we sin, we are yours, knowing your might;
we will not sin, knowing that we have been counted as yours.
3 For to know you is complete righteousness,
and to know your might is the root of immortality.
4 For neither the treacherous intention of humans has misled us,
nor the fruitless toil of painters,
a figure stained with various colors
5 from whose appearance comes into a reproach for fools,
and he longs for a lifeless form of a dead image.
6 Lovers of evil things and worthy of such hopes
are those who work and desire and worship them.
7 For also a potter, pressing soft earth, laboriously
forms each thing for our service,
but out of the same clay he forms
serving vessels for clean works
and for the opposite works all alike;
but what the different use of each of these is,
the clay worker is the one who decides.
8 And perversely he forms a fruitless god out of the same clay,
which shortly before was brought out of earth
and after a little while goes to that from which it was taken,
when the debt of the soul was demanded.
9 But it is of no concern to him that he will die,
or that he has a brief life;
rather, he competes with goldsmiths and silversmiths,
and he imitates bronze-workers,
and he considers it a glorious thing that he forms false things.
10 His heart is ashes, and his hope of less value than earth,
and his life more dishonored than clay,
11 because he did not know the one who formed him
and who inspired an energizing soul into him
and breathed in a living spirit.
12 But he considered our life to be a plaything
and life a profitable celebration,

for he says it is necessary to procure profit by any means,
    even if evil.

13 For this person knows that he sins beyond everyone,
    making fragile vessels and carved images from earthly wood.

14 But most foolish and more wretched than the life of an infant
    are all the enemies who oppress your people.

15 Because they also considered all the idols of the nations to be gods,
    which have no use of eyes for seeing
or nostrils for inhaling air
    or ears to hear
or fingers of the hands for touching,
    and their feet are ineffective for walking.

16 For a human made them,
    and one who borrows a spirit formed them;
    for no human has power to form a god like himself.

17 But being mortal, he makes a dead thing with lawless hands;
    for he is better than his objects of worship,
    because he lived, whereas those things never did.

*The Egyptian*
*Plagues*

18 But they worship even the most hostile animals,
    for when compared to the other animals, with respect to folly
        they are worse.

19 And even among animals they do not attain to beautiful
        appearance so much as to be desirable,
    but they escaped the praise of God and his blessing.

# 16

Because of this they were deservedly punished by similar things
    and tortured by a multitude of vermin.

2 Instead of that punishment you did good to your people,
    for the desire of the appetite, a strange taste,
    you prepared the quail as food,

3 so that those people might, when desiring food,
    because of what was shown of those that had been sent,
    and they might turn back even their urgent appetite;
but though they were in want for a little while,
    they partook also of the strange-tasting food.[a]

4 For it was necessary for unavoidable need to come upon those
        tyrants,
    but to these people only to be shown how their enemies were
        being tortured.

5 For also when the terrible wrath of the wild animals came upon
        them,
    and the bites of twisted serpents were destroying them,
    your anger did not remain until the end;

6 but for a warning they were troubled for a little while,
    having a sign of salvation as a reminder of your law's
        commandment.

---

[a] Lit. "partook also of the strange of taste"

7 For the person who turned himself was saved, not because of what
    was beheld,
  but because of you, the savior of all.

8 But also by this you persuaded our enemies
  that you are the one who rescues from every evil.

9 For they whom the bites of locusts and flies killed,
  and no healing was found for their soul,
  because they deserved to be punished by such things.

10 But the fangs of venomous serpents did not overcome your sons,
  for your mercy came to help and heal them.

11 For they were pricked as a reminder of your words
  and were delivered quickly,
  lest by falling into deep forgetfulness
  they might not be distracted by your kindness.

12 For also neither herbal remedy nor poultice healed[a] them,
  but your word, Lord, that cures all things.

13 For you have authority over life and death,
  and you lead down to the gate of Hades and you bring up.

14 But in his evil, a person kills,
  but he cannot return the departed spirit
  or release the soul that was taken.

15 But it is impossible to flee from your hand,

16 for by refusing to know you, the ungodly
  were whipped by the strength of your arm,
  pursued by strange rains and hail and unavoidable rainstorms
  and consuming fire.

17 For what is most unexpected,[b] in the water, which quenches
    all things,
  the fire burned[c] even more,
  for the world is a defender of the righteous.

18 For at one time the flame was restrained,
  lest it burn up the animals that were being sent against the
    ungodly,
  rather, that by seeing it, they might know that they were driven
    by the judgment of God.

19 But at another time it keeps burning in the midst of water with
    more power than fire,
  so that the produce of the unrighteous earth might be
    destroyed.

20 Because you fed your people the food of angels,
  and you sent them ready bread from heaven, without labor,
  having the ability to provide every pleasure, and agreeable to
    every taste.

21 For your provision showed your sweetness to your children,
  and, serving the desire of the one eating[d] it,
  it was changed to what anyone wished.

*Storms and
Manna*

---

[a] Lit. "attended to"  [b] Lit. "For the most paradoxical"  [c] Lit. "was at work"  [d] Lit. "bringing"

²² But snow and ice withstood fire and were not melted,
  so that they might know that
fire, burning in the hail and flashing in the rains, was destroying
  the crops of their enemies.
²³ But the fire*ᵃ* again had forgotten even its own power,
  so that the righteous might be fed.
²⁴ For creation, serving you who made it,
  exerts itself for punishment against the unrighteous
  and relaxes itself for the benefit of those who trust in you.
²⁵ Because of this also at that time, being mined for all,
  it was serving your all-nurturing gift
  for the desire of those in necessity,
²⁶ so that your sons whom you loved, Lord, might learn
  that it is not the production of fruits that feeds humanity,
  but your word preserves those who trust you.
²⁷ For what was not destroyed by fire
  was melted when simply warmed by a brief ray of sun,
²⁸ so that it was known that it is necessary to rise before dawn
    to thank you*ᵇ*
  and before daylight*ᶜ* to appeal to you.
²⁹ For the hope of an ungrateful person will melt like wintry frost
  and will flow like useless water.

*Darkness and*
*Light in Egypt*

**17** For your judgments are great and hard to explain;
  because of this, undisciplined souls were misled.
² For when lawless persons thought to oppress the holy nation,
  they were lying there as prisoners of darkness and captives
    of long night,
  shut in under their roofs, fugitives from eternal providence.
³ For thinking they were escaping notice in their secret sins
  under a dim veil of forgetfulness, they were scattered,
    terribly amazed
  and agitated by apparitions.
⁴ For not even the pit holding them would protect them fearlessly,
  but agitating sounds kept echoing around them,
  and sad apparitions with gloomy faces kept appearing.
⁵ And no force of fire was able to give light,
  and no brilliant flames of stars
  endured to shine on that horrible night.
⁶ But there appeared to them only
  a spontaneous fire, very fearsome,
  but, terrified, they considered the appearance of what was seen
    worse than what was unseen.
⁷ And delusions of their magical skill were ineffective,
  and there was a scornful rebuke of their boasting over
    wisdom.

---

ᵃ Lit. "this" ᵇ Lit. "to precede the sun for thankfulness of you" ᶜ Lit. "a rising of light"

8 For those who promised to drive away the fears and troubles
     of a sick soul
  were themselves sick with ridiculous fear.
9 For even if nothing terrifying was frightening them,
     yet, scared by the passing by of wild animals and by the hissing
       of reptiles, 10they were destroyed, trembling
  and refusing to look at the air, unavoidable from anywhere.
11 For wickedness is a cowardly thing, condemned by her own
     witness,
  and being constrained by conscience, it has always added
     difficulties.
12 For fear is nothing except abandonment of the helps that come
     from reason;
13 but anxiety, being lesser from within,
     reckons ignorance greater than the cause causing the
      torment.
14 But those who sleep the same sleep during the truly powerless
     night
  that comes out of the pits of powerless Hades,
15 some were driven by wonders of apparitions,
     and others were disabled by the abandonment of their soul,
  for sudden and unexpected fear came upon them.
16 So then whoever was falling down there
     was held prisoner, locked up in the prison not made of iron.
17 For whether one was a farmer or shepherd
     or a worker of labor in the desert,
  when caught, he would await inescapable distress,
18 for by one chain of darkness they all were bound.
     Whether a whistling wind,
     or the melodious sound of birds in wide-spreading branches,
  or the rhythm of forceful water,
19     or the harsh crash of stones being thrown down,
  or the unobserved running of leaping animals,
     or the sound of roaring wild beasts,
  or an echo, sounding back from the hollow of the mountains,
     they, by frightening them, paralyzed them.
20 For the whole world was illuminated with brilliant light
     and was held together by unhindered works;
21 but the burdensome night was spread on those alone,
     an image of the darkness about to receive them;
     but they were more burdensome to themselves than
      darkness.

# 18

But there was the greatest light for your holy ones,
whose voices they heard but whose forms they did not see then;
     they counted them blessed because they also had suffered;
2   they give thanks because, although previously wronged, they did
     not hurt them,

and they asked for pardon for having disagreed with them.

3 Because you provided a flaming pillar
    as a guide for the unknown journey,
    and a sun without harm for the glorious wandering.

4 For those people deserved to be deprived of light and imprisoned
        in darkness,
    those who kept your sons locked up,
    through whom the incorruptible light of the law was to be
        given to eternity.

5 When they had planned to kill the children of the holy people,
    and one child had been abandoned and rescued,
    for a rebuke, you removed a multitude of children from them
    and destroyed them together in mighty water.

6 That night was made known beforehand to our ancestors,
    so that they might rejoice because they assuredly knew the
        oaths in which they trusted.

7 The salvation of the righteous and the destruction of enemies
    were expected by your people.

8 For as you punished the opposing people,
    by this same means you also called and glorified us.

9 For the holy children of good people sacrificed secretly,
    and they established the divine law in unanimity,
    so, the saints would share alike with them,
        both good things and dangers,
        already singing before praises of the fathers.

10 But the discordant cry of enemies sounded,
    and the lamentable cry for pitiable children carried across.

11 But the slave was being punished with the same penalty along
        with the master,
    and the commoner was suffering the same things along with
        the king,

12 and they all together, in one kind of death,
        had countless dead;
    for there were not even enough living to bury them,
        since he utterly destroyed the most honored of their offspring
        in one decisive moment.

13 For although they disbelieved everything because of the sorcery,
    at the destruction of the firstborn, they acknowledged that this
        people was God's son.

14 For while gentle silence surrounded all things,
    and night in its swift course was in the middle of all things,

15 your all-powerful word leaped from the heavens off the royal
        throne,
    a relentless warrior into the middle of the doomed land,

16 bringing your sincere command as sharp sword;
    and it stood and filled all things with death,
    and it touched the heavens but stood on the earth.

17 Then immediately visions in dreams
　　threw them into confusion terribly,
　　and unexpected fears came upon them,
18 and one here, another there*a* thrown down half-dead
　　made known the cause of his death.
19 For the dreams that disturbed them forewarned them of this,
　　lest they be killed without knowing why they suffered badly.

20 But the experience of death touched also the righteous,
　　and slaughter came on the multitude in the desert,
　　but the wrath did not remain long.
21 For a blameless man hurried and fought as their champion,
　　bringing the weapon of his own ministry—
　　prayer and incense for atonement;
　he resisted the anger and put an end to the calamity,
　　showing that he was your servant.
22 He was victorious over the crowd not by strength of body
　　　or by the working of weapons,
　　but he subdued the punisher by word,
　　reminding him of the oaths and covenants of the ancestors.
23 For when the dead had already fallen on one another in heaps,
　　standing between them, he drove back the wrath
　　and cut off the way to the living.
24 For the entire world was on his full-length garment,
　　and the glories of the ancestors on a four-row engraving
　　　of stone,
　　and your greatness on the diadem of his head.
25 The destroyer yielded to these, and they were frightened
　　　of these things;
　　for just the attempt of anger was sufficient.

*The Threat of
Extermination
in the Desert*

# 19

But merciless wrath was set against the ungodly until the end,
　　for he had also known their future,*b*
2 that they, when they had turned to let loose
　　and had sent them forth with haste,
　　they would pursue them because they felt regret.
3 For still having grief in hands
　　and lamenting at the graves of the dead,
　they were drawn in by another foolish decision,
　　and those they had asked and thrown out, they pursued these
　　　as fugitives.
4 For the deserved distress was drawing them to this end,
　　and it threw them into forgetfulness of what had happened,
　so that they might fill up the punishment lacking in their
　　　torments,
5 　and your people might experience an unusual journey,
　　but those people might find a strange death.

*The Red Sea*

*a* Lit. "another in another place"　*b* Lit. "known of them also the coming things"

6 For the whole creation was fashioned again anew in its own kind,
    serving its commands,
  so that your children might be kept without harm.
7 The cloud was overshadowing the camp,
    and the emergence of dry land from where the water was seen
       before,
  an unhindered path out of the Red Sea,
  and a green field out of the violent wave;
8 through which those protected by your hand passed through
      as a whole nation,
  having seen amazing wonders.
9 For they ranged like horses
  and leaped like lambs,
  praising you, Lord, who delivers them.
10 For they had still remembered the events of their sojourn,
    how the earth produced flies instead of the birth of animals,
  and the river overflowed with an abundance of frogs
    instead of fish.*a*
11 But later they also saw a new kind of bird
  when, led by desire, they asked for luxurious meat.
12 For quails came up from the sea as encouragement to them.
13 And the punishments came upon the sinners
    not without signs having come by the force of the
      thunderbolt,
  for they were suffering justly by their own wickedness,
  for they also practiced a more cruel hatred of strangers.
14 For indeed some people would not receive unknown people
      when they came by,
  but these people would enslave strangers who were their
    benefactors.
15 And not only that, but some examination will be on them,
  since they would receive the strangers hatefully,
16 but they, after welcoming with celebrations
    those who had already shared of the same righteous things,
  mistreated them with terrible sufferings.
17 But they were also stricken with blindness,
    just as those at the door of the righteous one,
  when, surrounded by thick darkness,
    each one was looking for the way through his own doors.
18 For the elements are exchanged through one another,
    just as tones on a stringed instrument change the kind
      of rhythm,
  while remaining always in sound,
    which is to be inferred exactly from the accurate appearance
      of what had happened.
19 For land animals were changing into water animals,
  and swimming creatures were crossing over on the land.

---

*a* Lit. "watery things"

20 Fire was by its own power strong in water,
  and water forgot its fire-quenching power.
21 Flames, on the contrary, did not shrivel*a* the flesh of perishable
    animals walking among them,
  nor melt the easily thawed, ice-like kind of heavenly food.

22 For in everything, Lord, you exalted and glorified your people,       *Conclusion*
  and you have not neglected them, standing by them at every
    time and place.

*a* Lit. "quench"

*Introduction to*

# WISDOM OF SIRACH

Y EHOSHUA BEN SIRA WAS a scribe and head of a school in Jerusalem in the decades around the year 200 BC. He has left us a substantial sampling of his "curriculum" and, with it, important windows into the social practices, ethics, theological inquiries, and concerns of Judeans during this period. Ben Sira drew upon the Law of Moses, the narratives of the Hebrew Bible, the wisdom tradition of Israel, as well as traditions of wisdom and practical advice known from Egypt and Greece in the course of developing his own vision for a secure life and prosperous career. At the core of this vision, pushing quite hard against the hellenizing currents of the period, is a steadfast commitment to walking in the ways of the Jewish Law without deviation, without which a person can attain no genuine honor in life.

Ben Sira originally composed his work in Hebrew, and fragments of the Hebrew original have been discovered at Qumran and Masada, attesting to the popularity of his work in Essene and perhaps other circles. The whole has survived, however, only in the Greek translation undertaken by his grandson sometime after 132 BC for the benefit of Greek-speaking Jews in Ptolemaic Egypt. This was expanded over time with the result that two principal Greek editions have come down to us. The longer was used as the basis for the Latin Vulgate and, thus, became the dominant form known throughout most of church history. The shorter form, which is certainly the more original (as the Qumran and Masada fragments have demonstrated), survives in the principal fourth and fifth century codices and is represented in this translation. Ben Sira exercised significant influence on the generations of Jewish sages that followed him (including Jesus and James) and continued to be quoted in rabbinic literature. Alongside Wisdom of Solomon, Wisdon of Sirach has exercised the greatest influence on the Christian church of all the books of the Apocrypha.

—D. A. deSilva

# WISDOM OF SIRACH

*Sirach*
*Prologue* Many and great things to us through the Law and the Prophets and ²the others who followed after them have been given, for which it is proper ³to praise Israel for instruction and wisdom. And not only for them ⁴⁻⁵who read is it proper to become wise, but also for those who love learning to be able to be useful to outsiders, by both speaking and writing. ⁶My grand-father, Joshua, having given himself over much time to both the reading of the Law and the ⁷Prophets and the other books of our ancestors, and ⁸after obtaining sufficient skill in these, was himself also prompted to write something of the things pertaining to instruction and ⁹wisdom. It is fit-ting so that those eager to learn, having become acquainted with these things also, ¹⁰might make much more progress on account of the divine law of life. You are encouraged, therefore, ¹¹with goodwill and care to make a reading and to have patience for that which ¹²we might seem to lack power, as to some of the words that were lovingly labored over regard-ing their interpretation. ¹³For things do not have the same force in them when expressed in Hebrew and when ¹⁴translated into another tongue. But not only these, but even the Law itself ¹⁵and the Prophets and the rest of the books have no small difference ¹⁶when expressed in themselves. For having arrived in Egypt in the thirty-eighth year ¹⁷of King Euergetes, and spending some time, I found ¹⁸a copy of no small instruction. I myself set a most necessary duty to bring ¹⁹some diligence and love of labor to translate this book. ²⁰For much sleeplessness and skill has been brought to bear in the interval of time ²¹to bring the document to its end, to publish it also for those in exile ²²who are wishing to learn, being predisposed to live according to the customs in the law.

*Wisdom*
*and the Fear*
*of the Lord*

**1** All wisdom is from the Lord, and it is with him for eternity.
² Who will count the sands of the seas and the drops of rain and
    the days of eternity?
³     Who will search out the height of heaven and the breadth of
    the earth, and the abyss and wisdom?
⁴ Wisdom was created before everything,
    and prudent understanding from eternity.[a]
⁶ To whom has the root of wisdom been revealed?
    And who knows her great deeds?[b]
⁸ There is only one wise and very fearsome
    seated upon his throne.
The Lord ⁹himself created her
    and saw and measured her
    and poured her out upon all of his works,
¹⁰ together with all flesh, according to his gift;
    and he supplied her to those who love him.

[a] Swete lacks verse 5  [b] Swete lacks verse 7

11 The fear of the Lord is glory and honor
   and gladness and a crown of joy.
12 The fear of the Lord delights the heart
   and will give gladness and joy and length of days.
13 The one who fears the Lord will be well at the end,
   and he will find grace on the day of his death.
14 To fear God is the beginning of wisdom,
   and she was created in the womb along with the faithful.
15 And she built a foundation of eternity with humans,
   and she will be entrusted with their seed.
16 To fear the Lord is the fullness of wisdom,
   and she makes them drunk from her fruit.
17 She will fill her whole house with desirable things,
   and the storehouses with her products.
18 The fear of the Lord is a crown of wisdom,
   causing peace and health of healing to shoot up.
19 And he saw and numbered her;
   he poured out skill and knowledge of comprehension like rain,
   and he exalted the glory of those who take possession of her.
20 To fear the Lord is the root of wisdom,
   and her branches are length of days.*

22 Unrighteous wrath cannot be justified,          *Self-Control*
   for the tipping of his wrath is his fall.
23 A patient man will withstand until an opportune time,
   and later, merriment will burst forth for him.
24 He will hide his words until an opportune time,
   and the lips of the faithful will tell of his understanding.
25 In the treasuries of wisdom is the parable of knowledge,
   but the fear of God is an abomination to a sinner.
26 Having desired wisdom, observe the commandments,
   and the Lord will supply it to you.
27 For the fear of the Lord is wisdom and instruction,
   and his pleasure is faith and gentleness.
28 Do not resist the fear of the Lord,
   and do not come to him with a divided heart.
29 Do not be a hypocrite in the mouths of people,
   and keep watch over your lips.
30 Do not exalt yourself, lest you fall
   and bring dishonor to your soul,
   and the Lord will uncover your secrets,
   and he will throw you down in the middle of the congregation
   because you did not come in the fear of the Lord,
   and your heart was full of deceit.

**2** Child, if you come to serve the Lord God,          *Testing and*
   prepare your soul for temptation.          *the Fear of*
                                                *the Lord*

---

* Swete lacks verse 21

2 Make your heart right and be steadfast,
  and do not hurry in the time of distress.

3 Be joined to him, and do not turn away,
  so that you might be honored at your end.

4 Accept everything that would be brought upon you,
  and when you are changed into a state of humiliation,
    be patient;

5 because gold is tested in the fire,
  and acceptable people in the furnace of humiliation.

6 Trust in him, and he will support you;
  make your ways straight and hope in him.

7 You who fear the Lord, wait for his mercy,
  and do not turn aside lest you fall.

8 You who fear the Lord, trust in him,
  and your reward will never fail.

9 You who fear the Lord, hope for good things
  and for merriment of eternity and mercy.

10 Look at the ancient generations and see;
   who trusted the Lord and was put to shame?
   Or who abided in his fear and was forsaken?
   Or who called upon him, and he disregarded him?

11 For the Lord is compassionate and merciful,
   and he forgives sins and saves in the time of affliction.

12 Woe to the cowardly hearts and the neglectful hands
   and to the sinner who walks along two paths.

13 Woe to the faint heart, because it does not trust.
   Because of this, it will not be sheltered.

14 Woe to you who have lost patience!
   And what will you do when the Lord examines you?

15 Those who fear the Lord will not resist his words,
   and those who love him will observe his ways.

16 Those who fear the Lord will seek his approval,
   and those who love him will be filled with the law.

17 Those who fear the Lord will prepare their hearts
   and will humble their souls before him.

18 We will fall into the hands of the Lord and not into the hands
     of humans;
   for as is his majesty, so also is his mercy.

*Parents* **3** Children, listen to me, your father;
  and do this so that you might be saved.

2 For the Lord honors a father over his children,
  and he establishes the judgments of a mother over her sons.

3 The one who honors his father will make atonement for sins,

4   and the one who glorifies his mother is like one who stores up
      treasure.

5 The one who honors his father will be cheered by children,
    and the one who glorifies his mother is like the one who stores
      up treasure;

and he will be heard in the day of his prayer.

6 The one who honors his father will have length of days,
and the one who listens to the Lord will give rest to his mother;

7 and he will serve as masters those who engendered him.

8 Honor your father in deed and word
so that a blessing might come upon you from him.

9 For the blessing of a father strengthens the homes
of the children,
but the curse of a mother uproots the foundations.

10 Do not glory in the dishonor of your father,
for glory is not toward dishonor for you.

11 For the glory of a person comes from the honor of his father,
and a mother in disgrace is a reproach for children.

12 Child, help your father in his old age,
and do not grieve him in his life.

13 And should his mind fail, have patience,
and do not dishonor him in all of your strength.

14 For mercy for a father will not be forgotten,
and against sin it will be credited to you.

15 In the day of your affliction it will be remembered for you;
like fair weather on a frost, so your sins will be melted away.

16 The one who forsakes a father is like a blasphemer,
and the one who angers his mother has been
cursed by the Lord.

17 Child, accomplish your work in humility,          *Humility*
and you will be loved by an acceptable person.      *and Charity*

18 However great you are, humble yourself to that extent,
and you will find favor before the Lord.[a]

20 For great is the power of the Lord,
and he is glorified by the humble.

21 Do not seek what is too difficult for you,
and do not question that which is too strong for you.

22 Ponder these things that have been assigned to you,
for the secret things are not a concern for you.

23 Do not meddle with things beyond your works,
for things greater than the understanding of humans
have been revealed to you.

24 For their opinion has led many astray,
and evil suspicion has caused their thinking to slip.[b]

26 And the one who loves danger will fall into it.
A hard heart will be mistreated at the end;
A hard heart will be weighed down at the end.

27 A hard heart will be weighed down by toils,
and the sinner will add sin upon sin.

28 There is no healing for the distress of an arrogant man,
for a wicked plant has taken root in him.

[a] Swete lacks verse 19 [b] Swete lacks verse 25

<sup>29</sup> A wise heart will appreciate a parable,
    and the ear of a hearer is the desire of the wise.
<sup>30</sup> Water extinguishes a burning fire,
    and alms will make atonement for sin.
<sup>31</sup> The one who repays favors is reminded of the future,
    and in the time of a fall, he will find support.

*The Poor*

**4** My son, do not steal the life of the poor,
    and do not draw away the eyes of the needy.
<sup>2</sup> Do not grieve the hungry soul,
    and do not provoke a man in his need.
<sup>3</sup> Do not add to the troubles of a provoked heart,
    and do not delay a gift to the poor.
<sup>4</sup> Do not reject an afflicted suppliant,
    and do not turn your face back from the poor.
<sup>5</sup> Do not turn your eye back from the poor,
    and do not give any reason for a person to curse you.
<sup>6</sup> For if he curses you in the bitterness of his soul,
    the one who made him will hear his prayer.
<sup>7</sup> Make yourself beloved by the assembly,
    and bow your head before a nobleman.
<sup>8</sup> Incline your ear to the poor,
    and answer him with peaceable words in gentleness.
<sup>9</sup> Deliver the injured from the hand of the injurer,
    and do not be timid in your judgment.
<sup>10</sup> Be like a father to the orphans,
    and in place of a husband to their mother,
and you will be like a son of the Most High,
    and he will love you more than your mother does.

*Wisdom*
*Trains People*

<sup>11</sup> Wisdom raised sons for herself
    and takes hold of those who seek her.
<sup>12</sup> The one who loves her loves life,
    and those who eagerly seek her will be full of merriment.
<sup>13</sup> The one who grasps her will inherit glory,
    and the Lord will bless him wherever he goes.
<sup>14</sup> Those who serve her minister to the Holy One,
    and those who love her love the Lord.
<sup>15</sup> The one who obeys her will judge nations,
    and the one who has come to her will dwell confidently.
<sup>16</sup> If you entrust yourself, you shall obtain her,
    and his generations will be in possession.
<sup>17</sup> For at first, she walks inconsistently with him,
    but she will bring fear and cowardice upon him,
and she will torment him with her discipline
    until she entrusts herself to his soul,
    and she will test him with her duties.
<sup>18</sup> And then she will again return directly to him and cheer him,
    and she will reveal her secrets to him.

19 If he goes wrong, she will forsake him
   and hand him over to the hands of his fall.

20 Watch for an opportune time, and guard yourself from what is *Modesty,*
      wicked; *Speech, and*
   and do not be ashamed about your life. *Self-Control*

21 For there is a shame that brings on sin,
   and there is a shame that is glory and grace.

22 Receive no face against your soul,
   and do not show deference unto your fall.

23 Do not hinder a word in the time of salvation;

24    for wisdom will be made known by speech,
   and discipline by the words of the tongue.

25 Do not oppose the truth,
   and hesitate at your ignorance.

26 Do not be ashamed to confess your sins,
   and do not constrain the flow of a river.

27 And do not subject yourself to a stupid person,
   and do not receive the face of a ruler.

28 Fight to the death for the truth,
   and the Lord God will do battle for you.

29 Do not be rough with your tongue
   and lazy and neglectful with your work.

30 Do not be like a lion in your house
   while also indulging vain fancies among your household
      servants.

31 Your hand must not be stretched out to receive
   and closed to repay.

# 5

Do not hold on to your wealth,
   and do not say, "There is enough for me."

2 Do not follow your soul and your strength
   to walk in the desires of your heart.

3 And do not say, "Who shall control me?"
   For the Lord, when punishing, will punish you.

4 Do not say, "I have sinned, and has anything happened
      to me?"
   For the Lord is patient.

5 Do not be fearless about atonement,
   to add sin upon sin.

6 And do not say, "His compassion is great;
   he will make atonement for the multitude of my sins."
   For mercy and anger are from him,
   and his wrath will rest on sinners.

7 Do not wait to turn to the Lord,
   and do not delay day from day;
   for the anger of the Lord will come out suddenly,
   and you will be utterly destroyed at the time of vengeance.

8 Do not hold on to unrighteous possessions,
   for you will benefit nothing in the day of distress.

⁹ Do not winnow in every wind,
   and do not walk on every path;
   such is the double-tongued sinner.

¹⁰ Be strong in your understanding,
   and let your word be consistent.

¹¹ Be quick in your hearing,
   and speak an answer with patience.

¹² If you have understanding, answer your neighbor.
   But if not, let your hand be over your mouth.

¹³ In speaking there is glory and dishonor,
   and the tongue of a person is his downfall.

¹⁴ Do not be called a whisperer,
   and do not lie in wait with your tongue;
  for there is shame upon the thief
   and wicked condemnation upon the double tongued.

¹⁵ Do not be ignorant in things great or in things small,

# 6

   and do not be an enemy instead of a friend.
For a wicked name is a shame, and you will inherit reproach.
   Such is the double-tongued sinner.

² Do not lift up yourself in the counsel of your soul,
   lest your soul be torn to pieces like a bull.

³ You will devour your leaves,
   and you will destroy your fruit
   and leave yourself as dry wood.

*Friendship*

⁴ A wicked soul will destroy the one who acquires it,
   and it will make him an object of malicious joy to his enemies.

⁵ A sweet throat will multiply its friends,
   and an eloquent tongue will increase courteous greetings.

⁶ May those who are at peace with you be many,
   but your counselors be one in a thousand.

⁷ If you get a friend, get him by testing,
   and do not trust him quickly.

⁸ For there is a kind of friend who is so in his time,
   but will not remain on the day of your tribulation.

⁹ And there is a kind of friend who shifts to an enemy
   and will uncover strife to your reproach.

¹⁰ And there is a kind of friend who is a table partner
   but who does not remain on the day of your tribulation.

¹¹ And in your good times, he will be like you,
   and he will speak boldly over your household servants.

¹² If you are humbled, he will be against you
   and hide himself from your face.

¹³ Be separate from your enemies,
   and be on guard from your friends.

¹⁴ A faithful friend is a strong shelter,
   and the one who finds him has found a treasure.

¹⁵ A faithful friend cannot be bartered for,
   and there is no scale for his excellence.

<sup>16</sup> A faithful friend is the medicine of life,
  and those who fear the Lord will find him.
<sup>17</sup> The one who fears the Lord will direct his friendship,
  for as he is, so also is his neighbor.

<sup>18</sup> Child, choose discipline from your youth,                    *Learning*
  and you will find wisdom until your old age.                    *Wisdom*
<sup>19</sup> Like the one who plows and the one who sows,
  draw near to her and wait for her good fruit,
for in her work you will toil little,
  and soon you will eat of her produce.
<sup>20</sup> She is most quick to the uneducated,
  and the fool will not remain with her.
<sup>21</sup> She will be like a mighty stone of trial upon him,
  and he will not hesitate to cast her away.
<sup>22</sup> For wisdom is according to her name,
  and she is not evident to many.
<sup>23</sup> Listen, child, and accept my maxim,
  and do not reject my counsel.
<sup>24</sup> And put your feet into her fetters
  and your neck into her collar.
<sup>25</sup> Bow your shoulder down and bear her,
  and do not be irritated by her chains.
<sup>26</sup> Draw near to her with all your soul,
  and keep her ways with all of your power.
<sup>27</sup> Search out and seek her, and she will become known to you;
  and when possession takes place, do not let her go.
<sup>28</sup> For you will at last find her rest,
  and it will be turned into joy for you.
<sup>29</sup> And her fetters will be a mighty protection for you,
  and her branches a garment of glory.
<sup>30</sup> For there is a golden ornament upon her,
  and her chains are purple thread.
<sup>31</sup> You will put her on as a garment of glory,
  and you will place a crown of joy upon yourself.
<sup>32</sup> If you want, child, you will be disciplined,
  and if you give your soul, you will be clever.
<sup>33</sup> If you love to listen, you will receive,
  and if you incline your ear, you will be wise.
<sup>34</sup> Stand in the multitude of the elders,
  and cling to him who is wise.
<sup>35</sup> Desire to listen to every discourse of God,
  and do not let proverbs of understanding escape you.
<sup>36</sup> If you see a wise man, visit him early
  and let your foot wear out the threshold of his door.
<sup>37</sup> Ponder on the ordinances of the Lord,
  and meditate on his commandments at all times;
he will establish your heart,
  and the desire of your wisdom will be given to you.

*Miscellaneous Advice*

**7** Do no evil, and evil will never seize you.
2   Withdraw from unrighteousness, and it will turn from you.
3   Son, do not sow upon the furrows of unrighteousness,
     and you will never reap them sevenfold.
4   Do not seek a position of authority from the Lord
     or a seat of honor from a king.
5   Do not justify yourself in the presence of the Lord,
     and do not make yourself wise before a king.
6   Do not seek to become a judge,
       lest you be unable to take away unrighteousness,
     lest you become frightened by the face of the powerful,
       and you will place a stumbling block in your uprightness.
7   Do not sin against the multitude of the city,
     and do not throw yourself down among the crowd.
8   Do not repeat a sin,
     for you will not go unpunished for even one.
9   Do not say, "He will notice the multitude of my gifts,
     and when I offer them to the Most High God, he will accept them."
10  Do not be faint-hearted in your prayer,
     and do not neglect to do merciful deeds.
11  Do not laugh at a person who is in the bitterness of his soul,
     for there is one who humbles and exalts.
12  Devise no lie against your brother
     or do the same to a friend.
13  Don't want to tell any lie,
     for the persistence of it does not lead to good.
14  Do not chatter among the multitude of the elders,
     and do not repeat a word in your prayer.
15  Do not hate hard work
     and farming, created by the Most High.
16  Do not count yourself among the multitude of sinners;
     remember that anger will not delay.
17  Humble your soul very much,
     because the retribution of the ungodly is fire and worm.
18  Do not exchange a friend for what makes no difference
     or a dear brother for the gold of Ophir.
19  Do not dismiss a wise and good woman,
     for her favor is also beyond gold.
20  Do not mistreat a household servant who works with sincerity
     or the hired worker who gives his soul.
21  Let your soul love a good household servant;
     do not withhold freedom from him.

*Social Advice*

22  Do you have livestock? Look after them;
     and if they are useful to you, let them remain with you.
23  Do you have children? Discipline them
     and bend their neck from their youth.
24  Do you have daughters? Take care of their body,
     and do not brighten your face at them.

25 Give a daughter in marriage and you have completed a great work,
    and give her to an intelligent man.
26 Do you have a wife according to your soul? Do not throw her out.
27 With all your heart, honor your father,
    and do not forget the labor pains of your mother.
28 Remember that through them you came into being,
    and what will you repay them just as they did to you?
29 Fear the Lord with all your soul,
    and be in awe of his priests.
30 Love the one who made you with all your strength,
    and do not neglect his ministers.
31 Fear the Lord and honor the priest,
    and give him the portion as was commanded to you from the
        beginning,
  and the offering for sin and the portion of the arms
    and the sacrifice of consecration and the firstfruits.
32 And stretch out your hand to the poor
    so that your blessing might be complete.
33 The grace of a gift is in the presence of all who are living;
    do not withhold grace for the dead.
34 Do not lack from those who weep,
    and mourn with those who mourn.
35 Do not hesitate to visit the sick,
    for you will be loved for such things.
36 In all your words remember your end,
    and you will not sin for eternity.

# 8

Do not contend with a strong person       *Prudence*
    lest you fall into his hands.
2 Do not quarrel with a rich person
    lest he stand against your weight;
  for gold has destroyed many
    and perverted the hearts of kings.
3 Do not contend with a talkative person,
    and do not pile wood upon his fire.
4 Do not make fun of the ignorant
    lest your ancestors be dishonored.
5 Do not reproach a person who turns back from sin;
    remember that we are all valuable.
6 Do not dishonor a person in his old age,
    for some of us are also growing old.
7 Do not rejoice over the dead;
    remember that we all die.
8 Do not disregard the discourse of the wise,
    and engage yourself in their proverbs,
  because from them you will learn discipline
    and how to minister to nobles.
9 Do not dismiss the discourse of the elders,
    for they also learned from their fathers;

because from them you will learn understanding
and how to give an answer in a time of need.
10 Do not kindle the coals of a sinner
lest you be burned in the fire of his flame.
11 Do not rise because of the face of an insolent person,
lest he lie like an ambush for your mouth.
12 Do not lend to a person more powerful than you,
and if you lend to him, let it be as a loss.
13 Do not provide surety beyond your ability;
and if you do provide surety, be careful to pay it back.
14 Do not go to law with a judge,
for they will decide for him according to his honor.
15 Do not go on the way with a reckless person
lest he be burdensome upon you;
for he will act according to his will,
and you will perish with him for his folly.
16 Do not do battle with the hot-tempered,
and do not cross the desert with him,
because blood is as nothing in his eyes,
and he will cut you down where there is no help.
17 Do not take counsel with a stupid person,
for he cannot keep a word secret.
18 Do no secret thing in front of a stranger,
for you do not know what he will reveal.
19 Do not reveal your heart to every person,
and let him not return a favor to you.

*Women* **9** Do not be jealous of the wife of your embrace,
lest you teach an evil lesson against yourself.
2 Do not give your soul to a woman
for her to trample upon your strength.
3 Do not meet a woman escort,
lest you fall into her traps.
4 Do not continue with a singer,
lest you be caught in her attempts.
5 Do not stare at a virgin,
lest you stumble in her wages.
6 Do not give your soul to prostitutes,
lest you lose your inheritance.
7 Do not look around in the narrow streets of the city,
and do not wander into its deserted areas.
8 Turn your eye away from a shapely woman,
and do not gaze at another's beauty;
many have been misled by the beauty of a woman,
and from this, affection is kindled like a fire.
9 Do not sit with a married woman at all,
and do not share in wine with her
lest your soul turn away to her
and slip into destruction in your spirit.

10 Do not forsake an old friend, *Friends*
  for the recent friend is not his equal.
  A new friend is new wine;
  if it ages, you will drink it with joy.
11 Do not envy the glory of a sinner,
  for you do not know what his end will be.
12 Do not take pleasure in the pleasure of the ungodly;
  remember that they will never be justified, as far as Hades.
13 Keep far from a person who has the authority to murder,
  and you will never be anxious with the fear of death;
  and if you go near him, do not offend him,
  lest he take away your life;
  recognize that you are stepping among traps,
  and you are walking on the battlements of the city.
14 According to your strength, try to know your neighbors
  and consult with the wise.
15 And let your thoughts be with the intelligent
  and all your discourse in the law of the Most High.
16 Let righteous men be your table companions,
  and let your boast be in the fear of the Lord.
17 A work will be praised for the hand of the craftsmen,
  and the leader of people is wise for his word.
18 A talkative man is fearsome in his city,
  and one who is reckless in his word will be hated.

**10** A wise judge will discipline his people, *Government*
  and the leadership of the prudent will be well ordered.
2 According to the judge of his people, so also are his ministers,
  and according to the leader of the city are all those
    who dwell in it.
3 An undisciplined king destroys his people,
  and a city shall be settled by the understanding of the princes.
4 The government of the earth is in the hand of the Lord,
  and he will raise up over it one who is advantageous for
    the time.
5 The success of a man is in the hand of the Lord,
  and he will place his honor on the face of the scribe.

6 Do not cherish wrath against a neighbor for any wrong, *Pride and*
  and do nothing by works of insolence. *Honor*
7 Arrogance is hateful before the Lord and humans,
  and unrighteous things will offend from both.
8 A kingdom is transferred from people to people
  through unrighteousness and insolence and possessions.
9 Why are earth and ashes arrogant?
  Because I threw his entrails in life.*a*
10 A physician mocks a long illness,

---

*a* The meaning of the Gk. is obscure

and today a king, and tomorrow he will die.

11 For when a person dies, he will inherit creeping things and
beasts, worms.

12 The beginning of a person's arrogance is when he renounces
from the Lord,
and he has removed his heart from the one who made him,

13 because the beginning of arrogance is sin,
and the one who grasps it will pour out an abomination.
Because of this, the Lord appointed the miseries,
and he overthrew them in the end.

14 The Lord brought down the thrones of rulers,
and he seated the meek in their place.

15 The Lord has plucked out the roots of the nations,
and he has planted the humble in their place.

16 The Lord overthrew the territories of the nations,
and he destroyed them to the foundations of the earth.

17 He dried up some of them and destroyed them,
and their memory ceased from the earth.

18 Arrogance was not created for humans,
nor the anger of wrath for the offspring of women.

19 What sort of seed is honorable? Human seed.
What sort of seed is honorable? Those who fear the Lord.
What sort of seed is dishonorable? Human seed.
What sort of seed is dishonorable? Those who transgress the
commandments.

20 In the midst of brothers, their leader is honored,
and those who fear the Lord in his eyes.[a]

22 The rich and the noble and the poor—
their honor is the fear of the Lord.

23 It is not righteous to dishonor a poor person who is wise,
and it is not proper to honor a man who is a sinner.

24 The noble and the judge and the ruler will be honored,
and there is none of them greater than those
who fear the Lord.

25 The free will minister to a wise servant,
and an understanding man will not complain.

*Honor and
Wealth*

26 Do not act wise to do your work,
and do not be honored in the time of your difficulty.

27 Better in every way is the worker than the one who walks around
or who is honored and lacks bread.

28 Child, honor your soul in humility,
and give it the esteem corresponding to its worthiness.

29 Who will justify the one who sins against his soul?
And who will honor the one who dishonors his life?

30 The poor is honored for his knowledge,
and the rich is honored for his wealth.

[a] Swete lacks verse 21

³¹ But the one who is being honored in poverty, how much more
    also in wealth?
  And the one who is dishonored in wealth, how much more
    in poverty?

# 11

The wisdom of the humble exalts his head,
    and it will cause him to sit in the midst of nobles.

² Do not praise a man for his beauty,
    and do not detest a person for his appearance.

³ The bee is small among winged creatures,
    and her fruit is the first of sweet things.

⁴ Do not boast in the wearing of clothes,
    and do not lift up yourself in the day of glory;
  for the works of the Lord are wonderful,
    and his works are hidden among humans.

⁵ Many tyrants have sat on the ground,
    but the one who was not expected has worn a diadem.

⁶ Many princes have been very dishonored,
    and nobles have been given over into the hands
        of their comrades.

⁷ Do not blame before you examine;
    understand first, and then rebuke.

⁸ Do not answer before you hear,
    and do not insert yourself in the midst of words.

⁹ Do not argue about a matter that is no concern of yours,
    and do not hold a council at the judgment of sinners.

¹⁰ Child, do not let your deeds be about many things;
    if you multiply them, you will not go unpunished.
  And if you pursue them, you will never overtake them,
    and you will never escape them by fleeing.

¹¹ There is one who works and toils and hurries
    and lacks all the more.

¹² There is one who is lazy and in need of help,
    lacking in strength and abounding in poverty;
  and the eyes of the Lord look upon him for good things,
    and he set him aright from his humiliation

¹³ and raised up his head,
    and many were amazed at him.

¹⁴ Good things and bad, life and death,
    poverty and riches are from the Lord.ᵃ

*Prosperity
and Death*

¹⁷ The gift of the Lord remains with the godly,
    and his approval will prosper for eternity.

¹⁸ There is one who becomes rich by his care and greed,
    and this is his part of the reward:

¹⁹ When he says, "I have found rest,
    and now I will eat from my goods,"
  and does not know what time will pass by,

ᵃ Swete lacks verses 15–16

and he will leave them behind for others and will die.

20 Be firm in your covenant, and busy yourself in it,
    and grow old in your work.

21 Do not marvel at the works of a sinner;
    trust the Lord and remain in your labor,
    because it is easy in the eyes of the Lord to suddenly make
        a poor person rich through swiftness.

22 There is a blessing of the Lord in the reward of the godly,
    and in a quick hour he causes his blessing to flourish.

23 Do not say, "What is my need?
    And what good things will be mine now?"

24 Do not say, "I am self-sufficient,
    and how will I be mistreated now?"

25 In the day of prosperity, evil things are forgotten,
    and in the day of evil, prosperity is not remembered.

26 For it is light before the Lord in the day of death
    to repay a person according to his ways.

27 Affliction for an hour makes one forgetful of delight,
    and at the conclusion of a person his works are discovered.

28 Call no one blessed before death;
    a man will be known by his children.

*Caution and Benefit*

29 Do not bring every person into your house,
    for many are the traps of the deceitful.

30 A decoy partridge in a cage,
    so is the heart of the arrogant,
    and like the spy he watches for your downfall.

31 For he lies in wait, changing the good things into evil,
    and he places blame in what is preferred.

32 A heap of charcoal will grow from a spark of fire,
    and a sinful person lies in wait for blood.

33 Beware of a mischievous person, for he devises evil things,
    lest he give you blame for eternity.

34 Receive a stranger into your house, and he will turn you
        to troubles
    and alienate you from your own family.

**12** If you do good, know to whom you are doing it,
    and there will be grace for your good deeds.

2 Do good to a godly person, and you will find a reward,
    and if not from him, rather from the Most High.

3 There are no good things for the one who continues in evil
    and for the one who does not freely give alms.

4 Give to the godly, and do not help the sinner.

5 Do good to the humble, and do not give to the ungodly;
    hold back his loaves, and do not give them to him,
    lest he oppress you by them;
    for you will find twice the evil things
    in all the good things you would do for him.

6  For even the Most High hated sinners,
       and he will repay vengeance to the ungodly.
7  Give to the good and do not help the sinner.

8  A friend will not be punished in good times,          *Selecting*
       and an enemy will not be hidden in bad times.     *Friends*
9  In a man's good times his enemies are in grief,
       and in his bad times even his friend will depart.
10  Do not trust your enemy for eternity,
       for as copper becomes rusty so does his wickedness.
11  Even if he humbles himself and walks bent over,
       safeguard your soul and guard against him,
    and be to him like one who has wiped a mirror,
       and you will know that it was not completely tarnished.
12  Do not stand him beside yourself,
       lest, after overturning you, he stand in your place;
    do not sit him at your right hand,
       lest he seek after your seat,
    and at last you will recognize my words
       and be stung by my sayings.
13  Who will show mercy to a charmer bitten by a serpent,
       and all those who draw near to wild animals?
14  So it is for the man who associates with a sinner
       and becomes involved in his sins.
15  He will remain with you for a time,
       but if you fall away, he will not endure.
16  An enemy speaks sweetly with his lips,
       but in his heart he will plan to throw you into a pit.
    An enemy will shed tears with his eyes,
       but if he finds an opportunity he will not be satisfied with
          your blood.
17  If evil comes upon you, you will find him there ahead of you;
       and as if he is helping, he will trip your heel.
18  He will shake his head and clap his hands
       and whisper many things and change his face.

**13** The one who touches pitch will be stained,          *Peers*
       and the one who has fellowship with an arrogant person will
          become like him.
2  Do not take a burden that is beyond you,
       and do not associate with one stronger and richer than you.
    How will an earthen pot associate with a kettle?
       This one will knock against it, and this one will be smashed.
3  The rich does wrong and proceeds to be indignant;
       the poor has been wronged and he will be in need.
4  If you are useful, he will work with you,
       but if you are lacking, he will leave you behind.
5  If you have something, he will live with you
       and drain you, and he will not be distressed about it.

⁶ He has need of you and will deceive you
   and smile at you and will give you hope;
he will speak pleasantly to you
   and say, "What do you need?"
⁷ And he will shame you with his foods
   until he drains you two or three times,
   and at last he will mock you.
After these things, he will see you and leave you behind
   and shake his head at you.
⁸ Take care; do not be led astray,
   and do not be humbled by your merriment.
⁹ When a powerful person invites you, be reserved,
   and he will invite you so much more.
¹⁰ Do not be forward, lest you be pushed away,
   and do not withdraw far, lest you be forgotten.
¹¹ Do not hold yourself to speak with him as an equal,
   and do not trust his many words;
for he will test you with much talk,
   and as he smiles he will examine you.
¹² Merciless is the one who does not guard words
   and will not spare concerning affliction and chains.
¹³ Observe closely and take great care
   because you are walking with your downfall.ᵃ
¹⁵ Every living thing loves its like,
   and every person his neighbor.
¹⁶ All flesh gathers together according to kind,
   and a man will stick with the one like him.
¹⁷ What fellowship will a wolf have with a lamb?
   So is a sinner with the godly.
¹⁸ What peace does a hyena have toward a dog?
   And what peace does the rich have toward the poor?
¹⁹ Wild asses are the prey of the lions in the desert;
   so the poor are a pasture for the rich.
²⁰ Humility is an abomination to the arrogant,
   so the poor is an abomination to the rich.
²¹ A rich person who is shaken is supported by friends,
   but the humble who has fallen is pushed away by his friends.
²² When the rich stumbles, there are many protectors;
   he said unspeakable things, and they justified him.
The humble stumbled and they rebuked him;
   he spoke with intelligence and no place was given to him.
²³ The rich spoke and everyone was silent,
   and they exalted his word up to the clouds.
The poor spoke and they said, "Who is this?"
   And if he stumbles, they will overturn him.
²⁴ Wealth that has no sin is good,
   and poverty is evil in the mouths of the godly.

ᵃ Swete lacks verse 14

25 The heart of a person changes his face,
   whether to good things or to bad.
26 The sign of a heart in good times is a cheerful face,
   and the discovery of parables is reasoned through with toil.

**14** Blessed is the man who did not slip with his mouth                *Greed*
   and was not stung by the grief of sin.
2 Blessed is the one whose soul has not condemned him
   and who has not fallen from his hope.
3 Wealth is no good to a miserly man;
   and why does an envious person have possessions?
4 The one who gathers from his soul gathers for others,
   and others will live luxuriously in his good times.
5 To whom will the one who is evil to himself be good?
   And he will not be cheered by his possessions.
6 There is no one more evil than him who begrudges himself,
   and this is the repayment of his evil.
7 And if he acts well, he does it in forgetfulness,
   and at last he reveals his wickedness.
8 The one who begrudges with his eye is wicked,
   turning back his face and disregarding souls.
9 The eye of the greedy is not satisfied with his portion,
   and evil injustice will dry up the soul.
10 The evil eye is envious for bread,
   and it is lacking on his table.

11 Child, treat yourself well according to your means,                *Give While*
   and bring offerings to the Lord worthily.                         *You Can*
12 Remember that death will not delay,
   and the covenant of Hades has not been revealed to you.
13 Before you die, treat a friend well,
   and reach out and give to him according to your might.
14 Do not withdraw from a good day,
   and do not let a part of a good desire pass you by.
15 Will you not leave behind your toil to another,
   and your labors for distribution by lot?
16 Give and take, and deceive your soul,
   because in Hades there is no seeking of delight.
17 All flesh becomes old like a garment,
   for the covenant from eternity is, "By death you will die!"
18 Like a leaf growing on a bushy tree,
   some are cut down, while others grow;
   so is the generation of flesh and blood:
   one dies, and another is born.
19 Every decaying work comes to an end,
   and the one who does it will come to an end with it.

20 Blessed is the man who will die in wisdom                          *Happiness*
   and who will converse in his intelligence;                        *of the Wise*

²¹ the one who ponders her ways in his heart
    will also gain insight into her secrets.
²² Go out after her like a hunter
    and lie in wait at her entrances!
²³ The one who looks through her windows
    and listens at her doorway,
²⁴ who settles near her house
    and fixes a peg into the wall of her house,
²⁵ he will pitch his tent according to her hand
    and lodge in a good lodging place.
²⁶ He will put his children in her shelter
    and dwell under her branches.
²⁷ He will be protected by her from the heat,
    and he will lodge in her glory.

**15** The one who fears the Lord will do it,
    and the one who grasps the law will take hold of her.
² And she will meet him like a mother,
    and she will welcome him like a wife of virginity.
³ She will feed him the bread of understanding
    and give him the water of wisdom to drink.
⁴ He will be supported by her and he will not wobble,
    and he will be restrained by her and will not be disgraced.
⁵ And she will exalt him above his neighbors,
    and she will open his mouth in the midst of the assembly.
⁶ Gladness and a crown of rejoicing
    and an eternal name he will inherit.
⁷ Foolish people will never lay hold of her,
    and sinful men will never see her.
⁸ She is far from arrogance,
    and lying men will never remember her.

*Human*
*Freedom*
⁹ Praise is not beautiful in the mouth of a sinner
    because it was not sent from the Lord.
¹⁰ For praise will be proclaimed in wisdom,
    and the Lord will prosper it.
¹¹ Do not say, "I turned away on account of the Lord,"
    for you shall not do that which he hates.
¹² Do not say, "He led me astray,"
    for he has no need of a sinful man.
¹³ The Lord hated every abomination,
    and it is not beloved to those who fear him.
¹⁴ He made humanity from the beginning
    and left him in the hand of his counsel.
¹⁵ If you want, you will observe the commandments,
    and to perform faithfulness of goodwill.
¹⁶ He has set fire and water before you;
    you shall stretch out your hand to wherever you want.
¹⁷ Life and death is before humans,
    and whichever pleases him will be given to him.

18 For the wisdom of the Lord is great;
    he is mighty in dominance and he sees everything.
19 And his eyes are upon those who fear him,
    and he will recognize all of a person's work.
20 And he has commanded that no one act profanely,
    and he gave no liberty for anyone to sin.

# 16

Do not desire a multitude of useless children
    or make merry over ungodly sons;

*Curse and
Blessing*

2 if they multiply, do not make merry over them
    unless the fear of the Lord is with them.
3 Do not have trust in their life
    and do not hold on to their place;
for one is better than a thousand
    and to die childless than to have ungodly children.
4 For a city will be united*a* from one wise person,
    but a tribe of lawless people will be desolated.
5 I have seen many things such as this with my eyes,
    and my ear has heard things more powerful than these.
6 In an assembly of sinners a fire will be kindled,
    and anger will burn in a resistant nation.
7 He did not make atonement concerning the ancient giants
    who turned away in their might.
8 He did not spare—concerning Lot's exile—
    those whom he loathed on account of their arrogance.
9 He showed no mercy to a nation of destruction,
    to those who were taken away in their sins,
10 and so to six hundred thousand foot soldiers
    who gathered together in their hardness of heart.
11 Even if there is one stiff-necked person, this will be amazing
        if he will go unpunished;
for mercy and anger are with him,
    the master of atonements and the one who pours out anger.
12 According to his great mercy, so also his rebuke is great;
    he will judge a man according to his works.
13 The sinner will not flee with the spoils,
    and the patience of the godly will not come far behind.
14 He will make a place for all mercy;
    each will find according to his works.*b*
17 Do not say, "I will be hidden from the Lord;
    will anyone remember me from on high?
I will never be remembered among a great people;
    for what is my soul in the immeasurable creation?"
18 Look, the heavens and God's heaven of heavens,
    the deep, and the earth will be shaken at his visitation.
19 The mountains and the foundations of the earth together
    shake with trembling when he looks at them.

---

*a* Lit. "house together"  *b* Swete lacks verses 15–16

20 And no heart will think upon them,
   and who will ponder his ways?
21 And there is a tempest, which no person will see,
   and most of his works are in hidden places.
22 Who will announce works of righteousness?
   Or who will endure? For the covenant is far away.
23 The one who is lessened in his heart thinks these things,
   and a foolish and deceived man thinks stupid things.

*Order in Creation*

24 Listen my child, and learn understanding,
   and pay attention to my words in your heart.
25 I will reveal instruction with a weight,
   and I announce understanding with precision.
26 In the judgment of the Lord are his works from the beginning,
   and from the making of them he divided their parts.
27 He arranged his works for eternity
   and their offices for their generations;
   they do not hunger or grow weary,
   and they did not desist from their works.
28 Each one did not afflict his neighbor,
   and until eternity they will not resist his saying.
29 And after these things, the Lord looked upon the earth
   and filled it with his good things.
30 He covered its face with the soul of every animal,
   and they shall return into it.

*Creator and Judge*

**17** The Lord created a person from the earth,
   and he returned him to it again.
2 He gave them days of a number, and time,
   and gave them authority over the things on it.
3 He clothed them with might according to themselves,
   and he made them according to his image.
4 And he put the fear of him upon all flesh,
   even to dominate wild animals and birds.*
6 Counsel and tongue and eyes,
   ears and heart he gave to them to understand.
7 He filled them with the knowledge of understanding,
   and he showed them good and evil.
8 He put his eye upon their hearts
   to show them the splendor of his works,
9 so that they might proclaim his magnificent works
10 and they will praise the name of holiness.
11 He placed knowledge before them,
   and he gave them the law of life as an inheritance.
12 He established an eternal covenant with them,
   and he showed his judgments to them.

*a* Swete lacks verse 5

13 Their eyes saw a magnificent thing of glory,
   and their ears heard the glory of their voice.
14 And he said to them, "Beware of every unrighteous thing,"
   and he gave them each a command concerning their neighbor.
15 Their ways are before him always;
   they will not be hidden from his eyes.*
17 He appointed a leader for each nation,
   and Israel is the portion of the Lord.*
19 All of their works are before him like the sun,
   and his eyes are continually upon their ways.
20 Their injustices are not hidden from him,
   and all their sins are before the Lord.*
22 The alms of a man are with him like a signet ring,
   and he will closely guard a person's favor like the apple
      of his eye.
23 After these things, he will rise up and repay them
   and repay their recompense on their head.
24 But he gave return to those who repent,
   and he encouraged those who ran out of endurance.

25 Return to the Lord and abandon your sins;                    *Repentance*
   pray before his face and reduce the offense.
26 Turn back to the Most High and turn away from
      unrighteousness,
   and greatly hate abomination.
27 Who will praise the Most High in Hades
   instead of the living and those who give thanks?
28 Thanksgiving perishes from the dead like one who does not exist;
   the living and healthy will praise the Lord.
29 How great is the mercy of the Lord
   and forgiveness to those who turn to him!
30 For not everything can be among humans
   because the son of humanity is not immortal.
31 What is brighter than the sun? Even this comes to an end,
   and evil shall consider flesh and blood.
32 He examines the power of the height of the heavens,
   and all humans are earth and ashes.

# 18

The one who lives for eternity created everything in common.    *Greatness*
2 The Lord alone will be justified.*
4 He permitted no one to make his works known,
   and who shall search out his splendor?
5 Who will count the strength of his majesty?
   And who will add to recount his mercies?
6 There is no diminishing or increasing them,
   and there is no searching out the wonders of the Lord.

---

*a* Swete lacks verse 16  *b* Swete lacks verse 18  *c* Swete lacks verse 21  *d* Swete lacks verse 3

7 When a person finishes, then he is beginning,
    and when he ceases, then he will be at a loss.
8 What is a person, and what is his use?
    What is his good, and what is his evil?
9 The number of a person's days is many; a hundred years.
10 Like a drop of water from the sea and a grain of sand,
    so are a few years in the day of eternity.
11 Because of this the Lord was patient with them
    and kept pouring his mercy upon them.
12 He saw and recognized their destruction, that it was evil;
    because of this he multiplied his forgiveness.
13 The mercy of a person is upon his neighbor,
    but the mercy of the Lord is upon all flesh,
  reproving and instructing and teaching
    and turning them back like a shepherd turns his flock.
14 He has mercy upon those who receive instruction
    and those who are eager for his judgments.

*Caution*

15 Child, do not give blame with good deeds
    and grief of words with every gift.
16 Will not the dew relieve the burning heat?
    So a word is better than a gift.
17 Look, is not a word better than a good gift?
    And both are for a favored man.
18 A stupid person will revile ungraciously,
    and the gift of the grudging melts the eyes.
19 Learn before speaking,
    and attend to your health before sickness.
20 Scrutinize yourself before the judgment,
    and you will find forgiveness in the hour of visitation.
21 Humble yourself before you become sick,
    and show repentance in the time of sins.
22 Do not hold back from repaying a vow promptly,
    and do not wait until death to be justified.
23 Prepare yourself before praying,
    and do not be like a person who tests the Lord.
24 Remember wrath in the days of death
    and at the time of vengeance when he turns his face away.
25 Remember the time of famine in the time of plenty,
    poverty and want in the days of wealth.
26 Time changes from morning until evening,
    and all things are fleeting before the Lord.
27 A wise person will be cautious in everything,
    and in the days of sins he will take care against trespass.
28 Every wise person knows wisdom,
    and the one who finds her will give thanks.
29 The wise in words also made themselves wise,
    and they poured out accurate proverbs.

<sup>30</sup> Do not go after your desires,
  and restrain yourself from your appetites.
<sup>31</sup> If you will provide your soul with approval of desire,
  it will make you a laughingstock of your enemies.
<sup>32</sup> Do not make merry over great luxury;
  do not be bound by its expense.
<sup>33</sup> Do not become poor by feasting from borrowing,
  and you have nothing in your bag.

*Self-Control of Soul<sup>a</sup>*

# 19

<sup>1</sup> A drunken worker will not become wealthy;
  the one who scorns the few things will fall little by little.
<sup>2</sup> Wine and women will lead the intelligent astray,
  and the one who joins himself to prostitutes will be
    more reckless.
<sup>3</sup> Decay and worms will take possession of him,
  and a reckless soul will be taken away.
<sup>4</sup> The one who trusts quickly is light in heart,
  and the one who sins will do wrong to his soul.
<sup>5</sup> The one who makes merry will be condemned by his heart,
<sup>6</sup> and the one who hates talking will diminish evil.
<sup>7</sup> Never repeat a word,
  and you will never lose anything.
<sup>8</sup> Do not report it to friend or to foe,
  and unless it is sin to you, do not reveal it.
<sup>9</sup> For he has heard you, and he watched you,
  and in time he will hate you.
<sup>10</sup> Have you heard a word? Let it die with you.
  Take courage! It will never make you burst.
<sup>11</sup> A fool will go into labor from the face of a word,
  as she who gives birth from the face of a baby.
<sup>12</sup> An arrow sticking in a thigh of flesh—
  such is a word in the belly of a stupid person.

<sup>13</sup> Reprove a friend; perhaps he did not do it,
  and if he did do something, perhaps he would repeat it.
<sup>14</sup> Reprove a friend; perhaps he did not say it,
  and if he has said it, lest he repeat it.
<sup>15</sup> Reprove a friend, for often it becomes slander,
  and do not believe every word.
<sup>16</sup> There is one who slips, and not from his heart,
  and who has not sinned with his tongue?
<sup>17</sup> Reprove your neighbor before threatening him,
  and give a place for the law of the Most High.<sup>b</sup>

*Gossip*

<sup>20</sup> All wisdom is the fear of the Lord,
  and in all wisdom is doing the law.<sup>c</sup>
<sup>22</sup> And knowledge of evil is not wisdom,
  and prudence is not where the counsel of sinners is.

*True Wisdom and Speech*

<sup>a</sup> Swete includes section title  <sup>b</sup> Swete lacks verses 18–19  <sup>c</sup> Swete lacks verse 21

²³ There is a wickedness, and this is an abomination,
  and a fool is inferior in wisdom.
²⁴ Better is the one inferior in understanding who is fearful
  than the one who abounds in prudence and transgresses
  the law.
²⁵ There is a scrupulous craftiness, and this is unrighteous;
  and there is one who twists a favor to produce a judgment.
²⁶ There is a wicked person bent over in blackness,
  and he is full of deceit inside.
²⁷ Bending down his face and being deaf in one ear,
  he will outrun you where he is not recognized.
²⁸ And if he is hindered from sinning by lack of strength,
  if he finds an opportune time he will do evil.
²⁹ A man will be recognized by his appearance,
  and an intelligent person will be recognized by a meeting
  of the face.
³⁰ The clothing of a man and open-mouthed laugh[a] and the stride
  of a person report the things about him.

# 20

¹ There is a reproof that is not appropriate,
  and there is one who keeps silent, and he is prudent.

*Loss and Speech*

² How good it is to reprove rather than be wrathful,
  and the one who admits fault will be kept from loss.[b]
⁴ A eunuch's desire is to violate a young woman,
  so is he who makes judgments under threat of force.
⁵ There is one who keeps silent, being found wise,
  and there is one who is hated because of much talk.
⁶ There is one who keeps silent, for he has nothing to answer,
  and there is one who keeps silent because he knows
  the opportune time.
⁷ A wise person will be silent until the opportune time,
  but the swaggerer and fool will miss the opportune time.
⁸ The one who abounds in words will be detested,
  and the one who usurps authority will be hated.
⁹ A man has success in evil times,
  and there is unexpected fortune in loss.
¹⁰ There is giving that will not profit you,
  and there is giving whose return is double.
¹¹ There is loss for the sake of glory,
  and there is one who will raise his head from humiliation.
¹² There is one who buys many things with a little
  and repays them sevenfold.
¹³ The wise in word will make himself beloved,
  but the favors of stupid people will be poured out.
¹⁴ The giving of a fool will not profit you,
  for his eyes are many instead of single.

---

[a] Lit. "laughter of teeth"  [b] Swete lacks verse 3

15 He will give little and reproach much,
  and will open his mouth like a herald.
  Today he lends, and tomorrow he will demand return;
  hateful is such a person.
16 A fool will say, "I have no friend,
  and there is no thanks for my good deeds.
  Those who eat my bread are worthless with their tongues."
17 How often and how many will mock him?

18 A slip from the ground is better than from the tongue,                    *Careful Speech*
  so the downfall of the wicked will come with haste.
19 An ungracious person, an ill-timed story,
  will always be in the mouth of a fool.
20 A proverb from the mouth of a fool will be rejected,
  for he does not speak it in its opportune time.
21 There is one who is hindered from sinning because of need,
  and in his rest he will not be pierced to the heart.
22 There is one who destroys his soul through shame
  and will destroy it because of the face of a fool.
23 There is one who makes promises to a friend on account of shame,
  and has gratuitously made him an enemy.
24 A lie is an evil blot in a person;
  it will always be in the mouth of the undisciplined.
25 Better a thief than one who continues in a lie,
  but both will inherit destruction.
26 The disposition of a lying person is dishonorable,
  and his shame is with him continuously.

27 The wise in words will promote himself,                    *Proverbial*
  and a prudent person will please nobles.                    *Words*[a]
28 The one who works the land will raise his heap,
  and the one who pleases nobles will make atonement
      for injustice.
29 Hospitality and gifts blind the eyes of the wise,
  and turn him away from discipline like a muzzle in the mouth.
30 Hidden wisdom and unseen treasure—
  what benefit is there in both?
31 Better is a person who hides his folly
  than a person who hides his wisdom.

# 21

Child, have you sinned? Add to them no more,                    *Various Sins*
  and petition concerning your former ones.
2 Flee from sin as from the face of a serpent;
  for if you approach it, it will bite you.
  Its teeth are lion's teeth,
      destroying the souls of humans.
3 All lawlessness is like a two-edged sword;

---

[a] Swete includes section title

there is no healing for its wound.

4 Panic and insolence will desolate wealth;
  so, too, the house of the arrogant will be desolated.

5 The prayer of the poor person goes from his mouth to his ears,
  and his judgment comes with speed.

6 The one who hates reproof walks in the footprints of a sinner,
  and the one who fears the Lord will convert in his heart.

7 The one who is strong in tongue is known from afar,
  but the intelligent knows it when he slips.

8 The one who builds his house with the wealth of another
  is like one who gathers his stones in a storm.

9 The gathering of the lawless is like gathered flax,
  and their end is a flame of fire.

10 The way of sinners is leveled with stones,
  and at its end is the pit of Hades.

11 The one who keeps the law controls his thought,
  and the conclusion of the fear of the Lord is wisdom.

12 Whoever is not crafty will not be disciplined;
  there is a craftiness that increases bitterness.

13 The knowledge of the wise will increase like a flood,
  and his counsel is like a fountain of life.

14 The entrails of a stupid person are like a broken vessel,
  and he will not master any knowledge.

15 If an intelligent person hears a wise word,
  he will praise it and add to it;
  the indulgent person heard and it displeased him,
  and he turned it behind his back.

16 The explanation of a fool is like a burden on a journey,
  but grace will be found upon the lips of the intelligent.

17 The mouth of a prudent person will be sought in an assembly,
  and he will remember his words in his heart.

18 Like a destroyed house, so is wisdom to a stupid person,
  and the knowledge of the ignorant is unexamined words.

19 Fetters on the feet—discipline for the thoughtless,
  and like manacles on his right hand.

20 A fool raises his voice in laughter,
  but a clever man will scarcely smile softly.

21 Instruction is like a golden ornament to the thoughtful
  and like a bracelet on his right arm.

22 The stupid person's foot rushes into a house,
  but the experienced person will be ashamed by his face.

23 A fool peers into a house from the door,
  but a disciplined man will stand outside.

24 It is a person's ignorance to listen from the door,
  but the thoughtful will be weighed down by dishonor.

25 The lips of strangers will be weighed down by these,
  but words of the thoughtful will be set in a yoke.

26 The heart of the stupid is in their mouth,
  but the mouth of the wise is their heart.

27 When the ungodly curses the satan,
    he curses his own soul.
28 The whisperer defiles his own soul,
    and he will be hated in the neighborhood.

# 22

1 A lazy person was compared to a filthy stone,     *Degenerates*
    and everyone will hiss at his dishonor.     *and Friends*
2 A lazy person has been compared to the filth of manure:
    everyone who picks it up will shake off his hand.
3 The shame of a father is in an undisciplined child,
    but a daughter is born at a loss.
4 A thoughtful daughter will take possession of her husband,
    and she who is shamed becomes grief for the one who
        fathered her.
5 The bold woman shames a father and a husband,
    and she will be dishonored by both.
6 Music in mourning is like an ill-timed story;
    whips and discipline are of wisdom at every time.
7 The one who teaches a fool is one who glues pottery,
    who awakens a sleeper from a deep sleep.
8 The one who tells a story to a fool is one who tells a story
        to a sleeper,
    and at the conclusion he will say, "What is it?"[a]
11 Weep over the dead, for he has abandoned the light,
    and weep over the stupid person, for he has abandoned
        intelligence.
    Weep less bitterly over the dead, since he has found rest,
    but the evil life of a stupid person is beyond death.
12 There are seven days of mourning for the dead,
    but for a fool and the ungodly, all the days of his life.
13 Do not talk much with a fool,
    and do not go to a person without understanding.
    Keep away from him, lest you have trouble,
    and you will never be stained when he shakes himself.
    Turn away from him, and you will find rest,
    and you will not be wearied by his madness.
14 What will be weighed down more than lead?
    And what is the name for it except "fool"?
15 Sand and salt and a lump of iron
    are easier to carry than a person without understanding.
16 A beam of wood fastened into a building
    will not come loose in an earthquake;
    so the heart established by thoughts of a plan
    will not be afraid at the time.
17 A heart established on intelligent thought
    is like a plaster ornament on a polished wall.

---

[a] Swete lacks verses 9–10

<sup>18</sup> Fences laid on high ground
  shall not endure against the wind;
so a cowardly heart laid on the thought of a stupid person
  will never endure in the presence of every fear.
<sup>19</sup> The one who pricks the eye causes tears,
  and the one who pricks the heart reveals feelings.
<sup>20</sup> The one who throws a stone at birds scares them away,
  and the one who reviles a friend will break a
    friendship.
<sup>21</sup> If you draw a sword against a friend,
  do not despair, for there is a way back.
<sup>22</sup> If you open your mouth against a friend,
  do not worry, for there is reconciliation;
but reproach and arrogance and disclosing a secret and
    a deceitful wound—
  at these things, every friend will flee.
<sup>23</sup> Gain trust with your neighbor in poverty
  so that in his good times you might be filled together.
Remain by him in the time of affliction
  so that you might be a co-heir in his inheritance.
<sup>24</sup> Before a fire there is steam and smoke from a furnace;
  so, before blood there is abuse.
<sup>25</sup> I will not be ashamed to protect a friend,
  and I will not hide from his face.
<sup>26</sup> And if evil things happen to me because of him,
  everyone who hears it will keep away from him.

*Vigilance*   <sup>27</sup> Who will give me a guard over my mouth
  and a clever seal on my lips,
lest I fall because of it
  and my tongue destroy me?

**23** Lord, father and master of my life,
  do not abandon me to their plan;
do not leave me to fall among them.
<sup>2</sup> Who will set whips upon my thoughts
  and the discipline of wisdom over my heart,
so they might not spare over my mistakes
  and do not overlook their sins,
<sup>3</sup> so that my ignorance does not multiply,
  and my sins abound,
and then I will fall before my adversaries,
  and my enemy will rejoice over me?
<sup>4</sup> Lord, father and God of my life,
  do not give me lifting of eyes,
<sup>5</sup> and turn desire away from me.
<sup>6</sup> Do not let the appetite of the belly and lust take hold of me,
  and do not hand me over to a shameless soul.

7  Listen to the instruction of the mouth, children,           *Discipline*
   and the one who keeps watch will never be caught;    *of Mouth*[a]
 by his lips [8]he will be left behind,
   and the sinner and abuser and arrogant
   will be tripped up by them.

9  Do not accustom your mouth to an oath,
   and do not be accustomed to the naming of the Holy One.

10  For just as a household servant who is continuously scrutinized
   will not lack a bruise,
 so the one who always swears and takes the Name
   will never be clean from sin.

11  A man who swears often will be full of lawlessness,
   and the whip will not depart from his house.
 If he errs, his sin remains upon him;
   and if he disregards it, he has sinned doubly.
 And if he has sworn in vain, he will not be pronounced righteous,
   for his house will be full of misery.

12  There is a kind of speech clothed with death.
   Let it not be found among the inheritance of Jacob,
 for all these things will be far from the godly,
   and they will not be involved in sins.

13  Do not accustom your mouth to lewd ignorance,
   for in it is a word of sin.

14  Remember your father and mother,
   for you sit in council in the midst of nobles,
 lest you forget yourself before them
   and by your habit you become foolish,
 and you will wish you had not been born,
   and may you not curse the day of your birth.

15  A person who is accustomed to words of reproach
   will never be disciplined in all his days.

16  Two kinds multiply sins,                    *Impure Words*
   and the third will bring on anger.           *and Women*
 A hot soul is like burning fire;
   it will never be quenched until it is swallowed up.
 A fornicating person in the body of his flesh
   will never cease until the fire burns out.

17  To a fornicating person, all bread is sweet;
   he will not grow weary until he dies.

18  A person transgressing from his bed,
   says in his soul, "Who sees me?
 Darkness circles me, and the walls are covering me,
   and no one sees me. What do I have to fear?
   The Most High will never remember my sins."

19  And the eyes of humans are his fear,

---

[a] Swete includes section title

and he does not know that the eyes of the Lord are infinitely
 brighter than the sun,
 observing all the ways of humans and perceiving in
 the secret parts.

20 Before all things were created they were known to him;
 so also after they were completed.

21 This one will be punished in the streets of the city,
 and will be seized when he has not suspected it.

22 So also a woman who leaves her husband
 and presents him with an heir from a stranger.

23 For first of all, she has resisted in the law of the Most High;
 and second, she has committed an offense against her husband;
 and third, she has committed adultery by fornication;
 she presented children from a strange man.

24 This woman will be brought out unto the assembly,
 and there will be a visitation on her children.

25 Her children will not spread into root,
 and her branches will give no fruit.

26 She will leave behind her memory for a curse,
 and her reproach will not be wiped out.

27 And those who are left behind will recognize
 that nothing is better than the fear of the Lord,
 and nothing is sweeter than giving heed to the commands
 of the Lord.

*Praise of*
*Wisdom*
# 24
Wisdom will praise her soul,
 and in the middle of her people she will boast.

2 In the assembly of the Most High she will open her mouth,
 and in the presence of his power she will boast.

3 I came out of the mouth of the Most High,
 and I covered the earth like a fog.

4 I encamped in the lofty places,
 and my throne was in a pillar of cloud.

5 I alone surrounded the circle of heaven,
 and I walked in the depth of the abyss.

6 In the waves of the sea and in all the earth,
 and among every people and nation, I have acquired
 a possession.

7 With all of these I sought rest,
 and in whose inheritance shall I lodge?

8 Then the creator of all things commanded me,
 and the one who created me gave rest to my tent
 and said, "Encamp in Jacob,
 and take possession in Israel."

9 Before eternity, from the beginning he created me;
 and until eternity I will never come to an end.

10 I ministered in the holy tent before him,
 and thus I was established in Zion.

11 In the beloved city he likewise gave me rest,
   and my authority was in Jerusalem.
12 And I took root among an honored people,
   in a portion of the Lord, his inheritance.
13 I was raised up like a cedar in Lebanon
   and like a cypress in the mountains of Hermon.
14 I was raised up on the seashore like a palm tree
   and like rose bushes in Jericho,
   like a beautiful olive tree in the field,
   and I was raised up like a plane tree.
15 I gave a sweet smell like cinnamon and aspalathus,
   and I gave a sweet smell like choicest myrrh,
   like galbanum and onyx and myrrh oil,
   and like the vapor of frankincense in a tent.
16 I stretched out my branches like a terebinth tree,
   and my branches are branches of glory and grace.
17 I am like a vine sprouting grace,
   and my blossoms are fruit of glory and wealth.*a*
19 Come to me, you who desire me,
   and be filled by my produce.
20 For the memory of me is sweeter than honey,
   and my inheritance is sweeter than a honeycomb.
21 Those who eat me will hunger more,
   and those who drink me will thirst more.
22 The one who obeys me will not be put to shame,
   and those who work with me will not sin.
23 All these things are the book of the covenant of
       the Most High God,
   the law that Moses commanded
   as an inheritance for the congregation of Jacob:*b*
25 the one who fills wisdom like the Pishon,
   and like the Tigris in the days of new things;
26 the one who fills up understanding like the Euphrates,
   and like the Jordan in the days of harvest;
27 the one who reveals discipline like light,
   like the Gihon in the days of vintage.
28 The first person did not complete knowing her,
   and so, too, the last person could not search her out.
29 For her thought was filled by the sea,
   and her counsel by the great abyss.
30 I, too, am like a canal from a river,
   and I came out like an aqueduct into paradise.
31 I said, "I will water my garden
   and make my garden bed drunk,"
   and look, my brook became a river,
   and my river became a sea.
32 Yet I will make instruction shine like the dawn,

*a* Swete lacks verse 18  *b* Swete lacks verse 24

and I will reveal them to afar.

33 Still I will pour out discipline like prophecy,
and I will leave it for generations of eternity.

34 See that I labored not only for me,
but rather for all who seek her.

*Elders*

**25** I was beautiful by three things, and I stood beautiful before the
Lord and humans:
the unity of brothers, and the affection of neighbors,
and a woman and man living in harmony with themselves.

2 But my soul hates three kinds
and I was very irritated at their life:
an arrogant poor person, and a rich liar,
an old adulterer who lacks understanding.

3 If in youth you have not gathered,
and how can you find in your old age?

4 How beautiful is judgment in gray hairs
and recognizing counsel among elders.

5 How beautiful is the wisdom of the old,
and the understanding and counsel among the honored.

6 Experience is the crown of the old,
and their boast is the fear of the Lord.

*Blessedness*

7 I have blessed nine considerations in my heart,
and I will speak a tenth with my tongue:
a person who makes merry over children,
who lives and who sees the downfall of his enemies.

8 Blessed is the one who dwells with an intelligent wife
and who has not slipped with the tongue,
and who has not served someone unworthy of him.

9 Blessed is the one who finds prudence,
and the one who recounts into the ears of those who listen.

10 How great is the one who finds wisdom,
but there is no one better than the one who fears the Lord.

11 The fear of the Lord surpasses above all;
to whom can the one who masters it be compared?[a]

*A Wicked*
*Woman*

13 Any wound, and not a wound of the heart!
And any wickedness, but not the wickedness of a woman!

14 Any misery, and not the misery of those who hate!
And any vengeance, but not the vengeance of enemies!

15 There is no head beyond the head of a serpent,
and there is no wrath beyond the wrath of an enemy.

16 I would be pleased to dwell with a lion and a dragon
rather than dwell with a wicked woman.

17 The wickedness of a woman changes her appearance
and darkens her face like sackcloth.

[a] Swete lacks verse 12

18  In the midst of his neighbors her husband will sit,
     and when he listened, he groaned bitterly.
19  All evil is little compared to the evil of a woman.
     May the lot of a sinner fall upon her.
20  A sandy ascent by the feet of the elderly,
     so is a talkative wife to a quiet husband.
21  Do not stumble at the beauty of a woman,
     and do not desire a woman.
22  There is anger and shamelessness and great shame
     if a woman provides for her husband.
23  A humble heart and sad face
     and a wounded heart is a wicked wife;
     hands dropping to the side and weakened knees
     is she who does not bless her husband.
24  The beginning of sin was from a woman,
     and because of her we all die.
25  Do not give water an outlet
     or authority to a wicked woman.
26  Unless she walks according to your hand,
     cut her off from your flesh.

**26** Blessed is the husband of a good wife,     *A Good Wife*
     and the number of his days will be double.
2   A virtuous wife cheers her husband,
     and he will fill his years with peace.
3   A good wife is a good portion;
     she will be given as a portion for those who fear the Lord.
4   The heart of a rich or poor person is good;
     at every time his face is cheerful.
5   My heart felt dread from three things,
     and my face was bound at a fourth:
     an accusation of a city, and the assembly of a crowd,
     and slander; all are hardships beyond death.
6   A rival woman to a woman is heartache and grief,
     and she who shares with everyone is a scourging of the tongue.
7   A wicked wife is a yoke being shaken;
     the one who possesses her is like one who grasps a scorpion.
8   A drunken wife is great anger,
     and she will not cover her shame.
9   The fornication of a wife is in the haughtiness of her eyes,
     and it will be known by her eyelashes.
10  Keep a firm watch over your headstrong daughter,
     lest when she finds liberty for herself, she makes use of it.
11  Guard against a shameless eye,
     and do not marvel if she offends against you.
12  As a thirsty traveler opens her mouth
     and will drink from any water nearby,
     she will sit down before every tent peg,
     and she will open her quiver before the arrow.

13 The grace of a wife will delight her husband,
   and her skill will fatten his bones.
14 A quiet wife is a gift of the Lord,
   and there is no exchange for a disciplined soul.
15 A modest wife is grace upon grace,
   and there is no weight worthier than possession of the soul.
16 The sun rising up in the heights is the Lord's,
   and the beauty of a good wife is in the ornamentation
      of his house.
17 A shining lamp on the holy lampstand—
   also the beauty of the face on steady age.
18 Golden pillars on a base of silver—
   also beautiful feet on well-built chests.[a]

*Distressing*
*Things*
28 My heart has been distressed over two things,
   and wrath has come upon me over a third:
a warrior man in lack because of need,
   and wise men being held in contempt;
the one who turns from righteousness to sin,
   the Lord will prepare him for the sword.

*Commerce*
29 A merchant will hardly keep himself from deceit,
   and a huckster will not be justified from sin.

# 27

Many have sinned for what makes no difference,
   and the one who seeks to become rich will turn back his eye.
2 A peg will be driven between the joints of stones,
   and sin will be smashed between a sale and a purchase.
3 Unless one holds fast to the fear of the Lord
   hastily, without delay,
   his house will be overturned.
4 In the shaking of a sieve, the dirt remains;
   so the filth of a person in his reasoning.
5 The kiln tests the vessels of a potter,
   and the test of person is in his schemes.
6 Its fruit reveals a tree's cultivation;
   so speech reveals the reasoning of a person's heart.
7 Do not praise a man before reasoning,
   for this is the test of people.
8 If you pursue righteousness, you will take hold of it,
   and you will put it on like a robe of glory.
9 Birds will settle with the ones like them,
   and truth will return to those who practice it.
10 A lion lies in wait for prey;
   so do sins for those who practice unrighteousness.
11 The conversation of the godly is always wisdom,
   but the fool changes like the moon.

---

[a] Swete lacks verses 19–27

12 In the midst of those without understanding observe closely
    the time,
  but continue in the midst of those who consider.
13 The story of the stupid is offense,
  and their laughter is in wantonness of sin.
14 Profanity-laden talking will lift up hair,
  and their fight is a stopping up of the ears.
15 The strife of the arrogant is a shedding of blood,
  and their railing is grievous to hear.

16 The one who reveals secrets has destroyed trust,
  and will never find a friend for his soul.
17 Cherish a friend and keep faith with him,
  but if you reveal his secrets, do not follow after him.
18 For just as a person destroyed his enemy,
  so you have destroyed the friendship of your neighbor.
19 And as you set a bird free from your hand,
  so you have let your neighbor go, and you will not catch him.
20 Do not pursue him, for he has gone far away,
  and he has escaped like a gazelle from a snare.
21 For a wound can be bound,
    and there is reconciliation of abuse,
  but the one who uncovers secrets is without hope.
22 The one who winks the eye designs evil things,
  and no one will depart from him.
23 He will sweeten your mouth before your eyes,
    and he will be amazed at your words,
  but later he will twist his mouth,
    and he will give offense with your words.
24 I have hated many things, and I did not become like him,
  and the Lord will hate him.
25 The one who throws a stone up high throws it onto his head,
  and a deceitful blow will open wounds.
26 The one who digs a pit will fall into it,
  and the one who sets a trap will be caught in it.
27 The one who does evil, it will be rolled onto him,
  and he will never know from where it has come to him.
28 Mockery and reproach are from arrogant people,
  and vengeance will lie in wait for him like a lion.
29 Those who make merry at the destruction of the godly will be
    caught in a trap,
  and pain will consume them before their death.

*Secrets and*
*Hypocrisy*

30 Vengefulness and anger, these also are abominations,
  and a sinful man will be a possessor of them.
**28** The one who avenges will find vengeance from the Lord,
    and strengthening, he will strengthen his sins.
2 Forgive your neighbor his injustice,
  and then when you pray, your sins will be pardoned.

*Resentment*
*and Strife*

3 A person holds anger against a person—
    and he seeks healing from the Lord?
4 He has no mercy for a person like himself—
    and he petitions regarding his sins?
5 He, being flesh, harbors vengefulness—
    who will make atonement for his sins?
6 Remember the end, and stop being an enemy;
    remember destruction and death and be true to the commands.
7 Remember the commandments, and do not be vengeful to
        your neighbor,
    and remember the covenant of the Most High and overlook
        ignorance.

*Strife*  8 Abstain from a fight, and you will diminish sins,
    for a hot-tempered person will ignite strife.
9 And a sinful man will trouble friends,
    and he casts slander between those at peace.
10 According to the fire's wood, so it will burn;
    according to the person's strength will be his wrath.
    And according to his wealth, his anger will rise;
    and according to the obstinacy of the fight, so it will burn.
11 Hastened strife kindles a fire,
    and a hastened fight pours out blood.
12 If you blow a spark, it will be kindled,
    and if you spit on it, it will be put out;
    and both come from your mouth.

*The Tongue*  13 Curse gossips and the deceitful,
    for they have destroyed many who were at peace.
14 A third tongue has shaken many
    and scattered them from nation to nation
    and pulled down strong cities
    and overturned the houses of nobles.
15 A third tongue has driven out virtuous women
    and deprived them of their labors.
16 The one who gives heed to it will never find rest
    or encamp with quiet.
17 A blow of a whip makes bruises,
    but a blow of the tongue will crush bones.
18 Many have fallen by the mouth of swords,
    but not as many as those who have fallen because of the tongue.
19 Blessed is the one who is protected from it,
    who has not gone through in its wrath,
    who has not pulled its yoke
    and not been bound by its chains.
20 For its yoke is a yoke of iron,
    and its chains are chains of bronze.
21 Its death is a wicked death,
    and Hades is more profitable than it.

<sup>22</sup> It will not rule over the godly,
    and they will not be burned by its flame.
<sup>23</sup> Those who forsake the Lord will fall into it,
    and it will be kindled in them, and it will never be quenched;
it will be sent out upon them like a lion,
    and it will injure them like a leopard.
<sup>24</sup> Look! Build a fence around your property with thorns;
    tie up your silver and gold!
<sup>25</sup> And make a balance and scale for your words,
    and make a door and crossbar for your mouth.
<sup>26</sup> Beware lest you somehow slip in it;
    do not fall before those lying in wait.

**29** The one who does mercy will lend to his neighbor,    *Finances*
    and the one who strengthens with his hand keeps the
      commandments.
<sup>2</sup> Lend to your neighbor in his time of need,
    and repay your neighbor again at the proper time.
<sup>3</sup> Establish a word and be trustworthy with him,
    and you will find what you need every time.
<sup>4</sup> Many considered a loan as if it were unexpected fortune,
    and caused affliction for those who helped them.
<sup>5</sup> He will kiss his hands until he receives it,
    and he will lower his voice about his neighbor's possessions,
but at the time for repayment he will delay for time,
    and respond with words of indifference
    and complain about the time.
<sup>6</sup> If he has the power, he will recover hardly half,
    and he will count it as unexpected fortune;
but if not, he has robbed him of his wealth
    and made him an enemy not without cause;
he will respond to him with curses and abuse,
    and he will respond to him with dishonor instead of honor.
<sup>7</sup> Many have turned back for the sake of evil,
    fearing to be defrauded without cause.
<sup>8</sup> Nevertheless, be longsuffering over the humble,
    and you shall draw him aside over alms.
<sup>9</sup> Help a poor man for the sake of the commandment,
    and do not turn him away empty according to his need.
<sup>10</sup> Lose your silver for a brother and a friend,
    and do not let it rust under a stone for destruction.
<sup>11</sup> Set your treasure according to the commandments of the
      Most High,
    and it will profit you more than gold.
<sup>12</sup> Deposit alms in your storehouse,
    and this will deliver you from every affliction.
<sup>13</sup> More than a shield of strength and more than a spear of might,
    it will fight for you against your enemy.

14 A good man will be surety for his neighbor,
   but the one who has lost all shame will leave him.
15 Do not forget the favor of your supporter,
   for he has given his soul on your behalf.
16 A sinner will overthrow his supporter's goods,
17    and the ungracious in thought will forsake his rescuer.
18 Being surety has destroyed many who were prosperous,
   and has shaken them like a wave of the sea.
   It has exiled mighty men,
   and they wandered among foreign nations.
19 The sinner who has fallen into surety
   and pursues gain will fall into judgments.
20 Help your neighbor according to your ability,
   and take care that you not fall.

*Hospitality*

21 The beginning of life is water and bread and clothing
   and a house that covers shame.
22 Better is the life of the poor under the shelter of a beam
   than sumptuous meat among strangers.
23 Have satisfaction with little and great.
24 A wicked life is from house to house,
   and where it will lodge, it will not open its mouth.
25 You will entertain strangers and give drink to the ungrateful,
   and for the bitter you will listen to these words:
26 "Come, sojourner, set a table,
   and if there is anything in your hand, feed me."
27 "Away, sojourner, from a face of honor;
   my brother is being hosted by me; there is need
     of hospitality."
28 These things are burdens for a person having wisdom:
   criticism from the household and the reproach of
     a moneylender.

*Concerning Children*

**30** The one who loves his son will continue his scourge,
   so that he might make merry at last.
2 The one who disciplines his son will benefit by him,
   and he will boast about him among acquaintances.
3 The one who teaches his son will make his enemy jealous,
   and he will rejoice over him before his friends.
4 His father died, and it is like he had not died,
   for he has left after him one who is like him.
5 During his life he saw and rejoiced,
   and at his end he was not grieved.
6 He has left behind an avenger against enemies
   and one who repays kindness to friends.
7 He will bind up his wounds concerning souls of sons,
   and his insides will be troubled at every cry.
8 An untamed horse goes away stubborn,
   and a son let loose turns out unruly.

9 Nurture a child, and he will astonish you;
   play with him, and he will grieve you.
10 Do not laugh with him, lest you suffer with him,
   and at last you will grind your teeth.
11 Do not give him authority in his youth.
12 Bruise his side when he is young,
   lest he become stubborn and resist you.
13 Discipline your son and work with him,
   lest you stumble by your shame.
14 Better a poor person who is healthy and strong in
      constitution
   than a rich person who is whipped in his body.
15 Health and fitness are better than any gold,
   and a strong body than immeasurable wealth.

16 There is no wealth better than the health of the body, *Concerning*
   and there is no gladness surpassing joy of the heart. *Food*
17 Death is better than a bitter life or a chronic illness.
18 Like good things poured out on a closed mouth
   is laying an offering of food on a grave.
19 What benefit is a burnt offering to an idol?
   For it can neither eat nor smell.
   So is the one punished by the Lord,
20 seeing with his eyes and sighing,
   like a eunuch embracing a virgin and sighing.
21 Do not give your soul to grief,
   and do not afflict yourself with your own counsel.
22 Merriment of heart is the life of a person,
   and the rejoicing of a man is length of days.
23 Love your soul and encourage your heart,
   and remove sorrow far from you;
   for sorrow has killed many,
   and there is no profit in it.
24 Jealousy and anger shorten days,
   and anxiety brings old age before the proper time.*

**33** 13b A bright and gentle heart at table
       will benefit from its food.
**34** 1 Watchfulness of wealth wastes away the flesh,
       and anxiety of it drives away sleep.
2 Anxiety over sleeplessness will receive drowsiness in return,
   and a severe illness will carry off sleep.
3 The rich person toiled at amassing wealth,
   and in his rest, he fills himself with his luxuries.

---

*A section of the Greek text, Sirach 30:25–36:16a, is displaced in the ancient manuscripts. This material has been rearranged to correspond with the original order, as reflected in the Latin translation (which was made before the Greek material was displaced) and in the NRSV. However, the chapter/verse numbering remains aligned with Swete's edition, which differs from the NRSV: Swete 34:1–36:16a = NRSV 31:1–33:16; Swete 30:25–40 = NRSV 33:17–32; Swete 31:1–33:13a = NRSV 34:1–36:13

4 The poor person toiled in loss of life,
  and in his rest, he becomes needy.
5 The one who loves gold will not be justified,
  and the one who pursues destruction will himself be filled.
6 Many have been handed over to a calamity thanks to gold,
  and their destruction happened according to their face.
7 It is a stumbling block to those who sacrifice by it,
  and every fool will be captured by it.
8 Blessed is the rich person who was found blameless,
  and who has not gone after gold.
9 Who is he, and shall we bless him?
  For he has done wonders in his people.
10 Who has been tested by it and been made perfect?
  And let it become a boast.
  Who could transgress and did not transgress,
  and could do evil and did not do it?
11 His goods will be established,
  and the assembly will recount his charity.

*Banquet Etiquette*

12 Have you sat down at a great table?
  Do not open your throat over it,
  and do not say, "Indeed, how much is on it!"
13 Remember that the wicked eye is an evil thing;
  what was created more wicked than an eye?
  Because of this, there is weeping from every face.
14 Do not reach out your hand wherever you look,
  and do not press with him at the dish.
15 Consider your neighbor's things from your own,
  and ponder upon every deed.
16 Eat the things set before you like a human,
  and do not chomp, lest you be hated.
17 Be the first one to stop, thanks to discipline,
  and do not be insatiable, lest you cause offense.
18 And if you have sat among many,
  do not reach out your hand ahead of them.
19 How the little is sufficient for a disciplined person,
  and he does not gasp for breath upon his bed.
20 A healthy sleep depends upon a moderate gut;
  he rose early, and his soul with him.
  The labor of sleeplessness and cholera and colic are with
    the greedy man.
21 And if you were overpowered by delicacies,
  get up midway, and you will have rest.
22 Listen to me, child, and do not disregard me,
  and in the end, you will find my words.
  Become skillful in all your deeds,
  and no illness will ever encounter you.
23 Lips will bless him who is generous with bread,
  and the testimony of his excellence is trustworthy.

24 The city will mutter about the one who is stingy with bread,
   and the testimony of his stinginess is accurate.

25 Do not make a man of yourself with wine,                    *Wine*
   for wine has destroyed many.
26 The kiln tests steel with a dipping;
   so, too, wine tests hearts in the fight of the arrogant.
27 Wine is the equal of life for a person
   if you drink it in its moderation.
   What is life without wine?
   And it is created for people, for merriment.
28 Joy of heart and gladness of soul
   is sufficient wine drunk at the proper time.
29 Bitterness of soul is much wine drunk
   among irritation and conflict.
30 Drunkenness increases the anger of a fool to offense,
   diminishing might and producing wounds.
31 Do not reprove your neighbor at a wine-drinking party,
   and do not scorn him in his merriment.
   Do not say a word of reproach to him,
   and do not afflict him with a demanding for repayment.

# 35

1 Have they appointed you as head of a feast? Do not exalt     *Hosting a
        yourself;                                                Banquet*
   be among them like one of them;
   be considerate of them, and so sit down.
2 And when you have completed your every obligation, sit down
   so that you might make merry because of them
   and receive a crown thanks to your good conduct.

3 Speak, elder, for it is fitting for you,                     *Banquet
   with accurate knowledge, and do not hold back music.         Etiquette*
4 Wherever there is entertainment, do not pour out talking,
   and do not offer ill-timed wisdom.
5 A signet ring of ruby set upon a golden ornament
   is a concert of music at a wine-drinking party.
6 A signet ring of emerald in a golden setting
   is a piece of music with pleasant wine.
7 Speak, young man, if the need is yours,
   no more than twice if you are asked.
8 Summarize your speech; in few there are many;
   be like one who knows and is silent at the same time.
9 Do not make yourself equal in the midst of nobles,
   and when another is speaking, do not chatter much.
10 Lightning speeds ahead before thunder,
   and grace will go before the modest.
11 Rise up in the hour, and do not lag behind;
   run to home, and do not delay

¹² Amuse yourself there, and do the things you desire,
  but do not sin with an arrogant word.
¹³ And for these things, bless the one who made you
  and who fills you with his good things.

*Fear of*
*the Lord*

¹⁴ The one who fears the Lord will receive discipline,
  and those who seek eagerly will find approval.
¹⁵ The one who seeks the law will be filled by it,
  and the hypocrite will be tripped up by it.
¹⁶ Those who fear the Lord will find a judgment
  and will kindle duties like a light.
¹⁷ A sinful person will turn away conviction,
  and he will find an excuse according to his will.
¹⁸ A man of counsel will not disregard a thought;
  a strange and arrogant person will tremble before no fear,
  even after acting with him without counsel.
¹⁹ Do nothing without counsel,
  and when you act, do not repent.
²⁰ Do not go on a way of stumbling,
  and do not trip among the stones.
²¹ Do not trust in an unscouted path;
²² and guard against your children.
²³ In every deed trust your soul,
  for this also is the keeping of the commandments.
²⁴ The one who trusts the law gives heed to
    the commandments,
  and the one who trusts the Lord will suffer no loss.

**36** ¹ No evil will befall the one who fears the Lord,
  but even again he will be delivered in trials.
² A wise man will not hate the law,
  but the one who is hypocritical with it is like a boat in a storm.
³ An intelligent person will trust in the law,
  and the law will be faithful to him like the question of
    the righteous.
⁴ Prepare a word, and so you will be heard;
  bind the instruction together and answer.
⁵ The insides of a fool are the wheel of a wagon,
  and his thought is like an axle turning.
⁶ A mare for breeding is like a mocking friend:
  she neighs underneath all who sit upon her.
⁷ Why does one day surpass another day,
  when all the light of day of a year is from the sun?
⁸ They were separated by the knowledge of the Lord,
  and he made the changes of seasons and the feasts.
⁹ He exalted and consecrated some from them,
  and he established some from them for a number of days.
¹⁰ And all humans are from the ground,
  and Adam was created from the earth.

11 In the fullness of knowledge, the Lord separated them,
and he made the changes of their ways.
12 He blessed and exalted some from them,
and he consecrated and drew some from them to him;
he cursed and humbled some from them,
and he turned them from their position.
13 Like the clay of a potter in his hand,
all his ways are according to his pleasure;
so are humans in the hand of the one who made them,
to pay them back according to his decision.
14 Good is opposite evil,
and life is opposite death;
so, too, the sinner is opposite the godly.
15 And in this way, look at all the works of the Most High;
two by two, the one opposite the one.
16a And last of all, I was watchful,

**30** *a 25* like one who gleans after the harvest.
I arrived first by the blessing of the Lord,
and I filled the winepress like the harvester.
26 Observe that I have labored not for myself only,
but for all those who seek discipline.
27 Hear me, nobles of the people;
and leaders of the assembly, pay heed!
28 To a son or a woman, brother or friend,
do not give power over you during your life;
and do not give your possessions to another,
lest you regret it and ask for them.
29 As long as you still live and breath is in you,
do not exchange yourself for any flesh.
30 For it is better for children to ask you
than for you to look to the hands of your sons.
31 In all of your deeds, be one who excels;
do not put a flaw on your glory.
32 On the day of the completion of your life's days,
and at the time of death, pass on an inheritance.
33 Fodder and a rod and burdens for a donkey;
bread and discipline and work for a household servant.
34 Work in a servant, and you will find rest;
loosen his hands and he will seek freedom.
35 A yoke and thong will turn the neck,
and screws and torments for a mischievous household servant.
36 Put him to work lest he become idle,
37 for idleness has taught much evil.
38 Appoint him to works as are fitting for him,
and if he does not obey, add weight to his fetters.
And do not be overbearing over any flesh,
and do nothing without judgment.

*a* Swete 30:25–40 = NRSV 33:17–32

<sup>39</sup> If you have a household servant, let him be like you,
    since you have bought him with blood.
  If you have a household servant, treat him like yourself,
    for you will need him like your soul.
<sup>40</sup> If you mistreat him, and he leaves and runs away,
    in which way will you seek him?

*Dreams* **31** <sup>*a* 1</sup> Vain and false hopes belong to the senseless man,
    and dreams excite fools.
<sup>2</sup> Like one who grasps after a shadow and pursues wind,
    so is the one who pays attention to dreams.
<sup>3</sup> A vision of dreams is corresponding to this:
    the likeness of a face in front of a face.
<sup>4</sup> What will be cleansed from impurity?
    And what will speak the truth from lies?
<sup>5</sup> Divinations and omens and dreams are vain,
    and the heart fantasizes like that of a woman in labor.
<sup>6</sup> Unless they are sent from the Most High in a visitation,
    do not give your heart to them.
<sup>7</sup> Dreams have deceived many,
    and they have fallen away when they hope on them.
<sup>8</sup> Without lies the law will be completed,
    and wisdom in a faithful mouth is completeness.

*Journeys* <sup>9</sup> An educated man knows many things,
    and the one with much experience will announce
      understanding.
<sup>10</sup> He who has not been tested knows little,
<sup>11</sup>   but the one who has wandered will multiply prudence.
<sup>12</sup> I have seen many things in my wandering,
    and my understanding is greater than my words.
<sup>13</sup> Frequently I was in danger of death,
    and I was rescued thanks to these things.
<sup>14</sup> The spirit of those who fear the Lord shall live,
<sup>15</sup>   for their hope is upon the one who saves them.
<sup>16</sup> The one who fears the Lord will never dread
    and will never be afraid, because he is his hope.
<sup>17</sup> Blessed is the soul of him who fears the Lord.
<sup>18</sup>   For whom does he hold out? And who is his support?
<sup>19</sup> The eyes of the Lord are upon those who love him,
    a shield of strength and a support of might,
  a shelter from heat and a shelter from midday sun,
    a guard against tripping and a rescue from falling;
<sup>20</sup> who raises up the soul and lights the eyes,
    who gives health, life, and blessing.

---

*a* Swete 31:1–33:13a = NRSV 34:1–36:13

21 When one sacrifices from unrighteousness, the offering     *Sacrifices*
 is mocked,
22 and the mockeries of the lawless do not yield approval.
23 The Most High is not pleased with the offerings of the ungodly
 nor does he atone sin by an abundance of sacrifices.
24 One who slays a son before his father
 is the one who brings a sacrifice from the possessions of
 a poor person.
25 The bread of those in need is the life of the poor;
 the one who robs it is a person of blood.
26 One who murders his neighbor is one who takes away
 companionship,
27 and one who sheds blood is one who robs the pay of the
 hired worker.
28 One who builds and one who destroys,
 what did they profit more than labor?
29 One who prays and one who curses,
 whose voice will the Master hear?
30 One who immerses after touching a corpse and
 touches it again,
 what did he benefit by his bath?
31 So is a person who fasts over his sins
 and again goes and does the same things;
 who will listen to his prayer?
 And what did he benefit by being humbled?

**32** 1 The one who keeps the law abounds with offerings;
2 the one who gives heed to the commandments is one
 who sacrifices a peace offering.
3 The one who repays a favor is one who offers fine flour,
4 and the one who gives alms is one who sacrifices
 a praise offering.
5 Turning away from wickedness is pleasing to the Lord,
 and turning away from unrighteousness is atonement.
6 Do not appear in the presence of the Lord empty,
7 for all these things are the grace of the commandment.
8 The offering of the righteous enriches the altar,
 and its sweet smell is before the Most High.
9 The sacrifice of the righteous man is acceptable,
 and his memory will not be forgotten.
10 Glorify the Lord with a good eye,
 and do not belittle the firstfruit of your hands.
11 Brighten your face with every act of giving,
 and dedicate your tithe with gladness.
12 Give to the Most High according to his giving
 and with a good eye according to what is found in your hand.
13 Because the Lord is the one who repays,
 and he will repay you sevenfold.
14 Do not offer bribes, for he will not accept them;

15    and do not hold out for an unrighteous sacrifice.
      Because the Lord is judge,
        and there is no glory of face with him.
16    He will not receive a face against the poor,
        and he will listen to the prayer of the one who is wronged.
17    He will not disregard the supplication of an orphan
        or a widow if she pours out speech.
18    Do not the tears of the widow roll down over her cheek,
19        and is not her cry against the one bringing them down?
20    The one who attends with pleasure will be accepted,
        and his prayer will reach up to the clouds.
21    The prayer of the humble went through the clouds,
        and he is not comforted until it draws near.
      And it will never depart until the Most High examines it,
22        and he will judge justly and will render judgment.
      And the Lord will never delay
        or be longsuffering over them
      until he has crushed the loins of the merciless,
23        and he will repay vengeance to the nations;
      until he takes away the multitude of the insolent,
        and he will break the scepter of the unrighteous;
24    until he repays a person according to his practices,
        and the works of humans according to their thoughts;
25    until he judges the judgment of his people
        and cheers them with his mercy.
26    Beautiful is his mercy in the time of affliction,
        like clouds of rain in a time of drought.

*Prayer for Liberation*

# 33

¹ Have mercy upon us, Master, God of all, ²and look upon us,
      and put the fear of you on all the nations.
3     Lift up your hand against the foreign nations,
        and let them see your sovereignty.
4     Just as you are sanctified in us before them,
        so, too, may you be exalted before us in them.
5     And let them recognize you, just as also we recognize you,
        because there is no God except you, Lord.
6     Renew signs and change wonders;
7         glorify your hand and right arm.
8     Rouse anger and pour out wrath;
9         remove the adversary and wipe out the enemy.
10    Hasten the time and remember the oath,
        and let them recount your magnificent works.
11    Let the one who survives be devoured in the wrath of fire,
        and may those who harm your people find destruction.
12    Crush the heads of the enemy rulers,
        who say, "There is no one except us!"
13a   Gather all of the tribes of Jacob,

**36** <sup>a</sup> <sup>16b</sup> and you shall possess them just as from the beginning.

17 Have mercy on the people, Lord, who are called by your name,
and on Israel, whom you have made like your firstborn.

18 Have pity on the city of your holy place,
Jerusalem, the city of your rest.

19 Fill Zion with a celebration of your divine wonders
and your people with your glory.

20 Give testimony to your creations at the beginning,
and raise the prophecies that are in your name.

21 Give a reward to those who wait for you,
and let your prophets be trusted.

22 Listen, Lord, to the petition of your suppliants,
according to the blessing of Aaron for your people,
and all those on the earth will know
that you are the Lord, the God of the eternities.

*Discernment*

23 The belly will eat any food,
but there is a food finer than food.

24 The throat tastes food from a hunt;
so the intelligent heart lying words.

25 A twisted heart will give sorrow,
and a person with much experience will pay him back.

26 A woman will accept any male,
but there is a daughter better than a daughter.

27 The beauty of a woman brightens the face,
and it goes beyond any human desire.

28 If there is mercy and gentleness upon her tongue,
is not her husband like the sons of humans?

29 The one who acquires a wife enters upon an acquisition,
a helper corresponding to him and a pillar of rest.

30 Where there is no fence, property will be plundered;
and where there is no woman, he will sigh, wandering.

31 For who will trust a well-equipped thief
stumbling from city to city?
So is a person who has no nest
and lodges wherever he happens to be at night.

**37** Any friend will say "I, too, was his friend,"
but there is a friend who is a friend in name only.

*Friends,
Counsel, and
Restraint*

2 Is it not a sorrow until death:
a comrade and friend who turns to enmity?

3 O wicked inclination, how were you involved
to cover the dry land with deceit?

4 A comrade of a friend will delight in merriment
but will be against him in the time of affliction.

5 A comrade helps a friend thanks to his belly,
but in the midst of war he will take a shield.

---

<sup>a</sup> From here on, chapter/verse numbering matches the NRSV

⁶ Do not forget a friend in your soul,
   and do not be unmindful of him in your possessions.
⁷ Every counselor exalts counsel,
   but there is one who counsels for himself.
⁸ Guard your soul from a counselor,
   and know first what is his need;
   for he also will plan for himself,
  lest he throw the lot against you
⁹   and say to you, "your way is fine,"
   and he will stand across to see what happens to you.
¹⁰ Do not plan with one who looks suspiciously at you,
   and hide counsel from those who are jealous of you:
¹¹ with a woman of her rival,
   and with a coward concerning war,
  and with a merchant concerning business,
   and with one who buys concerning a sale,
  with a stingy man concerning gratitude,
   and with the merciless concerning generosity of spirit,
  with the lazy concerning any work,
   and with a hired worker far from home concerning
     finishing,
  to a lazy servant concerning much work—
   do not hold out over these concerning any counsel.
¹² But persevere with a godly man,
   whom you recognize is keeping the commandments,
  who in his soul is according to your soul
   and if you stumble will sympathize with you.
¹³ And establish the counsel of the heart,
   for you have no one more trustworthy than it.
¹⁴ For the soul of a man is sometimes accustomed to announce
   more than seven watchmen upon a lofty place, sitting
     upon a watchtower.
¹⁵ And above all these things, beg of the Most High
   that he might direct your way in truth.
¹⁶ Reason is the beginning of every work,
   and counsel before every deed.
¹⁷ The mark of a change in heart: ¹⁸Four portions arise,
   good and evil, life and death;
   and the tongue is the one constantly lording it over them.
¹⁹ A prudent man is also a trainer of many,
   but he is useless to his own soul.
²⁰ There is one who is wise in words yet hated;
   this one will lack all food.
²¹ For no grace was given to him from the Lord,
   because he was deprived of all wisdom.
²² There is one who is wise in his own soul,
   and the fruits of his understanding are trustworthy
     upon his mouth.

23 A wise man disciplines his own people,
    and the fruits of his understanding are trustworthy.

24 A wise man will be filled with blessing,
    and all those who see him will bless him.

25 The life of a man is in a number of days,
    but the days of Israel are innumerable.

26 The wise person among his people will inherit honor,
    and his name will live until eternity.

27 Child, in your life, test your soul,
    and see what is wicked to it, and do not give that to it.

28 For not everything is beneficial to everyone,
    and not every soul is pleased by everything.

29 Do not be insatiable in every luxury,
    and do not be poured out over delicacies.

30 For there will be affliction in many foods,
    and greediness will bring one to nausea.

31 Many die on account of greediness,
    but the one who gives heed will extend his life.

**38** Honor a physician for his services with honors,     *Illness*
    for the Lord created him also.

2 For healing is from the Most High,
    and he will receive a gift from the king.

3 The skill of a physician will exalt his head,
    and he will be admired before nobles.

4 The Lord created medicines out of the earth,
    and a prudent man will not be irritated at them.

5 Was not water made sweet by a piece of wood
    to make his power known?

6 And he gave humans skill
    to be glorified by his marvelous deeds.

7 By them he attended to and removed his pain;

8     the perfumer will make a mixture by these things.
And he will never complete his work,
    and peace from him is on the face of the earth.

9 Child, do not be negligent in your illness,
    but pray to the Lord, and he will heal you.

10 Stay away from error and direct your hands,
    and cleanse your heart from every sin.

11 Give a sweet-smelling offering and a memorial of fine flour,
    and pour the offering like one who does not exist.[a]

12 And give a place to the physician, for the Lord created him also,
    and let him not leave you, for there is need of him also.

13 There is a time when there is success also in their hands.

14     For they, too, will pray to the Lord,
that he might prosper them with rest
    and healing for the sake of preserving life.

---

[a] The meaning of the Gk. is unclear

¹⁵ May the one who sins before his maker
  fall into the hands of a physician.
¹⁶ Child, bring down tears over the dead,
  and begin the lament as if suffering terrible things,
  and dress his body according to his judgment,
  and do not disregard his burial.
¹⁷ Make weeping bitter and lament fervent,
  and perform mourning according to his worthiness,
  for a day or even two for the sake of slander,
  and then be comforted on account of your grief.
¹⁸ For from grief comes death,
  and the sorrow of the heart will bend strength.
¹⁹ Even sorrow passes by in separation,
  and the life of the poor passes down the heart.
²⁰ Do not give your heart unto grief;
  stay away from it, remembering the end.
²¹ Do not forget, for there is no way back,
  and you will not benefit this one, and you will harm yourself.
²² Remember that judgment is his, so also for you—
  yesterday for me, and for you today.
²³ In the rest of the dead, put his memory to rest,
  and be comforted by it in the departure of his spirit.

*Skilled* ²⁴ The wisdom of a scribe is in the time of leisure,
*Workers*   and the one who reduces his activity will become wise.
²⁵ How shall the one who grasps a plow become wise,
  and who boasts in the shaft of a goad,
  who drives oxen and engages in their work,
  and their discourse is among the sons of bulls?
²⁶ He gives his heart over to making furrows
  and his diligence to the feed of heifers.
²⁷ So, too, is every craftsman and master craftsman,
  who goes along by night as by day;
  those who carve engravings of seals,
  and his patience to making different embroidery;
  he gives his heart over to making a painting realistic
  and his sleeplessness to completing the task.
²⁸ So, too, the smith who sits near the anvil
  and looks intently at the inert iron;
  the vapor of the fire will pitch his flesh,
  and he will contend with the heat of the furnace;
  the sound of a hammer will renew his ear,
  and his eyes before a likeness of the vessel.
  He gives his heart over to completing the tasks
  and his sleeplessness to adorning to perfection.
²⁹ So, too, is a potter who sits at his work
  and turns a wheel with his feet,
  who always is set upon his work with care,
  and all of his work is numbered.

<sup>30</sup> With his arm he will form the clay,
  and he will bend its strength before his feet;
he will give his heart over to completing the favor
  and his sleeplessness to cleaning the furnace.

<sup>31</sup> All of these people relied on their hands,
  and each one is made wise in his work.

<sup>32</sup> Without them a city shall not be settled,
  and they shall not be sojourners or walk around;

<sup>33</sup> and they will not leap to prominence in the assembly,
  and they will not ponder a covenant of judgment.
They will not sit on the seat of a judge,
  and they will never display righteousness and judgment,
  and they will not be found in parables.

<sup>34</sup> But they will guard the creation of eternity,
  and their prayer is in the daily labor of their craft.

*The Scribe*

But the one who gave his soul freely
  and ponders on the law of the Most High
**39** will seek out the wisdom of all the ancients
  and be occupied in prophecies.

<sup>2</sup> He will preserve the tale of renowned men
  and will enter along with the turnings of parables.

<sup>3</sup> He will seek out the secrets of proverbs,
  and he will be conversant with the riddles of parables.

<sup>4</sup> He will serve among nobles
  and be seen before the ruler;
he will travel in the land of foreign nations,
  for he has experienced good and evil among humans.

<sup>5</sup> He will set his heart to rise early
  to the Lord who made him,
  and he will pray before the Most High,
and open his mouth in prayer,
  and he will pray concerning his sins.

<sup>6</sup> If the great Lord wants,
  he will be filled with the spirit of understanding;
he will pour forth words of wisdom,
  and he will confess to the Lord in prayer.

<sup>7</sup> He will direct his counsel and skill,
  and he will ponder in his hidden things.

<sup>8</sup> He displays the discipline of his teaching,
  and he will boast in the law of the covenant of the Lord.

<sup>9</sup> Many will praise his understanding;
  it will not be wiped out until eternity.
The memory of him will not depart,
  and his name will live for generations of generations.

<sup>10</sup> Nations will recount his wisdom,
  and the assembly will proclaim his praise.

<sup>11</sup> If he remains, he will leave a name greater than a thousand,
  and if he rests, he makes it in him.

*Praise God*

12 I will yet recount, because I have it in mind,
    and I am filled like the full moon.
13 Listen to me, pious sons, and sprout
    like a rose growing by a field stream,
14 and emit a sweet smell like frankincense,
    and blossom a blossom like a lily.
    Spread an odor, and praise with a song;
        bless the Lord for all his works.
15 Give majesty to his name,
    and give thanks in his praise
  with song of the lips and with harps;
    and this is what you shall say with thanksgiving:
16 "All the works of the Lord, because they are very good,
    and every command will be in its proper time.
17 One is not to say, 'Why is this? What is this for?'
    for all things will be sought in its proper time.
  At his word the water stood like a heap,
    and cisterns of water by the word of his mouth.
18 All that is pleasing is by his ordinance,
    and there is no one who can diminish his salvation.
19 The works of all flesh are before him,
    and it is not to be hidden from his eyes.
20 From eternity to eternity he has watched,
    and nothing is amazing before him.
21 One is not to say, 'Why is this? What is this for?'
    for all things have been created for their uses.
22 His blessing has covered like a river,
    and it has watered the dry land like a flood.
23 Thus the nations will inherit his anger,
    as he changed water into a salt marsh.
24 His ways are straight for the pious,
    so they are obstacles for the lawless.
25 Good things were created for the good from the beginning,
    so evil things for sinners.
26 The beginning of every need for a person's life is
    water, fire and iron, and salt and fine flour,
  wheat and honey and milk,
    the blood of grapes and olive oil and clothing.
27 These all belong to the godly for good things,
    so they will be turned into evil to sinners.
28 There are spirits that are created for vengeance,
    and they established their scourges in their wrath;
  and in the time of destruction they will pour out their strength,
    and the wrath of their maker will abate.
29 Fire and hail and famine and death,
    all these are created for vengeance.
30 The teeth of wild animals and scorpions and vipers
    and swords that avenge on the ungodly unto destruction—

31 they will make merry at his commandment,
>    and they will be prepared for service upon the earth,
>    and at their proper times they will not transgress a word."

32 Therefore, I was determined from the beginning
>    and planned it and left it in writing.

33 All the works of the Lord are good,
>    and he will supply every necessity in its time.

34 And one is not to say, "This is more evil than this,"
>    for all things will be shown to be of good repute in the
>        proper time.

35 And now, we have sung with all our heart and mouth,
>    and bless the name of the Lord.

# 40

Weighty labor has been created for every person,                    *Misery*
>    and a heavy yoke is upon the sons of Adam,
> from the day they come out from the womb of their mother
>    until the day upon the burial to the mother of all:

2    their schemes and fear of heart,
>    thought of anticipation, day of death.

3    From the one seated upon a throne in glory,
>    and to the one humbled in earth and ashes,

4    from the one who wears a hyacinth-colored cloth and a crown,
>    and up to the one who wears burlap cloth,

5    there is wrath and jealousy and trouble and disquiet
>    and fear of death and fury and strife.
> And in the time of rest upon a bed,
>    sleep at night makes his knowledge different.

6    A little is like nothing in rest,
>    and from that in sleep as in the day of keeping watch,
> being disturbed by the vision of his heart,
>    like one who has escaped from the face of war.

7    He was awakened at the time of his salvation,
>    even being amazed at no fear.

8    With all flesh from human to animal,
>    and upon sinners sevenfold to these:

9    death and blood and strife and sword.

10   All these things were created for the lawless,
>    and the flood came because of them.

11   All things that are from the earth return to the earth,
>    and from the water return to the sea.

12   All bribery and injustice will be wiped out,
>    but trust will remain for eternity.

13   The wealth of the unrighteous will dry up like a river
>    and will sound forth like loud thunder in rain.

14   When he opens his hands, he will make merry,
>    so those who transgress will come to an end completely.

15   The offspring of the ungodly will not multiply branches,
>    but they are unclean roots upon a sharp rock.

16 The achi[a] on any water and bank of a river
   will be plucked up before any grass.
17 Grace is like paradise in bounty,
   and alms will remain for eternity.
18 A life of an independent worker will be sweet,
   and above both is the one who finds a treasure.
19 Children and the building of a city establish a name,
   and above both is a wife reckoned blameless.
20 Wine and music cheer the heart,
   and above both is the love of wisdom.
21 A flute and harp make sweet parts,
   and above both is a pleasant tongue.
22 Your eye will desire grace and beauty,
   and above both the first shoot of the seed.
23 A friend and a companion who meet at a time,
   and above both is a woman with a man.
24 Brothers and help at a time of affliction,
   and above both alms shall rescue.
25 Gold and silver will make a foot stand,
   and above both a woman is esteemed.
26 Wealth and strength will exalt the heart,
   and above both is the fear of the Lord;
   there is no loss to the fear of the Lord,
   and one is not to seek help in it.
27 The fear of the Lord is like a paradise of blessing,
   and they covered him above any glory.
28 Child, do not live a life of begging;
   it is better to die than to beg.
29 A man who looks to the table of another,
   his way of life is not in the reckoning of life.
   He will pollute his soul with meat belonging to others,
   but the wise and disciplined man will guard himself.
30 Begging will be sweet in the mouth of the shameless,
   but a fire will burn in his belly.

*Death and Shame* **41** O death, how bitter is the remembrance of you
   to a person who lives in peace with his possessions,
   a man undistracted and prospering in everything,
   and yet being strong enough to receive food!
2 O death, your judgment is fine
   to a person who is in need and losing strength
   in old age and worried about everything
   and is resistant and has lost patience!
3 Do not fear the judgment of death;
   remember those earlier and later than you.
4 This is the judgment from the Lord for all flesh,
   and why would you reject the pleasure of the Most High?

[a] Transliteration of Heb. term meaning "reed grass"

Whether ten or a hundred or a thousand years,
  there is no reproving of life in Hades.
5 The children of sinners become disgusting children
  and living together in the exile of the ungodly.
6 The inheritance of the children of sinners will perish,
  and reproach will continue with their seed.
7 Children will blame an ungodly father,
  for they will be reproached on account of him.
8 Woe to you, ungodly men,
  who forsake the law of God Most High!
9 And if you are born, you will be born for a curse;
  and if you die, you will be apportioned for a curse.
10 All that is from the earth will depart into the earth;
  so the ungodly will go from a curse to destruction.
11 The sorrow of humans is in their bodies,
  but the no-good name of sinners will be wiped out.
12 Take thought for your name, for it will remain with you
  more than a thousand great storehouses of gold.
13 There is a number of days of a good life,
  and a good name will remain for eternity.
14 Preserve discipline in peace, children;
  but hidden wisdom and unseen treasure,
  what benefit is there in either?
15 Better is a person who hides his folly
  than a person who hides his wisdom.
16 Therefore show respect for my words;
  for it is not good to keep all shame,
  and not everything is highly esteemed to everyone in trust.
17 Be ashamed before father and mother concerning prostitution,
  and before a leader and sovereign concerning falsehood,
18 before a judge and ruler concerning an error,
  before a congregation and the people concerning lawlessness,
  before a partner and friend concerning wrongdoing,
19 and before the place where you sojourn concerning theft,
  and before the truth of God and the covenant
  and before reclining on your elbow at the loaves,
  before scorning, receiving and giving,
20 and before greeting, concerning silence,
  before seeing a companion woman,
21 and of turning your face from a relative,
  before taking away a portion and a gift,
  and before staring at a married woman,
22 before meddling with his servant girl—
  and do not set upon her bed—
  before friends concerning words of reproach—
  and do not reproach after giving—

**42** before gossip and a word of rumor,
  and before revealing secret words.
And you shall be truly modest,

and one who finds favor before every person.

Do not be ashamed about these things,
and do not receive face in order to sin:

2 concerning the law of the Most High and the covenant,
and concerning a judgment to justify the ungodly;

3 concerning a word of a partner and travelers;
concerning the giving of an inheritance of a comrade;

4 concerning exactness of balance and weights;
concerning property, many and few;

5 concerning a sale of no difference and of traders,
and concerning much discipline of children,
and to make the side bleed on a wicked household servant—

6 a seal is a fine thing on a wicked woman,
and lock up wherever there are many hands;

7 whatever you hand over in number and weight,
there is both giving and receiving for everyone in writing—

8 concerning the discipline of the unwise and stupid
and the aged contending with the young,
and you will be truly disciplined
and tested before every living person.

9 A daughter is hidden sleeplessness to a father,
and anxiety over her drives away sleep;
in her youth, lest she become past her prime;
or married, lest she be hated;

10 in virginity, lest she be defiled
and she become pregnant in her father's house;
when with a husband, lest she transgress;
and married, lest she be barren.

11 Keep a firm watch over a headstrong daughter,
lest she make you a laughingstock to your enemies,
a byword in the city and subject to appeal by the people,
and she will shame you in the multitude of many people.

12 Do not look at any person in beauty,
and do not sit in council among women.

13 For moths come out of a garment,
and the wickedness of a woman out of a woman.

14 Better is the wickedness of a man than a well-doing woman
and a woman who causes shame unto reproach.

15 I will recall the works of the Lord,
and I will declare what I have seen;
in the words of the Lord are his works.

16 The sun that shines looked down on everything,
and his work is full of his glory.

17 The Lord did not lay claim to the holy ones
to declare all his wonders,
which the Lord Almighty established,
for everything to be supported in his glory.

18 He examined the abyss and the heart,
   and I pondered on their great deeds;
   for the Lord knows all knowledge,
   and he has looked into the sign of eternity,

19 announcing the things that have passed and that will come,
   and revealing the marks of hidden things.

20 No thought has escaped him—
   not even one word has been hidden from him.

21 He has put the splendors of his wisdom in order,
   and he is before eternity and for eternity,
   and he was neither added nor taken away,
   and he had no need of any counselor.

22 How desirable are all his works,
   and they are like a spark to look at.

23 All these things live and remain for eternity
   in all services, and all obey.

24 All things are in pairs, one opposite the other one,
   and he has made nothing wanting.

25 One has established the good things of the other one,
   and who will be filled when he sees his glory?

**43** The pride of the height, the firmament of purity,
   the image of the heavens in a vision of glory!

2 The sun in its appearance, proclaiming in departing—
   a wondrous object, the work of the Most High.

3 It dries up a territory with its midday,
   and who can stand before its heat?

4 Though one guards a kiln in work of heat,
   the sun is three times hotter when it scorches mountains;
   when it blows in fiery vapors
   and shines forth rays, it dims the eyes.

5 Great is the Lord who made it,
   and it hastens along its journey at his words.

6 And the moon is among all things for its proper time,
   for a demonstration of times and a sign of eternity.[a]

7 A sign for a feast is from the moon,
   a light that wanes at the completion.

8 The month is according to its name,
   increasing marvelously in its coming change,
   an object of proverbs in the height,
   shining forth in the firmament of the heavens.

9 The beauty of the heavens, the glory of the stars,
   a shining ornament is the Lord in the heights.

10 By the holy words they will stand according to judgment,
   and they will never be weakened in their watch.

11 Look at the rainbow and bless the one who made it,
   very beautiful in its brightness.

12 It encircled the heavens in a circle of glory;

[a] The meaning of the Gk. is unclear

the hands of the Most High have strung it.

13 He stopped the snow by his ordinance,
   and speeds the lightnings of his judgment.

14 Therefore storehouses were opened,
   and clouds flew out like birds.

15 He strengthened clouds by his splendor,
   and hail stones are broken into pieces.

16 And the mountains will be shaken by his appearance;
   the south wind will blow by his will.

17 The sound of his thunder reproached the earth,
   and a storm from the north and a whirlwind.
   He scatters the snow like birds flying down,
   and its descent is like a lodging locust;

18 the eye will marvel at the beauty of its whiteness,
   and the heart will be amazed at its rain.

19 And he pours out frost like salt upon the earth,
   and when it freezes, the edges become points.

20 A cold north wind will blow,
   and ice will freeze from the water;
   it settles on every pool of water,
   and the water will put it on like a breastplate.

21 It will devour the mountains and burn the desert
   and wither the shoots like fire.

22 A mist is speedy healing of all things;
   dew that meets will refresh from burning heat.

23 By his reasoning he calmed the abyss,
   and Joshua planted it.

24 Those who sail the sea declare its danger,
   and we marvel at the reports of our ears.

25 And the incredible and wondrous works are there,
   a variety of all living things, a creation of sea monsters.

26 Because of him a sweet smell is his end,
   and all things hold together by his word.

27 We shall say much more, and we will never finish,
   and the end of words is "He is everything."

28 How will we be strong when we glorify him?
   For he is the one greater than all his works.

29 The Lord is fearsome and very great,
   and his sovereignty is marvelous.

30 When glorifying the Lord, exalt him
   as much as you are able, for he will excel even more.
   And when exalting him, increase in strength;
   do not grow weary, for you will never reach him.

31 Who has seen him and will recount it?
   And who has magnified him just as he is?

32 There are many hidden things greater than these,
   for we have seen few of his works.

33 For the Lord made everything,
   and he has given wisdom to the godly.

# 44

Now let us praise esteemed men
and our fathers by lineage.

2   The Lord created much glory,
his majesty from eternity.

3   Rulers in their kingdoms
and men famous in power,
they will plan in their intelligence—
those who have announced through prophecies;

4   leaders of the people in the counsel
and the intelligence of the scribal office of the people,
wise words in their discipline;

5   those who seek musical parts,
who set out words in writing;

6   rich men supplied with strength,
living prosperously in their foreign countries—

7   all these have been honored in their generations
and were an honor in their day.

8   There are some of them who left a name
for praises to be recounted.

9   And there are some of whom there is no memory,
and they were perishing as if they did not exist,
and they became as if they had not been born,
and their children after them.

10   But these were men of mercy,
whose righteous acts were not forgotten.

11   Their offspring will remain
as a good inheritance with their seed;*a*
in the covenants, ¹²their seed and their children
stood because of them.

13   Their seed will remain until eternity,
and their glory will not be wiped out.

14   Their body was buried in peace,
but their name lives for generations.

15   The people will recount their wisdom,
and the assembly will proclaim praise.

16   Enoch pleased the Lord and was transferred,
a model of repentance for the generations.

17   Noah was found perfect, righteous;
in the time of wrath he became a substitute.
Therefore, a remnant came to be on the earth;
therefore, the flood came to be.

18   Covenants of eternity were placed before him,
lest a flood destroy all flesh.

19   Abraham was a great father of a multitude of nations,
and none has been found similar in glory,

20   who kept the law of the Most High,
and came to be in a covenant with him;

---

*a* The meaning of the Gk. is unclear

and he established the covenant in his flesh,
and he was found faithful in a test.
21 Therefore he established by an oath with him
to bless the nations by his seed,
to increase him like the dust of the earth,
and to raise up his seed like the stars,
and to provide an inheritance for them,
from sea to sea,
and from river*a* to the edge of the earth.
22 And this he established with Isaac
on account of his father, Abraham,
a blessing for all humans and a covenant.
23 And he rested upon the head of Jacob;
he acknowledged him in his blessings
and gave him by an inheritance;
and he divided his portions;
he divided them among twelve tribes.
And he brought a man of mercy out from him,
who finds favor in the eyes of all flesh,

# 45

loved by God and humans,
Moses, whose memorial is with blessings.
2 He made him like the glory of the holy ones
and made him great in the fears of his enemies.
3 By his words he caused signs to cease;
he glorified him according to the face of kings;
he gave him commands for his people
and made known his glory to him.
4 He consecrated him in his faith and humility;
he chose him from all flesh.
5 He caused him to hear his voice
and led him into the darkness
and gave him the commandments face to face,
the law of life and of knowledge,
to teach Jacob the covenant
and Israel his judgments.
6 He exalted Aaron as a holy man like him,
his brother from the tribe of Levi.
7 He established him as an eternal covenant
and gave him the priesthood of the people.
He blessed him with decency
and girded him with a robe of glory.
8 He clothed him completely with honor
and strengthened him with tools of power:
undergarments and a robe and an ephod.
9 And he surrounded him with pomegranates,
many golden bells all around
(to sound forth a sound at his steps,

---

*a* That is, the Euphrates River

to make an audible sound in the sanctuary
for a memorial for the sons of his people),
10 with a holy vestment, with gold and hyacinth,
and purple, some works of embroidered things,
with an oracle of judgment, with manifestations*a* of truth,*b*
11 with twisted scarlet, the work of a craftsman,
with precious engraved stones of an engraved seal,
in a setting of gold, the works of a stoneworker,
for a memorial in engraved writing
according to the number of the tribes of Israel;
12 a golden crown atop the turban,
an inscription of a seal of the sanctuary,
a boast of honor, a work of power,
an adorned desire of the eyes.
Beautiful 13things such as these had not come into being
before him;
until eternity no foreigner put them on
except his sons alone,
and his offspring through all time.
14 His sacrifice shall be completely burned
each day, twice, continuously.
15 Moses ordained him*c*
and anointed him with sacred olive oil;
it became an eternal covenant with him
and with his seed, in the days of the heavens,
to minister to him and to serve as a priest at once,
and to bless his people by the Name.
16 He chose him from all who are living
to offer burnt offerings to the Lord,
incense and a sweet smell as a memorial,
to make atonement for your people.
17 He gave him, by his commandments,
authority in covenants of judgment,
to teach Jacob the testimonies
and to summon Israel with his law.
18 Foreigners gathered against him
and envied him in the desert—
men around Dathan and Abiram
and the assembly of Korah, in anger and wrath.
19 The Lord saw and was displeased,
and they died in the anger of wrath;
he performed signs for them,
to consume them by the fire of his flame.
20 And he added glory to Aaron
and gave him an inheritance;

*a* This term is used elsewhere to describe the Urim (Lev 8:8; Num 27:21; Deut 33:8) *b* This term is used elsewhere to describe the Thummim (Lev 8:8; Deut 33:8) *c* Lit. "Moses filled hands"

he dealt to them the firstfruits of the first products;
he prepared bread in abundance at the first.

21 For they also will eat the sacrifices of the Lord,
which he gave both to him and to his seed.

22 Moreover, he will receive no inheritance in the land of the people,
and there is no allotment for him among the people,
for he is your allotment, an inheritance.

23 And Phinehas son of Eleazar was third in glory,
when he was zealous in the fear of the Lord
and stood, when the people turned,
in the goodness of the eagerness of his soul;
and he made atonement for Israel.

24 Therefore a covenant of peace was established with him,
as head of the sacred things, and with his people,
so that he and his seed might have
the splendor of the priesthood for the eternities.

25 And the covenant with David, the son from the tribe of Judah,
an inheritance of a king, of a son from an only son,
an inheritance for Aaron and for his seed.

26 May he give you wisdom in your heart
to judge his people in righteousness,
lest their good things be destroyed
and their glory for all their generations.

**46** Joshua son of Nun was mighty in wars
and the successor of Moses in prophecies,
who became, according to his name,
great at the salvation of his chosen,
to avenge enemies when rising up,
so that he might inherit Israel.

2 How glorified he was when he lifted up his hands,
and turned away the sword against the cities.

3 Who before him stood in this way?
For the Lord himself brought the enemies on.

4 Was not the sun turned back by his hand,
and one day became as long as two?

5 He called on the Most High Sovereign
when enemies afflicted him all around;
and the great Lord listened to them
with hailstones of mighty power.

6 He made a war fall upon the nations,
and on a descent destroyed those who opposed him
so that the nations might know their armor,
because his war was before the Lord;
for he followed after the Sovereign One.

7 And in the days of Moses he performed mercy,
he and Caleb son of Jephunneh,
to stand up before the enemy,
to restrain the people from sin
and to stop the murmuring of wickedness.

8 And they, being two, were preserved
from six hundred thousand infantry
to lead them into an inheritance,
into a land flowing with milk and honey.

9 And the Lord gave Caleb strength,
and it remained with him until his old age,
to climb upon the height of the land,
and his seed obtained an inheritance

10 so that all the sons of Israel might see
that it is good to follow after the Lord.

11 And the judges, each one by his name,
whose heart had not prostituted itself
and who had not turned away from the Lord—
may their memory be for blessings.

12 May their bones shoot up again from their place
and their name be transferred onto their honored sons.

13 Beloved by his Lord,
a prophet of the Lord established the king
and anointed rulers over his people.

14 He judged the assembly by the law of the Lord,
and the Lord examined Jacob.

15 By his faithfulness he was proven to be a prophet,
and by his faithfulness he became known to be faithful
with a vision.

16 And he called on the sovereign Lord
when his enemies afflicted all around,
with an offering of a baby lamb.

17 And the Lord thundered from the heavens,
and he made his voice heard with a great sound.

18 And he rubbed out the leaders of the Tyrians
and all the rulers of the Philistines.

19 And before the time of his eternal sleep,
he bore witness before the Lord and the anointed one,
"I have received no possessions,
not even so much as a sandal, from any flesh,"
and no person accused him.

20 Even after he fell asleep, he prophesied
and showed the king his death
and lifted up his voice from the earth
in prophecy, to blot out the lawlessness of the people.

# 47

And after this man Nathan rose up
to prophesy in the days of David.

2 Just like fat set apart from the deliverance offering,
so was David from the sons of Israel.

3 He played with lions as if with young goats
and with bears as if with the little lambs of sheep.

4 In his youth, did he not kill a giant
and take reproach away from the people

when he lifted his hand with a stone of a sling,
and cut down the pride of Goliath?

5 For he called upon the Lord, the Most High,
and he granted strength into his right hand
to slay a person in war;
he will raise up the horn of his people.

6 So he honored him by myriads
and praised him with blessings of the Lord
when a crown of glory was offered to him.

7 For he destroyed enemies all around
and annihilated the opposing Philistines;
he broke their horn to this day.

8 In all his deeds he gave thanks
to the holy Most High with a word of glory;
he sang with his whole heart
and loved his maker.

9 And he set singers before the altar
also to make sweet parts by their voice.

10 He gave dignity to the feasts
and arranged the proper times until the end,
when they praised his holy name
and the sanctuary resounded from early morning.

11 The Lord took his sins away
and exalted his horn into eternity
and gave him the covenant of kings
and a throne of glory in Israel.

12 After this one a wise son arose,
and on account of him he lodged in spaciousness.

13 Solomon ruled in days of peace,
to whom God gave rest all around,
so that he might establish a house for his name
and prepare a sanctuary into eternity.

14 How wise you were in your youth,
and you were filled with understanding like a river.

15 Your soul covered the earth,
and you filled it with parables of riddles.

16 Your name reached to islands afar,
and you were loved in your peace.

17 For songs and proverbs and parables
and for interpretation, territories marveled at you.

18 In the name of the Lord God,
the one called the God of Israel,
you gathered gold like tin,
and you multiplied silver like lead.

19 You lay your flanks beside women,
and you were brought into subjection by your body.

20 You put disgrace in your honor,
and you profaned your seed,

making wrath come upon your children;
and I was pierced at your folly—

21 making the territory divided
and a disobedient kingdom rule from Ephraim.

22 But the Lord will never forsake his mercy,
and it will never be destroyed by his works,
and the offspring of his chosen one will never be wiped out,
and he will never take away the seed of those who loved him.
And he gave a remnant to Jacob,
and to David from his root.

23 And Solomon rested with his fathers
and left some of his seed after him,
a folly of the people, and one who lacked understanding:
Rehoboam, who turned the people because
of his counsel,
and Jeroboam son of Nebat, who caused Israel to sin
and gave Ephraim a way of sin.

24 And their sins were multiplied greatly,
making them depart from their land.

25 And they sought out every wickedness
until vengeance came upon them.

# 48

Then Elijah arose, a prophet like fire—
and his word burned like a torch—

2 who brought a famine upon them
and diminished them by his zeal.

3 He shut up the heavens by the word of the Lord;
so he brought down fire three times;

4 How glorious you were, Elijah, in your marvelous deeds!
And who is there to boast like you?

5 Who raised a corpse from death
and from Hades by the word of the Most High,

6 who brought kings down to destruction
and honored people from their bed,

7 who heard a rebuke at Sinai
and judgments of vengeance at Horeb,

8 who anointed kings for retribution
and prophets as successors after him,

9 who was taken up in a whirlwind of fire,
in a chariot of fiery horses,

10 who is recorded in reproofs at proper times,
to calm the wrath before the anger,
and to turn the heart of a father to a son,
and to set the tribes of Jacob in order.

11 Blessed are those who saw you
and those who have decorated with love,
for we also will live by life.

12 Elijah, who was covered by a whirlwind!
And Elisha was filled with his spirit,

and in his days he was not shaken by a ruler,
and no one exercised power over him.
13 No word surpassed him,
and his body prophesied in sleep.
14 He performed wonders in his life,
and his works were wondrous in death.
15 At all of these things the people did not repent,
and they did not turn away from their sins
until they were plundered from their land
and scattered in the whole earth.
And the people was left few in number,
and a ruler for the house of David.
16 Some of them did what is acceptable,
but others multiplied sins.
17 Hezekiah fortified his city
and brought Gog into the midst of them.
He dug the rock with iron
and built wells for waters.
18 In his days Sennacherib went up
and sent Rabshakeh and departed;
and he lifted his hand against Zion
and boasted in his arrogance.
19 Then their hearts and hands shook,
and they felt pangs like a woman giving birth.
20 And they called upon the Lord, the merciful one,
stretching out their hands to him,
and the Holy One quickly heard them from the heavens
and redeemed them by the hand of Isaiah.
21 He struck the army of the Assyrians,
and his angel destroyed them.
22 For Hezekiah did what was acceptable to the Lord
and was strong in the ways of David his father,
which Isaiah the prophet had commanded,
who was great and trustworthy in his vision.
23 In his days the sun turned back
and added life to the king.
24 By a great spirit he saw the final things
and comforted those who mourned in Zion.
25 He showed the things that will be until eternity,
and the hidden things before they happen.

**49** The memory of Josiah becomes a blending of incense
prepared by the work of a perfumer;
it will be sweet like honey in every mouth,
and like music at a wine banquet.
2 He did right in the turning of the people
and removed the abominations of lawlessness.
3 He directed his heart toward the Lord;
he strengthened godliness in the days of lawless people.

4 Except for David and Hezekiah and Josiah,
   all erred with error,
 for they forsook the law of the Most High;
   the kings of Judah came to an end.
5 For they gave their horn to others
   and their glory to a foreign nation.
6 It set the chosen city of the sanctuary on fire
   and desolated her streets
   by the hand of Jeremiah.
7 For they mistreated him,
   and he was consecrated a prophet in the womb,
 to root out and to mistreat and to destroy, likewise, to build
   and to plant.
8 Ezekiel, who saw a vision of glory,
   which he showed to him upon a chariot of cherubim.
9 For he remembered his enemies in a rainstorm,
   and to do good to those who direct their ways.
10 And may the bones of the twelve prophets
    shoot up again from their place.
 But he encouraged Jacob
    and redeemed them by the faithfulness of hope.
11 How shall we exalt Zerubbabel?
    Even he was like a signet ring upon the right hand.
12 So, too, Joshua the son of Jozadak,
    who in their days built the house,
 and they raised up people holy to the Lord,
    prepared for the glory of eternity.
13 And they graze on the plentiful memory
    of the one who raised the fallen walls for us
 and set up the gates and bars
    and raised up our building sites again.
14 And no one has been created on the earth like such a one
       as Enoch,
    for he also was taken up from the earth.
15 But Joseph became a man,
    a leader of his brothers, a support of the people,
    and they looked after his bones.
16 Shem and Seth were honored among humans,
    and above every living creature in creation was Adam.

**50** Simon the high priest, son of Onias,
    who repaired the house in his life
    and strengthened the temple in his days.
2 And the two-story height was laid by him as a foundation,
    the high fortified wall of the temple's enclosure.
3 In his days the cistern of water was brought down,
    copper like the perimeter of the sea—
4 the one who considered his people from downfall
    and strengthened the city for besieging.

⁵ How he was honored in the parade of people
  at the exit of the curtain from the house—
⁶ like the morning star in the middle of a cloud,
  like the full moon in the days,
⁷ like the sun shining forth upon the temple of the Most High,
  and like a rainbow shining in clouds of glory,
⁸ like a blossom of roses in days of new things,
  like a lily by outlets of water,
  like a shoot of Lebanon in the days of summer,
⁹   like fire and frankincense upon the censer,
  like an object of beaten gold
    decorated with every costly stone,
¹⁰ like olive trees sprouting fruit,
  and like a cypress rising in the clouds.
¹¹ When he put on the robe of glory
  and clothed himself in perfect honor,
  in the ascent of the holy altar
    he glorified the garment of the sanctuary.
¹² And when he received the parts from the hands of the priests,
  and he was standing beside the hearth of the altar,
  he was a crown of brothers all around,
    like a shoot of cedar in Lebanon,
    and they encircled him like the trunks of palm trees.
¹³ And all the sons of Aaron in their glory,
  and the offerings of the Lord in their hands
  before the whole assembly of Israel,
¹⁴ and ministering a conclusion upon the altars,
  to arrange the offering of the Almighty Most High.
¹⁵ He stretched out his hand for the offering cup
  and poured out an offering from the blood of the grape;
  he poured out at the foundations of the altar a sweet odor
    to the Most High King of all.
¹⁶ Then sons of Aaron cried out;
  they sounded with beaten trumpets;
  they made a great sound heard
    as a memorial before the Most High.
¹⁷ Then all the people hurried in common
  and fell on their face upon the earth
  to worship their Lord,
    Almighty God, the Most High.
¹⁸ And the psalmists praised with their voices;
  the part was sweetening in a great house.
¹⁹ And the people of the Lord Most High prayed
  with a prayer before the Merciful One,
  until the arrangement of the Lord was completed,
    and they finished his ministry.
²⁰ Then, going down, he lifted up his hands
  over all the assembly of the sons of Israel

to give a blessing to the Lord from his lips
    and to boast in his name.
21 And he repeated with obeisance
    to show the blessing from the Most High.
22 And now, bless God, everyone,
    him who does great things everywhere,
who raises our days from the womb
    and acts with us according to his mercy.
23 May he give you merriment of heart,
    for there to be peace in our days
    in Israel according to the days of eternity,
24 for him to entrust his mercy with us,
    and may he redeem us in his days.
25 My soul was irritated by two nations,
    and the third is not a nation:
26 those who sit on the mountain of Samaria, Philistines,
    and the stupid people who dwell in Shechem.

27 Instruction of understanding and knowledge         *Conclusion*
    I engraved in this scroll,
Joshua son of Sirach, Eleazar the Jerusalemite,
    who spouted wisdom from his heart.
28 Blessed is the one who will turn back by these things
    and place them on his heart and become wise.
29 For if he does them, he will become strong for anything,
    because the light of the Lord is his path.

**51** I will give thanks to you, Lord King,         *Prayer of*
    and I will praise you as God my savior.         *Joshua Son*
    I confess your name,         *of Sirach*
2 because you became a protector and helper for me,
    and you redeemed my body from destruction
    and from the snare of a slanderous tongue,
from the lips of the worker of falsehood,
    and before the bystanders
you became a helper, 3and you redeemed me
    according to the abundance of mercy and of your name,
from gnashings ready for food,
    from the hand of those who seek my soul,
    from the many tribulations which I had,
4 from the choking of fire all around
    and from the midst of fire that I did not kindle,
5 from the depth of the belly of Hades,
    and from an impure tongue and a false word.
6 The slander of an unrighteous tongue to the king;
    my soul praised unto the death,
    and my life was near Hades below.
7 They encompassed me from every side, and there was no helper;
    I looked for the help of humans, but there was none.

8 And I remembered your mercy, Lord,
  and your deeds from eternity,
  because you deliver those who wait for you,
  and you save them from the hand of the nations.

9 And I raised my supplication over the earth,
  and I prayed for deliverance over death.

10 I called upon the Lord, the father of my lord,
  not to forsake me in the days of affliction,
  in the time of the helplessness of arrogant acts.

11 I will praise your name continuously,
  and I will sing in confession.
  And my prayer was heard,

12 for you saved me from destruction,
  and you rescued me from the wicked time.
  Therefore, I will confess and praise you,
  and I will bless the name of the Lord.

*The Search*
*for Wisdom*

13 While I was still young, before I wandered,
  I sought wisdom openly in my prayer.

14 I asked for her before the temple,
  and I will seek her out to the last.

15 From the blossom as the ripening grape,
  my heart was cheered by her;
  my foot walked on rightness;
  I hunted after her from my youth.

16 I inclined my ear a little, and I received her,
  and I found for myself much discipline.

17 I had progress by her;
  I will give glory to the one who gives me wisdom.

18 For I purposed to practice her,
  and I was zealous for the good, and I will never be shamed.

19 My soul has contended with her,
  and I was exact in the doing of a famine.
  I stretched out my hands toward the height,
  and I grieved for her misfortunes.

20 I directed my soul to her;
  I acquired a heart with them from the beginning,
  and I found her in purification;
  therefore, I will never be forsaken.

21 And my belly was stirred up to seek her;
  therefore, I acquired a good possession.

22 The Lord gave me a tongue as my reward,
  and I will praise him with it.

*Invitation*
*to Instruction*

23 Draw near to me, undisciplined people,
  and dwell in the house of discipline.

24 And you say that you lack in these things,
  and your souls are very thirsty.

25 I opened my mouth and I said,
  "Buy for yourselves without silver;
26 place your neck under the yoke,
   and let your soul receive discipline;
   it is close to finding it."
27 See with your eyes that I have labored little
   and found much rest for myself.
28 Partake of instruction with a great amount of silver
   and gain much gold by her.
29 May your soul be cheered by his mercy,
   and do not be ashamed in his praise.
30 Do your work before its time,
   and he will give your reward at his time.

# *Introduction to*

# BARUCH

**B**ARUCH WAS KNOWN AS Jeremiah's associate and secretary (e.g., Jer 36:4–32) and thus became a fit authorial persona for one or more unknown later Jewish writers to assume as they sought to address the challenges of their own time. The book of Baruch may have developed in two or three stages, the earliest being the penitential liturgy that dominates its first half (Bar 1:1–3:8). This liturgy appears to depend upon the prayer found in Daniel 9:4–19 (which may itself have existed as an independent penitential prayer prior to the composition of Daniel), which it expands with images and content from Deuteronomy and Jeremiah. The second half of the book contains a wisdom poem, in which wisdom is identified with the Law of Moses and the path of wisdom with renewed covenant obedience (Bar 3:9–4:4). This poem draws inspiration from Job 28 and shares much in common with Ben Sira's similar equating of Wisdom with the Torah (Sir 24:8–12, 23). Baruch concludes with prophetic passages reminiscent of Isaiah (especially 40–66) assuring Jerusalem that she will be reunited with her children in glory. The book as a whole, while highly derivative, also makes a clear theological and pastoral statement: the way forward is always repentance, a return to covenant obedience, and, on this basis, reassurance of God's promises.

The first two parts of Baruch stand a very good chance of having been composed in Hebrew, even though the whole of Baruch has only survived in Greek and in translations derived from the Greek. The very general nature of the book makes dating the work even within a century difficult and speculative. Baruch came to be prized by early Christian writers especially for one passage (Bar 3:35–37) that was read as a prediction of the incarnation of the Messiah.

—D. A. deSilva

# BARUCH

**1** These are the words of the document that Baruch son of Neriah son of Maaseiah son of Zedekiah son of Hasadiah son of Hilkiah wrote in Babylon, ²in the fifth year in the seventh month at the time when the Chaldeans took Jerusalem and lit it on fire. ³Baruch read the words of this document before Jeconiah son of Jehoiakim, king of Judah, and before all the people who came toward the document, ⁴and in the ears of the dignitaries and sons of the king and in the ears of the elders and in the ears of all of the people from the least to the greatest of all who lived in Babylon near the river Sud. ⁵And they were weeping and fasting and praying before the Lord. ⁶They gathered money,ᵃ as the means of each allowed, ⁷and sent it to Jerusalem to Jehoiakim son of Hilkiah son of Shallum the priest and to the priests and to all the people who were found with him in Jerusalem, ⁸when he took the sanctuary instruments of the house of the Lord that had been carried out from the temple to return them to the land of Judah on the tenth day of Sivan, including the implements of silver that Zedekiah son of Josiah king Judah made, ⁹after Nebuchadnezzar king of Babylon deported Jeconiah, along with the rulers and the captives and the dignitaries and the people of the land away from Jerusalem and carried him into Babylon.

¹⁰Then they said, "Look, we have sent you money; and buy a burnt offering and the offering concerning sin and frankincense with the money, and make frankincense powder and offer it upon the altar of the Lord our God, ¹¹and pray for the life of Nebuchadnezzar king of Babylon, and for the life of Belshazzar his son, in order that their days might be like the days of heaven upon the earth. ¹²And the Lord will give strength to us and illuminate our eyes and we will live under the shadow of Nebuchadnezzar king of Babylon and under the shadow of Belshazzar his son, and we will serve them many days and find favor before them. ¹³Pray for us to the Lord our God because we wronged the Lord our God and have not turned back the anger of the Lord and his wrath from us even until this day."

¹⁴"You shall read this document that we sent to you, to explain in the house of the Lord in the day of the festival and in the days of the season. ¹⁵And you shall say, 'Righteousness belongs to the Lord God, but disgrace of faces belongs to us, as on this day, to the person of Judah, and to those who inhabit Jerusalem ¹⁶and our kings and our rulers and our priests and our prophets and our ancestors, ¹⁷because of what we have sinned in the presence of the Lord. ¹⁸We have resisted him and did not listen to the voice of the Lord our God to follow the commands of the Lord that he gave before our face. ¹⁹From the day when the Lord brought our ancestors from the land of Egypt until this day, we have been resistant to the Lord our God and have acted carelessly without regard to hearing his voice. ²⁰It has been following after us—the troubles and the curse that the Lord prescribed to

---

ᵃ Lit. "silver"

Moses his servant in the day when he led our ancestors to give us a land flowing with milk and honey as it is this day. <sup>21</sup>We did not obey the voice of the Lord our God according to all the words of the prophets whom he sent to us, <sup>22</sup>and each one pursued the intention of his evil heart to serve other gods, to do evil in the eyes of the Lord our God.'"

**2** "The Lord confirmed his word that he spoke to us and to our judges who judged Israel, and to our kings and to our rulers and to the people of Israel and Judah. <sup>2</sup>It has never been done under all the heavens as he did in Jerusalem in accordance with what was written in the law of Moses. <sup>3</sup>We ate, a person the flesh of his son, and a person the flesh of his daughter. <sup>4</sup>He granted them the authority of all the kingdoms surrounding us, to become a ruin and untraveled among all the surrounding peoples, where the Lord had scattered them. <sup>5</sup>They were subjugated and not promoted because we failed the Lord our God with regard to not obeying his voice." *Israel and Judah Subjugated*

<sup>6</sup>"Righteousness belongs to the Lord our God, but disgrace of faces belongs to us and our ancestors as on this day. <sup>7</sup>The things that the Lord spoke to us, all the troubles that came upon us. <sup>8</sup>But we did not entreat the face of the Lord by turning back, each person, from the thoughts of their wicked heart. <sup>9</sup>And the Lord kept watch over the evil things, and the Lord has brought them upon us because the Lord is righteous with all his works that he commanded us. <sup>10</sup>But we did not obey his voice to follow the commands of the Lord that he established as a contract before our face." *Confession of Unrepentance*

<sup>11</sup>"Now O Lord, the God of Israel who brought your people out of the land of Egypt with a strong hand, with signs and with wonders and with great power and with a high arm, and made a name for yourself to this day, <sup>12</sup>we have sinned, committed sacrilege, and acted unjustly, O Lord our God, concerning all your duties. <sup>13</sup>Turn your anger away from us because we remain few among the nations where you scattered us among them. <sup>14</sup>Hear, O Lord, our prayer and our entreaty and deliver us for yourself, and give us grace at the face of those who exiled us, <sup>15</sup>in order that the entire earth might learn that you are the Lord our God, because your name is invoked upon Israel and upon his descendants. <sup>16</sup>O Lord, look down from your holy house and consider us. Incline your ear, O Lord, and hear. <sup>17</sup>Open your eyes and see that the dead in the grave, whose spirit was taken from their guts, do not give glory and duty to the Lord. <sup>18</sup>But his soul that is sorrowing at the greatness, which walks bowed down and weakly, and the eyes that come to an end, and the soul that is hungry, offer you glory and righteous, O Lord. <sup>19</sup>Because we cast down compassion before your face not concerning the duties of our ancestors and of our kings, O Lord, our God, <sup>20</sup>because you sent your anger and your wrath upon us even as you said by the hands of your servants the prophets: <sup>21</sup>'Thus says the Lord, "Bow down your shoulder and serve the king of Babylon and remain upon the land that I have given your ancestors. <sup>22</sup>But if you will not obey the voice of the Lord to serve the king of Babylon, <sup>23</sup>I will make the sound of cheer and the sound of festivals, the sound of the bridegroom and the sound of the bride come to an end from the city of Judah and the area outside of Jerusalem, and the whole land will become untraveled, without inhabitants."' <sup>24</sup>And we did not obey your voice to serve the king of Babylon and you confirmed your words which you had spoken by means *Prayer for Deliverance*

of your servants the prophets: that the bones of our kings and the bones of our ancestors would be brought forth from their place. ²⁵Look, they were thrown out to the burning heat of the day and the frost of the night and they perished in painful anguish from hunger and from sword and from being dispatched. ²⁶You established the house, of which your name is invoked over it as on this day, on account of the evil of the house of Israel and the house of Judah."

*Reminder of God's Promise*
²⁷"You have acted for us, O Lord our God, with all of your fairness and with all of your great mercy, ²⁸just as you had spoken by the hand of your servant Moses in the day when you charged him to write your law before the sons of Israel, saying, ²⁹'If they will not obey my voice, cursed if this great mighty roaring crowd will not turn into a small one among the nations where I will scatter them. ³⁰Because I know that they will not obey me because the people are obstinate, yet they will return with their heart in the land of their exile, ³¹and they will learn that I am the Lord their God, and I will give them a heart and an ear for obeying. ³²They will praise me in the land of their captivity and will remember my name. ³³And they will turn away from their stiff back and from their wicked practices because they will remember the journey of their ancestors, who sinned before the Lord. ³⁴And I will return them to the land that I promised to their ancestors, to Abraham, Isaac and Jacob, and they will rule it and I will multiply them and they will not fade away. ³⁵I will confirm an eternal agreement with them: I will be a God to them, and they will be a people to me, and I will never again remove my people Israel from the land that I gave them.'"

*A Promise of Praise*
**3** "O Lord Almighty, God of Israel, a soul in difficulty and a spirit of weariness have cried out to you. ²Listen, O Lord, and show mercy, because we have sinned before you. ³For you are seated for eternity and we are being destroyed for eternity. ⁴O Lord Almighty, God of Israel, hear then, the prayer of those who have perished from Israel and of the sons of those who are sinning before you, who did not listen to the voice of you, their God and so evil followed us. ⁵Do not remember the offences of our ancestors, but remember your dominion and your name at this time, ⁶because you are the Lord our God and we will praise you, O Lord. ⁷Therefore, because of this you instilled fear of yourself within our heart also, so we might call your name. And we will praise you in our exile because we have turned back from our heart all the offenses of our ancestors who sinned before you. ⁸Look, today we are in our exile, in the place where you scattered us for a reproach and for a curse and for a punishment because of every injustice of our ancestors who departed from the Lord our God."

*A Poem in Praise of Understanding*
⁹"Hear,ᵃ O Israel, the commandments of life; pay attention to learn understanding. ¹⁰Why is it, O Israel, why is it that are you in a land of enemies? You have become old in a strange land; you have been defiled by the dead; ¹¹counted with those in Hades; ¹²you abandoned the source of wisdom. ¹³If you had followed the path of God, you would have dwelled

---

ᵃ The text shifts from prose to poetry for the remainder of the book; it is uncertain whether this reflects that the original was written in Hebrew or simply that the style of Hebrew poetry was adopted by an author writing in Greek

in peace eternally. ¹⁴Learn of where there is intelligence, where there is strength, where there is comprehension, so that you may know at the same time where there is longevity and life, and where there is light for eyes, and peace. ¹⁵Who has discovered her place and who has entered into her treasuries? ¹⁶Where are the rulers of the nations and the lords of the animals that are upon the earth; ¹⁷those who mock the birds in heaven and hoard silver and gold (in which humans trust and there is no end to their greed)? ¹⁸Because those who make and worry about money (and there is no searching their works) ¹⁹have been destroyed and descended into Hades, and others rise up in their place. ²⁰Young men have seen light and dwelt upon the earth, but they did not learn the way of knowledge ²¹nor understand her paths or even take hold of her. Their sons were far from their path. ²²And it was not heard in Canaan, or seen in Teman. ²³And the sons of Hagar who seek comprehension, who were upon earth, the traders of Merran and Teman, and the storytellers and seekers of comprehension did not know the way of wisdom or remember her paths."

²⁴"O Israel, how great is the house of God, and extensive the place of his possession. ²⁵It is great and has no end; it is high and immeasurable. ²⁶The giants who were famous from the beginning were born there, being very large and capable of war. ²⁷God did not select them or offer them the way of knowledge. ²⁸So they perished for not having understanding; they perished due to their lack of thought. ²⁹Who went up into heaven and took her and brought her down from the clouds? ³⁰Who crossed over beyond the sea and discovered her and who will bring her for choicest gold? ³¹There is no one who knows her way or ponders her path. ³²However, the one who comprehends everything knows her; he discovered her with his discernment. The one who created the earth into eternal time filled it with herds of four-footed animals. ³³The one who sends the light and it goes, he summoned it and it obeyed him with trembling. ³⁴And the stars twinkled brightly in their watches and were cheerful. ³⁵He called them and they said, 'We are here.' They twinkled brightly with cheer for the one who made them. ³⁶This is our God. No other can be compared with him. ³⁷He discovered every path of knowledge and gave it to Jacob, his child, and to Israel, who was loved by him. ³⁸After this she appeared upon the earth and lived among humans."

*God's Wisdom in Creation*

**4** "This is the document of the commands of God, and the law that is exists into eternity. All who hold her are destined for life, but those who forsake her will perish. ²Turn, O Jacob, and seize her, advance toward the glow before her light. ³Do not give another your glory or your profit to a foreign nation. ⁴Blessed are we, O Israel, because what is pleasing to God is known to us."

*Special Knowledge of God's Will*

⁵"Be courageous my people, memorial of Israel. ⁶You were sold to the nations not for annihilation, but because you angered God; you were given over to adversaries. ⁷For you provoked the one who made you, by sacrificing to demons and not to God. ⁸You forgot the Eternal God who raised you, and indeed you distressed Jerusalem who reared you. ⁹For she saw*ᵃ* the wrath come upon you from God and said,*ᵇ* 'Listen, neighbors of Zion!

*Wisdom Abandoned*

---

*ᵃ* Wisdom is still acting  *ᵇ* Wisdom speaks from this point until the end of the book

God brought great grief upon me. ¹⁰For I saw the captivity of my sons and daughters that the Eternal One brought upon them. ¹¹For I educated them with cheer, but sent them away with weeping and grief. ¹²Let no one rejoice over me, a widow and forsaken by many; I was abandoned because of the sins of my children, since they turned away from the law of God, ¹³and did not learn his duties or follow the paths of God's commands or set foot upon the tracks of his discipline in righteousness. ¹⁴Let the neighbors of Zion arrive and may they remember the captivity of my sons and daughters, which the Eternal One brought upon them. ¹⁵For he brought a far off nation upon them, a callous and foreign-speaking nation, because they did not respect the elderly or show mercy to a young child, ¹⁶and they led away the beloved of the widow and separated the lonely woman from her daughters. ¹⁷But how can I help you? ¹⁸The one who brought the troubles will deliver you from the hand of your enemies. ¹⁹Walk away, children, walk away, for I have been left lonely. ²⁰I have taken off the garment of peace, and I have dressed in sackcloth for my entreaty; I will cry out to the Eternal One for my days.'"

*Deliverance is Coming* ²¹"Take courage, children, cry out to God and he will deliver you from domination, from the hand of the enemy. ²²For I trust upon the Eternal One for your salvation, and joy has come to me from the Holy One at the mercy that will come to you quickly from your eternal savior. ²³For I sent you with sorrow and weeping, but God will return you to me with gladness and cheer for eternity. ²⁴Just as the neighbors of Zion have now seen your captivity, so in a short time they will see your salvation from God, which will come upon you with great glory and the splendor of the Eternal One. ²⁵Children, have patience about the anger that came upon you from God. The enemy pursued you, but you will see his destruction in a short time, and set your foot upon their necks. ²⁶My tender ones walked a rough path, carried away like a flock seized by an enemy."

*God Will Remember* ²⁷"Be brave, children, and cry to God, for there will be remembrance by the one who brought this upon you. ²⁸Even as your thought was to stray from God, return to seek him ten times as much. ²⁹The one who brought the troubles upon you will bring eternal cheer upon you with your salvation."

*Reversal of Fortunes* ³⁰"Be confident, O Jerusalem! The one who named you will comfort you. ³¹Wretched will be the ones who mistreated you and rejoiced at your fall. ³²Wretched be the cities in which your children were enslaved, wretched the one who received your sons. ³³Just as she rejoiced at your fall and was cheerful in your calamity, so will she grieve at her own desolation. ³⁴I will remove her satisfaction at her great population and turn her pride into to grief. ³⁵Fire will come upon her from the Eternal One for many days, and she will be occupied by demons for a long time."

*Return from Dispersion* ³⁶"Look toward the East, O Jerusalem, and see the cheer that is coming to you from God. ³⁷Look, your sons whom you sent forth are coming, gathered from east to west by the word of the Holy One, rejoicing in the glory of God."

*New Glory and Righteousness* **5** "Take off, O Jerusalem, the tunic of your sorrow and suffering, and put on the majesty from God's glory for eternity. ²Put on the cloak of righteousness from God; place the headband of the glory of the

Eternal One upon your head. ³For God will show your splendor every-where under the heavens. ⁴Your name will be called by God for eternity: 'Peace of Righteousness and Glory of Piety.' ⁵Arise, O Jerusalem, and stand upon the high place, and look to the east and see your children gathered from the west to the east by the word of the Holy One, rejoicing in the remembrance of God. ⁶For they departed from you on foot, carried away by enemies; but God is returning them to you, raised up with glory as on a kingdom's throne. ⁷For God ordered every high hill and permanent mound to be lowered, and the ravines to be filled for the leveling of the land, so that Israel might walk safely in the glory of God. ⁸And the forests and every fragrant tree have shaded Israel by the command of God. ⁹For God will go before Israel with cheer in the light of his glory, with the mercy and righteousness that is from him."

*Introduction to*

# LETTER OF JEREMIAH

J EREMIAH WAS KNOWN TO have given instructions to his people in exile (Jer 29) and so was chosen by an otherwise unknown Jewish writer as the authorial persona for this tirade against gentile religion, particularly idolatry. The author of the Letter of Jeremiah seeks to insulate Jews from the fervent religious devotion they see around them in the idolatrous practices of their gentile neighbors by undermining any sense of the genuineness of their religion, lest the Jews themselves begin to think that there might be something of value to the gentiles' gods and compromise their commitment to a single, aniconic Deity. In so doing, the author draws upon material found in Jeremiah (see especially Jer 10:2–15) as well as Israel's long history of anti-idolatry polemic (e.g., Ps 115:3–8; 135:15–16; Isa 46:6–7). The approach is reductionistic: the gentiles' gods are considered to be nothing other and nothing more than their sculpted representations, and, therefore, they are deaf to their worshipers and powerless to help either their worshipers or themselves.

The Letter of Jeremiah may have been composed originally in Hebrew and quite early (a date in the fourth century BC is not impossible). No fragments of a Hebrew original survive, however; even at Qumran the only fragment of the Letter discovered was already of the Greek translation. It remained an independent work until the Vulgate joined it to Baruch as its sixth chapter, a tradition followed by the King James Version. Early Christians valued the Letter of Jeremiah as a resource for their own ongoing work distinguishing their practice from the non-Christian majority's piety, for the sake of which those non-Christians applied great pressure upon their Christian neighbors to conform once again to the practices of worshiping the gods of the empire.

—D. A. deSilva

# LETTER OF JEREMIAH

<sup>a</sup>A copy of a letter that Jeremiah sent to those who were about to be carried away as captives into Babylon by the king of the Babylonians to declare to them just as was commanded to him by God.

*The Long Captivity* **6** <sup>1b</sup>You will be carried off to Babylon as prisoners under Nebuchadnezzar king of the Babylonians because of your sins that you sinned before God. <sup>2</sup>Therefore, after you have entered Babylon you will be there many years, a long time, up to seven generations, but after this, I will bring you out from that place with peace. <sup>3</sup>Now in Babylon you will see silver, golden, and wooden gods carried upon shoulders, showing fear to the nations. <sup>4</sup>Be cautious, then, lest you conform by conforming to the foreigners, and fear take you concerning them. <sup>5</sup>When you see a crowd before and following them, worshiping them, say with your mind, "It is necessary to worship you, O Master." <sup>6</sup>For my angel is with you and he is the one who searches your souls.

*Idols Cannot Clothe Themselves* <sup>7</sup>For their tongue is filed down by the carpenter, and they are gilded and silver-plated, but they are false, and they cannot speak. <sup>8</sup>And just like for a jewelry-loving virgin, taking gold <sup>9</sup>they create crowns upon the heads of their gods. And when the priests are embezzling the gold and silver from their gods, they spend it for themselves. <sup>10</sup>And they will give some from them to the prostitutes upon the roof. They dress them like humans with clothes, silver gods and golden gods and wooden. <sup>11</sup>But they cannot save themselves from tarnish and consumption, dressed with purple clothing. <sup>12</sup>They wipe their faces because of the dust from the house, which is thick upon them. <sup>13</sup>And he holds a scepter like a human judge from the region; however, he will not kill whoever sins against him. <sup>14</sup>And he holds a dagger in his right hand and an axe, but he cannot rescue himself from war and robbers. Thus they are known not to be gods; so then do not fear them.

*Idols Cannot Defend Themselves* <sup>15</sup>For even as a person's weapon is useless when crushed, <sup>16</sup>such are their gods, being set up in the houses. Their eyes are full of dust from the feet of those who enter. <sup>17</sup>Even as the courtyards are fenced around when someone has wronged a king, like one being led away to death, the priests fortify their houses with doors, cross pieces, and bars so they are not plundered by robbers. <sup>18</sup>They light many more lamps than for themselves; they<sup>c</sup> are unable to see any of them. <sup>19</sup>It is like a beam from the house, but their hearts, they say, are licked; when the reptiles of the earth devour them, they do not feel their clothing. <sup>20</sup>Their faces are blackened from the smoke from the house. <sup>21</sup>Bats, swallows, and hens fly near their body and upon

---

<sup>a</sup> 6:1 in some versions; throughout the book, versification varies across editions  <sup>b</sup> In the KJV and NRSV, the Letter of Jeremiah is included as the final chapter of Baruch (chapter 6); other editions include it as the final chapter of Lamentations (again, chapter 6) or as a separate book (chapter 1)  <sup>c</sup> The gods

their head; likewise also the cats. [22]Thus you shall know that they are not gods; so then do not fear them.

[23]If no one wipes the tarnish from the gold they wear for beauty, they will not shine, for they did not feel it even when they were molten. [24]Though they are purchased for every worship; no breath in them. [25]Since they are without feet, they are carried upon shoulders, revealing themselves to people as a dishonor. Also those who attend to them are dishonored, [26]because if they ever fall upon the earth, they do not get up by themselves, and if someone stands it upright, it cannot move itself, and if it is tipped over, it is not set straight, but rather, the gifts are presented to them as if to dead people. [27]And when they have made their sacrifices, their priests make full use of them. Likewise, also their wives salt the meat and do not share it with the poor or the weak. [28]The woman sitting apart and the woman in childbed touch their sacrifices! Therefore, knowing from these things that they are not gods, do not fear them.

*Idols Cannot Move Themselves*

[29]Why would they be called gods? Because women set food before silver, golden, and wooden gods. [30]And the priests sit in their houses, having torn shirts and shaved heads and beards, whose heads are uncovered. [31]They howl and cry out before their gods like some do during a dinner for the dead. [32]The priests will clothe their wives and children by taking some of their clothing.[a] [33]If they suffer evil from anyone or even good, they will not reward it, and they are unable to appoint or dethrone a king. [34]Likewise they are unable to give wealth or money. If someone who vows a vow to them does not deliver, they do not prosecute. [35]They cannot rescue a person from death or deliver the weak from the strong. [36]They are unable to convert a blind person to a sighted one; they cannot deliver a person who is in distress. [37]They do not show mercy to a widow or treat an orphan well. [38]They are wooden and gilded and silver-plated, being like the stones from the mountain, and those who attend to them will be ashamed. [39]How then are they considered or proclaimed to be gods?

*Idols Cannot Reward or Punish*

[40]Yet even the Chaldeans themselves dishonor them, those who when they see a mute person unable to speak, approaching Bel, they request that he speak, as if he could understand! [41]And they are unable to notice this and abandon them, for they have no common sense. [42]And the women, girded with ropes, sit in the paths to offer bran incense. [43]And whenever one of them is taken off by one of the passers-by to sleep with, she reproaches her neighbor because she was not worthy as herself and her rope was not torn. [44]Everything that happens to them is false. How then is it considered or proclaimed that they are gods?

*Idols Cannot Speak*

[45]They are created by woodworkers and goldsmiths. They cannot be anything other than that which the craftsmen wish them to be. [46]And even those who create them are not long lived, [47]so how indeed will it be for those constructed by them? For they left lies and disgrace for those who follow. [48]For whenever war and bad things come upon them, the priests plan among themselves how they might hide with them. [49]How then, is it not understood that they are not gods, who cannot save themselves from war and from bad things? [50]It will be known after these things that they

*Idols Cannot Save Themselves*

---

[a] That is, the gods' clothing

are false, since they are wooden and gilded and silver-plated. It will be evident to every nation and to the kings that they are not gods, but works of human hands, and no work of god is in them.

*Idols Cannot Judge Their Own Cause*

⁵¹So to whom is it known that they are not gods? ⁵²For they cannot establish the king of a region or give rain to the people. ⁵³They cannot judge their own judgment or be delivered from injustice, being powerless. ⁵⁴For they are just as a crow between the heavens and the earth. For also when fire presses upon a house of wooden or gilded or silver-plated gods, their priests will flee and escape, but they*a* are burned like middle beams. ⁵⁵They certainly cannot withstand a king and soldiers. ⁵⁶How then does one claim or consider that they are gods?

*Idols Cannot Do Any Good*

Neither wooden and silver-plated and gold-plated gods will certainly not run from thieves or from robbers, ⁵⁷of whom the strong remove the gold and silver and the clothing that is worn by them, and when they have these things they will disappear. They cannot possibly save themselves. ⁵⁸So that it is better to be a king who shows his own manliness, or a useful vessel in a house on which the owner will make use, than the false gods; or even a door in the house that preserves the things that are in it, than the false gods; or wooden pillars in a palace, than the false gods. ⁵⁹For even sun, moon and stars, which are bright, are obedient when sent upon a mission. ⁶⁰Similarly also lightning is seen whenever it strikes; the same way also the wind blows in every territory. ⁶¹And when a command is given by God to clouds to travel upon the entire world, they do what is required. ⁶²And fire that is sent from above to destroy mountains and forests does what was ordered. But these things are not comparable in their form or powers. ⁶³Therefore they are not to be considered nor called gods, because they are unable to judge a judgment or do good for humans. ⁶⁴Knowing, then, that they are not gods, do not fear them.

*Idols Cannot Help Themselves or Others*

⁶⁵They cannot curse or bless kings. ⁶⁶They cannot show signs in heaven for people; and they will not shine like the sun or glow like the moon. ⁶⁷The wild animals are better than they, since they can help themselves by escaping to shelter. ⁶⁸So it is in no way apparent to us that they are gods; therefore let us not fear them.

*Idols Will Ultimately Perish*

⁶⁹For as a scarecrow in a cucumber bed protects nothing, so are their wooden, gilded, and silver-plated gods. ⁷⁰Also in the same way, their wooden and gilded and silver-plated gods are like a thorn-bush in a garden, upon which every bird roosts; and also like a corpse thrown into the darkness. ⁷¹From the purple and the marble that rots upon them it will be known that they are not gods. And they will at last be eaten and be a reproach in the region. ⁷²Better, then, is a righteous person who does not have idols, for he will be far from reproach.

---

*a* The gods

*Introduction to*

# ADDITIONS TO DANIEL (OLD GREEK)

T HE GREEK VERSION OF Daniel contains two additional tales and expands the Daniel 3 episode of the three youths threatened with execution in the furnace with two liturgical pieces. The first additional tale, the story of Susanna, presents a pious young woman who is in danger of death because of the lust and perjury of two Jewish elders. Like the three youths and Daniel himself, Susanna becomes a model of committing oneself to do what is right in God's sight rather than secure temporary safety through compromising covenant obedience. The second additional tale shows an aged Daniel educating Cyrus concerning the emptiness of gentile religion, first by exposing the chicanery of the priests of Bel and then by exposing the mortality of a certain snake worshiped as a god. A lengthy prayer for forgiveness and rescue (the Prayer of Azariah) and an even lengthier psalm of praise (the Song of the Three Young Men) are inserted into the episode of Daniel 3. Apart from a single verse (3:88), the prayer and psalm might well have been composed and used independently of Daniel for some time prior to their incorporation into the narrative. The prayer and psalm took deep root in the liturgical practice of the Christian church; Susanna is read as a type of the Christian martyr and of the church itself, beset by her enemies; Bel and the Dragon enters the repertoire of early Christian anti-idolatry polemics.

Though no surviving Hebrew-Aramaic manuscript of Daniel includes any part of these additions, it remains almost certain that the liturgical pieces themselves were originally composed in Hebrew and likely that the additional tales were composed in either Hebrew or Aramaic. We cannot know if these additions were incorporated into Daniel prior to, or only at the time of, the translation of the whole into Greek. The following translation follows the Old Greek, or original Septuagint, version. This Old Greek version probably emerged in the second century BC.

—D. A. deSilva

# Additions to Daniel (Old Greek)[a]

## The Prayer of Azariah

**3** [24]In this manner, therefore, Hananiah and Azariah and Mishael prayed, and they sang to the Lord when the king commanded them to be thrown into the furnace. [25]And standing still, Azariah prayed in this manner, and when he opened his mouth he acknowledged the Lord together with his companions in the middle of the blazing fire, the furnace having been ignited by the Chaldeans very much with fire, and they said,

[26] "Blessed are you, O Lord, God of our fathers, and to be praised,
　　and glorious is your name into the eternities!
[27]　For you are righteous concerning all the things you have done
　　　　to us,
　　and all your works are true,
　　and your paths are right,
　　　and all your judgments are truthful.
[28]　And you have carried out accurate judgments
　　　according to all the things you have brought upon us,
　　and upon your holy city,
　　　the city of our fathers, Jerusalem,
　　because in truth and in justice
　　　you have done all these things on account of our sins.
[29]　For we have sinned in every way,
　　　and acted lawlessly by moving away from you,
　　　and we have done grievous wrong in every way.
[30]　And we have not listened to the commandments of your law.
　　　Neither have we closely observed
　　nor have we acted according to what you commanded to us,
　　　in order that it may go well for us.
[31]　And now, everything, whatsoever you have brought against us,
　　　and everything, whatsoever you have done to us,
　　　you have acted in truthful judgment.
[32]　Now you have given us over into the hands of our enemies,
　　　lawless and hostile rebels,
　　and to an unrighteous king,
　　　even to the most wicked king in all the earth.
[33]　And so now it is not permitted for us to open our mouth.
　　　Dishonor and disgrace has come to your servants,
　　　even those worshiping you.
[34]　Do not utterly give us over on account of your name,
　　　and do not turn from your covenant.

[a] This is a translation of the Old Greek (LXX) text of Daniel from Codex Chisianus

35 And do not remove your mercy from us on account of Abraham,
    the one loved by you,
and on account of your servant Isaac
    and your holy one Israel.
36 Just as you told them,
    saying that you would multiply their seed
as the stars of the heavens in abundance
    and as the sand along the shore of the sea.
37 For, O Master, we have been reduced
    more than any of the peoples,
and we are humbled throughout the whole earth today
    because of our sins.
38 Now there is not at this time a ruler nor a prophet
    nor a leader nor a whole burnt offering nor any offering
nor gifts nor an incense sacrifice nor a place to give an offering
        before you
    and thus to find mercy.
39 Yet, with a soul shattered and a spirit made low,
    we might be accepted,
40 just as though we came with whole burnt offerings of rams and
        bulls,
    and just as though we came with myriads of fat lambs.
So may our sacrifice be before you today,
    also to atone behind you,
since there is no shame for those who put confidence in you
    and completely follow you.
41 And now, we follow you earnestly with our whole heart,
    and we fear you,
and we seek your face;
42     do not shame us!
But have mercy with us according to your goodness
    and according to the abundance of your compassion.
43 And rescue us in accordance with your wonderful acts,
    and give honor to your name, O Lord.
44 And may they be shamed,
    all those who show forth against your servants their evil acts.
And may they be discredited from having any power,
    and may their authority be shattered!
45 Let them know that you alone are the Lord God,
    and notable and glorious over the whole inhabited world."

## Song of the Three Young Men

46 And those who threw them into the furnace, the servants of the king, those who were stoking the furnace, did not cease. And when they were casting the three at once, into the furnace, and as the furnace was blazing hot in accordance with its increased sevenfold heat, and when they cast

them in, those casting them in were above them, but those who fed the fire were below them with naphtha and flax and pitch and brushwood. ⁴⁷Then the flame shot forth high above the furnace by over forty-nine cubits. ⁴⁸And so it broke out of control and burned those it reached from around the furnace from the Chaldeans. ⁴⁹But a divine being of the Lord descended at the same time to the ones around Azariah, into the furnace, and dispersed the flame of fire from the furnace. ⁵⁰Then he made the middle of the furnace like a moist wind gently whistling, so that it did not touch them at all; and the fire did not cause pain and did not trouble them. ⁵¹And lifting up their voices, the three, as if out of one mouth, sang praises and extolled and praised and exalted God within the furnace, saying,

⁵² "Blessed are you, O Lord God of our fathers,
   and praiseworthy and to be exalted into the eternities.
And blessed is your glorious name, holy and praiseworthy,
   and to be exalted exceedingly into all eternities.
⁵³ Blessed are you within the temple of your holy glory,
   and to be highly exalted and wholly glorious into the eternities!
⁵⁴ Blessed are you upon the throne of glory of your kingdom,
   and to be praised and exceedingly exalted into the eternities!
⁵⁵ Blessed are you, the one who sees into the abyss,
   who sits upon the cherubim,
   and are to be praised and magnified into the eternities!
⁵⁶ Blessed are you in the firmament of the heavens,
   and to be praised and magnified into the eternities!
⁵⁷ Bless, O all works of the Lord, the Lord,
   praise and exalt him exceedingly into the eternities!
⁵⁸ Bless, O angels of the Lord, the Lord;
   laud and exalt him exceedingly into the eternities!
⁵⁹ Bless, O heavens, the Lord,
   laud and exalt him exceedingly into the eternities!
⁶⁰ Bless, O waters and all above the heavens, the Lord;
   praise and exalt him exceedingly into the eternities!
⁶¹ Bless, O all the power and hosts of the Lord, the Lord;
   laud and exalt him exceedingly into the eternities!
⁶² Bless, O sun and the moon, the Lord;
   laud and exalt him exceedingly into the ages!
⁶³ Bless, O stars of the heavens, the Lord;
   praise and exalt him exceedingly into the eternities!
⁶⁴ Bless, O all storms and dew, the Lord;
   laud and exalt him exceedingly into the eternities!
⁶⁵ Bless, O all winds, the Lord;
   praise and exalt him exceedingly into the eternities!
⁶⁶ Bless, O fire and scorching heat, the Lord;
   laud and exalt him exceedingly into the eternities!
⁶⁷ Bless, O shivering cold and cutting cold weather, the Lord;
   praise and exalt him exceedingly into the eternities!

68 Bless, O gentle dew and swirling snowstorm, the Lord;
   laud and exalt him exceedingly into the eternities!
69 Bless, the Lord, O frost and cold,
   laud and exalt him exceedingly into the eternities!
70 Bless, O hoar-frost and snow, the Lord;
   laud and exalt him exceedingly into the eternities!
71 Bless, O night time and day time, the Lord;
   sing a hymn and exalt him exceedingly into the eternities!
72 Bless, O light and darkness, the Lord;
   praise and exalt him exceedingly into the eternities!
73 Bless, O flashing lightning and stirring clouds, the Lord;
   laud and exalt him exceedingly into the eternities!
74 Bless, O earth, the Lord;
   sing forth and exalt him exceedingly into the eternities!
75 Bless, O mountain heights and high places of the hills, the Lord;
   laud and exalt him exceedingly into the eternities!
76 Bless, O everything that springs forth upon the earth, the Lord;
   sing a hymn and exalt him exceedingly into the eternities!
77 Bless, O rainstorms and running waters, the Lord;
   praise and exalt him exceedingly into the eternities!
78 Bless, O seas and rivers, the Lord;
   sing a hymn and exalt him exceedingly into the eternities!
79 Bless, O huge creatures of the sea
   and everything that moves in waters, the Lord;
   praise and exalt him exceedingly into the eternities!
80 Bless, O all the winged creatures of the heavens, the Lord;
   sing a hymn and exalt him exceedingly into the eternities!
81 Bless, O four-footed animals and beasts of the earth, the Lord;
   laud and exalt him exceedingly into the eternities!
82 Bless, O sons of humans, the Lord;
   laud and exalt him exceedingly into the eternities!
83 Bless, O Israel, the Lord;
   sing a hymn and exalt him exceedingly into the eternities!
84 Bless, O priests, the Lord;
   praise and exalt him exceedingly into the eternities!
85 Bless, O servants, the Lord;
   sing a hymn and exalt him exceedingly into the eternities!
86 Bless, O spirits and souls of the righteous, the Lord;
   praise and exalt him exceedingly into the eternities!
87 Bless, O holy and low ones in your heart, the Lord;
   sing a hymn and exalt him exceedingly into the eternities!
88 Bless, O Hananiah, Azariah, and Mishael, the Lord;
   praise and exalt him exceedingly into the eternities!
   For he has taken us out of Hades,
      and has saved us from the hand of death,
   and has rescued us from the middle of the raging flame,
      and from the fire he delivered us!
89 Acknowledge and give thanks to the Lord,
   For he is good, for his mercy continues into the eternities!

⁹⁰ Bless, all those who worship the Lord, God of the gods;
sing a hymn and acknowledge him fully,
for his mercy continues into the ages,
even into the age of eternities!"

## Susanna

¹Now there was a man dwelling in Babylon, and his name was Jehoiakim. ²And he took a wife whose name was Susanna, the daughter of Chelkios, a very beautiful woman and one fearing the Lord. ³And her parents were righteous and taught their daughter by the law of Moses. ⁴Now Jehoiakim was very rich, and he had an orchard adjacent to his house, and they brought to him the Judeans, because he was more honored than all.

*Susanna Is* ⁵Then two elders from the people were appointed as judges in that
*Accused by* year, about which the Master spoke, "Because lawlessness came from
*Evil Elders* Babylon, from elder judges, who seemed to guide the people." ⁶And disputes would come from other cities to them. ⁷These saw a woman graceful in appearance, wife of their brother among the sons of Israel, with the name of Susanna, daughter of Chelkios, wife of Jehoiakim, walking about in the orchard of her husband during the evening. ⁸And desiring her, ⁹they perverted their mind and turned away their eyes so as not to look to heaven nor to keep in mind righteous judgments. ¹⁰Now both of them were enthralled about her, but each one did not indicate to the other the wicked feeling which possessed them concerning her, nor did the woman know about this situation. ¹²And when early morning came, they came in haste to see who would appear to her first and speak with her. ¹³And look, this woman, according to her custom, was walking about. And one of the elders had arrived and look, the other one arrived, and one interrogated the other one, saying, "Why have you, so early in the morning, come out without taking me along?" ¹⁴And each confessed to each other his grief.ᵃ

¹⁹And one said to the other, "Let us go to her." And when they had agreed they went to her and they forced her.ᵃ

²²Now the woman of Judah said to them, "I see that if I do this, then death it is for me. And if I do not do it, I am still not able to escape from your hands. ²³It is better for me to not do this sin and so to fall into your hands than for me to sin before the Lord."ᵃ

²⁸And the lawless men turned back, terrified in themselves, and they were setting snares in order that they might kill her. And they came to the synagogue of the city where they were dwelling, and they were sitting and deliberating. Those who were there were all sons of Israel. ²⁹And when the two elders had stood up, then the judges said, "Send for Susanna, the daughter of Chelkios, who is wife of Jehoiakim." And they immediately summoned her. ³⁰And when the woman was present, along with her father and mother and her servants and maidens, there were five hundred in number; also, the four young children of Susanna. ³¹And the woman was exceedingly refined. ³²Then the wicked men commanded them to unveil her in order that they might be sated with her beauty, lusting after her.

---

ᵃ Swete does not include verses 15–18, 20–21, 24–27

³³And all the people with her wept, and as many as knew her. ³⁴And then the elders rose, and the judges placed their hands upon her head. ³⁵And her heart trusted in the Lord God, and lifting up her head to heaven she cried out within her, saying, ³⁵ᵃ"O Lord God, the eternal one who knows all things before their beginning, you know that I have not done this. You know what these lawless ones maliciously intend to do against me." And the Lord listened to her prayer. ³⁶And then the two elders said, "We were walking about within the orchard of her husband. ³⁷And as we were going around the walkway, we saw this woman reclining with a man. And, while standing still there, we watched them having intercourse with each other. ³⁸Now they themselves did not know that we were standing there. Then we talked to one another, saying, 'Let us find out who these people are.' ³⁹Then when we stepped forward, we recognized her, but the young man fled, veiled with a cloak. ⁴⁰And seizing this woman, we asked her, 'Who is the person?' ⁴¹But she did not inform us about who he was with respect to these things which we witnessed." And all the assembly believed them, since they were elders and judges of the people.ᵃ

⁴⁴⁻⁴⁵Now look, an angel of the Lord. As that woman was being led out to be executed, the angel gave, as he was commanded, a spirit of insight to a young man, Daniel.ᵃ ⁴⁸And Daniel, stirring up and dividing the gathering, and taking a stand in the middle of them, said, "In such a way as this, O foolish sons of Israel, are you not examining this closely nor recognizing the plain truth, that they killed a daughter of Israel?ᵃ ⁵¹And now, separate out for me these men from one another by a great distance, in order that I can test them." ⁵¹ᵃAnd when they were separated, Daniel said to the congregation, "Now, do not think because these men are elders, saying, 'they would not lie,' but I will examine them closely according to the things that fall under me." ⁵²And he summoned one of them, and they brought the elder to the young man. And Daniel said to him, "Hear, hear, you old relic of evil days, now your sins which you have committed in the past have come. ⁵³As one entrusted to hear and to give judgments, you have laid down the death penalty. And the innocent person you have condemned, but the guilty persons you are forgiving, while the Lord declares that the innocent person and the righteous person you will not slay. ⁵⁴Now, therefore, under what tree and in what part of the orchard did you see them present with each other?" And the ungodly man said, "Under the mastic tree." ⁵⁵And the young man said, "Right, you have lied to your own soul; for the angel of the Lord will tear apart your soul today." ⁵⁶Then, putting this man in another location, he said to bring forward to him the other man. Then to this man he said, "Why has your seed been perverted, as if stemming from Sidon, and not stemming from Judah? Beauty, a small lust, has seduced you. ⁵⁷And so thus you treated the daughters of Israel, and they feared to be in company with you. But no daughter of Judah consented to endure your disease in wickedness. ⁵⁸Now, therefore, tell me under what tree and in what place of the garden you caught them having intercourse with each other?" And the man said, "Under the evergreen oak." ⁵⁹Then Daniel said, "O sinful man, now the angel of the Lord has set it up, having a sword among the people. And he will utterly destroy you, in order that it may saw you asunder."

*Daniel Reveals the Truth*

---

ᵃ Swete does not include verses 42–43, 46–47, 49–50

⁶⁰⁻⁶²Then all the assembly cheered aloud for the young man, that out of each one's mouth, with agreement between them, they established both of them as false witnesses. And as the law states clearly, so they did to them. Just as they had acted wickedly toward a kinswoman, so they gagged them and, after leading them away, they threw them into a ravine. Then the angel of the Lord threw fire into the middle of them. And thus, innocent blood was saved on that day.

⁶²ᵃBecause of this, the young men are beloved of Jacob in their integrity. ⁶²ᵇAnd we indeed watch for able young sons who will live pious lives for young men. And there will be in them a spirit of understanding and knowledge and of insight and understanding for eternity of eternity.

## Bel and the Dragon

From the prophecy of Habakkuk, the son of Joshua, from the tribe of Levi.

²A certain man was priest, whose name was Daniel, the son of Abal, a confidant of the king of Babylon. ³Now there was an idol, named Bel, that the Babylonians worshiped. And there was lavished upon it each day the finest wheat flour, twelve artabas of flour, and four sheep, and six measures of olive oil. ⁴And the king revered it, and the king went forth each day and bowed himself to it. But Daniel prayed to the Lord. And the king said to Daniel, "Why don't you bow before Bel?" ⁵And Daniel said to the king, "I worship no one except the Lord God, who created the heaven and the earth, and the one who holds power and authority over all flesh."

⁶And the king said to him, "This, therefore, is not a god? Do you not see how much is consumed for him each day?" ⁷And Daniel said to him, "By no means let anyone deceive you! For this thing is on the inside mere clay, and on the outside it is bronze. I vow now to you by the Lord, the God of *Daniel* gods, that this has never eaten anything!" ⁸And having become angry, the *Exposes the* king summoned the attendants of the holy place and said to them, "Show *Deceitful* plainly the one who is eating the things being prepared for Bel! And if not, *Priests of Bel* indeed you will die, ⁹or Daniel, who affirms that these things are not being consumed by him." And they said, "Bel himself is the one who is consuming these things." And Daniel said to the king, "Let it be just so. If I do not show that Bel is not the one who is consuming these things, I will die, and all those who are mine."

¹⁰Now there were attached to Bel seventy priests, besides women and children. And so they brought the king into the idol's temple. ¹¹And the food was set before the king and Daniel, and mixed wine was brought in and set before Bel. And Daniel said, "You yourself see that these things are laid out, O king. You, therefore, set a seal on the keys of the temple when it is closed up." And the saying was pleasing to the king. ¹⁴Now Daniel ordered those with him, after forcing everyone from the temple, to mark clearly the whole temple with ashes, with no one of those outside of it observing, and then, sealing the temple, he ordered them to seal it up with the signet ring of the king, and with the seal rings of some of the most notable ones of the priests. And so, it was done, just in this manner.

15-17Then it happened on the next day that the king was present at the place. But the priests of Bel, by means of secret entrances, had entered in and eaten everything which had been placed beside Bel, and they had quaffed down the wine. And Daniel said, "Look closely at your seals to see whether they are still in place, O men and priests. And you yourself also, O king, take care lest something is suspicious in your opinion." Indeed, they found that the seal was unchanged, and they removed the sealed lock. 18And when they had opened the doors, they saw that all the things that had been set out were consumed, and the tables had nothing upon them, and the king was overjoyed and said to Daniel, "Great is Bel, and there is no deception with him."

19Then Daniel laughed out loud and said to the king, "Come here! See the deception of the priests!" And Daniel said, "O king, these footprints, whose are they?" 20And the king replied, "Of men and of women and of children!" 21Then he went to the house in which the priests were living and found the food for Bel along with the wine. And Daniel pointed out to the king the secret entrances through which the priests would enter and consume the things that had been set out for Bel. 22And the king led them from Bel's temple and handed them over to Daniel. And the expenses put out to run it he gave to Daniel, but he overthrew Bel.

23Now there was a dragon in the same place, and the Babylonians worshiped it. 24And the king said to Daniel, "You will certainly not say concerning this that it is merely bronze! Look, he lives and eats and drinks! Worship him!" 26And Daniel said, "O king, give me the power, and I will slay the dragon without sword or staff." And the king granted him authority and said to him, "I give it to you." 27And Daniel, taking thirty minas of pitch and hard fat and hair, boiled it together and made a lump from it and threw it into the mouth of the dragon. And, after consuming it, the dragon burst open. And he showed it to the king, saying, "Do not worship these things, O king!" *Daniel Destroys a Dragon*

28And all the men from the territories were gathered together against Daniel. And they asserted, "The king has become a Judean; he has overturned Bel and slayed the dragon." 30Now when the king saw that the multitude from the territory had gathered against him, he summoned his close companions and said, "I am giving Daniel over for destruction." 31-32And there was a den in which seven lions were being fed. To them were given those plotting against the king; and there was supplied to them each day two bodies of those who had been condemned to death. And the angry crowd threw Daniel into the den so that he would be devoured and so that not even a burial would take place. And Daniel was in the den six days. *Daniel Is Delivered from a Den of Lions*

33Now it was during the sixth day that Habakkuk had prepared some bread, crumbling it into a bowl with some soup, and a jar of mixed wine, and he was proceeding into the field to the reapers. 34And an angel of the Lord spoke to Habakkuk, saying, "These things the Lord God says to you, 'The meal that you have prepared, deliver it to Daniel in the den of lions in Babylon.'" 35Now Habakkuk said, "Lord God, I have not seen Babylon, and as for the den, I do not know where it is." 36And seizing Habakkuk by the hair of his head, the angel of the Lord put him beside the den in Babylon.

<sup>37</sup>Then Habakkuk said to Daniel, "Arise, eat the meal that the Lord God has sent to you."

<sup>38</sup>Then Daniel said, "The Lord God, the one who does not forsake those who love him, has remembered me." <sup>39</sup>And Daniel ate, and the angel of the Lord set Habakkuk down whence he had taken him on the same day. And the Lord God remembered Daniel.

<sup>40</sup>And after these things the king went out mourning for Daniel. And stooping down into the den he saw him sitting there. <sup>41</sup>And crying out loudly, the king said, "Great is the Lord God, and there is no other except him." <sup>42</sup>And the king led Daniel out from the den. And he threw those responsible for his destruction into the den in the presence of Daniel, and they were devoured.

*Introduction to*

# ADDITIONS TO DANIEL (THEODOTION)

D ANIEL CIRCULATED IN GREEK in two major editions—the Old Greek and the Theodotion versions. Theodotion was a second-century Christian whose name came to be attached to a revision of the Old Greek version of Daniel. The distinctive features of this revision predate Theodotion himself by more than a century, as both the authors of Hebrews and Revelation knew Daniel in a form much more akin to the Theodotion rather than the Old Greek version. This alternative text tradition associated with Theodotion, represented here in translation, is thus of great importance for the study of the New Testament and the version of Daniel with which its authors interacted. Theodotion is particularly richer in the telling of the story of Susanna (sixty-four verses as opposed to forty-seven in the Old Greek).

—D. A. deSilva

# ADDITIONS TO DANIEL (THEODOTION)[a]

## The Prayer of Azariah

**3** [24]They were walking in the midst of the flames, singing to God and praising the Lord. [25]Then presenting himself, Azariah prayed in this way, and opened his mouth in the midst of the fire, and said, [26]"Blessed are you O Lord, God of our ancestors, and your name is praiseworthy and glorified for eternity. [27]For you are righteous in everything that you have done, and all your works are genuine, and your ways are straightforward, and all your decisions are true. [28]You have performed judgments of truth according to everything that you have brought on us and on the sacred city of our ancestors, Jerusalem, because you have brought all these things in truth and judgment on account of our sins. [29]For we have failed, and we have acted lawlessly by rebelling against you, and we have sinned in everything.

[30]"And we did not listen to your commands. We have not kept them or done as you commanded us so that it would be well for us. [31]Everything you have brought on us and everything you have done to us you did by a true judgment. [32]You have delivered us into the power of lawless enemies and hated rebels and to a king that is unrighteous and the most evil in all the world. [33]And now it is not a disgrace for us to open our mouth; and it has become reproach to your slaves and to those who worship you. [34]Surely you have not delivered us completely, on account of your name, and do not reject your covenant. [35]Do not remove your mercy from us on account of Abraham, who was loved by you, and on account of Isaac, your servant, and Israel, your holy one, [36]to whom you spoke to multiply their seed, like the stars of the heavens and like the sand at the lip of the sea. [37]For, Master, we have become smaller than all the nations and we are humble in all the earth today on account of our sins. [38]At this time there is no ruler or prophet or leader or burnt offering or offering or gift or incense, no place to bear fruit before you and to find mercy. [39]However, with a shattered life and a spirit of humility, we may be accepted [40]as with the burnt offering of rams and bulls and with myriads of fat lambs. So let our offerings be before you today and accomplish behind you, because there shall be no disgrace for those who trust in you. [41]Now, we follow with our whole heart, and we fear you, and we seek your face. [42]Do not disgrace us, but treat us according to your goodness and according to the bounty of your compassion. [43]Rescue us according to your marvels and give glory to your name, O Lord. [44]May all those who show evil to your servants feel shame, and may they be disgraced by every dominion, and may their strength be shattered. [45]Let them learn that you are the Lord, God alone, and esteemed above all the world."

[a] This is a translation of Theodotion's Gk. translation of Daniel as found in Codex Vaticanus

## The Song of the Three Young Men

⁴⁶Now, those servants of the king who were throwing them in did not stop firing the furnace with naphtha and pitch and flax and brushwood. ⁴⁷The flame spread out above the furnace to forty-nine cubits in height ⁴⁸and shot out and set on fire those Chaldeans it found near the furnace. ⁴⁹But the angel of the Lord came down into the furnace together with those around Azariah and shook the flame of fire from the furnace ⁵⁰and made the midst of the furnace as if a moist breeze were whistling inside. Generally, the fire did not touch them and did not distress or cause them annoyance. ⁵¹Then the three began to sing as if from one mouth, and glorify and praise God in the furnace, saying:

52 "Blessed are you, O Lord God of our ancestors,
    and praiseworthy and highly exalted for eternities.
  Blessed is your glorious, holy name
    and to be highly praised and highly exceedingly for all
      eternities.
53 Blessed are you in the temple of your holy glory
    and highly extolled and highly glorious for eternities.
54 Blessed are you who look upon the abyss, sitting upon cherubim
    and praiseworthy and being greatly exalted for eternities.
55 Blessed are you upon the throne of your dominion
    and highly extolled and being greatly exalted for eternities.
56 Blessed are you in the foundation of heaven
    and praised and glorified for eternities.
57 Bless the Lord, all the labors of the Lord;
    sing and highly exalt him for eternities.
58 Bless the Lord, O heavens;
    sing and highly exalt him for eternities.
59 Bless the Lord, O angels of the Lord;
    sing and highly exalt him for eternities.
60 Bless the Lord, O waters, even all those above the heaven;
    sing and highly exalt him for eternities.
61 Praise the Lord, all powers;
    sing and highly exalt him for eternities.
62 Bless the Lord, O sun and moon;
    sing and highly exalt him for eternities.
63 Bless the Lord, O stars of the sky;
    sing and highly exalt him for eternities.
64 Praise the Lord, every thunderstorm and dew;
    sing and highly exalt him for eternities.
65 Bless the Lord, all spirits;
    sing and highly exalt him for eternities.
66 Bless the Lord, fire and burning heat;
    sing and highly exalt him for eternities.
69 Bless the Lord, cold weather and heat;
    sing and highly exalt him for eternities.

70 Bless the Lord, hoarfrost and snow;
   sing and highly exalt him for eternities.
71 Bless the Lord, nights and days;
   sing and highly exalt him for eternities.
72 Bless the Lord, light and darkness;
   sing and highly exalt him for eternities.
73 Bless the Lord, lightning and clouds;
   sing and highly exalt him for eternities.
74 Let the earth praise the Lord;
   let it sing and highly exalt him for eternities.
75 Bless the Lord, mountains and hills;
   sing and highly exalt him for eternities.
76 Bless the Lord, all the things produced in the earth;
   sing and highly exalt him for eternities.
77 Bless the Lord, springtime;
   sing and highly exalt him for eternities.
78 Bless the Lord, seas and rivers;
   sing and highly exalt him for eternities.
79 Bless the Lord, huge fish and everything that moves in the water;
   sing and highly exalt him for eternities.
80 Bless the Lord, everything that flies in the sky;
   sing and highly exalt him for eternities.
81 Bless the Lord, all wild beasts and herds;
   sing and highly exalt him for eternities.
82 Bless the Lord, O sons of humanity;
   sing and highly exalt him for eternities.
83 Bless the Lord, O Israel;
   sing and highly exalt him for eternities.
84 Bless the Lord, O priests;
   sing and highly exalt him for eternities.
85 Bless the Lord, O slaves;
   sing and highly exalt him for eternities.
86 Bless the Lord, O spirits and righteous souls;
   sing and highly exalt him for eternities.
87 Bless the Lord, O hallowed and humble in heart;
   sing and highly exalt him for eternities.
88 Bless the Lord, Hananiah, Azariah, and Mishael,
   sing praise and highly exalt him for eternities.
   Because he has taken us out from Hades and saved us from the
       hand of death,
   and he rescued us from the midst of the furnace of burning
       flame,
   and he rescued us from the midst of fire.
89 Acknowledge the Lord for kindness,
   because his mercy is for eternity.
90 Bless the God of gods, all those who worship the Lord;
   sing and acknowledge
   that his mercy is for eternity."

## Susanna

¹There was a man living in Babylon, and his name was Jehoiakim. ²He took a wife whose name was Susanna, daughter of Hilkiah, very beautiful and fearful of the Lord. ³Her parents were righteous, and they taught their daughter according to the law of Moses. ⁴Jehoiakim was very wealthy, and he had an orchard beside his house. And the Jews would come to him on account of him being held in higher esteem than all others.

⁵Two elders were assigned from the people as judges in that year, about whom the master said, "Lawlessness sprouted from Babylon, from elders, judges who were intended to guide the people." ⁶These were constantly in the house of Jehoiakim, and all those who needed a judge would come to them. ⁷And it happened when the people left in the middle of the day, Susanna would come in and walk around in the orchard of her husband. ⁸The two elders kept watching her entering and walking around according to the day, and they came to be in lust for her. ⁹They perverted their own mind, and they turned their eyes away to look not to the heavens or to remember righteous judgments. ¹⁰They were both deeply moved concerning her, but they did not report their distress to one another, ¹¹for they were ashamed to report their yearning because they wanted to be with her. ¹²They watched closely, eagerly, to see her according to the day. ¹³They said to one another,ᵃ "Let us go into home now because it is lunch time." And when they went out, they separated from one another. ¹⁴But returning, they came to the same place, and when they asked one another the reason, they confessed their yearning. Then, together, they arranged a time when they would be able to find her alone.

*Susanna and the Evil Elders*

¹⁵It happened that while they were watching closely for a convenient day, she once came in just like the day before and the third day before, alone with two girls. And she wanted to bathe in the orchard because it was scorching hot. ¹⁶There was no one there except the two elders, hidden and observing her. ¹⁷She said to the girls, "Now, bring me olive oil and soap and close the doors of the orchard so I can bathe." ¹⁸They did just as she said. They closed the doors of the orchard and went out at the side doors to bring the things assigned to them. They did not see the elders because they were hidden.

*The Evil Elders' Opportunity*

¹⁹And it happened when the girls left, the two old men got up and ran up to her, ²⁰and they said, "Look, the doors of the orchard are closed, and no one can see us. And we are in lust for you. Therefore, agree with us and be with us. ²¹But, if not, we will testify against you that a young man was with you, and you sent the maidens away from you on account of this." ²²And Susanna groaned and said, "I am confined on every side! For if I do this, it is death for me; and if I do not, I will not escape your hands. ²³It is preferable for me to fall into your hands by not taking part than to sin before the Lord." ²⁴And Susanna shouted out with a loud voice, but the two old men opposite her also shouted. ²⁵And one ran and opened the doors of the orchard. ²⁶But when they heard the shouting in the orchard, those from the house burst in through the side doors to see what had happened

---

ᵃ Lit. "the other to another"

with her. ²⁷But when the old men said their words, the servants were very ashamed because such a word as this had never been said about Susanna.

*The Cover-Up*  ²⁸And it happened on the next day, as the people assembled around her husband, Jehoiakim, the two old men came full of lawless thoughts against Susanna to put her to death. And they said before the people, ²⁹"Send in Susanna, daughter of Hilkiah, who is the wife of Jehoiakim." Then they sent for her. ³⁰And she came, and her parents and her children and all her relatives. ³¹But Susanna was very delicate and beautiful in shape. ³²Then the lawless ones ordered her to be uncovered, for she was veiled, so that they could be filled with her beauty. ³³Then those who were with her and all the ones who looked at her began crying. ³⁴The two old men arose in the midst of the people and put their hands on her head. ³⁵She wept and looked up into heaven because her heart had trusted in the Lord. ³⁶The old men said, "While we were walking alone in the orchard, she entered with two girls and closed the doors of the orchard and sent the girls away. ³⁷A young man who was hidden came to her, and he lay down with her. ³⁸But because we were in the corner of the orchard, upon seeing the lawlessness, we ran to them. ³⁹And when we saw them having sexual intercourse, we could not gain possession of that man because he was stronger than us and he opened the doors and leapt away. ⁴⁰But we seized this woman, and asked her who the young man was. ⁴¹And she did not want to tell us. We testify to these things." The assembly believed them, as they were elders of the people and judges, and they condemned her to die.

*Susanna's*  ⁴²But Susanna shouted out with a loud voice and said, "God Eternal, who
*Plea*  divines the hidden things, who knows everything before their beginning, ⁴³you realize that they have testified against me with lies. And look, I will die, doing nothing wrong that these men maliciously accuse against me."

*The Lord*  ⁴⁴And the Lord listened to her voice. ⁴⁵And while she was being led away
*Uses Daniel*  to be put to death, God roused the holy spirit of a young boy named Daniel, ⁴⁶and he cried out with a loud voice, "I am innocent of the blood of this woman!" ⁴⁷Then all the people turned toward him and said, "What is this word that you have spoken?" ⁴⁸As he stood in their midst, he said, "In this way you are stupid, O people of Israel! Without examining or recognizing what is clear, you have condemned a daughter of Israel! ⁴⁹Go back into the court, for these men have testified lies against her." ⁵⁰All the people returned quickly, and the elders said to him, "Come, sit in our midst and tell us, because God has given you the privilege of an elder." ⁵¹So Daniel said to them, "Separate them far from one another, and I will question them." ⁵²Then, when they were separated, the one from the other one, he called one of them and said to him, "O you who have become old of evil days, now your sins are present, which you continued to do before, ⁵³by judging unrighteous cases and condemning the innocent but dismissing the blameworthy, while the Lord says, 'You shall not kill an innocent and righteous person.' ⁵⁴Now, therefore, if you really saw this woman, tell us: Under what tree did you see them having sexual intercourse with one another?" He said, "Under the mastic tree." ⁵⁵Then Daniel said, "Rightly, you have lied against your own head—for the angel of God has already received the statement from God; he will split you in half." ⁵⁶After he had removed him, he ordered to bring the other and said to him, "Seed of Canaan and

not of Judah, beauty has deceived you, and lust has distorted your heart. <sup>57</sup>You used to act in this way to the daughters of Israel, and those women, since they were frightened, would have sexual intercourse with you, but a daughter of Judah did not tolerate your lawlessness. <sup>58</sup>Now, therefore, tell me: Under what tree did you seize them talking to one another?" So he said, "Under the evergreen oak." <sup>59</sup>Daniel said to him, "Surely, you also have lied against your own head; for the angel of God is waiting, holding a sword to cut you in half to destroy you."

<sup>60</sup>And all the assembly cried out with a loud voice and praised the God who delivers those who hope in him. <sup>61</sup>And they stood up against the two old men because Daniel had shown them from their own mouths they were false witnesses. And they did to them just as they had maliciously intended against the neighbor <sup>62</sup>by acting according to the law of Moses, and they killed them. And innocent blood was saved on that day. <sup>63</sup>Hilkiah and his wife praised for their daughter, with Jehoiakim her husband and all their kindred, because no unseemly action was found in her.

*Susanna's Honor Restored*

<sup>64</sup>Daniel became great before the people from day that and beyond.

## Bel and the Dragon

<sup>1</sup>And King Astyages was added to his ancestors, and Cyrus the Persian received his dominion. <sup>2</sup>And Daniel was a confidant of the king, and he was held in esteem above all his friends. <sup>3</sup>And the Babylonians had an idol whose name was Bel, and every day they would offer twelve measures of the finest wheaten flour and forty sheep and six measures of wine to it. <sup>4</sup>And the king would honor it and would go each day to bow before it. But Daniel kept bowing before his God. And the king said to him, "On what account do you not bow before Bel?" <sup>5</sup>Then he said, "Because I do not honor idols made by hand, but the living God who created the heavens and the earth and has dominion over all flesh." <sup>6</sup>And the king said to him, "Does Bel not seem to you to be a living God? Or do you not see what he eats and drinks every day?" <sup>7</sup>Daniel said, laughing, "Do not be deceived, O king, for this is clay inside and bronze on the outside, and he has never eaten." <sup>8</sup>And the king became angry and summoned his priests and said to them, "If you do not tell me who is the one consuming this expenditure, you will die. <sup>9</sup>But if you prove that Bel consumes them, Daniel will die because he has blasphemed against Bel." Daniel said to the king, "May it be according to your word." <sup>10</sup>And, there were seventy priests of Bel, excluding their wives and children. The king went with Daniel to the house of Bel. <sup>11</sup>And the priests of Bel said, "Look, we are departing outside, but you, O king, set out the food and place the wine after it is mixed and close the door and seal it with your signet. <sup>12</sup>And when you arrive in the morning, if you do not find everything eaten by Bel, we should die, or Daniel, the one who lies about us, should die." <sup>13</sup>They were acting contemptuously because they had made a hidden entrance under the table, and they were continually entering through it and consuming it. <sup>14</sup>And it happened as they departed, and the king set out food for Bel. And Daniel commanded his servants, and they brought ashes, and they scattered the ashes around the whole temple

*Daniel and the Priests of Bel*

before the king alone. And when they went out, they closed the door and sealed it with the signet of the king and departed. ¹⁵Then the priests and their wives and children came during the night according to their habit, and they devoured and drank everything.

¹⁶And the king woke early in the morning, and Daniel was with him. ¹⁷And he said, "Are the seals secure, Daniel?" And he said, "They are secure, O king." ¹⁸It happened at the same time the doors opened, when the king looked at the table, he shouted with a loud voice, "You are great, Bel! And there is none beside you, and not a single treachery." ¹⁹And Daniel laughed and grabbed the king so that he could not enter inside and said, "Indeed, see the ground and notice whose footprints these are." ²⁰And the king said, "I see the footprints of men and women and children." ²¹Infuriated, the king then assembled the priests and their wives and children. And they showed him the hidden doors through which they would go in and consume the things on the table. ²²And the king killed them, and he gave Bel to Daniel, and he destroyed it and its temple.

*Daniel Destroys a Dragon* ²³And there was a great dragon, and the Babylonians worshiped it. ²⁴And the king said to Daniel, "You cannot say that this one is not a living God; and bow before it." ²⁵And Daniel said, "I will bow before the Lord my God because he is a living God. ²⁶But you, O king, give me authority, and I will kill the dragon without a sword and staff." And the king said, "I give it to you." ²⁷And Daniel took pitch and fat and hair and boiled them together, and he made cakes and put them into the mouth of the dragon. And after it had eaten, the dragon tore open, and he said, "Behold, things for your worship!"

*Daniel Suffers the Wrath of the Bel Followers* ²⁸And it happened when the Babylonians heard, they were irritated, and they united together against the king and said, "The king has become a Jew! He has torn down Bel, and he killed the dragon and murdered the priests!" ²⁹And when they came to the king, they said, "Hand Daniel over to us, or else we will kill you and your house." ³⁰And the king saw that they were pressing him very much, and, since he was forced, he handed Daniel over to them. ³¹They threw him into the lions' den lions, and he was there six days. ³²There were seven lions in the den, and two bodies and two sheep were given to them daily, but then nothing was given to them so that they would consume Daniel.

*The Lord Saves Daniel* ³³And Habakkuk the prophet was in Judah. And he boiled vegetables, and he crumbled bread into a bowl, and he would go into the plain to bring food to the harvesters. ³⁴And an angel of the Lord said to Habakkuk, "Bring the meal that you have to Babylon to Daniel in the den of lions." ³⁵And Habakkuk said, "O Lord, I have not seen Babylon, and I do not know the den." ³⁶And the angel of the Lord seized his top, and as he gripped the hair of his head, he put him in Babylon above the den in the whizzing of his spirit. ³⁷And Habakkuk shouted, saying, "Daniel, Daniel, take the meal that God sent you." ³⁸And Daniel said, "For you have remembered me, O God, and you have not forsaken the ones who loved you." ³⁹And Daniel rose and ate. The angel of God immediately delivered Habakkuk to his place. ⁴⁰The king came on the seventh day to mourn for Daniel, and he went to the den and looked in and look, Daniel was sitting there. ⁴¹And he shouted aloud with a great voice and said, "You are great, O Lord, God of Daniel, and there is no other except you." ⁴²And he pulled him up, and threw those responsible for his destruction into the den, and they were devoured immediately before him.

*Introduction to*

# 1 Maccabees

FIRST MACCABEES PRESENTS A history of events in Judea and surrounding regions from about 175–141 BC, covering the hellenizing crisis and the Maccabean revolution that finally won political independence for Israel after four centuries of gentile rule. The book was probably written in Hebrew, in Israel, sometime after 134 BC and, given its positive view of Rome, sometime prior to 63 BC. The Hebrew original has not survived; the work has been transmitted primarily in Greek. The author wrote a history with a clear propagandistic purpose, namely, to increase the legitimacy of the Hasmonean dynasty in the eyes of their Judean subjects. It does this by emphasizing the pious character and the singular achievements of the aged Mattathias and his five sons—the most conspicuous of which was Judas Maccabaeus ("the Hammer")—on behalf of a grateful nation, which could only rightly show its gratitude by continuing to accord precedence and rule to their surviving descendants. Despite its rather obvious propagandistic aims, 1 Maccabees remains one of the most important sources for this watershed period in the life of Israel. It is especially important in the portrait that it paints of "zeal for the law" in action, often violent action against non-observant Jews, such as would later motivate a Saul of Tarsus as well as the Zealot revolutionary movement that plunged Israel into a futile and fatal revolt against Rome in AD 66.

—D. A. deSilva

# 1 MACCABEES

*Alexander*
*the Great* **1** And it happened after the victory of Alexander, the son of Philip, the Macedonian, who went out from the land of the Hittites and struck down Darius, king of the Persians and Medes, and ruled in place of him— earlier he ruled over Greece. ²And he participated in many battles and conquered strongholds and killed kings. ³And he passed through as far as the farthest point of the earth and took spoils from many nations. And the land was silent before him, and his heart was elated and stirred up. ⁴And he gathered a very mighty force and ruled over the territories, and nations, and tyrants,ᵃ and they became to him as tribute. ⁵And after this, he fell on his bed and perceived that he was going to die. ⁶And he summoned his esteemed servants who raised him from childhood and divided for them his kingdom while he was living. ⁷And Alexander ruled twelve years and then died. ⁸And his subordinates ruled, each in his place. ⁹And all of them put on crowns after his death, and their sons after them for many years. And they increased the amount of evil in the earth.

*Antiochus*
*Epiphanes*
*and*
*Hellenistic*
*Israel* ¹⁰And there came forth from them a sinful root: Antiochus Epiphanes, son of Antiochus, the king, who was a hostage in Rome. And he ruled in the one hundred and thirty-seventh year of the kingdom of the Greeks.ᵇ ¹¹In those days, the lawless son went out of Israel, and they persuaded many, saying, "We should go and make a treaty with the nations around us, because from that time we separated from them, much evil has found us." ¹²And the idea was attractive in their eyes. ¹³And some from the people were willing and went to the king, and they gave them authority to perform the duties of the nations. ¹⁴And they built a gymnasium in Jerusalem according to the customs of the nations. ¹⁵And they made a foreskin for themselves and discarded the holy covenant and joined with the Gentiles and were sold to act wickedly.

*Antiochus*
*Epiphanes*
*in Egypt* ¹⁶And the kingdom was prepared for Antiochus. And he decided to exercise his rule over the land of Egypt so that he might rule over the two kingdoms. ¹⁷And he went into Egypt in fierce force, with chariots and elephants and with cavalry and with a great navy. ¹⁸And he prepared for war against Ptolemy, the king of Egypt. And Ptolemy was shamed from his face and fled. And many casualties fell. ¹⁹And they captured the fortified city in the land of Egypt and took the spoils of the land of Egypt.

*Antiochus*
*Epiphanes*
*Overtakes*
*the Judeans* ²⁰And Antiochus turned after striking Egypt in the one hundred and forty-third year, and he went up against Israel and Jerusalem with a fierce army. ²¹And he entered the sanctuary in arrogance and took the gold altar and the lampstand for the light, and all its accessories, ²²and the table of presentation and the drink offering cups and the bowls and the golden censers and the veil and the crowns and the golden adornment applied to the face of the temple walls, and he peeled it all off. ²³And he took the gold and silver and the valuable accessories. And he

---

ᵃ Used for an absolute ruler, though not necessarily a despotic one  ᵇ This is 175 BC

took the hidden treasures that he found. ²⁴And having taken everything, he departed to his land. And he made a massacre and spoke with great arrogance. ²⁵And there was great mourning in Israel, in all their places. ²⁶And the rulers and elders groaned; virgins and young men lost their strength, and the beauty of women changed. ²⁷Every bridegroom took up a lament; she who stayed in the bridal chamber was in mourning. ²⁸And the land shook, for the inhabitants in it and the whole house of Jacob wore shame.

²⁹After two years of time, the king sent a chief of tribute collection to the cities of Judah. And he came to Jerusalem with fierce force. ³⁰And he spoke to them peaceful words with cunning. And they trusted him. But he fell upon the city suddenly and struck them with a great slaughter and destroyed many people from Israel. ³¹And he took the spoils of the city and burned it with fire and broke down its buildings and its surrounding wall. ³²And he took captive the women and children and took possession of the livestock. ³³And they built in the city of David a great wall and fortified towers, and it became for them as a fortress. ³⁴And they established there a sinful people, wicked men, and they became strong in it. ³⁵And they stored weapons and provisions and, gathering the spoils of Jerusalem, they put it away there. And he became a great threat. ³⁶And it became as an ambush against the sanctuary and as an evil menace to Israel through all time. ³⁷And they shed innocent blood all around the sanctuary and defiled the sanctuary. ³⁸And the inhabitants of Jerusalem fled because of them, and it became a settlement of foreigners, and it became foreign to the ones born in it, and its children abandoned it. ³⁹Her sanctuary was stripped bare like the wilderness; her feasts turned to grief, her Sabbaths to insult, her honor to contempt. ⁴⁰According to her glory, her dishonor was multiplied, and her majesty turned to grief.

*Jerusalem Is Occupied*

⁴¹And the king wrote to his whole kingdom that all should be as one people, ⁴²and each should abandon his customs. And all the peoples complied according to the word of the king. ⁴³And many from Israel consented to his service, and they sacrificed to idols and defiled the Sabbath. ⁴⁴And the king sent documents in the hands of messengers to Jerusalem and the cities of Judah, going after the customs of foreigners of the land, ⁴⁵and to withhold burnt offerings and sacrifice and drink offering from the sanctuary and to profane Sabbaths and festivals, ⁴⁶and to defile the sanctuary and holy things, ⁴⁷to build altars and shrines and idols and sacrifice pigs and common animals, ⁴⁸and to leave their sons uncircumcised, to make repulsive their souls with all impurity and profanation ⁴⁹so as to forget the law and to change all their duties. ⁵⁰And whoever should not act according to the word of the king would die. ⁵¹According to all these words, he wrote to his kingdom, and he appointed supervisors over all the people and ordered the cities of Judah to sacrifice according to city and city. ⁵²And many assembled from the people against them—namely, all who abandoned the law and did evil in the land ⁵³and put Israel in secret places, and in all kinds of hiding places, for their refuge.

*Installation of Gentile Cults*

⁵⁴And on the fifteenth day of Chislev, on the forty-fifth year, they built an abomination of desolation on the altar, and in the cities around Judah, they built altars. ⁵⁵And at the windows of their houses and in the streets,

they burned incense. ⁵⁶And the documents of the law that they found, they burned with fire, after cutting them up. ⁵⁷And where the book of the covenant was found with someone, and if that person should give approval to the law, the decree of the king was, "Execute him." ⁵⁸By their strength they did thus in Israel to the ones who were found during every month and month in the cities. ⁵⁹And on the fifth and twentieth of the month, they were sacrificing on the altar that was on the altar for burnt sacrifices. ⁶⁰And the women who had circumcised their children, they were executed according to the command. ⁶¹And they hung the infants from their necks and their family, as well as the ones who circumcised them. ⁶²And many in Israel were in suspense and determined among themselves not to eat what was common. ⁶³And they chose to die so that they might not be defiled by the food and not profane the holy covenant, and they died. ⁶⁴And there came a very great wrath upon Israel.

*Mattathias and His Sons React* **2** In those days rose up Mattathias son of John, the son of Simeon, a priest of the sons of Joiarib, from Jerusalem, and he settled in Modein. ²And to him there were five sons: John, who was called Gaddi; ³Simon, who was called Thassi; ⁴Judas, who was called Maccabeus; ⁵Eleazar, who was called Avaran; and Jonathan, who was called Apphus.

⁶And he saw the blasphemy happening in Judah and in Jerusalem. ⁷And he said, "Woe is me! Why was I born to see this affliction of my people and the affliction of the city of the holy and to stay here during its being given into the hand of enemies, and the sanctuary into the hand of foreigners? ⁸Her temple has become as a glorious man. ⁹The vessels of glory have been led away captive. Her children were killed in her streets, her young men by the enemy's sword. ¹⁰Which nation has not taken possession of her kingdom and not seized her spoils? ¹¹All her adornment was removed; instead of freedom, she became as a slave. ¹²And look, our holy things and our beauty and our glory have been desolated, and the nations defiled them! ¹³What reason is there for us to live any longer?" ¹⁴And Mattathias and his sons tore their robes and put on sackcloth and mourned very much.

*Refusing the Sacrifice at Modein* ¹⁵And from the king came those who were enforcing the defection in the city of Modein, that they might sacrifice. ¹⁶And many from Israel came to them, and Mattathias and his sons were assembled together. ¹⁷And those from the king responded and said to Mattathias, saying, "You are a ruler and honored and great in this city and supported with sons and brothers. ¹⁸Now come first and act on the command of the king, as all the nations and the rulers of Judah and those remaining in Jerusalem have done, and you and your house will be among the friends of the king, and you and your sons will be honored with gold and silver and many gifts." ¹⁹And Mattathias answered and said with a great voice, "If all the nations within the house of the king's rule have obeyed him, each departing from the service of their fathers and choosing among his commands, ²⁰yet I and my sons and my brothers will follow in the covenant of our ancestors. ²¹Mercy upon us should we discard law and duties! ²²We will not obey the law of the king to leave our service to the right or the left."

²³And as he finished speaking these words, a Judean man approached in the sight of everyone to burn incense upon the altar in Modein according to the command of the king. ²⁴And Mattathias saw and grew zealous, and

his insides trembled, and rage rose from judgment; and, rushing over, he killed him upon the altar. ²⁵And the man from the king who had forced him to sacrifice, he killed at that moment and tore down the altar. ²⁶And he was zealous for the law like Phinehas did to Zimri son of Shallum. ²⁷And Mattathias shouted in the city with a great voice, saying, "Everyone who is zealous for the law and supports the covenant, come out after me!" ²⁸And he and his sons fled into the mountains, and they abandoned everything they had in the city.

²⁹Then many who sought righteousness and justice went down into the wilderness to stay there, ³⁰they and their sons and their wives and their livestock, because evil pressed hard against them. ³¹And it was reported to the men of the king and the forces who were in Jerusalem, the city of David, that men who ignored the king's command had gone down to hiding places in the wilderness. ³²And many ran after them and, having overtaken them, they camped opposite of them and were drawn together for war against them on the Sabbath day. ³³And they said to them, "Enough! Now come out and act according to the word of the king, and you will live." ³⁴And they said, "We will not come out, nor will we follow the word of the king, profaning the Sabbath day." ³⁵And they rushed against them in attack. ³⁶And they did not respond to them nor hurl a single stone against them nor block their hiding places, ³⁷saying, "We should all of us die in our innocence. The heavens and the earth are testifying for us that you are slaughtering us unjustly." ³⁸And they rose against them in battle on the Sabbath, and they and their wives and their children and their livestock died, up to thousands of human lives.

*The Slaughter on the Sabbath*

³⁹And Mattathias and his friends learned what happened, and they mourned for them to the extreme. ⁴⁰And each man said to his neighbor, "If all of us act as our brothers did and do not fight against the nations for our life and our duties, now quickly they will slaughter us from the earth!" ⁴¹And they resolved on that day, saying, "Every person who should come to us in battle on the day of the Sabbath, we will fight against them, and we will not all die like our brothers died in their hiding places." ⁴²Then there gathered to them a congregation of Hasideans, a strong force from Israel, all who were devoted to the law. ⁴³And all the fugitives from the evil joined with them and became for them as support. ⁴⁴And they organized a force and struck sinners in their wrath and lawless men in their rage, and those who remained fled to the nations to escape. ⁴⁵And Mattathias and his sons went around and tore down the altars. ⁴⁶And they circumcised the uncircumcised young men, as many as were discovered in the borders of Israel, by force. ⁴⁷And they chased down the children of arrogance, and their work prospered in their hands. ⁴⁸And they rescued the law from the hand of the nations and from the hand of the kings, and they did not let the sinner have the upper hand.ᵃ

*The Decision to Fight*

⁴⁹And the days approached for Mattathias to die. And he said to his children, "Now arrogance and scorn are well established, and it is the time for destruction and raging wrath. ⁵⁰Now, children, be zealous for the law, and give your life for the covenant of our fathers. ⁵¹Remember the works of

*The Death of Mattathias*

---

ᵃ Lit. "did not give the horn to the sinner"

our fathers, which they did to their generations, and you will receive great glory and an eternal glory ⁵²Was not Abraham during his trial found faithful, and it was considered righteousness for him? ⁵³Joseph in the time of anguish, he kept the commandment and became lord of Egypt. ⁵⁴Phinehas, our father, in his striving for zeal received the covenant of the holy priesthood. ⁵⁵Joshua, by fulfilling God's word, became judge in Israel. ⁵⁶Caleb, by his bearing witness before the assembly, received the inheritance of the land. ⁵⁷David, by his compassion, inherited the throne of eternal kingship. ⁵⁸Elijah, by great zealousness for the law, was taken up as if into heaven. ⁵⁹Hananiah, Azariah, and Mishael, because they believed, were delivered from fire. ⁶⁰Daniel, by his innocence, was delivered from the mouth of lions. ⁶¹And in this way, you should consider according to each generation that all who hope on him will not be weak. ⁶²And from sinful man's words, do not fear, because his glory will be as filth and worms. ⁶³Today they will be exalted, and tomorrow they will not be found because they return to their dust, and their scheme perished. ⁶⁴And you, O children, be strong and be a man in your law, for in it you will be honored. ⁶⁵And look, here is Simeon, your brother. I know that he is a man of counsel. Listen to him all the days. He will be for you a father. ⁶⁶And Judas Maccabeus, he was strong in power from his youth. This one will be for you a ruler of the army, and you will fight the war against the peoples. ⁶⁷And you will gather among you everyone who observes the law and avenge with vengeance for your people. ⁶⁸You are to repay the nations with repayment and pay attention to commands of the law."

⁶⁹And he blessed them and joined with his ancestors. ⁷⁰And he died in the one hundred and forty-sixth year, and his sons buried him in his fathers' tombs in Modein, and all Israel mourned for him with great lamentation.

*Judas Succeeds Mattathias* **3** And Judas, who was called Maccabeus, his son, rose in his place. ²And all his brothers helped him, and everyone, as many as had joined his father. And they fought the battle for Israel with joy. ³And he extended the glory for his people. And he put on his breastplate like a giant and girded his armor for war, prepared for battle, protecting the camp with his sword. ⁴And he was like a lion in his deeds and like a lion's cub, roaring in the hunt. ⁵And he pursued, searching out the lawless; and those who troubled his people, he burned. ⁶And the lawless cowered in fear of him, and all doers of evil were confounded, and deliverance prospered in his hand. ⁷And he provoked many kings and made Jacob cheerful by his deeds, and until eternity, his memory will be blessed. ⁸And he passed through among the cities of Judah and destroyed the ungodly in them and turned back wrath from Israel. ⁹And he was known as far as the farthest part of the land, and he gathered together those who were being killed.

¹⁰And Apollonius gathered together the nations and a great force from Samaria to fight against Israel. ¹¹And Judas found this out and went out to meet them and struck and killed him. And many casualties fell, and those who remained fled. ¹²And they took their vessels, and Judas took the sword of Apollonius. And it was in battle with him all his days.

¹³And Seron, the ruler of the force of Syria, heard that Judas had gathered a multitude and assembly of faithful men with him and those who go out to war, ¹⁴and he said, "I will make a name for myself and obtain glory

in the kingdom, and I will fight Judas and those with him and those who scorn the word of the king." [15]And a strong company of the ungodly joined and went up with him to help him execute vengeance among the children of Israel. [16]And he came near to the ascent of Beth-horon, and Judas came out to meet him with a small group. [17]But as they saw the company coming to meet him, they said to Judas, "How will we be able, being few in number, to fight against so great a host? And we have grown weak from fasting today!" [18]And Judas said, "It is easy for many to be shut up in the hands of a few, and there is no difference before heaven to deliver by many or by a few; [19]because victory in battle is not in the size of your force, but rather the strength from heaven. [20]They came to us with an abundance of insolence and wickedness to destroy us and our wives and our children, to plunder us, [21]but we fight for our lives and our customs. [22]And he will break them before our face. But you must not be frightened of them!" [23]Now as he finished speaking, he began rushing upon them suddenly, and Seron and his company were crushed before him. [24]And they pursued them during the descent from Beth-horon as far as the plain, and there fell from them in the range of eight hundred men. The rest fled to the land of the Philistines. [25]And it began: the fear of Judas and his brothers. And terror was falling upon the nations surrounding them. [26]And his name came to the king. And every nation spoke about the battles of Judas.

[27]Now as the king, Antiochus, heard these words, he grew angry with rage and sent for and gathered all the forces of his kingdom, a very strong army. [28]And he opened his treasury and gave provisions to his force for the year and ordered them to be ready for every need for the year. [29]And he saw that the silver from the treasury had come to an end, and the tributes from the territory were small because of the sedition and slaughter that he had caused in the land by removing the customs that existed from the first days. [30]And he was afraid that he would not have as much as once and twice before for the expenses and the gifts that he gave previously with an abundant hand. [31]And he was very perplexed in his soul, and he resolved to go to Persia and to take tribute from the territory and gather much silver. [32]And he left Lysias, an honorable person and from ancestry of royalty, over the affairs of the king from the river Euphrates as far as the border of Egypt, [33]and to care for Antiochus, his son, until his return. [34]And he gave over to him half of the force and the elephant and commanded him about everything that he wished. And concerning all those who lived in the Judah and Jerusalem, [35]he was to send a force against them to cast out and remove the strength of Israel and the remnant of Jerusalem and take his memory away from the place [36]and settle foreign sons within all their borders and inherit their land. [37]And the king took the half of the forces that remained and departed from Antioch from the capital of his kingdom in the one hundred and forty-seventh year, and he crossed the Euphrates River and went through the northern territories.

[38]And Lysias chose Ptolemy son of Dorymenes, Nicanor, and Gorgias, mighty men of the friends of the king. [39]And he sent with them forty thousand infantry and seven thousand cavalry to go to the land of Judah and destroy it according to the word of the king. [40]And so they departed with his whole force, and they came and threw their tents beside each other

*Antiochus and Lysias*

*Lysias Prepares Forces for Battle*

near Emmaus in the land, the plain. ⁴¹And the merchants of the region heard their name and took very much silver and gold and servants and came to the camp to take the children of Israel as servants. And a force from Syria and from the territory of foreigners was added to them.

*The Judeans Prepare in Response* ⁴²And Judas and his brothers saw that their trouble had increased, and the forces were encamping within their borders. And they learned about the words of the kingdom that he ordered in order to prepare the people for their destruction and end. ⁴³And they said each to their neighbor, "We must raise up the ruin of our people and the holy place." ⁴⁴And the congregation gathered to be ready for battle and to pray and ask for mercy and compassion. ⁴⁵And Jerusalem was uninhabited like the wilderness; none were going in or out from her children, and the sanctuary was trampled, and children of foreigners were lodging in the citadel with the nations, and joy was removed from Jacob, and the flute and kinyra*ᵃ* came to an end. ⁴⁶And they gathered and went to Mizpah, opposite of Jerusalem, because there was formerly a place of prayer for Israel in Mizpah. ⁴⁷And they fasted on that day and put on sackcloth and ashes on their heads and tore their robes. ⁴⁸And they opened the document of the law, concerning which the nations consulted the images of their idols. ⁴⁹And they brought the robes of the priesthood and the firstfruits and the tithes and gathered the Nazirites who had completed their days. ⁵⁰And they cried out with their voices to heaven, saying, "What will we do with these, and where will we lead them? ⁵¹And your holy place has been trampled and is profaned, and your priests are in grief and humiliation. ⁵²And look! The nations have gathered against us to destroy us! You know what they are planning against us. ⁵³How will we be able to stand against their face if you do not help us?" ⁵⁴And they sounded the trumpets and shouted out with a great voice.

⁵⁵And after this, Judas appointed leaders over the people: commanders of a thousand and commanders of a hundred and commanders of fifty and commanders of ten. ⁵⁶And he told those who were building homes or engaged to women or planting vineyards or cowardly to return, each to his home, according to the law. ⁵⁷And the company departed, and they camped down south of Emmaus. ⁵⁸And Judas said, "Arm yourselves, and become as mighty sons, and be ready in the morning to fight among these nations who have gathered against us to destroy us and our holy place; ⁵⁹because it is better for us to die in battle than fix our eyes upon the evils against our nation and the holy place. ⁶⁰But as the will in heaven should be, likewise, he will do."

*The Battle at Emmaus* **4** And Gorgias took five thousand men and one thousand chosen horses, and the army departed in the night ²so as to pounce upon the army of the Judeans and strike them suddenly. And the people from the citadel were guides for him. ³And Judas heard, and he and the warriors departed to strike the forces of the king in Emmaus ⁴until the forces were dispersed from the camp. ⁵And Gorgias came into the camp of Judas in the night and found no one, and he sought for them in the mountains because he said, "They are fleeing from us." ⁶And as soon as day came, Judas appeared on the plain with three thousand men without armor, and they did not

---

*ᵃ Transliteration of Heb. "stringed instrument"*

have swords as they wished. ⁷And they saw the army of the nations, mighty, armored, and cavalry going around them, and these were experienced in war. ⁸And Judas said to the men with him, "Do not fear the great number of them, and you must not fear their fury. ⁹Remember how our fathers were delivered in the Red Sea when Pharaoh pursued them with his force. ¹⁰And now we must cry out to heaven, if he will desire us, and remember the covenant of the ancestors and destroy this army before our face today. ¹¹And all the nations will know that there is a redeemer and deliverer for Israel." ¹²And the foreigners raised their eyes and saw them possessing from the opposite side, ¹³and they came out from the camp to battle, and those with Judas trumpeted; ¹⁴and they engaged in battle and broke the nations, and they fled into the plain. ¹⁵But all the rear troops fell by the sword, and they pursued them as far as Gazara and as far as the plains of Judea and Ashdod and Jamnia, and they fell from them, to the man: three thousand.

¹⁶And Judas and the force returned from the pursuit following them. ¹⁷And he said to the people, "You must not desire the spoils because war is opposite our face, ¹⁸and Gorgias and his force are in the mountains near us. But stand now before our enemies and fight them. And after this, take plunder, and do it with boldness." ¹⁹While Judas was finishing this, a detachment of troops appeared coming out from the hill country. ²⁰And he saw that he had been put to flight, so they burned the camp, for the smoke that was seen made clear what happened. ²¹But having known this, they were very afraid, seeing also the army of Judas in the plain ready for battle. ²²They all fled to foreign land. ²³And Judas turned toward the plundering of the camp and received a great amount of gold and silver and hyacinth-colored cloth and purple dye from the sea and great wealth. ²⁴And upon returning, they sang songs and blessed to heaven:

> "Because he is good,
> for eternity[a] is his mercy."

²⁵And there was great deliverance in Israel on that day.

²⁶As many of the foreigners who escaped, after arriving, they reported to Lysias everything that happened. ²⁷But when he heard all these things, he grew confused and was disheartened because those same things he had not wanted were done to Israel, and not such things the king had ordered him to carry out.

²⁸And in the coming year, he gathered sixty thousand select infantry and five thousand cavalry so as to make war against them. ²⁹And they came to Idumea and camped at Beth-zur, and Judas met them with ten thousand men. ³⁰And he saw the strong army, and he prayed and said, "Blessed are you, the deliverer of Israel, who crushed the attack of the mighty in the hand of your servant David. And you handed over the army of the foreigners into the hands of Jonathan, son of Saul, and his armor carrier. ³¹Confine this force into the hands of your people Israel and let them be dishonored by their force and cavalry. ³²Give them cowardice, and melt their courage of strength, and let them tremble in their destruction. ³³Throw them down by

*First Campaign of Lysias*

---

[a] Lit. "into the ages"

the word of those who love you, and let them praise you, all those who look at your name, with hymns." ³⁴And they set up against each other, and there fell from the army of Lysias nearly five thousand men, and they fell across from them. ³⁵But Lysias saw what was happening, the rout of his troops, and of Judas being courageous, and how prepared they were whether they lived or died nobly. He departed to Antioch and enlisted mercenaries, and having made his army very great, again he went to Judas.

*Purification and Dedication of the Temple*

³⁶But Judas and his brothers said, "Look, our enemies are broken. We should go up to cleanse the holy place and to dedicate it." ³⁷And the entire army assembled and went up to Mount Zion. ³⁸And they saw our sanctuary stripped bare and the altar profaned and the gate burned. And in the courtyard, plants were overgrown like in a forest or like on one of the mountains, and the priest's chamber was torn down. ³⁹And they tore their robes and mourned with great lamentation and covered themselves with ashes upon their head. ⁴⁰And they fell on their face upon the land, and they sounded the trumpets, giving the signal, and they cried out to heaven. ⁴¹Then Judas ordered men to fight against those in the citadel until he had cleansed the holy place.

⁴²So he selected priests who were blameless, eager for the law, ⁴³and they cleansed the holy place and removed the stones that defiled it to an unclean place. ⁴⁴And they deliberated about the altar for the burnt offering, which was profaned: What should they do with it? ⁴⁵And good counsel fell to them to take it down, lest it might become for them as a disgrace because the nations defiled it. And they tore down the altar ⁴⁶and stored the stones on a mountain house in a suitable place until a prophet was available to report about them. ⁴⁷And they took unhewn stones according to the law and built a new altar just like the previous one. ⁴⁸And they rebuilt the holy place and the inside of the house and sanctified the courtyards. ⁴⁹And they made new holy vessels and brought the lampstand and the altar of whole burnt offerings and of incense and the table into the temple. ⁵⁰And they burned incense on the altar and kindled the lamps on the lampstand and they shone in the temple. ⁵¹And they put bread loaves on the table and spread out the curtain. And they completed all the work that they had begun.

⁵²And they rose early in the morning of the twenty-fifth of the ninth month, this is the month Chislev, the one hundred and forty-eighth year, ⁵³and they offered up sacrifices according to the law on the altar for the burnt offerings, the new one that they made. ⁵⁴According to the season, according to the day during which the nations defiled it, on that day, they dedicated it with songs and lutes and kinyrais*a* and with cymbals. ⁵⁵And all the people fell on their face and bowed and gave praise to heaven, which had caused them to prosper. ⁵⁶And they performed the dedication of the altar for eight days and offered up burnt offerings with cheer and sacrificed the deliverance and thanksgiving sacrifice. ⁵⁷And they decorated according to the face of the temple with gold crowns and small shields and consecrated the gate and the priest's chamber and fitted them with doors. ⁵⁸And a very great cheer took place among the people, and the

---

*a* Transliteration of Heb. "stringed instruments"

reproach of the nations was turned back. ⁵⁹And Judas and his brothers and the entire assembly of Israel established that the days of dedication of the altar should be celebrated during their times, year by year, for eight days beginning from the twenty-fifth of the month of Chislev, with cheer and joy. ⁶⁰And they built during that time, all around the mountain of Zion, high walls and strong towers, lest when they arrived, the nations would trample them down as they did before. ⁶¹And they set apart there a force to guard it, and they fortified Beth-zur to guard it so that the people would have a stronghold by the face of Idumea.

5And it happened when the surrounding nations heard that the altar had been rebuilt and the sanctuary dedicated like the previous one, they were made very angry. ²And they resolved to remove the descendants of Jacob who were in their midst, and they began executions among the people and destroyed them. ³And Judas fought against the descendants of Esau in Judea at Akrabattene because they were besieging Israel. And he struck them with a massive blow and humbled them and took their plunder. ⁴And he remembered the evil of the descendants of Beon, who were for the people like a snare and a stumbling block in their ambushes along the roads. ⁵And they were shut out by him in their towers, and he threw against them and focused on destroying them and burned their towers with fire with all the people inside. ⁶And he crossed over to the descendants of Ammon and found a strong hand and many people and Timothy leading them. ⁷And he engaged against them in many battles, and they were crushed before his face, and he struck them down. ⁸And he occupied Jazer and her daughter villages and returned to Judah.

⁹And the nations gathered together in Gilead against the Israelites who were within their borders to destroy them. But they fled*ᵃ* to Dathema, the stronghold. ¹⁰And they sent a letter to Judas and his brothers, saying, "The nations around us are gathering against us to destroy us! ¹¹And they are preparing to come and capture the stronghold into which we fled. And Timothy is leading their encampment. ¹²Now come, rescue us from their hand because a great number have fallen from us, ¹³and all our brothers who were in Tob are dead, and their wives and their children and the supplies have been captured, and they were killed there, as much as one thousand men."

¹⁴While the messages were being read, behold, other messengers arrived from Galilee with their robes torn, reporting according to these same words, ¹⁵saying that those from Ptolemais and Tyre and Sidon and all Galilee of the Foreigners had gathered against them "to annihilate us."

¹⁶When Judas and the people heard these words, a great assembly gathered together to resolve what they should do for their brothers who were in distress and being attacked by him. ¹⁷And Judas said to Simon, his brother, "Choose men for yourself, and go and rescue your brothers in Galilee. But I and Jonathan, my brother, we will go to Gilead." ¹⁸And he left behind Joseph the son of Zechariah, and Azariah, a leader of the people, with the remaining force in Judea to guard it. ¹⁹And he ordered them, saying, "Take care of these people, and you should not join in battle against the nations

*Wars against Neighboring Peoples*

*Rescue of Galilean Judeans*

―――――
ᵃ That is, the Israelites

until our return." ²⁰And they divided for Simon three thousand men to go to Galilee, but for Judas, eight thousand men to go to Gilead.

²¹And Simon went to Galilee and engaged in many battles against the nations, and the nations were crushed before his face. ²²And he pursued them as far as the city of Ptolemais, and they fell from the nations, as many as three thousand men, and he took their plunder. ²³And he took them from Galilee and in Arbatta with their wives and children. And everything, as much as there was with them, they also brought to Judah with great cheer.

*Judas and*   ²⁴And Judas Maccabeus and Jonathan, his brother, crossed over the
*Jonathan*   Jordan and traveled the road for three days in the wilderness. ²⁵And they
*in Gilead*   met the Nabateans. And they met them peacefully and described in detail to them everything that happened to their brothers in Gilead, ²⁶and that many from them were captured in Bozrah and Bezer, in Alema, Chaspho, Maked, and Karnain: "All these cities are fortified and great, ²⁷and in the remaining cities of Gilead, they are being held for tomorrow. They are stationed to camp against the strongholds and to overtake and destroy all of them in a single day." ²⁸And Judas and his army turned off the road into the wilderness to Bozrah suddenly and took the city and killed every male by the edge of the sword and captured all their plunder and burned it by fire. ²⁹And he departed from there in the night and went as far as over to the stronghold.ᵃ ³⁰And it happened at dawn that they lifted their eyes, and look, there were numerous people who could not be counted carrying ladders and siege machines to capture the stronghold, and they were fighting them. ³¹And Judas saw that the battle had begun, and the outcry of the city went up to heaven with trumpets and loud shouts, ³²and he said to the men of the force, "Fight today for our brothers!" ³³And he came out with three companies behind them, and he sounded the trumpets and cried out in prayer. ³⁴And the army of Timothy realized that it was Maccabeus, and they fled from his face, and he struck them with a great blow, and they fell before him on that day, to the number of eight thousand men. ³⁵And he turned aside to Maapha and fought them and captured them and killed every male in it,ᵇ and he took its plunder and burned it by fire. ³⁶From there he departed and seized Chaspho, Maked, Bezer, and the remaining cities of Gilead.

³⁷But after these events, Timothy gathered another army and camped according to the face of Raphon from beside the wadi. ³⁸And Judas sent men to spy on the army, and they reported to him, saying, "They are gathering to themselves all the nations around you—a very massive force. ³⁹And they have hired Arabs to help them, and they are camping beyond the wadi, ready to come over to you for battle." And Judas went to meet them. ⁴⁰And Timothy said to the rulers of his force, when Judas and his troops approached near the stream of water, "If he should cross over to us first, we will not be able to stand before him because in ability he will be strong against us. ⁴¹But if he should act cowardly and camp beyond the river, we will cross over to him." ⁴²But when Judas came near the stream of water, he stationed officers of the people at the wadi and ordered them,

---

ᵃ This is probably the stronghold of Dathema from v. 9   ᵇ That is, the city of Maapha

saying, "Do not permit any person to camp, but we all must go into battle." <sup>43</sup>And he crossed over to them first, and all his people before him; and they were crushed before his face, all the Gentiles, and they threw down all their weapons and fled to the shrine in Karnain. <sup>44</sup>And they captured the city and the shrine; they burned it with fire with all those who were inside it, and Karnain was subdued, and he was not able to stand any longer before the face of Judas.

<sup>45</sup>And Judas gathered every Israelite in Gilead, from young to old, and their wives and their children and belongings, a very large company, to come to the land of Judah. <sup>46</sup>And they came to Ephron. This was a great city with a very strong entrance. They could not go around from its right or left, but instead, through its middle they had to go. <sup>47</sup>And those from the city shut them out and blocked the gate with stones. <sup>48</sup>And Judas sent to them a peaceful message, saying, "Allow us to go through into your land in order to depart to our land. No one will do evil to you; we will only pass by on foot." But they did not wish to open the doors for him. <sup>49</sup>And Judas ordered a proclamation in the company: Each person should camp in whatever place he was. <sup>50</sup>And the men of the city camped, and they fought the city that entire day and the whole night, and the city was handed over into his hands. <sup>51</sup>And he killed every male by the edge of the sword and razed it[a] and took the plunder of the city and passed through the city over the dead. <sup>52</sup>And they crossed over the Jordan into the large plain according to the face of Beth-shan. <sup>53</sup>And Judas continued gathering together those lagging behind and encouraging the people along the entire road until they came to the land of Judah. <sup>54</sup>And they went up to Mount Zion in cheer and joy, and they offered burnt offerings because not one had fallen from among them, no one, until their return in peace.

<sup>55</sup>And on the day that Judas and Jonathan were in the land of Gilead and Simon, his brother, was in Galilee according to the face of Ptolemais, <sup>56</sup>Joseph the son of Zechariah, and Zechariah, rulers of the forces, heard about the bravery and the sort of battles they fought. <sup>57</sup>And they said, "We should make ourselves a name for ourselves also! And we will go to fight against the nations surrounding us." <sup>58</sup>And they ordered those from the force with them, and they went to Jamnia. <sup>59</sup>And Gorgias came out from the city, and his men also, to meet them in battle. <sup>60</sup>And Joseph and Azariah were routed, and they were pursued as far as the border of Judea, and they fell on that day from the people of Israel, as many as two thousand men. <sup>61</sup>And it was a great rout among the people because they did not listen to Judas and his brothers, imagining him to act bravely. <sup>62</sup>But they were not from the seed of those men through whom deliverance was given to Israel by their hand. <sup>63</sup>And the man Judas and his brothers were honored very much before all Israel and all the nations that heard their name. <sup>64</sup>And they gathered together to them to praise them.

*The Foolishness of Joseph and Azariah*

<sup>65</sup>And Judas and his brothers went out and fought the descendants of Esau in the land to the south, and he struck Hebron and her daughter villages and tore down her stronghold and burned her surrounding farms.[b]

*More Success for Judas*

---

[a] That is, the city   [b] The common sense of the Gk. word is "tower, watch tower," but the sense "farm building" is found and seems likely here

⁶⁶And he departed to go to the land of the foreigners and went through Samaria. ⁶⁷On that day, some priests fell in battle who were wishing to act bravely by going out to war ill-advisedly. ⁶⁸And Judas turned aside to Ashdod, the land of the foreigners, and tore down their altars and the carvings of their gods; he burned and plundered the spoils of the city and returned to Judea.

The Last Days<br>of Antiochus<br>Epiphanes

**6** And the king, Antiochus, was going through the northern regions, and he heard that there is in Elymais of Persia a city distinguished for wealth in gold and silver. ²And the temple in it was very rich, and there was golden armor and breastplates and weapons, which Alexander the son of Philip, the king of Macedonia, left behind there—he first ruled the Greeks. ³And he came and sought to overtake the city and plunder it and was not able because his plan was discovered by those from the city, ⁴and they rose up against him in battle, and he fled and departed from there with great disappointment to return to Babylon. ⁵And someone came reporting to him in Persia that the armies that went to the land of Judah had been routed. ⁶And Lysias went in first with a strong force and was overthrown from their face. And they were becoming stronger because of the weapons that they took from the armies that they defeated. ⁷And they had torn down the abomination that he had built on the altar in Jerusalem, and just as before, they surrounded the sanctuary with high walls, and also Beth-zur, his city. ⁸And it happened when the king heard these words, he became alarmed, and he was very shaken and fell on the bed and fell into sickness from the despair because nothing had happened to him as he planned. ⁹And he was there many a day because great despair continued in him, and he realized that he was dying. ¹⁰And he called all his friends and said to them, "Sleep has departed from my eyes, and I have become fallen in my heart from worry. ¹¹And I said in my heart, 'To what distress did they come? And a massive flood in which now I am!' Because I was kind and beloved during my rule. ¹²But now I remember the evils that I did in Jerusalem, and I took all the vessels, the silver, and gold in it and sent for the destruction of the inhabitants of Judah for no reason. ¹³I know that because of this, these evils found me; and look, I am dying from great despair in a foreign land." ¹⁴And he called Philip, one of his friends, and appointed him over all his kingdom. ¹⁵And he gave him the crown and his robe and the signet ring so that he might lead Antiochus, his son, and raise him to become king. ¹⁶And he died there, Antiochus, the king, in the year one hundred and forty-nine.ᵃ ¹⁷And Lysias learned that the king was dead, and he established Antiochus, his son, to become king in place of him, whom he raised from youth, and he called his name Eupator.

The Siege of<br>the Citadel<br>and the Battle<br>at Beth-<br>zechariah

¹⁸And those from the citadel were closing in upon Israel around the holy placesᵇ and seeking evil through all means and support for the nations. ¹⁹And Judas determined to remove them. And he assembled all the people to form a siege against them. ²⁰In the one hundred and fiftieth year, they built against them artillery machines and other war instruments. ²¹And some came out of it from the siege, and some of the ungodly from Israel joined them. ²²And they went to the king and said, "Until when

---

ᵃ 163 BC ᵇThe temple and its precincts

will you not make judgment and vengeance for our brothers? ²³We were willing to serve your father and to go by his words and to follow his commands. ²⁴For this reason, those of our people have become estranged from us; moreover, as many as are found among us they execute, and our possessions are plundered. ²⁵And it is not against us only that they stretch their hand, but also against everyone in their borders. ²⁶And look! They have camped today against the citadel in Jerusalem to capture it! And the sanctuary and Beth-zur they have fortified! ²⁷And if you should not capture them by speed, they will do more than these things, and you will not be able to stop them!"

²⁸And the king was enraged when he heard this. And he gathered all his friends—rulers of his force and those over the cavalry. ²⁹And from other kings and from islands of the sea, hired forces came to him. ³⁰And the total size of his force was one hundred thousand foot soldiers and twenty thousand horsemen and thirty-two elephants familiar with battle. ³¹And they came through Idumea and camped at Beth-zur, and they fought for many days and built instruments of war. And they came out*ᵃ* and burned them with fire and fought bravely. ³²And Judas departed from the citadel and camped in Beth-zechariah opposite the camp of the king. ³³And the king rose early in the morning and departed from the camp in its fury down the road to Beth-zechariah, and the forces prepared for battle and sounded the trumpets. ³⁴And to the elephants they showed juice of grapes and mulberries to arouse them for the battle. ³⁵And they divided the animals among the phalanxes and stationed for each elephant one thousand men, armed in chain mail and bronze helmets on their heads; and five hundred select horses were assigned to each animal. ³⁶These were ahead of time: wherever the animal should be, they would be, and wherever they should go, they went together; they did not depart from him. ³⁷And there were wooden towers on them, fortified covers on each animal, strapped on them with instruments, and on each there were thirty-two men who fought on them and an Indian to drive it. ³⁸And the remaining cavalry, they were stationed on one side and the other side, on the two parts of the army, for harassing, and protected by the phalanxes. ³⁹When the sun reflected on the gold shields, the mountains blazed because of them and lit up like flaming torches. ⁴⁰And a particular part of the army of the king was spread out over the high hills, and some were on the lower regions, and they were advancing steadily and orderly. ⁴¹And everyone was trembling who heard the noise of their host and of the marching of the host and of the clanking of their weapons. For the army was very large and strong. ⁴²But Judas and his army drew near into battle, and six hundred men fell from the king's army. ⁴³And Eleazar, called Sauaran, saw that one of the elephants was armed with royal armor and that it was higher than all the other elephants and saw that the king was on it. ⁴⁴And he sacrificed himself to deliver his people and keep alive for himself an eternal name. ⁴⁵And he ran at it boldly, into the middle of the phalanx, and killed men right and left, and they parted before him on both sides. ⁴⁶And he got under the elephant and stabbed the underside of it and killed it. And it fell upon the earth over him,

---

ᵃ That is, the Judeans

and he died there. ⁴⁷And they saw the strength of the king and the fury of the forces, and they retreated from them.

*The Siege of the Temple* ⁴⁸And from the army of the king, they went up to meet them in Jerusalem, and the king camped in Judah and in Mount Zion. ⁴⁹And he made peace with those from Beth-zur, and he came out from the city because there were no supplies for them there to close themselves in it,ᵃ because it was a Sabbath year for the land. ⁵⁰And the king captured Beth-zur and commanded a garrison there to hold it. ⁵¹And he camped at the sanctuary many days and built there siege towers and engines of war and fire machines and catapults and a scorpion for launchingᵇ arrows and slings. ⁵²And theyᶜ also made war machines to match their war machines, and they fought many days. ⁵³But there was no food in their holy place because it was the seventh year, and those who were rescued to Judah from the nations had devoured the remaining provisions. ⁵⁴And a few men were left in the holy places because the famine had prevailed over them, and they each dispersed to their places.

*A Hasty Peace* ⁵⁵And Lysias heard that Philip—whom the king, Antiochus, had appointed while he was alive to raise Antiochus, his son, for him to be king—⁵⁶had returned from Persia and Media, and the forces that went with the king were with him, and he was seeking to take over the affairs of the government. ⁵⁷And they went with all haste and said to the king, and the leaders of the force, and the soldiers, "We are coming to an end by the day, and our provisions are small, and the place where we camp is fortified, and the affairs of the king press against us. ⁵⁸Now then, we should give our right hand to these people, and we should make peace with them and with their whole nation. ⁵⁹And we should allow them to go and live by their customs as before. For it was because of their customs, which we abolished, that enraged them, and then they did all these things." ⁶⁰And the speech satisfied the king and the rulers, and he sent to them to make peace, and they accepted. ⁶¹And the king and the rulers made an oath to them. On the basis of these actions, he came out from the stronghold. ⁶²And the king entered into Mount Zion and saw the fortifications of the place. And he rejected the oath that he had sworn and ordered that the surrounding wall be torn down. ⁶³And they departed in haste and returned to Antioch and found Philip ruling the city. So he fought against him and captured the city by force.

*Bacchides and Alcimus* **7** In the fifty-first year, Demetrius the son of Seleucus came out from Rome, and he went up with a few men to a seaside city and ruled there. ²And it happened as he was entering into the royal house of his ancestors, his forces captured Antiochus and Lysias to bring them to him. ³And the action was made known to him, and he said, "Do not show their faces to me!" ⁴And so the forces killed them, and Demetrius sat upon the throne of his kingdom. ⁵And there came to him all lawless and the ungodly men from Israel; and Alcimus, who wished to be high priest, was going before them. ⁶And they informed on the people to the king, saying, "Judas and his brothers destroyed all your friends, and we have been driven from our land. ⁷Now then, send a man who you trust, and let him go to see all the destruction that he did to us and to the territory of the king, and he chastised them and all who helped them."

---

ᵃ That is, the city  ᵇ Lit. "throwing"  ᶜ That is, the Judeans

⁸And the king chose Bacchides, a friend of the king and governor in the province beyond the river and powerful in the kingdom and faithful to the king. ⁹And he sent him and the ungodly Alcimus, and they set him over the priesthood and ordered him to execute vengeance among the children of Israel. ¹⁰And he departed and came with a great force to the land of Judah, and he sent a messenger to Judas and to his brothers with peaceful words and with cunning. ¹¹And they paid no heed to their words, for they saw that they came with a large force. ¹²And a group of scribes gathered to Alcimus and Bacchides, seeking what is righteous, ¹³and the Hasideans were first among the children of Israel and asked for peace from them, ¹⁴for they said, "A person, a priest from the seed of Aaron, has come in the force, and he will not wrong us." ¹⁵And he spoke peaceful words with them and promised them, saying, "We will not seek evil against you and your friends." ¹⁶And they trusted him, and he seized from them sixty men and killed them on a single day according to the words that were written:

¹⁷ "The flesh of your saints and their blood
        they poured out around Jerusalem,
            and there was no one to bury them."

¹⁸And fear and trembling fell on them among all the people because they said, "There is no truth or justice in them. For they have broken the agreement and the oath that they swore." ¹⁹And Bacchides departed from Jerusalem and camped at Bethzaith and sent and seized many from those with him, men who had deserted, and some of the people and slaughtered them in a great pit. ²⁰And he appointed the territory to Alcimus and left with him a force to help him. And Bacchides departed to the king. ²¹And Alcimus fought for the high priesthood; ²²and they gathered to him, all who caused trouble for their people; and they gained control over the land of Judah and did great damage in Israel. ²³And Judas saw all the evil that Alcimus and those with him had done among the children of Israel. It was beyond what the nations had done. ²⁴And he went out in all the borders of Judea, and all around, and executed vengeance on the men and those who had deserted, and they were prevented from going into the territory. ²⁵But when Alcimus saw that Judas and those with him had grown strong, and he knew that he could withstand them, and he returned to the king and reported their so-called evils.

²⁶And the king sent Nicanor, one of his honored rulers and one who hated and detested Israel. And he ordered him to destroy the people. ²⁷And Nicanor came to Jerusalem with a large force and sent word to Judas and his brothers with deceitful words of peace, saying, ²⁸"Let there be no battle between me and you. I will come with a few men, that I can see you face to face with peace." ²⁹And he came to Judas, and they greeted each other peacefully; and the enemies were ready to kidnap Judas. ³⁰And the plan was made known to Judas—that with deceit he came against him. And he was terrified from him, and he did not wish to see his face again. ³¹And Nicanor learned that his plan was discovered, and he went out to meet Judas at Charpharsarama. ³²And there fell from those from Nicanor as much as five thousand men, and they fled to the city of David.

*Nicanor on a Mission to Destroy the Judeans*

*Nicanor Threatens the Temple* <sup>33</sup>And after these events, Nicanor went up to Mount Zion, and there came out from the priests from the holy place and from the elders of the people to greet him peacefully and to show him the burnt offering being offered on behalf of the king. <sup>34</sup>And he sneered at them and ridiculed them and defiled them and spoke arrogantly. <sup>35</sup>And he swore with rage, saying, "If Judas and his army is not handed over into my hands now or in the future, if I will return in safety, I will burn this house!" And he went out with rage. <sup>36</sup>And the priests went in and stood by the face of the altar and the temple and wept and said, <sup>37</sup>"You chose this house to be called by your name, for it to be a house for prayer and petition for your people. <sup>38</sup>Act with vengeance on this person and on his army, and let them fall by the sword; remember their blasphemies, and do not let them have life."

*Nicanor Crushed* <sup>39</sup>And Nicanor went out from Jerusalem, and they camped in Bethhoron, and the force from Syria met him. <sup>40</sup>And Judas camped in Adasa with three thousand men, and Judas prayed and said, <sup>41</sup>"Those from the king, when they spoke blasphemy, your angel went out and struck down among them one hundred and eighty-five thousand. <sup>42</sup>Likewise, crush this army before us today, and let those who remain know that he spoke wickedly against your holy place, and judge him according to his evil actions." <sup>43</sup>And the armies engaged in battle on the thirteenth of the month of Adar, and the army of Nicanor was crushed, and he fell first in the battle. <sup>44</sup>But when his army saw that Nicanor had fallen, throwing down their weapons, they fled. <sup>45</sup>And they closely pursued them a journey of one day from Adasa as far as to come to Gezer. And they sounded the signal after them with the trumpets. <sup>46</sup>And there came out from all the villages of Judah all around, and they outflanked them, and they returned to them; and all of them fell by the sword, and none were left behind from them, not even one. <sup>47</sup>And they took the spoils and the plunder, and they removed the head of Nicanor as well as his right hand, which he stretched arrogantly, and brought them and stretched them out for display near Jerusalem. <sup>48</sup>And the people were cheerful very much and observed that day as a day of great celebration. <sup>49</sup>And they established to observe this day yearly on the thirteenth of Adar. <sup>50</sup>And the land of Judah rested a few days.

*The Power of the Romans* **8** And Judas heard about the name of the Romans—that they were strong with might, and they found pleasure in all who joined with them and any that would continue with them, and as many as should approach them, they pledged to them friendship. <sup>2</sup>For they are strong in might. And it was described in detail to him their battles and bravery, which they displayed in Gaul, and that they had victory over them and held them by tribute; <sup>3</sup>and as much as they did in the territory of Spain, gaining control over the mines of gold and silver there; <sup>4</sup>and they gained control over the whole place by their planning and patience, even though the place was very far distant from them; and of the kings who came up against them from north of the land until they crushed them and struck down among them great blows, and those who remained gave them tribute each year. <sup>5</sup>And Philip and King Perseus of the Macedonians<sup>a</sup> and those who rose up against them, they crushed them in battle and gained control over them. <sup>6</sup>And Antiochus

---

<sup>a</sup> The Macedonians are here called "Kitians"

the Great, king of Asia, who went against them in battle, having one hundred and twenty elephants and cavalry and chariots and a very large force, and they were crushed by them. ⁷And they took him alive and decreed to him to give them—and also those who would rule after him—great tribute and give them hostages and territory. ⁸And the territory of India and Media and Audian, and from their best territories and taking them from them, they gave them to King Eumenes. ⁹And those from the Greeks had resolved to come and destroy them, ¹⁰and the plan was discovered by them, and they sent against them a single general, and they fought against them, and they fell from him many casualties, and they took prisoner their wives and their children and plundered them and took control over their land and took down their strongholds and plundered them and enslaved them until this day. ¹¹And the remaining kingdoms and islands, as many as ever stood up against them, they destroyed and enslaved them. ¹²But with their friends and those who relied on them, they maintained with them friendship. And they had victory over kings near and far, and as many as heard their name were terrified from them. ¹³Whoever should wish to help and to rule, they will rule; whoever should wish they would remove, and they have been exalted very much. ¹⁴And in all these actions, no one put a crown on themselves, nor do they wear purple so as to be exalted among them. ¹⁵And they built a senate chamber for themselves; and day by day, three hundred and twenty resolve, resolving for everyone concerning the populace to govern themselves well. ¹⁶And they entrust a single person to rule them each year and to be lord over all their land, and they all listen to the one man, and there is no malice nor jealousy among them.

¹⁷And so Judas selected Eupolemus son of John of Accos and Jason *An Alliance* son of Eleazar and sent them to Rome to establish with them a friend- *with Rome* ship and alliance, ¹⁸and to lift the yoke from them because they saw the kingdom of the Greeks oppressing Israel with slavery ¹⁹And they went to Rome, and the journey was very long, and they entered into the senate chamber and reported, ²⁰"Judas, also called Maccabeus, and his brothers and the population of the Judeans sent us to you to establish with you an alliance and peace, and that we might be written in with your allies and your friends." ²¹And the message was pleasing before them. ²²And this is the transcript of the writing that they wrote in response on a bronze tablet and sent to Jerusalem to be with them there as a memorial of the peace and alliance:

²³"May it be well for the Romans and the nation of the Judeans in the sea and on dry land into eternity; and the sword and enemy, may they be far removed from them. ²⁴If war should come to Rome first or any of their allies in all their power, ²⁵the nation of the Judeans will act as allies as the occasion should indicate to them with a full heart. ²⁶And to those who fight, they will not give nor supply grain, weapons, silver, or ships, as Rome has determined, and they will keep their obligations, receiving nothing in return. ²⁷By the same standards, if against the nation of the Judeans war should happen first, the Romans will act as allies from the soul as the occasion should indicate to them. ²⁸And to those fighting with the Judeans, there will be given no grain, weapons, or silver, as Rome has determined, and they will keep these obligations and do so with no deceit. ²⁹By these

words, thus, the Romans have established a treaty with the people of the Judeans. ³⁰But if after these words both parties should resolve to add or remove, they may do so from their free choice, and what they should add or remove will be authoritative. ³¹And concerning the wrongs that King Demetrius is doing against them, we have written to him saying, 'For what reason do you make heavy your yoke on our friends, the Judean allies? ³²If therefore they appeal again against you, we will show them judgment and will fight with you by sea and by dry land.'"

*Battle at Berea and the Death of Judas Maccabeus*
9 And Demetrius heard that Nicanor and his forces made war, and so he continued from a second time to send Bacchides and Alcimus to the land of Judah, and the right wing of the army with them. ²And they went by road to Gilgal and camped at Mesaloth in Arbela, and they captured it, and he destroyed many people's lives. ³And on the first month of the one hundred and fifty-second year, they camped in Jerusalem. ⁴And they departed and went to Berea with twenty thousand men and two thousand horses. ⁵And Judas was camping at Eleasah, and three thousand choice men were with him. ⁶And they saw the great number of the force, that they were many, and they became very afraid, and many slipped away from the army; only eight hundred of them remained. ⁷And Judas saw that his army had slipped away and the battle was pressing upon him, and he was crushed in his heart because he did not have time to gather them. ⁸And he grew weak and said to those remaining, "Let us rise, and let us go up against our enemies. If, then, we may be able to fight them." ⁹And they tried to turn him back, saying, "We are not able; rather, we should save our own lives now. We should return with our brothers and fight against them. But we are too few." ¹⁰And Judas said, "May it be never with me to do this deed, to flee from them. And our time has arrived, and we should die with courage for the sake of our brothers; and we should leave no basis for questioning our honor!" ¹¹And the force departed from the camp and took their positions to meet them. And the cavalry was divided into two parts, and the slingers and the bowmen went ahead of the force, and all the chief warriors did also. ¹²But Bacchides was in the right flank. And the phalanx advanced from the two parts, and they sounded the trumpets, and even those with Judas, they also sounded the trumpets. ¹³And the earth was shaken from their armies, and the battle was gathered from early morning until evening. ¹⁴And Judas saw that Bacchides and the foundation of the army were on the right, and so all those courageous in the heart gathered to him. ¹⁵And they crushed the right flank from them, and he pursued after them as far as Mount Ashdod. ¹⁶And those on the left wing of the army saw that the right wing had been crushed, and they turned after the feet of Judas and the men with him from behind. ¹⁷And the battle grew heavy, and many casualties fell from both sides. ¹⁸And Judas fell, and those who remained fled. ¹⁹And Jonathan and Simon lifted up Judas, their brother, and buried him in the tomb of their ancestors in Modein. ²⁰And they wept for him there, and all Israel mourned for him a great lamentation. And they mourned many days and said:

²¹ "How the mighty has fallen, the deliverer of Israel!"

<sup>22</sup>And the rest of the words of Judas and the battles and the brave deeds that he did, and his greatness were not written down because they were very many.

<sup>23</sup>And it happened after the death of Judas, the lawless emerged in all the borders of Israel, and all the doers of injustice rose up. <sup>24</sup>In those days there was a very great famine, and the territory switched sides with them. <sup>25</sup>And Bacchides chose the ungodly men and appointed them as lords of the territory. <sup>26</sup>And they were seeking and searching out for friends of Judas and brought them to Bacchides, and he showed vengeance against them, and they were mocking them. <sup>27</sup>And there was great distress in Israel, such that had never happened from that time when the prophet had ceased from being seen among them. <sup>28</sup>And all the friends of Judas gathered and said to Jonathan, <sup>29</sup>"From when your brother Judas died, there has not been a man like him to go out against the enemies and Bacchides and among those who detest our nation. <sup>30</sup>Now, therefore, we have chosen you today to be for us as our ruler instead of him, and our leader to fight our battle." <sup>31</sup>And Jonathan was chosen at that time for the command, and he rose in place of Judas, his brother.

<sup>32</sup>And Bacchides learned this and sought to kill him. <sup>33</sup>And Jonathan and Simon, his brother, and all those with him learned, and they fled into the wilderness of Tekoa and camped beside the water pool of Asphar. <sup>34</sup>And Bacchides found out on the day of the Sabbath, and he and his entire army went over the Jordan. <sup>35</sup>And he sent his brother as leader of the crowd and begged the Nabateans, his friends, to let them store their large amount of baggage with them. <sup>36</sup>And the sons of Jambri from Medeba went out and captured John and everything, as much as he had, and they departed having it. <sup>37</sup>After these events, they reported to Jonathan and Simon, his brother, "A son of Jambri is having a great wedding, and they are bringing the bride from Nadabath, a daughter of one of the great nobles of Canaan, with a great escort." <sup>38</sup>And they remembered John, their brother, and they went up and hid under the cover of the mountain. <sup>39</sup>And they lifted their eyes and saw, and look, there was a noisy procession and a large amount of baggage, and the bridegroom came out as well as his friends and his brothers to meet them with tambourines and musicians and many weapons. <sup>40</sup>And they rose against them from the ambush and killed them, and many casualties fell, and those who remained fled into the mountains, and they took back all their vessels. <sup>41</sup>And the wedding changed to grief, and the music of their musicians to lament. <sup>42</sup>And they avenged with vengeance their brother's blood and returned to the hills of the Jordan.

<sup>43</sup>And Bacchides heard and went on the day of the Sabbath as far as the flood plain of the Jordan with a large force. <sup>44</sup>And Jonathan said to his brothers, "We must rise now and fight on behalf of our lives! For it is not today like it was yesterday or the day before. <sup>45</sup>For look! The battle is before us and behind of us. But the water of the Jordan is on one side and on the other side, and there is the marsh and the forest! There is no place to turn. <sup>46</sup>Now, therefore, cry out to heaven so that you might be rescued from our enemies' hand." <sup>47</sup>And the battle began, and Jonathan stretched out his hand to strike Bacchides, and he turned aside from him to the rear. <sup>48</sup>And Jonathan and those with him jumped into the Jordan and swam across to

Jonathan Succeeds Judas

the other side, and they did not cross over the Jordan against them. ⁴⁹And about one thousand men perished from Bacchides' side on that day.

*Bacchides Fortifies Cities* ⁵⁰And they turned back to Jerusalem, and they built fortified cities in Judah—the stronghold in Jericho and Emmaus and Beth-horon and Bethel and Timnah and Pirathon and Tephon—with high walls and gates and bars. ⁵¹And they put a garrison in each of them to cause hostility against Israel. ⁵²And they fortified the city, both Beth-zur and Gazara and the citadel, and they put in them forces and provisions of food. ⁵³And they took the sons of the leaders of the territory hostage and put them in the citadel in Jerusalem in prison.

⁵⁴And in the one hundred and fifty-third year, in the second month, Alcimus ordered the wall of the courtyard of the interior sanctuary to be taken down, and he took down the works of the prophets. And he began to tear it down. ⁵⁵At that time, Alcimus was struck, and his work was hindered, and his mouth was stopped, and he was disabled and could not continue to speak a word and to give commands about his house. ⁵⁶And Alcimus died at that time with great torment. ⁵⁷And Bacchides saw that Alcimus had died, and he returned to the king; and the land of Judah rested for two years.

⁵⁸And all the lawless resolved, saying, "Look, Jonathan and those with him live in peace, confidently. Now, therefore, we will bring Bacchides, and he will capture them all in a single night." ⁵⁹And going, they consulted with him. ⁶⁰And he departed to come with a large force and sent messages secretly to all his allies in Judah so that they might seize Jonathan and those with him. And they were not able because their plan became known to them. ⁶¹And they captured from the men of the territory the leaders in this evil plan, about fifty men, and he killed them. ⁶²And Jonathan and Simon and those with him moved to Bethbasi in the wilderness and rebuilt what was torn down of it and made it firm. ⁶³And Bacchides found this out and gathered all his forces and sent orders to those from Judah. ⁶⁴And arriving, he camped against Bethbasi and fought it many days and built instruments of war. ⁶⁵And Jonathan abandoned Simon, his brother, in the city, and he went out into the territory and went with a small number of men. ⁶⁶And he beat down Odomera and his brothers and the sons of Phasiron in their home, and he began to attack and go up with the force. ⁶⁷And Simon and those with him came out from the city and burned the machines of war. ⁶⁸And they fought against Bacchides, and he was crushed by them. And they were afflicting him very hard because his plan and his expedition was a failure. ⁶⁹And they were made angry with rage against the lawless men who advised him to come to the territory, and they killed many of them and resolved to depart to his land. ⁷⁰And Jonathan learned and sent to him ambassadors to make a peace treaty with him and to obtain release of the captives to them. ⁷¹And it was accepted, and he did as he said, and he swore to him not to seek him out in evil all the days of his life. ⁷²And he restored the captives to him, which he had taken prisoner previously from the land of Judah. And turning back, he departed to his land and did not continue to still come to their borders. ⁷³And the sword of Israel rested, and Jonathan lived in Michmash. And Jonathan began to judge the people and rid the ungodly from Israel.

# 10

And in the one hundred and sixtieth year, Alexander the son of Antiochus Epiphanes went up and captured Ptolemais, and they welcomed him, and he ruled there. ²And Demetrius, the king, heard this and gathered very many forces, and he went out to meet them in battle. ³And Demetrius sent a letter to Jonathan in peaceful words, so as to honor him, ⁴for he said, "We should take advantage to establish peace with him before he should establish it with Alexander against us. ⁵For he will remember all the evils that we did to him and among his brothers and his nation." ⁶And he gave him authority to recruit forces and build weapons and to become his ally with him. And the hostages in the citadel, he said to hand them over to him.

*The Rise of Alexander, Jonathan as High Priest*

⁷And Jonathan came into Jerusalem and read the letter to the ears of all the people and those from the citadel. ⁸And they became afraid with a great fear when they heard that the king had given to them authority to recruit forces. ⁹And those from the citadel gave over to Jonathan the hostages and restored them to their parents. ¹⁰And Jonathan dwelled in Jerusalem and began to rebuild and restore the city. ¹¹And he said to those doing the work to rebuild the wall and surrounding Mount Zion using four-square stones for fortifications, and they did just that. ¹²And the foreigners who were in the stronghold that Bacchides built fled. ¹³And each left his place and departed to his land. ¹⁴Only in Beth-zur there remained some who had forsaken the law and the commandments. For it was to them a place of refuge.

¹⁵And Alexander, the king, heard about the promises, as many as Demetrius sent to Jonathan, and they described in detail to him the battles and the bravery that he and his brothers had performed and the troubles that they had experienced. ¹⁶And he said, "Could we never find such a man! And now we should make him our friend and ally." ¹⁷And he wrote letters and sent them to him in these words, saying,

¹⁸"King Alexander, to brother Jonathan: Greetings. ¹⁹We have heard about you, that you are a good man with might, and worthy to be our friend. ²⁰And now we have established you today as high priest of your nation and to be called a friend of the king"—and they sent him a purple robe and gold crown—"and you are to think about our affairs and maintain a friendship toward us."

²¹And Jonathan put on the holy robe in the seventh month of the one hundred and sixtieth year during the Festival of Booths, and he recruited forces and made many weapons.

²²And Demetrius heard about these words, and he was grieved and said, ²³"What is this we have done that Alexander has prevented us from forming a friendship with the Judeans for support? ²⁴I also will write them words of encouragement and praise and gifts, that they might be with me for support." ²⁵And he sent a letter to them in these words:

*Demetrius Sends a Letter to Jonathan*

"King Demetrius, to the nation of the Judeans: Greetings. ²⁶Since you have kept the agreement toward us and maintained our friendship and have not gone to our enemies, we heard of this and rejoiced. ²⁷And now, continue to stay to maintain the trust toward us, and we will repay you with good for what you do with us. ²⁸And we will permit you many immunities and give you gifts. ²⁹And now, we release you and exempt all Judeans from tribute and the salt tax*a* and from the crown. ³⁰And instead of the third of the grain, and instead of the half of the fruit of the trees added to me, to take, I release them from today and onward to take from the land of Judah and from the three districts added to her, from Samaria and Galilee, from this day and for all time. ³¹And Jerusalem will be holy and free, and also her borders, from tithes and taxes. ³²I am also releasing my authority over the citadel in Jerusalem and am giving it to the high priest so that he might station men in it whom he might choose to guard it. ³³And every life of a Judean who has been taken prisoner from the land of Judah to any part of my kingdom, I am releasing free as a gift, and all must release their tribute and livestock. ³⁴And all the festivals and Sabbaths and new moons and appointed days, and the three days before a festival and the three days after a festival, all shall be days of exemption and release for all the Judeans who are in all my kingdom. ³⁵And no one will have authority to accomplish and disturb anyone of them about any affair. ³⁶And let the Judeans be enrolled in the forces of the king to the number of thirty thousand men, and provisions be given to them as is appropriate for all the forces of the king. ³⁷And some of them will be stationed in the great stronghold of the king, and some of these will be set in positions of need in the kingdom, being in trust, and those over them also, their rulers, from them must be, and they must live by their law, just as also the king has prescribed in the land of Judah. ³⁸And the three districts added to Judah from the territory of Samaria, they must be added to Judah, for considering them as being under one ruler, to not obey any other authority but the high priest. ³⁹Ptolemais, and the land beside it, I have given as a gift to the sanctuary in Jerusalem for the necessary expenses of the sanctuary. ⁴⁰And I, I have delegated by the year fifteen thousand shekels of silver from the word of the king from the places they belong. ⁴¹And all the additional funds that are not returned from the necessity as in the previous years from now, they should be given for the service of the house. ⁴²And beyond this, five thousand shekels of silver, which they were receiving from the service as in the first year of the holy place from the account by year, also this I release because these belong to the priests who minister. ⁴³And any—if they should have fled to the temple in Jerusalem or in all its borders—who owe money to the king and all debts are to be released, and all, as much as is theirs, in my kingdom. ⁴⁴And the building and the restoring of the work of the sanctuary and the expense will be given from the account of the king. ⁴⁵And for the building of the wall of Jerusalem and fortifications all around, also the expense will be given from the account of the king, as well as for the building of the wall in Judah."

*Demetrius Rejected* ⁴⁶But when Jonathan and the people heard these words, they did not believe them or accept them because they remembered the great evil that he had done in Israel. And he had afflicted them very much. ⁴⁷And they found pleasure in Alexander because he was the leader who spoke peaceful words to them, and they were allied with him all his days. ⁴⁸And Alexander, the king, assembled great forces and camped opposite Demetrius. ⁴⁹And

---

*a* The sense "tax" is a figurative extension of the sense "honor, value." The "honor" was the value of a citizen's possessions for taxation purposes, but here the meaning has been generalized to any sort of tax

the two kings engaged in battle, and the army of Demetrius fled; and Alexander pursued him and prevailed over him. ⁵⁰And he pressed battle very much until the sun sank, and Demetrius fell on that day.

⁵¹And Alexander sent to Ptolemy, king of Egypt, ambassadors by these words, saying, ⁵²"Since I have returned to my kingdom and sit upon my father's throne and have established my rule, I crushed Demetrius and gained control over our territory. ⁵³And I engaged against him in battle, and he and his army were crushed beneath us, and we have sat upon the throne of his kingdom. ⁵⁴And we should gather to him a friendship. And now give me your daughter as my wife, and I will become a son-in-law to you, and I will give you and to her gifts that are worthy of you." ⁵⁵And Ptolemy, the king, answered, saying, "It is a good day on which you returned to your ancestors' land and sit upon their kingdom's throne. ⁵⁶And now I will do for you what you wrote, but you must meet me in Ptolemais so that we might see each other; and I will become a father-in-law to you, just as you said." ⁵⁷And Ptolemy went out from Egypt, he and Cleopatra, his daughter, and they arrived in Ptolemais in the one hundred and sixty-second year. ⁵⁸And Alexander, the king, met him, and he gave him Cleopatra, his daughter. And he performed her wedding in Ptolemais, just as kings with great glory do.

*Alexander Marries Cleopatra*

⁵⁹And Alexander, the king, wrote to Jonathan to come to meet him. ⁶⁰And he went with glory to Ptolemais and met the two kings and gave them gold and silver, as well as to their friends, and many gifts, and he found favor before them. ⁶¹And sinister men from Israel gathered against him, wicked men, to gain audience against him, and the king did not heed them. ⁶²And the king gave orders to them, and Jonathan took off his robe, and he put on him a purple robe, and they did so. ⁶³And the king sat him with him and said to his rulers, "Go out with him to the middle of the city and proclaim that no one is to bring charges against this one concerning any action, and that no one annoy him about any matter." ⁶⁴And it happened when those who would accuse him saw the honor shown to him just as they proclaimed, and that they clothed him with fine linen, and they all fled. ⁶⁵And the king honored him and enrolled him among his foremost friends and appointed him as general and governor. ⁶⁶And Jonathan returned to Jerusalem with peace and cheer.

⁶⁷And in the one hundred and sixty-fifth year, Demetrius, the son of Demetrius, came from Crete to his ancestors' land. ⁶⁸And King Alexander heard, and he was very vexed, and he returned to Antioch. ⁶⁹And Demetrius appointed Apollonius to be over Coele Syria, and he gathered a great force and camped in Jamnia. And he sent a message to Jonathan, the high priest, saying, ⁷⁰"You alone rise up against us. But I have become as a mockery and a disgrace because of you. Why do you exercise authority against us in the mountains? ⁷¹Now, therefore, if you have confidence in your forces, come down to us into the plain, and we will compare ourselves there, because the power of the cities is with me. ⁷²Ask and learn who I am and those who remain helping me. And they will say there is no standing on foot for you against our face because twice your ancestors were put to flight in their own land. ⁷³And now you will not be able to stand before the cavalry and such power in the plain where there is no stone nor pebble nor place to flee."

*Jonathan Defeats Apollonius*

⁷⁴But when Jonathan heard the words of Apollonius, he was roused in the mind and selected ten thousand men and went out from Jerusalem, and Simon, his brother, met him in order to help him. ⁷⁵And he camped at Joppa, and those from the city shut him out because of the garrison of Apollonius in Joppa. And they fought it. ⁷⁶And in fear, those from the city opened the gates, and Jonathan took control of Joppa. ⁷⁷And Apollonius heard about this and mustered three thousand cavalry and a large force, and he traveled to Ashdod as though he were going through. And at the same time, he led them into the plain, for he had a great number of cavalry, and he trusted upon it. ⁷⁸And he closely pursued after him to Ashdod, and the armies engaged in battle from behind him. ⁷⁹And Apollonius had secretly abandoned one thousand cavalry behind them. ⁸⁰And Jonathan knew that there was an ambush behind him, and they surrounded his army and showered arrows into the people from early morning until evening. ⁸¹But the people stood fast just as Jonathan ordered, and their horses grew tired. ⁸²And Simon drew forward his force and engaged against the phalanx because the cavalry were exhausted; and they were crushed by him, and they fled. ⁸³And the cavalry was dispersed on the plain. And they fled to Ashdod and entered into Beth-dagon, their idol's temple, for deliverance. ⁸⁴And Jonathan burned Ashdod and the cities around it, and he took their spoils and the sacred place of Dagon, and he burned its sacred place with fire. ⁸⁵And those who fell by the sword were, along with those burned, nearly eight thousand men. ⁸⁶And Jonathan departed from there and camped in Askalon, and those from the city came out to meet him with great honor. ⁸⁷And Jonathan returned with those with him, having much plunder. ⁸⁸And it happened when King Alexander heard these things, he continued to honor Jonathan. ⁸⁹And he sent him a golden buckle as it was custom to give to the kinsman of the king, and he gave him Ekron and all its borders to be his possession of land.

*Egypt Invades Syria*

**11** And the king of Egypt gathered many forces, like the sand from the seashore, and many ships, and he sought to take over the kingdom of Alexander by deceit and to add it to his kingdom. ²And he went out to Syria with peaceful words, and those from the cities opened their gates to him and met him because the command of Alexander the king was to meet him because of being his father-in-law. ³But when Ptolemy entered into the cities, he stationed the forces as a garrison in each city. ⁴Now when he came near to Ashdod, they showed him the temple of Dagon, which was burnt, and Ashdod and its surrounding villages that were destroyed, and the corpses thrown around, and the burnt bodies, which he had set on fire during the battle, because they built heaps of them along his road. ⁵And they set out the details to the king of what Jonathan had done, to blame him; and the king was silent. ⁶And Jonathan met the king in Joppa with honor, and they greeted each other and slept there. ⁷And Jonathan went with the king as far as the river called Eleutherus and then returned to Jerusalem. ⁸So King Ptolemy took control over the cities of the coast as far as Seleucia by the seaside, and he continued to devise evil plans against Alexander. ⁹And he sent ambassadors to King Demetrius, saying, "Come, we should make a treaty between ourselves, and I will give you my daughter, who Alexander possesses, and you will rule your father's kingdom. ¹⁰For

I regret giving him my daughter, because he tried to kill me." ¹¹And he blamed him because he desired his kingdom. ¹²And removing his daughter, he gave her to Demetrius; and the face of Alexander was altered, and their hostility became clear.

¹³And Ptolemy entered into Antioch and put round his head the crown of Asia; and he put two crowns on his head: the crown of Asia and of Egypt. ¹⁴But Alexander, the king, was in Cilicia during those times because the people from those places had revolted. ¹⁵And Alexander heard and moved against him in battle, and Ptolemy marched out and met him with a mighty hand and put him to flight. ¹⁶And Alexander fled to Arabia, and he hid there; but the king, Ptolemy, was exalted. ¹⁷And Zabdiel the Arabian removed the head of Alexander and sent it to Ptolemy. ¹⁸And King Ptolemy died on the third day, and those who were in his strongholds were destroyed by those in the strongholds. ¹⁹And so Demetrius ruled in the one hundred and sixty-seventh year.

²⁰In those days, Jonathan gathered those from Judah to attack the citadel in Jerusalem and built against her many war machines. ²¹And some wicked men who hated their nation went to the king and reported to him that Jonathan had laid siege to the citadel. ²²And hearing this, he grew angry. Now as soon as he heard, immediately marching, he went to Ptolemais and wrote to Jonathan to not continue the siege and to meet him to speak with him in Ptolemais quickly. ²³But when Jonathan heard, he ordered the siege to continue, and he chose some from the elders of Israel and the priests, and he placed himself in danger. ²⁴And taking gold and silver and clothing and many other gifts, he went to the king in Ptolemais, and he found favor before him. ²⁵And some lawless men from the nation attempted to obtain an audience against him. ²⁶And the king did for him just as those before him had done for him, and he honored him before all his friends. ²⁷And he confirmed him in the high priesthood, and in as many other honors as he had previously. And he made him the foremost friend to rule. ²⁸And Jonathan requested the king to make Judah free from tribute, and the three districts and Samaria, and promised him three hundred talents. ²⁹And the king approved and wrote Jonathan letters about all these things, having done it in this way:

³⁰"King Demetrius, to Jonathan his brother, greetings, and also to the nation of the Judeans. ³¹The copy of the letter that we wrote to Lasthenes our kinsman concerning you, we wrote also to you, so that you might know what it says.

³²"King Demetrius, to Lasthenes his father: Greetings. ³³To the nation of the Judeans, our friends and those who observe what is righteous to us, we have determined to do good because of their affection toward us. ³⁴Therefore, we have confirmed for them the borders of Judah, and the three districts of Aphairema and Lydda and Rathamin were added to Judah from Samaria, and all that border them, to all who sacrifice in Jerusalem rather than the revenues of the crown, which the king received from them previously by the year from the produce of the land and the fruit trees. ³⁵And the others belonging to us from now on—of the tithes and the taxes belonging to us, and those of the salt pits and the crowns belonging to us—all of

*Jonathan's Efforts at Diplomacy*

them we will grant release for them. ³⁶And nothing shall ever be rejected of these from now for all time.

³⁷"Now, therefore, take care to make a copy of this, and it must be given to Jonathan and placed on the holy mountain in a useful and notable place."

*Jonathan's* ³⁸And Demetrius, the king, saw that the land was quiet before him, and
*Forces Rescue* nothing stood against him; and so, he dismissed all his forces, each to
*Demetrius* his own place, except the foreign forces, whom he had enlisted from the islands of the nations. And all the forces who were from his ancestors hated them. ³⁹But there was Trypho of those from Alexander previously, and he saw that all the forces were complaining about Demetrius; and so he went to Imalkue the Arabian, who was raising Antiochus, the younger son of Alexander. ⁴⁰And he insisted to him that he should hand over him to him that he would rule instead of his father. And also, they reported to him as much as Demetrius had accomplished and about the hostility that his forces showed to him. And he stayed there many days.

⁴¹And Jonathan sent word to Demetrius, the king, that he might drive out those from the citadel from Jerusalem and those in the strongholds, because they were fighting Israel. ⁴²And Demetrius sent to Jonathan, saying, "Not only will I do this for you and your nation, but I will also honor you and your nation with glory should I find the opportunity. ⁴³Now, therefore, you will do well to send us men who will be allies to me, because all my forces have left me." ⁴⁴And Jonathan sent three thousand strong men with their might into Antioch, and they came to the king, and the king was cheerful at their arrival. ⁴⁵And those from the city gathered together in the middle of the city to the number of one hundred and twenty thousand men, and they wished to kill the king. ⁴⁶And the king fled into the palace; and those from the city took control of the streets of the city, and they began to make war. ⁴⁷And the king called for the Judeans for help, and they gathered to him all together and spread out in the city and killed in the city in that day up to one hundred thousand. ⁴⁸And they burned the city and took many spoils on that day and delivered the king. ⁴⁹And those from the city saw that the Judeans had gained control over the city as they wished, and they grew weak in their minds and cried out to the king with a petition, saying, ⁵⁰"Grant us your right hand and let stop the Judeans fighting us and the city." ⁵¹And they threw down the weapons and made peace. And the Judeans were honored before the king and before all of those in his kingdom, and they returned to Jerusalem, having many spoils. ⁵²And Demetrius, the king, sat on his kingdom's throne, and the land rested before him. ⁵³And he acted falsely about everything, as much as he had said, and he estranged himself from Jonathan and did not repay the favor that he had paid to him and afflicted him very much.

*Jonathan* ⁵⁴But after this, Trypho returned, and Antiochus, the young boy, was with
*and Simon* him. And he began to rule and put on the crown. ⁵⁵And he gathered to him all the forces whom Demetrius had discharged, and they fought against him, and he fled and was routed. ⁵⁶And Trypho took elephants, and he took control of Antioch. ⁵⁷And Antiochus the younger wrote to Jonathan, saying, "I confirm you in the high priesthood and set you over the four districts, and you are to be the friends of the king." ⁵⁸And he sent him a golden cup

and a table service and gave him the right to drink in golden cup and to be dressed in purple and to have a golden buckle. ⁵⁹And Simon, his brother, he appointed governor from the Ladder of Tyre as far as the borders of Egypt. ⁶⁰And Jonathan went out and went over the river and among the cities, and he gathered to him all of Syria's forces to ally. And he went to Askalon, and those from the city greeted him with honor. ⁶¹And he departed from there to Gaza, and those from Gaza shut him out, and so he camped against them and burned their surrounding fortifications with fire and plundered them. ⁶²And those from Gaza begged Jonathan, and he gave them his right hand and took their ruler's sons as hostages and sent them away to Jerusalem. And he continued through the territory as far as Damascus.

⁶³And Jonathan heard that the rulers of Demetrius had arrived in Kadesh in Galilee with many forces, wishing to turn him away from his office. ⁶⁴And he met them, but his brother, Simon, he left behind in the territory. ⁶⁵And Simon camped in Beth-zur and fought them many days and hedged in it. ⁶⁶And they begged him to receive his right hand, and he gave it to them and drove them out from there and took control of the city and set over it a garrison. ⁶⁷And Jonathan and his army camped beside the spring of Gennesaret. And they rose early in the morning to march to the plain of Hazor. ⁶⁸And look, the foreign army met them in the plain, and they set an ambush against them in the hills. They met from opposite each other. ⁶⁹But the ambush rose from their places and joined the battle. And all those from Jonathan fled; ⁷⁰not even one remained from them except Mattathias the son of Absalom and Judah the son of Chalphi, the rulers of the forces of the force. ⁷¹And Jonathan tore his robes and put dirt on his head and prayed. ⁷²And then he returned to them for battle and routed them, and they fled. ⁷³And those fleeing from him saw this and returned to him, and they pursued after him as far as Kedesh—as far as their camp— and they camped there. ⁷⁴And there fell from the foreigners on that day to the number of three thousand men. And Jonathan returned to Jerusalem.

**12** And Jonathan saw that the time worked for him and selected men and sent them to Rome to establish and to restore the friendship toward them. ²And to the Spartans and other places, he sent letters according to this. ³And they traveled to Rome and went into the senate chamber, and they said, "Jonathan, the high priest, and the nation of the Judeans sent us to renew the friendship with them and the alliance just as previously." ⁴And they gave them letters to the people by place that they sent before them to the land of Judah with peace. ⁵And this is a copy of the letter that Jonathan wrote to the Spartans:

⁶"Jonathan, high priest of the nation, and the council and the priests and the remaining people of the Judeans, to the Spartans, their brothers: Greetings. ⁷Still previously, letters were sent to Onias, the high priest from Arius, who ruled among you, that you are our brothers, as the copy given below shows. ⁸And Onias welcomed the man who was sent with honor and received the letters, in which it was quite clear concerning our alliance and friendship. ⁹We, therefore, being without need of these things since we have the encouragement of the holy books in our hands, ¹⁰we are endeavoring to send to you to renew brotherhood and friendship so that we might not be cut off from you. For much time has passed from

*Alliances with Rome and Sparta*

when you sent word to us. ¹¹We, therefore, during all time, remember you constantly during the festivals and on the remaining appropriate days, on which we bring sacrifices and in prayers, as it is necessary and fitting to remember brothers. ¹²We regularly are cheerful in your glory. ¹³But as for us, many afflictions and many battles have surrounded us, and kings around us have fought us. ¹⁴We do not wish, therefore, to disturb you nor our other allies and friends with these battles. ¹⁵For we have help from heaven aiding us, and we were rescued from our enemies, and our enemies were made low. ¹⁶We chose, then, Numenius of Antiochus and Antipater of Jason, and we have sent them to the Romans to renew the friendship to them and the earlier alliance. ¹⁷We commanded them also to go to you and to greet you and to give to you the letters from us regarding the renewal and our brotherhood. ¹⁸And now, please, make a reply to us to this."

¹⁹And this is the transcript of the message that they sent to Onias.

²⁰"Arius, king of the Spartans, to Onias, the high priest: Greetings. ²¹It was found in writing concerning both the Spartans and the Judeans that they were brothers and that they are from the ancestry of Abraham. ²²And now, from what we know of this, please act by writing to us concerning your welfare. ²³Also we write to you: Your livestock and your property are ours, and those of us are yours. We are ordering, therefore, that they should report to you about these things."

*Battles of Jonathan and Simon* ²⁴And Jonathan heard that the rulers of Demetrius had returned with many forces beyond the first to fight against him. ²⁵And he departed from Jerusalem and met them in the territory of Hamath. For he did not give them opportunity to invade in his own territory. ²⁶And he sent spies into his camp, and they returned and reported to him that they were stationed in such a way as to fall upon them during the night. ²⁷So when the sun had set, Jonathan commanded those beside him to be awake and to be at their weapons to prepare for battle for the whole night, and he placed advanced guards around the camp. ²⁸And the enemies heard that Jonathan and those beside him had prepared for battle, and they were afraid and cowered in fear in their hearts, and they kindled fires in their camp. ²⁹But Jonathan and those beside him did not know until morning, for they saw the lights burning. ³⁰And he closely pursued after them and did not overtake them, for they crossed over the Eleutherus river. ³¹And Jonathan turned aside against the Arabians, called the Zabadeans, and he struck them and took their spoils. ³²And marching, they came to Damascus and traveled through in the whole territory. ³³And Simon went out and marched as far as Askalon and the neighboring strongholds, and he turned aside to Joppa and captured it, ³⁴for he heard that they wished to give over the stronghold to those from Demetrius, and he stationed there a garrison so that they might guard it.

³⁵And Jonathan returned and assembled the elders of the people and resolved with them to build strongholds in Judah ³⁶and to build the walls of Jerusalem even higher and to set up a great barrier between the citadel and the city for separating it from the city so that it would be, accordingly, that people could neither buy nor sell. ³⁷And so they gathered to build. And the wall of the wadi from the east had fallen, and he repaired the part

called Chaphenatha. ³⁸And Simon built up Adida in the Shephelah, and he fortified gates and bars.

³⁹And Trypho sought to become king over Asia and put on the crown and stretched his hands upon Antiochus, the king. ⁴⁰And he was afraid lest Jonathan should not allow him and lest he should fight against him. So he sought a ford in order to capture and kill him; and departing, he went to Beth-shan. ⁴¹And Jonathan went out to meet him with forty thousand men selected for battle, and they went to Beth-shan. ⁴²And Trypho saw that he was present with many forces, and he was afraid to stretch his hands against him. ⁴³And he welcomed him with honor and commended him to all his friends and gave him gifts and commanded his friends and his forces to listen to him in like manner. ⁴⁴And he said to Jonathan, "Why did you smite all these people, with battle not having come to us? ⁴⁵And now, send them to their homes, and choose for yourself a few men who will be with you. And come with me to Ptolemais, and I will give it over to you and the remaining strongholds and the many forces and all those over the royal service. And turning, I will depart; for this reason, I am here." ⁴⁶And trusting him, he did just as he said and sent away the forces, and they departed to the land of Judah. ⁴⁷He kept behind with himself three thousand men, of which two thousand he left in Galilee, but one thousand went with him.

⁴⁸But when Jonathan entered into Ptolemais, the people of Ptolemais shut the gates and captured him; and everyone assembled with him, they killed with the sword. ⁴⁹And Trypho sent forces and cavalry to Galilee to the great plain to destroy all those from Jonathan. ⁵⁰And they learned that he had been captured, and they had also killed those with him. And they exhorted each other, and they continued marching, forming up, prepared for battle. ⁵¹And those pursuing them saw that it was about life for them, and they turned back. ⁵²And all of them came with peace to the land of Judah and mourned for Jonathan and those with him, and they became very afraid, and Israel mourned with great grief. ⁵³And all the nations around them sought to destroy them, for they said, "They have no man, ruler, or helper. Now, therefore, we should attack them and remove their memory from humanity."

**13** And Simon heard that Trypho had gathered a large force to come to the land of Judah to destroy it, ²and he saw the people, that they were trembling and terrified. And so, he went up to Jerusalem and assembled the people. ³And he encouraged them and said to them, "You know yourselves how much I and my brothers and my father's house have done for the laws and the sanctuary and the battles and the difficulties. ⁴For this reason, all my brothers were killed for the sake of Israel, and I alone am remaining. ⁵And now it is not for me to spare my life in any time of distress, for I am not better than my brothers. ⁶Except I will exact vengeance for my nation and for the sanctuary and for our wives and children, because all the nations are gathering to destroy us out of hatred." ⁷And the spirit of his people was revived when they heard these words. ⁸And they responded with a loud voice, saying, "You are our leader instead of Judas and Jonathan, your brother. ⁹Fight our battle, and everything, however much you should say to us, we will do." ¹⁰And he gathered all the men who were warriors and

*Jonathan Captured by Trypho*

*Simon Takes Command*

hurried to finish the walls of Jerusalem, and he fortified it all around. ¹¹And he sent Jonathan the son of Absalom, and with him an adequate force, to Joppa, and he drove out those who were in it and remained there, in Joppa.

*Trypho's*
*Treachery*
¹²And Trypho departed from Ptolemais with a large force to go into the land of Judah, and Jonathan was with him under guard. ¹³Simon camped at Adida, according to the face of the plain. ¹⁴And Trypho knew that Simon had risen up in the place of Jonathan his brother and that he was about to engage him in battle, and he sent to him envoys, saying, ¹⁵"Concerning the silver which Jonathan your brother owes to the royal treasury, through which he has royal offices, that is why we are detaining him. ¹⁶And now, send one hundred talents of silver and two of his sons as hostages so that when we release him, he might not revolt against us, and we will release him." ¹⁷And Simon knew that they were speaking deceit to him, and he sent the silver and the young men, lest he would cause great hostility toward the people, ¹⁸saying, "It was because he did not send him the silver and the sons that Jonathan was killed." ¹⁹And he sent the sons and the one hundred talents, and he was deceived, and Trypho did not release Jonathan. ²⁰And after this, Trypho came to invade into the city and to destroy it, and he surrounded the way to Adora and Simon, and his army marched along opposite him to every place that he was going. ²¹Now those from the citadel were sending envoys and urging him to come to him through the wilderness and to send them provisions. ²²And Trypho prepared all his cavalry to come. And during that night there was very much snow, and he did not come through the snow. And he departed and went to Gilead. ²³When he approached Baskama, he killed Jonathan. And he was buried there. ²⁴And Trypho returned and departed to his own land.

*Jonathan*
*Buried*
²⁵And Simon sent for and received the bones of Jonathan, his brother, and buried him in Modein, his ancestor's city. ²⁶And all Israel mourned for him with great mourning, and they mourned for him many days. ²⁷And Simon built upon the tomb of his ancestors and his brothers, and he raised it high to be seen, with polished stones from the back and from the front. ²⁸And he erected seven pyramids, one opposite of the other one, for his father and mother and four brothers. ²⁹And for these, he built an elaborate setting placed around the large pillars, and he built over the pillars suits of armor to be an eternal memorial, and beside the armor engraved ships for observance by all who sail the sea. ³⁰This is the tomb that he built in Modein; it is still there until this day.

*Simon and*
*Demetrius*
*Attain Peace*
³¹Now Trypho went with deceit with Antiochus, the young king, and killed him. ³²And he began to rule in his place, and he put on the crown of Asia and performed great misfortune upon the land.

³³And Simon built up the stronghold of Judah and walled them with high towers and great walls and towers and gates and bars and put food stores in the strongholds. ³⁴And Simon chose men, and he sent them to King Demetrius to provide debt relief for the territory because all Trypho did was plunder. ³⁵And Demetrius, the king, sent him according to these words and responded to him and wrote to him a message that looked like this:

³⁶"King Demetrius, to Simon, high priest and friend of kings, and to the elders and the nation of the Judeans: Greetings. ³⁷The gold crown and the palm branch that you sent, we have received, and we are ready to make

great peace with you and to write to those over the offices to permit you remission from tribute. [38]And as much as we have established to you, it remains set, and the strongholds that you have built, let them be for you alone. [39]We forgive you for errors and offenses to the present day and the crown tax that you owe; and if some other tax is collected in Jerusalem, no longer should it be collected. [40]And if some of you are suitable to be enrolled into those for us, let them be enrolled, and let there be between us peace."

[41]During the one hundred and seventieth year, the yoke of the nations was removed from Israel. [42]And the people of Israel began to write in the documents and contracts: "In the first year for Simon, the great high priest and governor and leader of the Judeans."

[43]On those days he camped at Gazara, and he surrounded it with sol- *Simon* diers and built siege equipment and brought it to the city and struck one *Captures* tower and captured it. [44]And those in the siege engine leaped out into the *Gazara* city, and there was a great uproar in the city. [45]And those in the city went up with their wives and children onto the wall, tearing their robes, and they cried out with a loud voice, begging Simon to give his right hand to them. [46]And they said, "Do not treat us according to our wickedness but according to your mercy!" [47]And Simon made an agreement with them, and he did not fight them, and he moved them out from the city and cleansed the houses in which there were idols. And this is how he entered into it: with hymns and praises. [48]And he removed from it all impurity and settled in it men who do the law, and he strengthened it and built a home for himself in it.

[49]Those from the citadel in Jerusalem were prevented from going out *Simon* into the territory and to buy or sell, and they were very hungry; and some *Occupies the* from them died because of the famine. [50]And they cried out to Simon to *Citadel in* receive his right hand. And he gave it to them, and he removed them from *Jerusalem* there and cleansed the citadel from the defilement. [51]And he entered into it on the twenty-third day of the second month of the one hundred and seventy-first year with praise and palm branches, and with lyres and with cymbals and with stringed instruments and with hymns and with songs, because a great enemy was crushed from Israel. [52]And he decreed according to the year to observe this day. And he strengthened the mountain of the temple beside the citadel, and he and those beside him lived there. [53]And Simon saw John, his son, that he was a man, and he stationed him over all the forces, and he lived in Gazara.

**14** And in the one hundred and seventy-second year, Demetrius, the *Demetrius* king, assembled his forces and went to Media to gain help for him- *Captured* self so that he could fight Trypho. [2]And Arsaces, the king of Persia and Media, heard that Demetrius came into his borders, and he sent one of his rulers to capture him alive. [3]And he went and struck the camp of Demetrius and captured him and brought him to Arsaces, and he placed him in prison.

[4]And the land rested all the days of Simon, and he sought good things *The Peace* for his nation; and his rule pleased them, and also was his honor all the *of Simon* days. [5]And with all his glory, he took Joppa to be a harbor and made an entrance to the islands of the sea. [6]And he extended the borders for his

nation and took control of the territory. [7]And he gathered many captives and ruled Gazara and Beth-zur and the citadel, and he removed the impurities from it. And there was no one who opposed him. [8]And they were farmers in their land with peace, and the land produced their crops, and the trees of the plains their fruit. [9]Old men sat in the streets; they all took counsel about good things, and the young put on honor and armor for battle. [10]He provided food for the cities and stationed them with equipment for defense wherever his glorious name was called, as far as the ends of the land. [11]He maintained peace over the land, and Israel was cheerful with great cheer. [12]And each person sat by his vine and his fig tree, and there was nothing terrifying them. [13]And there was an end of their battles over the land, and their kings were crushed in those days. [14]And he supported all the lowly ones among his people; he observed the law and removed all lawlessness and evil. [15]He made the sanctuary glorious and added more vessels for the sanctuary.

*Alliances with Rome and Sparta Renewed*
[16]And it was heard in Rome that Jonathan had died, and also as far as Sparta, and they were very grieved. [17]But when they heard that Simon, his brother, had become high priest in his place and was ruling over the territory and the cities in it, [18]they wrote to him on bronze tablets to renew with him the friendship and alliance that they had established to Judas and Jonathan, his brothers. [19]And they were read before the assembly in Jerusalem. [20]And this is the transcript of the message that the Spartans sent:

"The rulers of the Spartans and the city, to Simon, the high priest, and to the elders and the priests and the remaining people of the Judeans, brothers: Greetings. [21]The ambassadors sent to our people reported to us about your glory and honor, and we were cheerful over their arrival. [22]And we have recorded what was said by them in the counsels of the people as follows: 'Numenius of Antiochus and Antipater of Jason, ambassadors of the Judeans, came to us renewing the friendship to us. [23]And it pleased the people to welcome the men with honor and to put the transcript of their words in the public for the people, documents of memory that the Spartan people should have. But the transcript of these they wrote to Simon, the high priest.'"

[24]After this, Simon sent Numenius to Rome bearing a great golden shield weighing one thousand minas to establish to them the alliance.

*Official Honors for Simon*
[25]When the people heard these words, they said, "What favor will we return to Simon and his sons? [26]For they stood firm, he and his brothers and his father's house, and they fought the enemies of Israel away from them and established freedom for it." And he inscribed on bronze tablets and placed them in a pillar on Mount Zion. [27]And this is the transcript of the inscription:

"On the eighteenth day of Elul, of the one hundred and seventy-second year—and this is the third year for Simon, the high priest—[28]in Saramel over the great congregation of the priests and people and rulers of the nation and the elders of the territory, it was made known to us. [29]Since war often occurs in the territory, Simon the son of Mattathias, the son of the sons of Joiarib, and his brothers placed themselves in danger, and they stood against the enemies of their nation so that their sanctuary and the laws might be established. And they have honored their nation with great glory. ³⁰And Jonathan assembled their nation and became a high priest for them and added to his people. ³¹And their enemies wished to invade into their territory in order to destroy their territory and stretched their hands over their sanctuary. ³²Then Simon rose up and fought for his nation and expended much of his own money and armed the men of the force of his nation and gave them provisions. ³³And he fortified the cities of Judah and Beth-zur on the borders of Judah, where the weapons of the enemies were previously, and he stationed there garrisons of Judean men. ³⁴And Joppa, he fortified on the sea, and Gazara on borders of Ashdod, in which place our enemies lived there before. And he settled the Judeans there, and as much as was necessary for their restoration, he put in them. ³⁵And the people saw the faithfulness of Simon and the glory that he was resolved to create for his nation. And they appointed him as their ruler and high priest because of all these things he had done and the righteousness and the faithfulness that he maintained for his nation. And he sought out in every way to honor his people. ³⁶And during his days, there was prosperity in his hands to remove the nations from their territory, and those in the city of David in Jerusalem, as were those who built for themselves a citadel from which they went out and defiled the area around the sanctuary, and they did great damage in its purity. ³⁷And he settled in it Judean men and fortified it for the security of the territory and the city and built higher the walls of Jerusalem. ³⁸And King Demetrius confirmed him in the high priesthood on the basis of this. ³⁹And he made him one of his friends and honored him with great glory. ⁴⁰For it was heard that the Judeans were called by the Romans as friends and allies and brothers, and that they met the ambassadors of Simon with honor, ⁴¹and that the Judeans and the priests found pleasure in Simon being ruler and high priest over them to eternity until a faithful prophet should rise, ⁴²and that he should be over them as governor, and that he should take care for them regarding the sanctuary to appoint for them over their work and over the territory and over the weapons and over the strongholds, ⁴³and that he should take care for them regarding the sanctuary, and that he should be obeyed by all, and that all documents should be written in his name in the territory, and that he should wear purple and gold. ⁴⁴And it is not permitted for any of the people or the priests to reject any of this or to oppose anything spoken by him or gather an assembly in the territory without him or to put on a purple robe or put on a golden buckle. ⁴⁵But whoever should act against these resolutions or reject some of them, he will be liable to be punished. ⁴⁶And all the people were pleased to appoint Simon to act according to these words. ⁴⁷And Simon accepted and approved of being high priest and being governor and ruler of the Judeans and the priests and being protector over all."

⁴⁸And this inscription they said to put it on bronze tablets and set it on outer wall of the sanctuary in the trustworthy place, ⁴⁹but the copies of them, to put in the treasury so that Simon and his sons might have them.

**15** And Antiochus, son of Demetrius, the king, sent messages from the islands of the sea to Simon, the priest, and rulers of the Judeans and all the nation. ²And they were contained this way: *Letter of Antiochus VII*

"King Antiochus, to Simon, the high priest and ruler and to the nation of the Judeans: Greetings. ³Since some scoundrels gained control over the kingdom of my ancestors, I am resolving to reclaim the kingdom so that I might restore it as it was before. I have enlisted foreigners for a large number of forces and have built ships for war. ⁴Now I wish to land by the territory so that I can come over against those who have destroyed our territory and those who have desolated many cities in the kingdom. ⁵Now, therefore, I confirm to you all the tribute that the kings before me forgave you of and for as many other tributes they forgave you of, ⁶to mint your own currency of your territory. ⁷Now Jerusalem and the sanctuary are to be free, and all the weapons—as many as you build—and the strongholds that you build, which you control, they shall remain yours. ⁸And all royal debt and what will be royal debt from the present and into all time, it is forgiven to you. ⁹Now when we are appointed over our kingdom, we honor you and your nation and the temple with great glory so that your glory will become visible in all the earth."

¹⁰In the one hundred and seventy-fourth year, Antiochus went out into the land of his ancestors, and all the forces gathered together to him so that only a few there were with Trypho. ¹¹And Antiochus, the king, pursued him, and he came into Dor, fleeing near the sea. ¹²For he knew that evils had gathered against him, and the forces deserted him. ¹³And Antiochus camped against Dor, and with him were one hundred and twenty thousand warriors and eight thousand cavalry. ¹⁴And he surrounded the city, and the ships from the sea joined in, and he pressed the city from the land and from the sea. And he allowed no one to go out or to go in.

*Roman Support of the Judeans* ¹⁵And there came Numenius and those beside him from Rome with messages to the kings and the territories in which this was written: ¹⁶"Lucius, consul of the Romans, to King Ptolemy: Greetings. ¹⁷The ambassadors of the Judeans came to us as our friends and allies, renewing the ancient friendship and alliance, sending from Simon, the high priest, and the people of the Judeans. ¹⁸They brought a golden shield of a value of five thousand minas. ¹⁹Therefore, it pleased us to write to the kings and the territories that they should not seek evil against them and not fight them and their cities and their territories, and that they should not aid those who make war against them. ²⁰It seemed good to us to accept the shield from them. ²¹Therefore, if any scoundrels have fled from their territory to you, hand them over to Simon, the high priest, so that he may punish them according to their law."

²²And he wrote this same thing to Demetrius, the king, and Attalus and Ariarathes and Arsaces, ²³and to all the territories, and Sampsames, and to the Spartans and to Delos and to Myndos and to Sicyon and to the Caria and to Samos and to the Pamphylia and Lycia and to Halicarnassus and to Cos and to Side and to Aradus and to Rhodes and to the Phaselis and Gortyna and Cnidus and Cyprus and Cyrene. ²⁴A copy of them he wrote to Simon the high priest.

*Antiochus Challenges Simon* ²⁵Now Antiochus, the king, camped against Dor on a second occasion, bringing his hands against it constantly and making war machines and enclosing Trypho from going in and from going out. ²⁶And Simon sent him two thousand chosen men to be his allies, and gold and silver and suitable equipment. ²⁷And he did not want to accept them but rejected everything, as much as he had agreed with him previously, and he estranged himself from him. ²⁸And he sent to him Athenobius, one of his friends, to negotiate with him, saying, "You have taken control of Joppa and Gazara and the citadel in Jerusalem, cities of my kingdom. ²⁹Their borders you have desolated and have done great damage against the land. And you have taken control of many places in my kingdom. ³⁰Now, therefore, hand over the cities that you have captured and the tribute from the places where you have gained dominion outside the borders of Judah. ³¹But if not, give me instead of those five hundred talents of silver, both for the destruction that you have caused, and also for the tribute of the cities, another five hundred talents. If you do not, after coming, they shall make war against you."

³²And Athenobius, friend of the king, came to Jerusalem and saw the glory of Simon and the sideboard with golden cups and silver plates and magnificent display, and he was amazed and reported to them the words of the king. ³³And answering, Simon said to him, "Neither foreign land have we taken, nor foreign property have we taken control of, but our ancestor's inheritance was taken unjustly at one time by our enemies. ³⁴But we, having time, have regained our and our ancestor's inheritance. ³⁵Now regarding Joppa and Gazara, which you yourselves demand, they were causing among our people great damage and in our land; for them, we will give you one hundred talents." And he did not respond to him a single word. ³⁶But he returned with rage to the king and reported to him these words and the splendor of Simon and everything, as much as he had seen, and the king grew angry with great rage. ³⁷Meanwhile, Trypho entered a ship and fled to Orthosia. ³⁸And the king appointed Cendebeus viceroy of the coastal land and gave him infantry forces and cavalry. ³⁹And he ordered him to camp against the face of Judah and ordered him to build up Kidron and to fortify its cities and that he might fight the people. But the king pursued Trypho. ⁴⁰And Cendebeus arrived in Jamnia and began to provoke the people and to invade into Judah and to take prisoners from the people and to murder them. ⁴¹And he built up Kidron and stationed cavalry and forces there so that, going out, they might raid the roads of Judah, just as the king had directed him.

**16** And John went up from Gazara and reported to Simon, his father, what Cendebeus accomplished. ²And Simon called his eldest two sons, Judas and John, and said to them, "I and my brothers and my father's house have fought Israel's battles from youth until the present day, and everything has prospered in our hands, rescuing Israel many times. ³But now I am old, and you, by mercy, are sufficient in years. Be in my and my brother's place and, going out, fight for our nation. But from our heaven, may there be help with you." ⁴And John chose from the territory twenty thousand males of war and cavalry, and they marched against Cendebeus and slept at Modein. ⁵And rising in the morning, they went to the plain and look, a large force was to meet them, both infantry and cavalry; and a wadi was between them. ⁶And he camped by their face, he and his people, and he saw the people were afraid to cross through the wadi. And so, he crossed through first, and the men saw him, and they crossed after him. ⁷And he divided the people and situated the cavalry in the middle of the infantry, for the cavalry of the enemies was very numerous. ⁸And they sounded the trumpets, and Cendebeus and his army were routed, and many casualties

*Simon's Sons Victorious over Cendebeus*

fell among him; but the rest fled into the stronghold. ⁹At that moment, Judas, John's brother, was wounded, but John closely pursued them until coming to Kidron, which he had built up. ¹⁰And they fled into the towers in the field of Ashdod, and he burned them with fire, and there fell from them to the number of a thousand men. And then he returned to Judah with peace.

Simon and His Sons Slaughtered ¹¹And Ptolemy, the son of Abubus, was appointed governor for the plain of Jericho and had much gold and silver, ¹²for he was the high priest's son-in-law. ¹³And his heart was lifted, and he desired to take control of the territory, and he resolved treacherously against Simon and against his sons to remove them. ¹⁴Now Simon was visiting the cities in the territory and quickening their need with care, and he went down to Jericho, he and Mattathias and Judas and his sons, in the one hundred and seventy-seventh year, during the eleventh month—this is the month of Shebat.

¹⁵And the son of Abubus welcomed them with deceit into the small fortification called Dok, which he had built. And he made for them a great banquet and hid men there. ¹⁶And when Simon and his sons had become drunk, Ptolemy and those with him stood and took their weapons and rushed to attack Simon in the banquet and killed him and his sons and some of his servants. ¹⁷And he performed a great godlessness and repaid evil for good.

*John Succeeds Simon* ¹⁸And Ptolemy wrote about these things and sent it to the king so that he might send to him forces to help and hand over their territory and cities. ¹⁹And he sent others into Gazara to remove John; and to the commanders he sent messages for them to come to them so that he might give them gold and silver and gifts. ²⁰And others he sent to capture Jerusalem and the mountain of the temple. ²¹But running ahead, someone reported to John in Gazara that his father and his brothers had been killed and that he had sent men also to kill you. ²²And hearing these things, he was very shocked, and he captured the men who had come to kill him and executed them, for he knew that they sought to kill him.

²³And the rest of the acts of John and his battles and his bravery that he demonstrated and the construction of the wall that he built and his deeds, ²⁴look, these are written on the document of the days of his high priesthood, from when he became high priest after his father.

*Introduction to*

# 2 Maccabees

S ECOND MACCABEES OPENS ANOTHER window into Israel's history from about 175 to 161 BC. It differs from 1 Maccabees in giving a great deal more attention to the events of the hellenizing crisis and to the responsibility that the hellenizing party within Jerusalem bore for bringing on the crisis. Further, it explains the role of those Jews whose loyalty to the covenant led them to endure torture to the point of death rather than willingly renounce the covenant. It extends only as far as the death of Judas Maccabaeus. It is the result of its author's abridgement of a five-volume history of the period written in Greek by Jason of Cyrene, a diaspora Jew, perhaps shortly after the events that he purported to narrate. The abridgment was also executed in (very good) Greek, perhaps earlier than 124 BC (the date of the letter prefixed in 1:1–9), almost certainly earlier than 63 BC (again because of the positive portrayal of the Romans in the document). The abridger (or perhaps it was Jason himself) is less interested in supporting a particular dynasty than in the theological interpretation of the events he narrates. This is done through the lens of Deuteronomy, where neglect of the covenant leads to the withdrawal of divine protection of the nation and exemplary, renewed devotion to the covenant invites the return of God's favor and help.

Second Maccabees is particularly important also for the place that it gives to the resurrection of the dead, the hope for vindication that accounts for the martyrs' steadfastness. The martyrs of 2 Maccabees 6:18–7:42 have become important examples of faith and faithfulness in Christian tradition, starting as early as Hebrews 11:35b and picking up significant momentum in the third century when the prospect of a martyr's death faced a great many Christians.

—D. A. deSilva

# 2 MACCABEES

**1** To the Judean brothers, those down in Egypt: Greetings from the Judean brothers who are in Jerusalem and who are in the territory of Judea; great peace to you. ²And may God do good to you and remember his covenant that he made with Abraham and Isaac and Jacob, his faithful servants. ³And may he grant you a heart for everything to worship him and do his will with a strong heart and a willing soul. ⁴And may he open your heart to his law and to the ordinances, and may he make peace. ⁵And may he heed your prayers and reconcile you and not forsake you in an evil time.

⁶And now we are here praying concerning you. ⁷When Demetrius was reigning, in the one hundred and sixty-ninth year, we Judeans wrote to you in the affliction and in the culminating point that came against us in those years, after which Jason and those with him departed from the holy land and the kingdom. ⁸And they burned the gate and shed innocent blood, and we prayed to the Lord, and we obeyed. We offered a sacrifice and fine wheat flour, and we brought out the lamps and set out the loaves. ⁹And now, see that you observe the days of the Feast of Tabernacles in the month of Chislev ¹⁰in the eighty-eighth year in Jerusalem.

And those in Judea and the council of elders and Judah, to Aristobulus the teacher of Ptolemy, the king who is from the clan of the anointed priests, and to those Judeans in Egypt: Greetings and salutations. ¹¹Having been saved out of great dangers by God, we are giving thanks exceedingly to him, as those who make war against a king should. ¹²For he expelled those who make war against the holy city into Persia. ¹³For, having come, the leader and the force around him that seemed to be overwhelming were cut to pieces in the temple of Nanea, when the priests of Nanea used a deception. ¹⁴For, as if marrying her, both Antiochus and those friends with him arrived in the place for the sake of taking the great wealth in the temple as a dowry. ¹⁵And the priests of Nanea set them forth, and that one went with a few others into the enclosure of the shrine; they shut up the temple when Antiochus entered. ¹⁶After opening the hidden door of the coffered ceiling, casting stones, they struck the leader; and after cutting off the limbs and the heads, they were throwing them to those outside. ¹⁷May our God, who has given over those who act profanely, be blessed in every respect.

¹⁸Being about to observe the purification of the temple on the twenty-fifth day of Chislev, we deemed it necessary to instruct you plainly in order that you yourselves also might observe the Feast of Tabernacles and the fire*ᵃ* when Nehemiah, the one who restored at that time the temple and the altar, offered up sacrifices. ¹⁹For when our fathers were brought into Persia, the pious priests, having taken from the fire of the altar secretly, hid it in the hollow of a cistern—being a dry place—in which they sealed

---

*ᵃ* "The fire" refers to "the commemoration of the rekindling of the fire"; see verses 19–22 below for the account of the incident being referred to here

it up in order that the place would be unknown to everyone. ²⁰Now, after many years elapsed, when it seemed right to God, Nehemiah, being commissioned by the king of Persia, sent to the offspring of the priests who hid the fire for the fire. ²¹When they made it clear to us that they did not find fire but instead a thick liquid, he ordered them upon drawing some out to bring it back. And when the things of the sacrifices had been brought up, Nehemiah commanded the priests to sprinkle over the liquid both the wood and the sacrifices laid upon it. ²²And when it was done and time passed and the sun broke out anew, being cloudy, a great fire was kindled so that all marveled. ²³And the priests made a prayer while the sacrifice was being consumed. Both the priests and all the people prayed, with Jonathan leading and the rest of the people responding when Nehemiah responded. ²⁴And the prayer went like this: "Lord, God, the creator of all, the fearful and the mighty and righteous and merciful one, the only good king, ²⁵the only provider, the only righteous and almighty and eternal one, the one who saves Israel from all evil, the one who chose the fathers and who sanctified them, ²⁶accept the sacrifice on behalf of all your people, Israel, and protect and sanctify your portion. ²⁷Gather together our scattered people, set free those who are slaves among the Gentiles, look upon those who are being scorned and those who are abominable, and let the Gentiles know that you are our God. ²⁸Torment those who oppress and who are insolent in arrogance. ²⁹Plant your people in your holy place just as Moses said."

³⁰And the priests were singing the hymns. ³¹Now, as the parts of the sacrifice were consumed, Nehemiah commanded them to pour the remaining liquid over some large stones. ³²And when this came about, a flame was kindled, but it was expended when the light from the altar shone back. ³³Now as the event became known and was told to the king of the Persians that, in the place where those priests who were carried into captivity hid the fire, the liquid appeared, from which also Nehemiah's associates burned up the sacrifice, ³⁴the king, after verifying the event, erected a fence around the place and made it sacred. ³⁵And with these the king took many gifts, and he distributed them. ³⁶And Nehemiah's associates called this "nephtar," which is interpreted "purification," but it is called by many "Nephthar."

**2** Now it is found in the records that Jeremiah the prophet commanded those being carried into exile to take of the fire, just as has been noted, ²and that the prophet exhorted those being carried into exile, giving them the law in order that they might not forget the ordinances of the Lord and in order that they might not be led astray in their minds upon seeing the golden and silver idols and the ornamentation around them. ³And saying other things such as these, he admonished them to not send the law away from their heart. ⁴And it stands in the written report that the prophet ordered the tabernacle and the ark to accompany them, an oracle being received by him, and that he went out to the mountain from which Moses, upon ascending, beheld the inheritance of God. ⁵And when he arrived, Jeremiah found a cave-like house, and he brought in there the tabernacle and the ark and the altar of incense, and he blocked up the door. ⁶And some of those who accompanied Jeremiah went back in order to mark the path, and they were not able to find it. ⁷But when Jeremiah learned about it,

*Jeremiah Conceals the Tent, Ark, and Altar*

censuring them he said, "The place will be even unknown until God should bring together an assembly of the people, and there shall be mercy. [8]And then the Lord will reveal these things, and the glory of the Lord will appear, and the cloud, just as it was visible for Moses, as also Solomon prayed that the place be greatly sanctified." [9]And it was also made clear that because he possessed wisdom, Solomon offered up a sacrifice for the consecration and completion of the temple. [10]Just as also Moses prayed to the Lord and fire came down out of heaven and consumed the elements of the sacrifice, in the same way Solomon prayed to the Lord and, upon coming down, the fire consumed the whole burnt offerings. [11]And Moses said, "It was consumed because what is about the sin offering was not eaten." [12]In the same way also, Solomon observed the eight days.

*Nehemiah's Library*    [13]And the same things are related also in the records and in the memoirs according to Nehemiah, and that, upon founding a library, he gathered together the documents concerning the kings and the prophets and those of David and the epistles of the kings concerning dedicated items. [14]And in the same way also Judas gathered together these things that were spread abroad on account of our war,[a] and they are with us. [15]So then, if you have need of them, send some people to bring them back to you.

*Exhortation*    [16]Now then, because we are about to observe the purification, we write to you. Therefore you will do well to observe these days. [17]And God is the one who saved all his people and restored his inheritance to all and the kingdom and the priesthood and the consecration, [18]just as he promised through the law. For we hope in God that he will quickly show mercy to us and he will gather us together from under heaven into the holy place. For he delivered us out of great evils, and he purified the place.

*The Compiler's Preface*    [19]Now the things concerning Judas Maccabeus and the brothers of this one and the purification of the great temple and the dedication of the altar, [20]and further, the wars against Antiochus Epiphanes and the son of this one, Eupator, [21]and the manifestations that came about from heaven for those who were acting heroically and honorably on behalf of Judaism as, although being small in number, they plundered the entire territory, and they pursued the barbarous throngs, [22]and they recovered the temple renowned through all the inhabited world, and they freed the city, and they restored the laws about to be abolished because the Lord, with all graciousness, became merciful to them. [23]All these things, which are related by Jason of Cyrene in five documents, we shall attempt to abridge into one treatise. [24]For considering the outpouring of the quantity and the difficulty existing for those who want to plunge into the narrations of history on account of the abundance of the material, [25]we aimed to delight on the one hand those who wish to read it and on the other hand make it easier for those who are favorably disposed to memorize the record and benefit all those who happen to read it. [26]Even for us, the ones who undertook the painful labor of the abridgment, it was not easy; rather, it was a matter of sweat and sleeplessness, [27]just as it is not easy for one who prepares a banquet and one who seeks for the profit of others. Nevertheless, on account of the gratitude of many, we will endure the laborious toil gladly, [28]conceding

---

[a] Lit. "the war that happened to us"

on the one hand the detailed examination concerning these things to the author but on the other hand exhausted to come up with the outlines of the abridgment. ²⁹For as the master builder of a new house must take heed of the whole structure, but the one who endeavors to restore and draw scrutinizes the things necessary with the decorations, so also I think concerning us. ³⁰The entry into a subject and execution of a digression in the matter and the close inquiry in the matters part by part belongs to the originator of the account, ³¹but the right to pursue conciseness of expression and to avoid the full presentation of the narration of facts must be allowed to the one who makes the paraphrase.

³²From here, then, having added so much in the things mentioned previously, let us begin the narrative, for it is indeed foolish to increase the material before the narrative but shorten the actual narrative.

**3** While the holy city was dwelling in complete peace and the laws were being strictly observed on account of both the piety and hatred of evil of Onias, the high priest, ²it happened that the kings themselves honored the place and glorified the temple with the best gifts, ³so that even Seleucus, the king of Asia, provided for all the expenses accrued for the ministries of the sacrifices from his own revenue. ⁴Now Simon, a certain man from the tribe of Benjamin, having been appointed superintendent of the temple, fell out with the high priest over the clerk of the market in the city. ⁵Not being able to overcome Onias, he went to Apollonius of Tarsus, the governor at that time of Coelesyria and of Phoenicia, ⁶and he reported about the unspeakably great wealth filling the treasury in Jerusalem, so that the abundance of the gifts was countless and that it was not offered to the account of the sacrifices, but it might be possible that it fell under the authority of the king. ⁷Now Apollonius, upon meeting with the king, told him about the wealth that had been revealed to him. Then the king selected Heliodorus, who was over his affairs, and sent him off, giving him a command to carry out the removal of the aforementioned wealth. ⁸Heliodorus set off immediately on the journey with the pretense of inspecting the cities in Coelesyria and Phoenicia, but in actuality he went to execute the plan of the king. ⁹After arriving in Jerusalem and being warmly admitted by the high priest of the city, he explained concerning the information that had been divulged and made clear the reason why he was present. Then he inquired if in truth these things in reality were so. ¹⁰The high priest indicated that there were deposits both from widows and orphans, ¹¹and also that a certain Hyrcanus the son of Tobias, a man exceeding in dignity, was storing some money there. It was not as the impious Simon was misinforming; the total amount was four hundred talents of silver and two hundred of gold. ¹²And that wrongs should happen to those who trusted in the sanctity of the place and in the dignity and inviolability of the temple, which is honored throughout the whole world, was completely impossible. ¹³The other one, on account of the royal command that he had, was saying that surely these things must be confiscated for the royal treasury.

¹⁴Having set a day, he entered in, conducting the inspection of these things, and there was no small anxiety throughout the whole city. ¹⁵But the priests, after throwing themselves down in their priestly garb before

*Heliodorus Arrives in Jerusalem*

*Anguish in the Temple*

the altar, were invoking to heaven upon the one who gave the law concerning deposits, that he might keep them safe for those who had made deposits. ¹⁶Seeing the countenance of the high priest wounded the mind. For his countenance and the change of his complexion displayed the agony in his soul. ¹⁷For a certain fear and trembling of body had enveloped over the man, by which the pain present in his heart became clear to those who were watching. ¹⁸They were running out of their houses in droves for the sake of a common supplication because the place was not about to be brought into contempt. ¹⁹The women, having girded up sackcloth under their breasts, were flooding down into the streets. From those of the virgins who were kept inside, some were running together to the gates, and some to the walls, but others looked out through the windows. ²⁰But all the women held up their hands to heaven and were making supplication. ²¹It was miserable, the prostration of the diverse multitude and the great anxiety of the anguish of the high priest.

*The Temple* ²²So then, while they were invoking the all-powerful Lord to keep safe
*Protected* with complete security the things entrusted for those who had entrusted
*by the Lord* them, ²³Heliodorus was attempting to carry out the course already determined. ²⁴Now when he was already there in the treasury with his bodyguards, the Lord of the spirits and of all power made an amazing appearance with the result that all those who had dared to go in with him were astounded, and the power of God changed their boldness into feebleness and cowardice. ²⁵For a certain horse appeared to them, having a fearful rider and being adorned with excellent armor. Rushing up, it shook Heliodorus vigorously with its front hooves. The one who rode appeared as one having a suit of golden armor. ²⁶Then two other young men appeared to him, exceptional in strength but most excellent in language, and distinguished with respect to their raiment, who also stood by on each side and began flogging him continually, hitting him with many blows. ²⁷And suddenly falling to the ground and being enveloped by great darkness, his men picked him up and put him in a litter. ²⁸The one who entered the treasury shortly before with a great retinue and completely guarded, as was said earlier, they carried him completely helpless; clearly they acknowledged the lordship of God. ²⁹And he, on account of the divine action, lay prostrate, speechless, and completely deprived of hope of healing; ³⁰but the people were blessing the Lord, the one who treated his place with distinction. Also the temple, being full a little earlier of fear and tumult, was filling up with joy and cheer because the Almighty Lord appeared.

*The* ³¹Quickly some of the friends of Heliodorus's began begging Onias to
*Conversion* call upon the Most High even to grant life to the one lying down quite
*of Heliodorus* at his last breath. ³²The high priest, being worried in case the king held the opinion that some treachery concerning Heliodorus was being carried out by the Judeans, offered a sacrifice on behalf of the man's healing. ³³Now while the high priest was making the atonement offering, the same young men appeared again to Heliodorus dressed in the same raiment, and standing there, they said, "Have great gratitude for Onias the high priest, for because of him the Lord has granted you life. ³⁴Now that you have been flogged from heaven, go proclaim to all people the magnificent

power of God." And after saying these things, they became invisible. [35]Then Heliodorus, after he offered a sacrifice to God, and praying great prayers to the one who preserved his life and acknowledging Onias, took his soldiers back to the king. [36]And he bore witness to everyone with respect to the works of the great God, which indeed he had seen with his own eyes.

[37]But when the king asked Heliodorus what sort of person might be suitable to be sent once more to Jerusalem, he said, [38]"If anyone has hostile intentions or is plotting a deed against the king, send him there, and you shall welcome him back flogged—if he should even come through safely—because there is truly some power of God around the place. [39]For he who has a heavenly dwelling is the overseer and helper of that place, and he destroys those who come with ill intent by beating them down." [40]And that is how the matters concerning Heliodorus and the preservation of the treasury turned out.

4 But the aforementioned Simon, the one who became an informer about the wealth and against his country, spoke ill of Onias, saying that this was the one who terrified Heliodorus and the supervising architect of the calamities. [2]He dared even to say that the benefactor of the city and guardian of the nation and the one who was jealous for the laws was the one who plotted against the interests of the state. [3]Now as his hostility increased to such an extent that even murders were committed by a certain one of those who was approved by Simon, [4]Onias, realizing the danger of the dispute and that Apollonius of Menestheus, the governor of Coele Phoenicia and Syria, was encouraging the mischief of Simon, [5]he was regulated toward the king, not being a betrayer of the citizens but being a guardian with respect to the welfare for all the multitude, public and private. [6]For he saw that without royal attention, it was impossible in that state of affairs to find peace and that Simon would not cease from his folly. *Simon's Treachery*

[7]After Seleucus died and Antiochus, the one called Epiphanes, received the kingdom, Jason, the brother of Onias, procured the high priesthood by corruption, [8]promising the king by a petition of three hundred and sixty talents of silver and eighty talents from a certain other fund. [9]And in addition to these things, he promised also to pay out by draft another one hundred and fifty if a gymnasium be provided by his authority also for establishing youth with it and to register those from Antioch in Jerusalem. [10]And after the king granted these things and he took possession of the office, he changed his countrymen immediately to the Greek character. [11]Also, after setting aside the royal benevolence made valid for the Judeans by means of John the father of Eupolemus, who served as the ambassador for friendship and who made an alliance with the Romans, and destroying the lawful polity, he made new customs that were antithetical to the law. [12]Therefore he set up readily a gymnasium below the citadel itself, and he led around the best of those over us, compelling them to wear a petasus[a] hat. [13]Because of the surpassing wickedness of the profane Jason, who was not really a high priest, there was such a height of Hellenization and ascendance of the adoption of foreign customs [14]that the priests were no longer *Jason's Hellenistic Reforms*

[a] The petasus was a wide brimmed hat worn by adolescent boys as they exercised in the gymnasium, providing their faces with shade from the sun

eager with regard to the ministries of the altar, but rather despised the temple. And neglecting the sacrifices, they would hurry to participate in the unlawful publicly funded spectacle in the wrestling school after the summons of the gong. ¹⁵So they held the honor of their fathers as nothing, but they deemed Greek opinions as excellent, ¹⁶for the sake of which a dangerous calamity encompassed them. And the customs of those they were envying and were wanting to assimilate in every respect, those they had as their enemies and avengers. ¹⁷For to act profanely in regard to the divine laws is no easy thing. Certainly the period that followed will demonstrate these things.

¹⁸Now when the quinquennial*ᵃ* contest was being held in Tyre and the king was present, ¹⁹the vile Jason sent envoys as if from Jerusalem, Antiochenes, carrying three hundred drachmas of silver for the sacrifice of Hercules. Nevertheless, those carrying the money decided not to use it for the sacrifice. ²⁰For the sake of those present, for the construction of triremes.

²¹After Apollonius the son of Menestheus was sent to Egypt on account of the royal festival in honor of Philometor, the king, Antiochus, hearing that Philometer was becoming hostile toward his state, considered the security of his situation, whereupon being already in Joppa he went on to Jerusalem. ²²He was received magnificently by Jason and the city, being welcomed with torch bearers and joyful shouts. So then he encamped accordingly in Phoenicia.

*Menelaus*
*Becomes*
*High Priest*

²³Now after a time of three years, Jason sent Menelaus, the brother of the aforementioned Simon, as the one bearing the money to the king and as the one who could handle royal decrees for necessary state affairs. ²⁴But after being introduced to the king and praising himself as a face of authority, he secured the high priesthood for himself, outbidding Jason by three hundred talents of silver. ²⁵After receiving the royal commandments, he arrived bearing*ᵇ* nothing worthy of the high priesthood, but instead having the rages of a cruel tyrant and the wrath of a barbarous beast. ²⁶So also Jason, the one who undermined his own brother, was undermined by another and driven as a fugitive into the territory of Ammon. ²⁷Now Menelaus took possession of the office, but he did not make the regular payments of the money that was promised to the king. ²⁸When Sostratus, the commander of the citadel, was making demands for the money, because the job of collecting the revenue was given to him, the two were summoned by the king on account of this problem. ²⁹So Menelaus abandoned Lysimachus, his brother, as the deputy of the high priesthood, and Sostratus deputized Crates as the one over the Cyprian soldiers.

*The Murder*
*of Onias*

³⁰Now as these things were going on, it happened that Tarsus and Mallus revolted because these cities were given as a gift to Antiochis, the concubine of the king. ³¹Therefore the king went swiftly in order to settle matters, leaving in his place Andronicus, one from those who was positioned in rank. ³²But Menelaus, thinking he could take a convenient opportunity, stole some golden vessels from those of the temple. He gave them

---

*ᵃ* Or, "held every five years"  *ᵇ* Menelaus did not have any of the appropriate qualifications for the high priesthood

to Andronicus. He also obtained some others, selling them to both Tyre and the surrounding cities. ³³After Onias retreated to a safe place near Daphne, located near Antioch, he carried himself off when he found out the truth about them. ³⁴Therefore Menelaus received Andronicus privately and persuaded him to attack Onias. So he went to Onias and persuaded him with guile and greeted him warmly with an oath, giving him his right hand. Although Onias remained suspicious, he convinced him to come out of the sanctuary, and immediately he incarcerated him, having no respect for what is righteous. ³⁵For this reason, not only the Judeans but also many from other nations were indignant and angry about the unjust murder of the man. ³⁶After the king returned from the places around Cilicia, the Judeans in the city obtained an audience because of the unreasonable murder of Onias. The Greeks who felt a common hatred of evil also participated. ³⁷Therefore Antiochus, being grieved at heart deeply and being moved to compassion, even wept on account of the prudence and outstanding behavior of the one who died. ³⁸And burning with rage, he took off immediately the purple robe of Andronicus and tore off his inner garments, leading him around through the entire city to the very place where he acted wickedly toward Onias. There he executed the murderer, the Lord repaying him with a worthy punishment.

³⁹Now because of the great sacrilegious plunder that occurred against the city by Lysimachus with the approval of Menelaus and the spread of the news outside of the city, a multitude gathered together against Lysimachus, since many golden vessels had already been removed from the temple. ⁴⁰As the mobs were becoming excited and filling with rage, Lysimachus, having armed about three thousand men, commenced unjustified hostilities. A certain Auranus led the way, although he was advanced in years and no less also in ignorance. ⁴¹Having known the attack of Lysimachus, some from the crowd took up stones and some stout pieces of wood, and some gathered up ashes at hand. They hurled them in utter confusion at those around Lysimachus. ⁴²For this reason the mob inflicted many casualties on them, and they slew some. All of them they drove to flight. Then they killed the temple robber himself near the treasury.

*The Sacrilege of Lysimachus and Menelaus*

⁴³A judgment against Menelaus began because of these events. ⁴⁴When the king arrived in Tyre, three men who were sent by the council of elders presented a speech of justification before him. ⁴⁵But Menelaus, who was defeated, already promised great wealth to Ptolemy of Dorymenes in order to persuade the king. ⁴⁶Therefore Ptolemy, taking aside the king to a certain peristyle as if for refreshing, changed his mind. ⁴⁷So, he acquitted Menelaus, the one responsible for all the wickedness, of the charges. But those miserable people who would be delivered if they were pleading with Scythopolis, these innocent ones he separated to death. ⁴⁸Therefore those who spoke out for cities and districts and sacred vessels quickly suffered this unjust penalty. ⁴⁹For this reason, despising the wickedness, even the Tyrians provided magnificently for their funeral. ⁵⁰But Menelaus, who committed great treachery against the citizens continuing to cling to wickedness, remained in office because of the greediness of those in power.

Jason<br>Reasserts<br>Himself **5** Now about this time, Antiochus went on a second departure into Egypt. [2] It happened that throughout the entire city for almost forty days, horsemen having raiment interwoven with gold appeared running through the air and being fully armed by cohorts with spears [3] and waving swords. And troops of horses were set in array, and they were making attacks and counter attacks from both sides. And there was a brandishing of shields and an abundance of wrought weapons and flights of arrows and the shining forth of golden ornaments and manifold breastplates. [4] Therefore everyone was praying that the manifestation might be for good.

[5] Now a false report spread that Antiochus had lost his life. Jason, taking no fewer than a thousand men, made a sudden attack upon the city and those upon the wall were driven back. And at last, as the city was being overrun, Menelaus fled to the citadel. [6] And Jason unsparingly carried out a slaughter of his fellows of the city, not recognizing that military success with regard to kin is the greatest loss. Indeed, he seemed to be storing up trophies from enemies and not from his own people. [7] He did not take possession of the office of high priest. Instead, he passed by the completion of his plot, taking shame, namely another flight into the region of the Ammonites. [8] Finally he met an evil conclusion: Being shut in before Aretas, the tyrant of the Arabs, he succeeded in fleeing from city to city, though he was pursued and hated by everyone as a rebel against the laws and abhorred as the executioner of his country and citizens, he was driven into Egypt. [9] The one who banished many from his country was killed in a foreign land after having retired to the Lacedaemonians as if having found shelter with them on account of their kinship. [10] And the one who cast forth a multitude of unburied corpses was unlamented, and he had neither a funeral of any sort nor an ordinance of his fathers.

Pillage of<br>the Temple [11] But when it was made known to the king concerning the things that had happened, he assumed Judah was revolting. Therefore he broke camp and left Egypt, raging like a wild beast in his spirit. He took the city captive. [12] He also commanded his soldiers to slaughter without mercy those they happened upon and to slay those going up into the houses. [13] And there was the slaughter of young and old, the extermination of young men and women and children, and the butchery of both virgins and infants. [14] So in three full days, eighty thousand were lost, forty thousand who were slain by laws of hands, but no fewer than those were sold into slavery. [15] But not being satisfied with these things, he dared to enter into the most holy temple of all the earth, having as a guide Menelaus, who had become a betrayer even of the laws and of his country, [16] and took the sanctuary vessels with polluted hands, and with profane hands swept up the things being lifted up by many kings for the increase and glory and honor of the place. [17] And Antiochus was exalted in his thoughts, not realizing that the Master was briefly angry on account of the sins of those inhabiting the city. This is why punishment came to the place. [18] Now if it had not happened that they were involved in many sins, this one, upon advancing, would have been flogged immediately, diverted from his presumption just as Heliodorus was, who was sent by Seleucus the king for the inspection of the treasury. [19] For certainly the Lord did not choose the nation because of the place. Rather, he chose the place because of the nation. [20] Therefore even the place itself partook in the misfortunes that came upon the nation, afterward sharing in the benefits. And being overtaken by the wrath of the Almighty, it was restored again with all glory by the reconciliation of the great Master.

²¹Therefore Antiochus, after carrying off one thousand and eight hundred talents from the temple, departed swiftly into Antioch, imagining from his arrogance that he made the earth navigable and the open sea passable on account of the lifting up of his heart. ²²He also left magistrates to mistreat the nation. In Jerusalem he left Philip from the Phrygian nation, but he had a more barbarous manner than the one who appointed him. ²³In Gerizim he left Andronicus, and with these Menelaus, more wicked than the others. He lorded it over the citizens and had a hateful disposition toward the Judean citizens. ²⁴And he sent Apollonius the Mysian with an army of twenty-two thousand, commanding him to slaughter all those in manhood and to sell both the women and the boys. ²⁵Now this one, upon arriving in Jerusalem and pretending to be peaceful, kept his army in check until the holy day of the Sabbath. Then, finding the Judeans idle, he ordered those under him to take up arms. ²⁶And he stabbed all those coming because of the spectacle and, running into the city with his armed men, he appointed a great multitude. ²⁷But Judas, the one also called Maccabeus, was one of ten who were from there and who escaped. He lived in the mountains after the manner of wild beasts along with those with him and, eating the grass as food, they remained there in order to not share in the defilement.

**6** Now after not much time, the king sent an Athenian elder to compel the Judeans to depart from the laws of their fathers and to not live according to the laws of God, ²but to pollute themselves and even to call the temple in Jerusalem by the name of "Zeus who dwells on Olympus" and the one in Gerizim "Zeus the Guardian of Hospitality," just as those who inhabit the place happen to do. ³And the violence of wickedness was cruel and grievous in every respect. ⁴For the temple was being filled with debauchery and revelry by the Gentiles, who were carousing with companions and having sexual relations with women in the sacred enclosure and further, bringing inappropriate things inside. ⁵And the altar was filled with unlawful offerings, things forbidden by the laws. ⁶One could neither keep the Sabbath nor observe the festivals of the fathers nor even admit to being a Judean. ⁷By aid of bitter force they brought in the monthly day celebrating the king's birth by feasting on pagan sacrifices. And when the feast of Dionysus came, they were compelled to parade about while holding ivy for Dionysus. ⁸Then a decree went forth into the neighboring Greek cities, the city of Ptolemy suggesting it, that they observe the same policy against the Judeans and make them partake in pagan sacrifices, ⁹and to slaughter those who chose not to pass over to these Greek customs. Therefore one could see the actual misery that was present. ¹⁰For two women were brought forth because they circumcised their children. And after hanging the babies from the breasts of these two and publicly leading them around the city, they hurled them down from the wall. ¹¹And others who had run together into the caves nearby in order to observe the Sabbath secretly were revealed to Philip and burnt together because they held from reverently aiding themselves in accord with glory of the solemn day.

*Judaism*
*Repressed*

[12]So then, I beseech those reading this document not to be withdrawn because of these calamities, but to regard them as punishments, not for the destruction but rather for the training of our nation. [13]For to not permit much time to pass for those who act wickedly but instead to immediately incur the penalties is a sign of great kindness. [14]For as with the other nations, the Master waits with patience in order to punish them until they come to the filling up of the measure of their sins. He determined not to deal with us in this manner [15]in order that he might not decide finally concerning us after our sins have reached to their totality. [16]Therefore he never sends away his compassion from us. Instead, though disciplining us with calamity, he does not forsake his own people. [17]In any case, let these things proclaimed by us serve as a reminder, and let us return post-haste to the tale.

[18]Eleazar, a certain man who held a place of honor among the scribes, already being advanced in age and the appearance of his face was excellent, was being forced to open his mouth and eat the flesh of pigs. [19]But accepting death with good repute rather than life with defilement, he voluntarily went upon the rack. [20]But he spat it out, for concerning such a thing, one must approach it in the way as those who are determined to steer clear of things unlawful to taste simply because of one's strong desire to live. [21]Now those appointed with the unlawful task of forcing him to eat the portions of the sacrifice, on account of their acquaintance from old times with the man, taking him aside privately, he called him to carry meat that belonged to him and was prepared by him in order to use it, and to pretend that he was eating the portions of the flesh from the sacrifice commanded by the king, [22]in order that by doing this he would be delivered from death and, on account of his longstanding friendship with them, would obtain clemency. [23]But he adopted honorable reasoning, even reasoning worthy of his age and of the dignity of old age and of his acquired and evident citizenship and of excellent behavior from childhood and more, appropriate for the holy and God ordained legislation, and he displayed it without hesitation, saying to send him on his way to the grave. [24]For he said, "It is not befitting of my age to pretend to do such a thing so that many of the youth might suppose that the ninety-year-old Eleazar has turned to adopt foreign customs, [25]and they, because of my hypocrisy, even to live a short and brief amount of time longer, might be led astray on account of me, and I might gain defilement and a stain on my old age. [26]For even if in the present I might be delivered from the punishment of humans, yet whether in life or in death, will I escape from the hands of the Almighty? [27]Therefore courageously quitting life now, I will be shown worthy of my old age, [28]and for the youth I shall have left behind an excellent example of how to die willingly and bravely for our solemn and sacred laws." Then, after saying such great things, he went immediately up onto the rack. [29]Those who were bearing goodwill toward him a little earlier now bore enmity because of the madness, as they supposed, of the words mentioned earlier. [30]Now, being about to die from the blows, groaning he said, "It is clear to the Lord who possesses holy knowledge that though I was able to be delivered from death, I endured the hard suffering in my body while being whipped, but in my soul I am suffering these things gladly because of my fear of Him."

³¹So then Eleazar died in this way, leaving behind his death as an example of noble character and a memorial of virtue not only for the youth, but also for the great many of the nation.

7 Now it came about that seven brothers with their mother were also arrested, forced by the king to taste of the unlawful swine flesh and being tortured with whips and cords. ²One of them, acting as representative, said, "Do you intend to ask and learn from us? For we are prepared to die rather than transgress the laws of our fathers." ³Then, becoming angry, the king commanded some to heat pans and cauldrons. ⁴And as soon as they were heated, he commanded some to cut out the tongue of the one who was their representative and, after scalping him, to cut off his hands and feet while the rest of the brothers and his mother were watching. ⁵After rendering him incapacitated for the remainder, the king commanded some to bring him still alive to the fire and to fry him in the pan. And as the vapor from the pan was giving widely, they were exhorting one another together with their mother to die bravely, speaking thusly, ⁶"The Lord God is watching and truly is compassionate to us, just as Moses made quite clear through the song of witness against the people to their face, saying,

*The Martyrdom of the Seven Brothers*

'And to his servants he will be compassionate.'"

⁷Now after the first died in this way, they brought the second for mocking and, tearing away the skin of his head with his hair, they began asking, "Will you eat rather than have your body be punished limb by limb?" ⁸But answering in the language of his fathers, he said, "No!" Therefore even this one received the next torment like the first. ⁹But when he came to his last breath, he said, "You demon! You remove us out of the present life, but the king of the world will raise us, because we die on account of his laws, to an eternal resurrection of life."

¹⁰Then, after this, they began abusing the third one and, being ordered, he thrust out his tongue quickly and boldly stretched out his hands. ¹¹And nobly he said, "He called these from heaven, and on account of his laws, I disregard them, and from him I hope to receive them again." ¹²Therefore the king himself and those with him were amazed at the spirit of the young man, that he made his sufferings as nothing.

¹³Now after this one died, they tormented also the fourth, torturing him in the same way. ¹⁴And being near to death, he said the following: "Those who die as a choice by humans expect from God the hope to be raised up again by him. But there will not be a resurrection to life for you."

¹⁵And as soon as they brought the fifth brother, they began torturing him. ¹⁶But he, looking toward him, said, "Having authority among humans, though being corruptible, you do what you want. But do not think our race to have been abandoned by God. ¹⁷Instead, you wait and see! His magnificent strength, how it will torture you and your seed!"

¹⁸And after this, they brought the sixth son and, being about to die, he said, "Do not deceive yourself more; for we suffer these things because of our own fault; because we sinned toward our God, things worthy of

astonishment have happened. [19]But you, do not suppose yourself to be innocent, for you have attempted to fight against God!"

[20]Now the mother was exceedingly good and worthy of a noble memorial. Witnessing seven sons die in the span of one day, she suffered courageously because of her hope in the Lord. [21]And being filled with a noble spirit and stirring up her womanly reasoning with manly fury, she exhorted each of the people in the language of their fathers, saying to them, [22]"I do not know how you appeared in my belly, nor did I give breath and life to you. Also, I did not arrange the elements of each of you. [23]Now then, the creator of the world, the one who formed the family of humanity and who devised the generation of all things, will with mercy restore to you again both your spirit and your life because now you are disregarding yourselves on account of his laws."

[24]But Antiochus, imagining he was being despised and suspecting her reproachful voice, began exhorting the youngest, being alive, yet not only with reasons but also with trustworthy oaths both to make him rich and to make him most blessed, even changing from the ways of his fathers; also to hold him as a friend and to entrust him with an office. [25]But because the young man paid absolutely no attention, the king, after summoning the mother, exhorted her to be an adviser of the boy for his salvation. [26]And after he exhorted many things, she agreed to persuade her son. [27]But, leaning over him, scoffing the cruel tyrant, she spoke to her son in their native language as follows: "Son, show mercy to me, the one who carried you in the womb nine months and suckled you three years and reared and brought you to this age and sustained you. [28]I beg you, child, look up at the heaven and the earth and, seeing all the things in them, know that God did not make them from things that are. Even the race of humans comes about in this manner. [29]You should not fear this executioner, but becoming worthy of your brothers, accept death so that by his mercy I might receive you again together with your brothers."

[30]While she was still speaking, the young man said, "Why do you wait? I do not obey the command of the king. Rather, I obey the command of the law that was given to our fathers by Moses. [31]But you, having become an inventor of all kinds of wickedness against the Hebrews, you shall not escape from the hands of God. [32]For we are suffering on account of our own sins. [33]And if for the sake of reproof and training our living Lord is briefly angered, he will also be reconciled again to his servants. [34]But you, O unholy and most vile of all men, be not exalted in vain, being puffed up by uncertain expectations, calling curses with a hand against the heavenly children. [35]For you have not yet escaped the judgment of the almighty, all-watching God. [36]For, now my brothers, those bearing a brief affliction, have fallen heir to everlasting life under God's covenant, but you, by the judgment of God, will bear the righteous penalties of arrogance. [37]But I, just as my brothers, offer up both body and good fortune for the laws of my fathers, calling upon God quickly to be merciful to our nation and with afflictions and scourgings to make you acknowledge that only He is God, [38]because of me and also my brothers to cause the wrath of the Almighty that has come justly upon our whole nation to cease." [39]Now becoming angry, the king dealt with this one worse than the others, feeling bitter

because of his scorn. ⁴⁰So then even this one died spotlessly, having trusted completely upon the Lord. ⁴¹And the mother of the sons died last.

⁴²Therefore make these things plain concerning the eating of pagan sacrifices and even to such a great extent the surpassing torture.

**8** Now Judas, the one also called Maccabeus, and those who secretly infiltrated the villages with him began summoning their relatives and receiving also those who had remained in Judaism; they collected close to six thousand people. ²And they began to call upon the Lord to watch over the people who were being oppressed by all nations and also to have pity on his temple, which was profaned by impious people, ³and also to show mercy to the city, which was being destroyed and was about to be leveled, and to give ear to the blood crying out to him, ⁴and also to remember the lawless destruction of the innocent children and the blasphemies which had come to his name and to hate the wicked. ⁵Now Maccabeus, having put together a garrison, was becoming by this time an overwhelming force against the Gentiles, the wrath of the Lord being changed into mercy. ⁶And coming suddenly, he set on fire cities and territories, even regaining the strategic places and putting to flight not a few of the enemy. ⁷He took especially advantage of the nights for these assaults, and the report of his daring courage began to be spread everywhere.

*Judas Maccabeus Revolts*

⁸Now Philip, seeing the man moving toward progress little by little and then making rapid progress in his military successes, wrote to Ptolemy, the governor of Coelesyria and Phoenicia, so that he might come to aid in the affairs of the king. ⁹Without delay he selected Nicanor, the son of Patroclus, one of the king's first friends, and sent him off to destroy all of Judah, placing under his command no fewer than twenty thousand people, Gentiles of all sorts. And they gathered to him also Gorgias, a man who was a military commander and who was well experienced in the affairs of war. ¹⁰Nicanor resolved to make up for the king the tribute to the Romans, which was two thousand talents, from the captivity of the Judeans. ¹¹Immediately he sent to the maritime cities, making invitation for a sale of Judean individuals, promising to sell ninety people for one talent. He did not anticipate the punishment from the Almighty that was about to follow upon him. ¹²But it became known to Judas concerning the plan of Nicanor and, upon sharing with those who were with him regarding the arrival of the army, ¹³those who were cowardly and did not believe in the justice of God began running away on their own and fleeing. ¹⁴But those who stayed were selling all the things that remained, and with one accord they began to beseech the Lord to rescue those who had been sold by the impious Nicanor before a meeting in battle. ¹⁵And if not on account of them, yet on account of the covenants with their fathers, and because of the invocation upon them of his solemn and magnificent name.

*Philip's Military Response to Judas*

¹⁶But Maccabeus, gathering together those who were around him, six thousand in number, called them not to be terror-stricken by their captives nor to be afraid of the great number of Gentiles who were wrongfully drawing near against them and to fight nobly, ¹⁷holding before their eyes the insolence that was done impiously by them in the holy place and the abuse of the ridiculed city and further, the dissolution of their ancestral citizenship. ¹⁸"For they trust both in weapons and courage," he said, "But we

*Judas Defeats Nicanor*

trust in the Almighty God, who is able to overtake with one nod even those who are coming against us and the whole world." [19]And he also rehearsed to them the support that came to their ancestors, specifically the event in the time of Sennacherib, when one hundred and eighty-five thousand perished, [20]and the battle that occurred in Babylon with the Galatians, when fully eight thousand went into the business together with four thousand Macedonians. When the Macedonians were desperate, the six thousand destroyed one hundred and twenty thousand thanks to the help that came to them from heaven, and they took a great deal of spoil. [21]Rendering them bold with such accounts and ready to die on behalf of the law and their homeland, he separated the army into four parts, [22]appointing as leaders of each unit his brothers, Simon and Joseph and Jonathan, placing under each one fifteen hundred soldiers. [23]And further, he also appointed Eleazar to read publicly the sacred book. Then, after giving as a watchword "By God's help," and the first unit being led by himself, he engaged in battle with Nicanor. [24]And the Almighty became their ally. They slew more than nine thousand of the enemy, and wounded and maimed the greater part of Nicanor's army in the limbs and compelled the whole force to flee. [25]And they took the money of those coming for the sale of them,[a] and, after pursuing them for some time, they returned, being restrained from the territory. [26]For it was the justice before the Sabbath, for which reason they did not continue pursuing them. [27]And, after collecting arms from them and stripping off the spoils of their enemies, they began celebrating the Sabbath, blessing exceedingly and acknowledging the Lord, the one who saved them for this day, appointing a beginning of mercy. [28]Now after the Sabbath, they divided from the spoils some for those who were tortured and for the widows and orphans, themselves dividing the rest and some for their children. [29]After they completed these things and made a common supplication, they entreated the merciful Lord to become reconciled completely with his own servants.

Judas Defeats Timothy and Bacchides

[30]And contending with those around Timothy and Bacchides, they slew more than twenty thousand of them and came into possession of several exceedingly high fortresses, and they divided the many spoils equally among themselves, even with those who were tortured and with the orphans and with the widows. And further, they also did this for the elderly. [31]Now, after collecting the arms from them, they laid up carefully everything in opportune places. But they carried the rest of the spoils to Jerusalem. [32]And they killed the leader of those around Timothy, a profane man and one who had troubled many Judeans. [33]Then, observing a triumphal procession in their country, they burned those who set on fire the sacred gates and Callisthenes, who had fled into one little house and received the reward worthy of his impiety. [34]The thoroughly evil Nicanor, the one who brought three thousand slave merchants for the sale of the Judeans, [35]being made low with the help of the Lord by those considered, according to him, to be insignificant; after casting off his glorious clothing and making himself alone through the interior in the manner of a runaway slave, he came to Antioch, having been successful above all in

---

[a] The sale is that of the anticipated captives as slaves (cf. 8:10–11)

the ruin of his army. ³⁶And the one who undertook to collect successfully the tribute for the Romans from the captivity of those in Jerusalem, proclaimed that the Judeans had a defender and because the Judeans were invulnerable this way, because they follow the laws commanded by him.

**9** Now around that time, Antiochus happened to have departed in dishonor from the places around Persia. ²Therefore he entered into the city called Persepolis and attempted to rob its temples and control the city. Wherefore then they turned to the aid of weapons and a great number hastened forth. And it happened that Antiochus, being put to flight, was forced by the inhabitants to leave in shame. ³Now, being at Ecbatana, the things that happened concerning Nicanor and those with Timothy became known to him. ⁴But, being stirred up by rage, he also determined to repay the Judeans the affliction received from those who had banished him. Therefore he ordered his charioteer to put down the journey to Jerusalem by driving without ceasing. And in truth, the judgment of heaven followed him, for he arrogantly said the following: "I will make Jerusalem a burial ground of Judeans when I arrive there." ⁵But the all-seeing Lord, the God of Israel, struck him with an incurable and unseen plague. And, just as he finished speaking, incurable pains in the bowels took hold of him, and piercing torments racked his inner parts. ⁶And this was altogether just for one who tortured the bowels of others in many strange ways. ⁷But he in no way ceased from his arrogance. Instead he was full even more of his arrogance, breathing fire in his rage against the Judeans and ordering his charioteer to hasten the journey. But it came about that he fell from his chariot as it was tearing along, his body flying in an uncontrolled way, and, upon landing, every part of his body was horribly tortured. ⁸So he who thinks himself equal to the waves of the sea because of his superhuman arrogance, and imagining he could set in a balance the heights of the mountains, was now coming down to earth and was being carried on a sedan, displaying clearly to everyone the power of God. ⁹Therefore, too, worms broke out of the body of the impious one and, living in pain and suffering, his flesh rotted away. And the whole army was repulsed by the decay, due to his smell. ¹⁰And the one who thought a little earlier he could take hold of the stars of heaven, no one was able to carry on account of the unbearable burden of his smell. ¹¹Then, therefore, being enfeebled, he began to cease from the excess of his arrogance and to come to knowledge by the divine plague, suffering more intensely pain every moment. ¹²And, not being able to tolerate his own smell, he said this: "It is right to submit to God, and no mortal being should think himself arrogant." ¹³Then the vile man prayed to the Master, who would no longer show him mercy, accordingly saying ¹⁴that the holy city, which he was hastening to come to level and to turn into a place of burial, he proclaimed free, ¹⁵but the Judeans, as he had determined them unworthy of burial, to be destroyed with their children by wild animals, he would make all of them as carrion for birds, just like the Athenians. ¹⁶And the holy temple, which he previously plundered, he would adorn with precious votive offerings, and he would restore many times more all the sacred vessels, and he would provide for the things designated for the sacrifices by contributing from his own funds. ¹⁷And, in addition

*Antiochus*
*Epiphanes'*
*Last Days*

to these things, he would also become Judean and go to every inhabited place proclaiming the power of God.

[18]But, the afflictions in no way lessening, for the righteous judgment of God came against him, he despaired with respect to his concerns and wrote to the Judeans the letter copied below, which possessed the appearance of supplication. Now it read as follows:

[19]"To the benevolent Judeans, who are free citizens: Many greetings and salutations and good wishes from Antiochus, the king and commander. [20]You and your children are faring well, and your affairs will be for you according to your will, having hope in heaven. [21]I remember lovingly your honor and kindness. Returning from the places around Persia, I also came down with a distressing illness, on account of which I have deemed it necessary to take care of the common security of all of you. [22]I am not despairing of my concerns but am holding out great hope of being freed from this illness. [23]And considering that even my father, concerning those occasions when he marched out to camp in the northern places, appointed one to succeed him, [24]so that, if anything unexpected should happen or even some difficulty should arise, those throughout the territory, they might not be troubled because they knew to whom he bequeathed the affairs of the state. [25]Now in addition to these things, because I recognize that the adjacent rulers and neighbors to the kingdom are waiting for opportunities and watching to see how this might turn out, I have appointed my son, Antiochus, as king, whom I entrusted and introduced to many of you as I hurried many times to the upper provinces. And I have written to him the things written down here. [26]Therefore, I exhort you and beseech you, as you remember your benefits in public and in private, that each one maintain your present good will toward me and to my son. [27]For I am persuaded that he, being established with my own policy, will deal with you mercifully and lovingly."

[28]So then, the murderer and blasphemer, having suffered the most awful things just as he dealt with others, turned over his life in the mountains in a foreign land. [29]Philip, who had been raised with him, began to carry the body home. He, though, feared the son of Antiochus and crossed over into Egypt to Ptolemy Philometor.

**10** Now Maccabeus and those with him, the Lord going before them, obtained the temple and the city. [2]They destroyed the altars that had been built by the foreigners in the marketplace and also the shrines. [3]And they purified the temple; they made another altar and, upon striking a fire with flint stones and taking some fire from these, they offered up sacrifices and incense and lit the lamps, and they performed the presentation of the loaves after a span of two years. [4]And after doing these things, they fell upon their bellies and besought the Lord, pledging to never again fall away to such evil, but instead, if ever they should sin, by him with gentleness, and not to be handed over to blasphemers and barbarous Gentiles. [5]Now it happened on the day in which the temple was defiled by the foreigners, on that same day, the purification of the temple was made, the twenty-fifth of the same month, Chislev. [6]And they observed with cheer eight days in the manner of the Feast of Tabernacles, remembering how a little before, during the Feast of Tabernacles, they were grazing on the mountains and in the caves like wild animals. ⁷Therefore, holding ivy wreathed wands and branches with ripe fruit and still also date palm fronds, they were thankful to the one who helped to cleanse his own place. ⁸And with a common ordinance and vote, they decreed to the entire nation of the Judeans to observe ten days every year.

⁹So in this way the things concerning Antiochus, who was called Epiph- *Antiochus* anes, came to an end. ¹⁰Now we will discuss the things concerning Antiochus, *Eupator's Rise* the highest official, who was the son of the impious one, summarizing the *to Power* evils of the cities succinctly. ¹¹For this one, after inheriting the kingdom, appointed a certain Lysias over the affairs of state and prime governor of Coelesyria and Phoenicia. ¹²For Ptolemy, who was called Macron, preferred to act righteously with respect to the Judeans on account of the injustice that had come toward them and was continually seeking to manage matters with them peacefully. ¹³For this reason he was accused by the friends of Eupator, and he heard on all sides he was a traitor because he forsook Cyprus, having been entrusted with it by Philometor, and went over to Antiochus Epiphanes. And because he did not honorably exercise his noble office, he ended his life by giving himself poison.

¹⁴So Gorgias became the commander of these places. He hired mer- *Gorgias in* cenaries and, at every opportunity, stoked the feud toward their own. *Idumea* ¹⁵And, along with these, the Edomites, being in possession of strategically important fortresses, were harassing the Judeans and were welcoming those banished from Jerusalem, intentionally keeping up the feud. ¹⁶But those around Maccabeus, after making supplication and beseeching God to be allied with them, moved against the fortresses of the Edomites. ¹⁷And fiercely attacking them, they came into possession of these places, both defending themselves against all those who were fighting upon the wall and killing those who were attacking them. So they killed no fewer than twenty thousand. ¹⁸And no fewer than nine thousand took refuge in two very well fortified towers, and they possessed all the things necessary for a siege. ¹⁹Maccabeus himself, after abandoning Simon and Joseph and also Zacchaeus and those with him enough for the siege of the towers, departed for more pressing places. ²⁰Now those with Simon who were fond of money were persuaded by some of those in the towers. After receiving seventy thousand drachmas in silver, they permitted some to escape. ²¹But reporting to Maccabeus concerning what had happened, he gathered together the leaders of the people and told how they had sold their kinsfolk for silver by releasing their enemies against them. ²²Therefore, he slew those who became traitors and immediately overtook the two towers. ²³Succeeding at arms in everything in his hands, he killed more than twenty thousand in the two fortresses.

²⁴Now Timothy, who first was defeated by the Judeans, gathered *Judas Defeats* together foreign forces of vast size and assembled no small cavalry force, *Timothy* which came from Asia, and drew near as if to take Judah in war. ²⁵And as he approached, those around Maccabeus made supplication to God, sprinkling their heads with dirt and girding their loins with sackcloth. ²⁶Falling at the base before the altar, they were beseeching the one who was merciful to them to be at enmity with their enemies and to be an adversary to those who were being adversaries, just as also the law makes clear. ²⁷Then,

upon coming from the prayer, taking up their weapons, they advanced away from the city at a great distance. And drawing near to the enemy, they stopped. ²⁸And shortly before the dawn spread, they attacked each other; those, then, who have a surety of success and victory by aid of virtue, which is in the Lord; and the others, the leader of their efforts appointing their fury. ²⁹Now as the battle became fierce, five illustrious men upon horses with golden bridles appeared from heaven before opposing forces, and two were leading the Judeans. ³⁰And taking Maccabeus in the middle of them and sheltering him with their own armor, they were keeping him safe from harm. But they were repeatedly sending arrows and lightning toward the those opposite on account of which they were breached, being thrown into confusion with blindness and being completely disordered. ³¹And twenty thousand and five hundred soldiers and six hundred cavalry were slain.

³²But Timothy himself took refuge in a very good stronghold called Gazara; Chaereas commanded a fortress there. ³³And those with Maccabeus gladly besieged the fortress forty days. ³⁴But those within the fortress, trusting beyond measure in the strength of the place, were blaspheming and uttering godless words. ³⁵Now when the twenty-fifth day dawned, young men from those with Maccabeus, burning with rage on account of the blasphemies, attacked the wall bravely; and with savage fury they were slaughtering any who fell upon them. ³⁶Then, because of the distraction, others in like manner climbed up the towers and set fire to the inside and, kindling a fire, they were burning the blasphemers alive. But some others breached the gates and, gathering the rest of the army, they captured the city. ³⁷And they slew Timothy, who was hiding in a certain cistern, and Chaereas, the brother of this one, and also Apollophanes. ³⁸And when these things were completed, they began blessing the Lord, who showed exceeding kindness to Israel and gave the victory to them with hymns and thanksgiving.

*Lysias and the Siege of Beth-zur*

**11** Now after a very little time, Lysias, the guardian and relative of the king and the official over the affairs of state, being very displeased at the things that had happened, ²gathered about eighty thousand soldiers and cavalry in all and went to the Judeans, intending to make the city of Jerusalem a Greek city, ³and to make the temple subject to a levy just as the other shrines of other nations, and to put up the high priesthood for sale every year. ⁴He reckoned with in no way, however, the power of God, but was puffed up by the tens of thousands of foot soldiers and the thousands of horsemen and the eighty elephants. ⁵So after entering into Judah and drawing near to Beth-zur, being a fortified village about five measures away from Jerusalem, he began afflicting this town. ⁶But when those with Maccabeus heard of hisᵃ besieging the strongholds, they were beseeching together with the multitudes the Lord with lamentations and tears to send a good angel for salvation in Israel. ⁷Maccabeus himself first took up his weapons. He urged the others at the same time to make a desperate attempt with him to come to the aid of their kinfolk. And so with one accord they rushed out willingly. ⁸And there, while they were near Jerusalem, appeared one going before them on horseback in

ᵃ That is, Lysias

brilliant raiment brandishing golden weaponry. ⁹Then, with one accord, everyone blessed the merciful God, and they were encouraged in their souls, being prepared not only to attack humans but savage beasts and walls made of iron. ¹⁰They advanced in their armor, having their ally from heaven, because the Lord showed mercy on them. ¹¹And hurling toward their enemies, like lions they slew eleven thousand of them and sixteen hundred horsemen, and they forced all of them to flee. ¹²But the majority of them escaped wounded and unarmed. And even Lysias himself escaped by fleeing shamefully.

¹³Now Lysias was not without understanding. As he reflected to himself concerning the loss that came about for him, he realized the Hebrews were unconquerable because their powerful God was allied with them, sending them off. ¹⁴He convinced them to agree to everything righteous and that he would also persuade the king, compelling him to become a friend with them. ¹⁵So Maccabeus, considering that which was beneficial, consented to everything that Lysias proposed, for as much as Maccabeus gave to Lysias in writing concerning the Judeans, the scribe granted. ¹⁶Therefore, letters written to the Judeans from Lysias contained this content: *Lysias' Peace with the Judeans*

"Lysias to the multitude of the Judeans: Greetings. ¹⁷John and Absalom, those sent from you, delivered the petition copied below and are asking about the terms made known in it. ¹⁸So then, I made quite clear as much as was necessary to report to the king, and he granted what was possible. ¹⁹Therefore, if you observe good will toward the affairs of the state, then from now on I shall attempt to be partially responsible for your good. ²⁰Now concerning every part of these things, I have commanded both these men and those from me to discuss them with you. ²¹Be well. The hundred and forty-eighth year on the twenty-fourth day of the month of Zeus of Corinth."

²²The letter of the king contained the following:

"King Antiochus to his brother Lysias: Greetings. ²³Our father, having made his transition to the gods, and since we wish that those who are of the kingdom be undisturbed as regards the care of the Judeans, ²⁴having heard the Judeans are not consenting to the change of our father for the Greek customs, but are choosing their own customs, they beseech that their laws should be granted to them. ²⁵So then, preferring that even this nation exist without trouble, we determine both their temple be restored to them and they live as citizens according to the customs of their forefathers. ²⁶Therefore, you will do well to send messages to them and give our pledges of good faith, so that, knowing our policy, they might be both cheerful and might live gladly with the management of their own affairs."

²⁷The letter of the king to the nation was as follows:

"King Antiochus, to the council of the elders of the Judeans and to the other Judeans: Greetings. ²⁸Are you well? May it be as we wish. We ourselves are also well. ²⁹Menelaus explained to us that you were wishing to return to deal with your own affairs. ³⁰Therefore, pledges of good faith with safe conduct will be in effect for those who return home before the thirtieth of Xanthicus. ³¹For the Judeans are to deal with their own expenses and laws, just as even formerly, and none of them will be troubled in any manner for things done in ignorance. ³²Now I have sent also Menelaus, who will strengthen you. ³³Be well. The hundred and forty-eighth year on the fifteenth of Xanthicus."

³⁴Even the Romans sent a letter to them, having the following content:

"Quintus Memmius and Titus Manius, ambassadors of the Romans, to the Judean people: Greetings. ³⁵Concerning the things that Lysias, the cousin of the king, granted to you, we also give our consent. ³⁶Now, concerning those things he thought to report to the king, send someone immediately, after making an examination concerning these things, in order that we might hold as is satisfactory to us, for we are drawing near to Antioch. ³⁷Therefore, hasten and send some envoys to us, so that we also might find out what you have decided. ³⁸Be well. The hundred and forty-eighth year on the fifteenth of Xanthicus."

*Incidents and Joppa and Jamnia*

**12** Now when these agreements were settled, Lysias went to the king while the Judeans went about farming. ²But the governors in every place, Timothy and Apollonius the son of Gennaeus, and further, Hieronymus and Demophon, and with these Nicanor, the governor of Cyprus, were not allowing them to be stable and to observe peace. ³And the people of Joppa accomplished so great an impiety as inviting those Judeans who dwelt among themselves to embark with their women and children in boats that were equipped by them as if there were no ill will toward them. ⁴And this was after the public decree of the city. And when the Judeans accepted, as wanting to live in peace and having no suspicion, they were brought and drowned, being no fewer than two hundred people. ⁵Now Judas, after hearing about the cruelty that had happened to the people of his own race, summoned the men around him ⁶and, invoking the righteous judge, God, approached those murderers of his brothers. He set fire to their harbor at night and burned the boats and massacred those who took refuge in that place. ⁷Now the village was shut tight. He departed, planning to come again and root out the entire body of citizens of Joppa. ⁸But upon hearing that those in Jamnia were also wishing to accomplish the same action against the Judeans dwelling among them, ⁹falling upon the Jamnites at night, he set fire to their harbor together with their fleet so that brightness of the light shone on Jerusalem, although it was two hundred and forty stadia away.

*Judas Attacked*

¹⁰And departing from that place about nine stadia, while making the journey toward Timothy, no fewer than five thousand Arabians and five hundred cavalrymen lay upon him. ¹¹So a fierce battle broke out, and those who were with Judas were successful because of help from God. Being diminished, the nomads began beseeching Judas to give pledges of good faith to them. They were promising also to give them cattle and to assist them in other ways. ¹²Now Judas, supposing them as really useful in many ways, withdrew the peace to be made with them and, after receiving the pledges, they went back to their tents.

¹³Then he also fell upon a certain city, bridging over that which was fortified and enclosed with walls and inhabited by a variety of Gentile peoples. And its name was Caspin. ¹⁴But those within, trusting in the strength of its walls and in their store of food, began treating those with Judas rudely, harshly criticizing them and, even more, blaspheming and saying what is not lawful to say. ¹⁵But those with Judas, after invoking the great ruler of

the universe who, without battering rams and devices serving as instruments of war, threw down Jericho in the times of Joshua, savagely attacked the wall. ¹⁶And overtaking the city by the will of God, they carried out a massive slaughter, so that the adjacent lake, which had a width of two stadia, appeared to be filled, running with blood.

¹⁷And having moved away from there about seven hundred and fifty stadia, they arrived in Charax and came to the Judeans there called the Toubiani. ¹⁸Now they did not overtake Timothy in those places, who had departed by that time without success from those places, but had left a very well fortified garrison in a certain place. ¹⁹But Dositheus and Sosipater, who were commanders with Maccabeus, marched out and destroyed those who were left behind in the stronghold by Timothy, more than ten thousand men. ²⁰And Maccabeus, after he organized the army with him by cohorts, appointed them over the units and hastened toward Timothy, who had with him one hundred and twenty thousand foot soldiers and two thousand horsemen, also with seven thousand. ²¹And hearing of the approach of Judas, Timothy sent away the women and the other members of the household to the place called Carnaim, for it was hard to take by siege, and the place was difficult to access because of the narrowness of all of the places. ²²But when Judas' first division appeared, fear came upon their enemies, and fear came upon them from the manifestation of the one who beholds all things. They hastened to flee, being borne along here and there, so that many times they were hurt by their own comrades, and they were pierced by the points of their own swords. ²³And Judas was making a most vigorous pursuit, putting the wicked to the sword. And he killed thirty thousand men in number. ²⁴Now Timothy himself fell into the hands of those with Dositheus and Sosipater. He was entreating them with much trickery to set him free as unharmed because he indeed held the parents of many of them and the brothers of others, and it would happen that no regard would be paid to these. ²⁵And after he, by means of much pleading, established his oath to restore these prisoners unharmed, they released him for the sake of the deliverance of their brothers.

*Judas Prevails Over Timothy*

²⁶Then, heading out toward Carnaim and the temple of Atargatis, Judas slew twenty-five thousand people. ²⁷And after the rout and destruction of these, he also made war upon Ephron, a fortified city in which was a multitude of ethnicities within it. And young men who were strong of body, having taken positions before the walls, were resisting fiercely. They had there many provisions of engines of war and missiles. ²⁸And calling upon the ruler who, with might, crushes the weight of his enemies, they took the city in hand. And they slew in number twenty-five thousand of those within the city. ²⁹And departing from that place, they hastened on to the city of Scythopolis, which was a distance of six hundred stadia from Jerusalem. ³⁰But when the Judeans who were established in that place testified to the kindness that the people of Scythopolis had toward them and to their civilized response in times of misfortune, ³¹they gave thanks and exhorted them as well to be well disposed to their race from then on. They arrived in Jerusalem as the Feast of Weeks was imminent.

*A String of Victories for Judas*

³²Now after the feast, which is called Pentecost, they moved against Gorgias, the commander of Idumea. ³³And he came out with three thousand

*Judas Defeats Gorgias*

foot soldiers and four hundred horsemen. ³⁴And as they engaged the battle, it happened that a few of the Judeans fell. ³⁵But Dositheus, a certain ferocious cavalry man from those under Bacenor, took hold of Gorgias and, taking his cloak, he was bringing him by force, wishing to take the accursed one alive. But when one of the Thracian horsemen attacked him and cut off his arm, Gorgias fled to Mareshah. ³⁶Now when those with Esdris had been fighting a long time and were weary, Judas called upon the Lord to appear as their ally and appear as leader in the battle. ³⁷Then he began bellowing out with hymns in the language of his fathers, suddenly attacking those with Gorgias. He made a rout of them.

*Remembering the Fallen* ³⁸Now Judas, after regathering the army, went into the city of Adullam. And the Sabbath was upon them, so purifying themselves, in accordance with custom, he kept the Sabbath there. ³⁹But the next day, those with Judas went to pick up the bodies of those who had fallen, because of the time it had become necessary, and to restore them to the tombs of their fathers with kin. ⁴⁰But they discovered under the shirts of each of those who died amulets of the idols from Jamnia. The law kept the Judeans away from these. And it became clear to everyone that on account of this reason these men had fallen. ⁴¹Then everyone, after blessing the ways of the righteous judge, the Lord, who makes visible the things that have been hidden, ⁴²turned to supplication, entreating God that the sin that had come about be covered completely. And the noble Judas exhorted the multitude to keep themselves to be sinless, having seen with their eyes*a* the things that had come about on account of the sin of those who had fallen. ⁴³And after he made a collection of men, he sent off two thousand drachmas of silver to Jerusalem to offer a sacrifice for sin. He acted entirely rightly and honorably, considering about the resurrection. ⁴⁴For unless he expected those who had fallen to rise, to pray concerning corpses would be useless and silly. ⁴⁵And if he was considering the greatest gratitude that is reserved for those who fall asleep with godliness, the thought was holy and pious. Therefore, he made atonement for those who had died to be delivered from their sin.

*The Death of Menelaus* **13** Now in the one hundred and forty-ninth year, it became known to those with Judas that Antiochus Eupator came against Judah with a large force. ²And Lysias, his guardian and the official over the affairs of state, was with him. Each had a force of Greek foot soldiers numbering one hundred and ten thousand and five thousand and three hundred cavalry and twenty-two elephants and three hundred chariots bearing scythes. ³Then also Menelaus met with them and with great hypocrisy encouraged Antiochus, not for salvation of the country, but because he was imagining that he might be appointed to some office. ⁴But the King of kings stirred up the anger of Antiochus against the sinner, and, after Lysias pointed out that this one was responsible for the evils and everything, he commanded to bring him into Beroea to put him to death however is customary in that place. ⁵And there is in that place a tower fifty cubits high, full of ashes. But it had a steep contrivance surrounding it on all sides going down into the ashes. ⁶There the whole community pushes one who is liable for sacrilege

---

*a* Lit. "sight"

or those guilty of other excessive evils to their destruction. [7]So it happened that the lawless one, Menelaus, died such a death and did not happen to have a burial. [8]This was altogether just for, given that he performed many sins with respect to the altar, of which the fire and the ashes were holy, he received his death in ashes.

[9]Now the king, having become weighed down, was coming with inten- *The Battle* tions to exhibit against the Judeans things worse than those that had come *Near Modein* about in the time of his father. [10]But when Judas heard of these things, he commanded the people, who called upon the Lord through the day and night, that if ever at any time before, even now he might come to aid [11]those about to be deprived of the law and country and holy temple and to not allow the people who had revived now briefly to come into the hands of those blasphemous Gentiles. [12]So after everyone made the same petition with one accord and besought the merciful Lord with weeping and fasting, continually lying prostrate for three days, after encouraging them, Judas urged them to stand by. [13]And being with the elders, privately he planned to go out and settle the matter with the help of God before the army of the king entered upon Judah and came into possession of the city. [14]And giving the outcome to the Lord of the universe, he exhorted those with him to fight to the death bravely for the laws, the temple, the city, their country, and their way of life. And he set up the army near Modein. [15]And after giving those with him an agreed upon signal of "the victory of God," with the bravest, chosen young men, he fell at night upon the camp of the royal court. He slew two thousand men in number, and he placed the leader of the elephants along with the one who was in its accompanying house. [16]And the result was that they filled the camp with fear and confusion, and they escaped, being successful. [17]And this came about before the day dawned because the protection of the Lord came to aid him.

[18]But the king, having taken a taste of the courage of the Judeans, made *Antiochus* an attempt on their places by means of stratagems. [19]And he went up *Eupator* against Beth-zur, a small fortress of the Judeans. He was put to flight, was *Makes a* struck, and was defeated. [20]Then Judas sent necessities to those within *Treaty* the fortress. [21]And Rhodocus, who was from the Judeans' ranks, reported secrets to their enemies. He was sought for, arrested, and put in prison. [22]The king spoke a second time with those in Beth-zur. He gave and received a pledge of good faith, went away, [23]attacked those with Judas, and was defeated. He received notice that Philip, the one who had been left over the affairs of state, had abandoned him in Antioch. Being confounded, he summoned the Judeans, surrendered, and swore for all their legal rights. He came to a settlement and brought a sacrifice. He honored the temple and treated the place kindly. [24]And he accepted Maccabeus. He left Hegemonides as commander from Ptolemais to the regions of the Gerar. [25]He went to Ptolemais. The people of Ptolemais were angry concerning the agreements, for they were afraid beyond measure and wanted to break the arrangements. [26]Lysias came to the step and pleaded to the best of his ability and persuaded and pacified them and made them well disposed to the terms. He returned to Antioch. The things related to the king's invasion and retreat turned out in this manner.

**14** Now, after a period of three years, it became known to those with Judas that Demetrius, the son of Seleucus, had entered into Tripolis through the harbor with a mighty army and a fleet. ²Having taken possession of the territory, he slew Antiochus and his guardian, Lysias. ³Now a certain Alcimus, who was formerly the high priest, but who had defiled himself willingly during the times of purity, after he realized that for him there was no deliverance in any way and no further service before the holy altar, ⁴came to King Demetrius around the one hundred and fifty-first year, bringing to him a golden crown and a date palm and, in addition to these items, those considered as young shoots from the temple. And he held his peace at that time. ⁵But he received an opportunity for furthering his folly when he was summoned to the council by Demetrius and asked about what arrangement and plan the Judeans had established. Concerning these things he said, ⁶"Those of the Judeans who are called Hasideans, whom Judas Maccabeus leads, are keeping up the feud and stirring sedition. They are not allowing the kingdom to be at peace. ⁷Hence, separating myself from my ancestral glory—and saying, concerning the high priesthood—I have now come a second time. ⁸First, on account of thinking of what is due genuinely to the king, and second, also having regard for my fellow citizens, for the entirety of our race suffers no small misfortune by the recklessness of those mentioned above. ⁹You, O king, knowing each one of these things, observed the territory and our sorely tried race in accordance with that courteous benevolence you have toward all. ¹⁰For as long as Judas lives, it is impossible that the affairs of state will be at peace." ¹¹Now, after such things had been spoken by this one, at once the rest of the king's friends, who viewed with malice the things concerning Judas, incensed Demetrius even more. ¹²So he immediately selected Nicanor, who was the commander of the elephants, and, proclaiming him the commander of Judah, he dispatched him, ¹³giving him messages to kill Judas and to scatter those with him and appoint Alcimus as the high priest of the great temple. ¹⁴But those in Judah who had fled from Judas, the Gentiles, joined forces with Nicanor in droves, supposing the misfortunes and calamities of the Judeans would be their own prosperity.

¹⁵Now upon hearing of the approach of Nicanor and the attack from the Gentiles, the Judeans were sprinkling dirt upon themselves, entreating the one who established his own people until eternity and who helps always his own portion with an intervention. ¹⁶Then, after the one who was leading commanded, immediately breaking camp from that place, they met with their enemy near the village of Lessaou. ¹⁷Now Simon, the brother of Judas had joined battle with Nicanor and had slowly fallen back because of the stunning shock of their adversaries. ¹⁸Nevertheless, Nicanor, hearing of the bravery and the courage that those with Judas had in their struggles on behalf of their country, was somewhat worried about determining the judgment by means of bloodshed. ¹⁹Therefore he sent Posidonius and Theodotus and Mattithiah to offer and to receive pledges of good faith. ²⁰And after a thorough inspection of these matters was made and the one who was leading took counsel with the rest of his forces and equal voting concession was reached, they consented to the terms. ²¹And they appointed a day in which, in private, they would come to the same mind. And a chariot

advanced from each, and they set up seats. ²²Judas set prepared armed men in strategic places, in case treachery suddenly came about from their enemies, and they held a suitable conference. ²³Nicanor remained in Jerusalem and did nothing inappropriate. In fact, he sent away those mobs of people who had gathered around him. ²⁴He had even Judas continually in his face; he was genuinely inclined toward the man. ²⁵He exhorted him to marry and have children. He married, settled down, and participated in the common life.

²⁶But Alcimus, seeing their favor toward one another and taking the agreements that were made, he went to Demetrius and was saying to him that Nicanor was pondering hostilities against the state, for he appointed Judas, that plotter against the kingdom, as his deputy. ²⁷So the king, becoming angry and being provoked by the false accusations of the scoundrel, wrote to Nicanor on account of the agreements, saying he was displeased and ordering him to send Maccabeus in bonds to Antioch immediately. ²⁸Now when these things became known to Nicanor, he was troubled and began pondering grievously if he ought to reject the things agreed upon, for the man had done nothing wrong. ²⁹But since he was not able to act against the king, he began looking for a good time to accomplish by trickery. ³⁰But Maccabeus, perceiving Nicanor was managing the affairs with him more harshly, and was being more rude in their customary meeting, understood the gruff behavior was not from the best of motives. So, gathering together no small number of those with him, he hid himself from Nicanor.

*Nicanor Betrays Judas*

³¹Now when the other one*ᵃ* became aware that he had been excellently out strategized by the man, he went to the great and holy temple while the priests were offering the appropriate sacrifices. He commanded them to hand over the man. ³²But since they were swearing with oaths not to know where the one being sought was at any time, ³³he stretched forth his right hand toward the temple and swore these things: "If you do not hand over Judas to me in bonds, then I will make this shrine of God into a plain, and I will raze the altar to the ground and raise up a marvelous temple here for Dionysus." ³⁴Then, after saying such great threats, he departed. But the priests stretched forth their hands to heaven and called upon the continual defender of our nation and were saying these things: ³⁵"You, Lord of all, are not in need of possessions. You were pleased to establish a temple for your dwelling among us. ³⁶And now, O Holy One, Lord of all holiness, preserve undefiled into eternity this recently purified house."

³⁷Now a certain Razis, one of the elders from Jerusalem, was slandered before Nicanor. The man was a patriot and very well spoken of and, on account of his kindness, was called "father of the Judeans." ³⁸For in those earlier times of purity he was hauled to judgment for Judaism and risked with all zeal body and soul on behalf of Judaism. ³⁹Now Nicanor, wishing to make clear the ill will that he held toward the Judeans, sent more than five hundred soldiers to arrest him. ⁴⁰For he supposed by arresting that man, a calamitous thing would be done to them. ⁴¹But when the multitude were about to overtake the tower and were breaking down the door

*The Death of Razis*

---

*ᵃ* The "other one" is Nicanor

of the courtyard and calling to bring fire and to set fire to the doors, since he was surrounded on every side, he*a* fell upon his own sword, ⁴²wanting to die nobly rather than to fall into wicked hands and to be abused in a way unworthy of his own nobility. ⁴³But, because of the heat of the battle, the blow did not hit exactly. So, as the troops were charging into the doorways, he ran bravely upon the wall. He courageously threw himself down into the mobs. ⁴⁴But, when they quickly stepped back, an open space was created, and he came down into the middle of the space. ⁴⁵And being still alive and burning with fury, he stood up, blood gushing out like a spring and his wounds being grievous. He went through the troops, running, and stood up on a certain rocky precipice. ⁴⁶Being by this time completely drained of blood, he tore out his intestines and, taking them in each of his hands, flung them at the troops and called upon the one who is the Lord of life and of the spirit to restore it to him again. In this manner he died.

*Nicanor's Arrogant Blasphemy* **15** Now when Nicanor heard that those with Judas were in the places of Samaria, he resolved to fall upon them with all safety on the day of repose. ²But those Judeans who were accompanying him on account of force were saying, "You should certainly not kill cruelly and barbarously in this manner. But set apart in honor the day that has been honored above others with holiness by the one who observes everything." ³The thrice-guilty man inquired whether there is a ruler in heaven who had commanded to observe the day of the Sabbath. ⁴And they declared, "The living Lord himself is the ruler in heaven. He gave the command to keep the seventh day." ⁵Nicanor said, "And I, the one who gives the command to take up arms and to accomplish the royal business, am a ruler upon the earth." Nevertheless, he did not succeed in completing his wicked intention.

*Judas Rallies the Judeans* ⁶And Nicanor, showing off with all steadfastness, decided to make a public way from those with Judas. ⁷Maccabeus, on the other hand, was fully trusting, with all hope, to obtain help from the Lord. ⁸And he exhorted those with him not to fear the approach of the Gentiles, but, bearing in mind the assistance from heaven that had previously come to them, also to expect, with respect to the current situation, the victory from the Almighty would be theirs. ⁹And, by encouraging them from the law and the prophets, singing next to them of the battles that they had already fought, he made them more zealous. ¹⁰So, after rousing their spirits, he gave them orders, pointing out at the same time the faithlessness of the Gentiles and the breach of their oaths. ¹¹So he armed each of them, not with the safety of shields and spears, but with the encouragement in his good words. And he led toward a trustworthy dream on behalf of some and cheered everyone. ¹²And the spectacle of this was as follows: Onias, the one who was the high priest, an excellent and good man, modest in his demeanor and meek in his manner, and whose speech was full of grace and who had studied from childhood everything concerning the matters peculiar to virtue, this man stretched forth his hands in order to pray earnestly for the entire community of the Judeans. ¹³Then a man appeared in this manner: He excelled in old age and honor, and the dignity about him was a certain wonder and majesty. ¹⁴And responding, Onias said, "This is one who loves his kin,

---

*a* Razis is the implied subject

Jeremiah, the prophet of God, who prays much for the people and the holy city." ¹⁵Then, stretching forth his right hand, Jeremiah gave a golden sword to Judas and, while giving it, he spoke as follows: ¹⁶"Take this holy sword, a gift from God, by which you will smite your enemies."

¹⁷So, after being strengthened by the words of Judas, which were altogether excellent and able to stir up virtue and to make manly the souls of youths, they determined not to wage a war, but to rush in bravely and with all courage engage in order to decide matters, because the city and the holy things and the temple were at risk. ¹⁸For their fear for the women and children, and further for their brothers and relatives, was weighing on them in smaller part, and their greatest and first fear was for the consecrated temple. ¹⁹But there was also no small anxiety for those who were cooped up in the city, being troubled about the attack in the open air.

²⁰And, while everyone was already waiting for the judgment that would happen and their enemies had drawn near already and the army was lined up and the beasts had been brought into strategic position on the line and the cavalry was in place at the flank, ²¹Maccabeus, considering the arrival of the multitude and the manifold equipment of their arms and the savageness of the beasts, for the seasonable part, he lifted up hands to heaven. He called upon the wonder-working Lord, knowing that it is not by means of weapons, but, just as if it might be determined by him, he brings about the victory for those who are worthy. ²²And calling out, he was speaking in this way: "You, Master, sent your angel to Hezekiah, the king of Judah, and slew in number one hundred and eighty five thousand from the camp of Sennacherib. ²³And now, O Ruler of the heavens, send a good angel before us for fear and trembling. ²⁴May those who are coming against your holy people with blasphemy be terrified by the greatness of your strength." And this one ceased praying with these words.

²⁵Now those with Nicanor began advancing with trumpet blasts and battle cries. ²⁶Then those with Judas engaged their enemies with an invocation and prayers. ²⁷So fighting with their hands and praying in their hearts to God, they slew no fewer than thirty-five thousand, being cheered greatly by the care of God.

²⁸Now, after bringing an end to the business, and while departing with joy, they discovered Nicanor, who had fallen with his suit of armor. ²⁹So, after some shouting and confusion came about, they began blessing the Lord in the language of their fathers. ³⁰And the foremost fighter on behalf of his countrymen, in keeping with everything in his body and soul, the one who reserved the kindness of the prime of his life for his people, commanded them to cut off the head of Nicanor and a hand together with the shoulder, bringing them to Jerusalem. ³¹And after arriving there and inviting the people and setting up the priests before the altar, he summoned those from the Akra. ³²And after displaying the head of the vile Nicanor and the hand of the blasphemer, which he boasted with when he stretched it out against the holy house of the Almighty, ³³and, after cutting out the tongue of the impious Nicanor, he was saying by pieces to the birds but the wages of his folly would hang opposite the temple. ³⁴Then everyone blessed the distinguished Lord in heaven, saying, "Blessed be the one who preserved his own place undefiled." ³⁵So he hung the decapitated head of

*The Defeat and Death of Nicanor*

Nicanor from the Akra, a clear and visible sign to everyone of the help of the Lord. ³⁶And everyone decreed with a public proposal not to allow this day to go unnoticed but to hold it as a marked day, the thirteenth of the twelfth month, named Adar in the master language, one day before the day of Mordecai.

*The Compiler's Epilogue*     ³⁷So the things concerning Nicanor turned out in this manner. And from those times, the city was ruled over by the Hebrews. And I will bring to a close myself this account at this point. ³⁸And if it was good and compelling in its composition, this I was also wanting myself. But if it was poor and mediocre, this was what was attainable by me. ³⁹Just as drinking wine by itself, and, for that matter, also again water, can be unpleasant, yet, wine, after being mixed in its custom with water, already and renders a delightful attractiveness, so also the manner of the mixing of the style of the account delights the ears of those who read the composition. And here shall be the end.

*Introduction to*

# 1 ESDRAS

F IRST ESDRAS OFFERS AN alternative version of the events recounted in
1 Chronicles 35–36, Ezra, and Nehemiah 8, as well as an additional episode—the "Contest of the Three Bodyguards" in which a certain Zerubbabel
emerges as the winner and, as his prize, is granted the favor of leading a
group of Judeans back to Jerusalem to restore the temple and the city. The
purpose of the work appears to be less historical and more ideological,
elevating the character of Zerubbabel (to the total eclipsing of Nehemiah),
perhaps with a view to emphasizing the continuity of the house of David
in the postexilic period. That the author was particularly intent on making
room for the story of the three bodyguards is evident from the additional
historical problems he created in the process. The work may have been
composed originally in Greek or may have been translated into Greek from
a Hebrew or Aramaic original—no traces of which, however, have survived.
The Greek is thus our earliest and best witness to the original contents of
the book, particularly as preserved in Codex Vaticanus and Codex Alexandrinus. The date and place of composition are far from clear. Egypt has been
suggested on the basis of some political terms and customs reflected in the
text; a date anywhere in the two centuries before the turn of the era seems
plausible. While Josephus knew 1 Esdras, it left very little impact otherwise
on early Judaism. Early Christians appear to have been most interested in
the episode of the bodyguards and, especially, the final maxim: "Truth is
great, and it prevails over all" (4:41).

—D. A. deSilva

# 1 ESDRAS

*Josiah*
*Celebrates*
*the Passover*

**1** And Josiah led the Passover in Jerusalem to his Lord and sacrificed the Passover on the fourteenth day of the first month, ²after arranging the priests according to divisions for the daily temple service dressed in the temple of the Lord. ³And he explained to the Levites, temple-servants of Israel, that they should sanctify themselves to the Lord in the placing of the holy ark of the Lord in the house that Solomon, the son of David, had built. The king said, ⁴"It will not be for you to carry upon your shoulders. And now, minister to the Lord your God, and attend to his nation Israel, and prepare yourselves according to your families and tribes, according to the writing of David, king of Israel, and according to the majesty of his son Solomon. ⁵And standing in the holy place according to your paternal groupings, the Levites, who stand before your brothers, sons of Israel, ⁶in good order sacrifice the Passover, and prepare the sacrifice for your brothers. And make the Passover according to the ordinance of the Lord that was given to Moses." ⁷So Josiah presented to the people who were present thirty thousand lambs and kids, and three thousand calves; these, taken out of the royal possessions, were given according to a public promise to the people and to the priests and Levites. ⁸And Hilkiah and Zechariah and Jehiel, the overseers of the temple, gave to the priests two thousand and six hundred sheep and three hundred calves for the Passover. ⁹And Jeconiah and Shemaiah and Nathanael, his brother, and Hashabiah and Ochiel and Joram, the commanders over thousands, gave to the Levites one thousand sheep and seven hundred calves for the Passover. ¹⁰Now when these things were done in the proper order, the priests and the Levites, having the unleavened bread, according to the tribes and according to the groupings of the ancestors, stood before the people to offer to the Lord according to what is written in the document of Moses, and so they did in the morning. ¹¹And they roasted the Passover lamb with fire, as required, and the sacrifices they boiled in the copper cauldrons and kettles, with a sweet smell, and they carried them to all who were from the people. ¹²Now, after these things, they prepared for themselves and for the priests, their brothers, sons of Aaron. ¹³For the priests offered up the fat until night, and the Levites prepared it for themselves and for the priests, their brothers, Aaron's sons. ¹⁴And the temple singers, sons of Asaph, were in their order according to what was appointed by David, and Asaph and Zechariah and Eddinus, who were from the king. ¹⁵And the porters were at each gateway. It was not possible for anyone to deviate from their daily service, for their brothers, the Levites, prepared for them. ¹⁶And the things for the sacrifice of the Lord were completed in that day; the Passover was celebrated and the sacrifices were made upon the altar of the Lord according to the command of king Josiah. ¹⁷And the sons of Israel who were found at that time celebrated the Passover and the feast of unleavened bread for seven days. ¹⁸And no Passover such as this had been celebrated in Israel since the time of Samuel the prophet. ¹⁹And all the kings of Israel had not celebrated Passover such as the kind that Josiah celebrated, and the priests and the Levites and the Judeans and all Israel, who were found in their dwelling in Jerusalem. ²⁰This Passover was celebrated in the eighteenth year of the reign of Josiah. ²¹Now the deeds of Josiah were upright in the presence of his Lord, with a heart full of piety. ²²And even the things concerning him in the previous times were written, concerning those who sinned and acted impiously toward the Lord more than any nation and kingdom, and how they grieved him, and the words of the Lord rose against Israel.

²³And after all these deeds of Josiah, it happened that Pharaoh, king of Egypt, went to make war at Carchemish on the Euphrates, and Josiah went out to meet him. ²⁴And the king of Egypt sent a message to him, saying, "What exists between me and you, O king of Judah? ²⁵I have not been sent against you by the Lord God, for my war is at the Euphrates. And now the Lord is with me, and the Lord with me is urging me on; depart and do not oppose the Lord." ²⁶But Josiah did not turn himself back to his chariot, rather he attempted to fight, not heeding the words of Jeremiah the prophet from the mouth of the Lord. ²⁷And he joined with him in battle on the plain of Megiddo, and the rulers came down against king Josiah. ²⁸Then the king said to his servants, "Remove me from the battle, for I am very weak." And immediately his servants removed him from the line of battle. ²⁹And he mounted his secondary chariot, and he was restored to Jerusalem and changed his life and was buried in his ancestral tomb. ³⁰And in all Judah they mourned Josiah. And Jeremiah the prophet lamented for Josiah, and the chief men, together with women, lament him to this day. And this was published to take place always for all the nation of Israel. ³¹Now these things are recorded in the document of the stories concerning the kings of Judah, and every single thing accomplished of the deeds of Josiah, and of his splendor, and of his understanding in the law of the Lord, and the things done by him, and the things now, are recorded in the book of the kings of Israel and of Judah.

*The Death of Josiah*

³²Now when the men of the nation took Jeconiah, son of Josiah, they appointed him king in the place of Josiah his father, being twenty-three years old. ³³And he reigned in Israel and Jerusalem three months, and the king of Egypt dethroned*ᵃ* him from reigning in Jerusalem. ³⁴And he fined the nation one hundred talents of silver and one talent of gold. ³⁵Then the king of Egypt appointed king Jehoiakim, his brother, king of Judah and Jerusalem. ³⁶And Jehoiakim bound the nobles, but he seized his brother Zarius and brought him up out of Egypt.

³⁷Now Jehoiakim was twenty-five years old when he began to reign over Judah and Jerusalem, and he did what was evil before the Lord. ³⁸And Nebuchadnezzar, king of Babylon, went up against*ᵇ* him and bound him in a bronze bond and led him away to Babylon. ³⁹Then Nebuchadnezzar took some of the sacred vessels of the Lord and carried them away; he settled them in his temple in Babylon. ⁴⁰And the things recorded concerning him and his impurity and impiety are written in the book of the times of the kings.

*Nebuchadnezzar Conquers Jerusalem*

ᵃLit. "de-established" ᵇLit. "with"

⁴¹And his son Jehoiakim reigned in the place of him, for when he was appointed he was eight years old. ⁴²And he reigned three months and ten days in Jerusalem, and he did evil in the presence of the Lord.

⁴³Now after a year, Nebuchadnezzar sent and carried him to Babylon, together with the sacred vessels of the Lord. ⁴⁴And he appointed Zedekiah king of Judah and Jerusalem. Zedekiah was twenty-one years old, and he reigned eleven years. ⁴⁵And he did evil in the eyes of the Lord, and he did not feel shame on account of the word that was said by Jeremiah the prophet from the mouth of the Lord. ⁴⁶And although he had been made to swear by King Nebuchadnezzar, by the name of the Lord, he swore falsely. He revolted and hardened his neck and his heart and transgressed the statutes of the Lord God of Israel. ⁴⁷Now the men who lead the people and the priests committed many acts of impiety, and they committed more acts of lawlessness than all the impurities of all the nations, and they defiled the temple of the Lord that was dedicated in Jerusalem. ⁴⁸And the king of their ancestors sent through his messenger to recall them, because he would have spared them and his dwelling place. ⁴⁹But they sneered at his messengers, and on the day the Lord spoke, they were mocking his prophets until he, being made angry against his nation because of their ungodly acts, commanded to bring up against them the kings of the Chaldeans. ⁵⁰These killed their young men by sword round about the holy temple, and they did not spare young man or virgin or elder or younger but handed over all into their hands. ⁵¹And all the sacred vessels of the Lord, the great and the small, and the chests of the Lord, and the royal treasure chests, they took up and carried them to Babylon. ⁵²Then they set on fire the house of the Lord, and they broke down the walls of Jerusalem, and they set ablaze their towers with fire. ⁵³And they finished rendering useless all its glory, and they led away the survivors with the sword to Babylon. ⁵⁴And they were servants to him and to his sons until the reign of Persia, to fulfill the word of the Lord by the mouth of Jeremiah, ⁵⁵"Until the land is pleased with its Sabbaths, all the time of its desolation, it shall keep the Sabbath until the fulfillment of seventy years."

*The Decree of Cyrus* **2** In the first year Cyrus was king of the Persians, for the fulfillment of the word of the Lord by the mouth of Jeremiah, ²the Lord raised up the spirit of Cyrus, king of the Persians, and he proclaimed in all his kingdom, and at the same time through written form, saying, ³"Thus says Cyrus, the king of the Persians, 'The Lord of Israel, the Lord Most High, appointed me king over the world, ⁴and he indicated to me that I should build a house for him in Jerusalem, which is in Judah. ⁵Therefore, if anyone of you is from his nation, let his Lord be with him, and after going up to Jerusalem, which is in Judah, let him build the house of the Lord of Israel. This is the Lord who encamps in Jerusalem. ⁶Therefore, whoever lives in each place, let those who are in his place assist him with gold and with silver, and with gifts, with horses and livestock, together with the other things that are handed over as votive offerings for the temple of the Lord that is in Jerusalem.'"

⁷And they arose, the chiefs of the paternal families of the tribes of Judah and Benjamin, and the priests and the Levites, and all whose spirit the Lord raised, to go up to build a house for the Lord, which is in Jerusalem. ⁸And those surrounding them helped with everything, with silver and gold,

horses, flocks, and with as great a number of votive offerings from many whose mind was stirred. ⁹And King Cyrus brought out the holy vessels of the Lord that Nebuchadnezzar had transferred out of Jerusalem and had put them in his idol temple. ¹⁰And after carrying them out, Cyrus, king of the Persians, handed them over to Mithridates, his own treasurer, ¹¹and by this one they were handed over to Sheshbazzar, governor of Judah. ¹²Now the number of these was one thousand gold libation cups, one thousand silver libation cups, twenty-nine silver censers, thirty gold saucers, two thousand four hundred and ten silver bowls, and one thousand other vessels. ¹³And all the vessels were gathered in, gold and silver, five thousand four hundred and sixty-nine, ¹⁴and they were carried up by Sheshbazzar, together with the people from the captivity, out of Babylon to Jerusalem.

¹⁵Now in the time of Ahasuerus, the king of the Persians, Bishlam and Mithredath and Tabeel and Rehum and Beltethmus and Shimshai the scribe and the rest of those associated with them but living in Samaria and the other places wrote for themselves the letter written below concerning those who dwell in Judah and Jerusalem, ¹⁶"To King Ahasuerus, the lord, your servants Rehum the recorder and Shimshai the scribe and the rest of their council and those who are in Coele Syria, Syria, and Phoenicia. ¹⁷And now, let it be known to the lord king that the Judeans who went up from you to us, having come to Jerusalem, inhabiting the rebellious and evil city, they are attending to both its marketplaces and walls, and they are laying the foundations for a temple. ¹⁸Therefore, if this city is rebuilt and the walls are completed, they will not submit to give tribute, but they will also resist kings. And since the work on the temple is ongoing, we suppose it is not good to neglect a matter such as this, but to speak to the lord king in order that, if it seems good to you, an examination might be undertaken in the documents from your fathers. ¹⁹And you will find in the archives that were written concerning them, and you will learn that that city was rebellious, even troubling kings and cities, and the Judeans were rebels, and they were erecting a siege in it still from eternity, on account of which this city was laid waste. ²⁰Now therefore, we declare to you, O lord king, that if this city is rebuilt and these walls are raised, there will no longer be an exit for you into Coele Syria, Syria, and Phoenicia."

²¹Then the king replied to Rehum (who wrote up the events) and Beltethmus and Shimshai the scribe and to the rest who were associated with them and who live in Samaria and Syria and Phoenicia as follows: ²²"I read the letter that you sent to me. Therefore, I ordered a search to be made, and it was found that this city has opposed kings from eternity, ²³and the people accomplished rebellion and war in it, and strong and severe kings were masters in Jerusalem and were exacting tribute from Coele Syria, Syria, and Phoenicia. ²⁴Now, therefore, I have ordered that you prevent those people from building the city, and to take care that nothing more beside this be done, and that such wicked things do not continue, so as to annoy kings." ²⁵When the letter from king Ahasuerus was read, Rehum and Shimshai the scribe and the ones associated with them went with haste to Jerusalem with cavalry and army arrayed for battle, and they began to hinder those who were building. And the construction of the temple that is in Jerusalem ceased until the second year of the reign of Darius, the king over Persia.

*A Letter to Ahasuerus*

*The King's Response*

**3** Now King Darius gave a great banquet for all who were under him and for all born in his household and for all the nobles of Media and of Persia ²and for all the satraps and generals and governors who were under him in the one hundred and twenty-seven satrapies from India to Ethiopia. ³And they ate and drank, and when they were satisfied, they departed, but Darius the king departed to the bedroom and fell asleep but became awakened out of his sleep. ⁴Then the three young men, bodyguards who were watching the body of the king, said one to the other, ⁵"Let us state, each of us, one thing that is strongest, and whosoever his word seems wiser than the other, Darius the king will give him great gifts and great prizes of victory, ⁶and he shall be clothed in purple and drink from gold cups and sleep on gold and have a chariot with golden bridles and a turban of fine linen and a necklace around his neck. ⁷And he shall sit next to Darius because of his wisdom, and he shall be proclaimed kinsman of Darius." ⁸And then, after each one wrote his own statement, they sealed them and put them under the pillow of Darius the king. And they said, ⁹"When the king wakes up, they will give him what is written, and whatever the king decides, and the three nobles of Persia, because his statement is wisest, to him will be given the victory, just as it is written." ¹⁰The first wrote, "Wine is strongest." ¹¹The second wrote, "The king is strongest." ¹²The third wrote, "Women are strongest, but truth prevails beyond all things." ¹³Now when the king awoke, they took what was written and gave it to him, and he read. ¹⁴And he sent and summoned all the nobles of Persia and of Media and satraps and generals and governors and prefects, and he sat in the council chamber, and what was written was read in the presence of them. ¹⁵And he said, "Call the young men and they themselves will explain their statements." And they were called and entered. ¹⁶Then they said to them, "Explain to us about the writings." And the first, the one who spoke about the strength of wine, began and he declared thus,

¹⁷"O men, how does wine prove strongest? It leads astray all people who drink it, with respect to the mind. ¹⁸It makes the mind of both the king and the orphan equal, both of the servant and of the free, both of the poor and of the wealthy. ¹⁹And it turns every thought to feasting and cheer and does not remember any sorrow or any debt. ²⁰And it makes every heart rich and does not remember a king nor satrap and causes all to speak through talents. ²¹And they do not remember when they drink to act friendly with friends and brothers, and with not much they draw swords. ²²And when they awake from the wine, they do not remember what they have done. ²³O men, is wine not strongest since it forces people to act this way?" And he was thus silent after speaking.

**4** Then the second, the one who spoke about the strength of the king, began to speak, ²"O men, do not humans prove superior, ruling over the land and the sea and all the things in them? ³But the king proves strongest, and he is lord over them and master over them, and they obey everything he says to them. ⁴If he says to them to make war one against the other, they do it. And if he sends them against the enemy, they proceed and level mountains and walls and towers. ⁵They murder and are murdered, and they do not transgress the word of the king. And if they conquer, they bring to the king everything, whatever they plunder and everything else.

⁶And as many as do not serve in the army or fight, they instead till the land; in turn, whenever they sow and reap, they bring to the king, and one compels the other to bring tribute to the king. ⁷And yet he is alone! If he says to kill, they kill; he said to release, they release; ⁸he said to beat, they strike; he said to lay waste, they lay waste; he said to build, they build; ⁹he said to cut down, they cut down; he said to plant, they plant. ¹⁰And all his people and his forces obey. With these things he reclines, eats, and drinks, and sleeps, ¹¹but they keep watch all around him, and each one is not able to depart and do his own work, nor do they disobey him. ¹²O men, how is the king not strongest, since he is obeyed in this way?" And he was silent.

¹³Then the third, the one who spoke about women and truth (this is Zerubbabel), began to speak, ¹⁴"O men, isn't the king great, and aren't humans many, and doesn't wine prove superior? Who, then, is master over them, or who is lord of them? Is it not women? ¹⁵Women give birth to the king and all the people who are lord over the sea and the land. ¹⁶And from them they were born, and they reared those who planted the vineyards from which wine came into being. ¹⁷And they make the clothing of the men, and they bring about glory for men, and men are not able to exist apart from women. ¹⁸And if men gather gold and silver or any beautiful thing, and they see one woman lovely in appearance and beauty, ¹⁹then, leaving all these things, they gape at her, and opening their mouths wide they look at her, and all choose her rather than the gold or the silver or any beautiful thing. ²⁰A man forsakes his own father, who reared him, and his own country and clings to his own wife. ²¹And he lets his soul loose with his wife and neither remembers father nor mother nor territory. ²²And hence it is necessary for you to realize that women rule over you. Don't you work and labor and give and carry everything to women? ²³And a man takes his sword and goes to march out and rob and steal and sail to the sea and rivers, ²⁴and he faces the lion, and he proceeds in darkness, and when he steals and seizes and robs, he brings it to the woman he loves. ²⁵And a man loves his own wife much more than father or mother. ²⁶And many have lost all sense in their own mind because of women and have become slaves because of them. ²⁷And many have perished and stumbled and sinned because of women. ²⁸So now don't you believe me? Is not the king great in his authority? Don't all territories fear to touch him? ²⁹I have beheld him and Apame, the daughter of admirable Bartacus, the concubine of the king, sitting at the right hand of the king ³⁰and taking the diadem from the head of the king and putting it on herself, and slap the king with her left hand. ³¹And at these things the king, opening wide his mouth, would gaze at her. And if she laughs at him, he laughs; but if she is embittered at him, he flatters her, so that she may be reconciled to him. ³²O men, how are women not strong, since they act like this?" ³³And then the king and the nobles looked at one another. And he began to speak about truth, ³⁴"Gentlemen, are not women strong? The earth is big and the heavens high and the sun swift in its course, since it turns in the circuit of the heavens and again returns to its place in one day. ³⁵Isn't the one who does these things great? But truth is great and stronger than all. ³⁶All the earth calls upon truth, and heaven blesses her. And all its works quake and tremble, and with it there is nothing unrighteous. ³⁷Wine is unrighteous,

the king is unrighteous, women are unrighteous, all the sons of men are unrighteous, and all their works are unrighteous, all such things, and truth is not in them, and in their injustice they will perish. ³⁸But truth remains and is strong for eternity, and it lives and prevails for the eternity of eternity. ³⁹And there is no taking face with it, or difference; rather it does what is righteous instead of anything unrighteous or evil, and all approve of its deeds. ⁴⁰And there is nothing unrighteous in its judgment. And it has the strength and the kingship and the power and the majesty of all eternities. Blessed be the God of truth." ⁴¹And he stopped speaking, and all the people then shouted and said, "Truth is great, and it prevails over all.

*The King* ⁴²Then the king said to him, "Ask whatever you want beyond what is *Rewards* written and I will give it to you, whatever is custom. You were found to be *Zerubbabel* wisest, and you will sit next to me and be called my kinsman." ⁴³Then he said to the king, "Remember the vow that you prayed to build Jerusalem in the day that you received your kingship, ⁴⁴and all the vessels that were taken from Jerusalem also to send back, that which Cyrus removed when he vowed to destroy Babylon and vowed to send them back there. ⁴⁵And you also vowed to build the temple, which the Judeans burned when Judea was laid waste by the Chaldeans. ⁴⁶And now this is as much as I ask, O lord king, and what I request of you, and this is greatness from you. I ask, therefore, that you fulfill the vow that you vowed with your mouth to do for the king of heaven."

⁴⁷Then Darius the king rose and kissed him and wrote for him letters to all the governors and generals and satraps, that they should give safe conduct to him and those who were with him, all going up to build Jerusalem. ⁴⁸And to all the governors in Coele Syria, Syria, and Phoenicia, and those in Lebanon, he also wrote letters to transfer timber of cedar from Lebanon to Jerusalem, and that they should build the city with him. ⁴⁹And he wrote to all the Judeans who were going up from the kingdom to Judah in the interest of freedom, that no officer or satrap or governor or treasurer should come upon their door, ⁵⁰and that all the territory that they would seize should belong to them without tribute, and that the Chaldeans should free the villages of the Judeans that they held back, ⁵¹and that twenty talents per year should be given for the building of the temple until it is built, ⁵²and another ten talents per year for burnt offerings to be offered upon the altar of burnt offerings, to be offered every day, just as they have a command to offer seventeen offerings, ⁵³and that all who go up from Babylon to build the city should have freedom, both them and their children, and all the priests who go up. ⁵⁴Now, he also wrote concerning the expense and the priestly garment, in what way they would serve in it. ⁵⁵And he wrote to the Levites to give the expense until the days in which the house was completed and Jerusalem was rebuilt. ⁵⁶And to all those who guard the city he wrote to give them plots of land and provisions. ⁵⁷And he sent all the vessels that Cyrus had removed from Babylon, and all that Cyrus said he would do he indeed ordered to do, and to send to Jerusalem.

⁵⁸Now when the young man went out, he lifted up his face to heaven before Jerusalem and blessed the king of heaven, saying, ⁵⁹"From you comes victory, and from you comes wisdom, and yours is the glory, and I am your servant. ⁶⁰Blessed are you, who have given me wisdom, and I give

thanks to you, O master of the fathers." 61Then he took the letters and went out to Babylon and explained to all his brothers. 62And they blessed the God of their ancestors, for he gave them remission and release 63to go up and build Jerusalem and the temple, where his name is named on it, and they drank with music and rejoicing for seven days.

5 Now, after these things, the leaders of the house of the ancestral fami- *The Roster of* lies were chosen to go up according to their tribes along with their *Returnees* wives and sons and daughters and their male servants and female servants and their livestock. 2And Darius sent along with them a thousand cavalry until they returned to Jerusalem with peace and with music of drums and of flutes. 3And all their brothers were making merry, and he made them go up with those persons.

4Now these are the names of the men who went up, according to their patrilineal families for the tribes, over their groups: 5The priests, sons of Phinehas sons of Aaron; Joshua the son of Jozadak son of Seraiah and Jehoiakim the son of Zerubbabel son of Shealtiel, from the house of David, from the family Perez and the tribe Judah, 6who spoke wise words to Darius, the king of Persia, in the second year of his reign, in the month of Nisan, the first month. 7And these are those from Judah who went up from the captivity of sojourning, whom Nebuchadnezzar, the king of Babylon, deported to Babylon, 8and returned to Jerusalem and the rest of Judah, each to his own city. Those who came with their leaders Zerubbabel and Joshua, Nehemiah, Seraiah, Resaiah, Eneneus, Mordecai, Beelsarus, Aspharasus, Reeliah, Rehum, and Baanah. 9The number of those from the nation and their leaders: sons of Parosh, seventy-two thousand; 10sons of Arah, seven hundred and fifty-six; 11sons of Pahath-moab, with respect to the sons of Joshua and Rhoboab, two thousand eight hundred and two; 12sons of Elam, two; sons of Zattu, nine hundred and seventy; sons of Chorbe, seven hundred and five; sons of Bani, six hundred and forty-eight; 13sons of Bebai, six hundred and thirty-three; sons of Azgad, one thousand three hundred and twenty-two; 14sons of Adonikam, thirty-seven; sons of Bigvai, two thousand six hundred and six; sons of Adin, four hundred and fifty-four; 15sons of Ater son of Hezekiah; sons of Kilan and Azetas, sixty-seven; sons of Azaru, four hundred and thirty-two; 16sons of Annias, one hundred and one; sons of Arom; sons of Bezai, three hundred and twenty-three; sons of Arsiphurith; 17sons of Baiterus, three thousand and five; sons from Ragethlomon, one hundred and twenty-three; 18those from Netophah, fifty-five; those from Anathoth, one hundred and fifty-eight; those from Bethasmoth, Zammoth; 19those from Kiriatharim, twenty-five; those from Peiras and Beeroth, seven hundred; 20the Chadiasans and Ammidians, four hundred and twenty-two; those from Kirama Geba, six hundred and twenty-one; 21those from Macalon, one hundred and twenty-two; those from Betolio, fifty-two; sons of Niphish, one hundred and fifty-six; 22sons of Calamolalus and Ono, seven hundred and twenty-five; sons of Jerechus, two hundred and forty-five; 23sons of Senaah, three thousand three hundred and one. 24The priests: the sons of Jedaiah the son of Joshua, with respect to the sons of Sanabeis, eight hundred and seventy-two; sons of Immer, two hundred and fifty-two; 25sons of Pashhur, one thousand two hundred and forty-seven; sons of Charme, two hundred and seventeen. 26The Levites: sons of Joshua and Kadmiel and

Bannas and Sudias, seventy-four. ²⁷Temple singers' sons: sons of Asaph, one hundred and twenty-eight. ²⁸The porters: four hundred; the descendants of Ismaelou; the sons of Lakoubatou, one thousand; the sons of Tobeis, in all one hundred and thirty-nine. ²⁹The temple-servants: sons of Esau, sons of Hasupha, sons of Tabbaoth, sons of Keros, sons of Sua, sons of Padon, sons of Lebana, ³⁰sons of Akkub, sons of Uthai, sons of Ketab, sons of Hagabah, sons of Subai, sons of Hanan, sons of Cathua, sons of Geddur, ³¹sons of Jair, sons of Daisan, sons of Noeba, sons of Chezib, sons of Gezer, sons of Azaziah, sons of Phinoe, sons of Hasrah, sons of Basthai, sons of Hassenaah, sons of Maani, sons of Nephisim, sons of Acuph, sons of Hakupha, sons of Asur, sons of Pharakim, sons of Bazluth, ³²sons of Mehida, sons of Barkos, sons of Serar, sons of Temah, sons of Neziah, sons of Hatipha. ³³Sons of the servants of Solomon: sons of Assaphioth, sons of Peruda, sons of Jaalah, sons of Lozon, sons of Isdael, sons of Shephatiah, ³⁴sons of Agia, sons of Pochereth-hazzebaim, sons of Sarothie, sons of Masiah, sons of Gas, sons of Addus, sons of Subas, sons of Apherra, sons of Barodis, sons of Shaphat, sons of Allon. ³⁵All the temple-servants and the sons of the servants of Solomon, three hundred and seventy-two. ³⁶These came up from Tel-melah and Tel-harsha with Cherub and Immer leading them. ³⁷And they were not able to verify their paternal lineage or generations, that they were from Israel: sons of Asan the son of Baenan and sons of Nekoda, six hundred and fifty-two. ³⁸And from the priests, those who laid claim to priesthood but were not found: sons of Habaiah, sons of Accos, sons of Jaddus, who took as a wife Agia, one of the daughters of Barzillai, as a wife and was called by his name. ³⁹And, after inquiring of the family geneaology of these persons in the register and not finding it, they were removed from serving as priests. ⁴⁰And Nehemiah and Attharias said to them that they were not to share in the sacred things until the priest should arise wearing the Unveiling and the Truth.ᵃ

⁴¹And all Israel, from twelve years old, besides male servants and female servants: forty-two thousand three hundred and sixty; their male servants and female servants, seven thousand three hundred and thirty-seven; harpists and psalmists, two hundred and forty-five. ⁴²There were four hundred and thirty-five camels, seven thousand and thirty-six horses, two hundred and forty-five mules, and five thousand five hundred and twenty-five donkeys.

⁴³And some of those who led by patrilineal families, when they arrived at the temple of God that is in Jerusalem, vowed to erect the house upon its place according to their power ⁴⁴and to give to the temple treasury for the work one thousand minas of gold and five thousand minas of silver and a hundred priestly garments. ⁴⁵And the priests and the Levites and those who were of his people were settled in Jerusalem, and those who were in the territory,ᵇ and the temple singers and porters and all Israel in their villages.

*The Remnant Celebrates the Feast of Tabernacles* ⁴⁶Now when the seventh month came and the sons of Israel were each in their own home, they gathered with a single purpose at the spacious area of the first gateway, which was toward the east. ⁴⁷And, having taken their places, Joshua, the son of Jozadak, and his brothers the priests and

---

ᵃ Heb. "Urim and Thummim"  ᵇ In the vicinity of Jerusalem

Zerubbabel, the son of Shealtiel, and his kindred prepared the altar of the God of Israel, ⁴⁸to offer upon it burnt offerings in accordance with what is directed in the book of Moses, the man of God. ⁴⁹And some from the other nations of the land gathered with them and set up the altar in its place; because they were in enmity toward them, all the nations that were on the land that were stronger than they, and they offered sacrifices at the proper time and burnt offerings to the Lord in the morning and in the evening. ⁵⁰And they celebrated the feast of tabernacles, as it is commanded in the law, and offered sacrifices every day as to be fitting, ⁵¹and after these things, perpetual offerings and sacrifices on sabbaths and new moons and all consecrated feasts. ⁵²And as many as had vowed a vow to God began to offer sacrifices to God from the new moon of the first month, but the temple of God was not yet built. ⁵³And they gave silver to the stone cutters and carpenters, and drink and food, and the Sidonians and men of Tyre had joy, to deliver timber of cedar from Lebanon, to convey them on rafts to the Joppa harbor, and the command was written for them from Cyrus, the king of the Persians.

⁵⁴And in the second year after arriving at the temple of God in Jerusa- *The Remnant* lem, during the second month, Zerubbabel, the son of Shealtiel, and Joshua, *Rebuilds* the son of Jozadak, and their brothers, and the priests, the Levites, and *the Temple* all those who arrived from captivity in Jerusalem, began ⁵⁵and laid the *Foundation* foundation of the temple of God on the new moon of the second month of the second year after they came to Judah and Jerusalem. ⁵⁶And they appointed the Levites from twenty years old and up to the work of the Lord. And Joshua stood, along with his sons and his brothers, and Kadmiel his brother, and the sons of Joshua, Emadabun and the sons of Judah son of Iliadun, along with their sons and brothers, all the Levites, with a single purpose acting as taskmasters for the work on the house of the Lord. And the builders built the temple of the Lord, ⁵⁷and the priests stood, dressed in their garments, with musical instruments and trumpets, and the Levites, sons of Asaph, holding cymbals. They were singing hymns to the Lord and blessing according to the directions of David, king of Israel. ⁵⁸And they sung aloud with hymns, blessing the Lord, because his goodness and glory are upon all Israel for eternities. ⁵⁹And all the people trumpeted and cried out with a great voice, singing hymns to the Lord for the raising of the house of the Lord. ⁶⁰And some of the Levitical priests and some of those who presided over their paternal families, the old men who had seen the house before this one, came to the building of this one with crying and great weeping, ⁶¹and many with trumpets and joy with a great voice, ⁶²so that the people could not hear the trumpets because of the weeping of the people. For the crowd was trumpeting so loudly that it could be heard from far away.

⁶³Now when the enemies of the tribe of Judah and Benjamin heard, they came to learn what the sound of the trumpets meant. ⁶⁴And they learned that those who were from the captivity were building the temple for the Lord God of Israel. ⁶⁵And coming to Zerubbabel and Joshua and the leaders of the paternal families, they said to them, "We will build along with you. ⁶⁶For, like you, we have heard your Lord and have burned incense to him from the days of Esar-haddon, king of Assyria, who transferred us here."

⁶⁷And Zerubbabel and Joshua and the leaders of the paternal families of Israel said to them, "It is not for you to build the house for the Lord, our God, ⁶⁸for we alone will build for the Lord of Israel, in accordance with what Cyrus, the king over Persia, commanded us." ⁶⁹But the nations of the land overlaid*a* those in Judah and, besieging them, hindered the building. ⁷⁰And by making plans and persuasive rhetoric*b* and conspiracies, they hindered the production of the building all the time of the life of King Cyrus. And they hindered the building for two years until the reign of Darius.

*Haggai and*
*Zechariah*
*Motivate*
*the Remnant*
*to Finish*
*the Temple*

6 Now in the second year of the reign of Darius, the prophets Haggai and Zechariah, the son of Iddo, prophesied to the Judeans who were in Judea and Jerusalem, in the name of the Lord, God of Israel, who is over them. ²Then Zerubbabel, the son of Shealtiel, and Joshua, the son of Jozadak, stood and began to build the house of the Lord that is in Jerusalem, joining the prophets of the Lord and helping them. ³At the same time, Sisinnes, the governor of Syria and Phoenicia, and Sathrabuzanes and their companions, came to them and said to them, ⁴"Who ordered you that you are building this house and this roof and completing all these other things, and who are the builders who are completing these things?" ⁵And the elders of the Judeans obtained favor, on account of the providence of the Lord being done upon the captives, ⁶and they were not hindered in the building until a sign was given to Darius about them and a report was made.

⁷A copy of a letter that Sisinnes, the governor of Syria and Phoenicia, and Sathrabuzanes and their companions who were leaders in Syria and Phoenicia wrote to Darius and sent to King Darius: "Greetings! ⁸Let it be fully known to our lord the king that upon arriving in the territory of Judea and the city of Jerusalem, we found the elders of the Judeans of the captivity building in the city of Jerusalem a big new house to the Lord with polished stones, costly timber being laid in the houses. ⁹And that work is happening with haste, and the work is prospering in their hands and being completed with all splendor and care. ¹⁰Then we asked these elders, saying, 'By whose command to you are you building this house and founding these works?' ¹¹Therefore we questioned them in order to inform you and write to you about the people who are leading, and we asked them for the list of names of those who are guiding. ¹²And they answered us, saying, 'We are servants of the Lord who created the heavens and the earth. ¹³And the house was built many years ago by a great and strong king of Israel, and it was completed. ¹⁴But when our fathers, provoking him, sinned against the heavenly Lord of Israel, he gave them into the hands of Nebuchadnezzar, king of Babylon, king of the Chaldeans. ¹⁵They, having pulled down the house, both burned it and took captive the people to Babylon. ¹⁶But in the first year that Cyrus reigned over the territory of Babylonia, King Cyrus wrote that this house should be rebuilt. ¹⁷And the sacred gold and silver vessels that Nebuchadnezzar carried out of the house in Jerusalem and which are stored in his temple, in turn King Cyrus carried them out of the temple in Babylon and gave them to Zerubbabel and Sheshbazzar, the governor. ¹⁸And he ordered him, and he brought all these vessels and put them in the temple that is in Jerusalem and ordered that the temple of the

---

*a* Lit. "fell asleep upon"  *b* Lit. "leading the people"

Lord should be rebuilt on its place. [19]Then Sheshbazzar, after arriving, laid the foundation of the house of the Lord in Jerusalem, and from that time until now building has not yet received completion.' [20]Now therefore, if it is considered proper, O king, let a search be made in the royal archives of the lord king that are in Babylon, [21]and if it is found that the building of the Lord that is in Jerusalem occurred with the consent of King Cyrus and if it is considered right by the lord, our king, let him send directions to us about these things."

[22]Then King Darius commanded to search in the archives that lie in Babylon. And there was found in Ecbatana, the bastion that is in the territory of Media, a place in which this was recorded: [23]"In the first year of the reign of Cyrus, the king commanded that the house of the Lord that is in Jerusalem, where they make offerings with perpetual fire, should be rebuilt, [24]its height sixty cubits, its width sixty cubits, with three courses of polished stones and one course of new native wood, and the expense to be paid out of the house of King Cyrus. [25]And the sacred vessels of the house of the Lord, both the gold and silver ones, that Nebuchadnezzar carried out of the house that is in Jerusalem and brought to Babylon, should be restored to the house that is in Jerusalem, where they were housed previously, in order that they may be placed there." [26]Now, he commanded Sisinnes, the governor of Syria and Phoenicia, and Sathrabuzanes and their companions and those who were appointed in Syria and Phoenicia as leaders to take care to keep away from the place and to permit Zerubbabel, the servant of the Lord and lieutenant of Judea, and the elders of the Judeans to build that house of the Lord in its place. [27]"And I have also ordered that they build it completely and that they watch carefully that they cooperate with those who are from the captivity of Judah until the house of the Lord is completed, [28]and that from the tribute of Coele Syria, Syria, and Phoenicia a portion be carefully given to these people for sacrifices to the Lord, to the governor Zerubbabel for bulls and rams and lambs, [29]and likewise also wheat and salt and wine and olive oil, continually, per year, just as the priests who are in Jerusalem designate to use each day, without further question, [30]in order that libations may be offered to the Most High God for the king and his servants, so that they might pray for their lives." [31]And he commanded that if anyone should transgress or ignore the writings, a beam should be taken out of his own house, and upon it he should be hanged, and his belongings become property of the king. [32]"On account of the same things, also, may the Lord, whose name is invoked there, remove every king and nation that shall stretch out its hand to hinder or damage that house of the Lord that is in Jerusalem. [33]I, King Darius, have decreed that it be done carefully according to these things."

**7** Then Sisinnes, governor of Coele Syria, Syria, and Phoenicia, and Sathrabuzanes and their companions, carrying out the things commanded by King Darius, [2]supervised the temple work carefully, assisting the elders of the Judeans and the governor of the temple. [3]And the temple work proceeded without difficulty while the prophets Haggai and Zechariah were prophesying, [4]and they finished these things through a command of the Lord God of Israel, and with the consent of Cyrus and Darius and Ahasuerus, kings of Persia. [5]The house was completed by the twenty-third day of the month Adar, in the sixth year of King Darius. ⁶And the sons of Israel, even the priests and the Levites and the rest of those who were added from the captivity, did in accordance with what is in the book of Moses. ⁷And they offered at the dedication of the temple of the Lord one hundred bulls, two hundred rams, and four hundred lambs, ⁸and twelve male goats for the sin of all Israel, according to the number of the twelve tribal chiefs of Israel. ⁹And the priests and the Levites stood, dressed in their garments, by tribe, for the work of the Lord, God of Israel, in accordance with the book of Moses, and the porters were at each gate.

¹⁰And the sons of Israel, of those from the captivity, celebrated the Passover on the fourteenth of the first month, when the priests and the Levites were sanctified together, ¹¹even all the sons of the captivity that were sanctified, because all the Levites were sanctified together. ¹²And they sacrificed the Passover for all the sons of the captivity and their brothers, the priests, and themselves. ¹³And the sons of Israel who were from the captivity, all those separated from the abominations of the nations of the land, seeking the Lord, ate. ¹⁴They also celebrated the feast of unleavened bread seven days, rejoicing before the Lord, ¹⁵because he had changed the will of the king of Assyria concerning them, strengthening their hands for the work of the Lord, God of Israel.

*Ezra Returns to Jerusalem* **8** And there was a time after these things, when Ahasuerus, the king of Persia, was reigning, that Ezra came. He was the son of Saraias, son of Zechrias, son of Chelkeias, son of Shallum, ²son of Zadok, son of Ahitub, son of Amariah, son of Uzzi, son of Bukki, son of Abishua, son of Phinehas, son of Eleazar, son of Aaron, the first priest. ³This Ezra went up from Babylon as a scribe, skilled in the law of Moses, which was delivered by the God of Israel. ⁴And the king showed him honor, for he found favor before him in all his requests. ⁵And some of the sons of Israel and the priests and Levites and temple singers and porters and temple servants came up to Jerusalem ⁶in the seventh year of the reign of Ahasuerus, in the fifth month (this was the second year for the king), for they went out from Babylon on the new moon of the first month, and they arrived in Jerusalem due to the good journey given them by the Lord for him. ⁷For Ezra possessed much understanding, so that he omitted nothing from the law of the Lord or from the commands in teaching all Israel duties and judgments.

⁸Having come from King Ahasuerus to Ezra, the priest and reader of the law of the Lord, of which the following is a copy: ⁹"King Ahasuerus to Ezra, the priest and reader of the law of the Lord, greetings. ¹⁰Now having decided on a kind treatment, I commanded that those who wish of the nation of Judeans, having chosen to do so, and the priests and the Levites and those also in our kingdom, may go along with you to Jerusalem. ¹¹Therefore, let as many as so desire depart together, just as both I and the seven friends, who are my counselors, have decided, ¹²in order that they might examine the affairs concerning Judea and concerning Jerusalem in accordance with what is held in the law of the Lord, ¹³and bring gifts to the Lord that both I and the friends vowed for Jerusalem, and all the gold and silver that might be found in the territory of Babylon, for the Lord in Jerusalem, along with the gifts by the nation for the temple of their Lord that is in Jerusalem, ¹⁴to gather both the gold and silver for bulls and rams

and lambs and the things that go along with them, [15]so as to offer sacrifices upon the altar of their Lord that is in Jerusalem. [16]And everything you with your brothers wish to do with the gold and silver, complete it according to the will of your God, [17]also concerning your temple vessels that were given for the use of the temple of your God who is in Jerusalem. And the rest that might belong to you for the use of the temple of your God [18]you shall give out of the royal treasury. [19]And look, I, King Ahasuerus, have commanded the treasurers of Syria and Phoenicia that whatever Ezra, the priest and reader of the law of God Most High, sends for, they shall carefully give him up to one hundred silver talents, [20]and likewise also up to one hundred kors of wheat and one hundred measures of wine. [21]Let it be accomplished according to the law of God, for God Most High, so that wrath might not come upon the kingdom of the king and his sons. [22]And it is said also to you, that on any priests or Levites or temple singers or porters or temple servants or officials of this temple no tribute or any other plot should happen; no one has authority to add to them. [23]And you, Ezra, according to the wisdom of God, appoint judges and justices, that they might judge in the whole of Syria and Phoenicia all those who know the law of your God; you will also instruct those who do not know. [24]And all who transgress, both the law of your God and of the royal one, shall be strictly punished, whether by death or by physical punishment, not[a] by monetary[w] fine, or by imprisonment." [25]Blessed be the Lord alone, who placed these things in my heart, the king's, to glorify his house that is in Jerusalem, [26]and who honored me before the rulers[b] and all his friends and nobles. [27]And I became bold at the support of the Lord my God, and I assembled men from Israel to go up with me.

[28]Now these are the leaders, according to their paternal families and groupings, who went up with me from Babylon in the reign of King Ahasuerus: [29]From the sons of Phoros, Tarosotomos; from the sons of Ithamar, Gamael; the sons of David, [30]Phares, Zechariah, and with him from the register one hundred and fifty men; [31]from the sons of Pahath-moab, Eliehoenai son of Seraiah, and with him two hundred men; [32]from the sons of Zattu, Shecaniah son of Jahaziel, and with him two hundred men; the sons of Adin, Obed son of Jonathan, and with him two hundred and fifty men; [33]from the sons of Elam, Jeshaiah son of Gotholiah, and with him seventy men; [34]from the sons of Shephatiah, Seraiah son of Michael, and with him seventy men; [35]from the sons of Joab, Obadiah son of Jahaziel, and with him two hundred and twelve men; [36]from the sons of Bani, Shelomith son of Josiphiah, and with him one hundred and sixty men; [37]from the sons of Baier, Zechariah, Bebai, and with him twenty-eight men; [38]the sons of Azgad, Johanan son of Hakkatan, and with him one hundred and ten men; [39]from the sons of Adonikam, the last ones, these were their names: Eleiphelet son of Jeuel, and Shemaiah, and with them seventy men; [40]from the sons of Bigvai, Uthai son of Istalcurus, and with him seventy men.

[41]And, assembling them at the place called "River," we encamped there three days, and I inspected them. [42]And, not finding there any of the priests or Levites, [43]I sent word to Eleazar and Iduel and Maasmas and Elnathan

[a] Heb. text and some MSS omit "not"  [b] Or "kings"

and Shemaiah and Jarib, Nathan, Elnathan, Zechariah, and Meshullam, who were leaders and men of understanding. ⁴⁴And I told them to go to Iddo, the leader in the place of the treasury, ⁴⁵commanding them to discuss with Iddo and his brothers and the treasurers in the place to send us some to serve as priests in the house of our Lord. ⁴⁶A skilled man of the sons of Mahli son of Levi, son of Israel, namely Sherebiah, and his sons and his ten brothers, ⁴⁷from the sons of Hananiah and their sons, twenty men; ⁴⁸and from the temple servants, whom David and the leaders had given for the service of the Levites, two hundred and twenty temple servants, from all of these the list of names was indicated. ⁴⁹And I vowed there a fast for the young men before our Lord, ⁵⁰to seek from him a good journey both for ourselves and our children and livestock. ⁵¹For I was ashamed for the cavalry and the foot soldiers, which were an escort for security against those opposing us, ⁵²for we had said to the king that the strength of our Lord will be with those who seek after him for complete restoration. ⁵³And again we asked our Lord all these things, and we found him very merciful. ⁵⁴And I set apart from the tribal chiefs of the priests twelve men, both Sherebiah and Asabias, and ten men with them from their brothers, ⁵⁵and I weighed for them the silver and the gold and the temple vessels of the house of our Lord. In this way the king and his counselors and nobles and all Israel were presented. ⁵⁶And he gave to them, after weighing it out, six hundred and fifty talents of silver, and silver vessels of one hundred talents, and one hundred talents of gold, twenty golden cups, and copper vessels made of fine copper that glittered, ten vessels. ⁵⁷And I said to them, "You, too, are holy to the Lord, and the sacred vessels and the silver and the gold, as a vow to the Lord, the Lord of our fathers. ⁵⁸Be watchful and on guard until you deliver them to the tribal chiefs of the priests and the Levites and to the leaders of the paternal families of Israel, in Jerusalem, in the priest's chamber of the house of our Lord." ⁵⁹And the priests and the Levites who took the silver and the gold and the vessels that had been in Jerusalem carried them to the temple of the Lord.

⁶⁰Then, after breaking camp by the place Theras on the twelfth of the first month, they came into Jerusalem by the mighty hand of our Lord, which was upon us. He also rescued us from every enemy incursion, and they came to Jerusalem. ⁶¹And having been there three days, the silver and the gold were weighed and delivered in the house of the Lord to Meremoth son of Uriah, the priest. ⁶²And with him was Eleazar son of Phinehas; and also the Levites Jozabad son of Joshua and Moeth son of Binnui were with them. By count and weight all was delivered to them, and all the weight was recorded at that very time. ⁶³And those who had arrived from the captivity offered sacrifices to the God of Israel, the Lord, ninety-six rams, seventy-six lambs, and twelve male goats for deliverance, all as a sacrifice to the Lord. ⁶⁴And they delivered the command of the king to the royal treasurers and to the governors of Coele Syria and Phoenicia, and they honored the nation and the temple of the Lord.

*The Remnant Divorce Their Foreign Wives* ⁶⁵Now when these things were completed, the leaders came to me, saying, ⁶⁶"The rulers and the priests and the Levites have not separated from both the foreign nations and their impurities: Canaanites and Hittites and Perizzites and Jebusites and Moabites and Egyptians and Edomites.

⁶⁷For both they and their sons married some of their daughters, and the holy seed has been mingled with the foreign nations of the land, and the leaders and the nobles have shared in this lawlessness from the beginning of the matter." ⁶⁸And at the same time that I heard these things, I rent my garments and my sacred clothing. I pulled my head hair and my beard and sat gloomy and deeply grieved. ⁶⁹And as many as ever were moved at the word of the Lord of Israel gathered together to me while I was mourning at the lawlessness, and I sat deeply grieved until the evening sacrifice. ⁷⁰And when I rose from the fast, having rent my garments and my sacred clothing, when I bent my knees and stretched out my hands to the Lord, I was saying, ⁷¹"Lord, I am ashamed; I am embarrassed before your face. ⁷²For our sins have multiplied beyond our heads and our mistakes have surpassed the heaven. ⁷³From the time of our fathers and up to this day we are in great sin. ⁷⁴And because of our sins and our fathers' sins we were handed over, along with our brothers, along with our kings, and along with our priests, to the kings of the earth for sword and captivity and plunder with shame until this very day. ⁷⁵And now according to some measure mercy has come to us from the lord Lord, to leave behind for us a root and a name in this place of sanctuary, ⁷⁶and to uncover our light in the house of our Lord, to give us food in the time of our slavery. And in our slavery, we were not left behind by our Lord, ⁷⁷but he brought us into favor with the kings over Persia, to give us food, ⁷⁸and to honor our temple, and to arouse desolate Zion, to give us a stronghold in Judah and Jerusalem. ⁷⁹And now what shall we say, O Lord, having these things? They have transgressed your ordinances which you gave by the hand of your servants the prophets, saying, ⁸⁰'Because the land into which you are entering to take possession is a land stained with the pollution of the foreigners of the land, and they have filled it with their impurity, ⁸¹so now do not give your daughters in marriage to their sons, and do not take their daughters for your sons. ⁸²And do not seek to live peaceably with them at any time, in order that you may prevail and eat the good of the land, and give it as a possession to your sons until for eternity.' ⁸³And everything befalling us has happened because of our evil deeds and great sins. For you, O Lord, making light of our sins, ⁸⁴gave us a root such as this. Again, we have turned back to transgress your law by mingling with the impurity of the nations of the land. ⁸⁵Were you not angry enough with us to destroy us to the point of not leaving behind a root and a seed and a name for us? ⁸⁶O Lord of Israel, you are truthful; for we are left as a root on this very day. ⁸⁷Look, we are before you in our lawlessness, for we can no longer stand before you because of these things."

⁸⁸And when Ezra was praying, while confessing openly, weeping on the ground before the temple, there gathered to him from Jerusalem a very great crowd of men and women and youths, for there was great weeping in the multitude. ⁸⁹And calling out, Jeconiah son of Jehiel, of the sons of Israel, said to Ezra, "We have sinned against the Lord, and foreign women from the nations of the land have remained, but now Israel is above all. ⁹⁰On this let us swear an oath to the Lord to cast out all our wives who are from the foreigners, along with their children, as it was decided by you and as many as obey the law of the Lord. ⁹¹Arise, complete it, for the task is for you, and we are with you to make strength." ⁹²And standing up, Ezra put

the tribal chiefs of the priests and of the Levites of all Israel under oath to act according to this. And they swore an oath.

**9** And Ezra stood up from the court of the temple and went to the priest's chamber of Johanan son of Naseibou ²and spent the night there. He did not eat bread nor drink water, mourning over the great lawlessness of the multitude. ³And there was a proclamation in the whole of Judah and Jerusalem to all who were from the captivity to gather to Jerusalem. ⁴And whoever will not meet there within two or three days, in accordance with the judgment of the ruling elders, their livestock will be devoted for sacrifice, and he himself will be estranged from the multitude of the captivity.

⁵And those who were from the tribes of Judah and Benjamin gathered in three days to Jerusalem; it was the ninth month, on the twentieth day of the month. ⁶And all the multitude sat together in the wide-open space of the temple, shivering because it was the beginning of winter. ⁷Then Ezra stood up and said to them, "You have broken the law and married foreign women, adding to the sins of Israel. ⁸And now make confession and give glory to the Lord, God of our ancestors, ⁹and do his will, and be separated from the nations of the earth and from the foreign people." ¹⁰And the whole multitude shouted and said with a great voice, "We will do just as you have said, ¹¹but the multitude is large, and the hour is winter, and we will not be strong enough to stand in the open air, and we have not found it, and for us the task cannot be completed in one or two days, for we have sinned too much in these things. ¹²Let the leaders of the multitude stay, and let all those from our settlements who have foreign wives come at the appointed time, ¹³the elders and the judges of each place, until the wrath of the Lord is released from us over this thing." ¹⁴Jonathan son of Asahel and Jahzeiah son of Tikvah undertook the matter on these terms, and Meshullam and Levi and Shabbethai acted as arbitrators for them. ¹⁵And those from the captivity acted in accordance with all this.

¹⁶And Ezra the priest chose for himself men who were leaders of their paternal families, all of them by name, and they were confined on the new moon of the tenth month to examine the matter. ¹⁷And the cases concerning the men who were gathered together with foreign wives were brought to completion by the new moon of the first month. ¹⁸And of the priests who were gathered together and were found having foreign wives: ¹⁹of the sons of Joshua son of Jozadak and his brothers, Matthelas and Eleazar and Jarib and Jodan. ²⁰And they laid on their hands to cast out their wives and as an atonement to offer rams on account of their mistake. ²¹And of the sons of Immer: Hananiah and Zebadiah and Maaseiah and Shemaiah and Jehiel and Azariah. ²²And of the sons of Pashhur: Elioenai, Maaseiah, Ishmael, and Nathanael and Gedaliah and Salthas. ²³And of the Levites: Jozabad and Shimei and Kelaiah, that is, Kelita and Pethahiah and Judah and Johanan. ²⁴Of the temple singers: Eliashib and Zaccur. ²⁵Of the porters: Shallum and Telem. ²⁶Of Israel: of the sons of Parosh: Ramiah and Izziah and Malchijah and Maelus and Eleazar and Asebias and Benaiah. ²⁷Of the sons of Elam: Matanias and Zechariah and Jezrielus and Abdi and Jeremoth and Aedeias. ²⁸And of the sons of Zamoth: Eliadas, Eliashib, Othoniah, Jeremoth and Zabad and Zerdaiah. ²⁹And of the sons of Bebai: John and Hananiah and Zabbai and Emathis. ³⁰And of the sons of Mani:

Olamus, Mamuchus, Adaiah, Jashub and Sheal and Jeremoth. ³¹And of the sons of Eri: Naathus and Moossias and Laccunus and Naidus and Bescaspasmys and Sesthel and Belnuus and Manasseas. ³²And of the sons of Annan: Elionas and Asaiah and Malchijah and Sabbaias and Simon and Chosamaeus. ³³And of the sons of Husham: Mattenai and Mattithiah and Zabad and Eliphelet and Manasseh and Shimei. ³⁴And of the sons of Baani: Jeremiah, Momdius, Maerus, Joel, Mamdai and Bedeiah and Vaniah and Carabasion and Eliashib and Mamitanemus, Eliasis, Binnui, Elialis, Someis, Shelemiah, and Nethaniah. And of the sons of Ezora: Shashai, Azarel, Azael, Samatus, Zambris, and Joseph. ³⁵Of the sons of Nooma: Mazitias, Zabad, Iddo, Joel, and Benaiah. ³⁶All these lived together with foreign women, and they divorced them together with their children.

³⁷And the priests and the Levites and those from Israel settled in Jerusalem and in the territory. On the new moon of the seventh month, the sons of Israel were in their settlements, ³⁸all the multitude assembled with one accord in the spacious area toward the east temple gate. ³⁹And they told Ezra the priest and reader to bring the law of Moses that had been handed over by the God of Israel. ⁴⁰And Ezra, the chief priest, brought the law to all the multitude, from man to woman, and to all the priests, to hear the law on the new moon of the seventh month. ⁴¹And they read aloud in the place before the spacious temple gateway from dawn until midday in the presence of men and women, and everyone gave attention to the law. ⁴²And Ezra, the priest and reader of the law, stood upon the wooden platform that was constructed. ⁴³And he made stand by him Mattithiah, Shema, Hananiah, Azariah, Uriah, Hezekiah, and Baalsamus on his right, ⁴⁴and on his left Pedaiah, Mishael, Malchijah, Lothasubus, Nabariah, and Zechariah. ⁴⁵And when Ezra took up the document in the presence of the multitude, for he was seated in a place of honor in the presence of all, ⁴⁶when he unbound the law, they all stood upright and Azariah blessed the Most High, Almighty God. ⁴⁷And all the multitude shouted, "Amen, amen!" And lifting up their hands and falling upon the ground, they bowed before God. ⁴⁸The Levites Joshua and Anniuth and Sherebiah, Jadinus, Iarsouboos, Abtaios, Hodiah, Maiannas and Kalitas, Azariah, Katethzabdos, Hanan, and Pelaiah were teaching the law of the Lord and reading the law of the Lord to the multitude, putting meaning into the reading at the same time.

⁴⁹And Attharates said to Ezra, the chief priest and reader, and to the Levites who were instructing the multitude about everything, ⁵⁰"This day is holy to the Lord," and all were weeping at hearing the law, ⁵¹"therefore proceed, eat fats, and send off gifts to those who do not have. ⁵²For the day is holy to the Lord, and do not be sorrowful, for the Lord will exalt you." ⁵³And the Levites were commanding all the people, saying, "This day is holy; do not be sorrowful." ⁵⁴And all departed to eat and to drink and to rejoice and to give gifts to those who do not have and to rejoice greatly, ⁵⁵because they were also inspired by the words which they had been taught. And they gathered together.

*Introduction to*

# PRAYER OF MANASSEH

ACCORDING TO 2 KINGS, Manasseh, the king of Judah from 687–642 BC, so wickedly promoted the worship of other gods that he became ultimately responsible for God's determination to hand Judah over to Babylon. The author of 2 Chronicles, however, tells of Manasseh experiencing genuine repentance and reversing his policy in favor of promoting worship of the God of Israel alone. He even speaks of a written record of Manasseh's prayer of repentance in the "Annals of the Kings of Israel" (2 Chr 33:18–19). Though that document has not survived, a pious Jewish author composed a suitable substitute, leaving behind this marvelous prayer of humble confession. The prayer, rich in biblical language and allusions, appears to reflect knowledge of the Septuagint, and thus it is likely to have been composed in Greek sometime after 200 BC. It has been preserved in both Greek and Syriac manuscripts of the third century Apostolic Constitutions and in the fifth century Codex Alexandrinus, where it is included in a book of Odes. The book of Odes gathers prayers and psalms from the narrative books of both testaments (and beyond) into a kind of supplement to the Psalter. It does not appear to have enjoyed canonical status per se, but it was clearly used in the worship life of the early Christian church—a usage that it has continued to enjoy throughout Christian history. Attaching the prayer to the name of Manasseh makes it a testimony to the limitless mercy of God, who pardons all who truly repent.

—D. A. deSilva

# PRAYER OF MANASSEH

1 Lord Almighty, heavenly God of our fathers,
   of Abraham and Isaac and Jacob and their righteous seed;
2 you who made the heavens and the earth with all their order,
3 you who shackled the oceans by the word of your command;
   who closed off the abyss and sealed it by your awesome and
      honorable name;
4 at whom all shudder and tremble from the face of your power.
5 Because the magnificence of your glory cannot be endured,
   and overwhelming is the wrath of your anger upon sinners.
6 Immeasurable and also unsearchable is the compassion
      of your promise,
7 because you are the Lord Most High, compassionate, patient
      and full of mercy
   and repenting at the wickedness of humanity.
8 Therefore, you, O Lord the God of the righteous, did not establish
      repentance for the righteous—
   Abraham and Isaac and Jacob, the ones who have not sinned
      against you—
   rather you established repentance for me, the sinner.
9 Because I sinned beyond the number of grains of sand by the sea;
   because my lawless actions multiplied,
   and I am not worthy to gaze and see the heights of heaven
   because of the great number of my wrongdoings.
10 Being bent over by many a chain of iron so that I might reject
      my sins,
   and I have no release from them;
   because I provoked your anger
      and practiced evil before you by setting up idols and
         multiplying my offenses.
11 And now I bend the knee of my heart, begging kindness from you.
12 I have sinned, Lord, I have sinned.
   And my lawless actions I know.
13 I plead, begging you,
   "Release me, Lord, release me!
   May you not destroy me with my lawless actions;
      nor holding a grudge into eternity, keep my evil in mind,
   nor condemn me in the lowest parts of the earth,
      because you are the Lord, the God of those who repent."
14 And in me you make known your goodness;
      for unworthy though I am, you will save me according to your
         abundant compassion.
15 And I praise you through all the days of my life
      because the whole force of heaven is singing praises to you,
      and yours is the glory for eternities. Amen.

*Introduction to*

# PSALM 151

T HE MAJOR FOURTH AND fifth century Septuagint codices preserve
an additional psalm that celebrates two major events in the life of
David—his selection by God through the prophet Samuel and his victory
over Goliath that first brought him to public notice. The Greek psalm,
however, represents a conflation of two originally independent Hebrew
psalms, each focusing more fully on one of these events, preserved in their
fuller forms in the Psalms scrolls found among the Dead Sea Scrolls. The
psalms must predate the extermination of the Qumran community by the
Romans in AD 68. Linguistically speaking they may have been composed as
early as the Persian period to supply two obvious gaps in regard to psalms
connected with significant events in David's life.

—D. A. deSilva

# PSALM 151[a]

*I Was Small among My Brothers* THIS PSALM IS WRITTEN IN HIS OWN HAND BY DAVID, AND OUTSIDE OF THE NUMBER, WHEN HE FOUGHT IN SINGLE COMBAT AGAINST GOLIATH.

1   I was small among my brothers
     and the youngest one in the house of my father.
     I was shepherding the sheep of my father.

2   My hands made an organ;
     my fingers prepared a harp.

3   And who will report to my Lord?
     The Lord himself, it is he who will hearken.

4   He dispatched his messenger
     and raised me from the sheep of my father.
     He anointed me with the oil of his anointing.

5   My brothers were handsome and big,
     but the Lord was not well pleased with them.

6   I went out to a meeting against the foreigner,
     and he imprecated curses upon me with his idols.

7   But I, after drawing the sword from him, beheaded him
     and took away the reproach from the children of Israel.

[a] Heb. does not include Ps 151

# 3 MACCABEES

U NLIKE 1 AND 2 Maccabees, this book is not at all concerned with the Maccabean revolt or the events that precipitated it. Rather, it tells the story of one of the Ptolemies, the Hellenistic kings of Egypt, attempting to enter the inner shrines of the Jerusalem temple, meeting with human opposition, being thwarted by divine intervention, and returning to Egypt to take revenge on the Jewish population of his kingdom. The opening narrative does appear to have been inspired by the similar episode of 2 Maccabees 3, and the book as a whole might have been composed to show that the Jews of Egypt were no less bound to the fate of the temple than their Judean compatriots—even as their eventual deliverance shows God to be as concerned with their fate as with that of Jews in the land of Israel.

The contents of the book are generally regarded as more fiction than history. It was composed in Greek and likely written by a well-educated Jew in Egypt, perhaps even in Alexandria itself. Dates from the late Ptolemaic (100 BC) to early Roman (30 BC) periods have been suggested. While 3 Maccabees exercised almost no discernible influence on the early church, it does provide important windows into the hostility that Jews and gentiles often expressed toward one another and into the causes of their mutual disregard. It opens a window as well into the tensions experienced within the Jewish community between those who bore the costs of remaining faithful to their ancestral way of life and those who sought security, even advancement, at the cost of compromising or even renouncing that way of life.

—D. A. deSilva

# 3 MACCABEES

**1** Now Philopator, learning from those who returned that the places controlled by him were seized by Antiochus, giving orders to all his forces, infantry and cavalry, and taking along his sister, Arsinoë, he set out as far as the places toward Raphia, where those with Antiochus had encamped. ²But a certain Theodotus, intending to carry out the plot, taking with him the best of the Ptolemaic weapons having been assigned to him, crossed over alone by night to the tent of Ptolemy so as to kill him and in this way to end the war. ³But Dositheos, who was called the son of Drimylus, Judean by origin but who later turned away from their customs and became estranged from the ancestral doctrines, leading him away made a certain insignificant person to sleep in the tent who, it happened, bore the vengeance for that one.ᵃ ⁴When a fierce battle was taking place and things were going rather well for Antiochus, Arsinoë, going to the forces, began to exhort them with piteous wailing and tears, having loosed the braids of her hair, to rescue themselves both for their children and wives, confidently promising to give to each one two mina of gold if they prevailed. ⁵And thus it happened that the enemy was destroyed in hand-to-hand combat, and many captives were also seized. ⁶Now having overcome the plot, he decided to visit the nearby cities to encourage them. ⁷And doing this and granting gifts to their sacred precincts, he made his subjects of good courage.

⁸Now when the Judeans sent some persons to him from the council and the elders to greet him and to bring gifts of hospitality, and, rejoicing on account of the events that had occurred, it happened that he was all the more eager to come to them as soon as possible. ⁹And upon crossing over to Jerusalem and sacrificing to the trustworthy God and rendering thank offerings and doing what was befitting for the holy place and then appearing at the holy place, he was also amazed by its excellence and piety. ¹⁰And also marveling at the good arrangement of the temple, he considered planning to enter into the temple. ¹¹And when they said it was not proper to do this because the Gentiles do not enter in, nor all the priests, but only the chief priest, who is leader of all, and for this one once only during a year. But the king was by no means persuaded. ¹²Even after the law was read publicly, not even then did he abandon insisting that it was necessary for him to enter, saying, "Even if those ones are deprived of this honor, it should not be so for me." ¹³And he inquired why he was entering into every other sacred precinct, and none of those present prevented him. ¹⁴And someone without thinking said it was wrong to regard this as a portent. ¹⁵And he said, "Since this was done, why not by all means enter, whether they are willing or not?"

¹⁶Then the priests prostrated themselves in all their vestments and implored the supreme God to come to their rescue in the present situation and to avert the violence of the one wickedly imposing himself, filling

---

ᵃ That is, Ptolemy

the temple with wailing and with tears. ¹⁷Those who remained behind in the city, being agitated, rushed out, supposing something mysterious was happening. ¹⁸And the virgins, secluded in their chambers, rushed out along with those who bore them and gave themselves up to sprinkling their hair with dust, where also they began to fill the streets with moaning. ¹⁹And even those who had been recently arrayed for all those now appointed, and neglecting the modesty befitting them, they gathered together, running in a disorderly fashion. ²⁰And at this, the mothers and those nursing abandoned the newborn among the children, here and there—some in houses and others in the streets, heedlessly assembling together in the most high temple. ²¹And manifold was the petition of those who gathered in this place because of the things impiously being plotted by that man. ²²And with these, those who were emboldened concerning their compatriots would not tolerate his pressing for completion and the carrying out of his intended plan. ²³And crying out to make an assault with weapons and die courageously by the ancestral law, they created a great tumult in the holy place, and having been dissuaded with difficulty by both the old men and the elders, they arrived at the same posture of prayer. ²⁴And the crowd, indeed, as before these things, was occupied in praying, ²⁵but the elders near the king attempted in various ways to change his arrogant mind from the plan being conceived. ²⁶But being emboldened and having dismissed all already, even so he began to make his approach, already thinking to bring to completion the previously mentioned plan. ²⁷And so those who were near him, observing these things, they turned together with our people in order to call upon the one having all power in the present circumstances to defend them, not looking around at this lawless and arrogant deed. ²⁸Now from both the incessant and vehement outcry of the gathering crowds there was an immense roar. ²⁹For it seemed that not only the people but even the walls and the whole ground were ringing, in as much as in truth at that time all would take in exchange death rather than the profanation of the holy place.

2 ²"Lord, Lord, king of the heavens and master of the whole of creation, *Simon's* holy among the holy ones, only ruler, almighty, give heed to us who *Prayer* are being tormented by a wicked and impure one, who has become insolent with arrogance and power. ³For you are the creator of all things and who rules over everything, are a righteous master, and you judge those who do anything with insolence and arrogance. ⁴Those who previously did wrong—among whom were giants, who trusted in Rome and arrogance—you destroyed, bringing on them immeasurable water. ⁵You consumed with fire and brimstone the Sodomites who acted arrogantly, being unknown for depravities, making an example for those who come after. ⁶You made your power known, in addition to that which you made your great might known, upon testing the insolent Pharaoh, who enslaved your holy people Israel with manifold and many punishments. ⁷And when he pursued with chariots and a multitude of troops, you overwhelmed them with the depth of the sea; but those who trusted in you, the one holding power over the whole of creation, you carried over safely. ⁸And those who saw the works of your hand praised you, the Almighty. ⁹You, O King, who created the boundless and immeasurable earth, chose this city and consecrated this

place for your name, even though you have no need of anything, and you glorified it with a magnificent manifestation, making its structure for the glory of your great and honored name. [10]And, loving the house of Israel, you promised that if a reverse should happen to us and distress should overtake us, and coming to our place, we should pray, you would hear our prayer. [11]And indeed you are faithful and true. [12]And since frequently also when our ancestors were afflicted, you helped them in their humiliation, and you rescued them from great evils. [13]And now look, O Holy King, we are being tormented because of our many and great sins, and we have been subjected to our enemies, and we have become exhausted in our powerlessness. [14]But in our calamity, this arrogant and impure one is determined to insult wantonly the holy place on earth dedicated to your glorious name. [15]For your dwelling-place, the heaven of heaven, is inaccessible to humans. [16]But since you were pleased for your glory to be among your people Israel, you consecrated this place. [17]Do not punish us because of the uncleanness of these people, nor chastise us because of their profanation, in order that the lawless may not boast in their heart, nor exult in the arrogance of their tongue, saying, [18]'We trampled on the house of holiness as the houses of idols are trampled down.' [19]Wipe away our sins, and scatter abroad our faults, and show forth your mercy at this hour. [20]Let your mercies overtake us quickly, and cause praises in the mouth of those who have fallen and have been broken in spirit, bringing about peace for us."

*Ptolemy and the Wrath of God* [21]Then God, the overseer of all things, and primogenitor, holy among the holy ones, having heard the lawful entreaty, struck the one who exalted himself exceedingly with insolence and arrogance, [22]shaking him from one side and to the other like a reed is shaken by the wind, so that he lay powerless on the ground, and besides being paralyzed in his limbs, not even able to speak, being struck by a righteous judgment. [23]Then both his friends and bodyguards, seeing the severe chastisement that had overtaken him, even fearing lest he might lose his life, quickly dragged him out, having been struck with exceeding fear. [24]But later in time, when he came to himself, by no means did he come to repentance, though being punished with a threat; but he departed, being made bitter.

*Ptolemy's Bitterness Toward the Judeans* [25]And being carried back to Egypt, and his deeds of wickedness increased by both the previously mentioned drinking companions and comrades, who were separated from everything just, [26]not only was he not satisfied with his countless insolent deeds, but he also advanced to such a degree of audacious presumption that he contrived slanderous reports in those places. And many of his friends, gazing at the purpose of the king, also themselves followed the will of that man. [27]He proposed to disseminate publicly a censure against the Judean people. Erecting a stone pillar near the tower in the palace, he carved an inscription: [28]"Anyone who would not sacrifice in their temples shall enter, and all the Judeans shall be subjected to enrollment for poll tax and to servile status; and those who oppose this are to be brought by force to be killed.[a] [29]And those who are enrolled shall also be branded by fire on the body with the ivy-leaf marking of Dionysus and assigned before to their former limited status." [30]But in order that he might appear not to

---

[a] Lit. "to be removed *from* living"

be hated by all, he wrote under the inscription, "But if some from among them choose to live with those who have been initiated in accordance with mysteries, they shall have political rights equal with the Alexandrians."

³¹Some, detesting the approaches toward religious matters of the city on the surface, easily gave themselves up so as to share some of the great glory through having an association with the king. ³²But the majority, noble in spirit, remained strong and did not stray from piety, and by exchanging money for their life, they were attempting to rescue themselves without fear from the registration. ³³And they had restored good hope for obtaining help, and those departing from them, they were abhorring, and they were judging them as enemies of the people, and they were depriving them of communal association and help.

**3** And hearing these things, the impious man became angry to such an extent that he was angry not only with those Judeans throughout Alexandria, but he was opposed even more bitterly to those in the greater territory, and he ordered all to be gathered together hastily into one place, and to kill them[a] by the worst fate. ²But while these things were being organized, a hostile rumor was being cast out against the Judean nation by people who agreed together to do harm, a pretext being given for a report that perchance they were hindering them from practicing their customs. ³But the Judeans were maintaining unswerving goodwill and faithfulness toward the kings. ⁴And worshiping God and living his law, they used to practice separation with respect to foods, for which reason some used to appear to be hostile. ⁵But adorning their way of life with the good conduct of the righteous, they had established good repute with all people. ⁶Now while good conduct for the nation was common talk among all, foreigners by no means took account of it. ⁷But they were repeating over and over the differences concerning acts of worship and foods, saying that the Judean people were loyal neither to the king nor to the powers, but they were hostile and greatly opposed to the affairs of state, and they were taken by no ordinary fear.

*Ptolemy Opposes Judeans Everywhere*

⁸But the Greeks in the city, having in no way been wronged, upon seeing unexpected tumult around these men and unforeseen mobs forming, they did not have the power to help them, for their condition was one of tyranny. They were encouraging them, and feeling intolerably, and were thinking that these things would change. ⁹For so great a community should not be disregarded in this manner, since it had done nothing amiss. ¹⁰And already some neighbors and even friends and business associates, secretly drawing aside some of them, were offering assurances to support and to exhibit all diligence to defend them.

¹¹Then that person,[b] exulting in his prosperity for the moment and not regarding the power of the supreme God, but thinking to remain continually in the same plan, wrote this letter against them:

*Ptolemy's Decree*

¹²"King Ptolemy Philopator to the generals and soldiers throughout Egypt and in every place: Greetings and good health. ¹³And I myself am also in good health, and our affairs prosper. ¹⁴When our expedition into Asia took place, of which you yourselves also know, with the not lightly

---

[a] Lit. "remove *them from* living"  [b] That is, the king

given help of the gods, when it was brought to a conclusion according to plan, [15]we considered that we should nurture the nations inhabiting Coelesyria and Phoenicia, not with the violence of the spear, but with fairness and great benevolence, gladly doing well. [16]And upon distributing great revenues to the temples in all cities, we also went to Jerusalem, going up to pay honor to the temple of those wicked ones who never cease from their folly. [17]And they accepted our presence in word but disingenuously in deed. We were eager to enter into the temple itself and to honor it with extraordinary and beautiful gifts; [18]being carried away by ancient arrogance, they hindered our entry but were spared from our might on account of the benevolence that we have toward all humans. [19]But having established openly their enmity toward us, as the only one of the nations lifting their heads against kings and their benefactors, they are not willing to endure any action as legitimate.

[20]"But we accommodated ourselves to the folly of these people and also crossed over to Egypt, having dealt victoriously with all the nations benevolently, we acted just as it was fitting. [21]And among other things, making forgiveness toward their compatriots known to everyone, on account of both our alliance and the countless matters entrusted to them from the beginning, with sincerity, to make a change, we were also disposed to deem them worthy of Alexandrian citizenship and to make them participants of our perpetual priests. [22]But they received it to the contrary and, with innate meanspiritedness, rejected what is excellent. And continually turning aside to what is worthless, [23]they turned back not only the priceless citizenship, but also detest both with word and silence the few among them genuinely being disposed toward us, suspecting in every situation, in keeping with their shameful way of life, that we would swiftly overturn our policies. [24]Therefore, being persuaded rightly even by proofs that these people are ill-disposed to us in every way, and taking thought, in case a sudden disorder arise against us afterward, and we have these wicked traitors and barbarous enemies behind our back, [25]we have given an order that as soon as this letter arrives, immediately you are to send to us those living amongst you with their wives and children with insolence and cruel treatments, being locked up with chains made of iron on every side, for a cruel and infamous slaughter befitting enemies. [26]For when these people have been punished together, we comprehend that the affairs of state will be established for us perfectly in stability and in a more excellent condition, in a future time. [27]And whoever perchance shelters any of the Judeans, from an elderly person to a child, even to the nursing babes, shall be cruelly put to death with most hateful torments, along with their whole household. [28]And the one who wishes to give information, to whom will go the property of the one who falls under chastisement, will also receive two thousand drachmas from the royal money and will be rewarded with freedom. [29]But every place where, if by chance a Judean is detected who is being sheltered, without exception, shall be cordoned off and set ablaze, and to every mortal creature it shall appear completely useless for all time."

[30]And accordingly the content of the letter was written in this manner.

4 And in every place where this decree became known, a feast with loud *The Judeans* noise and joy at the public expense was organized for the Gentiles, as *Deported* perchance their enmity, having been hardened long beforehand in their *to Alexandria* minds, was now being revealed openly. ²But for the Judeans there was indescribable mourning and a most lamentable loud cry with tears; everywhere their hearts were aflame with groaning, bewailing the unexpected ruin suddenly being inflicted on them. ³What district or city, or what a most lamentable place without exception, or what streets were not filled up with lamentation and weeping for them? ⁴For in this way, with pitiless harshness of spirit by the commanders of the army in city after city, they were being dispatched with one mind so that, on account of their extraordinary punishments, even some of their enemies, receiving in front of their eyes the common object of pity and considering the uncertain conclusion of life, wept at their most miserable expulsion. ⁵For an old man, being covered full of gray hair from old age, was being led away, crooked with sluggishness of feet, with an impulse of violent ruin, without any respect, making full use of a swift march. ⁶And the young women just having entered the bridal chamber for a marital partnership of life exchanged joy to share in weeping and to mix hair wet with unguent with dust so as to defile it, and being led away unveiled, with one accord they began a dirge in place of a wedding song, as though having been rent asunder by the whelp of a foreign nation. ⁷And the captives were violently dragged away in public up to the entrance to the ship. ⁸And their husbands, in the full bloom of their youthful prime, wearing a noose instead of a garland around their necks, instead of feasting and amusement natural to youth, the remaining days of their wedding celebrations were spent in lamentation, seeing the grave already lying open at their feet. ⁹And they were led down like wild animals, taken forcibly with iron bonds for constraint, some fastened by the neck to the benches of the ship, and others made fast by the feet with unbreakable fetters. ¹⁰And further, with thick planking being fixed from above in such a manner that their eyes were totally darkened, during the whole voyage they received the treatment reserved for traitors.

¹¹And when these people were brought to the place being called Schedia, *The Judeans* and the aimless voyage was finished, just as had been decreed by the king, *Held in* he commanded them to encamp in the hippodrome, having established *Schedia* it outside the city with an immense circumference, and having made it very well situated for pointing out to public shame to all those returning to the city, and to those going from these cities into the territory for a trip abroad, so that they could not communicate with his forces, nor could they claim the enclosing wall at all. ¹²And when this was done, hearing their compatriots from the city were frequently going out in secret to bitterly lament the ignominious suffering of their brothers, ¹³becoming very angry, he also ordered these people to be treated diligently in exactly the same way as the others, not being spared in any way the punishment of the others. ¹⁴And all the race was to be registered by name, not for the kind of work already briefly explained, according to the way of servitude; but when they had been tortured with the outrages ordered against them, they were to be completely destroyed within the period of one day. ¹⁵Therefore

the registration of these people took place with bitter haste and zealous assiduity from the rising of the sun to its going down, the completion taking place over forty days, while remaining unfinished.

¹⁶And the king, having been filled greatly and continually with joy, organized drinking-parties at the locations of all of his idols, with a mind overflowing far from the truth, and with a profane mouth, praising mute things not even being able to speak or to give aid to them, but speaking improper things against God. ¹⁷And after the aforementioned interval of time, the clerks insisted to the king that they were able no longer to carry out the registration of the Judeans on account of the immeasurable multitude of them. ¹⁸Although the majority were still in the territory, some who had conspired were still in their houses, and others were even at that place, so that bringing the registration about was impossible for all the generals in Egypt. ¹⁹And after threatening them severely as though having been bribed to contrive a plan*a* of escape, it happened that he clearly became convinced about this matter ²⁰when they asserted with proof that even the stock of papyrus and writing reeds had already come to an end among those who used them. ²¹But this was the working of the unconquerable providence of the one giving aid to the Judeans from heaven.

*The Judeans Escape Execution— Twice*

**5** Then the king, completely inflexible, having been filled with cruel wrath and bitter anger, and summoning Hermon, the one close to the care of the elephants, ²he ordered him during the coming day to give all the elephants, being five hundred in number, abundant handfuls of frankincense and much unmixed wine to drink. And after making them wild with the copious abundance of the drink, to lead them in, for a meeting with the fate of the Judeans. ³Indeed, upon giving these orders, he turned to feasting, gathering together with those of his friends and the army who were exceedingly hateful toward the Judeans. ⁴And Hermon, the master of the elephants, punctually began to complete what was ordered. ⁵And the public servants near them,*b* going out in the evening, were fettering the hands of those enduring distress, and they took precautions for security around them through the rest of the night, supposing that with one blow the race would receive a deadly end. ⁶Now the Judeans, who appeared to the Gentiles to be without any protection on account of the tribulation accompanied with chains that befell them from all quarters, ⁷with a hard to silence cry of mourning accompanied with tears, they called upon all their Almighty Lord and merciful God and Father, who rules over every power, praying ⁸he would avert the wicked plan set against them and rescue them with a magnificent manifestation from the fate ready at their feet. ⁹And so their entreaty fervently went up to heaven. ¹⁰And Hermon, upon giving the pitiless elephants to drink so that they were filled with a great abundance of wine and also were filled with frankincense, arrived at the palace at daybreak to report to the king about these things. ¹¹But God sent to the king a portion of sleep, the precious creation from the time of eternity, being bestowed by night and day by the one giving it freely to whom all perchance he will be willing. ¹²And he was restrained from his unlawful purpose by a pleasant and deep sleep through the action of the

---

*a* Lit. "for a contrivance" *b* That is, the Judeans

Master, being utterly disappointed and being cheated out of his exceedingly unalterable plan. ¹³And the Judeans were praising their holy God, having escaped the hour that had been announced, and they entreated again the one who is easily appeased to show the power of the exceeding strength of his hand to the arrogant Gentiles. ¹⁴And being nearly the middle of the tenth hour by this time, the one who had been put in charge of the invitations, seeing the guests crowding together, approached the king and nudged him. ¹⁵And waking him with difficulty, he informed him the time of the banquet was slipping by already, making a report concerning these things. ¹⁶The king, after considering this and returning to his drinking party, commanded those who had arrived at the banquet to recline opposite him. ¹⁷And when this was done, he began to urge that, giving themselves to feasting, they spend the present part of the banquet in cheer, celebrating greatly. ¹⁸And after the conversation grew repugnant for a while, the king, summoning Hermon with a threat of bitterness, inquired why the Judeans had been allowed to survive through the present day. ¹⁹But when he pointed out that he had brought to completion what had been ordered at night, and his friends confirmed it, ²⁰having a savageness worse than that of Phalaris, he*a* said, "They*b* should be grateful for today's sleep, but without delay, at the fading day, prepare the elephants in the same way for the extermination of the lawless Judeans." ²¹And after the king had spoken, all those being present readily and joyously agreeing with one accord, each one departed to his own house. ²²And they did not use the nighttime so much for sleep as for devising all sorts of mocking for those who appeared miserable.

²³Now as soon as the cock had crowed at daybreak, then Hermon, having armed the beasts fully, began to move in the great colonnade. ²⁴And the multitude in the city had been gathering for the pitiable spectacle, waiting for the morning with eagerness. ²⁵And the Judeans, being at their last gasp because of the time being short, stretching out their hands toward heaven, with tearful supplication along with mournful strains, began to implore the supreme God to rescue them again quickly. ²⁶Now the rays of the sun were not yet inserted, and while the king was receiving his friends, Hermon, arriving, called on the king to go out: "You are showing that the desire of the king was laid in readiness." ²⁷Now, receiving the report and being astonished at the lawless exit, having been seized, he inquired with ignorance in regard to everything—because what was explained further to him had been accomplished zealously. ²⁸But this was the working of God, who is Lord over all things, who had put forgetfulness in his mind of the things previously contrived by him. ²⁹Hermon and all the friends were pointing out, "The wild animals and the forces have been prepared, O king, according to your assiduous plan." ³⁰But at these words, he was filled with fierce wrath because all his thought concerning these matters had been scattered in the providence of God; looking fixedly with menace, he said, ³¹"If your parents or the children of your children were present here, they would have prepared an abundant feast for the wild animals in place of the Judeans, who are without reproach to me and who are demonstrating

---

*a* That is, the king  *b* That is, the Judeans

a completely steadfast loyalty above others to my ancestors. ³²Albeit if it were not for the affection of common nurture and your service, you would have been deprived of life in place of them." ³³Thus Hermon endured an unexpected and dangerous threat, and he was downcast in his outward appearance and in his face. ³⁴And one by one the friends, sullenly slipping away, dismissed those who had assembled, each one to his own occupation. ³⁵And the Judeans, hearing the things spoken by the king, began to praise the manifest God, the Lord, the King who reigns, having also obtained this help from him.

³⁶And the king, having organized the whole banquet according to the same rules, invited the guests to return to their cheer. ³⁷And summoning Hermon with a threat, he said, "Now how many times is it necessary for you to give an order about these same things, you wretched person? ³⁸Now fully arm the elephants yet again for tomorrow for the extermination of the Judeans." ³⁹But those kinsmen who reclined together with him, marveling at his unstable mind, pleaded as follows: ⁴⁰"O king, how long*a* will you test us, commanding now a third time to destroy them and again canceling your opinions in a reversal concerning these matters? ⁴¹On account of these things, the city is in tumult because of its expectation and is now filled with tumultuous bands of people and altogether runs the risk of being plundered."

⁴²Whence the king, a tyrant in every way, being filled with recklessness and having almost no regard for the changes of heart coming about in him concerning the punishment of the Judeans, firmly swearing an oath without end to send these people to Hades without delay, being tormented by the knees and the foot of the beasts, ⁴³and marching against Judah, he will swiftly establish level ground with fire and with spear, and their temple, which had been inaccessible to us, quickly with fire to render it for all time of those who performed the sacrifice there. ⁴⁴Then the exceedingly glad friends and kinsmen, departing with confidence, began to assign the forces to the well-situated places of the city for the purpose of keeping watch. ⁴⁵And the master of the elephants, having driven the beasts nearly, so he said, into a condition like madness with fragrant draughts of wine mixed with frankincense, while having dressed them frighteningly with equipment, ⁴⁶about dawn, when the city had been already filled with countless hordes going toward the hippodrome, entering into the courtyard, he stirred up the king to the matter set before him. ⁴⁷But having his wicked heart filled full with cruel rage, he rushed out, with all fierceness along with the wild beasts, wishing in his invulnerable heart to behold even with the pupil of his own eye the painful and miserable destruction of the aforementioned people. ⁴⁸Now when the Judeans saw the cloud of dust and heard the roaring tumult of the elephants marching out against the gate, and of the following of the armed force, and of the marching of the horde, ⁴⁹thinking that moment to be the last one of life for them, the conclusion of their most miserable expectation, being turned to a cry of lamentation and wailing, they began to kiss one another, embracing their kinsmen on their necks, parents falling on children and mothers on young

---

*a* Lit. "until what"

women, and other women having newborn babies on their breasts drawing their last milk. [50] Nevertheless, upon considering the helps they previously received from heaven, throwing themselves prostrate with one accord, and separating the infants from the breasts, [51] they cried out with a very great voice, beseeching the Lord of all to have compassion on them with an intervention now, as they had come to the gates of death.

**6** Now a certain man, Eleazar, prominent among the Judeans from the territory, having now obtained stature with the privilege of age, and having been adorned with every virtue throughout his life, restraining the elders around him from invoking the holy God, and he prayed as follows, [2] "O King, mighty in power, most high, Almighty God, who governs the whole creation with mercy, [3] look upon the seed of Abraham, upon the children of the sanctified Jacob, the people of your consecrated portion, who are perishing unjustly as strangers in a strange land. [4] O Father, you destroyed Pharaoh, the former ruler of this Egypt, with his multitude of chariots,[a] who was presumptuous with lawless insolence and boasting tongue, along with his arrogant army, drowning them in the sea, displaying the light of your mercy to the people of Israel. [5] Sennacherib, cruel king of the Assyrians, who exalted himself with his innumerable forces, who had already taken the whole earth in his hand by the spear, and who was lifted up against your holy city, speaking grievously with boasting and arrogance, you, O Master, shattered him, showing your power openly to many nations. [6] The three companions in Babylon who had given their life to the fire of their own free choice, in order not to serve worthless things, you rescued them, to the point of a hair not being harmed, when you wet the fiery furnace with dew and sent a flame on all their enemies. [7] Daniel, who was thrown down into the earth to lions as food for the beasts on account of false accusations made from envy, you led up unharmed into the light. [8] And Jonah, who was wasting away in the belly of a sea monster living in the deep, who you looked on, showing him, O Father, unharmed to all his family members. [9] And now, you who hate insolence, who are plenteous in mercy, O judge of everything, show yourself swiftly to those holy ones of the race of Israel who are being spitefully treated by the abominable, lawless Gentiles. [10] And if our life has become entangled in impieties during our exile, rescue us from the hand of our enemies and destroy us, O Master, by whatever fate you choose. [11] Do not let the vain minded praise their vain gods for the destruction of your beloved, saying, 'Not even their God rescued them.' [12] And you, O Eternal One, who have all might and all power, watch over us now and have mercy upon us who are being deprived of life in the manner of traitors by the irrational insolence of lawless people. [13] Now let the Gentiles cower in fear today at your unconquerable force, O Revered One, you who have power over salvation of the family of Jacob. [14] The whole multitude of children and their parents beseech you with tears. [15] Let it be shown to all the Gentiles that you are with us, O Lord, and you have not turned back your face from us, but just as you have said, 'Not even when they were in the land of their enemies did I neglect them.' So accomplish it, O Lord."

*Eleazar's Prayer*

[a] Lit. "who multiplied his chariots"

<sup></sup>

*Glorified Angels Save the Judeans* [16]Now just as Eleazar was ending his prayer, the king marched into the hippodrome with the wild beasts and with all the insolence of his power. [17]And when the Judeans beheld it, they cried out to heaven loudly, so that even the valleys lying nearby reverberated, causing an uncontrollable fear in the whole army. [18]Then the very glorious and almighty and trustworthy God, showing forth his holy face, opened the heavenly gates, from which two glorified angels, terrible to behold, descended, visible to all except to the Judeans. [19]And they also opposed the power of the enemies; they filled them with confusion and cowardice, and they bound them in immovable fetters. [20]And even the body of the king was shuddering a little, and forgetfulness took his sullen insolence. [21]And the beasts turned back on the accompanying armed forces and began to trample and destroy them.

[22]And the wrath of the king was changed into pity and tears on account of the things previously devised by him. [23]For when he heard the wailing and saw them all prostrate for destruction, weeping with anger, he began to violently threaten his friends, saying, [24]"You are committing treason and have surpassed tyrants in cruelty, and you are attempting to deprive even me, your benefactor, of my rule now and my life, secretly devising things that are not advantageous to the kingdom. [25]Who has unreasonably gathered together here those keeping the fortresses of our territory faithfully, having driven each one from his home? [26]Who has beset so unlawfully with injurious treatments those who from the beginning differed from all the nations with goodwill toward us in every way, and who have often accepted the worst of human dangers? [27]Loosen and untie the unjust bonds; allow them to leave for their own homes in peace, asking pardon for the things being commanded. [28]Set free the sons of the almighty living God in heaven, who from our ancestors until now are producing an unimpeded stability with glory in our state affairs." [29]So indeed the king stated these things; and those who were unbound immediately[a] praised their holy savior God, having escaped now death.

*Celebration of Miraculous Deliverance* [30]So then the king, summoning to the city the one over the revenues, ordered him to supply both wine and the other necessities for feasting to the Judeans over seven days, having decided they should celebrate their deliverance in this matter with all cheer in the place in which they supposed they would receive destruction. [31]Then those who had previously been treated shamefully and were near death—or rather, who had stood at it—instead of a bitter and most miserable fate organized a feast of deliverance at the place having been prepared for their destruction and burial into a banquet, and they dispersed full of joy. [32]And ceasing their most lamentable strains of lament, they took up an ancestral song praising God, the deliverer of Israel and worker of wonders; having rejected all lamentation and wailing, they organized troops of dancers and singers as a sign of peaceful cheer. [33]And likewise also the king, bringing together a large banquet because of these events, began to ceaselessly give thanks magnificently to heaven for the unexpected deliverance happening to them. [34]And those who previously had appointed them for destruction and to be food for the birds, and who had registered them with joy,

---

<sup>a</sup> Lit. "in indivisible time"

groaned, having clothed themselves with shame and their fiery-breathing recklessness having been vigorously quenched. ³⁵And the Judeans, as we stated before, having organized the previously mentioned troop of dancers and singers, were celebrating with joyous thanksgiving and psalms accompanied with feasting. ³⁶And when they had ordained a communal ordinance concerning these matters for all their sojourning community for generations to come, they established the previously mentioned days for a cheerful celebration, not for the sake of a drinking party and gluttony, but on account of the deliverance by God that had happened to them. ³⁷And they appealed to the king, asking for release to return to their own homes.

³⁸And they registered them from the twenty-fifth day of the month of Pachon until the fourth day of Epeiph, for forty days, and they fixed their destruction from the fifth of Epeiph until the seventh, three days, ³⁹on which also the Lord of all, very gloriously displaying his mercy, delivered them together intact.

⁴⁰And they feasted, being provided with everything by the king, until the fourteenth day on which also they made petition concerning their release. ⁴¹And having approved it for them, the king wrote for them the written below letter to the commanders of the army in each city, generously containing his concern:

7 "King Ptolemy Philopator, to the commanders of the army in Egypt and to all those who have been put in charge over state affairs: Greetings and good health. ²And we are in good health ourselves and also our children, the great God guiding our ordinances just as we choose. ³Certain of our friends, frequently urging us through malice, joined in persuading us to gather together in order to punish the Judeans as a body under the control of the kingdom, with astonishing retribution as deserters, ⁴insisting that our affairs would never be stable on account of the enmity that these people hold toward the nations, until this might be accomplished. ⁵These, who also led them down in bonds with cruel treatment as slaves—or rather, as traitors—without any inquiry or close examination, they attempted to destroy them, crippling themselves with a savageness more cruel than the custom of the Scythians. ⁶But we, threatening them severely because of these deeds, in accordance with that tolerance we have toward all humans, granting their lives with difficulty, and having learned that the heavenly God surely has protected the Judeans through everything as a father fighting at their side for his sons, ⁷and taking into consideration the steadfast goodwill of friends that they have toward us and our ancestors, we have rightly acquitted them of every charge of whatever kind. ⁸And we have ordered all to return to their own homes, each one of them, no one in any way hurting them without exception, nor reproaching concerning the things contrary to reason that have happened. ⁹For you know that if we plot any evil against these people or we trouble them at all, we will not have a human being but the one who is Lord of every power, the most high God, as adversary for us, in vengeance for our deeds in everything without any possibility of escape throughout all time. Farewell."

¹⁰Now receiving this letter, they did not hurry immediately about their departure, but they petitioned the king that those from the Judean people

*Ptolmey's Letter Acknowledges God's Protection*

*The Judeans' Joyous Return Homeward*

who had transgressed against the holy God and the law of God of their own free choice should obtain deserved punishment through them. [11]They insisted that those having transgressed the divine commandments for the sake of the belly would never be favorably disposed to the ordinances of the king either. [12]And acknowledging and recommending the truth that they were speaking, he[a] granted to them permission of all sorts in order that they might utterly destroy those who had transgressed against the law of God in every place under his dominion with boldness, without any royal authority or oversight. [13]Then, after extolling him as was fitting, their priests and the whole multitude, crying out the hallelujah, departed with joy. [14]And these were killing and destroying on their way any compatriot falling before them from those who had defiled themselves, making an example of them. [15]And on that day, they slew over three hundred men, a day which they celebrated also with cheer accompanied with joy, having killed the profaners. [16]And the ones who clung to God to the point of death, having the complete release of deliverance, began to move off from the city, decked with all sorts of fragrant flowers, accompanied with cheer and loud cries in praise and hymns with all kinds of melodies, giving thanks to the holy God of their fathers, deliverer of Israel.

[17]When arriving in Ptolemais, named "Rose-bearing" on account of the particular character of the place, in which the fleet waited for them for seven days in accordance with their communal decision, [18]there they celebrated the deliverance with a drinking party, for the king supplied to them magnanimously all things for their departure to each person till the time when they should arrive at their own homes. [19]And when they had landed in peace with appropriate thanksgivings, even there they likewise established these days to celebrate in good cheer for the time of their sojourning, [20]which events having also devoted to writing on a pillar and dedicating a place of prayer at the site of the banquet, they departed unharmed, free, and overjoyed, having been rescued by land and sea and river by the command of the king, each to their [21]previous place. Possessing authority among their enemies, with honor and respect, they were extorted of their possessions by no one at all. [22]And they received back all their things in accordance with the registration, so that those possessing anything of theirs restored it to them with great tribute. The great God perfectly performed magnificent things for their deliverance.

[23]Blessed be the deliverer of Israel for all times! Amen.

---

[a] That is, the king

*Introduction to*

# 2 ESDRAS

S ECOND ESDRAS IS A composite work. Its core (chs. 3–14) is a Jewish apocalypse dating from about AD 100, probably originally written in Hebrew (often known as 4 Ezra). Writing in the guise of Ezra, a historical figure associated with the restoration of Jerusalem after its first destruction by Nebuchadnezzar in 587 BC, the author wrestles with God concerning the justice not merely of allowing Jerusalem to have been destroyed (again) by the Romans in AD 70 but also of allowing Rome—surely guilty of far worse offenses against God than his own people!—to continue to prosper for decades after the fact. The author must look to the future, to God's eventual punishment of Rome and restoration of Jerusalem, for God's justice, but his assurance that God's justice will manifest itself allows him to continue to affirm the value of a covenant-observant life. This Jewish apocalypse (chs. 3–14) provides an important comparative text for the study of the New Testament, particularly in its reflections on Adam's sin affecting the whole of humanity (cf. Rom 5) and in its portrayal of Roman imperialism (and God's forthcoming judgment) in terms stunningly similar to what one finds in Revelation 13–20.

This core apocalyptic text attracted two Christian additions (chs. 1–2, 15–16), both probably composed in Greek. Second Esdras 1–2 appears to have been written in the second century AD and is particularly interested in the relationship of the church to Israel. It reflects clear knowledge of Matthew and Revelation. Second Esdras 15–16 appears to have been composed in the third century AD and reflects a time of more serious persecution as well as the ongoing hope that the yoke of Rome would at last be thrown off the necks of the provinces they controlled (especially Asia, which is likely therefore to have been the author's location).

The composite work was preserved as an appendix to the Latin Vulgate, which provides the basis for this translation. It also survives in Syriac, Ethiopic, Armenian, and several other languages, all of which are important to consider alongside the Latin where recovery of the most original text is the goal.

—D. A. deSilva

# 2 Esdras[a]

Genealogy of Ezra **1** The second book of the prophet Ezra, the son of Saraiah, the son of Azaraiah, the son of Helkiah, the son of Shallum, the son of Zadok, the son of Ahitub, [2] the son of Ahijah, the son of Phinehas, the son of Eli, the son of Amariah, the son of Azariah, the son of Meraioth, the son of Arna, the son of Uzzi, the son of Borith, the son of Abishua, the son of Phinehas, the son of Eleazar, [3] the son of Aaron, of the tribe of Levi, who was captive in the land of the Medes, in the reign of Artaxerxes king of the Persians.

*Ezra's Call* [4] The word of the Lord came to me, saying, [5] "Go and announce to my people their sinful deeds, and to their children their wickedness which they have done against me, that they may tell their children's children, [6] because the sins of their fathers have increased in them, for they have forgotten me, and have offered sacrifices to foreign gods. [7] Did I not bring them out of the land of Egypt, out of the house of bondage? But they have provoked me to wrath and have despised my counsels. [8] So pull out the hair of your head and cast all evils upon them, for they have not been obedient to my law, but they are a rebellious people. [9] How long shall I endure them, to whom I have done so much good? [10] I have overthrown many kings for their sakes. I have struck down Pharaoh with his servants and all his army. [11] I have destroyed all the nations before them. In the east, I have scattered the people of two provinces, even of Tyre and Sidon, and have slain all their adversaries.

*God's Former Acts of Deliverance* [12] "Therefore, speak to them, saying: [13] The Lord says, truly I brought you through the sea, and where there was no path I made highways for you. I gave you Moses for a leader and Aaron for a priest. [14] I gave you light in a pillar of fire. I have done great wonders among you, yet you have forgotten me, says the Lord.

[15] "The Lord Almighty says: The quails were a sign for you. I gave you a camp for your protection, but you complained there. [16] You did not celebrate in my name for the destruction of your enemies, but even to this day you still complain. [17] Where are the benefits that I have given you? When you were hungry and thirsty in the wilderness, did you not cry out to me, [18] saying, 'Why have you brought us into this wilderness to kill us? It would have been better for us to have served the Egyptians than to die in this wilderness.' [19] I had pity on your mourning and gave you manna for food. You ate the bread of angels. [20] When you were thirsty, did I not split the rock, and water flowed out in abundance? Because of the heat, I covered you with the leaves of the trees. [21] I divided fruitful lands among you. I drove out the Canaanites, the Perizzites, and the Philistines before you. What more shall I do for you?" says the Lord.

---

[a] This translation is an adaptation of English versions in the public domain translated from the Vulgate; it largely follows the Clementine Vulgate

²²The Lord Almighty says, "When you were in the wilderness, at the bit- *Persistent* ter stream, thirsty and blaspheming my name, ²³I did not send fire upon *Sin Provokes* you for your blasphemies, but threw a tree in the water, and made the river *God's* sweet. ²⁴What shall I do to you, O Jacob? You, Judah, would not obey me. I *Judgment* will turn myself to other nations, and I will give my name to them, that they may keep my statutes. ²⁵Since you have forsaken me, I also will forsake you. When you ask me to be merciful to you, I will have no mercy upon you. ²⁶Whenever you call upon me, I will not hear you, for you have defiled your hands with blood, and your feet are swift to commit murder. ²⁷It is not as though you have forsaken me, but your own selves," says the Lord.

²⁸The Lord Almighty says, "Have I not asked you as a father his sons, as a mother her daughters, and as a nurse her young babies, ²⁹that you would be my people, and I would be your God, that you would be my children, and I would be your father? ³⁰I gathered you together, as a hen gathers her chicks under her wings. But now, what should I do to you? I will cast you out from my presence. ³¹When you offer burnt sacrifices to me, I will turn my face from you, for I have rejected your solemn feast days, your new moons, and your circumcisions of the flesh. ³²I sent you my servants, the prophets, whom you have taken and slain, and torn their bodies in pieces, whose blood I will require from you," says the Lord.

³³The Lord Almighty says, "Your house is desolate. I will cast you out as the wind blows stubble. ³⁴Your children will not be fruitful, for they have neglected my commandment to you, and done what is evil before me. ³⁵I will give your houses to a people that will come, who not having heard of me yet believe me. Those to whom I have shown no signs will do what I have commanded. ³⁶They have seen no prophets, yet they will remember their former condition. ³⁷I call to witness the gratitude of the people who will come, whose little ones rejoice with gladness. Although they see me not with bodily eyes, yet in spirit they will believe what I say."

³⁸And now, father, behold with glory, and see the people that come from the east: ³⁹to them I will give as leaders, Abraham, Isaac, and Jacob, Hosea, Amos, and Micah, Joel, Obadiah, and Jonah, ⁴⁰Nahum, and Habakkuk, Zephaniah, Haggai, Zechariah, and Malachi, who is also called the Lord's messenger.

2 The Lord says, "I brought this people out of bondage. I gave them my *Judgment of* commandments by my servants the prophets, whom they would not *God's People* listen to, but made my counsels void. ²The mother who bore them says to *and Woe to* them, 'Go your way, my children, for I am a widow and forsaken. ³I brought *Assyria* you up with gladness, and I have lost you with sorrow and heaviness, for you have sinned before the Lord God, and done what is evil before me. ⁴But now what can I do for you? For I am a widow and forsaken. Go your way, my children, and ask for mercy from the Lord.' ⁵As for me, O father, I call upon you as a witness in addition to the mother of these children, because they would not keep my covenant, ⁶that you may bring them to confusion, and their mother to ruin, that they may have no offspring. ⁷Let them be scattered abroad among the gentiles. Let their names be blotted out of the earth, for they have despised my covenant. ⁸Woe to you, Assyria, you who hide the unrighteous with you! You wicked nation, remember what I did to Sodom and Gomorrah, ⁹whose land lies in lumps of pitch and heaps

of ashes. That is what I will also do to those who have not listened to me," says the Lord Almighty.

¹⁰ The Lord says to Ezra, "Tell my people that I will give them the kingdom of Jerusalem, which I would have given to Israel. ¹¹ I will also take their glory back to myself, and give these the everlasting tabernacles which I had prepared for them. ¹² They will have the tree of life for fragrant perfume. They will neither labor nor be weary. ¹³ Ask, and you will receive. Pray that your days may be few, that they may be shortened. The kingdom is already prepared for you. Watch! ¹⁴ Call heaven and earth to witness. Call them to witness, for I have left out evil, and created the good, for I live," says the Lord.

¹⁵ "Mother, embrace your children. I will bring them out with gladness like a dove does. Establish their feet, for I have chosen you, says the Lord. ¹⁶ I will raise those who are dead up again from their places, and bring them out from their tombs, for I recognize my name in them. ¹⁷ Do not be afraid, you mother of children, for I have chosen you, says the Lord. ¹⁸ For your help, I will send my servants Isaiah and Jeremiah, after whose counsel I have sanctified and prepared for you twelve trees laden with various fruits, ¹⁹ and as many springs flowing with milk and honey, and seven mighty mountains, on which roses and lilies grow, with which I will fill your children with joy. ²⁰ Do right to the widow. Secure justice for the fatherless. Give to the poor. Defend the orphan. Clothe the naked. ²¹ Heal the broken and the weak. Do not mock a lame man. Defend the maimed. Let the blind man have a vision of my glory. ²² Protect the old and young within your walls. ²³ Wherever you find the dead, set a sign upon them and commit them to the grave, and I will give you the first place in my resurrection. ²⁴ Stay still, my people, and take your rest, for your rest will come. ²⁵ Nourish your children, good nurse, and establish their feet. ²⁶ As for the servants whom I have given you, not one of them will perish, for I will require them from among your number. ²⁷ Do not be anxious, for when the day of suffering and anguish comes, others will weep and be sorrowful, but you will rejoice and have abundance. ²⁸ The nations will envy you, but they will be able to do nothing against you, says the Lord. ²⁹ My hands will cover you, so that your children do not see Gehenna. ³⁰ Be joyful, mother, with your children, for I will deliver you, says the Lord. ³¹ Remember your children who sleep, for I will bring them out of the secret places of the earth and show mercy to them, for I am merciful, says the Lord Almighty. ³² Embrace your children until I come, and proclaim mercy to them, for my wells run over, and my grace will not fail."

³³ I, Ezra, received a command from the Lord on Mount Horeb to go to Israel, but when I came to them, they rejected me and rejected the Lord's commandment. ³⁴ Therefore I say to you, O nations that hear and understand, "Look for your shepherd. He will give you everlasting rest, for he is near at hand who at the end of the age will come. ³⁵ Be ready for the rewards of the kingdom, for the everlasting light will shine on you forevermore. ³⁶ Flee the shadow of this world, receive the joy of your glory. I call to witness my savior openly. ³⁷ Receive that which is given to you by the Lord, and be joyful, giving thanks to him who has called you to heavenly kingdoms. ³⁸ Arise and stand up, and see the number of those who

have been sealed at the Lord's feast. ³⁹ Those who withdrew themselves from the shadow of the world have received glorious garments from the Lord. ⁴⁰ Take again your full number, O Zion, and make up the reckoning of those of yours who are clothed in white, which have fulfilled the law of the Lord. ⁴¹ The number of your children, whom you long for, is fulfilled. Ask the power of the Lord, that your people, which have been called from the beginning, may be made holy."

⁴² I, Ezra, saw upon Mount Zion a great multitude, whom I could not *Ezra's* number, and they all praised the Lord with songs. ⁴³ In the midst of them, *Vision of the* there was a young man of a high stature, taller than all the rest, and upon *Crowned* every one of their heads he set crowns, and he was more exalted than they *Multitude* were. I marveled greatly at this. ⁴⁴ So I asked the angel, and said, "What are these, my Lord?"

⁴⁵ He answered and said to me, "These are those who have put off the mortal clothing, and put on the immortal, and have confessed the name of God. Now are they crowned, and receive palms."

⁴⁶ Then I said to the angel, "Who is the young man who sets crowns on them, and gives them palms in their hands?"

⁴⁷ So he answered and said to me, "He is the Son of God, whom they have confessed in the world."

Then I began to praise those who stood so valiently for the name of the Lord.

⁴⁸ Then the angel said to me, "Go your way, and tell my people what kind of things you have seen, and how the great wonders of the Lord God are, which you have seen."

**3** In the thirtieth year after the ruin of the city, I Salathiel, also called *Ezra's First* Ezra, was in Babylon, and lay troubled upon my bed, and my thoughts *Vision* came up over my heart, ² for I saw the desolation of Zion and the wealth of those who lived at Babylon. ³ My spirit was very agitated, so that I began to speak words full of fear to the Most High, and said, ⁴ "O sovereign Lord, *God's Work* did you not speak at the beginning when you formed the earth—and *in Primeval* that yourself alone—and commanded the dust ⁵ and it gave you Adam, *History* a body without a soul? Yet it was the workmanship of your hands, and you breathed into him the breath of life, and he was made alive in your presence. ⁶ You led him into the garden which your right hand planted before the earth appeared. ⁷ You gave him your one commandment, which he transgressed, and immediately you appointed death for him and his descendants. From him were born nations, tribes, peoples, and kindred without number. ⁸ Every nation walked after their own will, did ungodly things in your sight, and despised your commandments, and you did not hinder them. ⁹ Nevertheless, again in the course of time, you brought the flood on those who lived in the world and destroyed them. ¹⁰ It came to pass that the same thing happened to them. Just as death came to Adam, so was the flood to these. ¹¹ Nevertheless, you left one of them, Noah with his household, and all the righteous men who descended from him.

¹² "It came to pass that when those who lived upon the earth began to *God Chooses* multiply, they also multiplied children, peoples, and many nations, and *the Patriarchs* began again to be more ungodly than their ancestors. ¹³ It came to pass, when they acted wickedly before you, you chose one from among them,

whose name was Abraham. [14] You loved him, and to him only you showed the end of the times secretly by night, [15] and made an everlasting covenant with him, promising him that you would never forsake his descendants. To him you gave Isaac, and to Isaac you gave Jacob and Esau. [16] You set apart Jacob for yourself, but rejected Esau. Jacob became a great multitude. [17] It came to pass that when you led his descendants out of Egypt, you brought them up to Mount Sinai. [18] You bowed the heavens also, shook the earth, moved the whole world, made the depths tremble, and troubled the age. [19] Your glory went through four gates, of fire, of earthquake, of wind, and of ice, that you might give the law to the descendants of Jacob, and the commandment to the descendants of Israel.

*Persistence of* [20] "Yet you did not take away from them their wicked heart, that your law *the Evil Heart* might produce fruit in them. [21] For the first Adam, burdened with a wicked heart transgressed and was overcome, as were all who are descended from him. [22] Thus, disease was made permanent. The law was in the heart of the people along with the wickedness of the root. So the good departed away and that which was wicked remained. [23] So the times passed away, and the years were brought to an end. Then you raised up a servant, called David, [24] whom you commanded to build a city to your name, and to offer burnt offerings to you in it from what is yours. [25] When this was done for many years, then those who inhabited the city did evil, [26] in all things doing as Adam and all his generations had done, for they also had a wicked heart. [27] So you gave your city over into the hands of your enemies.

*The Sins of* [28] "Then I said in my heart, 'Are the deeds of those who inhabit Babylon *Babylon and* any better? Is that why it gained dominion over Zion?' [29] For it came to *of Zion* pass, when I came here, that I also saw impieties without number, and my soul saw many sinners in this thirtieth year, so that my heart failed me. [30] For I have seen how you endure them sinning, and have spared those who act in an ungodly manner, and have destroyed your people, and have preserved your enemies; [31] and you have not shown how your way may be comprehended. Are the deeds of Babylon better than those of Zion? [32] Or is there any other nation that knows you beside Israel? Or what tribes have so believed your covenants as these tribes of Jacob? [33] Yet their reward does not appear, and their labor has no fruit, for I have gone here and there through the nations, and I see that they abound in wealth, and do not think about your commandments. [34] Weigh therefore our iniquities now in the balance, and theirs also who dwell in the world, and so will it be found which way the scale inclines. [35] Or when was it that they who dwell on the earth have not sinned in your sight? Or what nation has kept your commandments so well? [36] You will find some men by name who have kept your precepts, but you will not find nations."

*The Angel* 4 The angel who was sent to me, whose name was Uriel, gave me an *Uriel Answers* answer, [2] and said to me, "Your understanding has utterly failed you *Ezra* regarding this world. Do you think you can comprehend the way of the Most High?"

[3] Then I said, "Yes, my Lord." He answered me, "I have been sent to show you three ways, and to set before you three problems. [4] If you can solve one for me, I also will show you the way that you desire to see, and I will teach you why the heart is wicked."

⁵ I said, "Keep speaking, my Lord."

Then said he to me, "Go, weigh for me the weight of fire, or measure for me a gust of wind, or call back for me the day that is past."

⁶ Then I answered and said, "Who of the sons of men is able to do this, that you should ask me about such things?"

⁷ He said to me, "If I had asked you, 'How many dwellings are there in the heart of the sea? Or how many springs are there at the fountain head of the deep? Or how many streams are above the firmament? Or which are the outgoings of paradise?' ⁸ perhaps you would say to me, 'I never went down into the deep, or as yet into hell, neither did I ever climb up into heaven.' ⁹ Nevertheless now I have only asked you about the fire, wind, and the day, things which you have experienced, and from which you cannot be separated, and you yet have given me no answer about them."

¹⁰ Furthermore, he said to me, "You cannot understand your own things that you grew up with. ¹¹ How then can your mind comprehend the way of the Most High? How can he who is already worn out with the corrupted world understand incorruption?"

¹² Then I said to him, "It would have been better if we were not here at all, than that we should come here and live in the midst of ungodliness, and suffer, and not know why." ¹³ He answered me, and said, "I went into a forest of the trees of the field, and they took counsel together, ¹⁴ and said, 'Come! Let us go and make war against the sea, that it may retreat before us, and that we may make ourselves more forests.' ¹⁵ The waves of the sea also in like manner took counsel together, and said, 'Come! Let us go up and subdue the forest of the plain, that there also we may gain more territory.' ¹⁶ The counsel of the wood was in vain, for the fire came and consumed it. ¹⁷ Likewise also the counsel of the waves of the sea, for the sand stood up and stopped them. ¹⁸ If you were judge now between these two, which would you justify, or which would you condemn?"

*Would Death Not Have Been Better?*

¹⁹ I answered and said, "It is a foolish counsel that they both have taken, for the ground is given to the wood, and the place of the sea is given to bear its waves."

²⁰ Then he answered me, and said, "You have given a right judgment. Why do you not judge your own case? ²¹ For just as the ground is given to the wood, and the sea to its waves, even so those who dwell upon the earth may understand nothing but what is upon the earth. Only he who dwells above the heavens understands the things that are above the height of the heavens."

²² Then I answered and said, "I beg you, O Lord, why has the power of understanding been given to me? ²³ For it was not in my mind to be curious of the ways above, but of such things as pass by us daily, because Israel is given up as a reproach to the gentiles. The people whom you have loved have been given over to ungodly nations. The law of our forefathers is made of no effect, and the written covenants are nowhere regarded. ²⁴ We pass away out of the world like locusts. Our life is like a vapor, and we are not worthy to obtain mercy. ²⁵ What will he then do for his name by which we are called? I have asked about these things."

*Why Is There No Understanding?*

²⁶ Then he answered me, and said, "If you are alive you will see, and if you live long, you will marvel, for the world hastens quickly to pass away.

²⁷ For it is not able to bear the things that are promised to the righteous in the times to come; for this world is full of sadness and infirmities. ²⁸ But about which you ask, I will say, for the evil has been sown, but its destruction has not yet come. ²⁹ If therefore that which is sown is not reaped, and if the place where the evil is sown does not pass away, the field where the good is sown will not come. ³⁰ For a grain of evil seed was sown in the heart of Adam from the beginning, and how much wickedness it has produced to this time! How much more it will yet produce until the time of threshing comes! ³¹ Ponder now by yourself, how much fruit of wickedness a grain of evil seed has produced. ³² When the grains which are without number are sown, how great a threshing floor they will fill!"

*When Will There Be Justice?* ³³ Then I answered and said, "How and when will these things come to pass? Why are our years few and evil?"

³⁴ He answered me, and said, "Do not hurry faster than the Most High; for you are hastening in vain to be above him, for your excesses are great. ³⁵ Did not the souls of the righteous question these things in their chambers, saying, 'How long shall I hope on this fashion? When does the fruit of the threshing floor come?' ³⁶ To them, Jeremiel the archangel answered, 'When the number is fulfilled of those who are like you. For he has weighed the world in the balance. ³⁷ By measure, he has measured the times. By number, he has counted the seasons. He will not move or stir them until that measure is fulfilled.'"

³⁸ Then I answered, "O sovereign Lord, all of us are full of ungodliness. ³⁹ Perhaps it is for our sakes that the threshing time of the righteous is kept back—because of the sins of those who dwell on the earth."

⁴⁰ So he answered me, "Go on your way to a woman with child, and ask her when she has fulfilled her nine months, if her womb may keep the baby any longer within her."

⁴¹ Then I said, "No, Lord, it is not able to."

He said to me, "In Hades, the chambers of souls are like the womb. ⁴² For just like a woman in labor hurries to escape the anguish of the labor pains, even so these places hurry to deliver those things that are committed to them from the beginning. ⁴³ Then you will be shown those things which you desire to see."

*Suffering Yet to Come?* ⁴⁴ Then I answered, "If I have found favor in your sight, and if it is possible, and if I am worthy, ⁴⁵ show me this also, whether there is more to come than is past, or whether the greater part has gone over us. ⁴⁶ For what is gone I know, but I do not know what is to come."

⁴⁷ He said to me, "Stand up on my right side, and I will explain the parable to you."

⁴⁸ So I stood, looked, and saw a hot burning oven passed by before me. It happened that when the flame had gone by I looked, and saw that the smoke remained. ⁴⁹ After this, a watery cloud passed in front of me, and sent down much rain with a storm. When the stormy rain was past, the drops still remained in it.

⁵⁰ Then said he to me, "Consider with yourself; as the rain is more than the drops, and the fire is greater than the smoke, so the quantity which is past was far greater; but the drops and the smoke still remained."

⁵¹ Then I prayed, and said, "Do you think that I will live until that time? *Will I See* Or who will be alive in those days?" *These Days?*

⁵² He answered me, "As for the signs you asked me about, I may tell you of them in part; but I was not sent to tell you about your life, for I do not know.

**5** "Nevertheless, concerning the signs, behold, the days will come when *The Signs* those who dwell on earth will be taken in a great number, and the way *of the End* of truth will be hidden, and the land will be barren of faith. ² Iniquity will be increased above what you see now, and beyond what you have heard long ago. ³ The land that you see ruling now will be a trackless waste, and men will see it desolate. ⁴ But if the Most High permits you to live, you will see that what exists after the third period will be troubled. The sun will suddenly shine in the night, and the moon in the day. ⁵ Blood will drop out of wood, and the stone will utter its voice. The peoples will be troubled, and the stars will fall. ⁶ He will rule, whom those who dwell on the earth do not expect, and the birds will fly away together. ⁷ The Sodomite sea will cast out fish, and make a noise in the night, which many have not known; but all will hear its voice. ⁸ There will also be chaos in many places. Fires will break out often, and the wild animals will change their places, and women will bring forth monsters. ⁹ Salt waters will be found in the fresh waters, and all friends will destroy one another. Then reason will hide itself, and understanding withdraw itself into its chamber. ¹⁰ It will be sought by many, and will not be found. Unrighteousness and lack of restraint will be multiplied on earth. ¹¹ One country will ask another, 'Has righteousness, or a man that does righteousness, gone through you?' And it will say, 'No.' ¹² It will come to pass at that time that men will hope, but will not obtain. They will labor, but their ways will not prosper. ¹³ I am permitted to show you such signs. If you will pray again, and weep as now, and fast seven days, you will hear even greater things than these."

¹⁴ Then I woke up, and an extreme trembling went through my body, *Ezra Awakens* and my mind was so troubled that it fainted. ¹⁵ So the angel who had come *from His* to talk with me held me, comforted me, and set me on my feet. *Vision*

¹⁶ In the second night, it came to pass that Phaltiel the captain of the people came to me, saying, "Where have you been? Why is your face sad? ¹⁷ Or do you not know that Israel is committed to you in the land of their captivity? ¹⁸ Get up then, and eat some bread, and do not forsake us, like a shepherd who leaves the flock in the power of cruel wolves."

¹⁹ Then I said to him, "Go away from me and do not come near me for seven days, and then you shall come to me." He heard what I said and left me.

²⁰ So I fasted seven days, mourning and weeping, like Uriel the angel *Ezra's Second* had commanded me. *Vision: Ezra*

²¹ After seven days, the thoughts of my heart were very grievous to me *Seeks Answers* again, ²² and my soul recovered the spirit of understanding, and I began to speak words before the Most High again. ²³ I said, "O sovereign Lord of all the woods of the earth, and of all the trees in it, you have chosen one vine for yourself. ²⁴ Of all the lands of the world you have chosen one pit for yourself. Of all the flowers of the world, you have chosen one lily for yourself. ²⁵ Of all the depths of the sea, you have filled one river for yourself.

Of all built cities, you have consecrated Zion for yourself. ²⁶ Of all the birds that are created you have named for yourself one dove. Of all the livestock that have been made, you have provided for yourself one sheep. ²⁷ Among all the multitudes of peoples you have gotten yourself one people. To this people, whom you loved, you gave a law that is approved by all. ²⁸ Now, O Lord, why have you given this one people over to many, and have prepared the one root above others, and have scattered your only one among many? ²⁹ Those who opposed your promises have trampled down those who believed your covenants. ³⁰ If you really do hate your people so much, they should be punished with your own hands."

*Uriel*  ³¹ Now when I had spoken these words, the angel that came to me the
*Responds*  night before was sent to me, ³² and said to me, "Hear me, and I will instruct you. Listen to me, and I will tell you more."

³³ I said, "Keep speaking, my Lord."

Then said he to me, "You are very troubled in mind for Israel's sake. Do you love that people more than the one who made them?"

³⁴ I said, "No, Lord; but I have spoken out of grief; for my heart is in agony every hour while I labor to comprehend the way of the Most High, and to seek out part of his judgment."

³⁵ He said to me, "You cannot."

And I said, "Why, Lord? Why was I born? Why was my mother's womb not my grave, that I might not have seen the travail of Jacob, and the wearisome toil of the people of Israel?"

³⁶ He said to me, "Count for me those who have not yet come. Gather together for me the drops that are scattered abroad, and make the withered flowers green again for me. ³⁷ Open for me the chambers that are closed, and bring out the winds for me that are shut up in them. Or show me the image of a voice. Then I will declare to you the travail that you asked to see."

³⁸ And I said, "O sovereign Lord, who may know these things except the one who does not have his dwelling with men? ³⁹ As for me, I lack wisdom. How then can I speak of these things you asked me about?"

⁴⁰ Then said he to me, "Just as you can do none of these things that I have spoken of, even so you cannot find out my judgment, or the end of the love that I have promised to my people."

⁴¹ I said, "But, behold, O Lord, you have made the promise to those who are alive at the end. What should they do who have been before us, or we ourselves, or those who will come after us?"

⁴² He said to me, "I will compare my judgment to a ring. Just as there is no slowness of those who are last, even so there is no swiftness of those who are first."

⁴³ So I answered, "Could you not make them all at once that have been made, and that are now, and that are yet to come, that you might show your judgment sooner?"

⁴⁴ Then he answered me, "The creature may not move faster than the Creator, nor can the world hold them at once who will be created in it."

⁴⁵ And I said, "As you have said to your servant, that you, who gives life, has given life at once to the creature that you have created, and the

creation will sustain them, even so it might now also support them to be present at once."

⁴⁶ And he said to me, "Ask the womb of a woman, and say to her, 'If you bear ten children, why do you do it at different times?' Ask her therefore to give birth to ten children at once."

⁴⁷ I said, "She cannot, but must do it each in their own time."

⁴⁸ Then he said to me, "Even so, I have given the womb of the earth to those who are sown in it in their own times. ⁴⁹ For just as a young child may not give birth, neither she who has grown old any more, even so have I organized the world which I created."

⁵⁰ I asked, "Seeing that you have now shown me the way, I will speak before you. Is our mother, of whom you have told me, still young? Or does she now draw near to old age?"

⁵¹ He answered me, "Ask a woman who bears children, and she will tell you. ⁵² Say to her, 'Why are they whom you have now brought forth not like those who were before, but smaller in stature?' ⁵³ She also will answer you, 'Those who are born in the strength of youth are different from those who are born in the time of old age, when the womb fails.' ⁵⁴ Consider therefore you also, how you are shorter than those who were before you. ⁵⁵ So are those who come after you smaller than you, as born of the creature which now begins to be old, and is past the strength of youth."

⁵⁶ Then I said, "Lord, I implore you, if I have found favor in your sight, *Visitation* show your servant by whom you visit your creation." *of God*

**6** He said to me, "In the beginning, when the earth was made, before the portals of the world were fixed and before the gatherings of the winds blew, ² before the voices of the thunder sounded and before the flashes of the lightning shone, before the foundations of paradise were laid, ³ before the fair flowers were seen, before the powers of the earthquake were established, before the innumerable army of angels were gathered together, ⁴ before the heights of the air were lifted up, before the measures of the firmament were named, before the chimneys of Zion were heated, ⁵ before the present years were reckoned, before the imaginations of those who now sin were estranged, and before they were sealed who have gathered faith for a treasure— ⁶ then I considered these things, and they all were made through me alone, and not through another; just as by me also they will be ended, and not by another."

⁷ Then I answered, "What will be the dividing of the times? Or when will *Division of* be the end of the first and the beginning of the age that follows?" *the Times*

⁸ He said to me, "From Abraham to Isaac, because Jacob and Esau were born to him, for Jacob's hand held Esau's heel from the beginning. ⁹ For Esau is the end of this age, and Jacob is the beginning of the one that follows. ¹⁰ The hand of man is between heel and hand. Ask nothing else, Ezra!"

¹¹ Then I answered, "O sovereign Lord, if I have found favor in your sight, *The End of* ¹² I beg you, show your servant the end of your signs which you showed me *the Signs* in part on a previous night."

¹³ So he answered, "Stand up on your feet, and you will hear a mighty sounding voice. ¹⁴ If the place you stand on is greatly moved ¹⁵ when it speaks do not be afraid, for the word is of the end, and the foundations

of the earth will understand ¹⁶that the speech is about them. They will tremble and be moved, for they know that their end must be changed."

¹⁷It happened that when I had heard it, I stood up on my feet, and listened, and, behold, there was a voice that spoke, and its sound was like the sound of many waters. ¹⁸It said, "Behold, the days come when I draw near to visit those who dwell upon the earth, ¹⁹and when I investigate those who have caused harm unjustly with their unrighteousness, and when the affliction of Zion is complete, ²⁰and when the seal will be set on the age that is to pass away, then I will show these signs: the books will be opened before the firmament, and all will see together. ²¹The children a year old will speak with their voices. The women with child will deliver premature children at three or four months, and they will live and dance. ²²Suddenly the sown places will appear unsown. The full storehouses will suddenly be found empty. ²³The trumpet will give a sound which when every man hears, they will suddenly be afraid. ²⁴At that time friends will make war against one another like enemies. The earth will stand in fear with those who dwell in it. The springs of the fountains will stand still, so that for three hours they will not flow.

²⁵"It will be that whoever remains after all these things that I have told you, he will be saved and will see my salvation, and the end of my world. ²⁶They will see the men who have been taken up, who have not tasted death from their birth. The heart of the inhabitants will be changed and turned into a different spirit. ²⁷For evil will be blotted out and deceit will be quenched. ²⁸Faith will flourish. Corruption will be overcome, and the truth, which has been so long without fruit, will be declared."

*Conclusion of the Second Vision* ²⁹And when he talked with me, behold, I looked little by little at him before whom I stood. ³⁰He said to me, "I came to show you these things for the time of the night to come. ³¹If therefore you will pray again, and fast seven days again, I will tell you greater things by day than I have heard. ³²For your voice has surely been heard before the Most High. For the Mighty has seen your righteousness. He has also seen your purity, which you have maintained ever since your youth. ³³Therefore he has sent me to show you all these things, and to say to you, 'Believe, and do not be afraid! ³⁴Do not be hasty to think vain things about the former times, that you may not hasten in the latter times.'"

*Ezra's Third Vision* ³⁵It came to pass after this, that I wept again, and fasted seven days in like manner, that I might fulfill the three weeks which he told me.

³⁶On the eighth night, my heart was troubled within me again, and I began to speak in the presence of the Most High. ³⁷For my spirit was greatly inflamed, and my soul was in distress.

*Creation for the Sake of God's Chosen* ³⁸I said, "O Lord, truly you spoke at the beginning of the creation, on the first day, and said this: 'Let heaven and earth be made,' and your word perfected the work. ³⁹Then the spirit was hovering, and darkness and silence were on every side. The sound of man's voice was not yet from you. ⁴⁰Then you commanded a ray of light to be brought out of your treasuries, that your works might then appear.

⁴¹"On the second day, again you made the spirit of the firmament and commanded it to divide and to separate the waters, that the one part might go up, and the other remain beneath.

⁴²"On the third day, you commanded that the waters should be gathered together in the seventh part of the earth. You dried up six parts and kept them, to the intent that of these, some being both planted and tilled, might serve before you. ⁴³For as soon as your word went out, the work was done. ⁴⁴Immediately, great and innumerable fruit grew, with many pleasant tastes, and flowers of inimitable color, and fragrances of most exquisite smell. This was done the third day.

⁴⁵"On the fourth day, you commanded that the sun should shine, the moon give its light, and the stars should be in their order; ⁴⁶and you gave them a command to serve mankind, who was to be made.

⁴⁷"On the fifth day, you said to the seventh part, where the water was gathered together, that it should produce living creatures, birds and fishes; and so it came to pass ⁴⁸that the mute and lifeless water produced living things as it was told, that the nations might therefore praise your wondrous works.

⁴⁹"Then you preserved two living creatures. The one you called Behemoth, and the other you called Leviathan. ⁵⁰You separated the one from the other; for the seventh part, namely, where the water was gathered together, might not hold them both. ⁵¹To Behemoth, you gave one part, which was dried up on the third day, that he should dwell in it, in which are a thousand hills; ⁵²but to Leviathan you gave the seventh part, namely, the watery part. You have kept them to be devoured by whom you wish, when you wish.

⁵³"But on the sixth day, you commanded the earth to produce before you cattle, animals, and creeping things. ⁵⁴Over these, you ordained Adam as ruler over all the works that you have made. From him came all of us, the people whom you have chosen.

⁵⁵"All this have I spoken before you, O Lord, because you have said that for our sakes you made the world. ⁵⁶As for the other nations, which also come from Adam, you have said that they are nothing, and are like spittle. You have likened the abundance of them to a drop that falls from a bucket. ⁵⁷Now, O Lord, behold these nations, which are reputed as nothing, being rulers over us and devouring us. ⁵⁸But we your people, whom you have called your firstborn, your only children, and your fervent lover, are given into their hands. ⁵⁹Now if the world is made for our sakes, why do we not possess our world for an inheritance? How long will this endure?"

**7** When I had finished speaking these words, the angel which had been sent to me the nights before was sent to me. ²He said to me, "Rise, Ezra, and hear the words that I have come to tell you."

*Uriel Responds: The Narrow Path*

³I said, "Keep speaking, my Lord."

Then he said to me, "There is a sea set in a wide place, that it might be deep and vast, ⁴but its entrance is set in a narrow place so as to be like a river. ⁵Whoever desires to go into the sea to look at it, or to rule it, if he did not go through the narrow entrance, how could he come into the broad part? ⁶Another thing also: There is a city built and set in a plain country, and full of all good things, ⁷but its entrance is narrow, and is set in a dangerous place to fall, having fire on the right hand, and deep water on the left. ⁸There is one only path between them both, even between the fire and the water, so that only one person can go there at once. ⁹If this city is now given to a man for an inheritance, if the heir does not pass the danger before him, how will he receive his inheritance?"

¹⁰ I said, "That is so, Lord."

Then said he to me, "Even so also is Israel's portion. ¹¹ I made the world for their sakes. What is now done was decreed when Adam transgressed my statutes. ¹² Then the entrances of this world were made narrow, sorrowful, and toilsome. They are but few and evil, full of perils, and involved in great toils. ¹³ For the entrances of the greater world are wide and safe, and produce fruit of immortality. ¹⁴ So if those who live do not enter these difficult and vain things, they can never receive those that are reserved for them. ¹⁵ Now therefore why are you disturbed, seeing you are but a corruptible man? Why are you moved, since you are mortal? ¹⁶ Why have you not considered in your mind that which is to come, rather than that which is present?"

*Judgment of the Righteous and the Wicked*

¹⁷ Then I answered and said, "O sovereign Lord, behold, you have ordained in your law that the righteous will inherit these things, but that the ungodly will perish. ¹⁸ The righteous therefore will suffer difficult things, and hope for easier things, but those who have done wickedly have suffered the difficult things, and yet will not see the easier things."

¹⁹ He said to me, "You are not a judge above God, neither do you have more understanding than the Most High. ²⁰ Yes, let many perish who now live, rather than that the law of God which is set before them be despised. ²¹ For God strictly commanded those who came, even as they came, what they should do to live, and what they should observe to avoid punishment. ²² Nevertheless, they were not obedient to him, but spoke against him and imagined for themselves vain things. ²³ They made cunning plans of wickedness, and said moreover of the Most High that he does not exist, and they did not know his ways. ²⁴ They despised his law and denied his covenants. They have not been faithful to his statutes, and have not performed his works. ²⁵ Therefore, Ezra, for the empty are empty things, and for the full are the full things.

²⁶ For behold, the time will come, and it will be, when these signs of which I told you before will come to pass, that the bride will appear, even the city coming forth, and she will be seen who now is withdrawn from the earth. ²⁷ Whoever is delivered from the foretold evils will see my wonders. ²⁸ For my son Jesus will be revealed with those who are with him, and those who remain will rejoice four hundred years. ²⁹ After these years my son Christ*ᵃ* will die, along with all of those who have the breath of man. ³⁰ Then the world will be turned into the ancient silence for seven days, like it was in the first beginning, so that no human will remain. ³¹ After seven days the world that is not yet awake will be raised up, and what is corruptible will die. ³² The earth will restore those who are asleep in it, and the dust those who dwell in it in silence, and the chambers will deliver those souls that were committed to them. ³³ The Most High will be revealed on the judgment seat, and compassion will pass away, and patience will be withdrawn. ³⁴ Only judgment will remain. Truth will stand. Faith will grow strong. ³⁵ Recompense will follow. The reward will be shown. Good deeds

---

ᵃ "Christ" means "anointed one"

will awake, and wicked deeds will not sleep.[a] 36 The place of torment will appear, and near it will be the place of rest. The furnace of Gehenna will be shown, and near it the paradise of delight. 37 Then the Most High will say to the nations that are raised from the dead, 'Look and understand whom you have denied, whom you have not served, whose commandments you have despised. 38 Look on this side and on that. Here is delight and rest, and there fire and torments.' Thus he[b] will speak to them in the day of judgment. 39 This is a day that has neither sun, nor moon, nor stars, 40 neither cloud, nor thunder, nor lightning, neither wind, nor water, nor air, neither darkness, nor evening, nor morning, 41 neither summer, nor spring, nor heat, nor winter, neither frost, nor cold, nor hail, nor rain, nor dew, 42 neither noon, nor night, nor dawn, neither shining, nor brightness, nor light, except only the splendor of the glory of the Most High, by which all will see the things that are set before them. 43 It will endure as though it were a week of years. 44 This is my judgment and its prescribed order; but I have only shown these things to you."

45 I answered, "I said then, O Lord, and I say now: Blessed are those who are now alive and keep your commandments! 46 But what about those for whom I prayed? For who is there among those who are alive who has not sinned, and who of the children of men has not transgressed your covenant? 47 Now I see that the world to come will bring delight to few, but torments to many. 48 For an evil heart has grown up in us, which has led us astray from these commandments and has brought us into corruption and into the ways of death. It has shown us the paths of perdition and removed us far from life—and that, not a few only, but nearly all who have been created."

*The Few Who Will Be Saved*

49 He answered me, "Listen to me, and I will instruct you. I will admonish you yet again. 50 For this reason, the Most High has not made one world, but two. 51 For because you have said that the just are not many, but few, and the ungodly abound, hear the explanation. 52 If you have just a few precious stones, will you add them to lead and clay?"

53 I said, "Lord, how could that be?"

54 He said to me, "Not only that, but ask the earth, and she will tell you. Defer to her, and she will declare it to you. 55 Say to her, 'You produce gold, silver, and brass, and also iron, lead, and clay; 56 but silver is more abundant than gold, and brass than silver, and iron than brass, and lead than iron, and clay than lead.' 57 Judge therefore which things are precious and to be desired, what is abundant or what is rare?"

58 I said, "O sovereign Lord, that which is plentiful is of less worth, for that which is more rare is more precious."

59 He answered me, "Weigh within yourself the things that you have thought, for he who has what is hard to get rejoices over him who has what is plentiful. 60 So also is the judgment which I have promised; for I will rejoice over the few that will be saved, because these are those who have made my glory to prevail now, and through them, my name is now honored. 61 I will not grieve over the multitude of those who perish; for these

---

[a] The passage from 7:36–105 was formerly missing but has been restored to the text in modern editions
[b] Following Syriac, Ethiopic, and Arabic versions. The Latin has "you will speak"

are those who are now like mist, and have become like flame and smoke; they are set on fire and burn hotly, and are extinguished."

*Lament Over the Coming Judgment* ⁶² I answered, "O earth, why have you produced, if the mind is made out of dust, like all other created things? ⁶³ For it would have been better that the dust itself had been unborn, so that the mind might not have been made from it. ⁶⁴ But now the mind grows with us, and because of this we are tormented, because we perish and we know it. ⁶⁵ Let the race of men lament and the animals of the field be glad. Let all who are born lament, but let the four-footed animals and the livestock rejoice. ⁶⁶ For it is far better with them than with us; for they do not look forward to judgment, neither do they know of torments or of salvation promised to them after death. ⁶⁷ For what does it profit us, that we will be preserved alive, but yet be afflicted with torment? ⁶⁸ For all who are born are defiled with iniquities, and are full of sins and laden with transgressions. ⁶⁹ If after death we were not to come into judgment, perhaps it would have been better for us."

⁷⁰ He answered me, "When the Most High made the world and Adam and all those who came from him, he first prepared the judgment and the things that pertain to the judgment. ⁷¹ Now understand from your own words, for you have said that the mind grows with us. ⁷² They therefore who dwell on the earth will be tormented for this reason, that having understanding they have committed iniquity, and receiving commandments have not kept them, and having obtained a law they dealt unfaithfully with that which they received. ⁷³ What then will they have to say in the judgment, or how will they answer in the last times? ⁷⁴ For how long a time has the Most High been patient with those who inhabit the world, and not for their sakes, but because of the times which he has foreordained!"

*The State of the Soul After Death* ⁷⁵ I answered, "If I have found grace in your sight, O Lord, show this also to your servant, whether after death, even now when every one of us gives up his soul, we will be kept in rest until those times come, in which you renew the creation, or whether we will be tormented immediately."

*The Fate of the Sinner* ⁷⁶ He answered me, "I will show you this also; but do not join yourself with those who are scorners, nor count yourself with those who are tormented. ⁷⁷ For you have a treasure of works laid up with the Most High, but it will not be shown to you until the last times. ⁷⁸ For concerning death the teaching is: When the decisive sentence has gone out from the Most High that a man shall die, as the spirit leaves the body to return again to him who gave it, it adores the glory of the Most High first of all. ⁷⁹ And if it is one of those who have been scorners and have not kept the way of the Most High, and that have despised his law, and who hate those who fear God, ⁸⁰ these spirits will not enter into habitations, but will wander and be in torments immediately, ever grieving and sad, in seven ways. ⁸¹ The first way, because they have despised the law of the Most High. ⁸² The second way, because they cannot now make a good repentance that they may live. ⁸³ The third way, they will see the reward laid up for those who have believed the covenants of the Most High. ⁸⁴ The fourth way, they will consider the torment laid up for themselves in the last days. ⁸⁵ The fifth way, they will see the dwelling places of the others guarded by angels, with great quietness. ⁸⁶ The sixth way, they will see how immediately some of them will pass into torment. ⁸⁷ The seventh way, which is more grievous than all the previously mentioned ways, because they will languish in confusion and be consumed with shame, and will be withered up by fears, seeing the glory of the Most High before whom they have sinned while living, and before whom they will be judged in the last times.

88 "Now this is the order of those who have kept the ways of the Most High, when they will be separated from their mortal body. 89 In the time that they lived in it, they painfully served the Most High, and were in jeopardy every hour, that they might keep the law of the lawgiver perfectly. 90 Therefore, this is the teaching concerning them: 91 First of all they will see with great joy the glory of him who takes them up, for they will have rest in seven orders. 92 The first order, because they have labored with great effort to overcome the evil thought which was fashioned together with them, that it might not lead them astray from life into death. 93 The second order, because they see the perplexity in which the souls of the ungodly wander, and the punishment that awaits them. 94 The third order, they see the testimony which he who fashioned them gives concerning them, that while they lived they kept the law which was given to them in trust. 95 The fourth order, they understand the rest which, being gathered in their chambers, they now enjoy with great quietness, guarded by angels, and the glory that awaits them in the last days. 96 The fifth order, they rejoice that they have now escaped from that which is corruptible, and that they will inherit that which is to come, while they see in addition the difficulty and the pain from which they have been delivered, and the spacious liberty which they will receive with joy and immortality. 97 The sixth order, when it is shown to them how their face will shine like the sun, and how they will be made like the light of the stars, being incorruptible from then on. 98 The seventh order, which is greater than all the previously mentioned orders, because they will rejoice with confidence, and because they will be bold without confusion, and will be glad without fear, for they hurry to see the face of him whom in their lifetime they served, and from whom they will receive their reward in glory. 99 This is the order of the souls of the just, as from henceforth is announced to them. Previously mentioned are the ways of torture which those who would not give heed will suffer from after this."

*Fate of the Righteous*

100 I answered, "Will time therefore be given to the souls after they are separated from the bodies, that they may see what you have described to me?"

101 He said, "Their freedom will be for seven days, that for seven days they may see the things you have been told, and afterwards they will be gathered together in their habitations."

102 I answered, "If I have found favor in your sight, show further to me your servant whether in the day of judgment the just will be able to intercede for the ungodly or to entreat the Most High for them, 103 whether fathers for children, or children for parents, or kindred for kindred, or kinsfolk for those who are most dear, or friends for those who are most dear."

*Intercession for the Ungodly on the Day of Judgment?*

104 He answered me, "Since you have found favor in my sight, I will show you this also. The day of judgment is bold, and displays to all the seal of truth. Even as now a father does not send his son, or a son his father, or a master his slave, or a friend him that is most dear, that in his place he

may understand, or sleep, or eat, or be healed, [105] so no one will ever pray for another in that day, neither will one lay a burden on another, for then everyone will each bear his own righteousness or unrighteousness."

[106] I answered, "How do we now find that first Abraham prayed for the people of Sodom, and Moses for the ancestors who sinned in the wilderness, [107] and Joshua after him for Israel in the days of Achan, [108] and Samuel, and David for the plague, and Solomon for those who would worship in the sanctuary, [109] and Elijah for those that received rain, and for the dead, that he might live, [110] and Hezekiah for the people in the days of Sennacherib, and many others prayed for many? [111] If therefore now, when corruption has grown and unrighteousness increased, the righteous have prayed for the ungodly, why will it not be so then also?"

[112] He answered me, "This present world is not the end. The full glory does not remain in it. Therefore, those who were able prayed for the weak. [113] But the day of judgment will be the end of this age, and the beginning of the immortality to come, in which corruption has passed away, [114] intemperance is at an end, infidelity is cut off, but righteousness has grown, and truth has sprung up. [115] Then no one will be able to have mercy on him who is condemned in judgment, nor to harm someone who is victorious."

[116] Then I answered, "This is my first and last saying, that it would have been better if the earth had not produced Adam, or else, when it had produced him, to have restrained him from sinning. [117] For what profit is it for all who are in this present time to live in heaviness, and after death to look for punishment? [118] O Adam, what have you done? For though it was you who sinned, the evil has not fallen on you alone, but on all of us who come from you. [119] For what profit is it to us, if an immortal time is promised to us, but we have done deeds that bring death? [120] And that there is an everlasting hope promised to us, but we have most miserably failed? [121] And that there are reserved habitations of health and safety, but we have lived wickedly? [122] And that the glory of the Most High will defend those who have led a pure life, but we have walked in the most wicked ways of all? [123] And that a paradise will be revealed, whose fruit endures without decay, in which is abundance and healing, but we will not enter into it, [124] for we have lived in perverse ways? [125] And that the faces of those who have practiced self-control will shine more than the stars, but our faces will be blacker than darkness? [126] For while we lived and committed iniquity, we did not consider what we would have to suffer after death."

[127] Then he answered, "This is the significance of the battle which humans born on the earth will fight: [128] if they are overcome, they will suffer as you have said, but if they get the victory, they will receive the thing that I say. [129] For this is the way that Moses spoke to the people while he lived, saying, 'Choose life, that you may live!' [130] Nevertheless they did not believe him or the prophets after him, not even me, who have spoken to them. [131] Therefore there will not be such heaviness in their destruction, as there will be joy over those who are assured of salvation."

[132] Then I answered, "I know, Lord, that the Most High is now called merciful, in that he has mercy upon those who have not yet come into the world; [133] and compassionate, in that he has compassion upon those who turn to his law; [134] and patient, in that he is patient with those who have

sinned, since they are his creatures; [135] and bountiful, in that he is ready to give rather than to take away; [136] and very merciful, in that he multiplies more and more mercies to those who are present, and who are past, and also to those who are to come— [137] for if he was not merciful, the world would not continue with those who dwell in it— [138] and one who forgives, for if he did not forgive out of his goodness, that those who have committed iniquities might be relieved of them, not even one ten thousandth part of mankind would remain living; [139] and a judge, for if he did not pardon those who were created by his word, and blot out the multitude of sins, [140] there would perhaps be very few left of an innumerable multitude."

**8** He answered me, "The Most High has made this world for many, but the world to come for few. [2] Now I will tell you a parable, Ezra. Just as when you ask the earth, it will say to you that it gives very much clay from which earthen vessels are made, but little dust that gold comes from. Even so is the course of the present world. [3] Many have been created, but few will be saved."

[4] I answered, "Drink your fill of understanding then, O my soul, and let my heart devour wisdom. [5] For you have agreed to listen, and are willing to prophesy, for you have only been given a short time to live. [6] O Lord over us, grant to your servant that we may pray before you, and give us seed for our heart and cultivation for our understanding, that fruit may grow from it, by which everyone who is corrupt, who bears the place of a man, may live. [7] For you alone exist, and we all are one workmanship of your hands, just as you have said. [8] Because you give life to the body that is now fashioned in the womb, and give it members, your creature is preserved in fire and water, and your workmanship endures nine months as your creation which is created in it. [9] But that which keeps and that which is kept will both be kept, and when the time comes, the womb returns what has grown in it. [10] For you have commanded that out of the parts of the body, that is to say, out of the breasts, be given milk, which is the fruit of the breasts, [11] that the body that is fashioned may be nourished for a time, and afterwards you guide it in your mercy. [12] Yes, you have brought it up in your righteousness, nurtured it in your law, and corrected it with your judgment. [13] You put it to death as your creation, and make it live as your work. [14] If therefore you destroy him which with so great labor was fashioned by your commandment, to what purpose was he made? [15] Now therefore I will speak. About man in general, you know best, but about your people for whose sake I am sorry, [16] and for your inheritance, for whose cause I mourn, for Israel, for whom I am heavy, and for the seed of Jacob, for whose sake I am troubled, [17] therefore I will begin to pray before you for myself and for them; for I see the failings of us who dwell in the land; [18] but I have heard the swiftness of the judgment which is to come. [19] Therefore hear my voice, and understand my saying, and I will speak before you."

The beginning of the words of Ezra, before he was taken up. He said, [20] "O Lord, you who remain forever, whose eyes are exalted, and whose chambers are in the air, [21] whose throne is beyond measure, whose glory is beyond comprehension, before whom the army of angels stand with trembling, [22] whose service takes the form of wind and fire, whose word is sure, and sayings constant, whose ordinance is strong, and commandment

*Ezra Affirms God's Rule Over Life and Death*

*Ezra's Plea for God's Mercy and a Response*

fearful, ²³ whose look dries up the depths, and whose indignation makes the mountains melt away, and whose truth bears witness— ²⁴ hear, O Lord, the prayer of your servant, and give ear to the petition of your handiwork. ²⁵ Attend to my words, for as long as I live, I will speak, and as long as I have understanding, I will answer. ²⁶ Do not look at the sins of your people, but on those who have served you in truth. ²⁷ Do not regard the doings of those who act wickedly, but of those who have kept your covenants in affliction. ²⁸ Do not think about those who have lived wickedly before you, but remember those who have willingly known your fear. ²⁹ Let it not be your will to destroy those who have lived like cattle, but look at those who have clearly taught your law. ³⁰ Do not be indignant at those who are deemed worse than animals, but love those who have always put their trust in your glory. ³¹ For we and our fathers languish with such diseases, but you are called merciful because of us sinners. ³² For if you have a desire to have mercy upon us who have no works of righteousness, then you will be called merciful. ³³ For the just, which have many good works laid up with you, will be rewarded for their own deeds. ³⁴ For what is man, that you should take displeasure at him? Or what is a corruptible race, that you should be so bitter toward it? ³⁵ For in truth, there is no man among those who are born who has not done wickedly, and among those who have lived, there is none which have not done wrong. ³⁶ For in this, O Lord, your righteousness and your goodness will be declared, if you are merciful to those who have no store of good works."

³⁷ Then he answered me, "Some things you have spoken rightly, and it will happen according to your words. ³⁸ For indeed I will not think about the fashioning of those who have sinned, or about their death, their judgment, or their destruction; ³⁹ but I will rejoice over the creation of the righteous and their pilgrimage, their salvation, and the reward that they will have. ⁴⁰ Therefore as I have spoken, so it will be. ⁴¹ For as the farmer sows many seeds in the ground, and plants many trees, and yet not all that is sown in its season is saved, neither will all that is planted take root, even so those who are sown in the world will not all be saved."

⁴² Then I answered, "If I have found favor, let me speak before you. ⁴³ If the farmer's seed does not come up because it has not received your rain in due season, or if it is ruined by too much rain and perishes, ⁴⁴ likewise man, who is formed with your hands and is called your own image, because he is made like you, for whose sake you have formed all things, even him have you made like the farmer's seed. ⁴⁵ Do not be angry with us, but spare your people and have mercy upon your inheritance, for you have mercy upon your own creation."

*God's Care for His Creation*

⁴⁶ Then he answered me, "Things present are for those who live now, and things to come for those who will live hereafter. ⁴⁷ For you come far short of being able to love my creation more than I. But you have compared yourself to the unrighteous. Do not do that! ⁴⁸ Yet in this will you be admirable to the Most High, ⁴⁹ in that you have humbled yourself, as it becomes you, and have not judged yourself among the righteous, so as to be much glorified. ⁵⁰ For many grievous miseries will fall on those who dwell in the world in the last times, because they have walked in great pride. ⁵¹ But understand for yourself, and for those who inquire concerning the glory

of those like you, ⁵²because paradise is opened to you. The tree of life is planted. The time to come is prepared. Plenteousness is made ready. A city is built. Rest is allowed. Goodness is perfected, and wisdom is perfected beforehand. ⁵³The root of evil is sealed up from you. Weakness and moth are hidden from you, and corruption flees into hell into oblivion. ⁵⁴Sorrows have passed away, and in the end, the treasure of immortality is shown. ⁵⁵Therefore ask no more questions concerning the multitude of those who perish. ⁵⁶For when they had received liberty, they despised the Most High, scorned his law, and forsook his ways. ⁵⁷Moreover they have trodden down his righteous, ⁵⁸and said in their heart that there is no God—even knowing that they must die. ⁵⁹For, as the things I have said will welcome you, so thirst and pain which are prepared for them. For the Most High did not intend that men should be destroyed, ⁶⁰but those who are created have themselves defiled the name of him who made them, and were unthankful to him who prepared life for them. ⁶¹Therefore my judgment is now at hand, ⁶²which I have not shown to all men, but to you, and a few like you."

Then I answered, ⁶³"Behold, O Lord, now you have shown me the mul- *When Will* titude of the wonders which you will do in the last times, but you have not *the Last Day* shown me when." *Come?*

**9** He answered me, "Measure diligently within yourself. When you see that a certain part of the signs are past, which you have been told beforehand, ²then you will understand that it is the very time in which the Most High will visit the world which was made by him. ³When earthquakes, tumult of peoples, plans of nations, wavering of leaders, and confusion of princes are seen in the world, ⁴then will you understand that the Most High spoke of these things from the days that were of old, from the beginning. ⁵For just as with everything that is made in the world has a beginning and an end, and the end manifest, ⁶so also are the times of the Most High: the beginnings are manifest in wonders and mighty works, and the end in effects and signs. ⁷Everyone who will be saved, and will be able to escape by his works, or by faith by which they have believed, ⁸will be preserved from said perils, and will see my salvation in my land and within my borders, which I have sanctified for myself from the beginning. ⁹Then those who now have abused my ways will be amazed. Those who have cast them away despitefully will live in torments. ¹⁰For as many as in their life have received benefits, and yet have not known me, ¹¹and as many as have scorned my law, while they still had liberty and when an opportunity to repent was open to them, did not understand, but despised it, ¹²must know it in torment after death. ¹³Therefore do not be curious any longer how the ungodly will be punished, but inquire how the righteous will be saved, those to whom the world belongs, and for whom the world was created."

¹⁴I answered, ¹⁵"I have said before, and now speak, and will say it again *Those* hereafter, that there are more of those who perish than of those who will *Perishing* be saved, ¹⁶like a wave is greater than a drop." *Are More*

¹⁷He answered me, "Just as the field is, so also the seed. As the flowers *Numerous* are, so are the colors. As the work is, so also is the creation on it. As is the *Than Those* farmer, so also is his threshing floor. For there was a time in the world *Saved* ¹⁸when I was preparing for those who now live, before the world was made for them to dwell in. Then no one spoke against me, ¹⁹but when the world

was made, both now and then the manners of every one created were corrupted by a never failing harvest, and a law unsearchable 20 So I considered
my world, and behold, it was destroyed, and my earth, and behold, it was in
peril, because of the plans that had come into it. 21 I saw and spared them,
but not greatly, and saved myself a grape out of a cluster, and a plant out
of a great people. 22 Let the multitude perish then, which were born in vain.
Let my grape be saved, and my plant, for I have made them perfect with
great labor. 23 Nevertheless, if you will wait seven more days—however do
not fast in them, 24 but go into a field of flowers, where no house is built,
and eat only of the flowers of the field, and you shall taste no flesh, and
shall drink no wine, but shall eat flowers only— 25 and pray to the Most
High continually, then I will come and talk with you."

*Ezra's Fourth*    26 So I went my way, just as he commanded me, into the field which is
*Vision* called Ardat. There I sat among the flowers, and ate of the herbs of the
field, and this food satisfied me. 27 It came to pass after seven days that I
lay on the grass, and my heart was troubled again, like before. 28 My mouth
was opened, and I began to speak before the Lord Most High, and said,
29 "O Lord, you showed yourself among us, to our fathers in the wilderness,
when they went out of Egypt, and when they came into the wilderness,
where no man treads and that bears no fruit. 30 You said, 'Hear me, O Israel.
Heed my words, O seed of Jacob. 31 For behold, I sow my law in you, and it
will bring forth fruit in you, and you will be glorified in it forever.' 32 But
our fathers, who received the law, did not keep it, and did not observe the
statutes. The fruit of the law did not perish, for it could not, because it was
yours. 33 Yet those who received it perished, because they did not keep the
thing that was sown in them. 34 Behold, it is a custom that when the ground
has received seed, or the sea a ship, or any vessel food or drink, and when
it comes to pass that that which is sown, or that which is launched, 35 or
the things which have been received, should come to an end, these come
to an end, but the receptacles remain. Yet with us, it does not happen that
way. 36 For we who have received the law will perish by sin, along with our
heart which received it. 37 Notwithstanding the law does not perish, but
remains in its honor."

*Vision of a*    38 When I spoke these things in my heart, I looked around me with my
*Mourning* eyes, and on my right side I saw a woman, and behold, she mourned and
*Woman* wept with a loud voice, and was much grieved in mind. Her clothes were
torn, and she had ashes on her head. 39 Then I let go of my thoughts with
which I was occupied, and turned to her, 40 and said to her, "Why are you
weeping? Why are you grieved in your mind?"

   41 She said to me, "Leave me alone, my Lord, that I may weep for myself
and add to my sorrow, for I am very troubled in my mind, and brought
very low."

*The Barren*    42 I said to her, "What ails you? Tell me."
*Woman*    43 She said to me, "I, your servant, was barren and had no child, though
*Gives Birth* I had a husband thirty years. 44 Every hour and every day these thirty years
I made my prayer to the Most High day and night. 45 It came to pass after
thirty years that God heard me, your handmaid, and saw my low estate,
and considered my trouble, and gave me a son. I rejoiced in him greatly, I
and my husband, and all my neighbors. We gave great honor to the Mighty

One. ⁴⁶ I nourished him with great care. ⁴⁷ So when he grew up, and I came to take him a wife, I made him a feast day.

**10** ¹ "So it came to pass that when my son had entered into his wed- ding chamber, he fell down and died. ² Then we all put out the lamps, and all my neighbors rose up to comfort me. I remained quiet until the second day at night. ³ It came to pass, when they had all stopped consoling me, encouraging me to be quiet, then rose I up by night, and fled, and came here into this field, as you see. ⁴ Now I do not intend to return to the city, but to stay here, and not eat or drink, but to continually mourn and fast until I die." *The Death of Her Son*

⁵ Then I left the reflections I was engaged in, and answered her in anger, ⁶ "You most foolish woman, do you not see our mourning, and what has happened to us? ⁷ For Zion the mother of us all is full of sorrow, and much humbled. ⁸ And now we all mourn, and we are sad, since we are all in sorrow, but are you sorrowful for one son? ⁹ Ask the earth, and she will tell you that it is she which ought to mourn for so many that grow upon her. ¹⁰ For out of her, all had their beginnings, and others will come; and, behold, almost all of them walk into destruction, and the multitude of them is utterly doomed. ¹¹ Who then should mourn more, she who has lost so great a multitude, or you, who grieve for one? ¹² But if you say to me, 'My lamentation is not like the earth's, for I have lost the fruit of my womb, which I brought forth with pains, and bare with sorrows; ¹³ but it is with the earth after the manner of the earth. The multitude present in it has gone as it came.' ¹⁴ Then I say to you, 'Just as you have brought forth with sorrow, even so the earth also has given her fruit, namely, people, ever since the beginning to him who made her.' ¹⁵ Now therefore keep your sorrow to yourself, and bear with good courage the adversities which have happened to you. ¹⁶ For if you will acknowledge the decree of God to be just, you will both receive your son in time, and will be praised among women. ¹⁷ Go your way then into the city to your husband." *Ezra Rebukes the Mourning Woman*

¹⁸ She said to me, "I will not do that. I will not go into the city, but I will die here."

¹⁹ So I proceeded to speak further to her, and said, ²⁰ "Do not do that, but allow yourself to be persuaded by reason of the adversities of Zion; and be comforted by reason of the sorrow of Jerusalem. ²¹ For you see that our sanctuary has been laid waste, our altar broken down, our temple destroyed, ²² our lute has been brought low, our song is put to silence, our rejoicing is at an end, the light of our candlestick is put out, the ark of our covenant is plundered, our holy things are defiled, and the name that we are called is profaned. Our free men are despitefully treated, our priests are burned, our Levites have gone into captivity, our virgins are defiled and our wives ravished, our righteous men carried away, our little ones betrayed, our young men are brought into bondage, and our strong men have become weak. ²³ What is more than all, the seal of Zion has now lost the seal of her honor, and is delivered into the hands of those who hate us. ²⁴ Therefore shake off your great heaviness, and put away from yourself the multitude of sorrows, that the Mighty One may be merciful to you again, and the Most High may give you rest, even ease from your troubles."

Mourning
Woman
Transforms
into a City
²⁵ It came to pass while I was talking with her, behold, her face suddenly began to shine exceedingly, and her countenance was flashing, so that I was very afraid of her, and wondered what this meant. ²⁶ Behold, suddenly she made a great and very fearful cry, so that the earth shook at the noise. ²⁷ I looked, and behold, the woman appeared to me no more, but there was a city built, and a place shown itself from large foundations. Then I was afraid, and cried with a loud voice, ²⁸ "Where is Uriel the angel, who came to me at the first? For he has caused me to fall into this great trance, and my end has turned into corruption, and my prayer a reproach!"

Interpretation
of the Vision
of the Woman
²⁹ As I was speaking these words, behold, the angel who had come to me at first came to me, and he looked at me. ³⁰ Behold, I lay as one who had been dead, and my understanding was taken from me. He took me by the right hand, and comforted me, and set me on my feet, and said to me, ³¹ "What ails you? Why are you so troubled? Why is your understanding and the thoughts of your heart troubled?"

³² I said, "Because you have forsaken me; yet I did according to your words, and went into the field, and, behold, I have seen, and still see, that which I am not able to explain."

³³ He said to me, "Stand up like a man, and I will instruct you."

³⁴ Then I said, "Speak on, my Lord; only do not forsake me, lest I die before my time. ³⁵ For I have seen what I did not know, and hear what I do not know. ³⁶ Or is my sense deceived, or my soul in a dream? ³⁷ Now therefore I beg you to explain to your servant what this vision means."

³⁸ He answered me, "Listen to me, and I will inform you, and tell you about the things you are afraid of, for the Most High has revealed many secret things to you. ³⁹ He has seen that your way is righteous, because you are continually sorry for your people, and make great lamentation for Zion. ⁴⁰ This therefore is the meaning of the vision. ⁴¹ The woman who appeared to you a little while ago, whom you saw mourning, and began to comfort her, ⁴² but now you no longer see the likeness of the woman, but a city under construction appeared to you, ⁴³ and she told you of the death of her son, this is the interpretation: ⁴⁴ This woman, whom you saw, is Zion, whom you now see as a city being built. ⁴⁵ She told you that she had been barren for thirty years because there were three thousand years in the world in which there was no offering as yet offered in her. ⁴⁶ And it came to pass after three thousand years that Solomon built the city and offered offerings. It was then that the barren bore a son. ⁴⁷ She told you that she nourished him with great care. That was the dwelling in Jerusalem. ⁴⁸ When she said to you, 'My son died when he entered into his marriage chamber,' and that misfortune befell her, this was the destruction that came to Jerusalem. ⁴⁹ Behold, you saw her likeness, how she mourned for her son, and you began to comfort her for what has happened to her. These were the things to be opened to you. ⁵⁰ For now the Most High, seeing that you are sincerely grieved and suffer from your whole heart for her, has shown you the brightness of her glory and the attractiveness of her beauty. ⁵¹ Therefore I asked you to remain in the field where no house was built, ⁵² for I knew that the Most High would show this to you. ⁵³ Therefore I commanded you to come into the field, where no foundation of any building was. ⁵⁴ For no human construction could stand in the place in which the

city of the Most High was to be shown. ⁵⁵ Therefore do not be afraid nor let your heart be terrified, but go your way in and see the beauty and greatness of the building, as much as your eyes are able to see. ⁵⁶ Then will you hear as much as your ears may comprehend. ⁵⁷ For you are more blessed than many, and are called by name to be with the Most High, like only a few. ⁵⁸ But tomorrow at night you shall remain here, ⁵⁹ and so the Most High will show you those visions in dreams of what the Most High will do to those who live on the earth in the last days."

So I slept that night and another, as he commanded me.

**11** It came to pass the second night that I saw a dream, and behold, an eagle which had twelve feathered wings and three heads came up from the sea. ² I saw, and behold, she spread her wings over all the earth, and all the winds of heaven blew on her, and were gathered together. ³ I saw, and out of her wings there grew other wings near them; and they became little, tiny wings. ⁴ But her heads were at rest. The head in the middle was larger than the other heads, yet rested it with them. ⁵ Moreover I saw, and behold, the eagle flew with her wings to reign over the earth and over those who dwell therein. ⁶ I saw how all things under heaven were subject to her, and no one spoke against her—no, not one creature on earth. ⁷ I saw, and behold, the eagle rose on her talons, and uttered her voice to her wings, saying, ⁸ "Do not all watch at the same time. Let each one sleep in his own place and watch in turn; ⁹ but let the heads be preserved for the last."

*The Rise of Alexander, Jonathan as High Priest*

¹⁰ I saw, and behold, the voice did not come out of her heads, but from the midst of her body. ¹¹ I counted her wings that were near the others, and behold, there were eight of them. ¹² I saw, and behold, on the right side one wing arose and reigned over all the earth. ¹³ When it reigned, the end of it came, and it disappeared, so that its place appeared no more. The next wing rose up and reigned, and it ruled a long time. ¹⁴ It happened that when it reigned, its end came also, so that it disappeared, like the first. ¹⁵ Behold, a voice came to it, and said, ¹⁶ "Listen, you who have ruled over the earth all this time! I proclaim this to you, before you disappear, ¹⁷ none after you will rule as long as you, not even half as long." ¹⁸ Then the third arose, and ruled as the others before, and it also disappeared. ¹⁹ So it went with all the wings one after another, as every one ruled, and then disappeared. ²⁰ I saw, and behold, in course of time the wings that followed were set up on the right side, that they might rule also. Some of them ruled, but in a while they disappeared. ²¹ Some of them also were set up, but did not rule.

²² After this I saw, and behold, the twelve wings disappeared, along with two of the little wings. ²³ There was no more left on the eagle's body, except the three heads that rested, and six little wings. ²⁴ I saw, and behold, two little wings divided themselves from the six and remained under the head that was on the right side; but four remained in their place. ²⁵ I saw, and behold, these under wings planned to set themselves up and to rule. ²⁶ I saw, and behold, there was one set up, but in a while it disappeared. ²⁷ A second also did so, and it disappeared faster than the first. ²⁸ I saw, and behold, the two that remained also planned between themselves to reign. ²⁹ While they thought about it, behold, one of the heads that were at rest awakened, the one that was in the middle, for that was greater than the two other heads.

³⁰ I saw how it joined the two other heads with it. ³¹ Behold, the head turned with those who were with it, and ate the two under wings that planned to reign. ³² But this head held the whole earth in possession, and ruled over those who dwell in it with much oppression. It had stronger governance over the world than all the wings that had gone before.

³³ After this I saw, and behold, the head also that was in the middle suddenly disappeared, like the wings. ³⁴ But the two heads remained, which also reigned the same way over the earth and over those who dwell in it. ³⁵ I saw, and behold, the head on the right side devoured the one that was on the left side.

*The Lion and the Eagle*  ³⁶ Then I heard a voice, which said to me, "Look in front of you, and consider the thing that you see."

³⁷ I saw, and behold, something like a lion roused out of the woods roaring. I heard how he sent out a man's voice to the eagle, and spoke, saying, ³⁸ "Listen and I will talk with you. The Most High will say to you, ³⁹ 'Are you not the one that remains of the four animals whom I made to reign in my world, that the end of my times might come through them? ⁴⁰ The fourth came and overcame all the animals that were past, and ruled the world with great trembling, and the whole extent of the earth with grievous oppression. He lived on the earth such a long time with deceit. ⁴¹ You have judged the earth, but not with truth. ⁴² For you have afflicted the meek, you have hurt the peaceful, you have hated those who speak truth, you have loved liars, destroyed the dwellings of those who produced fruit, and threw down the walls of those who did you no harm. ⁴³ Your insolence has come up to the Most High, and your pride to the Mighty. ⁴⁴ The Most High also has looked at his times, and behold, they are ended, and his ages are fulfilled. ⁴⁵ Therefore appear no more, you eagle, nor your horrible wings, nor your evil little wings, nor your cruel heads, nor your hurtful talons, nor all your worthless body, ⁴⁶ that all the earth may be refreshed and relieved, being delivered from your violence, and that she may hope for the judgment and mercy of him who made her.'"

*The Destruction of the Eagle*  **12** It came to pass, while the lion spoke these words to the eagle, I saw, ² and behold, the head that remained disappeared, and the two wings which went over to it arose and set themselves up to reign; and their kingdom was brief and full of uproar. ³ I saw, and behold, they disappeared, and the whole body of the eagle was burned, so that the earth was in great fear.

*Interpretation of the Vision of the Eagle*  Then I woke up because of great perplexity of mind and great fear, and said to my spirit, ⁴ "Behold, you have done this to me, because you search out the ways of the Most High. ⁵ Behold, I am still weary in my mind, and very weak in my spirit. There is not even a little strength in me, because of the great fear with which I was frightened tonight. ⁶ Therefore I will now ask the Most High that he would strengthen me to the end."

⁷ Then I said, "O sovereign Lord, if I have found favor in your sight, and if I am justified with you more than many others, and if my prayer has indeed come up before your face, ⁸ strengthen me then, and show me, your servant, the interpretation and plain meaning of this fearful vision, that you may fully comfort my soul. ⁹ For you have judged me worthy to show me the end of time and the last events of the times."

[10] He said to me, "This is the interpretation of this vision which you saw: [11] The eagle, whom you saw come up from the sea, is the fourth kingdom which appeared in a vision to your brother Daniel. [12] But it was not explained to him, as I now explain it to you or have explained it. [13] Behold, the days are coming when a kingdom will rise up on earth, and it will be feared more than all the kingdoms that were before it. [14] Twelve kings will reign in it, one after another. [15] Of those, the second will begin to reign, and will reign a longer time than others among the twelve. [16] This is the interpretation of the twelve wings which you saw. [17] As for when you heard a voice which spoke, not going out from the heads, but from the midst of its body, this is the interpretation: [18] That after the time of that kingdom, there will arise no small contentions, and it will stand in peril of falling. Nevertheless, it will not fall then, but will be restored again to its former power. [19] You saw the eight under wings sticking to her wings. This is the interpretation: [20] That in it eight kings will arise, whose times will be short and their years swift. [21] Two of them will perish when the middle time approaches. Four will be kept for a while until the time of its end approaches; but two will be kept to the end. [22] You saw three heads resting. This is the interpretation: [23] In its last days, the Most High will raise up three kingdoms and renew many things in them. They will rule over the earth, [24] and over those who dwell in it, with much oppression, more than all those who were before them. Therefore they are called the heads of the eagle. [25] For these are those who will accomplish her wickedness, and who will finish her last actions. [26] You saw that the great head disappeared. It signifies that one of them will die on his bed, and yet with pain. [27] But for the two that remained, the sword will devour them. [28] For the sword of the one will devour him that was with him, but he will also fall by the sword in the last days. [29] You saw two under wings passing over the head that is on the right side. [30] This is the interpretation: These are they whom the Most High has kept to his end. This is the brief reign that was full of trouble, as you saw.

[31] "The lion, whom you saw rising up out of the forest, roaring, speaking to the eagle, and rebuking her for her unrighteousness, and all her words which you have heard, [32] this is the anointed one, whom the Most High has kept for them to the end. He will reprove them for their impieties and for their injustices, and will heap up their contemptuous dealings before them. [33] For at first he will set them alive in his judgment, and when he has reproved them, he will destroy them. [34] For he will deliver the rest of my people with mercy, those who have been preserved throughout my borders, and he will make them joyful until the coming of the end, even the day of judgment, about which I have spoken to you from the beginning. [35] This is the dream that you saw, and this is its interpretation. [36] Only you have been worthy to know the secret of the Most High. [37] Therefore, write all these things that you have seen in a book, and put it in a secret place. [38] You shall teach them to the wise of your people, whose hearts you know are able to comprehend and keep these secrets. [39] But wait here yourself seven more days, that you may be shown whatever it pleases the Most High to show you." Then he departed from me.

*Interpretation of the Eagle's Heads and Wings*

*Interpretation of the Lion*

⁴⁰It came to pass, when all the people heard that the seven days were past, and I had not come again into the city, they all gathered together, from the least to the greatest, and came to me, and spoke to me, saying, ⁴¹"How have we offended you? What evil have we done against you, that you have utterly forsaken us, and sit in this place? ⁴²For of all the prophets, only you are left to us, like a cluster of the vintage, and like a lamp in a dark place, and like a harbor for a ship saved from the tempest. ⁴³Are the evils which have come to us not sufficient? ⁴⁴If you will forsake us, how much better had it been for us if we also had been consumed in the burning of Zion! ⁴⁵For we are not better than those who died there." Then they wept with a loud voice. I answered them, ⁴⁶"Take courage, O Israel! Do not be sorrowful, you house of Jacob; ⁴⁷for the Most High remembers you. The Mighty has not forgotten you in the struggle. ⁴⁸As for me, I have not forsaken you. I have not departed from you; but I have come into this place to pray for the desolation of Zion, and that I might seek mercy for the humiliation of your sanctuary. ⁴⁹Now go your way, every man to his own house, and after these days I will come to you."

⁵⁰So the people went their way into the city, as I told them to do. ⁵¹But I sat in the field seven days, as the angel commanded me. In those days, I ate only of the flowers of the field, and my food was from plants.

**13** It came to pass after seven days, I dreamed a dream by night. ²Behold, a wind arose from the sea that moved all its waves. ³I saw, and behold, ᵃthis wind caused to come up from the midst of the sea something like the appearance of a man. I saw, and behold,ᵃ that man grew strong with the clouds of heaven. When he turned his face to look, everything that he saw trembled. ⁴Whenever the voice went out of his mouth, all who heard his voice melted, like the wax melts when it feels the fire.

⁵After this I saw, and behold, an innumerable multitude of people was gathered together from the four winds of heaven to make war against the man who came out of the sea. ⁶I saw, and behold, he carved himself a great mountain, and flew up onto it. ⁷I tried to see the region or place from which the mountain was carved, and I could not.

⁸After this I saw, and behold, all those who were gathered together to fight against him were very afraid, and yet they dared to fight. ⁹Behold, as he saw the assault of the multitude that came, he did not lift up his hand, or hold a spear or any weapon of war; ¹⁰but I saw only how he sent out of his mouth something like a flood of fire, and out of his lips a flaming breath, and out of his tongue he shot out sparks and storms. ¹¹These were all mixed together: the flood of fire, the flaming breath, and the great storm, and fell upon the assault of the multitude which was prepared to fight, and burned up every one of them, so that all of a sudden an innumerable multitude was seen to be nothing but dust of ashes and smell of smoke. When I saw this, I was amazed.

¹²Afterward, I saw the same man come down from the mountain, and call to himself another multitude which was peaceful. ¹³Many people came to him. Some of them were glad. Some were sorry. Some of them were bound, and some others brought some of those as offerings.

ᵃ The words from "this wind" to "and behold" are added from the Syriac

Then through great fear I woke up and prayed to the Most High, and said, <sup>14</sup> "You have shown your servant these wonders from the beginning, and have counted me worthy that you should receive my prayer. <sup>15</sup> Now show me also the interpretation of this dream. <sup>16</sup> For as I conceive in my understanding, woe to those who will be left in those days! Much more woe to those who are not left! <sup>17</sup> For those who were not left will be in heaviness, <sup>18</sup> understanding the things that are laid up in the latter days, but not attaining to them. <sup>19</sup> But woe to them also who are left, because they will see great perils and much distress, like these dreams declare. <sup>20</sup> Yet is it easier for one to be in peril and to come into these things, than to pass away as a cloud out of the world, and not to see the things that will happen in the last days."

*Interpretation of the Vision of the Man*

He answered me, and said <sup>21</sup> "I will tell you the interpretation of the vision, and I will also open to you the things about which you mentioned. <sup>22</sup> You have spoken of those who are left behind. This is the interpretation: <sup>23</sup> He that will bear the peril in that time will protect those who fall into danger, even those who have works and faith toward the Almighty. <sup>24</sup> Know therefore that those who are left behind are more blessed than those who are dead. <sup>25</sup> These are the interpretations of the vision: Whereas you saw a man coming up from the midst of the sea, <sup>26</sup> this is he whom the Most High has been keeping for many ages, who by his own self will deliver his creation. He will direct those who are left behind. <sup>27</sup> Whereas you saw that out of his mouth came wind, fire, and storm, <sup>28</sup> and whereas he held neither spear, nor any weapon of war, but destroyed the assault of that multitude which came to fight against him, this is the interpretation: <sup>29</sup> Behold, the days come when the Most High will begin to deliver those who are on the earth. <sup>30</sup> Astonishment of mind will come upon those who dwell on the earth. <sup>31</sup> One will plan to make war against another, city against city, place against place, people against people, and kingdom against kingdom. <sup>32</sup> It will be, when these things come to pass, and the signs happen which I showed you before, then my Son will be revealed, whom you saw as a man ascending. <sup>33</sup> It will be, when all the nations hear his voice, every man will leave his own land and the battle they have against one another. <sup>34</sup> An innumerable multitude will be gathered together, as you saw, desiring to come and to fight against him. <sup>35</sup> But he will stand on the top of Mount Zion. <sup>36</sup> Zion will come, and will be shown to all men, being prepared and built, like you saw the mountain carved without hands. <sup>37</sup> My Son will rebuke the nations which have come for their wickedness, with plagues that are like a storm, <sup>38</sup> and will rebuke them to their face with their evil thoughts, and the torments with which they will be tormented, which are like a flame. He will destroy them without labor by the law, which is like fire.

<sup>39</sup> Whereas you saw that he gathered to himself another multitude that was peaceful, <sup>40</sup> these are the ten tribes which were led away out of their own land in the time of Josiah the king, whom Salmanansar the king of the Assyrians led away captive, and he carried them beyond the River, and they were taken into another land. <sup>41</sup> But they made this plan among themselves, that they would leave the multitude of the gentiles, and go out into a more distant region, where mankind had never lived, <sup>42</sup> that there they might keep their statutes which they had not kept in their own land.

⁴³ They entered by the narrow passages of the river Euphrates. ⁴⁴ For the Most High then did signs for them, and stopped the springs of the River until they had passed over. ⁴⁵ For through that country there was a long way to go, namely, of a year and a half. The same region is called Arzareth.ᵃ ⁴⁶ Then they lived there until the latter time. Now when they begin to come again, ⁴⁷ the Most High stops the springs of the River again, that they may go through. Therefore you saw the multitude gathered together with peace. ⁴⁸ But those who are left behind of your people are those who are found within my holy border. ⁴⁹ It will be therefore when he will destroy the multitude of the nations that are gathered together, he will defend the people who remain. ⁵⁰ Then will he show them very many wonders."

⁵¹ Then I said, "O sovereign Lord, explain this to me: Why have I seen the man coming up from the midst of the sea?"

⁵² He said to me, "As no one can explore or know what is in the depths of the sea, even so no man on earth can see my Son, or those who are with him, except in the time of hisᵇ day. ⁵³ This is the interpretation of the dream which you saw, and for this only you are enlightened about this, ⁵⁴ for you have forsaken your own ways, and applied your diligence to mine, and have searched out my law. ⁵⁵ You have ordered your life in wisdom, and have called understanding your mother. ⁵⁶ Therefore I have shown you this, for there is a reward laid up with the Most High. It will be, after another three days I will speak other things to you, and declare to you mighty and wondrous things."

⁵⁷ Then I went out and passed into the field, giving praise and thanks greatly to the Most High because of his wonders, which he did from time to time, ⁵⁸ and because he governs the time, and such things as happen in their seasons. So I sat there three days.

*Ezra's Seventh Vision: A Voice from the Bush*

**14** It came to pass upon the third day, I sat under an oak, and, behold, a voice came out of a bush near me, and said, "Ezra, Ezra!"

² I said, "Here I am, Lord," and I stood up on my feet.

³ Then he said to me, "I revealed myself in a bush and talked with Moses when my people were in bondage in Egypt. ⁴ I sent him and led my people out of Egypt. I brought him up to Mount Sinai, where I kept him with me for many days. ⁵ I told him many wondrous things, and showed him the secrets of the times and the end of the seasons. I commanded him, saying, ⁶ 'You shall publish these openly, and these you shall hide.' ⁷ Now I say to you: ⁸ Lay up in your heart the signs that I have shown, the dreams that you have seen, and the interpretations which you have heard; ⁹ for you will be taken away from men, and from now on you will live with my Son and with those who are like you, until the times have ended. ¹⁰ For the world has lost its youth, and the times begin to grow old. ¹¹ For the age is divided into twelve parts, and ten parts of it are already gone, and the half of the tenth part. ¹² There remain of it two parts after the middle of the tenth part. ¹³ Now therefore set your house in order, reprove your people, comfort the lowly among them, and now renounce the life that is corruptible, ¹⁴ and let go of the mortal thoughts, cast away from you the burdens of

---

ᵃ That is, "another land"
ᵇ From the Syriac. The Latin omits "his"

man, put off now your weak nature, ¹⁵ lay aside the thoughts that are most grievous to you, and hurry to escape from these times. ¹⁶ For worse evils than those which you have seen happen will be done after this. ¹⁷ For look how much the world will be weaker through age, so much that more evils will increase on those who dwell in it. ¹⁸ For the truth will withdraw itself further off, and falsehood will be near. For now the eagle which you saw in vision hurries to come."

¹⁹ Then I answered and said before you, O Lord. ²⁰ Behold, I will go, as you have commanded me, and reprove the people who now live, but who will warn those who will be born afterward? For the world is set in darkness, and those who dwell in it are without light. ²¹ For your law has been burned, therefore no one knows the things that are done by you, or the works that will be done. ²² But if I have found favor before you, send the Holy Spirit to me, and I will write all that has been done in the world since the beginning, even the things that were written in your law, that men may be able to find the path, and that those who would live in the latter days may live."

²³ He answered me and said, "Go your way, gather the people together, and tell them not to seek you for forty days. ²⁴ But prepare for yourself many tablets, and take with you Saraia, Dabria, Selemia, Ethanus, and Osiel, these five, which are ready to write swiftly; ²⁵ and come here, and I will light a lamp of understanding in your heart which will not be put out until the things have ended about which you will write. ²⁶ When you are done, some things you shall publish openly, and some things you shall deliver in secret to the wise. Tomorrow at this hour you will begin to write."

²⁷ Then I went out, as he commanded me, and gathered all the people together, and said, ²⁸ "Hear these words, O Israel! ²⁹ Our fathers at the beginning were foreigners in Egypt, and they were delivered from there, ³⁰ and received the law of life, which they did not keep, which you also have transgressed after them. ³¹ Then the land of Zion was given to you for a possession; but you yourselves and your ancestors have done unrighteousness, and have not kept the ways which the Most High commanded you. ³² Because he is a righteous judge, in due time, he took from you what he had given you. ³³ Now you are here, and your kindred are among you. ³⁴ Therefore, if you will rule over your own understanding and instruct your hearts, you will be kept alive, and after death you will obtain mercy. ³⁵ For after death the judgment will come, when we will live again. Then the names of the righteous will become manifest, and the works of the ungodly will be declared. ³⁶ Let no one therefore come to me now, nor seek me for forty days."

*Ezra Assembles the People and Makes a Proclamation*

³⁷ So I took the five men, as he commanded me, and we went out into the field, and remained there.

³⁸ It came to pass on the next day that, behold, a voice called me, saying, "Ezra, open your mouth, and drink what I give you to drink."

³⁹ Then opened I my mouth, and behold, a full cup was handed to me. It was full of something like water, but its color was like fire. ⁴⁰ I took it, and drank. When I had drunk it, my heart uttered understanding, and wisdom grew in my breast, for my spirit retained its memory. ⁴¹ My mouth was opened, and shut no more. ⁴² The Most High gave understanding to the five men, and they wrote successively the things that were told them,

*God Reveals His Words to Ezra and the Five*

in characters which they did not know, and they sat forty days. Now they wrote in the day-time, and at night they ate bread. ⁴³As for me, I spoke in the day, and by night I did not hold my tongue. ⁴⁴So in forty days, ninety-four books were written.

⁴⁵It came to pass, when the forty days were fulfilled, that the Most High spoke to me, saying, "The first books that you have written, publish openly, and let the worthy and unworthy read them; ⁴⁶but keep the last seventy, that you may deliver them to those who are wise among your people; ⁴⁷for in them is the spring of understanding, the fountain of wisdom, and the stream of knowledge."

⁴⁸I did so.

*God Pronounces Judgment on the Wicked*

**15** "Behold, speak in the ears of my people the words of prophecy which I will put in your mouth," says the Lord. ²"Cause them to be written on paper, for they are faithful and true. ³Do not be afraid of their plots against you. Do not let the unbelief of those who speak against you trouble you. ⁴For all the unbelievers will die in their unbelief.

*Egypt Punished*

⁵"Behold," says the Lord, "I bring evils on the whole earth: sword, famine, death, and destruction. ⁶For wickedness has prevailed over every land, and their hurtful works have reached their limit. ⁷Therefore," says the Lord, ⁸"I will hold my peace no more concerning their wickedness which they profanely commit, neither will I tolerate them in these things, which they wickedly practice. Behold, the innocent and righteous blood cries to me, and the souls of the righteous cry out continually. ⁹I will surely avenge them," says the Lord, "and will receive all the innocent blood from among them. ¹⁰Behold, my people is led like a flock to the slaughter. I will not allow them now to dwell in the land of Egypt, ¹¹but I will bring them out with a mighty hand and with a high arm, and will strike Egypt with plagues, as before, and will destroy all its land."

¹²Let Egypt and its foundations mourn, for the plague of the chastisement and the punishment that God will bring upon it. ¹³Let the farmers that till the ground mourn, for their seeds will fail and their trees will be ruined through the blight and hail, and a terrible tempest. ¹⁴Woe to the world and those who dwell in it! ¹⁵For the sword and their destruction draws near, and nation will rise up against nation to battle with weapons in their hands. ¹⁶For there will be sedition among men, and growing strong against one another. In their might, they will not respect their king or the chief of their great ones. ¹⁷For a man will desire to go into a city, and will not be able. ¹⁸For because of their pride the cities will be troubled, the houses will be destroyed, and men will be afraid. ¹⁹A man will have no pity on his neighbors, but will assault their houses with the sword and plunder their goods, because of the lack of bread, and for great suffering.

*Oppressors of God's People Punished*

²⁰"Behold," says God, "I call together all the kings of the earth to stir up those who are from the rising of the sun, from the south, from the east, and Libanus, to turn themselves one against another, and repay the things that they have done to them. ²¹Just as they do yet this day to my chosen, so I will do also, and repay into their bosom." The Lord God says: ²²"My right hand will not spare the sinners, and my sword will not cease over those who shed innocent blood on the earth. ²³A fire has gone out from his wrath and has consumed the foundations of the earth and the sinners, like burnt

straw. ²⁴ Woe to those who sin and do not keep my commandments!" says the Lord. ²⁵ "I will not spare them. Go your way, you rebellious children! Do not defile my sanctuary!" ²⁶ For the Lord knows all those who trespass against him, therefore he will deliver them to death and destruction. ²⁷ For now evils have come upon the whole earth, and you will remain in them; for God will not deliver you, because you have sinned against him.

²⁸ Behold, a horrible sight appearing from the east! ²⁹ The nations of the dragons of Arabia will come out with many chariots. From the day that they set out, their hissing is carried over the earth, so that all those who will hear them may also fear and tremble. ³⁰ Also the Carmonians, raging in wrath, will go out like the wild boars of the forest. They will come with great power and join battle with them, and will devastate a portion of the land of the Assyrians with their teeth. ³¹ Then the dragons will have the upper hand, remembering their nature. If they will turn themselves, conspiring together in great power to persecute them, ³² then these will be troubled, and keep silence through their power, and will turn and flee. ³³ From the land of the Assyrians, an enemy in ambush will attack them and destroy one of them. Upon their army will be fear and trembling, and indecision upon their kings. *Assyria Punished*

³⁴ Behold, clouds from the east, and from the north to the south! They are very horrible to look at, full of wrath and storm. ³⁵ They will clash against one another. They will pour out a heavy storm on the earth, even their own storm. There will be blood from the sword to the horse's belly, ³⁶ and to the thigh of man, and to the camel's hock. ³⁷ There will be fearfulness and great trembling upon earth. They who see that wrath will be afraid, and trembling will seize them. ³⁸ After this, great storms will be stirred up from the south, from the north, and another part from the west. ³⁹ Strong winds will arise from the east, and will shut it up, even the cloud which he raised up in wrath; and the storm that was to cause destruction by the east wind will be violently driven toward the south and west. ⁴⁰ Great and mighty clouds, full of wrath, will be lifted up with the storm, that they may destroy all the earth and those who dwell in it. They will pour out over every high and lofty one a terrible storm, ⁴¹ fire, hail, flying swords, and many waters, that all plains may be full, and all rivers, with the abundance of those waters. ⁴² They will break down the cities and walls, mountains and hills, trees of the forest, and grass of the meadows, and their grain. ⁴³ They will go on steadily to Babylon and destroy her. ⁴⁴ They will come to it and surround it. They will pour out the storm and all wrath on her. Then the dust and smoke will go up to the sky, and all those who are around it will mourn for it. ⁴⁵ Those who remain will serve those who have destroyed it. *Babylon Punished*

⁴⁶ You, Asia, who are partaker in the beauty of Babylon, and in the glory of her person— ⁴⁷ woe to you, you wretch, because you have made yourself like her. You have decked out your daughters for prostitution, that they might please and glory in your lovers, which have always lusted after you! ⁴⁸ You have followed her who is hateful in all her works and inventions. Therefore God says, ⁴⁹ "I will send evils on you: widowhood, poverty, famine, sword, and pestilence, to lay waste your houses and bring you to destruction and death. ⁵⁰ The glory of your power will be dried up like a flower *Asia Punished*

when the heat rises that is sent over you. ⁵¹ You will be weakened like a poor woman who is beaten and wounded, so that you will not be able to receive your mighty ones and your lovers. ⁵² Would I have dealt with you with such jealousy," says the Lord, ⁵³ "if you had not always slain my chosen, exalting and clapping your hands, and saying over their dead, when you were drunk?

⁵⁴ Beautify your face! ⁵⁵ The reward of a prostitute will be in your bosom, therefore you will be repaid. ⁵⁶ Just as you will do to my chosen," says the Lord, "even so God will do to you, and will deliver you to your adversaries. ⁵⁷ Your children will die of hunger. You will fall by the sword. Your cities will be broken down, and all your people in the field will perish by the sword. ⁵⁸ Those who are in the mountains will die of hunger, eat their own flesh, and drink their own blood, because of hunger for bread and thirst for water. ⁵⁹ You, unhappy above all others, will come and will again receive evils. ⁶⁰ In the passage, they will rush on the hateful city and will destroy some portion of your land, and mar part of your glory, and will return again to Babylon that was destroyed. ⁶¹ You will be cast down by them as stubble, and they will be to you as fire. ⁶² They will devour you, your cities, your land, and your mountains. They will burn all your forests and your fruitful trees with fire. ⁶³ They will carry your children away captive, and will plunder your wealth, and mar the glory of your face."

*God Pronounces Judgment on the Nations*

**16** Woe to you, Babylon, and Asia! Woe to you, Egypt and Syria! ² Put on sackcloth and garments of goats' hair, wail for your children and lament; for your destruction is at hand. ³ A sword has been sent upon you, and who is there to turn it back? ⁴ A fire has been sent upon you, and who is there to quench it? ⁵ Calamities are sent upon you, and who is there to drive them away? ⁶ Can one drive away a hungry lion in the forest? Can one quench a fire in stubble, once it has begun to burn? ⁷ Can one turn back an arrow that is shot by a strong archer? ⁸ The Lord God sends the calamities, and who will drive them away? ⁹ A fire will go out from his wrath, and who may quench it? ¹⁰ He will flash lightning, and who will not fear? He will thunder, and who would not tremble? ¹¹ The Lord will threaten, and who will not be utterly broken in pieces at his presence? ¹² The earth and its foundations quake. The sea rises up with waves from the deep, and its waves will be troubled, along with the fish in them, at the presence of the Lord, and before the glory of his power. ¹³ For his right hand that bends the bow is strong, his arrows that he shoots are sharp, and will not miss when they begin to be shot into the ends of the world. ¹⁴ Behold, the calamities are sent out, and will not return again until they come upon the earth. ¹⁵ The fire is kindled and will not be put out until it consumes the foundations of the earth. ¹⁶ Just as an arrow which is shot by a mighty archer does not return backward, even so the calamities that are sent out upon earth will not return again. ¹⁷ Woe is me! Woe is me! Who will deliver me in those days?

*Calamities Upon the Earth*

¹⁸ The beginning of sorrows, when there will be great mourning; the beginning of famine, and many will perish; the beginning of wars, and the powers will stand in fear; the beginning of calamities, and all will tremble! What will they do when the calamities come? ¹⁹ Behold, famine and plague, suffering and anguish! They are sent as scourges for correction. ²⁰ But for

all these things they will not turn them from their wickedness, nor be always mindful of the scourges. <sup>21</sup> Behold, food will be so cheap on earth that they will think themselves to be in good condition, and even then calamities will grow on earth: sword, famine, and great confusion. <sup>22</sup> For many of those who dwell on earth will perish of famine; and others who escape the famine, the sword will destroy. <sup>23</sup> The dead will be cast out like dung, and there will be no one to comfort them; for the earth will be left desolate, and its cities will be cast down. <sup>24</sup> There will be no farmer left to cultivate the earth or to sow it. <sup>25</sup> The trees will give fruit, but who will gather it? <sup>26</sup> The grapes will ripen, but who will tread them? For in all places there will be a great solitude; <sup>27</sup> for one man will desire to see another, or to hear his voice. <sup>28</sup> For of a city there will be ten left, and two of the field, who have hidden themselves in the thick groves, and in the clefts of the rocks. <sup>29</sup> As in an orchard of olives upon every tree there may be left three or four olives, <sup>30</sup> or as when a vineyard is gathered, there are some clusters left by those who diligently search through the vineyard, <sup>31</sup> even so in those days, there will be three or four left by those who search their houses with the sword. <sup>32</sup> The earth will be left desolate, and its fields will be for briers, and its roads and all her paths will grow thorns, because no sheep will pass along them. <sup>33</sup> The virgins will mourn, having no bridegrooms. The women will mourn, having no husbands. Their daughters will mourn, having no helpers. <sup>34</sup> Their bridegrooms will be destroyed in the wars, and their husbands will perish of famine. <sup>35</sup> Hear now these things, and understand them, you servants of the Lord. <sup>36</sup> Behold, the Lord's word: receive it. Do not doubt the things about which the Lord speaks.

<sup>37</sup> Behold, the calamities draw near, and are not delayed. <sup>38</sup> Just as a woman with child in the ninth month, when the hour of her delivery draws near, within two or three hours great pains surround her womb, and when the child comes out from the womb, there will be no waiting for a moment, <sup>39</sup> even so the calamities will not delay coming upon the earth. The world will groan, and sorrows will seize it on every side. *Judgment Is Near*

<sup>40</sup> "O my people, hear my word: prepare for battle, and in those calamities be like strangers on the earth. <sup>41</sup> He who sells, let him be as he who flees, and he who buys, as one who will lose. <sup>42</sup> Let he who does business be as he who has no profit by it, and he who builds, as he who will not dwell in it, <sup>43</sup> and he who sows, as if he would not reap, so also he who prunes the vines, as he who will not gather the grapes, <sup>44</sup> those who marry, as those who will have no children, and those who do not marry, as the widowed. <sup>45</sup> Because of this, those who labor, labor in vain; <sup>46</sup> for foreigners will reap their fruits, plunder their goods, overthrow their houses, and take their children captive, for in captivity and famine they will conceive their children. <sup>47</sup> Those who conduct business, do so only to be plundered. The more they adorn their cities, their houses, their possessions, and their own persons, <sup>48</sup> the more I will hate them for their sins," says the Lord. <sup>49</sup> Just as a respectable and virtuous woman hates a prostitute, <sup>50</sup> so will righteousness hate iniquity, when she adorns herself, and will accuse her to her face, when he comes who will defend him who diligently searches out every sin on earth. *Like Strangers Upon the Earth*

<sup>51</sup> Therefore do not be like her or her works. <sup>52</sup> For yet a little while, and iniquity will be taken away out of the earth, and righteousness will reign

over us. ⁵³ Do not let the sinner say that he has not sinned; for God will burn coals of fire on the head of one who says "I have not sinned before God and his glory."

*Sinners Cannot Hide from God*

⁵⁴ Behold, the Lord knows all the works of men, their imaginations, their thoughts, and their hearts. ⁵⁵ He said, "Let the earth be made," and it was made, "Let the sky be made," and it was made. ⁵⁶ At his word, the stars were established, and he knows the number of the stars. ⁵⁷ He searches the deep and its treasures. He has measured the sea and what it contains. ⁵⁸ He has shut the sea in the midst of the waters, and with his word, he hung the earth over the waters. ⁵⁹ He has spread out the sky like a vault. He has founded it over the waters. ⁶⁰ He has made springs of water in the desert and pools on the tops of the mountains to send out rivers from the heights to water the earth. ⁶¹ He formed man, and put a heart in the midst of the body, and gave him breath, life, and understanding, ⁶² yes, the spirit of God Almighty. He who made all things and searches out hidden things in hidden places, ⁶³ surely he knows your imagination, and what you think in your hearts. Woe to those who sin, and try to hide their sin! ⁶⁴ Because the Lord will exactly investigate all your works, and he will put you all to shame. ⁶⁵ When your sins are brought out before men, you will be ashamed, and your own iniquities will stand as your accusers in that day. ⁶⁶ What will you do? Or how will you hide your sins before God and his angels? ⁶⁷ Behold, God is the judge. Fear him! Stop sinning, and forget your iniquities, to never again commit them. So will God lead you out, and deliver you from all suffering.

*God's Wrath for Sinners and Mercy for His Elect*

⁶⁸ For, behold, the burning wrath of a great multitude is kindled over you, and they will take away some of you, and feed you with that which is sacrificed to idols. ⁶⁹ Those who consent to them will be held in derision and in contempt, and be trodden under foot. ⁷⁰ For there will be in various places, and in the next cities, a great insurrection against those who fear the Lord. ⁷¹ They will be like mad men, sparing none, but spoiling and destroying those who still fear the Lord. ⁷² For they will destroy and plunder their goods, and throw them out of their houses. ⁷³ Then the trial of my elect will be made known, even as the gold that is tried in the fire. ⁷⁴ Hear, my elect ones, says the Lord: "Behold, the days of suffering are at hand, and I will deliver you from them. ⁷⁵ Do not be afraid, and do not doubt, for God is your guide. ⁷⁶ You who keep my commandments and precepts," says the Lord God, "do not let your sins weigh you down, and do not let your iniquities lift themselves up." ⁷⁷ Woe to those who are choked with their sins and covered with their iniquities, like a field is choked with bushes, and its path covered with thorns, that no one may travel through! ⁷⁸ It is shut off and given up to be consumed by fire.

*Introduction to*

# 4 Maccabees

FOURTH MACCABEES WAS ALSO known in antiquity as "On the Supremacy of Reason," a title far more appropriate for the book's actual contents. The author, a faithful Hellenistic Jew well-schooled in Greek language, rhetoric, ethics, and literature, took up a common topic of Greek ethical philosophy, namely, that a person's rational faculty ought to exercise mastery over the desires, emotions, and sensations that might come over him or her. His distinctive emphasis, however, falls on the power of the Jewish law to train a person's rational faculty to exercise such mastery—both by teaching the value of piety and by providing consistent exercise in choosing a virtuous course over a self-indulgent one. After a brief review of how particular commandments in the Law of Moses work to restrain particular passions, the author focuses on the example of the martyrs who endured the most brutal tortures to the point of death rather than willingly yield to impiety during the hellenizing crisis of 167–166 BC (see 2 Macc 6:18–7:42). These martyrs show just how completely, and against what extreme pressures, training in the Law of Moses empowers the individual to resist—specifically, the feelings and pains that potentially subvert commitment to act in line with virtue. The book (which very much resembles an oration) thus provides a demonstration that the person who is most faithful to the Jewish law will also be the person who most perfectly fulfills the Greek ethical ideal of self-mastery. It is likely that the author wrote to shore up his fellow Jews' commitment to the covenant and to insulate them against the contempt in which non-Jews typically held their way of life. The book was written in well-crafted Greek, probably in the vicinity of Syria or Cilicia, in the middle of the first century AD. Fourth Maccabees was valued in the church first as a source of encouragement to endure martyrdom and then, after the legalization of Christianity, as an encouragement to master the desires and impulses that tend toward sin.

—D. A. deSilva

# 4 MACCABEES

*Reason as Master of Emotions* **1** Being about to demonstrate an especially philosophical subject—whether devout reason is absolute master of the emotions—I should probably advise you rightly so that you all might readily pay attention to the philosophy. ²For the subject is also necessary for everyone to attain knowledge, and otherwise, it includes the praise of the greatest virtue—I mean, indeed, wisdom. ³If then reason appears to rule over the emotions that hinder moderation, both gluttony and lust, ⁴but also reason appears to control the emotions that impede righteousness, such as malice, and the emotions that impede courage: anger and pain and fear, ⁵how then, some people might perhaps ask, if reason rules the emotions, why does it not rule over forgetfulness and ignorance? Attempting to speak this way is ridiculous. ⁶For reason does not rule its own emotions, but the emotions that are contrary to righteousness and courage and moderation and wisdom, and it rules these emotions not for the purpose of destroying them, but rather for the purpose of not yielding to them.

⁷Therefore I could certainly demonstrate to you with many examples and from other places that pious reason is the complete master of the emotions, ⁸but I could show this much better from the bravery of both Eleazar and seven brothers, and their mother, who died for the sake of virtue. ⁹For every one of these people, who showed disdain for those pains to the point of death, demonstrated that reason rules over emotions. ¹⁰Therefore it is certainly set before me to praise for their magnificent acts the men who died with their mother for the sake of their moral character upon this occasion, but I also would consider them blessed for their honors. ¹¹For those being admired because of their courage and perseverance, not only by all people but also by those torturing them, these accused ones caused the tyranny against their nation to be destroyed, defeating the tyrant by their perseverance for the purpose of cleansing the country through them. ¹²But it will also be proper to speak about this presently in just a moment, beginning with the proposal that I am accustomed to do; and in this way, I will turn to the story about them, giving glory to the all-wise God.

*Defining the Task* ¹³So then we are investigating whether reason is the complete master of the emotions. ¹⁴Let us judge then what exactly is reason, and what is emotion, and how many forms of emotion exist, and whether reason rules over all of these. ¹⁵Now, therefore, reason is indeed a mind that with a morally upright life prefers a word of wisdom. ¹⁶Now, therefore, wisdom is the knowledge of divine and human matters and the cause of these. ¹⁷Accordingly, now, this is the discipline from the law, through which we learn about divine subjects reverently and about human subjects profitably.

¹⁸And they have caused the forms of wisdom to be good judgment and righteousness and courage and moderation. ¹⁹Good judgment is supreme over all, because of which indeed reason rules over the emotions. ²⁰The two overarching kinds of emotion are both pleasure and pain; and each of these have also grown around the soul. ²¹And even regarding pleasure

and pain, the emotions that follow from them are many. <sup>22</sup>So then, desire is before pleasure; but gladness is with pleasure. <sup>23</sup>And fear is before pain; grief is with pain. <sup>24</sup>Anger is an emotion sharing pleasure and pain, if someone recognizes when they encounter it. <sup>25</sup>There is even a malicious propensity in pleasure, since it is the most complicated of all the emotions. <sup>26</sup>In regard to the soul, there are arrogance and love of money and love of glory and love of conflict and malice; <sup>27</sup>but with regard to the body, there is indiscriminate eating and gluttony, and eating alone. <sup>28</sup>Therefore, just as both pleasure and pain are two growths from the body and the soul, there are many offshoots from these emotions, <sup>29</sup>of which each master gardener—namely, reason—by weeding and pruning and binding up and watering and irrigating in every direction, tames the forest of habits and emotions.

<sup>30</sup>For while reason is the guide of the magnificent acts, it is the absolute master of the emotions. Therefore you should first also examine by the restraining power of self-control that reason is absolute master of the emotions. <sup>31</sup>Now then, self-control is mastery over the desires, <sup>32</sup>and of the desires, some are mental, whereas the others are physical, and reason seems to rule over both of these. <sup>33</sup>Otherwise, how is it that, being attracted toward the forbidden foods, we turned away the pleasure from them? Is it not because reason is able to rule over the appetite? I certainly imagine so. <sup>34</sup>Therefore, while desiring seafood and birds and animals (all kinds of food are forbidden to us according to the law), we abstain because of the mastery of reason. <sup>35</sup>For the emotions of the appetite are guarded by the sensible mind being bent back and all the movements of the body rivaled by reason.

**2** And who is amazed if the desires of the soul toward the beautiful union are set aside? <sup>2</sup>By this, therefore, the sensible Joseph is praised because by reason, by thinking he maintained control over physical pleasure. <sup>3</sup>For being young and ripe for sexual intercourse, he held back by reason the mad desire of his emotions. <sup>4</sup>Not only is reason seen to rule over the mad passion of physical pleasure, but also over all desire. <sup>5</sup>Therefore the law says, "You will not desire the wife of your neighbor nor anything your neighbor has." <sup>6</sup>And so when the law has told us not to desire, I could likely convince you of much more that reason is able to rule over the desires, just as it even rules over the emotions that hinder righteousness. <sup>7</sup>Otherwise how can a person who eats alone, and someone who is by habit both gluttonous and a drunkard, be educated in a different way of life, if it is not evident that reason is lord over the emotions? <sup>8</sup>Therefore, for example, when living by the law, even if a person was a lover of money, he is constrained to his path, lending to the people who are poor without interest and cutting down the debt when the seventh year arrives. <sup>9</sup>And if someone was selfishly frugal, then by the law he rules through reason, neither gleaning the harvest nor gathering grapes from the vineyard. And on the other matters, he is to acknowledge this: that reason is the ruler over the emotions. <sup>10</sup>For the law rules even over the affection toward parents, not abandoning virtue because of them. <sup>11</sup>And it rules over the love toward the wife, convicting her for breaking of the law. <sup>12</sup>And it masters the love of children, punishing for their evil deeds. And it is master over the loving friendship, convicting

*The Law and Reason*

them for wickedness. ¹³And you should not consider it to be surprising where even reason is able to rule over hatred because of the law, ¹⁴nor cutting down the cultivated plants of the enemy, but rather rescuing the possessions of the hated from the ones destroying and helping to raise up what has fallen.

¹⁵And reason is even seen to rule because of the more violent emotions such as desire for power and conceit and arrogance and pride and slander. ¹⁶For the sensible mind rejects all these malicious emotions, just as it even rejects anger; for it is master even over this. ¹⁷When Moses was quite angry against Dathan and Abiram, he did nothing against them in anger, but by reason he controlled his anger. ¹⁸For the sensible mind, as I said, is capable to be the best against the emotions and to correct some of them and even to set aside the others. ¹⁹Otherwise, why did our all-wise father Jacob accuse the households of Simeon and Levi who unreasonably cut the throats of the Shechemite people, saying, "May their anger be greatly cursed"? ²⁰For if reason is not able to rule anger, he would not speak in that way. ²¹For at the time God made humans, he implanted their emotions and habits. ²²And at that time, he enthroned the mind as the sacred guide among the sensory organs over all the rest. ²³And he gave to this the law, according to which the one who lives will be king over a sensible kingdom and a righteous, good, and courageous one.

²⁴Therefore, someone might possibly say how, if reason is strong among the emotions, does it not rule over forgetfulness and ignorance? **3** But the reason is entirely absurd. For reason is not shown to rule over its own emotions, but the one related to the body. ²No person among you is able to remove such a desire, but reason can make it possible to not be enslaved by desire. ³None of you is able to remove anger from the soul, but it is possible to deal with anger. ⁴No person among you is able to remove malice, but reason can help in not yielding to malice. ⁵For reason is not the uprooter of emotions, but their challenger.

*The Example of David's Thirst* ⁶So then this is to be considered more clearly by the story of David the king's thirst. ⁷For being attacked by the foreigners through the whole day, David killed many of them with the soldiers of his nation. ⁸Then when evening came, sweating and very exhausted, he went into the royal tent around which the entire army of the ancestors was encamped. ⁹So then everyone else was at dinner. ¹⁰And the king, as he was very thirsty, though having plentiful springs, he was not able to satisfy the thirst by them. ¹¹But some irrational desire for water from the enemy territory, tormenting him, was inflaming and undoing him, and it was consuming him. ¹²Therefore, when the protectors were complaining about the desire of the king, two young, fierce soldiers, respecting the desire of the king, put on themselves suits of armor and, taking a pitcher, they began to climb over the defenses of the enemy. ¹³And avoiding notice by the guards of the gate, they passed through, being found through the entire camp of the enemy. ¹⁴And, bravely finding the spring, they filled the drink for the king from it. ¹⁵But even being parched with thirst, he considered it to be a terrible danger to the soul, considering the drink of equal value to blood. ¹⁶Therefore, setting desire against reason, he poured out the drink to God. ¹⁷For the sensible mind is able to conquer the compulsions of the emotions, and to quell the flames of desire, [18]and to overthrow the sufferings of the body that are to an extreme degree, and by the noble character of reason to reject all domination of the emotions.

[19]Now the time calls us to the demonstration of the narrative of sensible reason. [20]For when our ancestors were having deep peace because of their observance of the law and were achieving prosperity, so that even the king of Asia, Seleucus Nicanor, also marked off money for the temple service for them and recognized their state, [21]then at that time certain people, attempting a revolution against the public unity, caused various disasters. *A Demonstration of Reason*

4 Now there was a man called Simon who was a political opponent against Onias, who held at the time the high priesthood for life. He was a good and honorable man. When making accusations of all kinds before the nation, Simon did not succeed to injure Onias; he left, fleeing his country and betraying it. [2]Having come to Apollonius, the governor of Syria and also Phoenicia and Cilicia, he said, [3]"Being sympathetic to the affairs of the king, I have come informing you of many thousands of private money in the Jerusalem treasury to be stored up for the temple, not being shared, but these are to belong to Seleucus the king." [4]Apollonius, upon learning each and every one of these things, indeed applauded Simon for the service to the king and, going up to Seleucus, made known the treasury of the money. [5]And receiving authority over this matter, he came quickly into our country with the abominable Simon and a formidable army. [6]Coming by the command of the king, he said he came in order to take the private money from the treasury. [7]And the nation, complaining to the statement and opposing, considered it to be terrible if the ones who entrusted deposit to the temple treasury were deprived, and as such, they were trying to prevent it. [8]But with a threat, Apollonius went away into the temple. [9]While the priests with women and children in the temple were praying to God to protect the place from being desecrated, [10]and when a fully armed army was going up with Apollonius for the capture of the money, angels from heaven appeared on horseback, flashing around weapons and implanting much fear and also trembling in them. [11]Then, falling half dead on the courtyard of the temple open to all nationalities, Apollonius stretched out his hand to heaven and, with tears, begged the Hebrews so that, praying for him, they might satisfy the heavenly army. [12]For he said he had sinned so as to be deserving to die and, being saved, he would sing the blessedness of the holy place to all people. [13]By these heavy words, Onias the high priest, although otherwise discreet, in case Seleucus the king considered them to be from a human plot and not that Apollonius had been done away with by divine justice, prayed for him. [14]And the one who was preserved quite unexpectedly went to report to the king what happened to him.

[15]But when Seleucus, the king, passed away,[a] his son, Antiochus Epiphanes—an arrogant, terrible man—took up the rule, [16]who, after removing Onias from the high priesthood, appointed Jason, his brother, as high priest, [17]who agreed to give annually three thousand six hundred and sixty talents if Antiochus would allow him the rule as high priest. [18]So *Antiochus Persecutes the Judeans*

[a] Lit. "ended"

the king allowed him to be the high priest and to lead the nation. ¹⁹He even sought out the nation and modified the government in violation of the entire law ²⁰so that not only at the very citadel of our country did he build a gymnasium, but he also removed the service for the temple. ²¹On account of these deeds, the divine justice, having been angered, surely instigating him, Antiochus fought. ²²For when he was making war against Ptolemy in Egypt, he heard that because of a rumor being passed around about his death, the people of Jerusalem would be rejoicing as much as possible. He marched quickly upon them. ²³And as he plundered them, he issued a decree so that if any among them should be seen living by the ancestral law, that person should be put to death. ²⁴And when he was in no way able to end by decrees the nation's goodwill, but he saw all of his own threats and punishments were being disregarded ²⁵so that even women, because they circumcised their children, were thrown down from a cliff with their infants, knowing ahead of time that they would experience this, ²⁶when therefore his decrees were disregarded by the people, he himself through torture compelled each one of the nation to renounce Judaism by means of tasting defiled food.

*Antiochus*
*Provokes*
*Eleazar* **5** Sitting with his advisors on a certain high place, the tyrant Antiochus, with their armed soldiers standing around, ²commanded the guards to divert each one of the Hebrews and to compel them to eat pig meat and food sacrificed to idols. ³But if anyone should not want to eat unclean food, being tortured, they were to be put to death. ⁴So after many had been seized, one—first from the group, a Hebrew named Eleazar, a priest by ancestry, his training in the law, and his age advanced, and familiar to many of those around the tyrant because of his age—he was led before him. ⁵And looking at him, Antiochus said, ⁶"Before I begin the torture against you, O elderly man, I would probably advise this to you, that by tasting the pig you might save yourself. For I respect your age and grey hair, which having for so long a time, it does not seem to me that you love knowledge since you consult the Judean religion. ⁷For by what reason, when nature grants us a beautiful thing like this creature, do you detest the eating of meat? ⁸For even this is senseless, not enjoying pleasant things without disgrace. And it is not right to turn back the gifts of nature. ⁹But it seems to me that you will do something even more senseless if, by holding a useless view concerning the truth, ¹⁰you still despise me at your own punishment. Will you not wake up from this nonsense philosophy of yours ¹¹and throw aside your futile reasoning and, taking up a mind worthy of your age, pursue knowledge according to the truth that is beneficial ¹²and, by honoring my benevolent exhortation, show mercy to your old age? ¹³For reflect also on this as even if there is some power watching over this religion it would excuse you for all because of the compulsion that causes a violation of the law."

*Eleazar*
*Explains*
*His Defiance* ¹⁴After the tyrant urged on this way regarding the unlawful eating of meat, Eleazar requested a word. ¹⁵And after receiving permission to speak, he began to address the people in this way: ¹⁶"We, Antiochus, who have been convinced to live by the divine law, consider no compulsion to be more forceful than our ready obedience toward the law. ¹⁷Therefore, now in no way do we consider it worthwhile to break the law. ¹⁸Indeed, if on

the basis of truth our law were not divine, as you assume, but otherwise, we consider it to be divine, it is not permitted for us in this way to disregard our reputation for piety. ¹⁹Therefore you should not consider this to be small sin if we should eat unclean food! ²⁰For the breaking of the law in small and large matters is the same. ²¹For in either case, the law is treated in the same way. ²²You mock our philosophy as if living by it was not with prudence. ²³But it thoroughly teaches us good judgment so as to rule over all the pleasures and desires and courage; to train so as to endure willingly all pain. ²⁴And it educates us in righteousness so as to act fairly through all habits and to teach piety, so as to worship the only God who exists reverently. ²⁵Therefore, we do not eat unclean food. For because we believe the law to have been appointed by God, we know that, according also to nature, the Creator of the world has sympathy for us by making the law. ²⁶He permitted us to eat that which is suitable for our soul, but he forbade us to eat meat that would be opposed to this. ²⁷But it would be tyrannical to force us not only to break the law, but also to eat so that you may still laugh at this hated eating of unclean food of ours. ²⁸But you must not laugh this laughter at me, ²⁹and I will not disregard the sacred oath of the ancestors concerning the keeping of the law, ³⁰not even if you will cut out my eyes and melt my entrails. ³¹As you can tell, I am not so old and cowardly that because of piety my reason is not young. ³²Toward this aim, prepare the torture wheel and fan the fire hotter. ³³Thus, I should not have pity for my old age such that I break the ancestral law by myself. ³⁴I will not lie to you, law, my teacher, nor cry to you, beloved self-control. ³⁵I will not disgrace you, philosophical reason; nor will I disown you, precious priesthood and knowledge of the law. ³⁶I will neither defile my dignified mouth of old age nor my age that was lawfully lived. ³⁷My ancestors will accept me in innocence because I do not fear your torture, even to death. ³⁸For although you will tyrannize the ungodly, you will be master over me with pious reason neither by word nor by deed."

6 After he responded this way to the exhortation of the tyrant, the soldiers who were standing by cruelly dragged Eleazar to the torture chamber. ²And first they stripped the old man, adorned with the elegance of piety. ³Then, after binding both hands, with a whip they wounded him severely ⁴while a herald opposite of him cried out, "Be convinced by the commands of the king!" ⁵But the high minded and noble man, as truly Eleazar was, as if being tortured in a dream, in no way changed his mind. ⁶But while lifting his eyes high to heaven, the old man was being torn in his flesh by the whip and was flowing with his blood, and on his sides he was gouged open. ⁷And although falling to the ground from his body, not being able to bear the sufferings, he held his reason upright and unwavering. ⁸Then one of the guards, leaping upon him, beat him with his foot sharply in the area below the ribs, so that he would stand up after falling. ⁹But he endured the pain and ignored the use of force and endured the torments to the end. ¹⁰And just like an excellent athlete being beaten, the old man prevailed over the torturers. ¹¹So, with his face sweating and breathing exceedingly hard, he was marveled at by the torturers for his good luck. ¹²Therefore, partially having pity on his old age, ¹³partially in sympathy of being an acquaintance, and partially from admiration at the

*The Torture of Eleazar*

endurance attributed to him, some people of the king said, [14]"Why destroy yourself thoughtlessly by this evil, Eleazar? [15]We will serve you boiled meat. Now as for you, save yourself by pretending to taste the pig."

[16]And Eleazar, as if being tormented more cruelly by the counsel, shouted loudly, [17]"May the children never think of Abraham in this evil way, so as being cowardly enough to fake an act so unfitting to us. [18]For it would be especially irrational if, although having lived a life until old age for truth and having guarded lawfully a reputation upon them, we should change our ways presently. [19]And we ourselves indeed should become an example of ungodliness to the young, so that we become a precedent for the eating of unclean food. [20]For it would be shameful if we were to survive a little longer and be a mockery for this to all for our cowardice [21]and be despised by the tyrant as cowardly, while also not defending our divine law until death. [22]For this reason, you, O children of Abraham, die nobly for the sake of your faith! [23]So, guards of the tyrant, what are you waiting for?"[a]

[24]Thus, in seeing him being so high minded toward the torture, and not being turned quickly by their compassion, they brought him to the fire. [25]Then, burning him with maliciously produced tools, they threw him down and poured stinking liquids into his nose. [26]And by this time, being burnt to his bones and about to pass out, he stretched his eyes toward God and said, [27]"You know, God, although it is possible[b] for me to save myself from fiery torture, I am dying for the law. [28]Be merciful to your nation, this being sufficient for our punishment concerning them. [29]Make my blood their purification, and take my soul in exchange for their life." [30]And after saying this, the holy man nobly died in the torture, and he resisted until the tortures of death by his reason for the law. [31]Therefore, pious reason is undeniably the master of the emotions. [32]For if the emotions had ruled over his reason, I might yield the evidence of their superiority to them. [33]But now reason, having conquered the emotions, we attribute appropriately the authority for governing to it. [34]And it is right for us to recognize the strength to be reason, where it rules over even the external sufferings [35]since it is also laughable. For I have demonstrated that reason rules not only over pain but also rules over pleasure and never does it give in to it.

*Eleazar's Death an Example of Reason Prevailing over Emotion* **7** For just like a good helmsman, the reason of our father Eleazar, steering the ship of piety in the sea of emotions, [2]and although being beaten by the threats of the tyrant and swept by the huge waves of the tortures, [3]in no way changed the rudder of his piety until that moment he sailed into the harbor of victory of death. [4]No city has held out even in such a way against the many and various machines while being besieged as that most holy person. Although being consumed in his holy life by tortures and racks, he removed the ones who besieged him through the protection of pious reason. [5]For stretching out his mind as an overhanging cliff, our father Eleazar broke the furious waves of emotion.

[6]O priest worthy of the priesthood, you did not defile your holy teeth, nor did you share your stomach, which makes room for service to God and purification in eating unclean food. [7]O man living in harmony with the law and philosopher of divine life! [8]It is necessary that men like this be the

---

[a] Lit. "what are you expecting?" [b] Lit. "available"

ones who practice the law by their own blood and noble sweat until death, protecting it from the emotions. ⁹You, father, established firmly our observance of the law through your endurance unto glory, and you did not abandon the ritual service that you praise. And by your deeds, you confirmed the words of philosophy. ¹⁰O old man more forceful than torture; O elderly man more vigorous than fire and greatest king over the emotions, Eleazar.

¹¹For like our father Aaron, being armed with a censer, running through the great crowds, conquered the fiery angel, ¹²in the same way the son of Aaron, Eleazar, being consumed by the fire did not turn from his reason. ¹³And so it was most marvelous that although being an old man, the labors of his body already being loose and his muscles being relaxed and his tendons also being worn out, he became young. ¹⁴By the spirit of reason and by the reason of Isaac he made the many-headed rack useless. ¹⁵O man of blessed old age and dignified gray hair and life of lawfulness whom the faithful seal of death has perfected.

¹⁶If accordingly an old man disregards tortures until death by piety, then pious reason is undeniably the ruler over the emotions. ¹⁷Now, perhaps some might say not all have full command over the emotions because not all have prudent reason. ¹⁸But as much as people have regard for piety with their whole heart, these alone are able to rule the emotions of the flesh. ¹⁹Because they believe that they do not die to God, just as our patriarchs Abraham, Isaac, and Jacob believed, but live for God. ²⁰Therefore it is not contradictory to appear for people to be governed by passion because of their weak reason. ²¹For who, being a philosopher in a godly manner by the whole standard of philosophy, and having believed in God, ²²and having known that it is a blessing to endure all pain because of virtue, would not have full command over the emotions by godliness? ²³For only the wise and temperate courageous one is lord over the emotions. ²⁴So indeed because of this, even young children, when following their philosophy according to the pious reason, have triumphed over the harshest instruments of torture.

**8** For when, in spite of the first attempt, the tyrant was conquered on all sides, not being able to force the old man to eat unclean food, ²then at that point, in extreme rage, he commanded to lead others from the prime of life of the Hebrews, and if they were to eat unclean food, to set them free after eating, but if they were to oppose, to torture them most cruelly. ³With the tyrant ordering these things, seven brothers who were handsome and also modest and honorable and gifted in every way, being led with their elderly mother, were brought into his presence, ⁴whom after the tyrant saw surrounding their mother in the middle just as in a choir, he took delight at them and being amazed by the dignity and nobility, he smiled at them, and calling them near, he said, ⁵"O young men, I kindly marvel at each one of you, greatly honoring the handsomeness and the impressive number of brothers. Not only do I not advise you to show madness—the same madness by the old man who was tortured before—⁶but also I encourage you to yield to me to enjoy my friendship. For just as I would be able to punish the ones who resist my commands, in the same way also I would be able to do good to the ones who show obedience to me. ⁷Therefore trust me, and you will receive a government position of authority in my affairs if

*The Example of the Seven Brothers*

you renounce the ancestral laws of your nation. [8]And by taking part in the life of a Greek and changing your ways, revel in your youth. [9]Otherwise, if you cause my anger by your resistance, you will compel me with dreadful punishments to destroy each one of you by tortures. [10]Therefore have compassion for yourselves, whom even I, your enemy, pity—especially your age and your handsome appearance. [11]Will you not consider this, that nothing is reserved for you who resist except on the rack to die?" [12]So after saying this, he ordered the guards to put out the instruments of torture in front of them, so that by fear he might also convince them to eat unclean food. [13]So both torture wheels and instruments for setting limbs, torture racks and bone-crushers and catapults and cauldrons, frying pans and finger sheaths and iron claws and wedges and embers from the fire—the guards brought all of these into their presence, resuming again, and the tyrant spoke, [14]"Boys, be afraid, and whatever justice you worship, it will be merciful to you since you are breaking the law out of compulsion."

[15]But after hearing the incentives and seeing the dreadful instruments, not only were they not afraid, but they also held their opposing perspective against the tyrant; and by means of their prudence, they overcame his tyranny. [16]And further, let us consider if some had been fainthearted and cowardly among them, what kind of arguments might they have used. Would they not be these? [17]"O we are wretched and so senseless! When the king summoned and called us with kind treatment, would we not obey him? [18]Why do we make ourselves cheerful in useless intentions and dare to act on resistance that brings death? [19]Men, brothers, do we not fear the instruments of torture and consider the threats of tortures and retreat from this conceit and arrogance that brings destruction? [20]Let us have pity for our age and show compassion for the old age of our mother, [21]and we should consider well that by resisting, we will die. [22]So also divine justice will agree with us since we feared the king by compulsion. [23]Why should we cast ourselves out of a pleasant life and deprive ourselves of the sweet world? [24]We should not struggle against compulsion nor hold useless views in view of the rack that would torture us. [25]Not even the law itself would willingly put us to death, in fearing the instruments of torture. [26]How is such great contentiousness sunk deep into us, and how can fatal endurance please us when we can stay to live quietly by obeying the king?" [27]But the young men about to be tortured said nothing like this, not even remotely considering such thoughts. [28]For they were ignoring their emotions and held control over their sufferings [29]so that at the moment the tyrant stopped advising them to eat unclean food, all of them with one voice, together as from the same soul, said as follows:

*The Brothers Stand Firm*

**9** "What are you about, O tyrant? For we are ready to die rather than disobey our ancestral commandments. [2]For we also clearly dishonor our ancestors if we do not demonstrate ready obedience for the law and knowledge to our advisor. [3]Tyrant and advisor of lawlessness, in hating us, do not pity us beyond ourselves. [4]For we consider your compassion by our lawless preservation to be more troublesome than death itself! [5]You are terrifying us with death by torture, threatening us as though you did not learn from Eleazar shortly earlier. [6]If the old men of the Hebrews died because of their piety and in spite of enduring torture, we, the young men, more likely rightly desire to die, despising the tortures of your compulsion, which even the elderly teacher conquered. ⁷Therefore O tyrant, test also if you will put to death our lives because of our piety; do not consider us injured by being tortured. ⁸For indeed we, through this distress and endurance, we will bring the prize of virtue. ⁹But you, because of the despotic murder of us, you will endure, by divine justice, eternal torture by fire."

¹⁰After they said these things, not only was the tyrant frustrated at these resistant young men, but he was also filled with rage at these ungracious boys. ¹¹Therefore, after giving the order, the scourger brought the oldest of them; and after tearing his tunic, they bound his hands and arms with leather straps on each side. ¹²But as they were beating him with the whip, they grew tired; having accomplished nothing, they placed him up on the torture wheel, ¹³around which having been stretched, the noble young man's limbs were dislocated. ¹⁴And with all his limbs being torn from their sockets, he accused, saying, ¹⁵"Most bloodstained and savage tyrant and enemy of the justice of heaven, you are wounding me in this way not because I am a murderer, not even because I behaved profanely, but because I defend the divine law." ¹⁶And the guards were saying, "Agree to eat, so that you might be set free from the torture." ¹⁷He said, "Your way is not mighty in such a way, O polluted servants, so as to break my reason! Cut off my arms and legs! And burn up flesh! And twist my limbs out of joint! ¹⁸For through all the torture I will convince you that only the children of the Hebrews are unconquered for the sake of virtue." ¹⁹Saying these words, still they spread fire, and provoking greatly, further tightened the torture wheel. ²⁰The torture wheel was stained all over with blood, and the pile of charcoal was quenched by his dripping bodily fluids, and flesh flowed around the axle of the machine. ²¹And already having the ligaments of his bones melted, the young man, high minded and worthy of Abraham, did not groan. ²²But as being transformed by fire into immortality, he nobly endured the rack. ²³"Imitate me, brothers," he said. "Do not desert my eternity nor renounce my high spirited brotherhood with you. Fight the holy and noble fight concerning godliness ²⁴through which the righteous providence of our fathers in being merciful to our nation might aid us against the accursed tyrant." ²⁵And after saying this, the holy young man gave up his life.

²⁶After everyone was amazed by his strength of spirit, the guards led the second youth according to the age of the first and, fitting irons on his hands, they attached him with sharp claws to the machine and catapult. ²⁷Before the torture, inquiring as to whether he would wish to eat, they heard his noble decision. ²⁸After dragging across the iron claws from his tendons even up to his chin, all his flesh, these beasts like leopards scraped off the skin of his head as well. But he, enduring this suffering with difficulty, said, ²⁹"How sweet is every manner of death for our ancestral faith!" He also said to the tyrant, ³⁰"Do you not think, most savage tyrant of all, that you are being tortured more than I, now seeing the arrogant reason of your tyranny being defeated by our endurance for our faith? ³¹For I indeed relieve the pain by the pleasure that comes through virtue, ³²but you are

*The Torture of the First Brother*

*The Torture of the Second Brother*

tortured by the threats of ungodliness, and you will not escape, depraved tyrant, the punishments of the divine wrath."

The Torture
of the Third
Brother

**10** And after this young man endured a death to be remembered, the third brother was led out, being much encouraged by many so that by tasting the meat he might save himself. ²But he, shouting loudly, said, "Don't you know that the same father begot me with the ones who died, and the same mother conceived me, and on the same teachings I was raised? ³I do not renounce the noble kinship of brotherhood. ⁴As regards these things, if you have some instrument of correction, bring it to my body; for my soul you will not set on fire should you want it." ⁵Then the ones who bitterly bore the frankness of the man with joint-wrenching machines, his hands and feet began to dislocate and dismember him by forcing his limbs out from their sockets. ⁶And his fingers and toes and arms and legs and elbows were dragged about. ⁷And prevailing by not even one way to overwhelm him, tearing away the skin with their fingernails, they began scalping him. So immediately they moved him onto the wheel ⁸around which, while being dislocated from his vertebrae, he saw his own flesh being torn all over and flowing with drops of blood down his entrails. ⁹Then, being about to die, he said, ¹⁰"We clearly, O depraved tyrant, are suffering this because of our training and virtue for God. ¹¹But you, because of your ungodliness and blood guilt, you will perpetually endure tortures."

The Torture
of the Fourth
Brother

¹²And when this one died fittingly for a brother, they compelled the fourth, saying, ¹³"You, then, do not act madly with the same madness as your brothers did, but rather by being convinced by the king, save yourself." ¹⁴But he said to him, "For that to convince me, you do not have your fire hot enough for me, so as to make me a coward. ¹⁵No! By the blessed death of my brothers and the eternal destruction of the tyrant and the praiseworthy life of piety, I will not renounce my noble brotherhood. ¹⁶Contrive, O tyrant, tortures so that also through these you might learn that I am a brother of those tortured previously." ¹⁷After hearing this, the bloodthirsty and stinking and entirely abominable Antiochus ordered his tongue to be cut out. ¹⁸But he said, "Even if you take away my voice organ, God hears those who are mute. ¹⁹Look, my tongue has been loosened; cut it out! For besides this, you will not silence our reason. ²⁰Gladly, for God, we allow the mutilation of our bodies' limbs. ²¹But God will quickly come after you, for you are cutting out a musical tongue of the divine hymns."

The Torture
of the Fifth
Brother

**11** As this one also died, being severely wounded from the tortures, the fifth leaped forward, saying, ²"I am not about to be excused, tyrant, from torture for the sake of virtue. ³But I have come myself on my own so that by murdering me as well, you might deserve punishment by heavenly justice for your many crimes. ⁴O hater of virtue and hater of humanity, for what act are you destroying us in this way? ⁵Does it seem bad to you? Or is it because we live in devotion to the Creator of all things and live according to his virtuous law? ⁶But these actions are worthy of honor, not torture, ⁷if you really were perceiving human longing and had hope of deliverance from God. ⁸Now see, being a stranger from God, you make war against those living for God." ⁹While he was saying these words, the guards, after binding him, dragged him onto the catapult, ¹⁰on which, binding him by the knees and fitting on them iron clamps, they twisted his waist upon the torture wheel wedge, on which, in the manner of a scorpion, his entire body was being bent backward upon the wheel; they dislocated his limbs. ¹¹In this condition, and his breathing having restricted, and having squeezed his body, ¹²he said, "Excellent favors you are granting to us O involuntary tyrant; excellent through these honorable sufferings, you make available to us an opportunity to demonstrate our endurance to the law."

¹³And also when this one passed away, the sixth was led out, a young *The Torture* boy, who, after the tyrant inquired whether he would be willing to eat to *of the Sixth* be released, the boy responded, ¹⁴"Although by age I am younger than my *Brother* brothers, but in mind I am their equal. ¹⁵For both being born and being nourished in the same way for the same purpose, we ought to die in like manner. ¹⁶Therefore, if it seems best to you to torture me for not eating unclean food, then torture me!" ¹⁷As he said these words, they were leading him onto the wheel, ¹⁸on which, stretching him tight with stout limbs and dislocating his vertebrae, they built a fire underneath him. ¹⁹And they were applying a burning sharp little skewer to his back and, piercing through to his ribs, they burned through his entrails. ²⁰But the boy being tortured, he said, "O holy eternity, in which, because of piety we many brothers being summoned have not been defeated in the contest of suffering. ²¹For pious knowledge, O tyrant, is invincible. ²²I also, being equipped with noble character, will die with my brothers. ²³And I myself am bringing a great avenging spirit against you, inventor of tortures and enemy of those who truly live in devotion. ²⁴Being six boys, we destroyed your tyranny. ²⁵For your ability to neither change our minds regarding our reason nor to force us to the eating of unclean food; is this not the dissolution of your rule? ²⁶Your fire is cold to us, and your catapult causes no pain, and your force has no strength. ²⁷For it is not the guards of the tyrant, but the guards of divine law that are set before us; because of this, unconquered, we hold onto reason."

**12** As also this one happily died after being thrown into a cauldron, *The Torture* the seventh, the youngest of all, came up, ²whom the tyrant had *of the Seventh* compassion for even though he was reproached dreadfully by his broth- *Brother* ers. ³When he saw the boy already wearing the imprisoning bonds, he had brought him near and tried to exhort him, saying, ⁴"You see the conclusion from the senselessness of your brothers, for because of their resistance, being tortured, they died. If indeed you do not obey after being tortured wretchedly, you yourself will also die before your time. ⁵But, by being convinced, you will be a friend and lead the affairs in the kingdom." ⁶And after exhorting the boy with these words, he sent for the child's mother, so that in showing mercy to her after depriving her of so many sons, he might urge her to make her remaining son obedient for his salvation. ⁷But the boy, when his mother urged him by the Hebrew language, as we will tell little later, ⁸"Release me!" he said, "Let me speak to the king and to all the friends with him." ⁹And rejoicing exceedingly on the promise of the youth, they quickly loosed him. ¹⁰Running over to the nearest frying pans, he said, ¹¹"O profane one," he said, "and worst of any ungodly tyrant, were you not ashamed, having received good things and your kingdom from God, to murder his attendants and to torture the one who practices piety? ¹²Because, he reserved divine justice for you, constant and eternal fire and tortures, which for the whole time will not send you out. ¹³Were you ashamed, not being human, you wild beast, to cut out the tongues of those who have the same feelings and are made from the very same basic materials and to torture by disfiguring them in such a manner? ¹⁴But indeed, the ones who died nobly have fulfilled their devotion to God. ¹⁵But you, you will wail loudly and terribly to kill the champions of virtue for no reason." ¹⁶Therefore because he was also about to die, he said, ¹⁷"I do not desert the testimony of my brothers; ¹⁸rather, I appeal to our ancestral God that he might be merciful to my race. ¹⁹But he will also punish you in the present life and in death." ²⁰And after earnestly praying these words, he threw himself down into the frying pans, and in this way he gave up his life.

*The Seven Brothers' Example of Reason* **13** If the seven brothers accordingly despised sufferings until death, all kinds of people will agree that pious reason is sovereign over the emotions. ²For just as those being enslaved to their emotions had eaten unclean food, for we would say they had been defeated by these emotions. ³But now this is not how it is. Rather, by the reason that is applauded by God, they prevailed over the emotions, ⁴and a person is not to ignore this chief command of the mind. For it rules over both emotion and sufferings. ⁵How, then, is a person not to acknowledge the blessed self-restraint by these men, who definitely did not turn away from the agonies from fire? ⁶For like towers jutting out over the harbor driving back the threats of waves, they maintain the calm for those who sail into the anchorage. ⁷In the same way, the seven-towered prudence of the youths, securing the harbor of piety, conquered the reckless abandon of the emotions. ⁸For standing as a holy choir of piety, they encouraged each other, saying, ⁹"Brothers, may we die as brothers for the sake of the law. Let us imitate the three, the youths in Syria, who despised the equally afflicting furnace. ¹⁰We must not be cowardly regarding the showing forth of our piety." ¹¹So the first one said, "Take courage, brother." Then another, "Endure nobly." ¹²And still another said, "Remember from where we came and by the hand of which father Isaac remained under to be slaughtered because of devotion." ¹³Then each one, and together all looking at one another, cheerful and exceedingly bold, said, "We will consecrate ourselves to God, the one who gave our souls from our whole hearts and let us use our bodies to guard concerning the law. ¹⁴We should not fear the one who intends to kill us. ¹⁵For great is the contest of the soul, and the danger in eternal torture lies before the ones who disobey the command of God. ¹⁶Therefore, let us equip ourselves in the self-control of divine reason. ¹⁷If we suffer in this way, Abraham and Isaac and Jacob will welcome us, and all our ancestors will commend us." ¹⁸And as each one of the brothers were being dragged away from the rest, the remaining ones said, "Do not disgrace us, brother, nor disappoint those who died before."

¹⁹You are not ignorant of the bond of abstract humanity, the very thing which the divine and all wise Providence distributed through our ancestors to their descendants and planted through our mother's womb, ²⁰in which the brothers dwelt for the same amount of time and being formed in the same length of time, and developing from the same blood and being born from the same person. ²¹And being born through the same

time and drinking milk from the same source from where brotherly loving souls are nourished with embraces. ²²And they grow stronger through common nurturing and their friendship daily and both a general education as well as our training in God's law. ²³So then in this way, the sympathizing of brotherly love having been appointed accordingly, the seven brothers had more sympathy for harmony toward each other. ²⁴For being educated by the same law and being trained in the same virtue and raised together in righteous living, they brought upon themselves more than ever. ²⁵For the common zeal for a noble character strengthened their unity for each other. ²⁶For with piety, he was building for them a great desire for brotherly love. ²⁷But, although like the nature and friendship and magnificent habits had strengthened the bond of brotherhood for them, the ones being left behind held themselves up because of their piety, while looking at their brothers who were being disfigured, being tortured until death.

**14** Beyond that, urging them ever onward to the torture, so as not only to disregard their agony but also to control the emotions of brothers' brotherly love.

²O reason, more royal than a king and more free than a freeman. ³O, the holy and harmonious music coming from the piety of the seven brothers! ⁴Not one out of the seven boys were afraid; not even in the face of death did they hesitate, ⁵but all of them, as though running on the road to immortality, were sped onward to death by means of torture. ⁶For just as hands and feet move harmoniously in the same way by the guidance of the soul, those holy boys, as by an immortal soul of devotion, agreed together to move toward death for the sake of it. ⁷O most holy seven harmonious brothers, for just as there were seven days of creation around the piety, ⁸in the same way, dancing, the boys encircled around the sevenfold fear of torture, destroying it. ⁹Now we, hearing about the oppression of these young men, are shaken up; they—not only seeing, and not even merely hearing the immediate threatening words, but also while suffering—they were steadfast even in this: by the agonies through fire. ¹⁰Regarding that, what could be more painful? For the power of fire, being intense and swift, quickly dissolved their bodies.

¹¹And do not consider it surprising, if reason has full command over those men in their tortures, since indeed the mind of woman also despises agonies even more. ¹²For the mother of the seven youths endured the rack inflicted upon each one of her children. ¹³But pause to think about how complex the affection of maternal love is, dragging everything toward the emotion deep inside her. ¹⁴Since indeed even the irrational animals have sympathy and affection with the ones that were conceived from them, like people have. ¹⁵For also of the birds—indeed, the tame ones that roam over the mountains protect their young chicks on the top of buildings, ¹⁶and the ones on the mountain tops and clefts of ravines and in tree holes and making a den in the highest parts of these are born and fend off the one who might approach. ¹⁷But even if they are not able to prevent this, by flying in circles around them grieving in their affection, calling with their own voices, by which way they are able, they help their children. ¹⁸And why is it necessary to demonstrate sympathy toward children by unreasoning creations, ¹⁹since indeed even bees, around the time of making honeycombs,

*The Mother's Example of Reason*

defend themselves against the ones who would approach and, as if with an iron dart, sting those who come near to their hive and are warded off until death? <sup>20</sup>But sympathy for children did not move the mother of the youth who was of one mind with Abraham.

**15** O reason of the children, tyrant over emotions, and piety, more desirable to the mother than her children! <sup>2</sup>The mother, having set two options before her—piety and the temporary preservation of her seven sons according to the tyrant's promise—<sup>3</sup>she loved piety more, which saves toward eternal life according to God.

<sup>4</sup>O what way should I describe the emotions of parents loving a child, impressing a marvelous likeness of soul and also form in the small type of child, mostly because the mothers are established more sympathetically for the offspring than the fathers! <sup>5</sup>For as much as mothers are both weaker souls and bear many children, so much more do they love those children. <sup>6</sup>But the mother of the seven was one who loved her children more than all mothers; during seven pregnancies, each of which caused her to be implanted with tender affection toward them, <sup>7</sup>and because of constraining many pains with each of them, she had affection for them. <sup>8</sup>Because of her fear toward God, she disregarded the fleeting safety of her children. <sup>9</sup>Not even that, but also because of the noble character of her sons and their ready obedience toward the law, she developed greater tender affection for them. <sup>10</sup>For they were righteous and also sensible and courageous and high spirited and loved their brothers and their mother in such a way so as to obey her even until death by keeping the law. <sup>11</sup>But, nevertheless, although so many things pulled the mother to her feelings regarding maternal love, in none of them were the various tortures strong enough to turn her away from her reason. <sup>12</sup>But, on top of that, with regard to each child individually as well as all of them together, the mother urged them onward to death for the sake of piety.

<sup>13</sup>O sacred nature and parental bond and affection for parents and nurture and unbroken emotions of mothers! <sup>14</sup>Seeing them being tortured one by one and burned up, the mother did not change position because of her piety <sup>15</sup>She saw the flesh of her children around the fire being consumed and the toes of their feet and hands quivering on the ground and the flesh of their heads to the point around the chin being exposed as if it was a mask. <sup>16</sup>O mother, tested now by more bitter sufferings than even the pains of childbirth for them! <sup>17</sup>O woman who gave birth alone to complete devotion! <sup>18</sup>It did not change your mind when the firstborn breathed his last nor the second, looking pitiable in tortures, nor the third, when he stopped breathing. <sup>19</sup>Nor did you weep when you looked boldly at the eyes of each one of them as they looked in their tortures, at the same mistreatment, and saw their noses, which predicted their death. <sup>20</sup>Seeing the cut-off flesh of children piled upon the flesh of other children, and chopped off hands upon hands, and decapitated heads upon heads, and fallen corpses upon corpses, and seeing the place for mass burial of your children because of their tortures, you did not weep. <sup>21</sup>As we have seen, neither the siren's song nor the voice of a swan draws the ones who hear to pleasant listening, O voices of children in their tortures calling to their mother. <sup>22</sup>How great and how much, then, the mother of the sons who were tortured by the

wheel and also by the branding iron was tortured by their torture. ²³But the devout reason, as she took courage in the same emotions, intensified her guts to overlook her maternal love for a time. ²⁴Although seeing the destruction of seven children and the complex variety in racking them, embracing them, the noble mother departed through her trust in God. ²⁵For it was like seeing terrible advisers in the council chamber within her own soul: nature and family and maternal love and the racking of her children, ²⁶the mother prevailed over two votes:ᵃ one that brings death and another deliverance for her children. ²⁷She did not approve of the saving of her seven sons for a little time of safety. ²⁸But this daughter remembered the God-fearing endurance of Abraham.

²⁹O mother of the nation, vindicator of the law, and protector of the faith, and victor of the contest through the heart. ³⁰O more noble than males regarding endurance and more courageous than men regarding steadfastness! ³¹For just as Noah's ark, carrying the world during the worldwide flood, endured the fierce waves, ³²in the same way you, guardian of the law, being overwhelmed from all directions in the flood of emotions and the fierce winds, the tortures of your sons, holding together nobly, you endured the winter of the faith.

**16** So then if a woman, old and a mother of seven children, endured seeing the tortures of her children until death, then undeniably pious reason is the absolute master over the emotions. ²Therefore, I have shown that not only have men ruled over the emotions, but woman also despises the greatest of tortures. ³And in the same way, the lions around Daniel were not as wild, nor the burning furnace of Mishael a furious fire as that nature of her maternal love burned, seeing her seven sons being tortured. ⁴But by reason of piety, the mother quenched so great and so large emotions. ⁵For also consider this: that if this woman was fainthearted, though being a mother, she would have likely mourned over them and probably might have spoken these things in this way, ⁶"O worthless I am and thrice unhappy many times over who, bearing seven children, have become the mother of none! ⁷O seven vain pregnancies and seven useless gestations and barren nurturing and miserable nursing. ⁸In vain I endured many birth pains for you, O children, and difficult care for your education. ⁹O for my children, some unmarried, others married uselessly; neither will I see your children nor will I be blessed by being called grandmother. ¹⁰O the one with many beautiful children, I, a woman, am now a widow and alone with great sorrow. ¹¹And when I die, I will have none of my sons burying me." But the holy and God-fearing mother bewailed no one with this lamentation, ¹²nor did she avert any of them so that they would not die nor, as they were dying, did she grieve. ¹³Rather, as though having an adamant mind and giving birth again for the entire number of her sons into immortality, she urged them forward, imploring them onward to death for the sake of piety.

¹⁴O mother, soldier of God for piety, an elder and a woman, by endurance you conquered even a tyrant, and by deed and word you were found more mighty than even a man. ¹⁵For even when you were arrested together

*The Proof of the Excellence of Reason*

*Praise for the Mother*

ᵃ Lit. "pebbles"

with your children, you stood, seeing Eleazar being tortured, and said to your children in the Hebrew language, ¹⁶"O children, noble is the contest in which, being called for your testimony for the nation, you must contend readily on behalf of the law of the fatherland. ¹⁷For it would also be shameful if the old man were to endure this agony because of his faith, but you, the younger, were to be astounded by the tortures. ¹⁸Remember that because of God you had a share in the world and enjoyed life, ¹⁹and on this account you ought to endure all suffering for God. ²⁰Because of which also our father Abraham was zealous to sacrifice his son Isaac, the ancestor of the nation. And when he saw his father's hand bearing a sword coming down upon him, he did not cower in fear. ²¹And Daniel the righteous was thrown to lions, and Hananiah and Azariah and Mishael were hurled into a furnace of fire, and they endured because of God. ²²You, therefore, since you have the same faith in God, you were not distressed. ²³For it is irrational for those who know piety to not stand against sufferings."

²⁴By these words the mother of seven children, encouraging each one of her sons, persuaded them to die rather than disobey the command of God. ²⁵And still also knowing this, that those who die for God are alive to God, just as Abraham and Isaac and Jacob and all the patriarchs did.

*The Death of the Mother* **17** And some of the guards also say as when she was about to be seized and she was put to death, in order that no one would touch her body, she threw herself down into the flames.

²O mother with seven children, you destroyed the force of the tyrant and canceled his evil plans and exhibited the nobility of faith! ³For just as you, nobly setting an unwavering roof on the pillar of children, you endured the shock caused by the tortures. ⁴Take courage, therefore, O mother with a pious soul, nobly holding the hope of endurance toward God. ⁵The moon in the heaven with the stars are not set to be as dignified in such a way as you, a guiding light for your star-like seven children toward piety, set in honor before God and firmly established in heaven with them. ⁶For your bearing of children was from the child of Abraham.

*The Effect of the Deaths of the Brothers and Their Mother* ⁷If it was being permitted for us to paint as upon some surface the godliness of your account, would not the observers shudder at the mother of seven children, because of piety, enduring various tortures until death? ⁸For it would also be honorable to inscribe even over their tomb these words also for the ones from our nation as a reminder, saying, ⁹"Here is buried an elderly priest and an old woman and seven sons because of the violence of a tyrant who wanted to destroy the Hebrew nation. ¹⁰They also avenged their nation, looking away toward God and enduring the tortures until death." ¹¹Truly what was brought about by them was a divine contest. ¹²For then virtue gave awards after testing them by endurance. The prize was in immortality in endless life. ¹³So Eleazar fought first. Then the mother of the seven sons struggled bravely, and the brothers contended for the prize. ¹⁴The tyrant struggled against them, and the world and the life of humans were observers. ¹⁵Godliness was the victor, crowning its own athletes. ¹⁶Who did not marvel at the athletes of true legislation? Who was not amazed?

¹⁷Indeed, surely the tyrant himself and their whole council marveled at their endurance, ¹⁸because of which they also now stand around the

divine throne and live in eternal blessing. ¹⁹For even Moses says, "And all the ones who are consecrated are under your hand." ²⁰And so these, being consecrated by God, therefore are honored not only with this honor, but also by this: Because of them, enemies did not rule over our nation, ²¹and the tyrant was punished, and the country was cleansed, ²²as if they had become a recompense for the sin of the nation. And through the blood of those pious ones and the atoning sacrifice of their death, Divine Providence rescued Israel, who had been afflicted before. ²³For when the tyrant looked at the courage of their virtue and their endurance during the tortures, Antiochus proclaimed to his soldiers as an example to the endurance of those who died. ²⁴And that made them noble and courageous in battle and siege, and by pillaging, he conquered all his enemies.

**18** O descendants of the seed of Abraham, Israelite children, obey this law and practice piety in every way, ²knowing that pious reason is master over the emotions—and not only the internal emotions, but also external sufferings. ³For which, because of piety in bringing forward their bodies to those tortures, not only did they cause astonishment in the people but also were recognized as worthy of divine portion. ⁴And through them the nation found peace. And renewing the observance of the law in the country, they made their enemies surrender. ⁵And the tyrant Antiochus was both punished on earth and chastised in death. For in no way whatsoever was he strong enough to compel the inhabitants of Jerusalem to adopt foreign customs and to force them to change their ancestral nations. ⁶Then indeed, departing from Jerusalem, he encamped against Persia.

The righteous mother of the seven sons also said these things to her children: ⁷"I was a pure virgin and did not go beyond my father's house. But I guarded the rib out of which woman was built. ⁸No seducer of the desert or destroyer in the field destroyed me, nor did the destroyer, the deceitful serpent, maltreat my innocent virginity. At the time of my maturity I remained with my husband. ⁹But when these sons became adults, the father passed away. That man was happy indeed, for seeking after a life blessed with children, he did not grieve a time of childlessness. ¹⁰He used to teach you, still being with us, the law and the prophets. ¹¹He read to us the murder of Abel by Cain and the sacrifice of Isaac as well as the story of Joseph in prison. ¹²He told us about the zeal of Phinehas. Then he taught you about Hananiah and Azariah and Mishael in the fire. ¹³He also extolled Daniel, whom he also considered fortunate, in the pit of lions. ¹⁴He reminded you of the writing of Isaiah, the text that says, 'Even if you go through flames of fire, it will not burn you.' ¹⁵He sang the songs of the psalmist David to us who says, 'Numerous are the afflictions of the righteous.' ¹⁶He spoke Solomon's proverbs to us, who says, 'The tree of life is for all those who do his will.' ¹⁷He confirmed the question of Ezekiel, who said, 'Will these dry bones live?' ¹⁸For he did not forget the song that Moses taught, the one teaching, 'I kill, and I make to live. ¹⁹This is your life and the blessedness of your days.'"

*The Mother Tells of Her Children's Upbringing*

²⁰O bitter was the day, and yet not bitter, when the bitter tyrant of the Greeks, inflaming the fire in his cruel cauldron and in his boiling rage, leading the seven children of the daughter of Abraham onto the catapult

and back again for his tortures. ²¹He mutilated the pupils of their eyes and cut out their tongues and, by various tortures, he killed them; ²²for which the divine justice pursued and will continue to pursue the accursed. ²³But the children of Abraham with their victorious mother are gathered together into the ancestral country, pure and immortal souls receiving from God, ²⁴to whom be glory for eternities of eternities. Amen.

*Introduction to*

# PSALMS OF SOLOMON

T HE COLLECTION OF PRAYERS known as Psalms of Solomon was not
embraced as "canonical" by any major Christian body. It appears, however, to have been included at the end of Codex Alexandrinus as a kind of
appendix along with 1 and 2 Clement (it is listed in the table of contents,
but the back pages of the codex have been lost), and the work survives in a
number of Greek manuscripts from the eleventh century and later. Several
of these psalms preserve responses to particular events, notably Pompey's
intervention in the Judean civil strife of 63 BC, his siege of Jerusalem, and
bold entrance into the sanctuary itself (2:1–3; 8:12–24; 17:13–15). One looks
back upon the assassination of Pompey in 48 BC, celebrating it as God's
vengeance upon the gentile encroacher (2:27–33). A number of the psalms
must therefore date from the early period of Roman oversight in Judea,
though it is not clear if the collection as a whole was composed within
such a short period. Although preserved primarily in Greek and Syriac,
they were almost certainly originally written in Hebrew. Besides their witness to sentiments in Jerusalem against the last Hasmonean rulers and
the Roman "peacekeepers," the psalms are important for their witness to
the piety, ethical standards, and messianic hopes of mid-first century BC
Judea. They indirectly bear witness to the impact of the canonical Psalms
upon the style and diction of fresh Jewish liturgical compositions.

—D. A. deSilva

# PSALMS OF SOLOMON

*Oppressors* **1** I cried to the Lord when I was afflicted completely,
    to God when sinners made an attempt against me.
2 Suddenly a cry of war was heard before me.
    He will hear me, because I was full of righteousness.
3 I considered in my heart that I was full of righteousness
    when I thrived and became great with children.
4 Their wealth was spread through to all the earth,
    and their glory unto the end of the earth.
5 They were lifted high unto the stars;
    they said, "They will never fall."
6 And they were arrogant with their goods,
    and they did not bring.
7 Their sins were in hidden places,
    and even I did not know them.
8 Their lawless acts were beyond the nations before them;
    they profaned the holy things of the Lord with profanation.

*Concerning* **2** A PSALM OF SOLOMON CONCERNING JERUSALEM.
*Jerusalem* 1 When the sinner acted arrogantly, with the battering ram
    he struck down strong city walls,
    and you did not restrain him.
2 Foreign nations went up against your altar.
    They trampled it down with their shoes in arrogance.
3 Because the sons of Jerusalem defiled the holy place of the Lord,
    they profaned the gifts of God with lawless acts.
4 Because of these things he said, "Cast them far away from me."
    It has not prospered them, the beauty of his glory.
5 It is disdained before God.
    It was dishonored until the end.
6 Sons and daughters are in a wicked captivity.
    Their neck is in a seal, notable among the nations.
7 He dealt with them according to their sins,
    because he forsook them into the hands of those
        overpowering them.
8 For he turned his face away from mercy of them,
    young and old and their children at one time,
9 because they did evil things at one time, by not listening.
10 And the heavens were weighted down, and the earth was
    disgusted with them,
11 because no person upon it had done what they did.
12 And the earth will know all your righteous judgments, God.
13 They set the sons of Jerusalem for mockery because of the
    prostitutes in her.
    Everyone going entered opposite the sun.

They were ridiculing their lawless acts,
14 just as they used to do before the sun they made an example of
their injustices.
And the daughters of Jerusalem were profane according to your
judgment,
15 because they defiled themselves with the mess of intercourse.
I toil over these things in my belly and my inward parts.
16 I will justify you, God, in uprightness of heart,
because your righteousness is in your judgments, God.
17 For you repaid the sinners according to their works
and according to their very wicked sins.
18 You uncovered their sins that you might show your judgment.
19 You wiped out the memory of them from the earth.
God is a righteous judge and will not be impressed by a face.
20 For nations reviled Jerusalem by trampling;
he pulled her beauty down from the throne of glory.
21 She girded herself with sackcloth instead of a decent garment,
a rope around her head instead of a crown.
22 She removed the headband of glory that God had placed
around her;
23 her beauty was cast away upon the earth in dishonor.
24 And I saw and I beseeched the face of the Lord, and I said,
"Let it be enough, Lord, that your hands weigh Israel down
by the nations' invasion,
25 because they ridiculed and they did not refrain in wrath and
anger with rage;
26 and they will be finished, unless you, Lord, rebuke them in
your wrath.
27 Because they did not act in jealousy but in the desire of the soul
28 to pour out their wrath against us in plunder.
And do not delay, God, to repay them upon their heads,
29 to speak the arrogance of the dragon in dishonor."
30 And I did not delay until God showed to me his insolence,
a man pierced on the mountains of Egypt,
being scorned more than the smallest upon the earth and
the sea,
31 his body being carried over the waves in great insolence;
and there was no one to bury it
32 because he rejected him in dishonor.
He did not consider that he was a human,
and he did not consider what comes later.
33 He said, "I will be lord of earth and sea!"
And he did not acknowledge that God is great,
mighty in his great strength.
34 He is King over the heavens
and the one who judges kings and rulers,
35 who raises me[a] into glory

---

[a] An emphatic form of the pronoun

and puts the arrogant to sleep for eternal destruction
in dishonor,
because they did not know him.

36 And now see, great ones of the earth, the judgment of the Lord,
because the King is great and righteous, judging the earth
under the heavens.

37 Bless God, you who fear the Lord in understanding,
because the mercy of the Lord is on those who fear him, with
judgment,

38 to separate between the righteous and the sinner,
to repay sinners for eternity according to their works,

39 and to show mercy to the righteous one because of lowliness
by the sinner,
and to repay the sinner because of the things he did to
the righteous one.

40 Because the Lord is good to those who call upon him in patience,
to act according to his mercy to his holy ones,
to be present always before him in strength.

41 Blessed be the Lord for eternity before his servants.

*The Righteous*  **3** A PSALM OF SOLOMON CONCERNING THE RIGHTEOUS ONES.
1 Why do you sleep, soul, and not bless the Lord?
2 Sing with hymn and praise to the praiseworthy God.
Sing and watch for his watching,
because a psalm to God from a good heart is good.
3 The righteous will remember the Lord always,
in thanksgiving, and he will justify the judgments of the Lord.
4 The righteous who is disciplined by the Lord will not show
contempt.
His goodwill is always before the Lord.
5 The righteous stumbled and vindicated the Lord.
He fell and watches what God will do for him.
6 He looks steadily whence salvation will come for him.
7 The truthfulness of the righteous is before God their savior.
Sin upon sin does not dwell in the house of the righteous one.
8 The righteous one examines his house continually
to remove injustice done by his transgression.
9 He made propitiation concerning ignorance with fasting and
lowliness of his soul,
10 and the Lord cleanses every holy man and his house.
11 The sinner stumbled and curses his life,
the day of his birth and the labor pangs of his mother.
12 He added sins upon sins to his life.
13 He fell, because his downfall was wicked, and he will not arise.
The destruction of the sinner is for eternity,
14 and he will never be remembered whenever he examines
the righteous.

15 This is the portion of the sinners for eternity.
16 But those who fear the Lord will arise into eternal life,
  and their life will never come to an end in the light of the Lord.

# 4

A DISCOURSE OF SOLOMON TO THE PEOPLE PLEASERS.

*People-*
*Pleasers*

1 Why do you, profane one, sit in the holy assembly,
  and your heart has moved far from the Lord,
  provoking the God of Israel with transgressions?
2 Excessive in words, more excessive in a sign than anyone,
  is the one who is severe in words in condemning sinners
    in judgment.
3 And his hand is among the first people against him as if in zeal,
  and he is guilty with a variety of sinners, in acts of
    self-indulgence.
4 His eyes are on every woman without distinction;
  his tongue is false in a contract with an oath.
5 He sins at night and in hidden places as if not seen;
  he speaks with his eyes to every woman in an arrangement
    of evil.
6 He is quick in his entrance into every house with cheerfulness
    as if innocent.
7 Remove, God, those who live in hypocrisy with holy ones,
  his life by the destruction of his flesh and poverty.
8 May God reveal the works of people-pleasing persons,
  his works in derision and scorn.
9 And may the holy ones justify the judgment of their God,
  when he removes sinners from the face of the righteous one,
10 the people pleaser who speaks only with deceit.
11 And their eyes are upon the house of a man in stability like
    a serpent,
  to dissolve the wisdom of one another by lawless words.
12 His words are frauds
  for acting on desires for unrighteous things.
13 He did not stop until he prevailed to scatter as in orphanhood.
  And he desolated a house because of lawless desire.
14 He defrauded with words, because there is no one who sees and
    judges.
15 He was filled with lawlessness in this,
  and his eyes were upon another house to destroy it with
    words of clamor.
  His soul is not satisfied, like Hades, at all these things.
16 Lord, may his portion be in dishonor before you,
  his departure in groanings, and his entrance in a curse.
17 May his life be with pains and poverty and perplexity, Lord.
  May his sleep be in sorrows and his awakening with
    perplexities.
18 May sleep be taken away from his temples at night.
  May it fall away from every work of his hands.

<sup>19</sup> And may his house be lacking everything that will satisfy his life.
<sup>20</sup>    May his old age be in the persistence of childlessness until
            his removal.
<sup>21</sup> May the flesh of people-pleasing persons be scattered by beasts,
            and the bones of the lawless before the sun in dishonor.
<sup>22</sup> May ravens strike out the eyes of those who act hypocritically,
<sup>23</sup>    because he desolated many houses of people in dishonor
            and scattered their desire.
<sup>24</sup> And they did not remember God,
            and they did not fear God at all these things.
<sup>25</sup> And they provoked God, and they irritated him;
            may he remove them from the land,
            because they acted hypocritically with deception toward
                the souls of the innocent.
<sup>26</sup> Blessed are those who fear the Lord in their innocence.
<sup>27</sup>    And the Lord will rescue them from deceitful people and sinners
            and rescue us from every lawless obstacle.
<sup>28</sup> May God remove those who do every injustice with arrogance,
            because the Lord our God is a great judge and mighty
                in righteousness.

<sup>29</sup> May your mercy, Lord, be upon all those who love you!

*A Psalm of*    **5** A PSALM OF SOLOMON.
*Solomon*    <sup>1</sup>    Lord God, I will praise your name with rejoicing
            in the middle of those who understand your righteous
                judgments.
<sup>2</sup>    For useful and merciful is the refuge of the poor.
<sup>3</sup>        When I cry out to you, do not pass me over in silence.
<sup>4</sup>    For one will not take spoils from a powerful man,
<sup>5</sup>        and who will take from all which you made, unless you yourself
            give it?
<sup>6</sup>    For a person and his portion are from you on a scale;
            he will not add to it for it to abound beyond your judgment, God.
<sup>7</sup>    When we are afflicted, we will call for help,
            and you will not turn our entreaty away,
            because you are our God.
<sup>8</sup>    Do not weigh your hand down upon us,
            lest we sin because of distress.
<sup>9</sup>    And even if you do not restore us, we will not be far off,
            but we will come to you.
<sup>10</sup>    For if I will be hungry, I will cry out to you, God,
            and you will give to me.
<sup>11</sup>    You yourself feed the birds and the fish;
            when you give rain to the deserts for the rising of shoots,
            you prepared food in the desert for every living thing,
<sup>12</sup>        and if they hunger for you, they will lift up their face.
<sup>13</sup>    You feed kings and rulers and peoples, God,
            and who is the hope of the poor and the needy if not you, Lord?

14 And you will hear, because who is good and fair but you,
    to cheer the soul of the low when your hand opens in mercy?
15 The goodness of a human is in thrift, also tomorrow;
    and if he repeats it without murmuring, you should marvel
        at even this.
16 But your gift is abundant with goodness, and rich,
    and where hope is upon you, it will not be lacking a gift.
17 Your mercy is over all the earth, Lord, in goodness.
18 Blessed is he whom God remembers in due proportion
    to sufficiency;
19 if the person abounds too much, he sins.
20 Moderation in righteousness is sufficient,
    and in this is the blessing of the Lord for satisfaction
        in righteousness.
21 Those who fear the Lord were cheerful with good things,
    and your goodness was upon Israel your kingdom.
22 Blessed be the glory of the Lord,
    because he is our King.

# 6 IN HOPE, OF SOLOMON. *In Hope*

1 Blessed is the man whose heart is ready
    to call upon the name of the Lord;
2 when he remembers the name of the Lord, he will be saved.
3 His ways are directed by the Lord,
    and the works of his hands are guarded by the Lord his God.
4 He will not be troubled by a vision of his wicked dreams;
5 his soul will not be terrified of the crossing of rivers and
    the surging waves of the seas.
6 He stood up from his sleep
    and blessed the name of the Lord.
7 He praised the name of God in the stability of his heart.
    And he beseeched the face of the Lord concerning everything of
        his house.
8 And the Lord heard the prayer of everyone in the fear of God,
    and the Lord will fulfill every request of the soul that hopes
        in him.
9 Blessed be the Lord who enacts mercy to those who love him
    in truth.

# 7 OF SOLOMON ON CONVERSION. *Conversion*

1 Do not move away from us, God,
    lest those who hated us gratuitously attack us.
2 For you rejected them, God.
    Do not let their foot trample the inheritance of your sanctuary.
3 As for you, discipline us by your will!
    And do not give us to the nations.
4 For if you send death, you will command it concerning us.
    For you are merciful and will not be angry to bring us to an end.

⁵ When your name dwells in the middle of us, we will be shown
mercy,
⁶ and no nation will be strong against us;
for you are our protector.
⁷ And we will call upon you, and you will hear us.
⁸ For you will have mercy on the race of Israel for eternity, and
you will not reject it.
And we are under your yoke for eternity,
and the whip of your discipline.
⁹ You will direct us in the time of your help,
to show mercy to the house of Jacob for the day you promised
them.

*Victory*  **8** OF SOLOMON FOR VICTORY.
¹ My ear heard affliction and the sound of war,
the sound of the trumpet sounding slaughter and ruin,
² the sound of a great people like a very great wind,
like a storm of a great fire carried through the desert.
³ And I said in my heart,
"Where then will God judge him?"
⁴ I heard a sound in Jerusalem, the city of the sanctuary.
⁵ My loins were crushed at the report. My knees were paralyzed.
⁶ My heart was afraid. My bones were shaken like linen.
⁷ I said, "They will direct their ways in righteousness."
I considered the judgments of God from the creation of
the heavens and earth.
I vindicated God in his judgments that are from eternity.
⁸ God exposed their sins before the sun.
All the earth knew the righteous judgments of God.
⁹ Their iniquities are in secret underground places, in provocation;
¹⁰ a son with his mother and a father with his daughter mingle
together.
¹¹ Each one committed adultery with the wife of his neighbor.
They arranged pacts with themselves with an oath concerning
these things.
¹² They plundered the sanctuary of God
as if there were no redeeming heir.
¹³ They trampled the altar of the Lord from every uncleanness,
and they defiled the sacrifices with menstrual blood*ᵃ* like
profane meat.
¹⁴ They left no sin undone that they did not do worse than the
nations.
¹⁵ Therefore God mixed them a spirit of error.
He gave them a drinking cup of unmixed wine to drink, for
drunkenness.
¹⁶ He led the one from the end of the earth, the one who strikes
strongly.

---

ᵃ Lit. "menstruation of blood"

<sup>17</sup> He decided on war against Jerusalem and her land.
<sup>18</sup> The rulers of the earth met him with joy.
 They said to him, "Your way is welcome! Come, enter with peace!"
<sup>19</sup> They leveled rough ways from his entrance.
 They opened the gates in Jerusalem; they crowned her walls.
<sup>20</sup> He entered with peace, like a father into the house of his sons.
 He established his feet with great security.
<sup>21</sup> He captured her fortresses and the wall of Jerusalem,
<sup>22</sup>  because God led him with security during their error.
<sup>23</sup> He destroyed their rulers and every man wise in counsel.
 He poured out the blood of the inhabitants of Jerusalem like
  water of uncleanness.
<sup>24</sup> He led away their sons and daughters
 that they had borne in profanation.
<sup>25</sup> They acted according to their impurities, just as their fathers did.
<sup>26</sup>  He defiled Jerusalem and the things sanctified in the name of
  God.
<sup>27</sup> God was justified in his judgments among the nations of the
  earth,
<sup>28</sup>  and the holy ones of God are like lambs, in innocence in the
  midst of them.
<sup>29</sup>  The Lord who judges all the earth in his righteousness is worthy
  of praise.
<sup>30</sup> Look now, God; you have shown us your judgment in your
  righteousness.
<sup>31</sup>  Our eyes have seen your judgments, God.
 We have vindicated your honored name into eternities,
<sup>32</sup>  because you are the God of righteousness who judges Israel
  with discipline.
<sup>33</sup> Convert, God, your mercy upon us and have pity upon us!
<sup>34</sup>  Gather the diaspora of Israel with mercy and goodness.
<sup>35</sup> Because your faithfulness is with us, and we stiffened our neck,
  and you are the one who disciplines us.
<sup>36</sup> Do not overlook us, our God,
 lest nations devour us, as if there were no one who redeems.
<sup>37</sup> And you are our God from the beginning,
 and our hope is on you, Lord.
<sup>38</sup> And we are not far from you,
 because your judgments are good to us.
<sup>39</sup> We and our children have your goodwill for eternity;
 Lord our savior, we will not be afflicted anymore for eternal
  time.
<sup>40</sup> The Lord is praiseworthy in his judgments in the mouth of the
  holy ones,
 and blessed be Israel by the Lord for eternity.

# 9

OF SOLOMON FOR REBUKE.     *For a Rebuke*
<sup>1</sup> When Israel was led away in exile into a foreign land,
 when they fell away from the Lord who redeemed them,

2 they were expelled from the inheritance that the Lord had given
them.
The diaspora of Israel was in every nation according to
the word of God,
3 so that you would be vindicated, God, in your righteousness
by reason of our lawlessness acts,
4 because you are a righteous judge over all the peoples
of the earth.
5 For no one who does unrighteous things will be hidden from your
knowledge,
6 and the righteous acts of your holy ones are before you, Lord.
And where will a person be hidden from your knowledge, God?
7 Our works are in the choosing and authority of our soul,
to do righteousness and unrighteousness by the works
of our hands.
8 And in your righteousness you examine the sons of humans.
9 The one who performs righteousness stores up life for
himself before the Lord.
And the one who performs injustice is himself blameworthy
of the soul in destruction.
10 For the judgments of the Lord are against man and house
in righteousness.
11 To whom will you show goodness, God, if not to those who call
upon the Lord?
12 You will cleanse the soul with sins in thanksgiving, in
confession,
13 because we and our faces have disgrace concerning everything.
14 And for whom will he forgive sins if not for those who
have sinned?
15 You will bless the righteous ones, and you will not set straight
concerning those who sinned,
and your goodness concerning those who sin in repentance.
16 And now you are God, and we are your people whom you loved.
See and have pity, God of Israel, because we are yours;
and do not send your mercy from us,
lest they attack us.
17 For you selected the seed of Abraham rather than all the nations,
18 and you placed your name upon us, Lord.
And you will not stop for eternity.
19 You made a covenant with our fathers concerning us,
and we will hope on you with the conversion of our soul.
20 The mercy of the Lord that is upon the house of Israel
is for eternity and further.

*Among the*
*Hymns*

# 10 AMONG THE HYMNS OF SOLOMON.

1 Blessed is the man whom the Lord remembered in reproof
and encompassed from an evil way with a whip,
to be cleansed from sin, to not multiply it.
2 The one who prepares his back for scourges also will be cleansed.

    For the Lord is good to those who wait for discipline.

3   For he will set upright the ways of the righteous,
    and he will not be conspicuous in discipline.

4   And the mercy of the Lord is upon those who love him in truth.
    And the Lord will remember his servants in mercy.

5   For the testimony is in the law of the eternal covenant.
    The testimony of the Lord is on the ways of people in visitation.

6   Our Lord is righteous and holy in his judgments for eternity,
    and Israel will praise the name of the Lord in cheerfulness.

7   And the holy ones will give thanks in the gatherings of the people,
    and God will show mercy to the poor in the cheerfulness
      of Israel.

8   For God is good and merciful for eternity,
    and the gathering of Israel will glorify the name of the Lord.

9 The salvation of the Lord is upon the house of Israel for eternal self-control

# 11

OF SOLOMON FOR EXPECTATION.           *Expectation*

1 Sound the trumpet in Zion with the signal trumpet of the
    holy ones.

2   Proclaim in Jerusalem the voice of the one who brings good news,
    because God had mercy on Israel in his examination of them.

3   Stand, Jerusalem, upon the height, and see your children
    gathered at once from the east and the west by the Lord.

4   They are coming from the north to the cheer of their God.
    God gathered them from islands afar.

5   He brought high mountains low into level ground for them.

6   The hills fled at their entrance.
The woods shaded them at their passage.

7   God raised every tree of sweet smell for them,
    that Israel might pass along at the examination of the glory
      of their God.

8   Put on, O Jerusalem, the garments of your glory.
    Prepare the robe of your sanctuary,
because God has spoken good things for Israel,
    forever and for eternity.

9   May the Lord do what he spoke of regarding Israel and Jerusalem!
    May the Lord raise up Israel in the name of his glory!
The mercy of the Lord be upon Israel
    for eternity and further.

# 12

BY SOLOMON IN THE TONGUE OF THE LAWLESS.    *The Tongue*

1 Lord, deliver my soul from a lawbreaking and wicked man,  *of the Lawless*
    from a tongue that breaks the law and whispers and speaks
      false and deceitful things.

2   The words of the tongue of an evil man are in diversity
      of twisting.
Just like a fire lighting up its beauty among a people

3   is its exile, to fill houses with a lying tongue,

for lawbreakers to cut down trees of burning cheer,
4      to demolish lawbreaking houses in battle with whispering lips.
   May God remove the lips of lawbreakers from the innocent
         inperplexity,
      and may the bones of the whisperers be scattered by those who
         fear the Lord;
5   may a slanderous tongue be destroyed by the holy ones with
      the fire of flame.
6   May the Lord guard the quiet soul that hates the unrighteous,
      and may the Lord guide the man who makes peace in the house.
7   The Lord's salvation be on Israel his servant for eternity,
8      and may sinners be destroyed from the face of the Lord at once,
      and may the holy ones of the Lord inherit the promises.

*Encouragement
of the
Righteous* **13** A PSALM OF SOLOMON; ENCOURAGEMENT OF THE RIGHTEOUS ONES.
1   The right hand of the Lord sheltered me.
      The right hand of the Lord spared us.
2   The arm of the Lord saved us from the sword that passes through,
      from hunger and the death of sinners.
3   Wicked beasts ran at them.
      They plucked their flesh with their teeth,
      and they were breaking their bones with their molars.
   And the Lord rescued us from all these things.
4   The ungodly was troubled on account of his transgressions,
      lest he be taken along with the sinners;
5   because the overthrow of the sinner is fearsome,
      and not one of all these things will touch the righteous one.
6   Because the discipline of the righteous in ignorance
      and the overthrow of the sinner are not alike.
7   The righteous is disciplined in his cloak,
      lest the sinner rejoice at the righteous.
8   Because he will admonish the righteous like a son of affection,
      and his discipline is like that of a firstborn.
9   For the Lord will spare his holy ones,
      and he will wipe out their transgressions by discipline.
   For the life of the righteous is for eternity.
10      But sinners will be removed into destruction,
      and their memory will no longer be found.
11   But the mercy of the Lord be upon the holy ones,
      and his mercy upon those who fear him.

*Hymn* **14** A HYMN OF SOLOMON.
1   The Lord is faithful to those who love him in truth,
      to those who wait for his discipline,
   to those who walk by the righteousness of his commands,
      in the law which he commanded us for our life.
2   The holy ones of the Lord will live in it for eternity.
      His holy ones are the orchard of the Lord, the trees of life.
3   Their planting is rooted for eternity.

They will not be plucked up all the days of the heavens,
because the portion and inheritance of God is Israel.
4 And not so the sinners and lawbreakers,
who loved a day in the sharing of their sin.
Their desire was for smallness of corruption.
5 And they did not remember God.
Because the ways of humans are always known before him,
and he knows the inner chambers of the heart before
they happen.
6 Therefore their inheritance is Hades and darkness and destruction,
and they will not be found in the day of mercy of the righteous.
But the holy ones of the Lord will inherit life in cheerfulness.

# 15 A PSALM OF SOLOMON WITH A SONG.                    *With a Song*
1 When I was afflicted I called on the name of the Lord;
I hoped for the help of the God of Jacob, and I was saved,
2 because you, God, are the hope and refuge of the poor.
3 For who is strong, God, unless they give thanks to you in truth?
4 And why is a person strong unless they give thanks to
your name?
5 A new psalm with a song in the cheer of the heart,
the fruit of lips in a prepared instrument of the tongue,
the first fruits of lips from a holy and righteous heart—
6 the one who does these things will not be shaken by evil
for eternity.
The flame of fire and the wrath of the unrighteous will not
touch him
7 whenever it comes out upon sinners from the face of the Lord,
to destroy all the substance of sinners.
8 For the sign of God is upon the righteous ones for salvation.
Famine and sword and death are far from the righteous.
9 For they will flee from the holy ones like those pursued in battle,
and they will pursue and capture sinners.
And those who do lawlessness will not escape the judgment of
the Lord;
they will be captured as if by experienced warriors,
10 for the sign of destruction is upon their forehead.
11 And the inheritance of the sinners is destruction and darkness,
and their lawless acts will pursue them to Hades below.
12 Their inheritance will not be found for their children.
13 For the sins will desolate the houses of sinners;
and sinners will perish in the day of the judgment of the Lord
for eternity,
14 whenever God examines the earth in his judgment.
15 But those who fear the Lord will be shown mercy in it,
and they will live in the mercy of their God;
and sinners will perish for the eternal time.

## 16 A HYMN BY SOLOMON FOR HELP TO THE HOLY ONES.

1 When my soul slumbered from the Lord,
  I slipped a little in the descent of sleep.

2 Far from God my soul was poured out a little to death,
  near the gates of Hades with a sinner;

3 when my soul was carried away from the Lord, the God of Israel,
  unless the Lord helped me with his mercy for eternity.

4 He pricked me like a horse prod at his watch;
  my savior and helper saved me every time.

5 I will give thanks to you, God, because you helped me
    for salvation
  and did not reckon me for destruction with the sinners.

6 Do not remove your mercy from me, God,
  or the memory of you from my heart until death.

7 Restrain me, God, from wicked sin
  and from every wicked woman who trips up the foolish.

8 And do not let the beauty of a lawbreaking woman deceive me,
  or that of anyone liable to useless sin.

9 Guide the works of my hands in your place,
  and protect my steps in the memory of you.

10 Clothe my tongue and my lips in words of truth;
  make wrath and speechless anger be far from me.

11 Distance from me murmuring and timidity in oppression,
  if I sin when you discipline for conversion.

12 But strengthen my soul in good pleasure with cheerfulness,
  when you strengthen my soul; what is given to me will be
    enough.

13 For unless you strengthen, who will endure discipline in poverty?

14 When a soul is reproved by the hand of his corruption,
  your testing is in his flesh and in the oppression of poverty.

15 When the righteous one remained in these things, he will be
    shown mercy by the Lord.

## 17 A PSALM OF SOLOMON WITH A SONG TO THE KING.

1 O Lord, you are our King for eternity and further,
  because in you, our[a] God, our soul will boast.

2 And what is the time of a person's life upon the earth?
  According to his time is also his hope in it.

3 But we will hope in God our savior,
  because the strength of our God is for eternity with mercy,

4 and the kingdom of our God is for eternity over the nations.

5 You, Lord, selected David as king over Israel,
  and you swore to him concerning his seed for eternity,
  that his royal place would not come to an end before you.

6 And sinners rose up against us because of our sins;
  they laid hold of us and expelled us.

[a] Refers back to "time"

Those to whom you did not promise removed us with force,

⁷    and they did not glorify your honored name;

with pomp they set a royal place because of their loftiness;

⁸    they desolated the throne of David in arrogance of a cost.

And you, God, will cast them down and remove their seed from
        the earth,

⁹    when a person foreign to our race rises up against them.

¹⁰ You will repay them according to their sins, God,

so that it will be found against them according to their works.

¹¹ God will show them no mercy;

he searched their seed and let not one of them go;

¹²    the Lord is faithful in all his judgments that he makes upon the
        earth.

¹³ The lawless one desolated our land from its inhabitants.

They destroyed a young man and old woman and their
        children together.

¹⁴ He dismissed them to the west in the wrath of his beauty,

and the rulers of the land to a mockery; and he did not relent.

¹⁵ With estrangement the enemy acted, with arrogance;

and his heart was foreign from our God.

¹⁶ And all the things he made in Jerusalem,

just as the nations also in the cities make their gods.

¹⁷ And the sons of the covenant controlled them in the middle of
        the mixed nations.

There was no one who acts with mercy and truth in the middle
        of them in Jerusalem.

¹⁸ Those who love the gatherings of the holy ones fled from them.

They were scattered from their bed like sparrows.

¹⁹ They were misled in deserts, for their souls to be saved
        from evil,

and a soul saved from them is a prized thing in the eyes of
        the sojourn.

²⁰ Those who love the gatherings of the holy ones fled from them.

Their scattering by the lawless was into all the earth,

because the heavens withheld the dropping of rain upon the
        earth.

²¹    The eternal springs were stopped out of the abysses from
        high mountains,

because there was no one among them who was doing
        righteousness and justice.

From their rulers and the least of the people, they were in every
        sin;

²²  the king was in lawbreaking, and the judge in disobedience,

and the people in sin.

²³ See, O Lord, and raise up their king for them,

a son of David,

for the proper time that you see, God,

to rule over Israel your servant.

<sup>24</sup> And undergird him with strength to shatter unrighteous rulers.

<sup>25-26</sup> Cleanse Jerusalem from the nations that trample it in destruction,
   to expel sinners from the inheritance in wisdom,
      in righteousness,
   to rub out the arrogance of the sinner like a potter's vessel,
   to crush all their support with an iron rod;

<sup>27</sup> to destroy lawless nations by the word of his mouth,
   for gentiles to flee from his face at his threat,
   and to reprove sinners by the word of their heart.

<sup>28</sup> And he will gather a holy people whom he will lead
      in righteousness,
   and he will judge tribes of the people sanctified by the Lord
   its God.

<sup>29</sup> And he will no longer permit injustice to dwell among them,
   and no person who sees wickedness will dwell with them.

<sup>30</sup> For he will know them, because all of them are sons of God,
   and he will divide them among their tribes upon the earth.

<sup>31</sup> And no longer will an expatriate or foreigner dwell among them;
   he will judge peoples and nations by the wisdom of
      his righteousness.

*Musical interlude*

<sup>32</sup> And he will have peoples of nations to serve him under his yoke,
   and he will glorify the Lord notably over all the earth.

<sup>33</sup> And he will cleanse Jerusalem with sanctification, as also from
      the beginning,

<sup>34</sup> for nations to come from the edge of the earth to see
      his glory,
   bringing as gifts its utterly weakened sons,

<sup>35</sup> and to see the glory of the Lord that God glorified.
   And he is a righteous king over them, taught by God,

<sup>36</sup> and there is no injustice in his days in the middle of them;
   because they all are holy, and their king is the anointed Lord.

<sup>37</sup> For he will not hope in horse and rider and bow,
   or multiply gold nor silver to himself for battle,
   and he will not gather hopes for many for the day of war.

<sup>38</sup> The Lord himself is his King, the hope of the one who is mighty
      by the hope of God,
   and he will show mercy to all the nations before him in fear.

<sup>39</sup> For he will bring down the earth with the word of his mouth
      for eternity.

<sup>40</sup> He will bless the people of the Lord by wisdom with cheer.

<sup>41</sup> And he will be clean from sin, to rule over great peoples,
   to reprove rulers, and to remove sinners by the strength of
      his word.

<sup>42</sup> And he will not be weak in his days upon his God,
   because God made him strong by the Holy Spirit
   and wise by the counsel of understanding, with strength
      and righteousness.

<sup>43</sup> And the blessing of the Lord will be with him in strength,

44  and his hope in the Lord will not be weak;
    and who will be strong against him?
        Strong in his works and mighty in the fear of God,
45  shepherding the flock of the Lord in faithfulness and
            righteousness,
        and he will not permit any among them to be weak in their
            pasture.
46  He will lead them all with equality,
        and there will be no arrogance among them for any among
            them to be oppressed.
47  This is the propriety of the king of Israel that God knew,
        to raise him up over the house of Israel, to discipline it.
48  His words have been purged in fire more than first-rate gold.
        He will judge the tribes of the sanctified people in
            the assemblies.
49  His words are as words of holy ones in the middle of sanctified
            peoples.
50  Blessed are those who are born*a* in those days,
        to see the good things of Israel in the gathering of tribes;
            may God do it.
51  May God speed his mercy upon Israel;
        he will rescue us from the impurity of profane enemies.
        The Lord himself is our King for eternity and further.

# 18

A PSALM OF SOLOMON: ANOTHER ONE OF THE CHRIST OF THE LORD.   *The Anointed*
1   Lord, your mercy is upon the works of your hands for eternity,   *of the Lord*
2       your goodness upon Israel with a rich gift,
        your eyes looking down upon them,*b* and none of them will lack
            anything.
3       Your ears hear the entreaty of the poor in hope;
        your judgments are upon all the earth with mercy,
4       and your love is upon the seed of Abraham, the sons of Israel.
        Your discipline is upon us like a firstborn unique son,
5       to return an obedient soul from rudeness in ignorance.
6       May God cleanse Israel for the day of mercy with blessing,
        for the day of election when he brings up his anointed one.
7   Blessed are those who are born*c* in those days,
        to see the good things of the Lord, which he will do for
            the coming generation
8   under the rod of discipline of the anointed one of the Lord, in
            the fear of his God,
        in the wisdom of spirit and righteousness and strength,
9   to direct men in works of righteousness by the fear of God,
        to establish them all before the Lord.
10  A good generation in the fear of God in the days of mercy.
                        *Musical interlude*

---

*a* Lit. "become"  *b* I.e., the gifts  *c* Or "become"

11 Great is our God and of glorious, dwelling in the highest places,
12    who appointed stars in course for occasions of times from
      days to days,
   and they did not transgress from the way that you commanded
      them.
13 Their way is in the fear of God each day,
   from the day God created them and until eternity.
14 And they were not led astray from the day he created them;
   they were not removed from their ways from ancient
      generations,
   unless God commanded them by the command of his servants.

*Introduction to*

# 1 ENOCH

T HE BOOK KNOWN AS 1 Enoch is a composite text that grew over the course of at least two centuries. It was authoritative for the Qumran community, as fragments of twenty manuscripts were discovered in the caves surrounding the Qumran settlement. As these fragments were all written in Aramaic, it is believed that Aramaic (and not Hebrew) was the original language of composition. First Enoch was known to Jude, whose brief letter includes a quotation of 1 Enoch 1:9 and several references to the story of the fate of the Watchers, the errant angels now kept in chains in deep darkness. The book rose to canonical status in the Ethiopic Orthodox Church, which can be credited with the preservation of the whole book for posterity (the complete text survives only in Ethiopic translation). A Greek manuscript containing almost the whole of 1 Enoch 1–36 (the "Book of the Watchers") was discovered in a Christian grave in the city of Panopolis in Upper Egypt, and this forms the basis for the following translation. The "Book of the Watchers" is an imaginative expansion of the mysterious episode in Genesis 6:1–4 wherein heavenly beings mate with human females to bring forth a race of giants. In 1 Enoch, the angels also teach forbidden arts (like working metals into weapons, using cosmetics and potions, and mining for gold and silver) to humanity, giving rise to violence, lust, and greed. Their giant offspring wreak havoc on the earth until God decrees their death, after which their souls become the demons that plague humankind. The book thus offers an account for the origins of human evils, promotes a worldview with a significant population of spirit beings, and nurtures strong expectations of God's future interventions to judge the wicked and vindicate the righteous.

—D. A. deSilva

# 1 ENOCH[a]

*The Sayings of Enoch on the Elect and Wicked*

**1** Enoch's word of blessing that blessed the righteous chosen, who will be present in the day of tribulation when all enemies are removed; for the righteous shall be saved.

²Taking up his proverb, Enoch said: "The man is righteous: the vision from God was opened to him. He possesses the vision of the Holy One and heaven." He showed this to me, and I heard holy holy-speakers, and as I listened to everything from them; and watching, I knew. And I did not intend these things for the current generation; rather I speak at the generation that is far off.

³About the chosen ones I speak now, and concerning them I take up my proverb:

"My Holy Great One will come out from his dwelling place.
4    And the God of eternity will walk upon the earth, upon
       Mount Sinai.
    He will appear from his encampment
    and shine forth in the power of his strength from the heaven
       of heavens.
5    All will be afraid and the watchmen will believe.
   They will sing hidden in all the high places of the earth.
    And all the high places of the earth will shake;
    trembling and great fear will take them unto the end
       of the earth.
6    And they will shake and fall;
    the high mountains shall break up
    and the high hills will be made low to slip through
       the mountains.
   They will melt like beeswax from the face of the fire in flame.
7    And the earth will be divided, a division like grapes.
    As much as is upon the earth will destroy itself
    and judgment will be against everyone.
8    With the righteous he will make peace
   and upon the chosen there will be preservation and peace.
    Upon them mercy will come and they all shall belong to God;
    and he shall give approval to them and will bless them all.
   He will help them all and help us;
    light will shine on them and he will make peace over them.
9    For he comes with his ten thousands
    and his holy ones to enact judgment against all.

---

[a] This translation is based on the Greek text found in Codex Panopolitanus

He will destroy everyone who is ungodly
and reproach all flesh concerning all works of the ungodly:
    the things they did impiously,
    the harsh words that they spoke
    and all that ungodly sinners spoke against him."

**2** Observe all the works in heaven, how they do not change their ways; and the luminaries that are in heaven, how all things rise up and set, each being arranged in the appointed time. Their festivals are brought to light, and they do not pass up their own order. ²See the earth and be reminded of the works that are happening in her from the beginning until the completion, how they are perishable, how nothing upon the earth changes, but all the works of God appear to you. ³See the summer and the winter.

**3** Observe well and see all the trees,ᵃ

**5** how the trees are covering themselves in green leaves and all their fruit for honor and glory. Be reminded and know about all his works, and perceive that God who lives made these things in this way, and he lives unto all the eternities. ²All his works that he made for the eternities, they all go on in this way from year to year, all the works that they produce for him: their works do not change. But in accordance with his command all things come to be. ³See how the sea and the rivers in like manner produce and their works do not change from his words.

⁴But you did not persevere nor obey according to his commands; instead you turn away and loudly speak out a great, harsh word with your unclean mouth against his greatness. Because you speak boldly with your lies, O hard-hearted ones, peace is not in you. ⁵Therefore you call down curses upon your days: the years of your life will be destroyed and the years of your destruction will be increased with the curse of eternities. There will be no mercy and peace for you.

⁶At that time your name will be for an eternal curse for all the righteous. All those calling down curses will call them down upon you. All sinners and ungodly ones will swear over you and all the innocent will rejoice. For them there will be a release of sins, and all mercy, peace, and equity. Salvation will be a good light for them, and they will inherit the earth. For all of you sinners, salvation will not be present, but upon all of you dissolution and a curse. ⁷And for the chosen there will be light and grace and peace, and they will inherit the earth. But for you, the ungodly, there will be a curse.

⁸Then light and grace will be given to the chosen, and they will inherit the earth. Then wisdom will be given to all the chosen, and all these will live, and they shall no longer sin, neither against truth nor according to arrogance, and there will be a light among an enlightened person, and thought for a knowing person, and they shall not go wrong, ⁹nor shall they sin all the days of their life, and they shall not die in the wrath of anger, rather the number of the days of their life will be abundant. Their life will

---

ᵃ The content of chapter 4 as found in the Ethiopic version is not attested in the Greek versions of Enoch

increase in peace, and the years of their joy will increase in great joy and peace of eternity for all the days of their life.

*The Sons* **6** And it happened that when the sons of humans multiplied in those
*of Heaven* days, they fathered good and beautiful daughters. ²And the angels,
*and the Evil* the sons of heaven, saw them and desired them and said to one another,
*Deeds of Their* "Come let us choose for ourselves women from among the humans and
*Children* bring forth children for ourselves." ³And Semiaza, who was their ruler, said to them, "I fear you may not wish to do this deed and I alone will be responsible for a great sin." ⁴Therefore they all answered him, "Let us all swear by an oath, and devote one another to mutual destruction, not to turn back from this decision until we complete it and do this deed." ⁵Then they all made a vow together and put each other under a curse in regard to this.

⁷These are the names of their rulers: Semiaza (this was their ruler of all the angels), Arathak, Kimbra, Sammane, Daniel, Arearos, Semiel, Iomiel, Chochariel, Ezekiel, Batriel, Sathiel, Atriel, Tamiel, Barakiel, Ananthna, Thoniel, Rhamiel, Aseal, Rhakiel, Touriel. ⁸These are the chiefs of tens among them.

**7** Then they took for themselves women, each of them choosing a woman for themselves. They began to go to them and defile them. And they taught them sorcery and enchantments and cutting of roots and explained herbs to them.

²But those who became pregnant*a* brought forth great giants from three thousand cubits. ³These giants ate up the produce of the humans. When the humans were not able to provide for them, ⁴the giants had courage against them and ate up the humans. ⁵And they began to sin against birds and wild animals and reptiles and fish, and each one of them ate up the flesh and drank the blood. ⁶Then the earth brought up charges against the lawless ones.

*The Fallen* **8** Azael taught the humans to make swords, weapons, shields, and
*Angels Teach* breastplates—the lessons of the angels; and they showed them their
*Humans* mining and craftsmanship, anklets and adornment, powders and painted
*Magical Arts* eyes, and all kinds of choice stones and dying. ²Much ungodliness and prostitution happened, and they were led astray and ruined in all their ways. ³Semiaza taught enchantments and cutting of roots; Armaros, spells of healing; Rhakiel, astrology; Chochiel, the science of symptoms; Sathiel, watching the stars; Seriel, the course of the moon. ⁴Therefore the cry of the utterly destroyed people went up unto heaven.

*The* **9** Then Michael, Uriel, Raphael, and Gabriel, looking on from heaven, saw
*Archangels* much blood poured out upon the earth. ²And they said to one another,
*Appeal to God* "See: a voice crying aloud upon the earth unto the gates of heaven." ³The
*for Vengeance* souls of the humans made an appeal, saying, "Bring our judgment to the Most High."

⁴And they said to the Lord, "You are Lord of lords and the God of gods and King of the ages. The throne of your glory lasts unto all the generations of eternity, and your name is holy and great and blessed unto all the eternities. ⁵For you made all things and having all power and all things before you uncovered and open to sight. ⁶And you see all things that Azael

---

*a* Lit. "conceived in the womb"

made, who taught all the wrongdoing upon the earth and made visible the mysteries of eternity that are in the heaven, and which humans pursue and know. ⁷And Semiaza, to whom you gave power to rule those who are together with him. ⁸And they went to the daughters of the humans of the earth and slept with them*ᵃ* and they were defiled, and they revealed all the sins to them.*ᵃ* ⁹And the women bore giants under whom the whole earth was filled with blood and wrongdoing. ¹⁰And now behold, the souls of the dead shall cry aloud and make an appeal unto the gates of heaven. And their groaning went up, and it was not able to go from the face of the transgression happening upon the earth. ¹¹And you know everything before it came to be, and you see these things and you allow them; you do not say to us what must be done for them about this."

**10** Then the Most High, the Great Holy One, spoke about these things; and he sent Istrael*ᵇ* to the son of Lemech and said: ²"Say to him on behalf of my name, 'Hide yourself,' and reveal to him the end that is coming, that the whole earth is destroyed, and a flood is about to happen among all the earth and utterly destroy everything that is in it. ³And teach him that he should flee, and his seed will remain in all the generation of eternity."

*God's Commandments to the Archangels*

⁴And he said to Raphael, "Bind Azael hand and foot, and throw him into the darkness; open the desert that is in the Daduel and throw him there. ⁵And place under him the rugged and sharp stones, and let darkness cover him. Let him live there for the eternities: cover up his appearance and let no light be seen. ⁶For in the day of great judgment he will be led away into the burning. ⁷And the earth that the angels removed will be healed, and reveal the healing of the earth, so that they may heal the injury, lest all the sons of the humans be destroyed with the whole mystery that the watchmen ordered and showed to their sons. ⁸And the whole earth was destroyed and laid waste by the works of Azael's teaching. Ascribe to him all sins."

⁹And the Lord said to Gabriel, "Go against the bastards, against the base ones and the sons of fornication, and destroy the sons of the watchmen among the humans; send them into the battle of destruction. For they do not have length of days, ¹⁰and their fathers will not have any questioning even concerning them, because they hoped to live an eternal life, and because each of them will live five hundred years."

¹¹Then Michael said, "Go and make known to Semiaza and to those remaining with him, those women with whom they mixed, being defiled by them in their uncleanness. ¹²Should their sons ever be slaughtered and see the destruction of their beloved ones, bind them for seventy generations in the wooded vales of the earth until the days of their judgment and consummation, until the judgment of the eternity of eternities is completed. ¹³Then they will be led away into the gaping abyss of fire and into the torment and into the jail, being shut up from eternity. ¹⁴And whoever is burned up and destroyed from the present, they will be bound up together

---

*ᵃ* The pronoun is feminine, referring to the daughters of the people of the earth  *ᵇ* The Greek text found in the Chronography of Georgius Syncellus has "Uriel" instead of "Istrael"

with them until the completion of the generation. ¹⁵Destroy all the spirits of the frauds and the sons of the watchmen on account of wronging the humans. ¹⁶Destroy all wrongdoing from the earth, and every work of wickedness will be coming to an end. Let the plant of righteousness and truth be revealed into the eternities. It will be planted with joy.

¹⁷"And now all the righteous ones will flee, and they will be the living ones until they father thousands, and all the days of their youth and their Sabbath rest will fill with peace. ¹⁸Then the whole earth will work in righteousness, and the tree will be planted in it and be filled with blessing. ¹⁹And all the trees of the earth will rejoice exceedingly. It will be planted, and they will be planting vines. The vine that they plant will make pitchers of wine; according to each of the sown seeds it will make a thousand measures of olives. It will make up to ten jugs.

²⁰"And you, make the earth clean from all uncleanness and from all wrongdoing and from all sins, ungodliness and uncleanness that is upon the earth. Wipe it away. ²¹And all the people will be serving and blessing and worshiping me. ²²And the whole earth will be made clean from all defilement and from all uncleanness, wrath, and suffering. I will never send it upon them again unto all the generations of the ages."

**11** And then I will open the chambers of the blessing that are in the heavens, also to bring them down upon the deeds, upon the toil of the sons of humans. ²And then truth and peace will share together for all the days of eternity and for all the generations of the humans.

*Enoch Is Taken Up into Heaven* **12** Before these words were spoken Enoch was taken, and none of the humans knew where he was taken and where he was and what had happened to him. ²And his works were with the watchmen, and his days were with the holy ones.

³And standing there, I, Enoch, was blessing the Lord of greatness, the King of the eternities; and behold the watchmen of the Holy Great One called me: ⁴"Enoch, scribe of righteousness, go and speak to the watchmen of heaven—any who abandoned the high heaven, the holy eternal place, who were defiled with the women and just as the sons of the earth did, they did the same also, and took for themselves women. You have brought great destruction on the earth. ⁵And there will be no peace for you, nor remission of sins. And though they rejoice in their children, ⁶they will see the murder of their beloved ones, and they will groan over the destruction of their children. They will be bound for eternity, and there will be for them no mercy and peace."

*Enoch's Message to the Fallen Angels* **13** Enoch said to Azael, "Go: There will be no peace for you; great judgment has come out against you to bind you. ²There will be neither pause nor questioning for you about which wrongs you made known and about all works of ungodliness, wrongdoing, and sin, all that you declared to the humans."

³Then I went and spoke to all of them. They all were terrified: trembling and fear took hold of them. ⁴They request that I should write to them records of questioning so that there might be a remission of sins for them, and that I might read to them the record of questioning before the Lord of heaven. ⁵For they are not yet able to speak nor lift their eyes to the heaven from the shame of their sin; so they were condemned.

⁶Then I wrote the record of their questioning and the prayer concerning their spirits and what they are asking, how there should be for them a remission of sins and length of days. ⁷Then I went and sat upon the waters of Dan in the land of Dan, which is from the right side of Hermon toward the west. I read the record of their prayer. ⁸As I was put to sleep, suddenly dreams came upon me, and visions fell upon me, and I saw visions of wrath. Then a voice came, saying, "Speak to the sons of heaven to reprove them." ⁹And when I became awake I came to them, and they all gathered together and were sitting mourning in Ebelsata (which is between Lebanon and Senisel), covering their faces. ¹⁰Before them also I reported to them all the visions that I saw in my sleep. And I was beginning to speak words of righteousness, reproving the watchmen of heaven.

**14** The book of the words of righteousness and reproving of the watchmen of eternity, according to the commandment of the Great Holy One in this vision. *Enoch's Heavenly Vision*

²I saw in my sleep what I now say with a fleshly tongue with the spirit of my mouth, which the Great One gave to humans to speak to each other, and he will perceive hearts; ³who created and gave to reprove watchmen, the sons of the heavens.

⁴I wrote your request from the angels and in my vision I was shown this: your request was not received, ⁵namely, that you may no longer go up to heaven for all time; and you are bound with the chains of the earth for all the eternities. ⁶Also, in the same way you may see the destruction of your beloved sons. Because their profit will not be for you, but they will fall before you by the sword. ⁷And there will be no questions from you about them, nor about your own. Though you are weeping and praying and not speaking every word from the writing that I wrote.

⁸And the following was shown to me in the vision: behold, the clouds called me, and the mists summoned me. The running across of the stars and flashings were very earnest and troubling to me, and the winds in my vision were spread out to me. ⁹And they lifted me up and carried me into heaven. I went until I was brought near a wall built with hailstones and tongues of fire surrounding them, and they began to alarm me.

¹⁰And I went into the tongues of fire and was brought into a great house built with hailstones. The wall of the house was like flat stones, and all were from snow and a ground of snow. ¹¹The roofs were like the running across of stars and lightning, and between them cherubs of fire and the heaven above like water. ¹²Burning fire surrounded the walls, and its doors were like burning fire. ¹³I went into the house which is hot as fire and cold as snow, and it had no sustenance of life. Fear covered me and trembling took me. ¹⁴I was shaking and trembling, and I fell.

I looked again at my vision, ¹⁵and behold, another door opened in front of me. This was a great house and all was built with tongues of fire. ¹⁶It was all worth more in glory and honor and greatness such that I am not able to point out to you its glory and its greatness. ¹⁷Its ground was of fire and its upper part was lightning and the spreading out of stars, and its roof was burning fire.

¹⁸I looked, and I saw a high throne, and its appearance was like crystal, a wheel like the sun shining brightly and a mountain of cherubs. ¹⁹And below

the throne, burning rivers of fire were going out, and I was not able to see. ²⁰And the great glory was seated upon it, its covering like the appearance of the sun, brighter and whiter than all snow. ²¹And all the angels were not able to go into this house and see his face because of the honored and esteemed one. And all flesh was not able to see him. ²²The fire was burning in a circle, and the great fire stood beside it. No one comes near to him in the circle; numberless ten thousands stood before him, and all of his reason is a work. ²³The holy ones of the angels who come near to him do not withdraw with the night, neither do they leave him.

²⁴Until then I was cast upon my face and trembling. And the Lord called me with his mouth and said to me, "Come here, Enoch, and hear my word." ²⁵And one of the holy ones came to me and woke me, and stood me up, and brought me to the door; I bowed my face down.

*The Lord Gives a Prophecy to Enoch*

**15** And answering, he said to me, "The true human, a human of the truth, the scribe." Then I heard his voice say, "Don't be afraid, Enoch, a true human and scribe of the truth. Come here and hear my voice. ²Go and say to those who sent you, 'It was necessary for you to ask about the humans, and not the humans about you. ³On what account did you abandon the high, holy heavens of eternity, and sleep with the women and be defiled with the daughters of humans, and take women for yourselves? You acted just like the sons of the earth, and you fathered children for yourselves, giant sons. ⁴And you were holy, living, eternal spirits. But then you were defiled with the blood of the women, and with the blood of the flesh you brought forth children and you desired the blood of humans, just as any of those of flesh and blood do, those who die and are destroyed.'

⁵"Because of this I gave women to them in order to be impregnated and procreate children by them this way, and so that not every work comes to an end for them upon the earth. ⁶You were living eternal spirits and not dying into all the generations of eternity. ⁷And because of this I did not make wives available for you; but the spirits of heaven, their dwelling is in heaven. ⁸And now the giants who are born from the spirits, even the strong spirits of flesh upon the earth, their dwelling will be on the earth. ⁹Evil spirits went out from their body, for they came from the higher places, and the beginning of their creation and foundation is from the watchful holy ones. They will be called evil spirits. ¹⁰And so for the spirits of heaven, their dwelling will be in heaven, and the spirits that are born upon the earth, their dwelling will be upon the earth.

¹¹"The spirits of the giants were doing unjustly, destroying, attacking, and wrestling with each other and thrown together upon the earth, the hard spirits of the giants. They are making courses, and no one is eating, but they are fasting and thirsting and stumbling spirits. ¹²These will rise up against the sons of men and women because they have gone forth from them.

**16** "During the days of slaughter, destruction, and death, when the spirits are proceeding from the life of their flesh, there will be destruction without judgment. Thus they will be destructive until the last day of the great judgments, in which the great eternity will be completed.

²"And now to the watchmen whom you sent to ask about those who were in heaven: ³'You were in heaven and you knew every mystery that is

not uncovered for you and the mystery that is coming from God. Now you reveal this to the women in your hardness of heart, and by this mystery the women and men increase evil upon the earth.' ⁴Say therefore to them, 'There is no peace.'"

**17** And they took and led me away into a certain place, in which those who were there become like burning fire and, whenever they desire, they appear as humans. ²Then they led me away into an opaque place and to a mountain where its peak went up to heaven. ³There I saw a place of luminaries and the treasure of stars and thunder, and into the depths of air where there is a bow of fire, arrows and their housings, and all kinds of lightning.

*The Archangels Show Prophetic Wonders to Enoch*

⁴And they led me away to living waters and to the fire of the setting sun that also causes all the settings of the sun. ⁵And I came up to a river of fire in which the fire runs down as water and flows into the great sea of the setting sun. ⁶I saw the great river and went up to the great river and to the great darkness, and I departed to where no flesh walks around. ⁷I saw the winter winds of the darkness and the outflow of the depth of all waters. ⁸I saw the mouth of the earth of all the rivers and the mouth of the deep.

**18** I saw the treasures of all the winds; I saw that in them he ordered all creation and the foundation of the earth. ²And I saw the stone of the corner of the earth. I saw the four winds lifting the earth and the firmament of the heaven. ³And they stood between earth and heaven. ⁴I saw the winds of the heavens turning and completing the wheel of the sun and all the stars. ⁵I saw the winds upon the earth lifting up with the cloud. I saw the limits of the earth and the support of the heaven above.

⁶I passed by and I saw a place being set on fire night and day, where there are seven mountains made from costly stones, three placed in the east and three in the south. ⁷And the ones toward the east were from colored stone, and the other one was from pearl stone, and another from stretched stone, and the one against the south from red stone. ⁸The middle one of these was in heaven like the throne of God from alabaster stone and the head of the throne from sapphire stone. ⁹And I saw burning fire beyond these mountains. ¹⁰There is a place at the end of the great earth: there the heavens will be completed. ¹¹And I saw a great chasm in the pillar of fire going down, and there was no measure to it, neither in depth nor in height. ¹²And beyond this chasm I saw a place where there was neither firmament of heaven above nor earth having lain a foundation below it. Neither was there water under it, nor birds; but there was a place desolate and terrifying. ¹³There I saw seven stars like great burning mountains about which I inquired. ¹⁴The angel said, "This place is the end of heaven and earth; this prison was in the stars and in the powers of heaven. ¹⁵And these stars rolling along in the fire are those passing beside the ordinance of the Lord in the beginning of their rising (for the outer place of heaven is empty), because they do not go in their time." ¹⁶And he was angry with them and bound them up for ten thousand years, until the time of completion of their sins.

**19** Then Uriel said to me, "Here the angels who are mixing with the women shall stand, and their spirits, becoming multiform, shall treat the humans with indignity. And they will lead them astray to burn incense to the demons until the great judgment in which they will be judged so as to bring about perfection. ²And their women whom angels led astray will be as Sirens." ³And I, Enoch, alone saw the visions, the limits of all things, and not even one human shall see as I saw.

*The Names of*
*the Archangels*

**20** These are the angels of powers: ²Uriel, one of the holy angels, who is over the world and the Tartarus;*ᵃ* ³Raphael, one of the holy angels, who is over the spirits of humans; ⁴Raguel, one of the holy angels, who avenges the world of luminaries; ⁵Michael, one of the holy angels, who was appointed over the good ones of the people and over the chaos; ⁶Sariel, one of the holy angels, who is over the spirits who sin in the spirit; ⁷Gabriel, one of the holy angels, who is over orchard and the dragons and cherubim. These are the seven*ᵇ* names of the archangels.

*Enoch Visits*
*More Places*
*of Wonder*

**21** Then I visited an unprepared place. ²There I beheld an awesome work: I saw neither heaven above, nor did I behold the established earth, but an unprepared and fearful place. ³And there I beheld seven of the stars of heaven bound and thrown into it like great mountains burning with fire. ⁴Then I said, "For what reason were they bound, and on what account were they thrown here?" ⁵Then Uriel, who is one of the holy angels who was with me (and who went before the angels), said to me, "Enoch, for what reason do you ask, and why are you zealous for the truth? ⁶These are from the stars of heaven, those passing by the command of the Lord. And they were bound here until the fulfillment of countless years, the time served for their sins."

⁷From there I visited another place that is more fearful, and I beheld awesome works. In that place a great fire was alighted and burning. And the place had a crevice into the deep, full of pillars of great fire going down. Neither measure nor breadth was I able to see or conjecture. ⁸Then I said, "How fearful is this place and how terrible in appearance!" ⁹Then one of the holy angels who was with me answered, saying to me, "Enoch, why are you terrified and trembling in this way?" And I answered, "Because of this fearful place and because of the appearance of this terror." ¹⁰And he said, "This place is a prison of angels. They will be held together here until the eternity of eternity."

**22** From there I traveled to another place, and he showed to me another great and high mountain of stiff rock in the west. ²There were four hollow places in it having depth and exceeding smoothness, three of them dark and one shining with a spring of water coming between it. And I said, "How smooth are these hollows, great depths and dark places in the vision!"

³Then Raphael, who is one of the holy angels who was with me, answered and said to me, "These places are hollow in order to gather together the spirits of the dead souls. For this very thing they were judged, to gather together here all the souls of humans. ⁴And these places for their reception were made until the day of their judgment, until the division and limitation of time, in which the great judgment will be with them."

---

ᵃ the netherworld  ᵇThe Greek has "seven" though only six names are listed; the seventh name is Remiel, attested in some versions

5I looked on the dead humans who were petitioning, and their voice went up to heaven pleading. 6Then I asked Raphael, the angel who was with me, saying to him, "This petitioning spirit, from whose voice does it go up to heaven, petitioning in this way?" 7And he replied to me, saying, "This spirit comes from Abel, whom his brother Cain murdered. Abel petitions him until Cain's seed is destroyed from the face of the earth and his seed is removed from the seed of humans."

8Then I asked about the whole circumference, why the one is separated from the other. 9And he answered me, saying, "These three were made to separate the spirits of the dead; and so it is separated for the spirits of the righteous, where the spring of water is shining in it; 10and so it was created by the sinners, when they die and are buried in the earth, and judgment has not happened to them in their life, 11their spirits are separated here for this great torture until the great day of judgment, by whips and tortures of the accursed; it was a recompense of the spirits until eternity; he will bind them there until eternity. 12In this way there is a separation for the spirits of those petitioning, any who are revealed concerning the destruction, when they were murdered in the days of the sinners. 13And in this way it is created for the spirits of the humans, any who will not be holy but sinners, any who are ungodly; and they will be companions with the lawless. But the spirits, because the oppressors here punish the smaller of them, they will not be punished in the day of judgment, nor will they rise from there."

14Then I blessed the Lord of glory, and I said, "Blessed are you, O Lord, the ruler of righteousness who rules for eternity."

**23** From there I visited another place toward the west of the ends of the earth. 2And I gazed at the fire running across that was neither stopping nor leaving the course, but at the same time remaining by day and night. 3And I asked, "What is the thing that has no rest?" 4Then Raguel, who is one of the holy angels who was with me, answered, "This course of fire that is toward the west is the fire chasing away all the luminaries of heaven." *The Mountains of Burning Fire and the Sweet-Smelling Tree*

**24** And he showed me mountains of burning fire at night. 2And beyond them I went and gazed at seven mountains, all of them glorious, each differing from each other, the stones of which were honored in beauty, and all of them honored and glorious and well shaped, three were set upon the east with the one and three upon the south with the one. There were also deep and rugged ravines, never one coming close to the other one, 3and to the mountain, the seventh mountain between these, and it was held above the height like the seat of the throne, and well-shaped trees were around it. 4And there was a tree among them that I had never smelled and no one else was cheered by it, and none other was like it; it had a sweeter-smelling fragrance than all other sweet spices, and its leaves and blossom and wood do not wither for eternity; concerning the fruit, they were like clusters of date palms. 5Then I said, "How beautiful and sweet-smelling is this tree; beautiful are its leaves and blossom, beautiful is its appearance." 6Then Michael, one of the holy angels who was with me, answered me, and he went before them.

**25** And he said to me, "Enoch, why do you ask and why do you wonder at the smell of the tree, and why do you want to learn the truth?" ²Then I answered him, "I want to know about all things, and especially about this tree."

³And he answered, saying, "This high mountain, of which the head is like the seat of the throne of God, upon this the great holy Lord of glory, the King of eternity, sits whenever he goes down to consider the earth with goodness. ⁴⁻⁵And as for this sweet-smelling tree, no flesh has power to touch it until the great judgment, in which there is vengeance for all and a completion until eternity. Then its fruit will be given to the righteous and holy chosen ones for life and for food; and it will be transplanted to the holy place from the house of God, King of eternity. ⁶Then the cheerful will be cheered and will rejoice. And they will go to the holy place. Its fragrance is in its bones, and they will live much more life upon earth, such as your fathers lived. And in their days, torments and blows and whips will not touch them."

⁷Then I blessed the God of glory, the King of eternity who prepared such things for righteous humans. He created them and declared that he would give to them.

*The Holy Mountain and the Ravine* **26** And from there I traveled to the middle of the earth, and I saw a blessed place, in which there were trees having lasting budding branches from a pruned tree. ²There I beheld a holy mountain; below the mountain there was water out of the east, and it headed west to the south. ³And I saw toward the east another mountain higher than this: between it, a deep ravine having no breadth; and water went through it, below under the mountain. ⁴And toward the west another mountain lower than this and having no height, with a deep ravine and a dry place between them, and another deep ravine and a dry place upon the highest point of the three mountains. ⁵And how many are the deep ravines from the stiff rock with no tree planted upon them. ⁶And I wondered about the ravine: I wondered deeply.

**27** And I said, "On what account is this land blessed and all full of trees, yet there is this cursed ravine?"

²"The accursed land is for those who are cursed until eternity. Here all those accursed ones will be gathered together, any who will speak with their mouth in an unfitting voice against the Lord. For they speak harsh things about his glory. They will be gathered together here, and the dwelling place will be here. ³In the last eternities, in the days of true judgment against the righteous for all time, here the pious will bless the Lord of glory, the King of eternity. ⁴In the days of their judgment they will bless him with mercy as he divides them." ⁵Then I blessed the Lord of glory, and I manifested his glory and sang magnificently.

**28** And from there I went into the middle of Mandobara, and I saw a desert in it. It was alone ²and full of trees. And the water is born from above without rain from the seeds, ³like abundant water brought forth toward the northwest, it brought up water and dew everywhere.

**29** Yet from there I went into another place in Babdera, and toward the east of this mountain I departed. ²And I saw trees of judgment blowing sweet aromas of Lebanon and myrrh; and their trees were like nut-bearing trees.

**30** And beyond these I departed far off toward the east, and I saw another great place, a ravine of water ²in which there was also a colored tree of sweet aromas like a mastich tree. ³Also from the lip of these ravines I saw a cinnamon tree of sweet aromas; and beyond these I departed toward the east.

*More Sweet-Smelling Trees and the Tree of Wisdom*

**31** And I saw other mountains and among them groves of trees and nectar going out of them, which is called sarra and galbanum. ²And beyond these mountains I saw another mountain toward the east of the ends of the earth, and it was all full of trees at once in the likeness of almond trees ³when they were crushed: indeed, they were more sweet-smelling than every sweet aroma.

**32** Into the northeast I looked upon seven mountains full of good nard, mastic trees,ᵃ cinnamon, and pepper.

²And from there I went up to the beginnings of all these mountains, which are far off, a long way toward the east of the earth. And I stepped across above the Red Sea, and I departed over the highest point. From here I stepped across above Zotiel. ³I came toward the orchard of righteousness, and I saw far beyond these trees, many more great trees. Two that were there were very great and beautiful, held in esteem and magnificent, and also the tree of wisdom from which holy ones eat the fruit and know great wisdom. ⁴That tree is like the fir tree in its height, its leaves like the carob tree, its fruit like very cheerful clusters of the vine, and its smell was carried away, far off from the tree. ⁵Then I said, "How beautiful the tree and how pleasing to behold!" ⁶Then Raphael, the holy angel who was with me, answered, "This is the tree of wisdom from which your father ate."

---

ᵃ See Susanna 54